An Ordered Love

An Ordered Love 🜹 Sex Roles and Sexuality in Victorian Utopias— the Shakers, the Mormons, and the Oneida Community

by Louis J. Kern

The University of North Carolina Press 🜹 *Chapel Hill*

© 1981 The University of North Carolina Press

All rights reserved

Manufactured in the United States of America

Cloth edition, ISBN 0-8078-1443-1
Paper edition, ISBN 0-8078-4074-2

Library of Congress Catalog Card Number 80-10763

Library of Congress Cataloging in Publication Data

Kern, Louis J   1943–
  An ordered love.

  Bibliography: p.
  Includes index.
    1. Free Love—United States—History—19th century.
  2. Sex customs—United States—History—19th
  century. 3. Sex role. 4. Shakers—United
  States—History. 5. Mormons and Mormonism in the
  United States—History. 6. Oneida Community—
  History. I. Title.
  HQ967.U6K47   306.7   80-10763
  ISBN 0-8078-1443-1
  ISBN 0-8078-4074-2 pbk.

TO SUSAN

Amamus ergo sumus

In Memoriam

ALICE M. KEENE

(1917–1980)

She sustained us all.

Contents

PART III
Celestial Marriage: Mormon Sexuality and Sex Roles in Ideology
and Practice

PART IV
"In the Eden of Heart-Love": Sexuality and Sex Roles of the
Oneida Community in Ideology and Practice

PART V
Distinguishing the Church from the World: Sectarian
Communitarianism and Nineteenth-Century America

Preface

*Les utopies ne sont souvent que des
vérités prematurées*
[Utopias are frequently but premature truths].

   —Lamartine

The mass of men lead lives of quiet desperation.

   —Henry David Thoreau, *Walden*

*T*he utopian tradition has been an important strain in the American mind throughout our history. It has acted as a goad to slumbering conscience, a call to action. Utopian thought has not influenced the main currents of our political and economic life extensively, but has played a significant role in keeping alive the spirit of perfectibility, the belief that man can improve his circumstances as well as himself. In that respect, utopian societies have performed a social function analogous to that of third parties in American politics.

Third parties have never succeeded in controlling the policies of the major political parties in the United States, nor have they wielded significant power on the national level; but they have served as political gadflies to call attention to the abuses and shortsightedness of orthodox politicians, and thereby sufficiently to awaken them from their lethargy to achieve some measure of reform. Seen in the long view, utopianism has served a similar social function, especially insofar as it has stimulated middle-class advocates to take up reform causes.

Postmillennial utopians, who believed in the radical and immediate perfectibility of man, were concerned with an exceptionally broad range of reform issues. Oneida Perfectionists, for example, were pacifists and antislavery and temperance advocates and sought reform in health, dietary practice, hygiene, education, and, in a wider sense, the whole of social life as it related to labor, economic production and distribution, the family, marriage, and divorce. Through articles in various reform journals and private correspondence with reform leaders (John H. Noyes, head of the Oneida Community, corresponded with William Lloyd Garrison, for instance), they helped to keep these issues before the public, proposed alternative solutions to them, and reinforced the effect of the organized reform groups that operated within the context of mainstream society.

With the exception of slavery, no area of nineteenth-century life commanded as much attention and consumed as much reform energy as questions of sex, marriage, and the family. This work provides a detailed examination of the response of three nineteenth-century utopian communities to social ambivalence and normative uncertainty in the area of familial and sexual relations. These three communities, the pantagamous Oneida Community (1848–79), the polygamic Mormons (1843–90), and the celibate Shakers (1779–1890), consciously sought to provide social alternatives to monogamous marriage. Clearly, each of these utopian societies was a total social environment; it answered all the basic needs of its members. I am therefore not arguing for a sexual reductionism in the examination of these communities. All three were profoundly religious organizations; their particular economic, political, and social theories arose directly out of the theological matrix.

Earlier studies of communitarian societies have emphasized their communistic economic and authoritarian political elements, while providing only cursory attention to the sexual aspects of utopianism. Unlike these antecedent works, the present study maintains the critical importance of considerations of sexuality and sexual behavior in these communities. It also insists that these communities must be seen within the context of nineteenth-century perfectionist sectarianism. Essentially, what I am concerned with here is demonstrating that questions of sexuality and sexual behavior were an integral part of life in these three communities and that they were intimately related to their theological and ideological foundations.

Implicit also in this argument is a critique of the assumption that economic and political affairs are *preeminently* important in the historical process. Demographers and historians of the family have emphasized the fact that the onset of major changes in family organization, fertility rates, sexual behavior, and sexual ideology in America predated the industrial revolution or the process of large-scale urbanization. Furthermore, the process of culture formation, as the Structuralists have argued, is not a closed, linear progression of causation with a fixed hierarchy of causal agents. The historical study of cultural morphology involves the attempt to understand contexts, to reach an awareness of the complex interrelations between the various culture elements (political and social life, for example), as well as the different levels within a given culture (predominant culture, counterculture, subculture, and so on).

As well as being influenced by other cultural forms, family life and patterns of sexual behavior often have considerable effects on economic, industrial, political, and intellectual life. The study of utopian sexuality thus has a dual relevance. In the first place, because a culture is a unified whole, the alternative modes of organizing the common elements of that culture help us to understand more clearly the assumptions behind the dominant cultural manifestations. Utopian sexuality expresses the obverse side of Victorian sexual mores and behavior. In addition, insofar as the various cultural forms are interrelated and together comprise the totality of a culture's self-expression, the study of utopian sexual life provides an alternative vision, a different perspective from which to view not only sectarian utopian culture but the culture of Victorian America as a whole.

Significant as the study of utopian sexuality may be to an understanding of broader cultural themes, however, it remains true that the direct influence of utopianism on the dominant culture of Victorian America was minimal. The primary contribution of these sectarian communities is to be found in their influence on the lives of the individual men and women who committed themselves to a vigorous social code, often requiring mortifying self-denial and renunciation, in order to further human perfectibility. The people who entered such communities were alienated from mainstream society; they were most frequently evangelical Protestants whose expectations of a truly moral society had been cruelly disappointed by a refractory, materialistic world. They were objects of derision in a practical, none-too-squeamish world, often struggling along on the periphery of economic failure.

Individuals who saw themselves as social outcasts, the oppressed and dispossessed, found a home, mutual support, and an organization self-consciously devoted to creating a morally perfect society on earth in these sectarian communities. The broader society had no use for these people; without the utopian impulse they would have been consigned to the rubbish bin of history. Utopianism gave a purpose, a meaning, a direction to the lives of people who formed part of the vast, indistinguishable mass of humanity that is born unremarked, passes without notice, and is anonymously interred in the historical record.

Westminster Station, Vt.   L J K
July 1979

Acknowledgments

*I*t would have been impossible to complete a book of this length without the assistance of many people. The staffs of numerous libraries, but especially those of the New York Public Library Annex, the Rare Books and Manuscript Division of the Firestone Library of Princeton University, Speer Library of the Princeton Theological Seminary, and the Rare Book Room of the Syracuse University Library were most helpful in locating materials and facilitating the process of research. Special thanks are due to Ruth Beasley of the Institute for Sex Research at Indiana University for providing photocopies of the papers of Anita N. McGee relating to the Oneida Community. Elaine Dixon of the Putney Historical Society, Putney, Vermont, graciously provided access to the small collection of letters from Noyes family members housed there.

The whole project was encouraged by and profited enormously from many fruitful discussions with Warren Susman, who also read the manuscript at various stages of completion. I am indebted to him for calling my attention to the unique body of manuscript material on the Oneida Community located in the Institute for Sex Research. Helpful comments were also provided by Gerald Grob, Walter Bezanson, and Philip Greven. I am especially grateful for the careful, detailed reading given the manuscript in its later stages by Laurence Veysey. His kind encouragement and constructive suggestions have contributed materially to making this a stronger book.

My greatest debt is to my wife, for her many sacrifices and her commitment to seeing the project through to its conclusion with me. For her courage and determination to persevere, I am most grateful.

An Ordered Love

I will love thee as the gods love—
The Father God and Mother,
Whose intermingled Being is
The Life of every other.

   —"Free Marriage" (1870)

For in the resurrection they neither
marry nor are given in marriage, but are
as the angels of God in heaven.

   —Matthew 22:30

Introduction

*Sexuality is the center around which revolves
the whole of social life as well as the inner life
of the individual.*

  —Wilhelm Reich, *The Function of the Orgasm*

*Love, work and knowledge are the well-springs
of our life. They should also govern it.*

  —Wilhelm Reich, *The Function of the Orgasm*

*I*n the late eighteenth and nineteenth centuries, over one hundred
utopian communities were established in the United States. Of this
number, nearly seventy were communistic societies founded as conscious alternatives to the socioeconomic structure then prevalent in
America. Their members were primarily drawn from the lower-middle-
class ranks of farmers, artisans, and craftsmen. Their leaders were either
particularly able charismatic figures from the same class or more solidly
middle-class individuals whose discontent with the prevailing value system would have excluded them from positions of leadership to which
they might otherwise have aspired.

It has become customary in discussions of nineteenth-century communal societies to follow the typology set forth in John Humphrey Noyes's
classic contemporary account, *History of American Socialisms* (1870). Noyes divided the seventy-eight communities he cataloged
and described into two categories. The first, predominantly secular and
of European origin (the Owenite and Fourieristic phases of American
socialism), he called "Socialism." The second, pervasively religious and
American to the core, he designated "Revivalism." As Noyes himself
realized, this categorization was largely heuristic since the two streams
were convergent and confluent rather than discretely parallel.[1]

Both branches of American socialism were imbued with a millennial
fervor which, although religious in its inception, had become an article
of secular faith by the 1830s. Within the communitarian setting, however, the traditional millennial formulation, which maintained that under

divine guidance the historical process would inevitably result in the triumph of Christian principles (progress) and the subsequent establishment of a holy utopia, was inverted. Utopians believed that their communities would be the cause rather than the result of progress; theirs was a messianic vision of social and moral reform.

Millennial utopianism also differed from what one clergyman called the "millennium of republicanism"[2] in that it assumed that the agency of progress was a select vanguard of despised and often persecuted "saints," rather than the united moral force of the nation. As a minority set apart by its self-proclaimed purity and its voluntary assumption of the duty of leadership in meliorative reform, utopians found themselves at odds with the established society of antebellum America.

There were many subtle differences between the communities founded by various utopian groups, but they found themselves in broad general agreement in their opposition to the economic arrangements, the moral code, and the social organization of the broader American society of which they were a part. Their dissatisfaction centered about the capitalist system of production, the immorality they felt was consuming the vitals of nineteenth-century American society, and the institutions and social roles which characterized that society.

Despite their rejection of the established social order, however, both religious and secular communitarians tended to deemphasize the apocalyptic thrust inherent in primitive chiliasm. Indeed, the theosophy of most sectarian utopians can best be described as postmillenarian—that is to say, they believed that the awesome Second Coming had already occurred and that they were the living incarnation of the glorified Kingdom of God on earth. This doctrine was central to the social cohesion of the religiously based communities because it served to enhance the isolation and sense of separateness and specialness of their members. Heightened alienation from accepted social norms and mores intensified communal commitment.[3]

Most religious communists were perfectionists who believed that they had progressed so far morally that they were literally incapable of sin. In theological terms they had achieved perfect sanctification. Their postmillenarian stance, however, saved them from a harshly self-righteous antinomianism or an aggressively antisocial Adventism that breathlessly awaited the violent purging of the sinful world. On one level they remained concerned with the rehabilitation of mankind, even though their physical and moral alienation from the world rendered their perception of the utopian redemptive role highly ambiguous. The majority of perfectionist utopias opted for a passive strategy toward the broader society and settled for a paradigmatic rather than a participatory role in the reform process.[4]

Perfectionism, a version of sectarian antinomianism, had always raised the specter of sexual license. In traditional society, the question of sexual behavior and morality was a bench mark of the moral worth of the individual man or woman. But the doctrine of radical sinlessness, the belief that individual believers were no longer subject to civil or ecclesiastical law, forced perfectionists to come to grips with a socially unregulated sexual impulse.[5] Logically, there were four alternatives open to them. First, they might adopt a doctrine of complete sexual freedom for the individual. This was the solution the majority of their enemies assumed they had uniformly adopted, a behavior pattern they called licentiousness. Perfect freedom, however, is not consistent with social organization of any kind, and insofar as religious utopians attempted to institutionalize perfection in a communal setting, they rejected this option. A second possibility, which was chosen by many sectarian utopians, was to accept the conventional monogamous system as a basis for communal sexual behavior. The other two alternatives found in nineteenth-century communitarian societies were total rejection of overt sexuality and some form of communally regulated sexual relation that differed from the monogamic.

The focus of this work is the detailed analysis of three communities that are representative of the latter two options. These communities, whose social theories differed dramatically from those of mainstream American society, as well as from those of a broader cross section of the communitarian movement, are among the most interesting examples of the utopian experimentation of the day.

Historians have considered these communities primarily agents of an abortive liberal reformism. They have tended to see them as communities whose ideals of male-female relationships, and to some extent sexuality in general, were much more in tune with modern attitudes than with those of the rest of nineteenth-century American society. At the same time, they have concentrated their attention on the economic and political realities of these utopian societies, often evincing greater concern with why communism has failed in the United States than with a study of what caused individuals to choose to live in such alternative societies, or how they structured their social lives.[6]

In recent years, the sociological school of historical research and sociologists themselves, doubtless because of the recrudescence of communal life-styles in the 1960s, have become increasingly interested in the historical study of utopian movements and have brought a fresh approach and new insights to the problem. These social experiments have come to be examined as phenomena in their own right and are treated with dignity as valid social alternatives seeking to alter the accepted social arrangements and thus enhance the quality of human life, rather than as anomalous and altogether ineffectual, if mildly amusing, aberrations from the accepted social norm.[7]

Sexual aspects of communal life have, nevertheless, received only passing attention. Only one book has been written on the history of sexuality in utopian societies, and in a very real sense the sexual aspects still remain of peripheral interest in that work. The persistent ideological question of why socialism failed to take root in American culture and a rather self-satisfied complacency about the failure of reform to affect the American consensus inform this study.[8]

An increased concern with sex roles and sexual behavior, part of a new consciousness that followed in the wake of the women's liberation movement, has brought about some reconsideration of these utopian societies. Nevertheless, we have yet to have a work that elucidates the significance of sexuality and sexual behavior in them. The sexual doctrines of these communities were not adventitious; they were an integral part of their ethical, theological, and ideological structure. We have yet to have an investigation of the ways in which individuals sought to solve social and moral problems related to the family, marriage, and sex roles within the context of such ethically oriented social organizations.

The questions of the degree of change in the accepted male-female roles, the ideological assumptions that underlay sexual attitudes, and the relative attractiveness of the various nonmonogamic sexual arrangements to males and females in these utopian societies have also been ignored. It is hoped that this work will serve to stimulate interest in these topics, as well as contributing to righting the balance that has too long devalued the fundamental importance of sexual behavior, sexual ideology, and sexuality in the context of utopian social experimentation.

The term "ideology" as used in this study is not intended as a value judgment. It should be kept in mind that an ideology can, and often does, express the parochial viewpoint of a particular country, ethnic group, class, or even sex. But from a broader sociological perspective, an ideology is assumed to be a universal cultural phenomenon which implies a conscious ideational construct that is not only a response to, but also a tool for coming to grips with, social reality and historical change. The psychological roots of ideologies grow out of collective needs, interests, desires, and beliefs. To the extent that these psychic elements are part of the collective unconscious and are raised to the level of consciousness by ideological formulation, an ideology serves the function of collective wish fulfillment. But ideology is not a mere collective expression of individual drives, for the nature of social reality at any given point assures that certain problems will preoccupy people's minds. The formation of ideologies is thus both a function of the individual as collective man and a social process.

Social ideologies provide formalized codifications of expected behavior and socially acceptable ideals; they set forth visions of reality that define the nature and preferred behavior of, and the interrelationship between, man and society. Ideologies arise in a particular sociohistorical context; when that context changes, the system of norms and prescriptive behavior patterns associated with a given ideology ceases to be congruent with reality. At any given point in time different social groups may have different perceptions of and various devices for dealing with reality; in short, cultural alternatives. But on the level of individual consciousness, these cultural alternatives, whether they aim at maintaining social ·stability or seek to promote radical change, cut two ways. Ideology is at once a source of security in its delineation of proper behavior, whether it be in normative terms (morality) or social terms (sexual roles, for example), and a well of anxiety and ambiguity when it fails to provide a comfortable fit with social and historical reality.[9]

People become uneasy when they perceive that historical change either lags behind or leaps ahead of their ideological formulations. This dissatisfaction finds expression in attempts either to arrest the flow of time or to push the temporal sluggard ahead faster than it wants to go. In the former instance, as Karl Mannheim expresses it, "in certain situations the collective unconscious of certain groups obscures the real condition of society both to itself and to others and thereby stabilizes it."[10] On the other hand, in a more radical denial of the reality of the historical moment, "the collective unconscious, guided by wishful representation and the will to action, hides certain aspects of reality. It turns its back on everything which would shake its belief or paralyze its desire to change things."[11]

The situation is complicated by the fact that different aspects of the social ideology of a given group (for instance, sexual, economic, religious) may simultaneously manifest different degrees of adjustment to sociohistorical reality. Thus, economic ideology might be progressive while sexual ideology remains retrogressive. Insofar as modern historical analysis of nineteenth-century American utopian communities has heretofore focused largely on the economic and political aspects of their ideological spectra, it has provided a reductionist vision of their social and intellectual aspects. It has derived their liberal or radical nature primarily from their communistic economic principles and has assumed that other aspects of their overall ideological positions must also have been radical. Too little attention has been paid to the discontinuities among the different elements of their ideological structures.

One area that has received scant attention in the past is utopian sexual ideologies. The term "sexual ideology" is used in this study to indicate that part of the ideological spectrum which is particularly concerned with the social and personal dimensions of human sexuality. It bears a dialectical relation to sexual behavior. Values function, as J. E. Crowley has observed in another context, "as responses to behavior, as efforts to understand, define, and shape it, and therefore as manifestations of the mediation of experience and consciousness."[12] Sexual ideology, from this point of view, serves to assuage the guilts, anxieties, and ambiguities that individuals feel about sexual intercourse and changing sexual mores, as well as to stabilize the social position and routinize the roles of the respective sexes. It finds expression most frequently in accepted "truths" that dictate behavior during intercourse, sex-role models, and sexual power relationships.

Contemporary sexual ideology, for instance, includes the cult of mutual or simultaneous orgasm and the belief that sensual pleasure in a sexual act can and should be separated from other aspects of sexuality, like tenderness, psychological needs, and of course reproduction. Contemporary American society has accepted the statistical authoritativeness of the work of Masters and Johnson, with its emphasis on the physical differences between the sexual responses and capabilities of the sexes and the consequent annihilation of the myth of the vaginal orgasm. In a society in which pleasure has been widely accepted as the chief end of sexual intercourse, mutual orgasm is a device for "legitimizing" or justifying one's own pleasure and avoiding a self-seeking hedonism.

But given a potentially insatiable female sex drive, the male is faced with the likelihood of his failure to provide adequate sexual release for the female, while she is encouraged to be ever challenging orgasmic frontiers. This leads to a metrical vision of sexuality. Affection and warmth or the quality of the sexual experience become unimportant. The honing of technique and the measurement of performance largely in quantitative terms have become the dominant sexual values.[13] The belief persists that once technical mastery is achieved, sexuality becomes a universal panacea. And yet this ideological stance has led to a decline in the physical closeness possible in sexual relations. Increasingly, men and women are encouraged to turn to the products of a technological society to provide uninvolved, essentially autoerotic sexual release as a means of preserving self-esteem. For those women who do not have the multiple orgasmic experience they are told is the essence of femaleness, for those men who feel inadequate to satisfy what is believed to be a ravenous feminine sexual appetite, the alternative is sexual isolation and loneliness.

Despite, or perhaps because of, the increasing isolation in the sex act, society sanctions the increased physical contact of the sexes and an omnipresent overt expression of sexuality. On the social level, modern sexual ideology increasingly maintains that there are really no significant differences between the mental abilities and physical capabilities of the sexes.

This belief, that the sexes, apart from their sexual drives and responses, are quite similar in composition and needs, facilitates the acceptance of female equality.

The roots of these changes in sexual attitudes and behavior lie in late eighteenth- and early nineteenth-century America. Recent historians of women and the family have emphasized that the period from 1780 to 1850 was one of rapid and significant change in sex roles and behavior. During these years the roles of middle-class men and women were increasingly differentiated, as industrialization drew male attention to the affairs of the marketplace, while married women's work remained centered in the home. The ideological formulation of this change, the "cult of domesticity," and the doctrine of separate "spheres" of male and female competence, served to codify sex-role assumptions in a highly conscious fashion. Ironically, with the dwindling importance of household manufactures and the growth of a market economy, and as the scope of woman's role shrank to child-centered activities, women were increasingly told how indispensable their contribution was. For men, home became an Edenic retreat from the amoral, competitive struggle of the world of work, while the institutionalization of motherhood conferred upon women the aura of tutelary deities.[14]

Within the marriage relation between 1740 and 1830 historians have discovered, at least for the New England states, a trend toward a greater degree of personal freedom in mate selection. This new ideal of romantic love in marriage was reflected in greater premarital sexual activity as well. Prior to 1740, as Lawrence Stone notes, the rate of premarital pregnancy was very low; after 1740 it shot up to over 40 percent of all brides.[15] This rise in premarital pregnancy seems to have been indicative of a collapse of control over courtship and perhaps also an increasing privacy available to courting couples. The triumph of the doctrine of romantic love in marriage (the belief that a special affinity existed between two lovers that tied them together while it separated the couple from the rest of the world) led to the expectation of marital happiness or, more precisely, erotic satisfaction as a justification for sexual intercourse. From about 1790 on, the declining importance of the reproductive aspect of sexuality was reflected in a declining birthrate and reduced average household size. These trends were related to both an increased concern with the uniqueness of the individual child, which was quite evident by the 1820s, and the desire, which seems to have been expressed in the greater use of contraception, for more intimate dyadic and familial intimacy. Also indicative of the rise in emotional expectations from marriage was the liberalization of divorce laws in the years between 1815 and 1875, and the consequent steady increase, especially after mid-century, in the divorce rate.[16]

The ideological dimension of nineteenth-century sexuality, as represented by marital advice manuals and the sentimentalization of romantic love, provided a counterthrust to the behavioral trends outlined above. Sexual advisers cautioned against the dangers of marital excess, decried the rising level of degeneracy and indecency, and advocated a greater emphasis on female modesty and virtue as a means of dealing with marital sexuality. From the first decade of the nineteenth century, but with increasing stridency after 1820, moralists began to stress the purity and piety of the "true woman,"[17] a doctrine that countered the behavioral trend (already underway by the late eighteenth century) toward increased erotic sexuality. The growing advocacy of a shrinking feminine sensibility, withdrawn from and repelled by the grosser world of male sensuality, paralleled the separation of women from the marketplace and the sanctification of domesticity. It found expression in the literary mode of sentimentalism. Femininity was cultivated to the exclusion of feminism: "Modesty without decency, love without sex, affection without passion—these were the prudish ingredients with which the sentimentalists worked."[18]

Although sentimentalism, modesty, submissiveness, and domesticity clearly excluded women from the male world, they heightened their influence within the feminine sphere. The cult of the true woman represented an altered social division of labor. Paradoxically, male preemption of the business and political domains achieved logical ideological coherence only with the ascription of the religious, cultural, and domestic realms to the female. Historians concerned with feminism have pointed out the growth of "domestic feminism," a novel creation of the early nineteenth century springing from the central importance attached to the conjugal family and the dramatic stresses accompanying economic modernization. As Daniel Scott Smith describes it, "By defining the family as community, this ideology allowed women to engage in something of a critique of male, materialistic, market society and simultaneously proceed to seize power within the family. Women asserted themselves within the family much as their husbands were attempting to assert themselves outside the home."[19]

The ambiguous response generated by an ideology that equated femaleness with domesticity, docility, and devotion and that emphasized the importance of mutual attraction in the conjugal relation found expression in the literature of cultural criticism. Most of this literature was written by males, many of whom were clergymen, and appeared as an undercurrent in the marital-advice genre. Male anxiety about nineteenth-century sex roles issued in a preoccupation with female fashions and with such deviations from the established norm of feminine behavior as the rising incidence of prostitution and divorce (assumed to be initiated by the wife in the overwhelming majority of cases) and the alarming decline in the fertility rate among the native-born population. The crusade for fashion reform was doubly significant because behavior in this area threatened to undermine the ideological imperatives of purity and motherhood. Tight-laced fashions that crushed the abdomen threatened to destroy the fecundity of the womb, and supposedly provocative dress undermined prescriptive feminine virtue and presented a menacing challenge to the whole structure of sentimental romanticism so carefully constructed to control the erotic potential of sexuality.[20]

Female anxiety and dissatisfaction with Victorian role prescriptions found an outlet in certain aggressive responses that, like male responses, operated within the context of the dominant cultural patterns. As Ann Douglas has so aptly demonstrated, middle-class women during the years 1820–75 were attempting to establish what Harriet Beecher Stowe called a "Pink and White Tyranny," a matrimonial mana energized by "the drive of nineteenth-century American women to gain power through the exploitation of their feminine identity as their society defined it."[21] Though the evidence is far from conclusive, Daniel Scott Smith has convincingly argued that women began to play a central role in family planning in the nineteenth century and that female moral power extended to the control of marital sexual intercourse as recommended in middle-class advice manuals.[22]

The realm of moral value and standards of taste, fashion, and beauty—in short, the whole of religious and cultural life—was feminized in the period from 1820 to 1875. Insofar as it was women who made up the vast majority of consumers of literature, fashion, and religion, their tastes and preferences became dominant in these areas. Women's social aggression and cultural and moral power was objectively expressed in their domination of the ministerial class. Evangelical Protestant ministers, who like women had lost status as a result of the emphasis on a competitive business ethic in industrializing America, and whose power was even further eroded by religious disestablishment (1777–1833), were increasingly forced to accommodate themselves to feminine moral standards and cultural tastes. Indeed, it appears that ministers internalized (though not without a great deal of anxiety and ambiguity) a middle-class feminine role model.[23] No doubt this represented in part an accommodation to the religious sentiments and social opinions of the majority of their parishioners so commonly noted in democratic American religion from the late eighteenth century on; but the current of feminization ran deeper than this.

Broad doctrinal changes indicative of a shift from a patriarchal to a matriarchal conception of the godhead and of the agency of salvation had occurred by the early nineteenth century. An affective, matriarchal vision of God had been superimposed on the older patriarchal, authoritarian Christian substratum. In the iconographic representation of Christ feminine characteristics came to predominate, underlining yet again the confusion and ambiguity inherent in Victorian gender roles. By the 1860s, Harriet Beecher Stowe had clearly perceived the tendency of these cultural and religious changes. In her fictional productions and her occasional essays she expressed the apotheosis of woman as an object of worship. In her later writings woman became synonymous with the church, and not only determinative of the character and characteristics of Christ, but his moral superior.[24] In a piece on the Virgin Mary, entitled "The Blessed Woman," she underscored the connection between purity and the power of woman, and the necessity of female mediation in the process of male salvation. The uniqueness of Christ, she asserted, was that "He had no mortal father. All that was human in him was her nature; it was the union of the divine nature with the nature of pure woman. Hence there was in Jesus more of the pure feminine element than in any other man. It was the feminine element exalted and taken into union with divinity."[25]

Within the family, feminine dissatisfaction with and aggression against role expectations were manifested in a hysterical response. Hysteria, defined largely as a female illness in the nineteenth century, allowed women to seek escape in the sickroom from the oppressively cloying and emotionally exhausting aspects of the feminine role. Maternal illness also readjusted the intrafamilial balance of power by converting the mother, who had previously been the servant of all, into the cynosure of attention, concern, and special consideration.[26]

Both within and without the home, then, female discontent and aggression against sex-role prescriptions found expression. But throughout the nineteenth century most women seem to have accepted their roles and the sphere of activity assigned them. As one feminist historian sums up the feminine response to the world of Victorian gender roles, "They had little objective reason and still less subjective cause to envision advancement (or even comfort) outside it."[27] Nevertheless, however widespread the acceptance of these social norms may have been, there were those of both sexes who found them inadequate, degrading, and psychologically destructive. They developed behavioral alternatives (for instance, organized feminism, free love, and utopian sexuality) even though their sexual value systems often preserved significant elements of the more widely accepted social norms.[28]

In the sphere of sexuality—sexual ideology, mores, behavior, and roles—the connection between social reality and ideology is highly dynamic. Occasionally ideology leaps ahead of behavioral change, but more characteristically changes in values are reactions to changes in behavior.

The frequent conservatism of the pace of change in sexual ideologies underlines the human desire for order and certainty in the relationship between the sexes, and the amount of attention given and the agonizing concern devoted to questions of normative change is a reflection of the fundamental importance of sexuality in social and individual life. At the same time, however, the role of sexual ideologies must be seen in a broader perspective. They are part of a larger complex of social ideologies —religious, political, economic. All these aspects of the ideological position constitute the collective mind of a culture trying to define itself, its limits, and its potentialities.

This study concentrates on the sexual ideologies and behavior of three utopian communities, considering them not as countercultures or subcultures but as alternative cultures. The problems faced by these communities were identical with those faced by the broader society from which they were drawn. As a response to those problems, utopian communities made certain changes, primarily in the simple dyadic form of monogamous marriage and in the nature of the role of woman and the family. In what ways and to what extent were the ideological assumptions that these communitarians shared with nineteenth-century American society changed? What were the bases for the changes in behavior that were manifested? How extensive were these behavioral changes, and to what extent did they necessitate ideological changes? These questions indicate that we are dealing with a situation in which the confrontation between the process of social change and the natural resistance of ideological assumptions to change can be viewed in microcosm. The connection between the individual and social response to change or perceived disorder (the anxiety-generating perception of intolerable discontinuity between values and behavior), as well as the relationship between different levels of that social response, can be studied, and the extent of instituted change, the pragmatic response to perceived historical change, can be evaluated.

These three utopian societies have been chosen for study because they represent the three major alternatives to monogamy: celibacy, polygamy, and pantagamy. Promiscuity, prostitution, and fornication are not considered cultural alternatives to monogamy because they are structurally isomorphic with it. These are acceptable deviations *within* the system of established sexual norms. As long as they can be constrained by moral obloquy so that they do not become excessive in individual life, or too widespread in the culture as a whole, they are functional as outlets for individual unhappiness in sadly mismated pairings, sexual frustration, and aggressive antispouse feelings. They leave the basic institutions of monogamy and the family untouched and do not question the legal and moral validity of the marriage tie. In channeling off discontent and tension generated in the intimacy of the conjugal relation, these deviant responses not only left the behavioral and normative aspects of the Victorian family unchanged and unchallenged, but may well have contributed to the stability of the cultural system. The changes in the marriage system advocated by utopians, on the other hand, bore an allomorphic relation to mainstream nineteenth-century American culture. They offered true cultural alternatives, in both a behavioral and an ideological sense. They represented a challenge to, rather than a confirmation of, the structural integrity of the Victorian cultural definition of the sexual relationship.

The members of all three communities were largely from the farming and artisan classes. Their religious background was heavily evangelical Protestant, and conversion from one denomination to another or to more radical sectarian groups was a common feature of the experience of many communitarians. At Oneida, for example, about nine of every ten individuals in 1849 had come from an evangelical denomination, about one in twenty-five from a rationalistic or freethinking background, and one in twenty from a more militantly millennial sect like the Millerites. Baptist, Methodist, Congregationalist, and Presbyterian religious backgrounds are most frequently encountered among both Shakers and Mormons. Among the Mormons the first three denominations contributed approximately 30 percent each, and the Presbyterian around 10 percent, of the total membership. For Shakers, Baptists and Presbyterians combined probably constituted as much as 60 to 65 percent of all converts.[29]

These three communities, all of which tended to be missionary to some extent, therefore came in conflict with precisely those elements of the American religious establishment that constituted the very heart of its power in the nineteenth century. Their missionary activities threatened the similar but more institutionally oriented activities of a fervent evangelical Protestantism.[30] To the extent that they maintained a parasitic relationship with the missionary activities of dominant Protestantism (early Shaker revivals paralleled the revivals of Baptists and Presbyterians quite closely), they were a threat to the very heart of the dominant Protestant denominations. Their potential effect on nineteenth-century morals and social life through conversions was no doubt miniscule; but the effects of their printed material in an age with a mania for religious literature, as well as the attacks on them by members of the Protestant religious establishment both in the pulpit and in print (which indirectly diffused specific knowledge of their doctrines and practices), must have been much more widespread.[31] Furthermore, utopians affected precisely that part of the religious spectrum whose members were most highly susceptible to ever more emotionally radical conversion experiences. With the increasing participation and influence of women in these evangelical

denominations,[32] the sexual threat of utopians, posed by their alternative systems of sexual relationships, was multiplied in the minds of the
Protestant establishment.

These three utopian communities were also the most outspoken about
their sexual beliefs and practices, and they therefore provide the greatest
body of material on these topics for the researcher. The sexual practices
of most utopian societies certainly do not present as spectacular a vista as
those of the Shakers, Mormons, and Oneidans; but most alternative
communities gave serious attention to the relationship between the sexes.
This study could well have been done on the basis of a broader survey,
but that approach would have drastically crippled the attempt to integrate the study of individual and social levels of thought and behavior.
These three communities were by far the most obnoxious and celebrated
in the public press and popular mind of their day. Contemporaries considered them not as proponents of alternative solutions to social problems, but as part of the problems themselves. They are central to the
communal experience of sexuality, then, not merely in retrospect, but
considered solely from the point of view of their own era.

Biographical introductions on the founders of each of these communities are included in order to suggest the connection between individual
and social manifestations of thought and behavior. Detailed information
about the personal lives and formative experiences of the rank-and-file
members of these communities is rare, so we cannot with any precision
say that the followers of a given figure were necessarily psychologically
similar to their leader. The fact that association with these communities
was voluntary, however, argues that they were concerned with the same
social problems and approved the solutions to them offered in the communitarian setting. Community founders, furthermore, set up the ideological and behavioral structure (primarily in terms of theology) that
became a given for those who came to the communities in later years.
Indeed, the leaders kept a tight rein on the selection of members, thus
insuring their immediate control over the kind of people admitted to
membership and the overall balance and composition of the community.

Only those experiences of these charismatic, theocratic leaders that
seem to have had a direct bearing on their decisions to found alternative
communities and their choices of particular sexual patterns for those
communities have been included here. These biographies are not intended
to be complete but rather suggestive of the relationship between the
experiences of individuals and the ideological and structural dimensions
of the communities they founded. They are capsule psychobiographies,
grounded in Freudian psychological assumptions.[33] Others did not necessarily have similar psychological experiences (although many communitarians may have); but the particular experiences of the charismatic

leaders were such that they were more acutely aware of the tensions, ambiguities, and anxieties of the age, and therefore the systems they devised (initially perhaps to cope with personal problems as much as broader social ones) appealed to others as a way of shaping and ordering their own personal experiences.[34]

Emphasis on the psychological development of communitarian leaders, despite their charismatic power, should not be taken as an attempt to reduce the significance of utopianism to a psychohistorical dimension. As we noted above, the Oneida, Shaker, and Mormon communities were quite homogeneous in composition. The overwhelming majority of Shakers, for instance, had a common ethnic, religious, regional, and class background. Among the three communities, only the tendency toward immigrant Saints among the Mormons diverges significantly from this pattern. The collective or sociological dimension of the formative process in these communities is also reflected in what Neil Smelser has called the "structural strain" generated by the discontinuity between values and behavior in the broader society. This strain was clearly evident in the fears and ambiguities built into the sexual norms of nineteenth-century America. Among those who chose to pursue personal solutions in the context of an alternative cultural value system, there was also a predominant sense of what Smelser has called "the failure of social control," the belief that the normative structure and behavioral prescriptions of society are not functioning adequately in the empirical world.[35]

Motivations for voluntary communal association were highly complex, but the level of consciousness and commitment required of individual communitarians testified to the seriousness of their concern with social values and their alienation from the accepted behavioral models of their culture. Utopian societies offered the promise of a resolution of psychological and social tensions and alternative modes of ordering experience that many of their adherents hoped would provide more cooperation and less conflict and antagonism in interpersonal relations. In the main body of this work we shall have an opportunity to see to what extent the promise of cultural alternatives was realized in the area of sexual relations and sex roles among the Shakers, the Mormons, and members of the Oneida Community.

Part I 🥀 The True Plan of Life: Nineteenth-Century American Attitudes toward the Self and Sexuality

Chapter 1 🎐 The Problem of the Self

It is allowed, that the cause of most actions, good or bad, may
be resolved into the love of ourselves; but the self-love of
some men, inclines them to please others; and the self-love of
others is wholly employed in pleasing themselves. This makes
the great distinction between virtue and vice. Religion is the
best motive of all actions, yet religion is allowed to be the
highest instance of self-love.

—Jonathan Swift, "Thoughts on Various Subjects, Moral
  and Diverting"

In marriage, a man becomes slack and selfish, and undergoes
a fatty degeneration of his moral being.

—Robert Louis Stevenson, *Virginibus Puerisque*

*T*he problems presented by sexual behavior, sexuality, and sex
roles were, of course, not unique to utopian societies. They were
problems of vital interest as well to the broader social context of
which communitarians formed a part. This concern was an expression of
a profound malaise about the place of sex in human life, the socially most
acceptable form of relationship between men and women, the proper
balance between the social and personal dimensions of human experience, and the nature and direction of the progress of civilization. Utopians, through their frank espousal of definite solutions to problems such
as abortion, prostitution, and the rising incidence of divorce, helped to
keep these matters before the public eye and, through the opposition they
generated by their proposed solutions, served to clarify the positions
taken on these questions by the broader society. Nevertheless, both
utopians and their opponents remained essentially ambivalent in the
attitudes and feelings that underlay their particular stands.

At bottom, sexual questions were an integral part of a broader ethical-
social problem that went to the heart of nineteenth-century American

culture. This was the question of the role of the self in society and culture. What were the individual's rights and responsibilities vis-à-vis social institutions? How should conflicts between individual desires and social needs be decided? What role could the individual play in the progress of civilization? The exceptional interest exhibited in sexual questions in the nineteenth century reflected the realization that such questions were intimately bound up with interpersonal relations and that certainly no other social act was more closely linked to the individual self. The realization that sexual relationships and concepts of sexuality were in a state of flux, and that therefore basic assumptions about the relationships between the self and society were also being questioned, only heightened that interest.

Perhaps the best way to approach this background to the sexual questions of such immediate interest to utopians and their opponents alike is through a conceptual reading of the literature (mainly admonitory and hortatory) of those who sought to defend society from what they perceived as destructive changes in sexual behavior and concepts of sexuality.

At the heart of much of this writing is the concept of "selfishness," with its concomitant concern with the nature of the "true" or normatively positive self. This concern was associated with the Puritan tradition in America and represented a confluence of the religious tradition of the Reformation (and especially the England of the Puritan Revolution) with the rationality of eighteenth-century utilitarian ethics.

The Reformation presented the problem of the self in its modern form: the assertiveness of self (autonomy) versus the agony of self (responsibility). As one student of the period expressed it, "The Protestant reformation begins a vast new experiment in the culture of the self and the systems of self-direction."[1] With its doctrine of the priesthood of all believers, the authority of ecclesiastical institutions was undermined; and in its place arose the idea of the sufficiency of individual understanding and intuition to establish religious truth. At the same time the terror of the isolated self, the burden of salvation resting squarely on the shoulders of each individual, created ambiguous feelings about the moral autonomy of the self.

A recent study by Michael Zuckerman contends that the relationship between the individual and society "became markedly more tortured in the late sixteenth and seventeenth centuries. Something seems to have come unhinged in the ways people were wont to live with one another and in their aspirations for, and anxieties about, group life. Something seems to have driven them simultaneously to seek a new purity of personal identity and covenanted community alike."[2] Zuckerman argues that the dynamic tension between the values of self and community, rooted in an excessive concern for morality and purity and a hypersensitivity to sin and purification in this period, issued in a new conception of selfhood: "In many ways it was from the concern for distinguishing, say, the saved from the damned or the civilized from the savage, and upon the structures of guilt which were built on that concern, that the modern idea of the self emerged."[3]

In the eighteenth century the focus of the problem of the self shifted dramatically. With the acceptance of an increasingly secular basis for morality and individual behavior, the autonomy of the self was taken for granted. The social nature of the problem—the responsibility of the individual not to God or to the church but to his fellows—became paramount. Utilitarian ethics, following the lead of Hobbesian psychology, accepted selfishness as the irreducible essence of human nature and the primary motive of all conduct. Even those who rejected a secularized approach shared the belief of Bernard de Mandeville and Adam Smith that self-interest was the driving force behind all ethical and social behavior.

Jonathan Edwards, for example, maintained that "self-love" was "the entity of the thing" and that therefore a sentient being would presume to be good only that "which agrees immediately and directly with its own being."[4] Self-love for Edwards becomes essential to both social and religious life, personal well-being, and moral obligation: "Self-love is a man's love to his own good. . . . Any good whatsoever that a man any way enjoys, or anything that he takes delight in—it makes it thereby his own good. . . . 'Tis impossible that a man should delight in any good that is not his own, for to say that would be to say that he delights in that in which he does not delight."[5] The essence of this eighteenth-century position is sensibility, the source of what Edwards called the "affections," or the broadly conative quality of the mind. Self-love, grounded in the affections, was the force that moved the will to action. Without it man remained inert and passive and thus incapable of relating to God.[6]

Less religious figures shared Edwards's moral position, but preferred to call the foundation of the morality of self-interest the passions. "Passions" was a broadly conceived term that included not only all aspects of bodily pleasure, but also such intangible desires as the need for honor and power. But whereas the Edwardean system assumed that rational pursuit of self-love would naturally lead to pure love (or love of God), since an individual would always choose that which was most perfectly capable of satisfying his affectional nature, secular thinkers assumed that there would be conflicts between individual desires.

By the late 1740s, Americans had developed a social ethic of enlightened self-interest based on the frank acceptance of individual acquisitiveness. The persistence of an older value system, however, tempered the ethic of self-interest. Traditional values led, on the one hand, to an insistence on the need to restrain the excesses of private interests in order to preserve public order and, on the other, to a belief that the virtue of benevolence (the desire to promote the good of others) would moderate the new ethic in practice.[7]

The Madisonian political system of "checks and balances" is representative of the most widely accepted eighteenth-century solution to the problem of social egotism. Single-minded pursuit of self-interest was deemed to be the nature of man. The secular solution was to balance individual interests through the very operation of self-interest itself. If each individual were to pursue his own self-interest vigorously, a rough equilibrium would be established. "Ambition," Madison wrote, "must be made to counteract ambition." Within the context of a Lockean social contract, the social egoism of individuals, or its organized expression in "faction," could be directed toward constructive ends. As Madison expressed it, "The inference . . . is that the *causes* of faction cannot be removed, and that relief is only to be sought in the means of controlling its *effects*."[8]

The question of personal autonomy as opposed to religious or ethical responsibility was of prime importance to the conception of self and selfishness. The latter term seems to have been first used in 1640, and its initial use—"a carnal, selfish spirit"—suggests that it was linked to matters of bodily pleasure from the outset. The related terms "self-pollution" and "self-abuse," synonyms for masturbation that came into use about 1628 and 1728, respectively, provide additional evidence that the sexual self was increasingly coming to be considered an ethical problem. During the early years of the eighteenth century, masturbation came to be a problem of social significance,[9] and the corresponding assertion of the self to provide ballast for the unsteady skiff of human sexuality found expression in such terms as "self-determination" as a synonym for "free will," which was first used in 1683, and the even more apposite "self-control," coined by the moralist Lord Shaftesbury in 1711.[10]

In the sexual life of Enlightenment Europeans, the need for such control or balance was apparent in the Continental peregrinations of the erotomanic Jacques Casanova de Seingalt (1725–98) and the phenomenal sexual exploits of James Boswell (1740–95), which issued in almost incessant afflictions with gonorrhea. It was even more immediately manifest in the life and philosophic speculations of the Marquis Donatien de Sade (1740–1814), whose excesses not only asserted the right of the individual to nullify the self-interest of others (if not their very existence), but also maintained the absolute freedom of the individual even to the point of the destruction of the self through the degradation and enslavement of the will.

The Enlightenment assertion of the value of the individual and the function of the assertive self in maintaining a balance, an equilibrium in the life of man, remained important in the nineteenth century. But below this lay another layer of meaning, which revealed the intellectual distance separating the nineteenth century from the eighteenth. The problem was no longer simply a concern that the independent self develop the internal powers to control its own desires and physical responses, or moral balance within the self; it was now a question of egoism out of control, the social threat of the autonomous individual. The image of the self-sufficient individual, who owed little or nothing to society, gave rise to a literary figure, part romantic innocent and part solitary outcast, that was the dialectic focus of the cultural myth embodied in the Daniel Boone saga and the Leatherstocking Tales.

Timothy Flint's biography of Boone was one of the essential elements in creating the vision of the Kentucky frontiersman that came to predominate in the popular mind of Jacksonian America. Boone was depicted as at once one of nature's noblemen and an opponent of civilization. "He presents himself to us," Flint wrote, "as a new man, the author and artificer of his own fortunes, and showing from the beginning rudiments of character, of which history has recorded no trace in his ancestors."[11] But the backwoodsman as "solitary individual" has an antisocial streak, too. He has removed to the Kentucky wilderness to find a life in which "the indulgence of none but natural desires and pure affections would not be deadened by the *selfishness*, vanity, and fear of ridicule, that are the harvest of what is called *civilized and cultivated* life."[12]

The Boone myth is part of a broader literary tradition reflecting the cultural transition from a value system emphasizing innate moral values common to all men to one based on the power of the individual will to master the passions and shape the unique moral individual. As the sense of control and power, the dynamic force of the will in organizing the personality, grew with the spread of democratic ideology and the acceleration of industrialism in the Jacksonian era, the eighteenth-century value system based on virtue passed over into the character-oriented one so characteristic of the nineteenth century. As Marvin Meyers has brilliantly demonstrated, however, Jacksonian Americans remained ambivalent about the dramatic changes their society was undergoing. They expressed their anxieties about social, economic, and cultural change in a body of nostalgic literature that emphasized the purity of the agricultural life industrialism was destroying, the temptations and galling restraints of civilization, and a sentimental longing for a more clearly defined and, in their oversimplified formulation, less demanding moral code.[13]

The anxiety generated by the new normative system based on character (the psychological fear of standing alone as the isolated, naked self) and fundamental doubts about the capacity of the individual to create the moral self in a rapidly changing world came together in the mythic concept of the frontiersman. The traditional formulation of the myth allayed fears of moral incapacity, and assuaged guilt feelings arising from the sense of having betrayed parental values, by combining character and virtue in the person of the frontiersman as culture hero.

The moral nature of the mythic Daniel Boone confirms this cultural expression. He is faced with an archetypal environment that heightens his isolation, the necessity for moral self-creation, and the consequent temptation to pride and self-absorption. He survives in the primitive world of the id because he is "a man of the kindliest nature, and of the tenderest affections."[14] In other words, he is a man of virtue. His innate moral capacity finds expression in benevolence, which serves as a check to self-interest. At the same time, however, in a world in which the self is in perilous danger of drowning in the pool of its own reflection, mere virtue is not sufficient to salvation. To overcome "the heathen rivalry and selfishness of the present generation," the force of character, the "utmost exertion of self-possession and fortitude," will be required.[15]

That preoccupation with individual "force of character" was clearly a dominant concern in nineteenth-century America. This was indicated by two key phrases, "self-culture" (which became part of American speech patterns through an address of William Ellery Channing in 1837) and "self-made man" (which entered the language in 1832). As John Cawelti has demonstrated, it was Ralph Waldo Emerson, apostle of the self-culture cult, who was the chief artificer of the synthesis of the success ethic and self-improvement. Ironically, "believing in the tremendous creative power inherent in all individuals, the self culture movement was, in many respects, far more sympathetic to individual mobility and social innovation than moralistic apostles of the Protestant ethic like Henry Ward Beecher and T. S. Arthur."[16]

Even though a certain romantic belief in the value of the self and of consciousness as the heightened expression of that self inheres in the Transcendentalist tradition associated with Channing, the actions of the grasping, greedy self of the industrial order and the existence of southern chattel slavery raised serious doubts about the social value of selfhood in nineteenth-century American thought. Although the self-made man became a staple character in the American social imagination after 1850, the concept remained, even in its classical formulation, highly equivocal.

This ambivalence comes out very clearly in the self-help guidebooks in which the authors, largely Protestant clergymen, sought to provide the keys to ethical success. As John Cawelti characterizes the underlying assumptions of these "apostles of self help," they found themselves "caught in a curious paradox: men must be encouraged to pursue individual economic advancement, but they must do so without wishing to be rich or to rise dramatically in social status. The man who did not work diligently to improve his condition was corrupt and degraded, but the real purpose of industry was not wealth but moral merit."[17] Man was not to build a fortune, but to build character.

The underlying sense of moral doubt evident in the doctrine of the self-made man was also clear in Horace Greeley's attack on individualism at mid-century. "This is predominantly an age of Individualism," he wrote, "(it would hardly be polite to say Egotism), wherein 'the Sovereignty of the Individual'—that is the right of every one to do pretty nearly as he pleases—is already generally popular, and visibly gaining ground daily."[18] He was less equivocal in his condemnation of the same phenomenon a decade later:

> The will of our age, the main source of its aberrations, is a morbid Egotism, which overrides the gravest social necessities in its mad pursuit of individual, personal ends. . . .
> . . . Nor do I regard the strong tendency of our time to wild, ultra Individualism, as an element of any Progress, but that made by Eve at the serpent's suggestion. . . . Admit the legitimacy of egotism, or the selfish pursuit of happiness by each Individual, and a government of despotism seems to me a logical and practical necessity. . . .
> . . . [In the moral realm people are] throwing themselves on their Individual Sovereignty, and trampling on every dictate of Duty, in subserviency to their own selfish lusts.[19]

This was the essence of what Robert V. Remini has called "go-ahead" Jacksonian democratic America. The responsibilities of individuals were "to themselves and their own goods. Never mind the neighbors. Let neighbors keep their distance and mind their own business. The needs of the community in maintaining a stable society were problems for 'others' to bother about—whoever those others might be."[20] The extent of this concern with the self and the sense of power egoism evoked, as well as its connection with industrialism, were clear in the plethora of "self" words that entered the American vocabulary after mid-century. Self-rakers (1857), the self-cocker for firearms (1863), self-rising flour (1865), self-feeders for stamps (1876), and the self-binder (1879) are a few examples of this trend. By the 1880s the concern with the problem of selfishness had given rise to two new constructions, "selfward" (1887) and "selfwardness" (1889).[21]

This tendency toward self-absorption was widely noted in the accounts of foreign travelers who visited antebellum America. They were most outspoken about the breakdown of traditional values and the lack of discipline in American child-rearing practices. Much of this critique was inferred from observed behavior—the hyperactivity, utter disregard of traditions of deference, and outright defiance of authority characteristic of American children. The Scotsman William Chambers, who traveled widely in the United States in the 1850s, was so vexed by the ubiquitous presence of children in American hotels (resulting from the widespread practice of young families taking up semipermanent residence there) that he declared: "Everywhere these youngsters are a sore trial of temper to the guests generally. Flying up and down the passages with hoops, yelling, crying, and tumbling about in everybody's way, they are clearly out of place, and constitute an unhappy and outré feature of American hotel life."[22]

Frederick Marryat, who visited some two decades earlier, gave an account of resolute disobedience in a three-year-old boy, commenting that it was "one instance of a thousand which I witnessed during my sojourn in the country."[23] "How is it possible," he asked, "for a child to be brought up in the way that it should go, when he is not obedient to the will of his parents?"[24] He was repelled by "such remarkable specimens of uncontrolled will in children" and contended that "the principal cause of it is the total neglect of the child by the father, and his absence in his professional pursuits, and the natural weakness of most mothers when their children are left altogether to their care and guidance."[25]

The result was that Europeans found Americans "egoistic, stubborn, and self-seeking."[26] The general aura of cupidity that characterized public life in America, as one traveler remarked, was reflected in "the tone of callous selfishness which pervades the conversation, and the absence of all pretensions to pure and lofty principle. The only restraint upon these men is the law, and he is evidently considered the most skillful in his vocation who contrives to overreach his neighbor, without incurring its penalties."[27] From the European point of view, the fundamental causes of American egoism remained a faulty upbringing and the "youth of America being under no control." Frederick Marryat best expressed the overall repugnance American society evoked in the cultivated European: "The self-will arising from this fundamental error [permissive child rearing] manifests itself throughout the whole career of the American's existence, and consequently it is a self-willed nation *par excellence*."[28]

Although it was admitted that the evils of self-absorption threatened the self-reliant, nineteenth-century American culture felt that it had two antidotes which could preserve the balance, the moral tone of the individual: self-control, or the power of the individual will; and self-culture, or social control, which frequently merged with the power of the example of the totally selfless woman of romantic mythology. Willpower was another of the shibboleths of popular nineteenth-century moral thought. It reinforced the essential insistence upon the primacy of self in society;

the essentially theological nature of the problem; and the competence of the unaided self to accomplish all things. Theoretically, the power of the will was a built-in regulator that ensured that the appetitive and aggressive nature of the assertive ego would remain within socially acceptable bounds.[29]

But beneath the superficial level of assertion of the power of the ego lay a very deep disquiet about the nature of that self and the possibility that it could successfully set its own limits. This found expression in what was one of the most powerful metaphorical images of the nineteenth century—slavery. Certainly the growing awareness of the political and moral problems inherent in southern chattel slavery contributed to the heightened popular sensitivity to the levels of meaning drawn from the literal institution; but in a society in which freedom and self-assertion were such central values, slavery was a particularly prepotent figurative device. It had wider cultural significance as well. The metaphorical use of slavery broadened and deepened the abolitionist critique of the slave system while it helped to focus and intensify sectional animosities in the antebellum years through the implicit ascription of a deviant cultural role to the plantation South. The South functioned as an inverted image of the cultural ideal of the North, upon which all the aggression rooted in hatred of the self for its failure to live up to the ideal could be projected.

The slavery metaphor expressed at the same time the fear of a social threat to the autonomy of the ego and the realization of the weakness of the independent self to control its antisocial impulses or, on its most basic level, to preserve itself from destruction. In the former instance it was applied to all individuals or groups whose autonomy was restricted by larger or more powerful social units. In the latter case, slavery served as a figurative expression of the impotence of the will, the failure of self-control in the face of extreme temptation.

This was generally the case in reform literature: temperance, antidrug, antitobacco, antiprostitution, and feminist. In the temperance field, for instance, the connection between alcohol addiction and slavery was continually made. One of the more forthright statements of this connection was that of George W. Bungay in a pamphlet entitled *Freemen, or Slaves?* There is, he maintained,

> more than one kind of slavery, and the man who is a drunkard, whether he be black or white, is a slave, and habit—the habit of drinking—is his master. . . . You cannot see the chains which entangle him . . . because they are not outside—they are liquid chains, and he has poured them down his throat. But you see that he is not free; his feet are bound in fetters so that he cannot walk; his hands are hampered with gyves, so that he can not use them to

advantage; even his brains and his tongue feel the effects of this degrading slavery. He does not think like a freeman, he does not talk like a freeman, he does not walk like a freeman; he is a poor slave, the slave of a tyrant who takes away his money and refuses to give him any food or clothing or shelter in return.[30]

The use of the slavery trope in relation to marriage was also quite common at mid-century, as was its use in castigating the feminine abuse of *la mode*, as the current term "slaves of fashion" indicates. By the 1840s the idea of slavery, not only as physical but also as "mental bondage," the sufferings of "enslaved minds," had been extended by feminists to stand as a synecdoche of the feminine condition.[31]

American literature of the period 1830–70 was concerned in a very immediate way with the problems of self versus social institution and democracy versus strident individualism, and with the threat to personal autonomy posed by strong social and religious institutions (especially Roman Catholicism and alternative communities) requiring unquestioning loyalty. The question of free will and control of the will by others was clearly at issue here; and animal magnetism, as in Nathaniel Hawthorne's *Blithedale Romance*, was used as a variation on the slavery metaphor.

Perhaps the best example of the genre, however (particularly because it was consciously structured to fit the accepted iconography of this type of literature by a self-conscious stylist), was Walt Whitman's *Franklin Evans* (1842), which poignantly weaves together a tale of the degradation of slavery and enslavement to alcohol. A similar use of the slavery metaphor provided the ironic dimension of Harriet Beecher Stowe's *Uncle Tom's Cabin* (1852). The white master class is really the enslaved group. Augustine St. Claire, although a "good" man, lacks the willpower to free himself from the economic shackles of slavery; Simon Legree is the debased slave of his passions. Only the lowly slave, Uncle Tom, is really free, because he has control over his own will. His body is unfree; his soul (or will) is free.

The belief that the individual will often failed to provide the necessary restraint in the face of temptation, which served as the foundation for the popularity of the metaphoric use of slavery, was also reflected in the note that it was deemed necessary to add to the definition of "will" in Webster's unabridged dictionary for 1850: "*Will* is often quite a different thing from *desire*."[32] The anxiety generated by the contemplation of selfishness in the world and the tremendous emphasis placed upon unselfishness also indicate that the former was the rule in social behavior and the latter was the exception. This is scarcely surprising, and one would expect such a state to have prevailed in most Western industrialized, capitalist societies; but nineteenth-century Americans were extremely concerned about the discrepancy and considered it to be the chief social problem they faced. In their minds redressing the balance between self and society became a matter of grave import for the progress, if not the survival, of civilization itself. Some sense of the seriousness of the problem can be gathered from the capsule homily contained in the definition of "selfishness" in Webster's 1850 edition:

> the exclusive regard of a person to his own interest or happiness; or that supreme self-love or self-preference which leads a person in his actions, to direct his purposes to the advancement of his own interest, power, or happiness, without regarding the interest of others. Selfishness in its worst or unqualified sense, is the very essence of human depravity, and stands in direct opposition to BENEVOLENCE, which is the essence of the divine character. As God is *love*, so man in his natural state, is selfishness.[33]

That the human depravity observed by Webster was very attractive to Americans of the age of Jackson was underscored by the romantic cult of Byron, or American Don Juanism, which grew up in the decade 1830–40. A burgeoning industrial economy, the rapid development of transportation and communications systems, and restless westward migration provided almost incredible physical evidence to support the optimistic faith in human capacity and potentiality. Given this environment, the general confidence in the power of the individual to establish values and make judgments predicated on the pure force of his own personality, often in defiance of established authority and convention, became increasingly pervasive. This self-centered optimism was reflected in nineteenth-century religious life in the emotional revivalism centered on individual salvation, which provided the basis for the romantic belief in the perfectibility of the self—for ultimate sanctification in *this* life. Transcendentalism, with its belief in the spark of divinity in every man that must be nourished and liberated, was a secular expression of this belief in the ultimate perfectibility of man.[34]

The romantic solution to the problem of the self in American culture was at once less pessimistic than the eighteenth-century belief in the need to balance competing self-interests and more restrictively structured than the feeling of illimitable grandeur the Byronic model offered. Its more optimistic aspect was represented by the concept of self-culture, which was very closely allied with the idea of the self-made man. But even in the act of exercising what William Ellery Channing called the "self-forming power," a tension was generated between self-realization and self-control, between self-interest and social duty. Thus, Channing could at one point describe self-culture as "the care which every man owes to himself, to the unfolding and perfecting of his nature," in order that we be enabled to "see in ourselves germs and promises of a growth to which no bounds can be set, to dart beyond what we have actually gained to the idea of Perfection as the end of our being."[35]

This mood of limitless secular perfection is tempered, however, by a nagging anxiety about the egocentric force of the "free, illimitable soul" of man. Channing's solution to the dilemma of the unfettered self is to assert the omnipotence of the process of self-culture; if man makes himself, he must complete his handiwork in a disciplined, organized way, so that duty remains of more importance than inclination. The belief that duty will triumph over selfishness, though, remains an article of emotional, romantic faith. "No man," Channing writes, "however narrowed to his own interest, however hardened by selfishness, can deny, that there springs up within him a great idea in opposition to interest, the idea of Duty."[36] Self-culture became the handmaiden of duty, or social conscience: "No part of self-knowledge is more important than to discern clearly these two great principles, the self-seeking and the disinterested; and the most important part of self culture is to depress the former and to exalt the latter, or to enthrone the sense of duty within us."[37]

But there were many who lacked faith to credit the ability of the unaided self to accomplish the internalization of virtue, or a social conscience. They shared the romantic faith to the extent that they abhorred any overt external restraint on the freedom of the individual, yet they felt the necessity of a broader reinforcement of societal values. The perspective of most of this group was primarily religious, and consequently they saw the problem in theological terms: how to reestablish the link between man and God. Because the individual will was too often enslaved and impotent, the answer had to come from outside the self.[38] It is not surprising that in a society whose religious life was dominated by evangelical Protestant groups, in which the religious role of women (always important) had become central by the mid-nineteenth century, the putative solution was found in the socioethical power of woman. Or, to be more specific, the solution lay in the "true woman" in her maternal and uxorial roles: woman the savior of man and thus of civilization.[39] This was reiterated (no doubt in the hope of getting people to believe it) in innumerable instances in the manners and marriage manuals so popular in the nineteenth century. One example will suffice. The exhortation to self-denial goes out to all from this secular pulpit:

> That which separates us from God, and produces all the mental
> disorders under which we labor, is selfishness. There is no means of
> returning to God, and to true order, except by denying self; and this
> we do when we seek, in all the various relations of life, to discharge
> our duties for the sake of good to others. Of ourselves we cannot act

from this high motive; it comes from God, who alone is good, and from whom all good flows. But we can shun the evil of selfishness, by denying it the gratification of its inordinate desires, and compelling ourselves faithfully to do whatever useful thing comes in our way; and then the love of doing good will flow in our minds, and we shall feel a higher delight than ever before thrilled through our bosoms.[40]

But those chosen are women, who are peculiarly suited to the arduous but essential task. In her capacities of wife and mother,

> self-denial and regard for the good of others she is now more than ever called upon to exercise; and in their exercise she can alone find true peace of mind. All turning of thought inward upon self as an object of primary consideration, all looking to the attainment of selfish ends and selfish gratification, will react upon her with a disturbing force; for she cannot do this without interfering in some way with the comfort or happiness of those in whose comfort and happiness her own is inextricably involved. The mother who neglects her child in the eager pursuit of some phantom of pleasure, or for the attainment of ease, will make that child unhappy, and herself doubly so; for she can no more expel from her mind a consciousness of having wronged that child, than she can prevent being disturbed by the evidences of her neglect. The same will be true if she think more of her own ease and pleasure than she does of her husband's comfort.[41]

The conclusion was plain to even the dullest of readers; "true happiness" lies in the observance of this code for the female, and salvation for *everyone* lies in emulating that code of behavior. The romantic and evangelical religious traditions merged at this point, and the doctrine of love (selfless and holy), personified in the ethereal ideal of womanhood, became the key to the destruction of selfishness, the last great obstacle to the attainment of human moral and social perfection. For

> to act thus brings more than an earthly reward; by such a life, she is prepared for heavenly felicities, which consist alone in the delight that springs from doing good. In heaven *no one* thinks of self, nor seeks his own gratification; but *all*, from genuine love, seek the good of others, and their happiness consists in the delight that springs from the attainment of their ends. If we wish to come into a heavenly society at death, we must act from heavenly principles here. There is no other way. This is the straight and narrow path that leads to eternal felicity, and *all* who wish to gain that desirable state must walk therein.[42]

The feeling that the old patriarchal god is moribund, if not yet quite deceased, and a resigned, though not openly avowed, sense of the secularization of society lie behind this attitude. The pervasive invocation of the musty relics of the pagan lares and penates was a pathetically futile effort to fill the void left by the neglect of a god who had failed to keep in step with the material progress of civilization. Lip service was paid to these chthonian deities; they were identified with woman, the last pure hope of mankind; and they were endowed with all those qualities in which nineteenth-century America knew itself to be sadly lacking.

This is clearly delineated in the popular Horatio Alger tales, in which the conflict between social obligation and self-assertiveness in the business world becomes central. It is virtue and service that in the end justify success; but the implication that some social sacrifice is necessary to the achievement of success is also obvious. This sacrifice or martyrdom is most often that of the mother, or of the family of origin of the waif who seeks to "re-create" himself. The family, and especially the mother, are necessary to the foundation of the values that will preserve him during his quest, but he must be free of them if social mobility is to be possible. The reflection of the feminization of virtue in the romantic ideal of the selfless woman, therefore, especially as represented in motherhood, forms the ideological basis of Alger's conception.[43]

The extreme concern of nineteenth-century culture about selfishness represented an expression, on a broader level, of the chief sexual problem that faced society. It was preeminently a moral question: whether there was any value in the erotic aspect of sexual intercourse apart from its accepted reproductive function. This was clearly demonstrated in one book of manners in the belief that newlyweds are peculiarly subject to the hereditary sin and "perverting influence" of selfishness. "If they give themselves up," the nubile reader is admonished, "to a mere life of pleasure, they will commit a great mistake, for *pleasure*, sought as an end, always defeats itself. To do this is to act from mere selfishness—a motive entirely unworthy of the human mind."[44]

Sex for purposes of reproduction was "natural," "true," and acceptable; all other sexual behavior was perverse. The key to the unnaturalness of pleasurable sex was selfishness. In fact, so integrally related were selfishness and the problems of sexual morality in the nineteenth-century mind that masturbation became with some writers a vast synecdoche for a whole catalog of sexual deviancy. As one writer expressed it, late in the century:

> Onanism is a term of comprehensive meaning, applicable in a broad sense to all forms of sexual stimulation employed by either sex, singly or mutually, to produce orgasm in *unnatural* ways—i.e.,

otherwise than by coitus. The onanistic acts are as follows: "Withdrawal," or the offence of Onan; "coitus in os"; "coitus inter femora"; pederasty; bestiality; "mutual masturbation"; "self-pollution" (masturbation, auto-sexual indulgence), etc. *None of these acts have in view the perpetuation of the species, and all are therefore perversions.*[45]

No clearer expression of the urgent need for social values to counter unrestrained self-interest can be found. Hawthorne's serpentine force of egotism[46] had penetrated even the bosom of the family; the polluted self threatened the perversion and subversion of all moral value. For nineteenth-century American culture, in the struggle between self and society, civilization hung in the balance.

Chapter 2 🦪 The Violation of Truth and Nature: Some Anxieties and Ambiguities of Nineteenth-Century American Culture about Sexuality and the "True" Woman

A *perfect Woman, nobly planned,*
To warn, to comfort, and command;
And yet a Spirit still, and bright
With something of angelic light.

—Wordsworth, "She was a Phantom of Delight"

In der Rache und in der Liebe ist das Weib barbarischer als
der Mann [In vengeance and love woman is more barbarous
than man].

—Friedrich Nietzsche, *Jenseits von Gut und Böse*

*T*he failure of moral self-confidence in nineteenth-century American culture was expressed not only in terms of the problem of selfishness but also, in light of the romantic-evangelical emphasis on the preeminent feminine moral capacity, in a deep-seated uncertainty about the "real" nature of woman and a fear that her supererogatory moral goodness might be insufficient to achieve social perfection. Fundamental doubt about feminine selfishness, and, at the same time, the need to believe in woman as moral angel, was one of the most frequent themes of nineteenth-century advice literature.

Chief among the concepts that expressed this mixture of credulity and distrust with which woman was viewed, as well as doubts about the inevitable moral progress of civilization, was another of the major catchwords of the era—"true"—with all its synonyms and amplifications: "pure," "selfless," "ideal," and "loyal." From a broader social perspective, the central moral concern with the true and its antonymous reflections in society—deceit, hypocrisy, and falsehood—indicates the realization of the disparity between ideal and real in nineteenth-century America; the awareness that despite persistent spiritual belief, materialism and relativism were really central to their vision of the world.

Although the term "true" retained its original sense of loyalty to a code in nineteenth-century speech (witness the origin of the phrase "true grit" in the 1840s), which gave it secure roots in the Puritan tradition, its usefulness to social ideology of the period was vastly expanded in the 1840s and 1850s.[1] In its usage as a normative adjective applied to the social code, it supported the idea that there were established "spheres" or "stations in life," which delimited the boundaries of the possible for individuals in a social context. Faithful observance of class, sex, and age distinctions constituted the standard ideal of behavior; a person legitimately held a position in society, had a public identity, only insofar as he observed the limitations laid out for the particular sphere to which he (or she) was born. The true was that which was consonant with the standard pattern. This was essentially a reinforcement of bourgeois virtue, which seems to have been derived from the doctrine of the "calling." It was directly related to questions of fashion control (the enactment of sumptuary laws among the Puritans was a model), based on attacks against luxury as a violation of the idea of order and regularity, and to the failure of self-control and willpower discussed in the last chapter.

The chaos and single-minded self-centeredness necessary for success in the business world meant that the burden of remaining true to the social code again fell squarely on the shoulders of women. They were continually admonished "to do everything in its proper time, to keep everything in its right place, and to use everything for its proper use."[2] This order and regularity would preserve the gains made by the male against a refractory, treacherous, wild, filthy, and disorderly world. A major part of that feminine order required a woman to know her place both within the family and in society at large: "Many persons are so adroit in purchasing, in cutting and contriving, that they can obtain articles at a much cheaper rate than others: but perhaps when reduced by those means to their lowest cost, the amount not only exceeds what ought to be afforded, but the article so obtained ill accords with the rank in life, or confined income of the purchaser, and only exposes her to ridicule or censure."[3]

Reinforcing this initial level of meaning, especially after mid-century, were other connotative significations that associated the term "true" with "natural" and "real." The latter concern was of central importance to American culture down to the end of the century. Of the nine definitions for "true" listed in Webster's unabridged dictionary for 1850, for instance, five are concerned with that which is "genuine, pure, real, not counterfeit, adulterated, or false." Two others equate "true" with "right." This extreme concern for the "true" as antonym of "false" indicates, as we have suggested, a society in which a vast disparity is perceived between appearances and reality, ideals and practice. Such a society is a society in transition, in which old moral values, although still publicly enunciated as the norm, are privately ignored if not consistently countermanded. This concern with hypocrisy and the inveterate distrust it revealed found their classic expression in the growing concern over confidence men and their nefarious practices in duping the unwary. The term "confidence man" first entered American popular speech in 1849, and "confidence game" dates from the period directly after the Civil War. By the mid-1870s the concern had spawned a verbal form, "to confidence," or practice the confidence game on someone.

Neil Harris has commented on the way Americans flocked to see the hoaxes of P. T. Barnum, expressing at once, like children who had lost their innocence, the need to believe and the deep-seated distrust of the great prestidigitator. Harris writes: "They [hoaxers] understood, most particularly Barnum understood, that the opportunity to debate the *issue* of falsity, to discover how deception had been practiced, was even more exciting than the discovery of fraud itself. The manipulation of a prank, after all, was as interesting a technique in its own right as the presentation of genuine curiosities. Therefore, when people paid to see frauds, thinking they were true, they paid again to hear how the frauds were committed."[4] The deep psychological attraction of the fraud to the nineteenth-century mind is clear in this delineation of the psychology of Barnum's operation.

Foreign travelers noted with alarming regularity the prevalence of swindlers, humbugs, and quacks. In Boston in the late 1830s, according to one account, public notices could be seen announcing: "Bank notes made here to any pattern." Just such an announcement led one Englishman to comment on the open and extensive practice of fraud and counterfeiting in America. "There is no part of the world where forgery is carried to such an extent as it is in the U.S., chiefly in the western country. . . . But the eastern banks are seldom forged upon. Counterfeit money is also very plentiful."[5] As far as most foreign observers were concerned, American preoccupation with "the almighty dollar" was responsible for what they considered an extraordinary pandemic of sharpers and rogues. "Mammon is the idol which the people worship," a cultivated Englishwoman wrote; "the one desire is the acquisition of money; the most nefarious trickery and bold dishonesty are invested with a spurious dignity if they act as aids to the attainment of this object.

Children from their earliest years imbibe the idea that sin is sin—*only when found out.*"[6]

The more discerning travelers, whose ears were attuned to the subtler shadings of cultural nuance, observed that the American obsession with roguery and attraction to charlatanism was embedded in the popular language and folk humor of the nation. Of the tall tales she heard in the 1850s, Isabella Bird remarked that the narrative burden was almost exclusively "some clever act of cheating." She found American colloquial speech full of references to shysters and scoundrels. She heard them referred to in such approbatory terms as "a wide-awake feller," a " 'cute' chap," and "a 'cute' coon." The art of cozening the careless, of "sucking a greenhorn," was referred to as "a smart sell, that." There is even more open admiration for the perpetrator and contempt for the victim in the observation "That coon had cut his eye-teeth."[7] Just over a decade earlier, Frederick Marryat had found a predominance of the same concern in American humor. "If there required any proof," he wrote, "of the dishonest feeling so prevalent in the United States, arising from the desire of gain, it would be in the fact that almost every good story which you hear of an American is an instance of great ingenuity and very little principle."[8]

Herman Melville's novel *The Confidence Man* (1857) was a brilliantly mordant satire on this aspect of the American character. The need to believe in the ideal (an ordered social reality), in the face of the suspension of all belief in a world in which it is no longer possible to believe, continually allows the Confidence Man to take advantage of those who are profoundly distrustful of everything else. Melville has put his finger on the pulse of the mid-century American and given us an exceptionally insightful reading of the ambiguities, fears, hopes, and ironies of his world.

In terms of the moral outlook of the nineteenth-century male, the most successful confidence "man" of the entire era was woman.[9] It was she to whom man looked as a moral arbiter, a source of salvation from the grimy materialistic world; and at the same time it was she who was the source of the continual distrust and uncertainty he felt about morality and the social order. This idea found expression in the veil metaphor, which was so popular in American polemical literature throughout the century. It was not accidental that an article of feminine apparel, that which concealed or disguised the face, the key to the nature of the true self, was chosen to represent the deceit and hypocrisy attributed to one's opponents. The association between groups perceived as detrimental and threatening to social order and the female is clearly present on the subliminal level in these constant references to "unveiling" with the intent of uncovering, disclosing to view, stripping the cover from.[10]

Anxiety about the true or real woman, the actually "genuine, not artificial, counterfeit or fictitious; not affected or assumed,"[11] revealed the precariousness of gender roles and an extensive insecurity about the permanence of moral values during most of the nineteenth century, but especially after 1850. Much of this concern centered about the question of sex roles, marriage, and the family. It frequently found its objective correlative in the critique of women's fashions as the overt expression of concealed deceit and treachery. This distrust was present in a wide variety of books of the period, from medical treatises to books of advice and manuals of beauty. The goal of most of this literature, an unmasking or unveiling, was clearly expressed in a chapter title from a work of the latter class. Chapter 21 of *The Ladies' Guide to Perfect Beauty* (1861) is entitled "External Indications; or Art of Determining the Precise Figure, the Degree of Beauty, the Mind, the Habits, and the Age of Woman, notwithstanding the Aids and Disguises of Dress."[12] The ability to look behind the mask, to "read" the fripperies of fashion as the essential cheats they were, to distinguish the true woman, was the object of the work. We are told, for example, that

> persons with waists too large render them less before by a
> stomacher, or something equivalent, and behind by a corresponding
> form of the dress, making the top of the dress smooth across the
> shoulders, and drawing it in plaits to a narrow point at the bottom
> of the waist. Those who have the bosom too small, enlarge it by the
> oblique folds of the dress being gathered above, and by other means.
> Those who have the lower posterior part of the body too flat, elevate
> it by the top of the skirt being gathered behind and by other less
> skillful adjustments, which though hid, are easily detected.[13]

The connection between such artifices and the generally flaccid moral tone of society was explicitly delineated: "Deceit and hypocrisy are so universal in our day, that, by other than a scientific analysis of the brain and face, surface indications and manners go for little."[14]

The consummate art of the most skilled and artful confidence "man" —woman—reflected the reality of a world in flux and the difficulty of discriminating between reality and illusion. The challenge, the uncertainty, and the terror of that world of unceasing kinesis made changes in status and the social order, especially in the realm of sex roles (and class structure, the "forms" of human societal life), unpalatable. The realization that such changes were in fact already occurring and were largely welcomed in the economic and political realms, that the very doctrine of progress itself necessitated and assumed continual change, only rendered opposition to such deviation more vehement and intractable. The sensation of being sucked into a vortex of mutability, the doubt that all change was beneficial, and the feeling of a social order cut adrift from its moorings in the natural order gave rise to powerful sexual ambivalence and anxiety. The sexual nightmare of a Victorian physician and social critic provides a striking projection of this dubiety and dread:

> If a man, perfectly possessed both of feeling and sight—conversant with, and sensible to the charms of women—were even to be in contact with what he conceived to be the most beautiful and lovely of the sex, and at the moment when he was going to embrace her, he was to discover *that the parts which he touched only were feminine or human*; and that, *in the rest of her form, she was an animal of a different species, or a person of his own sex* . . . [there would be a] total and instantaneous change of his sentiments from one extreme to another.[15]

The consciousness of the discrepancy between the natural and the social, the ideal and the real, gives rise to a thoroughgoing feeling of aesthetic and moral repugnance, for

> in detecting an imposture of this kind, admiration would give place to disgust, [which] only proves that the external qualities which were admired were the natural and appropriate signs of the internal qualities expected to be found under them, and that they now cease to interest only because they have become, not *naturally* less the signs of these qualities, but because they have by a mere trick been rendered insignificant, because *truth and nature have been violated*, and because the mind feels only disgust at the imposture.[16]

As the terms of this "unnatural" nightmare indicate, sexual problems in a rapidly changing society, especially those of the respective roles of male and female and the question of the erotic life of the latter, were immediately relevant to the sense of betrayal and discomfort males felt in an increasingly materialistic world that belied their professed ideals. Perceptions of the true and natural were opposed to the hypocrisy of everyday sexual life.

Were virtue and the perfectibility of man merely illusions? Was woman, the temple of virtue, but an animal under the skin, as this nightmare suggested? These questions were crucial to the man of nineteenth-century America. We can understand the reasons for his malaise more fully if we briefly survey the changes in behavior that underlay the frenetically neurotic ideological level of the culture.

The trend in popular morality, as might be expected, was precisely in the direction of nonreproductive sexuality. Not that any of the "perversions" that sought to avoid reproductive sex were new to humanity (even a cursory reading of the Bible confirmed that); but advancing scientific, technological, and demographic developments—in short, the evolutionary progress of civilization—had facilitated erotic sexuality in certain ways. Concurrently, however, the persistence of traditional sexual morality—a legitimation of sexual intercourse by an appeal to reproductive necessity rather than to the pleasure nexus—meant that contemporaries experienced at once a sense of rapid and disconcerting change in sexual mores and a discomfiting discontinuity between behavior and values.

In demographic terms, William L. Langer has recently pointed out the significance of the European population explosion of the years 1750–1850. Greater availability of food and relative freedom from disease laid the foundation for the boom. A similar demographic and social phenomenon seems to have been going on in America at about the same time. David H. Fischer has pointed out that the years after 1780 saw a stabilization in the death rate in New England. As mortality became stable, fertility began to decline in the decade 1810–20, a trend that continued through the first quarter of the twentieth century. American population increase, then, resulted more from a higher survival rate (a rise in life expectancy coupled with a fall in infant mortality) than from increased reproduction. Increased longevity was primarily a function of improved diet and sanitation.[17] Although it is clear that modernization and industrialization did not cause the demographic trends outlined above, it appears that the agricultural and transportation revolutions of the period 1815–60 in the United States may well have had a multiplier effect on the population explosion during the years 1830–70, in which the aggregate population more than tripled.

In any case, in America as well as Europe, increased population in turn created pressure on the means of subsistence and public health. Psychological reluctance to relinquish the better life that an increased food supply afforded led to widespread practice of birth control, abortion, infanticide, and abandonment of children. One aspect of improved health and alimentary conditions, therefore, seems to have been an increasingly common rather haphazard use of sex and a growing tendency to separate its reproductive from its pleasurable aspect.[18] Technological discoveries helped to further this behavioral trend, even though ideological assumptions remained rooted in an earlier moral tradition.

In the scientific and industrial world, for example, the discovery of the vulcanization process for rubber (1837); the development of the instantaneous or cold-cure process for vulcanization in 1846 (which made possible the rapid production of thin, delicate articles); the construction of the first oil refinery (1860); and the development of the coal-tar industry in the 1850s and 1860s set the stage for advances in contraceptive technology and medical treatment of venereal diseases. Concurrent developments in the application of technology to biology, the premier science of the nineteenth century, especially in the area of microscopy—the development of the achromatic lens (1847); the use of coal-tar or aniline dyes for staining the protoplasm (1868); and the development of oil-immersion lenses and better sectioning techniques in the 1870s—accelerated the process.

The developments most directly associated with this technological and scientific progress, which greatly increased the possibility for pleasurable sexual intercourse apart from reproductive necessity, were the rise of large-scale production of inexpensive rubber condoms, which had become a booming business in the United States by the 1850s; the invention of the flexible vaginal diaphragm (late 1850s); and the discovery of the gonococcus, the bacteriological agent of gonorrhea, by A. Neisser in 1879, which, combined with the development of the gram stain (1884), laid the foundation for control of this dreaded venereal disease.[19] Ironically, then, while biology, as J. Wilson has effectively demonstrated, was establishing the ubiquitous influence of cellular reproduction during the decades from 1830 to 1880,[20] its exertions in ameliorating some of the more common hazards contingent upon the sex act may well have contributed to a movement of popular mores away from a reproductive *justification* for sexual intercourse.

Behavioral indices to this shift in mores, however, are primarily indirect. The main question of sexual behavior in the nineteenth century was how to reconcile its erotic and reproductive aspects. Pleasure as a raison d'être of intercourse was increasingly being accepted; the problem for moralists was what to do about it. It was not a question of sex for pleasure (sex had always had its erotic dimension), but an argument over the normative side of the problem: how ought sex to be used; and what was its "true" justification?

The issues of birth control, abortion, prostitution, pornography, and divorce were inseparably bound up in the nineteenth-century mind with the issue of rampant eroticism. This was a predominantly patriarchal reading of the realities of sexual life, for it ignored, for the most part, the legitimate feminine grievances that underlay the rising incidence of contraception and abortion, the mistreatment and oppression many women experienced in marriage, and the economic realities that were part of the cause of prostitution. With the caveat, therefore, that these five issues of contention reflected male concern with sexual morality more accurately than female, we may briefly examine developments in these areas as indicators of the conflict between the rising tendency to accept the erotic nature of sexual life as its most important characteristic in the realm of behavior and the anxiety to create a more stringent and effective value system to check that tendency.

In the realm of contraception, not only the rubber condom and the vaginal diaphragm, but also the discovery by Oldham in 1849 that the fertile period was precisely two weeks after the onset of a woman's period (which made possible an intelligent and surreptitious use of the rhythm method of birth control), were significant innovations.[21] The rise of *tableaux vivants*, or *poses plastiques*, in the 1840s, and the trickle of salacious writings and illustrations, which grew out of the mass printing industry in the 1830s and 1840s and had become a flood by the mid-1860s, indicate the rise of a pornography industry in this period. So great did public indignation become in some quarters that in 1842 Congress was forced to pass a law forbidding the importation of pornographic books and pictures. In 1865 an additional law forbidding the mailing of pornographic matter was passed (the Collamer bill, S. 390), and in 1872 the infamous Comstock Law was promulgated.[22] Anthony Comstock became a special agent for the postal service the next year, assiduously ferreting out what he considered to be objectionable material.

Comstock's career as a muckraker and exposer of vice meshed very neatly with the concern of the age for unmasking or unveiling hypocrisy and paralleled its paranoia about the declining state of morality. This was clearly reflected in the titles of two works he wrote after entering the Postal Department. The earliest was *Frauds Exposed; or, How the People Are Deceived and Robbed, and Youth Corrupted: Being a Full Exposure of Various Schemes Operated through the Mails, and Unearthed by the Author in a Seven Years' Service as a Special Agent of the Post Office Department and Secretary and Chief Agent of the New York Society for the Suppression of Vice* (1880). The other was entitled—ironically, in view of Comstock's use of decoy letters, blinds, and harrassment of "pornographers" until many committed suicide out of desperation—*Traps for the Young* (1883).

Prostitution remained the viable business enterprise it had become by the second decade of the nineteenth century, but if figures for New York City (considered by contemporaries a veritable den of iniquity) are representative, its growth does not appear to have been excessive throughout the century. Figures of the Magdalen Society for 1830 estimated that there were some twenty thousand women, one-third of all those of marriageable age, engaged in prostitution. The life expectancy of the average prostitute was estimated at three to five years after first taking up the occupation. Over 50 percent of the male population of the city was said to have recourse to prostitutes; they averaged three visits each per week. Figures for 1890 indicated a body of thirty to forty thousand whores, one of every fifty-five persons in the city.[23] But in view of the increase of population during these years, the latter figure represented an absolute decline in the ratio of prostitutes to total city population. Nevertheless, the argument about the legitimacy of erotic sexuality found one of its foci in the prostitution issue; it became a symbolic issue (as did pornography): an evil to mount a crusade against for its opponents, and a form of eroticism to be defended against the cant and hypocrisy of the moral crusaders by those who, if they cannot be said to have openly advocated it, certainly excused it.[24]

A recent historian of abortion in America contends that it was widely practiced in the first quarter of the nineteenth century. Abortifacients and information on techniques not only were a part of American folklore but were available from midwives, herb doctors, quacks, and regular physicians. There were no legal statutes regulating abortion in the United States prior to 1821, and American practice therefore followed English common-law tradition. Under this rubric abortive practices that occurred before "quickening" (the first perceived motion of the child, variously established at four to five months *in utero*) were neither a criminal offense nor a misdemeanor; they simply did not come under the purview of the law.[25]

In the matter of abortion legislation, a New York State law that went into effect in 1830 declared any abortion subsequent to quickening a criminal offense. This initial provision was qualified in a later section, which provided for imprisonment (for up to one year) and a fine (not to exceed five hundred dollars) for those who "administered, prescribed, advised, procured, or sought" abortions. Essentially, this legislation was merely a codification of the common-law practice that had prevailed earlier, but two new provisions were added, which qualified the postquickening abortion. These were that the abortion "shall have been necessary to preserve the life" of the woman "or shall have been advised by two physicians to be necessary for that purpose."[26]

In the 1840s, Americans became acutely concerned with abortion, the incidence of which was believed to be increasing at an alarming rate. The consensus of medical opinion, expressed in a flood of articles and reports that appeared in the professional literature between 1850 and 1900, upheld this popular belief. One alarmed observer, for example, cited a statistical study that he identified only as the Report of the Special Committee on Abortion [the "Report on Criminal Abortion" by D. A. O'Donnell and W. L. Atlee, authorized and adopted by the American Medical Association in 1871?], which asserted that in the 1840s 17 percent of all pregnancies were aborted and that there were approximately one hundred thousand abortions per annum in the United States. What made the matter so shocking to contemporaries was the demographic shift in the kinds of women seeking abortions. Whereas, previously, lower-class women who had conceived out of wedlock and sought to destroy the evidence of their shame had constituted the bulk of those who attempted to terminate pregnancies, after 1840 abortion was increasingly used by respectable middle- and upper-class women as a contraceptive measure. Moralists were aghast at reports that 75 to 90 percent of all abortions were procured by married women.[27]

Legislative response was rapid. The New York law of 1846 effectually retained the provision that felonious abortion depended on the judgment of the court as to whether the aborted fetus was quick, but defined the consequent death of either woman or fetus as second-degree manslaughter and raised the penalties for violation. Significantly, another section of the act provided that any woman who sought or performed an abortion on herself was liable to a fine and prison term. New Hampshire (1849) and Wisconsin (1858) also passed laws striking down the traditional common-law immunity of the woman in abortion cases. The Massachusetts law of 1847 went further and made an explicit link between abortion and contraception, declaring illegal all practices and materials "obtained for the purpose of causing or procuring the miscarriage of a woman pregnant with child or [of] preventing, or which is represented as intended to prevent, pregnancy."[28] New York introduced similar legislation, designed to limit both abortion advertisements and readily available contraceptive information, in 1868.

During the period 1860–80, abortion laws rejected the quickening standard. New York legislation, passed in response to the petitioning of the state medical society in 1869, was typical. It reiterated the liability of the woman and reflected the distrust and anxiety about the place of woman in American society contained in one of the legislative petitions. The petitioners called for the enactment of any legislation that would "arrest the flagrant corruption of morality among women, who ought to be and unquestionably are the conservators of morals and of virtue."[29] Abortion, then, in the years 1830–80, seems to have been both a widespread practice and a focal point of the unabated social and moral concern that was rooted in a desire to believe in the true-woman ideology, coupled with a simultaneous distrust of female virtue.

Changing attitudes toward divorce in nineteenth-century America were indicated by a general liberalizing of the laws regarding absolute separation. With the exception of the southern states, which generally occupied a very conservative position on this issue, and New York, which allowed divorce *a vinculo* for adultery alone through most of the century, a gradual expansion in allowable causes for divorce characterized the period 1815– 75. The supplemental causes most frequently added to divorce laws during these years were primarily concerned with the rights of women in the marriage relation: cruel treatment, indignities, failure to provide, abandonment, habitual drunkenness, and extended imprisonment. Increasingly, prohibitions on the remarriage of divorced persons declined, even in the case of the party legally at fault, except in the instance of proceedings initiated because of adultery.[30]

Many contemporary observers saw the broadening of divorce legislation as a sign not only of moral decadence but also of rampant, asocial egotism. They shared Horace Greeley's belief that marriage "concerns not only the men and women who contract it, but the State, the community, mankind."[31] Especially those who lived in New York, with its biblically based divorce law, were concerned about the divorce racket, which employed private detectives and agents provocateurs, and often secured final decrees which were the first indication to the defendants that proceedings had been initiated. The states of Connecticut, Maine, Indiana, and Utah (for the period 1875–78) became infamous as "divorce mills" in which those from outside the state could receive expeditious and legal divorces, in the more egregious cases without even having set foot in the state.

A careful student of divorce trends from 1867 to 1886, however, noted that only about 20 percent of the total number of divorces were granted to individuals who had not been married in a given state. This figure was on the whole less than the prevailing level of general population migration.[32] Connecticut and Utah, with their "omnibus" clauses governing divorce, and Maine and Utah, both of which lacked residence requirements for divorces, apparently did figure in a marginally legal divorce market. Indiana, however, was unjustly maligned, because its divorce law required two years' residency. The case of Utah became notorious in the 1870s, and in Maine the out-of-state divorce rate exceeded the immigration rate by 8 percent.[33]

The available evidence indicates that contemporaries were right in their belief that the divorce rate was increasing at a rapid rate. In the decade 1870 to 1880, for example, while the population of the United States increased by 30 percent, divorces increased by nearly 80 percent. Whereas there were 666 married couples to 1 divorce in 1870, the ratio was 481 to 1 in 1880.[34] The contemporary belief that women were largely responsible for the increase also seems justified. During the years 1867–86, almost two-thirds of the total number of divorces were granted to women. This was largely a function of the increasingly liberalized divorce laws, as an analysis of the causes of successful divorce actions in this period indicates. Of every five divorces, two were granted for desertion; drunkenness and cruelty were the next most significant causes, followed by adultery. Significantly, of divorces granted for adultery, 56 percent were granted to men.[35] Although contemporaries argued that the rising divorce rate was a reflection of erotic sexuality, statistics do not bear out their contention. Changing mores and legislation caused great anxiety (especially among men); it found expression in the irrational fear of a destructive, egocentrically motivated flood of divorce.

In all five of the areas we have briefly surveyed, the debate over the erotic nature of sexuality was central. The dizzying pace of change in mores brought confusion, and sexual ideology was an attempt to regain stability—not that such changes were universally accepted, but they were becoming more and more the standard of private practice despite publicly voiced moral positions. A statistical study by a woman doctor, begun in 1892, makes this change in mores clear. The very assumptions that underlie the study—the belief that woman has a sex drive and that the physical enjoyment of the sex act is important to woman's sexual life, the tacit assumption that birth control is widely practiced, and concern with the frequency of intercourse—indicate that the pleasure nexus is considered a vital aspect of human sexuality. Of the forty-seven women surveyed (all of whom were married in the 1870s, 1880s, and 1890s), 85 percent admitted that they or their husbands practiced some form of birth control. The condom, pessary, and withdrawal were the most common. Nearly all these women (93 percent) acknowledged that they regularly experienced sexual desire (usually immediately prior to or after their menses); nearly 70 percent found sex "agreeable," as the questionnaire expressed it; and fully 86 percent experienced regular orgasms during intercourse. The frequency of intercourse among this group averaged more than once a week (4.7–5.13 times per month), and sexual activity well into pregnancy was admitted by nearly 80 percent of those replying.

The portion of the survey that reveals most about mores in transition, however, is the replies to the question on the proper justification for intercourse. Almost half of these women replied categorically that reproduction was the *only* reason for sexual activity; 17 percent found that *male* pleasure provided some justification; and only a little over a third considered *female* gratification of any significance. There is some indication that these women felt their behavior would be viewed with disapprobation by an authority figure such as the researcher (female though she was), and that they therefore provided the answer they thought was expected. This impression is strengthened when we consider the fact that of seven women who answered "always" or "usually" to the question about orgasms, six, or 87 percent, asserted that reproduction was the primary purpose of sexual intercourse.[36]

Behavioral practices as revealed in this survey were clearly in contradiction to the advice of most moralists as expressed in guidebooks of the era. The technological, social, and demographic changes that had made the wider enjoyment of sexual indulgence possible ran counter to accepted sexual ideology. Most moral pundits recommended an average of one sexual experience per month (preferably less), forbade intercourse during pregnancy, and opposed most forms of birth control other than abstinence. Clearly, this was the ideal; for as the relatively liberal reformer Charles Knowlton (one of the pioneers of the movement for contraception in America) revealed frankly in his admonitions against sex during pregnancy, intercourse for pleasure was quite common; the female sex drive was acknowledged if not accepted; and women were apparently experiencing orgasms regularly. This was the basis for the attack on sex during pregnancy among all those who tried to improve the moral tone of their society.[37] In medicohygienic literature, the debate over eroticism took the form of competing sexual ideologies, which, although primarily male oriented, were also adapted to female sexual behavior. The two main ideologies here were "spermatic economy," or the belief that vitality, intelligence, creativity, and energy inhered in the semen and that passing the seed would therefore debilitate, desiccate, and ultimately destroy the organism; and "seminal repletion," the belief that a temperate indulgence of the sex instinct and the concomitant passing of the seed were essential to preserving the tone and vigor of the body.[38]

The key to moral control was firmly in the hands of the male in *both* ideological systems. This was an ideological expression of the fear generated by changing sexual mores and especially the concern about the fate of the family and the place or role of woman in society. The whole body of thought that dealt with sexual behavior and mores was an inchoate attempt at social eugenics or human control of the evolution of society, employing assumptions derived from a more stable and rational eighteenth-century scientific outlook coupled with social assumptions that went back to the Puritan tradition of the seventeenth century. Each sex had its calling, its sphere, but that of males had become more individualized with the development of an industrial-business society, whereas that of women had retained a corporate ideal, fundamentally subserving the commonweal. The "rational" order of things was "natural"; it functioned smoothly and seemed to provide order in social life. It was this stable, orderly, completed world that the change in sexual mores, the corresponding "woman problem," and the decline of the family threatened directly. This is quite clear when we consider the statements on the place of women in society, especially those that postdate the rise of the organized women's movement in America. One example will indicate the general tenor of these statements: "The laws of nature and the instincts of the sex imperiously demand of woman to do what is feminine; those who would defy both are, therefore, untrue to themselves. It is in harmony with reason and the fitness of things, that woman's appropriate sphere of life—the domestic—should be defended against the Utopian schemes and aggressions of the faction who so fiercely contend for her 'political rights,' thus placing her in the attitude of a rival instead of a companion of man."[39]

The rebellion of woman represented a threat not only to the stability of the social order but to civilization as well. Anxiety about sexual and moral change was reflected in concern about the direction social change was taking. The concept of civilization was still bound up with the baroque mode of thought that had given it birth; it was deemed to be a rational, orderly human construct. It implied control over nature (instinct, sexuality) and the taming or *domestication* of the wild (the animalistic, the bestial).

The way in which George Bancroft (1800–1891) used the term "civilization" in his monumental *History of the United States* (1834–74) is exemplary. For Bancroft, civilization was a vigorous, driving, masculine, ordering force, in opposition to the "feeble barbarians," who had left the natural world "an unproductive waste," a veritable desert of "useless vegetation." The rationalizing, instrumental, structuralizing connotations of civilization are clear here.[40] The increasing use of the term "civilization" in the nineteenth century and the rise of bastardized forms ("civilizational" in 1848 and "civilizee" in 1868) indicate the importance the concept assumed during this period.[41]

Clearly, insecurity about gender roles and sexual behavior lay at the bottom of this concern about civilization; the problems of a system of mores in transition were being expressed through reference to established symbols and modes of thought. When we recall the physician's nightmare of the beast beneath the female form, and the insistence on the domestic sphere of woman, coupled with the emphasis placed upon self-control, the will, and self-limitation, can there be any doubt about the underlying sexual foundation considered essential to civilization? These problems, anxieties, and ambiguities found their objective correlative in the social alternatives offered by the various utopian societies. As one observer expressed it, "Oneida communities and such like experiments are legitimate outgrowths from this slimy region of our theory [i.e. insistence on the right to follow the lead of impulse without concern for the consequences] and they have their genteel parallels in civilized society—which will practice what it will never avow."[42]

To the self-appointed male guardians of social virtue it seemed that their civilization was beleaguered by a perfidious (though necessary) feminine element from within and by a more clearly inimical utopian element from without. Although some social critics could accept this situation with equanimity and philosophical detachment, as "a phase of our social experience which we must pass through, very disagreeable, very disgusting, very alarming, but incidental after all, and transient,"[43] others were more deeply distressed. They liked to think, but could not believe on the basis of their reading of social change, that "we have no fear that marriage is about to be abolished. It has too many friends among the wise and prudent to be exposed to a dangerous peril."[44] It was this group, concerned about a society in transition, but uncertain, timorous, about the durability of their cultural values, that supplied most of the critics of the social experimentation associated with utopian societies. It is their ideology and symbolism, the connecting tissue between the general body of sexual ideology and the specific ideological framework of the three utopian communities, that forms the subject of the next chapter.

Chapter 3 🎋 "Get Thee Behind Me, Satan": Contemporary Critical Perspectives on the Shakers, Mormons, and Oneida Community

Vice is a monster of so frightful mien,
As to be hated, needs but to be seen;
Yet seen too oft, familiar with her face,
We first endure, then pity, then embrace.
But where the extreme of vice, was ne'er agreed:
. . . .
No creature owns it in the first degree,
But thinks his neighbour farther gone than he.

   —Alexander Pope, *An Essay on Man*

We have just enough religion to make us hate, but not enough
to make us love one another.

   —Jonathan Swift, "Thoughts on Various Subjects, Moral
   and Diverting"

*T*he French Structuralist anthropologist Claude Lévi-Strauss has given us a striking metaphorical representation of the process of culture formation. Culture, he argues, is like a card game; there are only a finite number of cards in the deck, and of the total number, each individual can use only those he is dealt. This is the "culture fix," the hereditary "hand" that all members of a given culture hold. Given this common set of cards, however, the reactions of different players to the flow of the game, whether brought about by personality differences or differing perceptions of the course of the game, may well lead to alternative strategies of play. It is frequently those players who hold the same hand, but choose to play it differently, who become the most vehement enemies. This is especially true, when, as in nineteenth-century America, the players experience ambiguity, an uncertainty about the best "style of play."

This was clearly the case in the altercations and mutual recriminations that separated those who entered the utopian societies we are concerned with and those who did not. Many values or ends were common to both groups, but their "styles of play" were quite different. The debate was one of form or system (the tactics of play), rather than content (the "hand" or established rules of the game).[1] We can therefore best examine the general background and the moral and cultural assumptions (or rather the procedural prescriptions considered indispensable for their realization; the ideology, if you will) against which utopians were rebelling by considering the specific objections, fears, and objurgations of their critics. An analysis of critical reactions to utopian sexual and social ideologies (or strategies of play) reveals the tensions between mainstream ideology and changing mores.

It is at such points of impingement that cultural-ideological fissures become most apparent; and therefore such an approach to the comparative dimension of cultural modes within and without these utopian communities aids in the discrimination of those attitudes, feelings, and ways of behavior that, in view of the challenge utopians presented to established mores, were deemed of crucial importance by the nonutopian populace.

The homologous relationship of utopians to antiutopians is clear when we consider that both critics and members of the communities came from similar religious, geographic, and social backgrounds.[2] Assuming that these critics reflect the general cultural attitudes of their classes, religions, and regions, we should have a more accurate and meaningful basis for comparison of utopian and antiutopian cultural assumptions and responses to social change than we would have with a randomly selected group from the broader society.

The most immediate response of these critics was a sense of violated propriety, the decorous tone of which ill concealed the growing anxiety that underlay it. This pervasive substratum of fear was grounded in an uncertainty about the function of the family and the role of woman in modern industrial society. Significantly, the bulk of opposition to utopian communities came from males (many of whom were clergymen)[3] who felt that nineteenth-century American society was losing its moral tone. They shared a faith in the prevailing popularization of Enlightenment ideas that supported the status quo and firmed up key social institutions. Whereas love, a force that operated on a personal level, was central to the doctrine of evangelicals and led them to visions of a highly individualized perfection, more conservative religious figures operated on a social level, concentrating their energies on the obligation to forward the progress of civilization. Both evangelicals (whose emotional approach to religious behavior was shared by Oneidans, Mormons, and Shakers) and their less emotionally oriented opponents sought progress; but the former concentrated on individual experience, whereas, to the latter, social duty was central.

In its most grandiloquent form, the rhetoric of communal opponents associated alternative perceptions of the "right" way to overcome the evils of increasing divorce, abortion, and prostitution, and to achieve a transcendently pure relationship between the sexes and healthy, moral children, with uncivilized, lawless, predatory male behavior. The argument was joined essentially over the issue of what was to be done with women in a society that was in evolutionary transition. What was the meaning of progress in the realm of the relationship between the sexes? Could changes in woman's roles and position in society be reconciled with her maternal role? In sexual behavior, could there be any other *justification* for intercourse than mere reproductive necessity? Wasn't there a natural limit to the evolutionary progress of social development, which provided that certain fixed boundaries of decency could not be exceeded without dire consequences? The very nature of the questions asked indicates that such changes were considered to be already in train; and the fact that utopians became so frequently the prime targets of those who sought to defend civilization against the animalistic and asocial forces of *perverted* change indicates that they were perceived as prime movers in the process.

For the most part, these critics do not seem to have been particularly well informed as to the detailed sexual ideologies and practices of the communities they attacked; but they were quite well aware (as twentieth-century observers have only infrequently been) of the importance of sexual questions to these communities. Their perception of these social alternatives was at once eristic and symbolic; they saw them as objective correlatives of moral and social declension. So, whether they attacked the celibate Shakers or the polygamous Mormons, their arguments were virtually identical. In the case of the pantagamous Oneida Community, whose sexual arrangements bore a certain superficial resemblance to those of the Mormons, an even closer correlation is observable. John Humphrey Noyes noticed that whenever the antipolygamy animus ran high in central New York, there was a corresponding rash of anti-Oneida feeling not long afterward.[4]

Written condemnations of these three social alternatives stretched from 1783 to the end of the nineteenth century and, despite variations of intensity, appear to have enjoyed a notable consistency of argument throughout the entire period. It will be most convenient and logical, therefore, in dealing with these critics, who served as the vanguard of the crusade against all the social and sexual evils utopian societies were thought to incarnate, to consider their ideas as a unified body of thought.

In the minds of their opponents, fanaticism, the failure of control, an improper balance between the mental and the physical, and an overwhelming sense of disorder characterized the three communities under consideration. Lurking behind this emotional response was an anxious trepidation that these qualities of life might be attributable not only to communitarian attempts to change society, but to the very dynamics of the inevitable process of change itself in a rapidly evolving society. "Ultraism," as one writer called it, had become "the disease of the age. . . . We are running," he wrote, "into extremes upon almost everything we undertake."⁵

Such fanaticism denied the need for balance and order both in individual and in social life. The response to this perceived "extremism" was the kind of hysterical paranoia David Brion Davis found in nineteenth-century anti-Catholic literature. A similar psychological projection, by which subconscious wish fulfillment and the exorcising of guilt through transferring the forbidden desires and clandestine practices of one's own social group to a more peripheral, less respectable social group, was clearly functioning in the case of the acrimonious critics of the Shakers, Mormons, and Oneidans as well.⁶

Interestingly enough, the resemblance between the anti-Catholic and anticommunitarian arguments went far beyond their psychological foundation. In a predominantly Protestant, sectarian society that still held to the Puritan distaste for popery and the Enlightenment rationalism which condemned "priestcraft," moral virtue, republican good sense, and the future of human civilization all inhered in a handful of denominations— precisely those that were most outspoken in their opposition to the utopians. They were also the denominations that were most aggressively anti-Catholic. It is not surprising, therefore, that one of the most frequent charges (which was not without some basis in fact) hurled against these utopian societies was that they were tyrannical, governed by a theocratic priestcraft. They were considered secret societies, specifically, although in some unspecified and nefarious way, related to the Roman Catholic church. Hypocrisy, displaced from the antiutopians and their society to the alternative social orders they criticized, became one of the central characteristics in the tendentious delineation of these challengers of the values and mores of Protestant America. What Shakers or Mormons said they were doing, the justifications they provided for the changes they had initiated in their sexual lives, were nothing but a smokescreen, a "veil" that concealed the base lasciviousness behind all such attempts. The insinuatingly indirect style of most of the "revelations" of what was really going on in these communities was exemplified in the charge of hypocrisy made against the Shaker Elders. "We have as much reason, to say the least of it," a typical antagonist wrote, "to believe in the sincerity of the Roman Catholic Priesthood, as in that of the Shaker Priesthood. And their corruption in this respect is too notorious to be denied."[7] In short, Shakerism presented the phenomenon of "a Society, founded by fanaticism, supported by enthusiasm, and governed by the principles of deceitful priest craft."[8]

In addition to the anti-Catholic nexus, opponents of the Mormons and the Oneida Community also linked these bêtes noires to their more salient Semitic parallels—Judaism and Mohammedanism. The anti-Semitism of a self-righteous Protestant culture, which considered it an act of missionary mercifulness to attempt the conversion of the benighted Jews, was brought into play to underscore the danger inherent in the utopian-sectarian challenge to mainstream Christian denominationalism. That challenge was considered to be preeminently foreign, blatantly sexual, and representative of a much lower level of civilization than that attained in nineteenth-century Protestant America. The Mormons in particular had dared to compare themselves with the Jews as the "chosen people," a direct denial of the exclusive birthright mainstream Protestant America had received from its Puritan forebears; a kind of ecclesiastical escheat of a hereditary aura of morality and right. Critics of the Mormons reversed the game on them, however, maintaining that, yes, the Mormons were the direct descendants of the Jewish chosen people, but that latter group had been no better than it should have been. "As they were merely *outward* in all things of religion and worship," one writer noted about the Jews, "so, too, they were grossly licentious, and presented the lowest plane of human degradation into which the Divine could descend, and work out the salvation of the human family. In all these respects the Jews were a *chosen people*; but the idea that Christians are to revive the practices of Jewry would be as startling and absurd as to command the mature and fruit-bearing tree to sink back into its own roots."[9]

Mohammedanism, however, was a much more expressive metaphor, because Arabic lands still preserved the practice of polygamy. That the comparison among "Mahometanism, Mormonism, Perfectionism, and a long catalogue of other *isms*" proved so effective and popular, as opposed to the much more infrequently used Judaic parallel, indicates that they were believed to be "all of a kindred character . . . but the varied species of the same genus,"[10] the primary taxonomic characteristic of which was base sexual behavior. In this connection Mormonism was referred to as "Yankee Mahometanism," whereas Oneidans were depicted as maintaining a "harem."[11]

A conscious attempt at prurient titillation pervades many of the works of the opponents of these three communities. Little concrete information is provided about actual sexual practices, nor is a thorough exposition of the ideology that informs such practices thought necessary. Oblique references, innuendo, double entendre, and cheap typographical devices such as a "censored" paragraph of asterisks, or references to matters "too delicate" to discuss in mixed company, abound.

William Jarman, excerpts from whose book appeared under the title "Mormonism Uncovered" in the "Illustrated Lectures" section of the *Police Gazette* in the 1880s, instructed the typesetter: "Printer, put in some stars here and skip the next eight lines. It will never do for the readers of this book."[12] Another instance of prurience masquerading as prudery was this evaluation of the writings of the founder of the Oneida Community: "Mr. Noyes . . . has descended so low, and unblushingly published sentiments so sensual and debasing in their character and tendency, and in some instances used language so very obscene and vulgar that it is extremely difficult and almost impossible to present the subject in a just light, without transgressing the common rules of propriety."[13]

Such circumlocutions aroused the curiosity and whetted the voyeuristic appetite for more revealing detail. Always avoiding a direct description, these works provided darkly veiled hints of the vilest perversions, couched in such vague terms that the reader's imagination was stimulated to complete the fantasy for himself. Author and reader thus became partners in the creation of a fantasy, ostensibly rooted in repulsion and loathing, but involving a dynamic that insured the release of repressed desire through subliminal cathexis and wish fulfillment.[14]

John H. Beadle, who served briefly as editor of one of the few Gentile, or non-Mormon, newspapers in Utah, the *Salt Lake City Reporter*, exemplifies the more tantalizing aspects of anticommunitarian rhetoric. Describing the ceremony of initiation into the Second Estate of the Melchizedek priesthood, which took place in the Endowment House in the Mormon Temple in Salt Lake City, he quotes "eyewitness accounts" by three apostate Mormon women. The essence of the ritual, we are told, involves a reenactment of the Edenic temptation, in which those who portray Adam and Eve wear very little clothing. The "temptation consists of gestures and hints 'not to be described.'" And yet we are treated to further allusions: "I cannot mention the *nature* of the fruit, but have left more unsaid than the imagination held with the loosest possible rein would be likely to picture . . . the reality is too monstrous for human belief, and the moral and object of the whole is socially to unsex the sexes."[15]

The authors of these works are obviously most uncomfortable dealing with sexual matters; and perhaps because they realize that the morality of their own groups is not, objectively considered, very much different from that of the communities whose practices they find so heinous, they do not dare to describe it in too much detail. They are manifestly writing for an audience that considers itself pious in reading "religious," "morally uplifting" books, but that enjoys the fantasies and visions of forbidden pleasure evoked by the veiled suggestions of these critics. One wonders, in fact, whether these critics are not really playing devil's advocate in a subtle attempt to criticize the immorality and hypocrisy of *all* nineteenth-century American society, that of their readers as well as that of their ostensible antagonists.[16]

This impression is strengthened when one considers the fury with which the utopians were attacked and the hyperbolic rhetoric that was used to describe the danger they presented to the general society. The exaggerated response suggests that utopian critics perceived these communities as wielding a potentially dangerous, if not catastrophic, influence over the morals and behavior of men and women who had never even been near an alternative society. The fears behind this response are obviously grounded in the assumption that the moral position and sexual practices of these communities are perhaps quite similar to behavior that is, although not openly avowed, not at all uncommon in their own society. They are considered particularly attractive to women. An analysis of the content of this antiutopian literature bears out this assertion. It is directed primarily at women and is largely an exhortation to conservatism and the acceptance of traditional values, addressed to a potentially revolutionary class.

The primary motif of most of this literature was borrowed from the anti-Catholic literature of the 1830s, which in turn had taken it from the earlier gothic and confessional-epistolary novels of the eighteenth century.[17] This remained true whether the work in question was frankly fictional or pretended to objective reportage by providing a patent gloss of tables, figures, and "facts." The central character in the piece remained outraged womanhood; the true woman, inveigled, seduced, and enchained. The innocence of woman, according to this romantic vision, made her the ideal victim; sadistically tortured, enslaved, led into lascivious orgies because of misguided religious zeal, practicing abortion and birth control at the behest of her brutal masters, she forms the central concern of these books and pamphlets.

Among critics of the Shakers, for example, eyewitness accounts of sadistic beatings were a staple item. One young woman, who confessed a purely chaste partiality for an Elder's son, was seized by that worthy, a man "naturally of an austere and tyrannical character [who] extorted several answers from the girl, and then upon these, he thought himself justifiable in stripping her and putting her into a tub of cold water. It would be proper to remark in as modest a manner as possible, that certain circumstances, concurrent with her age (which was eighteen years), were then ruling, and the effect of the water was such, that for some time her life was despaired of."[18] "What augments the turpitude of this affair," an eyewitness continues, "is his stripping her naked, and then whipping her in a manner, that would be too unpleasant to relate: suffice it to say, the effect of this treatment was such, that she was unable to make up her bed for more than a year."[19]

What held the victim in the power of her sadistic master was her superstition and credulousness and the servitude this sentimental weakness of character made inevitable. It was in the period from 1840 to 1860 that the connection between Negro slavery and the abasement and abuse suffered by many women became increasingly common in print; and slavery became a synecdoche that expressed at once the fear of a whole gamut of change (deterioration, our critics would have said) in the relationship between the sexes and the desire to reverse the direction of that perceived change, or to punish those who, through excess of sensibility and affectivity, had dared overstep the bounds of generally acceptable sexual behavior. The metaphorical use of the white-slavery trope, although the phrase itself seems to have been current only sub rosa, was quite widespread during these decades and became even more popular with the termination of the Civil War, which destroyed its abortive twin, black slavery.[20]

Shaker recruiting practices, for instance, which purportedly led to splitting families, were compared to "Negro stealing." The system of Shakerism, it was claimed, was "nothing more or less than a system of slavery, carried on by cunning and fraud. A game perpetrated upon the innocent and unsuspecting by the crafty . . . toil is unremitting, and unrequited, [they] can call nothing their own, and submission to the elders is as complete as a slave's to his master."[21]

Among the Mormons, missionaries were accused of purchasing wives both for themselves and for the faithful at home in Zion. The fate of these women was depicted as a life of drudgery and chattel slavery. As one of the most outspoken and flauntingly pornographic of their critics expressed it, making quite explicit the connections between white and black slavery, and between polygamy and prostitution:

> Utah's WHITE SLAVES pitifully cry, "Wake up and free us!" America *talks in her sleep*, and answers: "N-O! W-H-I-T-E T-R-A-S-H a-i-n-t s-o i-m-p-o-r-t-a-n-t a-s N-i-g-g-e-r-s." Actions speak louder than words. Oh! Americans, chop your Liberty Poles into kindling wood! or wake up and free your WHITE SLAVES IN THE WEST, held *now* in a slavery of body and soul, worse than ever existed in the South, and *far more filthy*. Burn that *dear* old Cap, declare to the World

you no longer love liberty, decency, law, and order: that America is the filthiest, most lawless, and slavish country in the world, unless you *at once* clean out THE NASTY FILTH existing and growing in your midst, and which ruins the bodies and souls of hundreds of thousands.[22]

But prostitution was the least of the crimes promoted by those who sought to overturn the monogamic system of marriage. Their opponents considered these alternative systems of sexual relationship to be grounded in nothing but hypocritically concealed, flagitious lust. Both Oneidans and Mormons were accused of practicing seduction through the medium of animal magnetism, and the leaders of both communities, as well as the founder of Shakerism, Ann Lee, were considered characters of the most lewd and lascivious nature, who pandered to the concupiscent desires of their followers and were themselves victims of satyriasis and nymphomania. The slavery metaphor was thus extended to include all the members of these communities in a vast enslavement to lust. There was no crime in the whole catalog of social vices that was too gross for their commission. Ann Lee was accused of habitual harlotry, incest, and group sex; of being a camp follower; and, in an indirect reinforcement of the slavery metaphor, of having had sex with a black servant for three hundred dollars. In the latter case, to render the moral putrefaction of her character more forcefully, the objective correlative of her turpitude is revealed to the reader in the words of the testifier: "She in return gave him such a disorder, that he rotted alive, as his master told me. It was said, she brought this from the sailors, when she returned from the shipping, and for which she was doctored in Concord."[23] "Mormon ribaldry" under the "American Mahomet" (Joseph Smith) and "Bigamy Young" included, according to one particularly vicious critic, "debauchery, lasciviousness, bestiality . . . fornication, adultery, rape, incest."[24] The docket of Oneida's sexual crimes, its "systematized licentiousness," was quite similar.[25]

What lay at the heart of this attack, however, was a generalized sense of malaise. Social critics feared the "new woman" and had particularly ambiguous feelings about female sexuality; they were uneasy about the possibility that their values were none too stable. One hostile observer, for instance, reported that a Shaker sister [reputedly under inspiration], had accused another of masturbation with a kitchen utensil. The accuser cried: "Oh, what abomination! what corruption! what filth! gratifying your lusts with a cleaver." To further underscore the unnatural lust and depraved venery of the act, we are told that "the cleaver was of iron, and about three feet long; handle two feet."[26]

Critics saw their fondest beliefs about woman, their dearest myths about sexuality, being openly challenged. They reacted with an aggression born of an inveterate fear of woman. On the one hand, they graphically portrayed the punishments meted out to those women who dared to question their biologically and socially established roles (note the sadistic tortures and sufferings endured by the "victims" [sinners?] in the utopian societies); and on the other, they attacked those women who successfully adjusted to an alternative mode of life as depraved creatures of lust, vile prostitutes, and selfish harridans.

This hostility and aggression, grounded in the perception of utopians as sexual deviants and moral reprobates, was most graphically expressed in two images that responded to popular fears about Shaker and Mormon life. These were, respectively, a sudden and total amenorrhea and brutal emasculation. One young woman, for instance, testified that as a result of her experiences in a Shaker community, "the constitution of my nature ceased, or—[*mores feminarum totales mutantur*]."[27] The implication here is that such a condition resulted from brutal rape by a community Elder, or from venereal disease, which was assumed to have reached epidemic proportions among the Shakers. A Mormon exposé described the castration of a rebellious young man who stood in the way of the sexual designs of a Mormon high priest on a young woman: "The lights were then put out. An attack was made on the young man. He was severely beaten, and then tied with his back down on a bench, when Bishop [Warren] Snow took a bowie-knife, and performed the operation in a most brutal manner, and then took the portion severed from his victim and hung it up in the school-house on a nail, so that it could be seen by all who visited the house afterwards."[28]

These expressions of sexual aggression are central to the antiutopian vision. They reveal at once the fear that energizes this literature, and the threat of dire consequences that impend for those who disregard its menacing warnings. Castration and amenorrhea are simultaneously expressive of animosity against those who dare to thwart traditional sexual norms and of fear of utopian social life as an attack on reproductive sexuality and, by extension, on the centrality of the family in American life. The minatory burden of this imagery is clear: the threat of savage violence against the individual communitarian; the consequent physical alteration of the biologically determined roles of the sexes; and the potential of racial sterility for any society that accepts a nonreproductive sexuality.[29]

Monogamy, the nuclear family, and pronatalism, then, were the essential values of civilization. But more candid observers refused to accept the irrational fears detailed above and argued instead that demographic pressures had given rise to lax morals in modern society and that consequently the older values had been undermined. A British writer who traveled widely in America observed that if the problem of the demographic surplus of females could be solved,

> domestic trouble in America would cease for want of aliment. Most of their trouble may be traced directly to the disparity of the sexes. If the males and females were so fairly mixed, that every man who felt inclined to marry could find a wife, he would be likely to leave his neighbor's wife alone. If every woman had the chance given her by nature to secure one man's preference, and no more, she would be less dreamy and ideal, less exercised about her rights and wrongs, less moved about her place in creation. A woman with one mate, and no visible temptation to change her partner for another, and still another, would pay scant heed to those quacks of either sex, who come to her with their jargon about affinities and passionals. She would want no higher laws, and seek no greater freedom than her English mothers have enjoyed in wedded-love.[30]

Yet note that the underlying assumption, even in this more "objective" account, places the blame for the decline in American virtue squarely on the shoulders of American women. Women had been seduced, yes; but they had been susceptible to such influences only because they had already ceased to believe in the virtues of marital fidelity and motherhood. For the critics of alternative social orders, the ideal of womanhood, woman the "cheerful giver,"[31] was biologically determined; any attempt to restructure the role or function of woman in society was unnatural. The essence of this position was pronatalist and was based on the observation that the birthrate among native white Americans was steadily declining. This was considered the fault of American women, who sought to be something other than mothers. The same British traveler quoted above made this point most effectively, noting that "women began to doubt whether it was well for them to love their husbands and nurse their children. Some ladies set the fashion of laughing at mothers; nay, it became in Boston, Richmond, and New York, a sign of high breeding to be known as a childless wife. Wretches arose in every city of the land, some of them men, more of them women, who professed to teach young wives the secret arts by which . . . the laws of nature have often been set aside."[32]

Women were considered a threat, then, to the perpetuation of the species, a barrier to progress. They were more directly threatening to man because through birth control or abortion they could deny the physical evidence of his masculinity; they could in effect "castrate" or "unsex" man within the confines of the only legitimate channel through which his potency could be socially acknowledged. References to women who practiced such restriction of pregnancies and who refused to bear children are quite common in the anticommunity literature. Writers of these works obviously believed that the practice was becoming ever more prevalent, and they found it personally (and sexually) very threatening. It was to be expected, in an era concerned about the question of whether sexual intercourse for pleasure was justifiable, that women who practiced birth control should be seen, not as attempting to protect themselves from the burden of incessant gestation, but as abandoned profligates, pursuing their forbidden pleasures at the expense of their better or truer natures, as well as the expense of society. Much of the rhetorical attack on women that permeates this literature is manifestly concerned with the transference of guilt generated by the realization that many sex acts had been motivated by pleasure rather than reproductive necessity. The continual assertion that women who rejected motherhood had unsexed themselves ironically reveals this transference mechanism. If those who rebelled against pronatalism did so primarily for gratification without the natural consequences, they were unsexed; that is, they became men. Ergo, to pursue sexual goals for pleasurable ends was masculine.[33]

Opponents of the Mormons, for example, spoke of "Female Roosters," or "that class of females who indulge their sensual propensities, without restraint, whether married or single, by the express permission of the Prophet."[34] The fear expressed here seems to be of the sexually aggressive woman, who, it was believed, would be the natural result of the demise of double-standard morality. Another critic of polygamy makes this point through the assertion that the natural end of polygamy is polyandry: "Polygamy poisons everything, it seems to break down all the barriers of female virtue. . . . A dozen women, the common property of one man, some of them divorced from other men, lodged under the same roof, and often more than one in the same room, soon begin to feel that they might as well be the common property each of a dozen men."[35] In other words, women would begin to demand the same rights of sexual gratification that were being offered to men. The same situation was thought to prevail in the Oneida Community, where "the women have given themselves over to this species of debauchery, rarely making any effort to resist their fate. On the contrary, the most of them, having their appetites whetted by the life they lead, enjoy the variety at their command, and would seriously object to any interruption in the rotation system."[36]

The utopian communities under consideration, then, were considered both debauchers of pure womanhood and proponents of the "new woman," a fractious, rebellious creature, who rejected the quiet role of "cheerful giver" in favor of the strident role of self-assertive individualism. Utopian opponents considered these communities hotbeds of woman's-rights agitation, which served only to exacerbate the already widespread feeling of female dissatisfaction. This, of course, was another way in which woman was unsexed by her aberrant behavior (she was not a true woman); and precisely insofar as she deviated from the ideal, just so far did she become less feminine. The external appearance of these women, their dress, their very physiognomy, provided a visible index to their true character. Uniformly, then, critics commented on the plainness of dress and the unattractiveness of utopian women. It was not simple hard-featured drabness but a negative quality, a lack of "sweet womanliness," which, one commentator noted, "I have yet to see in any of the perfect creatures in short skirts and breeches."[37] The fear of female rebellion, its serious challenge to the social order, its reification in the appearance of women who asserted their rights, and the psychological fear of castration at the hands of a "masculine" woman all came together in Artemus Ward's folksy, cracker-barrel philosophy. He noted of a Shaker woman that she was "a solum female, lookin sumwhat like a last year's bean-pole stuck into a long meal bag."[38] He went on to exhort his female audience: "O, woman, woman! ... you air a angle when you behave yourself; but when you take off your proper appairel & (metyforically speaken)—get into pantyloons—when you desert your firesides, & with your heds full of wimin's rites noshuns go around like roarin lyons, seekin whom you may devour someboddy—in short, when you undertake to play the man, you play the devil and air an emfatic noosance."[39]

Specifically, utopian communities were accused of furthering the rebellion of women by providing a means of ready divorce and social alternatives to marriage, encouraging and actively abetting the breakup of families, and practicing birth control. In all these respects the Shakers, Mormons, and Oneidans were considered asocial groups composed of individuals who had "been disappointed in life, and have thus withdrawn themselves from the rest of mankind, unable to bear up and strive against the adversities of their lot as true Christians,"[40] and who, moreover, actively sought the overthrow of accepted American mores. Anxiety about the collapse of the family, evidently based on the perception of a declining birthrate, reinforcing the fear of rebellious woman, was central to the vision of utopian critics who considered these communitarians dangerous antinomian renegades.

The depths that popular affection for the home, motherhood, and the nuclear family plumbed were quite palpable in acerbic, emotional tirades against communitarian "home-wreckers." The vitriolic denunciation of the Shakers, who brought about "the wrecks of domestic happiness, . . . the abandonment of *wives* and *children*, who had been deprived of their natural guardians and protectors, and thrown upon the cold charities of the world," was typical.[41] Opponents called upon legislators and public officials to "stop these Shakers from creeping about, like the Serpent of old, destroying many a fair Eden of domestic happiness. There is no relation existing in society, of which the law is more jealous and watchful, than that which exists between husband and wife, and it remained to be seen . . . [if they would] permit this people called Shakers to continue their ravages upon Society without any check or restraint."⁴²

Opponents of the Mormons were even more explicit about the need for positive, energetic measures to combat that threat to the peace and integrity of the family. The clarion call of one proponent of the happy hearth is exemplary: "Either all our views of the sacredness of the marriage relation, the unity of the family circle, and the present laws of morality, must be overthrown, or the lawbreakers of Utah must be taught that law is law, right is right, and crime is crime, in Utah just the same as in any other part of the U.S."⁴³

In broader perspective, opponents of these alternative societies saw the family as central to the moral progress of society. The family was the source of all values, all good. A society was only as good as the basic social units (monogamous families) that made it up; families were only as good as their ethical-religious centers (mothers). But the monogamous nuclear family was at the same time the bulwark of the ideological position of communal critics, and its essential weakness. The highly ambivalent attitude toward woman's capacities and her performance in her prescribed role found expression here, as did the tension that the assertion of the self created in nineteenth-century morality. The dilemma was diabolically simple: on the one hand, the ideal of womanhood was selfless abnegation; on the other, the monogamous relationship required strong self-assertion to protect the sanctity of the home and matrimonial alliance from interlopers. In a religious sense, these were the sacred and secular aspects of the female character. In a social sense, they represented the requirements of the female role and the assurance that the reward of the selflessness it prescribed—a limited and socially functional selfishness (which aimed at preserving the family and home intact)—would be provided. The female reward for "cheerful giving" in this ideological structure, her hedge against dissatisfaction and discontent, was, ironically, a reinforcement of the ties that bound her to that system. In a psychological sense, the dilemma was a reflection or projection of that which faced the male, but was less often expressed.

His religious nature, the charitable, loving side of his character, was in conflict with the self-assertive, acquisitive nature of the socioeconomic order of burgeoning capitalism. The "Christian gentleman"⁴⁴ equated charity-unselfishness and the monogamous family–capitalistic economic structure. The ambiguous feelings he had about his own balance, his own failure to achieve selflessness, exacerbated the ambivalence he felt about the new woman and what seemed to him a direct threat to civilization.

The necessity for romantic selfishness was latently expressed in a mis-construed description of the functioning of pantagamy in the Oneida Community penned by the free-love critic John Ellis. He wrote: "There must be no partialities, no selfishness. You may love a woman most devotedly—but you must be ready to yield her to the embrace of any brother Saint who seeks her society. Any reluctance on your part is selfish and sinful, and must be criticized out of you. And you, my fair sister, must be ready to accept the love of any brother. You have no right to dislike him. He has a right to your love, and to every privilege involved in it. You can have no preference for anyone."[45]

The problem was a failure of social egotism; "No woman has a hus-band *of her own* and no man a wife."[46] Foes of Mormon polygamy, however, gave this conception of monogamic selfishness its clearest ex-pression. A "high and holy affection," one such source asserts, in "its very essence is duality; a divided affection is utterly at war with 'that sweet egoism of the heart called love,' that divine selfishness of choosing *one* being apart from all the world, perhaps the *only* form in which selfishness is approved of God."[47]

The dilemma was resolved, inasmuch as it was susceptible of resolu-tion by an artificial individual-social dichotomization. Selfishness in the individual, for personal ends (including sexual intercourse for pleasure rather than reproduction, its social ramification), was wrong and had to be eradicated at all costs. Social egotism, on the other hand, fulfilled a purpose beyond the individual and was therefore permissible. Viewed from this perspective, monogamous love became the foundation of the entire socioethical order, the premier value of all civilized nations. "Its public benefits," as one writer expressed it, "are in the founding of families and establishment of communities, and by it alone can the State be established, on aught approaching sure foundations. In this view, then, marriage is not, as certain theorists would persuade us, a matter strictly between individuals; the State has the highest interest in its regu-lation, and justly determines from the experience of the past what is best for the stability of our institutions."[48]

Criticism of utopian sexuality in its most expansive expression, there-fore, took the form of a crusade against insinuating, irruptive, and incursive forces that were perceived as alien and actively hostile. The similar threats that seemed embodied in foreign immigration with its hordes of "barbarous" foreigners (also people who represented alterna-tive social and religious values) suggested an equation between communi-tarian movements and immigrants. Both groups were quintessentially un-American. They did not share (or at least it was *believed* that they did not) the sense of the givenness of American institutions, the inherent nature of republican virtue that was the legacy of the eighteenth century.

They did not seem to share the current belief in American progress and the inevitable spread of the wings of the American eagle in his flight of manifest destiny. They failed to understand the extent to which Americans identified their peculiar socioethical values with the natural order, the pure distillation of divine inspiration.

Staid nineteenth-century America was perceived by critics of utopias as a society beleaguered, defending virtue and right in a last-ditch stand against a barbaric conspiracy of the new woman, foreigners, Catholics, and communitarians in an unholy alliance. This reading of the seriousness of perceived changes in social behavior was expressed time and time again by opponents of these alternative societies. The concatenation of circumstances that seemed to be destroying the old republic of virtue was clearly set forth.

Reviewing the statistics of the Bureau of Education published in 1873, for example, one concerned writer concluded: "This paper shows that the birth-rate is declining in America from year to year; not in one State only, but in every State. The decline is constant and universal. . . . The birth rate is admitted to be larger among the immigrants than among the natives; yet the average, thus increased by strangers, is lower than that of any country in Europe."[49] In a tone of premonitory foreboding, the same writer called Protestant America to action. Was not "the rapid displacement of the old American stock" evident? "The Irish and the Germans rush into every vacant space. Is it pleasant for any one to consider that in three or four generations more there may be no Americans left on the American soil? In the presence of such a possibility, have the noble churches, the many conservative schools of New England, no mission to assume?"[50] A more militant, religiously inclined observer blamed the decline in native fertility on the rising incidence of birth control and abortion and the hostility to maternity among American-born women. He most feared abortions because, as he put it, if "Protestants continue to practice foeticide to such an extent as is at present done, there is no reasonable doubt why the Roman Catholic Church will not ultimately attain ascendency on this continent, and so hold the balance of power in its management—truly not a desirable prospect."[51]

It was precisely here, at the maternal node, that the doctrine of individual self-abnegation and the social egotism of the dyadic matrimonial unit were in most glaring conflict. The new woman concluded that if she were entitled to proprietorial rights to one man, she had to protect her investment from embezzlement. Her duty was to preserve intact the basic dyadic social unit at all costs. The opinion expressed by a young New England woman that "nothing should ever be allowed to come between these two" was considered by many frightened male observers to be the reason why "America is wasting for the want of mothers."[52] Lest we miss the drift of the author's argument, we are explicitly informed that such women "while proudly insisting on woman's rights . . . abandon all woman's duties."[53]

The conjunction of militant Protestant anti-Catholicism, nativism, patriarchal antifeminism, and distrust of "ultraist" social alternatives is clear throughout the literature critical of these utopian communities. Perhaps because they carried a time-honored, built-in response and provided a popular literary genre in which to encompass their arguments, critics tended to emphasize anti-Catholicism and nativism. In the latter case, they argued that foreigners were the leaders of most of these communities and in fact made up the overwhelming majority of their membership. The visceral fear of the un-American nature of these communal societies was expressed by the anti-Mormon Judge Goodwin. "The Mormon Church," he declared, "is a foreign kingdom, hostile in all its features to a representative form of government; it is guided and controlled by foreigners, and depends on foreigners and the children of foreigners for future expansion and power. *It is absolutely un-American in all its attributes*."[54] Fear of the more fertile and (it was believed) hypersexualized foreigners is never far from the surface in this literature. Temperance and control of the passions were the keys to republican virtue; their opposites, fanaticism and sensuality, characterized those groups (Catholics, immigrants, strident women's-rights advocates) that utopian critics felt threatened by. One of the more obdurate opponents of the Oneida Community made these assumptions explicit when he spoke of

> that tide of sensuality which is setting in with a strong current upon the land, and which, if not turned back, will, it is to be feared, roll on with accumulating strength and accelerating velocity, and before long acquire a momentum, against which all efforts would be unavailing; which would carry away, as with a flood, all opposing influences, and fearfully sweeping, like a devastating tornado, over the land, spreading devastation around on every hand, and making a moral waste of many of the fairest portions of our happy country, and work the temporal and eternal ruin of thousands and millions of our race.[55]

This vast wave of barbarism, ostensibly external but recognized at bottom as largely domestic, was, furthermore, an antidemocratic force opposed to the dominant views of ineluctable progress for America. These utopian communities at best were merely perverse but more frequently were considered positive obstacles to the full realization of American social and economic progress (equated with the capitalistic system) and manifest destiny. In the 1880s, for example, a group of Methodist, Presbyterian, Episcopal, and Congregational divines from Salt Lake City issued a militant statement on the nature and scope of the Mormon problem. "We, in common with the masses of American people," they concluded, recognize that the Mormon church "is *antagonistical to American institutions*, and that there is *an irrepressible conflict between Utah Mormonism and American republicanism*; so much so that they can never abide in harmony. We also believe that the growth of this anti-republican power is such that if not checked speedily it will cause serious trouble in the near future."[56] The echoes of Seward's stand on slavery were taken up by other opponents of Mormonism. By 1882, when anti-Mormon agitation reached its apogee, many hard-line opponents of polygamy were supporting the argument that

> there is an irrepressible conflict between the Mormon power and the principles upon which our free institutions are established, and one or the other must succumb. The arguments, the dogmas, and the whole line of defense of this system are so similar to those used years gone by by the defenders of the system of slavery, that it is, indeed well-named the "Twin Sister." And now I say to the American people that, if something is not done soon to stop the development of this law-breaking, law-defying fanaticism, either our free institutions must go down beneath its power, or, as with slavery, it must be wiped out with blood.[57]

This recalls statements at the 1878 anti-Oneida meeting (convened on the campus of Syracuse University), which employed such language as "extinguish," "eradicate," "demolish," and "wipe out" in reference to proposed solutions to the Oneida problem.[58] Ultimately, the Syracuse meeting came out in favor of legislative action, and the way to a solution to the problem of Mormon polygamy was provided by the passage of the more efficient and stringent Edmunds bill in 1882; but the violent animus against both communities had bordered on a crusading war mentality for a time. The seriousness of these threats to American institutions was evidenced by the militant and unyielding stance of their opponents.

Especially in the case of the Mormons, but to a lesser degree in that of the Oneida Community as well, the equation was drawn between barbarian, unnatural hordes and communitarians. Mormons were compared to the American Indians, the quintessence of savagery, from whom they were thought to have borrowed the essential elements of the polygamic system. Oneidans were likened to wild beasts under the sway of unnatural passions. In short, they were too concerned with the self and lacked all regard for society. The Shakers, on the other hand, were condemned for valuing a social group over the American tradition of individualism.[59] All these communitarians lacked a temperate balance;

they were ultraists who threatened not only the social fabric and the essence of the American republican polity, but the very existence of civilization itself. This argument can best be summarized by a brief look at an anti-Mormon pamphlet that made the assumptions implicit in all anti-communitarian literature quite clear. Polygamy, it argued, "is not Republican. . . . monogamy is the true basis of all Democratic institutions. . . . If that root is rendered corrupt, the whole fabric of society becomes polluted."[60] All opposition to monogamy, then, tends to undermine solid republican virtue: "Search out the cause of decay of every perished Republic, and you will find it was *licentiousness*, or the desecration of the primal law of marriage, which was the canker-worm at the root of the sacred tree of liberty, causing its fall, and thus crushing out the life of free institutions by destroying the fundamental basis on which civil freedom must rest, to wit, justice and purity in the marriage relation."[61]

Opposition to Mormonism, and indeed to *all* alternative communities that did not abide by the republican virtue of monogamy, became a Christian duty of citizenship. All loyal Christian (read Protestant) Americans (read nativists) were called to be "Paladins, battling against the fiercest foes of Woman; Patriots, upholding the dearest rights of Freedom; Christians, advocating the holiest duties of Humanity."[62]

It seemed to these utopian critics that a whole way of life, a whole culture, stood on the brink of frightful change. The old values, the familiar social and sexual relationships, seemed to be crumbling all around. A new woman had arisen, and with her the claim to a new femininity and consequently a new masculinity, which many men found terrifying. The literature of communal opposition was both an exhortation to the faithful to resist such change and a defiant attrition that sought to conceal its fundamentally defensive anxieties beneath an aggressive literary bravura. Underneath lurked the nagging realization that change in sexual behavior and values was inevitable; that in fact it had already begun; and that the seeds of that change had been planted in the normative soil that they knew had nurtured, but denied had sustained, such unnatural and rank undergrowth. We shall see in the following chapters to what extent the fears and anxieties of these communitarian opponents were justified, and how these same problems were confronted by the utopians themselves.

Part II 🜨 Hymenius Bound: Shaker Sexuality in Ideology and Practice

Introduction 🜨 Parousia in Toad Lane: Ann Lee, Founder of the Shakers

What a loving tender Mother
We have in this gospel day,
And if we are subject to her,
We shall never go astray,
She is our kind mediator,
And has taught us what to do,
She has ever been our Saviour,
And our tender Parent too.

—Shaker hymn, "Pure Vessels"

Now stand, and let the Queen of glory in
The Dual Christ upon the cloud now sits
Sickle in hand, to thrust, and reap the world!
The clusters of earth's vine to gather home.

—Shaker poem, "The New Song"

Jeremiah, the somber prophet, warned the Israelites that "the Lord hath created a new thing in the earth" and predicted that in the latter days "a woman shall compass a man" (Jeremiah 31:22). The Shakers believed that this prophecy had been fulfilled in the person of Ann Lee (1736–84), daughter of a Manchester, England, blacksmith, whom they, with reverent affection, called "Mother." Certain it is that her experience played a central role in the shaping of Shaker theology and attitudes toward sexual intercourse.[1]

Lee apparently had deep feelings of guilt and shame about her sexuality almost from her first awareness of the functioning of the reproductive process; for "in early youth, she had a great abhorrence of the fleshy cohabitation of the sexes; and so great was her sense of its impurity, that she often admonished her mother against it; which coming to her father's ears, he threatened and actually attempted to whip her; upon which she threw herself into her mother's arms and clung round her to escape his strokes."[2] The pattern of her response to sex was set in this brief childhood encounter. She experienced continual anxiety about sexual intercourse, begged her parents to be allowed to remain single, and evinced a habitual and somewhat prurient interest in the sexual lives of others. Her adoption of the title "Mother" also takes on additional meaning in the light of this incident. Lee seems to have seen herself assuming the role of her own mother, shielding poor young women who wished to become celibate or remain virginal from the wrath of the men whose sexual desires were frustrated by such behavior.

Apparently Lee had strong maternal instincts as well as a strong sex drive, which, coming into conflict with her inveterate sense of sexual guilt, caused her terrible anxiety. Prior to her marriage, she experienced a series of visions that deeply impressed her with "the odiousness of sin, especially the impure and indecent nature of sexual coition *for mere gratification*."[3] "But nature in her, prone to the earthly, demanded indulgence, and contrary to the teachings of her earlier visions, she yielded, through the importunities of others, and was married" in about 1753 to Abraham Standley, a blacksmith.[4] She underwent eight pregnancies, four of which ended in stillbirths. None of her children lived beyond infancy, the most fortunate surviving but six years. There is a tradition which maintains that all her children were brought forth only after hard labor and that her last child was taken by forceps, or even cesarean section, but no positive evidence to that effect exists.[5] Having begun married life with "the inclination to gratify the evil and corrupt nature of the flesh . . . beyond what . . . [was] ever found to exist in any mortal from that day to this,"[6] yet convinced that intercourse should be primarily for reproduction, Lee's marital experience led her to reject sexual intercourse altogether. That her dissatisfaction with her sexual experience was grounded in the difficulties she had experienced with her pregnancies became part of the traditional hagiographic lore which grew up about her. In a putative visionary appearance in 1849, she discussed her marital experience in these revealing words: "Then I found my soul plunged into the depths of hell. . . . In this state I had to overcome the power of death, and travel out by great struggles, and the most severe sufferings, that I might be enabled to bring souls from thence, into the resurrection from dead works."[7] The association of gestation and birthing with travail (often written "travel"), a favorite word of the Shakers, and the giving of life with death make the attitude of Lee and her followers toward pregnancy and birth quite clear.

Lee's revulsion from sexual intercourse, reinforced by her association with a society of Shaking Quakers led by James and Jane Wardley in

1758 and by her bitter experiences in childbirth, was increased even more, according to orthodox Shaker accounts, by the subsequent behavior of her husband. After marriage, her visions continued, and the conviction that sexual intercourse was a grievous sin grew upon her. Some time in 1770 she informed her husband of her belief and her desire to discontinue cohabitation. He complained of her behavior to the church, which in turn rebuked her, but her antinomian spirit was uncowed. She began to have the physical manifestations of a religious fanaticism: breaking out in uncontrollable cold sweats, perspiring blood, becoming extremely emaciated, and shaking so violently as to set the bed rocking beneath her. She remained in this state (a perverse inversion of the normal course of pregnancy), she tells us, "until my soul broke forth to God; which I felt as sensibly as ever a woman did a child, when she was delivered of it. Then I felt an unspeakable joy in God, and my flesh came upon me, like the flesh of an infant."[8]

It is interesting to note that even in the process of receiving the power to stand out boldly for her choice of a celibate life against her husband and the world, she expressed her figurative rebirth in terms that directly echo the process of natural childbirth. Obviously, her maternal instincts ran very deep. But her visionary experiences go even beyond this. She became in her ecstasy both child and mother at the same time; in a virgin rebirth, she became her own mother.

Her relationship to her husband after 1770 also suggests the maternal more than the uxorial. She looked after him in sickness and health and was "willing to take the most tender care of him," but refused all sexual intimacy.[9] Standley seems to have felt the need for more carnal enjoyments, for after five years of enforced sainthood, he ran off with a prostitute whom he married in 1775.[10]

Inspired by a vision, Lee had led a small band of the faithful to the American colonies in the summer of 1774. But it was not until a year after her break with Standley that she went to Niskeyuna, New York, and established the first Shaker community just outside that place at Watervliet. She was accompanied by a group of her followers, among whom was her brother, William. Her maternal attitude toward this seminal group, especially her brother, is clearly reflected in William's statement, "I love my Mother—altho' she is my sister; yet she has become my Mother."[11] Her successor as spiritual leader of the Shakers was her adopted son, James Whittaker, whose natural mother was a distant cousin of Mother Ann's also named Ann Lee.[12]

Although the evidence is very scanty, there seems little doubt, then, that Ann Lee was strongly attracted to her father and both identified with and sought to displace her mother as the dominant maternal figure in her family.[13] It is likely that jealousy of her mother's sexual prerogatives, as well as concern for the life of her mother, led her to suggest the termination of sexual relations between her parents. Her feelings for her father would also have helped to generate deep feelings of anxiety and guilt about sex, while at the same time leaving her with a gnawing sense of sexual frustration that would provide the impetus for an extremely powerful, if not overwhelming, sex drive. Her marriage to Abraham Standley was both a solution to her problem and a threat to the cherished child-parent relationship. Standley, like her father, was a blacksmith, and thus could serve as a kind of surrogate father-husband. The ambiguity of his role was enhanced by the living arrangement the young couple adopted. They lived in Lee's parental home, allowing her to be simultaneously daughter, wife, and mother.[14] Her experiences in childbirth, though apparently harrowing and exhausting on a physical level, could only have enhanced the feelings of guilt and inferiority she already felt about her sexuality on a psychological level. Her family of origin was fairly large—eight children—and her own failure to be as productive as her mother might have caused her to have feelings of inferiority about her femininity, complicated by a sense of frustration at being unable to displace her mother in the affections of her father, owing to her procreative inadequacies. On another level, her frequent pregnancies by her father-husband would only have increased her sense of guilt in the sex act.

Ann Lee's sense of guilt and the physical suffering that childbirth entailed could only have been heightened by her experience with her family of origin. As one of eight children who worked in the industrial mills of Manchester, she had direct experience of the evils of overpopulation. Henri Desroche suggests that her mother (who died while Ann was still living at home) probably died in childbirth.[15] Given a certain jealousy of her mother and a deep sense of guilt caused by the wish fulfillment her death represented, as well as a tendency to identify with her, Ann's feelings of guilt and shame and her fear of the sexual act become more understandable.

The celibate alternative she adopted allowed her to become a universal mother (thus exceeding her own mother's procreative capacities), while at the same time avoiding the risks of pregnancy and the sense of guilt the act of sexual intercourse always aroused in her. She found satisfaction in a spiritualization of her sex drives, or a kind of pansexual spiritualism. She called herself, and was considered by her followers, the "Second Appearing of Christ," or the "Lamb's Bride." As a female Christ she stood in the place of spiritual mate to the male Christ. She is reputed to have told the Elders on one occasion that Christ "is my Lord and Lover" (a spiritual lover impregnating her with the lives of regenerated souls). "I feel the blood of Christ running through my soul and body, washing me; Him do I acknowledge as my head and Lord."[16] Her spiritual pregnancy was evidenced when she said: "I have had new fruit to eat this morning; such as I never had before! I am full, like a vessel that is ready to burst! My soul is running over!"[17] Thus, Shaker theology revered motherhood but abhorred sexual intercourse.

But her simultaneous antipathy and attraction to the subject of sex remained one of Lee's dominant characteristics. If she succeeded in sublimating her sexual energies in part by establishing a relationship with a spiritual lover, she did so in a more immediate way through her voyeuristic obsession with the sexual irregularities of others, her meddling in their lives, and her curt frankness about sexual matters. Her initiation of auricular confession, which became an established theological principle of the Shakers, allowed her free rein in this perverse redirection of her sexual energies.

Her prurient concern encompassed not only heterosexual relations but homosexuality, masturbation, and animal aberrations as well. Her frankness was on many occasions offensive, and its effect was heightened by an apparent gift of clairvoyance. Her own feelings of guilt and shame led her to adopt a rather sadomasochistic attitude towards the sexual activities of others. On one occasion she attacked the reputation of a young woman living in a house where she herself was a guest. "Are you a Christian," she cried to her host, "and think that girl is chaste and honest? You are deceived—She lives in whoredom with married men, young men, black men, and boys."[18] She attacked another young woman of unblemished reputation, calling her "you filthy whore!"[19] The woman was subsequently found to be pregnant by a married man. Lee removed a plague from the cattle of Joseph Bennett when she forced a confession from a lad who had been guilty of "defiling himself with the cattle."[20]

Lee was masochistic in her obsession with sex, and sadistic in her revelation of the sins of others and in her projection of her own guilt and shame upon others, for whom she could devise fearful punishments to be anticipated. The hell she depicted was a torture chamber for sexual offenders, a dungeon where "those who live in the gratification of their lusts, will be screwed through those parts and tormented."[21] In her Dantesque vision of hell, the punishment would be suited to the crime. Thus, those guilty of animal aberrations would find their souls "transformed into the shape of beasts in hell. . . . They appear in the shape of such beasts as they committed sin with; and this is laid upon them as a punishment of that sin."[22]

We have then, finally, a method of achieving sexual enjoyment through voyeurism, while at the same time punishing the projection of the self passively invested in the vicarious sexual experience by proposing the punishment of those actively involved in the act. The Shakers' pattern of sexual ideology and behavior was thus established *ab initio* in the experience and "travel" of their founder, Ann Lee.

Chapter 4 🐛 "Flesh Is the Forbidden Fruit": The Theological Background and Its Relationship to Sexual Ideology

Ye have no resurrection otherwise, except ye continue chaste, and defile not the flesh but keep it pure.

—New Testament Apocrypha: Acts of Paul 2:12

Multi quidem facilius se abstinent ut non utantur, quam temperent ut bene utantur [To many, total abstinence is easier than perfect moderation].

—St. Augustine, *De bono conjugali*

*T*he rudiments and basic orientation of the Shakers' sexual ideology were directly derived from the oral tradition about Ann Lee, which became an integral part of their holy books. Insofar as it went beyond their philosophical system, their sexual ideology was constructed of elements of popular nineteenth-century thought combined with their reading of Lee's experience.

At the heart of their theological system was a pervasive dualism, which envisioned the universe as an arena in which the conflict between an uncreated good (pure spirit) and an uncreated evil force (pure matter) was played out. In order to bridge the gap between these two antipodal forces, they posited a hierarchy within which mankind was divided into two classes or "orders," an Adamic and a Divine, which were totally separate and "organically different," with discrete systems of laws. The Adamic order was subject to natural law and the cycle of procreation and death, whereas the Divine order was above all law, subject only to God, and emancipated from birth and death.[1] By the 1870s this doctrine of hierarchies was expressed in terms of spiritualistic thought (inner and outer, spiritual and material, and higher and lower spheres), which took on a very specific yet at the same time very all-encompassing meaning for Shaker sexuality.

The legacy of Ann Lee was evident both in the absolutist morality implied in this dualistic system and in the energizing of that system from its very inception by a pansexual force. Shakers accepted the biblical account of the origin of man, framed in the image of God, and insisted "that it is the male and female in man that is peculiar to the 'image of God.'"[2] All nature was dual, "the action of *two forces*, the positive and the negative, whose forms, in the vegetable kingdom, gradually resolve themselves into male and female types. . . . The Shakers believe that the distinction of sex is eternal, that it inheres in the soul itself, and that no angels or spirits exist who are not male and female."[3] Given the pervasive duality of the universe, we are ineluctably led to the conclusion that the hypostases of the godhead are also male and female. Lee becomes the female Christ.

The necessity for a female Christ arose out of the Shakers' perception of the radical nature of gender differences, as well as the impossibility of transcending the innate sexual division that characterized the universe. Both a male and a female Christ were necessary to their theology, not only because it was impossible for them to conceive of a generation or a "regeneration" in any other than sexual terms, but also because it was only "through these [that] the male and the female find each their corresponding relation to the great first cause, *from whom* all order and perfection flows, and their joint union and relation to each other in the work of redemption."[4] Male and female have separate intermediaries because they are of radically different orders; their natures are completely different, though complementary. They are driven by separate and opposite forces: the male by an active, positive force, and the female by a passive, negative force. Like everything else in the Shaker system, male and female are diametric opposites in a duality that finds perfection only in an all-encompassing unity, that of a male-female godhead.[5]

Not only did the fundament of the universe rest upon the sexual duality, but the force that made the worlds turn was sexual in nature. Shakers considered the sex drive a natural force of overwhelming power, a force that required all their mental and physical energies to keep at bay, for "that desire of carnal enjoyment, that mutually operates between male and female, is far more powerful than any other passion in human nature. . . . Surely then, that must be the fountain head, the governing power, that . . . stupefies the sense to all other objects of time or eternity, and swallows up the whole man in its own peculiar enjoyment."[6]

Like other dualists, they were obsessed with the evil force in the universe, an evil force grounded in the power and allurement of sexuality. Others might find sex a harmless pleasure, but for Shakers the indulgence of the sexual appetite was the original sin and literally the head of all subsequent ones. In the primeval garden, the metaphorically represented act of Adam and Eve in "eating the forbidden fruit, was the *very act* by which *Adam knew Eve his wife*, when she conceived and brought forth a murderer." From that time onward, Shakers remarked in a tongue-in-cheek parody of the sexual mores of worldly people, "the very seat and fountain head of all sin and corruption, might have been discovered at once to view, by no more than the bare removal of a *fig-leaf*."[7]

Sex, as the source of all lust, lost its association with sociability and companionship; it became the ultimate form of selfishness, a totally asocial and anarchistic force. "The nature of fallen man," as they expressed it, "is selfish, being wholly bent on selfish gratifications. His desires are selfish; because they are directed solely to objects which tend to gratify his selfishness. His love is selfish; because it is confined to those who indulge and please his selfishness. In short, the gratification of *self* is the great object of all his pursuits."[8] It is not surprising, then, that the language the Shakers used to describe lust was permeated with references to other kinds of asocial behavior—drug addiction, alcoholism, and criminal activity—and that their description of the effects of sexual indulgence was often couched in the lurid imagery of nineteenth-century masturbation literature. Masturbation was, after all, the "solitary vice," the ultimate in selfish sexual gratification, and a blatant declaration that sex was to be used not for reproduction but for pleasure alone. This is clearly illustrated in a Shaker sermon dealing with "the abuse of amativeness": "All the propensities and appetites are excited and inflamed beyond the natural antagonistical control of the moral powers . . . [This leads to] irregularity and depravity of appetite; all manner of cravings, gnawings, and perversions, paving the way for flesh, grease, narcotics, stimulants, excitants, irritants, etc.; by connection with perverted taste one of the principal foundations for chewing tobacco, betel, opium, etc."[9]

The Shakers continually maintained that they were not opposed to sex in the abstract, or in its proper "order"; and their skill in the breeding of domestic animals and success in founding one of the earliest garden-seed industries in America lend credence to this claim. What they were opposed to was the inversion of what they perceived to be the natural order. As it applied to man, "The *order* of his creation was, for the *animal* organization, which connected him with the external world, to be directed and governed by the powers of his superior part, or living soul; and for the *spirit* to be under the guidance of the Divine laws of his being."[10] Lust inverted the order of creation by rendering man bestial. As the Shakers' unusual concern for regulations governing the relationships between animals and human beings illustrates, they felt that man was continually threatened by the animal nature both within and without. It is not surprising, therefore, that another of the key Shaker metonymies for lust, along with masturbation, was bestiality.

The only way to survive amid the swirl of animality and the seducing power of sexuality was to reestablish the natural order through an iron control of the will, a control so thorough that all desire would be crushed out. The Shakers saw themselves as radical reformers who, through the control of their passions, could achieve perfection and freedom from sin. To their minds, lust was a drug with addicting properties, and the analogy which most readily occurred to them was that between sex and alcohol. The very tone with which they discussed the battle for self-control was that of nineteenth-century temperance literature: "No sensualist can be reformed by a moderate sensuality. Badly as we may hate it, total abstinence . . . is the only sure remedy."[11] "Considering the weakness of human nature, it cannot rest safely half way. To taste is to drain the cup—to drain the cup is to die. Therefore, my words to the world are, handle not—touch not that which defileth; but . . . practice virgin celibacy not only in *deed*, but in word and thought."[12]

The goal of Shaker ethics was instinctive obedience to the rational, ethical aspect of nature and, consequently, a complete freedom from everything instinctual, bestial, and terrestrial. Transcendence of the body through sheer willpower, the attainment of a state beyond all physical need and desire, a Western nirvana, was to be accomplished through "a perfect obedience to the law of Christ . . . denying *self* of every actual and sensual gratification, as he did, [which] released every member of his body from all the external obligations of those carnal ordinances."[13]

The aggressive nature of the Shakers' "taking up the cross" against the flesh is evident in the imagery they used to describe the experience of self-denial and their strident insistence on the analogy between circumcision and a celibate life-style. The underlying sadomasochistic longing for castration as a release from the desires of the body is quite clear in many of these statements. The more rational level of this kind of imagistic argument maintained that "emasculation is like Paul's circumcision, of the heart, in the spirit, and not in the letter (Rom., ii, 29). Outward emasculation would avail nothing, but in the heart everything. The eunuchs for the kingdom of heaven's sake are such as in *heart* deny themselves, not such as externally incapacitate themselves and retain an adulterous heart."[14] This was the official position: circumcision of the heart but not of the body, a church of spiritual but not physical eunuchs. The militancy of the Shakers' celibacy, however, often was not conducive to such a restrained mode of expression; and the underlying hatred of man's sexual nature, and perhaps the frustration of a daily, hourly, struggle for the mastery of their own sexual desires, led them to adopt a much more aggressive rhetoric.

The extreme hatred they felt for their own sexual natures often took the form of an almost scatological equation of the sex organs with filth and ordure, blood, disease, and death. Describing the experience of redemption from married life, for example, a female visionary clearly expressed this metaphorical tradition: "Never could any one, who had become besmeared from the crown of the head to the soles of the feet with the most loathsome nuisance, be found more engaged to be set free, than was my soul engaged to dig out of the pit into which I had fallen, and be set at liberty and purified from the defilements which I had gathered."[15] "Pollution" and "defilement" are key words in their description of the organs of generation. Perhaps the best example of this kind of rhetoric is to be found in a discussion of the taboos of the Mosaic law. According to the Shaker reading, under this legal code,

> the sexes were wholly prohibited from cohabitating on pain of being excommunicated, for a time, from the congregation of such as were counted clean. . . . There was no possible case, in which a man and woman could lie together, with seed of copulation, and hold their union with the congregation within the camp of Israel. The very act cut them off, and exposed them to the reproaches of those who were unclean without the camp. Nor could they be again accepted until they were cleansed: for nothing unclean could abide in the camp.[16]

It is not the passage itself but, even more significantly, the documentation of it that reveals the Shaker attitude. What is highly significant here is the association of ideas set up in the use of the particular passages chosen and the idea of the uncleanliness of sex and the organs of sex evidenced in the passage cited above. Leviticus, chapter 20, is a statement of the blood taboo as it relates both to avoiding sex with a menstruating female and to observing lines of descent so as to avoid incestuous relationships. Numbers 19:20–21 deals not with sex but with uncleanliness resulting from touching the dead. Numbers 12:14 is about Miriam's uncleanness as a leper. Significantly, the only passages that have anything directly to do with sexual matters are concerned not with intercourse but with the uncleanliness of the excretions of the body. Deuteronomy 23:10–11 and Leviticus 15:17 refer to nocturnal emissions and condemn them not because they are a manifestation of man's sexual nature but because they are excretions of the body, and as such unclean.[17]

The depth of meaning Shakers attached to such terms as "wallowing in the filth of sexuality" and "corrupting the fountain of his existence" through concupiscence[18] becomes much more understandable in the light of such a passage and the associations evoked by its panoply of biblical allusions. The selection of biblical passages to buttress their argument, as well as their frequent reference to "pollution" when referring to sexual matters, also reveals a probable source for at least a portion of their aggressive, destructive attitudes toward the sexual organs themselves. Nocturnal emissions, perhaps only half understood, would have been a source of shame and deep guilt among militantly celibate men. Was I responsible through lust in my heart? Even in sleep, was my will not sufficiently under my rational control? Was clandestine, unconscious masturbation involved? For a community of virgin celibates, these were not idle fears. When coupled with the fear of losing their masculinity through the loss of semen, which will be discussed below, these fears and feelings of guilt must have been a powerful force in generating the extreme desire to be rid of sexual problems forever, a desire which is obviously behind the castration imagery that is such an integral part of their writings.

The language used in describing the eschewal of the sexual life of the world has a fierceness all its own. "Cutting off," "reaping," "burning up," and "rooting out" are favorite phrases. The need for suffering in the sexual organs themselves as a punishment for concupiscence is clear:

> The circumcision of the male in the flesh of his foreskin, was a signal mark of mortification in that particular member of the flesh in which is found the seat of its pleasures. . . . it was very plainly manifested that the seal of the covenant in Christ, was to consist in the *cutting off, and total rejection of fleshy lust*, by a life of self-denial and the cross. . . . This not only wounded the flesh in such a manner that the mark remained visible ever after; but it took blood, which is the life of the flesh, from that very member in which is found the seat and center of all the pleasures of lust.[19]

Redemption for man came only through "cutting him off and severing him from the work of generation," "the ax being first applied to the root and first cause of human depravity."[20]

The logical extension of such imagery, coupled with the desire to be free from sexual desire, to transcend sexuality, was the desire for emasculation. This sense of identification with those who were physically beyond the sins of the flesh not infrequently burst to the surface in Shaker religious writings. The vision that preceded Frederick W. Evans's conversion was a classic statement of the association of perfectionism with the total extirpation of the sex organs: "I saw a great fire, and a nude man, perfect in his physical organism, standing by it, he stepped into its very midst, the flames completely encircled his whole body. The next thing I observed was, that while he was perfect in *living beauty*, he was so organically changed that no 'fig leaf' covering was required."[21]

The emphasis in all of this castration imagery is, not surprisingly in a female-founded religion, aggressively antimale. The obvious assumption was that if the male could succeed, through the powers of his will, in mastering and crushing out his sexual nature, and "if sexual coition ceases in the male, it must cease in the female of course."[22] Interestingly, the main emphasis was upon male self-control; women were considered to be weaker in this respect. It should not be assumed, however, that this meant that the primary guilt for lust lay with the male, or that an aggressively antifemale attitude was not inherent in Shakerism. The point to be noted here is rather that Shaker dualism extended the doctrine of spheres or orders to separate functions for the sexes (will being that of the male), and that statements expressing aggression against the female genitals were comparatively rarer than those expressing an emotional longing for emasculation.

Metaphorical expressions of the extirpation of the female generative organs are extant—for example, Frederick Evans's statement that "the testimony of the Christ Spirit pierced, as a sword, through the bowels or womb of the Virgin Mary"; or the vision of the damned in hell, where "their torment appears like melted lead, poured through them, in the same parts where they have taken their carnal pleasure"[23]—but they are not as unequivocal as those directed against males. This is suggestive of a certain indecision among the Shakers about the role and place of women in society, an ambiguous perception of their nature and abilities.

Shaker attitudes toward women are an exceedingly complex mixture of theological, social, and sexual attitudes. They take their departure from the Edenic fall that came upon Adam and Eve as a result of consummated desire. In Shaker mythology, the female of the species seems to have been literally seduced by the devil. As a Shaker didactic poem has it:

> The woman was beguiled
> And got the serpent's seed you know;
> And though she was defiled
> The harlot took the lead you know.[24]

What is continually emphasized is that woman was first in sin; that she is less human than man; and that she, because more animalistic, rebelled against God and overthrew the rationally established order of things. Woman becomes, for the Shakers, a dangerous anarchistic force, a demon of chaos, which must be controlled if progress toward civilization and the perfection of humanity is to be achieved. The implications of this position are clearly delineated in this extract from their general theological principles:

> The woman was overcome. She yielded to the evil influence which, through the subtlety of the serpent, wrought upon her animal propensities, and infused into her mind the filthy passion of *lust*. The woman being thus enticed and overcome, enticed her husband, and through the same evil influence overcame him. Thus the noble order of creation was reversed. Man having yielded to the temptation, and receiving and indulging an evil propensity, his power was gone. And having been once overcome, by yielding to the insinuations of an authority inferior to his own, he had henceforth no control over the inferior creation, any further than by the permission of his Creator.[25]

There are two important corollaries implicit in this theological position, which became central elements in the Shaker attitude toward women. First, woman is less rational, less able to control her emotional responses, and more of a sexual creature than man. Secondly, woman is a temptress; a force, if not positively evil in itself, certainly allied with all that most immediately threatens the virtuous life of the male.

The female is the chief repository of the sexual drive, according to Shaker sexual ideology. Sexual passion itself was considered to be an attribute of the female nature, a manifestation of those "effeminate desires, and sensual pleasures" shunned by all good Shakers.[26] In an extension of their aggression against their own sexual natures manifested by a desire for emasculation, Shakers found that sexual desire "UNMANS the man."[27] The root of this kind of argument (as well as that which considered the female a temptress) seems to have been men's anxieties and guilt feelings about their own sexuality. These fears and misgivings were projected onto women, who thus became the scapegoats who would atone for the original and, in the Shaker interpretation, all subsequent sin. As we shall see later, it is this mechanism of psychological projection that explains in great measure the ability of the Shakers to view woman as simultaneously an evil temptress and threat to the universe, and the only possibility of ultimate salvation through perfection. For the moment, however, to illustrate more clearly the way this projection mechanism operated, let us consider the associations that Shakers evoked in other uses of the term "effeminate." The testimony of one Reuben Rathbone, a quondam Shaker, provides an excellent example: "I never have had any unlawful connection with any woman; and from the time I first knew the Shakers to this time, *I never defiled myself with what is called among you effeminacy.* . . . As to the woman who is now my wife, *I never knew whether she was male or female* until after I was legally married to her."[28] The reference was even more unequivocally pointed when Thomas Brown, a sympathetic observer, speaking of a Shaker sermon, made reference to a group, "one of whom is the *effeminate* ———," a phrase that delicacy prohibited him from completing.[29] The obvious association in both passages was with homosexuality, and Brown's citation of 1 Corinthians 6:9 made this unmistakable. It is evident that when the Shakers used the term "effeminate," one of the major connotations they attached to it was that of the passive partner in a male homosexual relationship.[30] Their use of the term in this sense was a literal one; men who behaved in this manner literally became women, and objects of contempt in their minds. The association between "lust" and "effeminacy" in the Shaker mind is quite obvious on this level of usage. Because the only sexual behavior that was even vaguely justifiable in their minds was for reproduction alone, homosexuality, which like masturbation was for pleasure alone, could be naught but lust.

Shaker males seem to have been obsessed with a fear of the power of women. In their own terms, in a universe in which perfection meant a unified bisexual whole, this could only mean that what they feared was the feminine nature within themselves (which they externalized as fear of homosexuality) and that part of the masculine nature (the sexual) which most readily responded to the feminine. One of the dominant motifs employed in the description of feminine characteristics, therefore, was that of the temptress. In many instances there was an implication that the fate of those who fell into the hands of this Jezebel was death or, on a less conscious level, castration. The expression of sexual guilt and especially the need for an ostensible punishment for the projection of one's own sexual responsibility onto the opposite sex (the temptress) appears to have been what made the metaphor of the temptress such an attractive and powerful one to the minds of Shaker males. The wickedness imputed to the carnivorous female is obvious in the Shaker admonition to an "adulterous generation" to "flee . . . from the habitations of the rude, and of the witty charmer, whose flattering words and fair speeches are as a net drawn to gather her prey, and wait for blood; therefore beware . . . that ye be not cut off in the days of your youth, and in the midst of your uncleanness, to meet the reward of the filthy."[31]

The functioning of the projection mechanism in the context of the temptress imagery is best illustrated by the Shaker treatment of the story of the triangular relationship of Sarai-Abram-Hagar. They believed that Abram, in taking Hagar to wife, had been "deceived through Sarai, as Adam was deceived through Eve."[32] The assumption made here was that the sexual union of Abram and Hagar was lust, as evidenced by the offspring of the union, Ishmael, the antitype of Cain. But Abram gives no evidence of having been seduced in the biblical account (Genesis, chapter

16). On the contrary, he seems quite amenable to the proposed relationship with Hagar (Genesis 16:7–9). The Shakers in their interpretation
characteristically identified with the male, patriarchal figure; assumed
the reason for punishment to be lust (after all, sex was the root of all
evil); refused to accept consciously any male guilt for that putative sin;
and chose instead to project that guilt upon Sarai, the wife of Abram.
The female thus became a creature of infinite lust and seduction, the male
an innocent victim.

What defense did the Shakers offer the male against this seductress? In
essence, they suggested that it should be the male rather than the female
who controlled sexual morality. They expressed this idea in a neat
couplet: "By Man's example led, / Woman to the flesh is dead."[33] In
accordance with their perception of the two sexes as separate orders with
different attributes, they provided for the dual government of their communities. Under this arrangement, "the male and female elements are
equally balanced in the leaders. The *former* has reference to, and operates
more specifically upon, the *rational* faculty in human nature; the *latter*,
to the affectional."[34]

In the natural order of things, the female was obviously considered to
be inferior. Female qualities were those most closely associated with
matter, whereas those of the male were ethereal and spiritual.[35] It was
for this reason that the Shakers did not consider Mary the true mother of
Christ. Their aggressive attack upon the female character and especially
upon the value of the institution of maternity is striking:

> Mary was a fallen creature, possessed of the same corrupt nature
> with other women. . . . It is evident that in Christ Jesus was no sin,
> that he did no evil. . . . therefore it follows, that he derived no part
> of his substance from a sinful woman, any more than the substance
> of the human soul is derived from the dust of the ground. That
> which he took upon him through the medium of a woman, he never
> owned as any part of his divine substance, but crucified it unto *the
> death*. . . . the conception of the Son of God was merely in Mary, as
> the medium of his existence on earth, and not *of* her substance;
> hence he was conceived by the *Holy Ghost*, which came upon her,
> and was begotten by the power of the *Highest*, which over-
> shadowed her; and therefore the *Holy Ghost* was the real and true
> Mother of our Lord.[36]

Because Shakers considered women to be of a totally different order
from men, they felt that a special heavenly dispensation was necessary
for the salvation of the female. Ann Lee was the female Christ both in a
universal sense and in the more limited sense of a savior of women, for
"in her was first wrought the complete redemption of the female, and

through her ministration a way was opened for the restoration of the female character to its proper lot and dignity, from which it had been degraded by the transgression of the first woman."³⁷ A female Christ was necessary for the special salvation of women because Christ (as man) had triumphed over human sexuality without ever really being involved in the life of the physical body. The male incarnation of the Christ-spirit was born and remained chaste, pure, and godlike; the female was chthonic, filthy, and lustful in its inception, with a nature that must perforce be transcended. It was necessary, therefore, that the female manifestation of Christ "should come in a vessel who had been immersed in this stream of sorrow, that she might be enabled, in her compassion, to reach beneath the depth of all human depravity."³⁸

But the female Christ was necessary to the final salvation of man as well, for no "spiritual union and relation [could] exist in order, between the sexes, until the woman was raised up, in her appointed season, to complete the order in the foundation of the new creation, for the redemption of both man and woman. . . . The woman was the *first* in the transgression, and therefore must be the *last* out of it; and by her the way of deliverance must be completed."³⁹ Woman becomes, then, in the Shaker system, a highly ambiguous entity: at once Jezebel and foundation stone of the new order; harlot and saint.

Yet despite this ambiguity, the final impression the Shakers' writings create is one of profound distrust and fear of the feminine nature. Again, their anxieties are most clearly revealed in the field of associations they set up by their use of biblical references. Asserting the need for a dual Christ, so that "the male and female might both have their proper and equal lot and place, in the work of redemption,"⁴⁰ they immediately cite 1 Corinthians 11:3, 7–12, which maintains that "the head of the woman is the man." This makes clear their rendering of the phrase "equal lot and place." The fear of woman as a usurper and the necessity of keeping the unruly creature under control are perfectly illustrated in a typical Shaker venture into typological exegesis. Female subjection to male authority was presaged by the fact that Eve,

> "the figure of *her* that was to come," was not created out of the dust of the earth, as Adam was, but was formed of his substance, and taken from his body; therefore she was dependent on him, and it was her duty to be subject to him as her head and lord. Had the woman been created in the same manner that the man was, there would have been two separate heads of the creation; and as neither of them could have had pre-eminence; so neither of them could have been placed in a state of subordination to the other. So also, agreeable to this figure, the second Eve was not brought forth in the

same manner that the second Adam was; but, as to her person, she came into the world as all other women do. But as the substance of the first woman was taken from the body of the first man; so that Divine Spirit with which the second woman was endowed, and which constituted her the second Eve, was taken from the Spirit of the second Adam, the Lord Jesus Christ; therefore she was necessarily dependent on him, as her head and lord.[41]

Woman remains the "glory of man" (1 Corinthians 11:7) at all levels of the hierarchy of creation. Even the angels are male and female, cherub and seraph, the latter characterized as "most glorious." Lest we are left with any illusions, we are told in a footnote: "N.B. The word *glorious* alludes to the heavenly beauty of the female as the glory of the male."[42]

But at bottom, male Shakers remained uneasy about their ability to control the female of the species; no doubt on some level they recognized their own guilt and responsibility for the sin of lust, no matter how often they reiterated the dogma of the female seductress. In the 1870s, when the Shakers were swept up in what was perhaps the most powerful effluence of nineteenth-century feminism, Frederick Evans, in a paroxysm of reform rhetoric, could declare that the regulation of human sexuality was "contrary to nature; for in all the animal creation the female governs and rules in the work of reproduction, except amongst the human race. Man rules over woman, to her loss and damage, and to his own confusion of face."[43] The more typical reaction, however, seems to have been an inveterate fear that the female of the species *might* gain control of social mores.

The sexual allure of women, therefore, threatened weakness, insanity, and ultimately death for the individual; and for society, the usurpation of man's place by women, and indeed the final demise of civilization. It was this fear of the female that provided the basis for Shaker ideas about the physical relations between the sexes. These ideas were derived from a sexual ideology Shakers shared with noncommunitarian Americans of the nineteenth century—"spermatic economy," rooted in an anxiety over "spermatic *loss*, with its concomitant losses of will and order."[44]

In the Shaker mind the threat to male potency through sexual intercourse became associated with the feminine overthrow of the natural order of created things and beings, through another use of the term "effeminate." When used specifically in its reference to this male anxiety, it appears to mean "render voluptuous or self-indulgent," or "enervated and wrecked in mind and body";[45] in short, considering the typical assumptions made in the nineteenth century, literally to convert the male into a female. This association is clear, when lust is attacked as that which "not only effeminates the mind, but enervates the body; which not only distaineth the soul, but disguiseth the person."[46] A man had to be careful: the relationship between the sexes could not be considered mere dalliance or childish disporting; it was in deadly earnest. If the male yielded to what Shakers considered to be the stronger sexual drives of the female, he stood to lose his position of precedence, his moral authority, and his very sexual identity. The male was, after all, subject to sexual dehydration; he could easily become the withered, "sapless tree."[47] An article in the *Shaker*, entitled "Regeneration," makes the point most cogently: "Every atom of nervous force he allows to be wasted, in the pleasurable excitements of . . . animal indulgences and intoxications, subtracts directly from that unreplenishable stamina of body and mind by which he is to effect his final exaltation to a higher plane."[48]

In this ideological formulation, which was largely a product of post-1850 Shaker thought, the body was clearly considered a closed system, maintained by the control of the will, governed by the principle of conservation of matter and energy. The Shakers seem to have adopted this ideology more or less as a whole from physiological texts like John Cowan's *The Science of a New Life* (1874) and spiritualist-phrenological doctrine, especially that of Andrew Jackson Davis (1826–1910).[49] The problem posed by this ideology was the danger of sexual drain, which "taxes severely every part of the vital economy. Man cannot evade this law, nor the penalties of violation. The sole cure is abstinence; hence unchastity causes in the aggregate, a tremendously expensive, inane and profitless drain upon the vital forces. It penetrates every part of the system and drains therefrom the finest essence of brain and blood and nerve, the seeds of health, vigor, life and motion and expels them as food for demons of darkness that feed on the vices of mortals."[50] "Virgin celibacy" was the Shakers' unique solution to this problem, but it did not prevent them from considering the sexual problems of the world outside their communities from this ideological point of view.

Shakers always maintained that they were not against the practice of marriage in its "proper order." They meant, of course, that it was all right for those who were not Shakers and who were living an unregenerated life anyway. They insisted, however, that sexual intercourse be used for generative purposes only. Frederick Evans made the connection between this Shaker tenet and their sexual ideology explicit: "The primal purpose of Amativeness is not gratification nor pleasurable intoxication, but the 'replenishing of the earth.' All more than this is wasted expenditure; and Nature hurls terrible penalties at those who thus destroy their vital forces. The legitimacy of the generative plane, under the guidance of the wisdom principle [will] is admissible."[51] This doctrine had certain ramifications that were expressed in the form of recommended sexual behavior. Evans proposed a reform in the legal structure to provide that "children [be] nursed three years, during which time the woman was free."[52] Their system further interdicted all sexual congress during menstruation and pregnancy, as well as for a postpartum period of at least eighty days.[53] Shakers were also opposed to sexual activity among the elderly, because it violated their law of "times and seasons," predicated upon the ideological assumption that sex was for generative purposes only.[54]

A grudging acceptance of sexuality for procreation only led to an exceptionally frank discussion of a whole catalog of sexual sins that were (they assumed) chiefly pleasurable. Adultery, prostitution, and bigamy were proscribed as a matter of course. They admonished all to "cease to mingle in fleshly defilement with the beasts of the field, or with your domestic animals. Cease to gratify your carnal desires with your own sex, man with man and woman with woman; neither become defilers of your own bodies, working self-pollution in ways which are unseemly, and against the law of nature."[55]

Retribution awaited all who violated the order of nature; but the fate of those in the normal marriage relation was perhaps the worst. If intercourse were indulged in for pleasure rather than reproduction, the lust of the act would be transferred to the progeny. Whatever sensation influenced the parental minds (especially that of the mother) at the moment of conception would determine the character of the child.[56] This rudimentary understanding of the principles of heredity and genetic transmission was common among all the individuals I have encountered who subscribed to the spermatic-economy doctrine. It was very intimately related to the importance attached to control of the will, its obvious corollary being that man could control the course of genetic inheritance by exerting the spiritual power of his mind, or as the phrenologists called it, the cerebral power, at the moment of ejaculation.[57]

Ultimately, for the Shakers, man's existence in this life, his hope for improvement, and his reward or punishment in the next life hung upon his sexual conduct. The universe was energized by an awesome sexual force. Man could render it beneficent only through his willpower, by controlling his relation to it. If he failed, it would destroy him. This vision of the universe, rooted in a profoundly sexual vision of the behavior of man and God, permeated all facets of Shaker life. The Shakers' frugality in economic matters and even their craftsmanship were closely related to this body of thought. The link between their sexual ideology and domestic economy is obvious when we consider that Shakers were urged to eschew "all manner of wastefulness, use the things of this world as not abusing them, and consider that it is a command of your Lord to gather up the fragments, that nothing be lost."[58] The strict control of the will required of Shaker craftsmen, in order to avoid the prodigality of adornment in furniture, a control perceived as a subordination of one's will to the will of God as expressed in the inherent design of the emergent article, was a reflection of the Shaker sexual ideology on both the purely economic and the artistic levels.[59]

Above all else, however, the Shakers' sexual system brought the possibility of perfection within their grasp and insured reform and the continuing moral progress of the species. Celibacy afforded Shakers the opportunity to become angelic, a vanguard of the regenerated while still on earth through the full realization of their natural potential:

> Nature's great law is PROGRESS, carrying up and sublimating each lower grade of being to subserve the grade above. Nature's law of reproduction is only a *sub*-law, subservient to the grand law of progress. Those portions of seeds which are reserved for reproduction can rise to no higher use than merely to *propagate and die*! This is an inflexible law of Nature. . . . [Those] . . . which yield up their organs of reproduction, enter into nobler uses, and higher grades of life; forming blood, muscle, bone, nerve, brain, and thus subserving, if not actually constituting, the sublime mentality of the human intellect.[60]

Man and woman in their parallel and separate orders, by conquering every vestige of sexual desire, would become the next stage in the evolutionary progress of the race—"creatures new formed."[61] In a communal setting, where lust and selfishness could be more completely overcome, they would become part of "a galaxy of sainted, virgin souls."[62]

Chapter 5 🜹 Under the Fig Leaf: Sexual Regulations and Practices among the Shakers

Lust ist Lust. Es its einerlei, bezogen in dem Ehestande oder aussen demselben [Lust is lust. It is the same, whether in connection with the marriage state or outside it].

—Giles Avery, *Eine Kurtze Beschreibung des Glaubens und Praktischen Lebens*

Quid si, inquiunt, omnes velint abomni concubitu abstinere, unde subsistet genus humanum? Utinam omnes hoc vellent! dumtaxat in caritate, de corde puro, et conscientia bona, et fide non ficta: multo citius Dei civitas compleretur et acceleraretur terminus mundi [What if, they say, everyone were to abstain from all coition; how then would the human race survive? Oh, that all wanted to abstain! provided only that it were done in love (caritas), from a pure heart, with a good conscience, and unfeigned faith; then the City of God would be compassed much more rapidly, and the end of the world hastened].

—St. Augustine, *De bono conjugali*

Shakers were postmillenarians, religious perfectionists, and vigorous social reformers. Their meliorative concerns not only included marriage, divorce, prostitution, birth control, abortion, and all sorts of sexual problems, but also extended to temperance, women's dress, pacifism, dietary questions, the use of tobacco, adulterated food, and a host of lesser matters.[1] As "radical reformers," however, they believed that if lust were once conquered, all other problems would solve themselves. Eradicate the root; the branches will wither away.

Shakers accepted the postmillenarian position, considering themselves free from sin, while at the same time advocating universal reform. They were "progressive perfectionists," who combined the older religious tradition of millennial perfection with the secular, optimistic belief in progress that was so characteristic of the nineteenth century. As a Shaker text expressed it:

> The idea which most people have of perfection, is a state in which there can be no increase for the better. This is a mistaken idea; such a state will never be attained, neither in time nor eternity: for the very life of all things which have life . . . consists in an increasing growth of some kind or other. Stop that increase or growth in any thing, and its life will immediately begin to decay, and it must at length die. . . . Therefore, tho' a soul in the progress of faithful obedience to the increasing light and work of God, may become divested of all sinful desires and propensities; yet his life and happiness must and will consist in a further and progressive growth in the knowledge and nature of God, to the endless ages of eternity. And yet a soul who is perfectly obedient to the revealed will of God, is equally perfect before God, in every step of his travel, according to his capacity and God's requirement. . . . the real nature of perfection . . . consists in nothing more nor less than in doing what God requires of us, which is to improve all our faculties in doing good, according to the best of our understanding and capacity: and in so doing every person who sincerely desires and rightly pursues it, *may attain to perfection.*[2]

This kind of doctrine presented a problem for the Shakers very similar to one of the central difficulties the seventeenth-century Puritans had faced. All men are not saints. Within the communal setting, there were three "orders," the Novitiate, Junior, and Senior. Each order might have its "perfection," but the hierarchical structure of Shaker society was predicated upon the assumption that the apogee of human perfection was to be attained in the Senior Order, most especially among the even more select group of the Ministry and Elders. The problem, then, was to insure the highest possible standard of perfection for the community as a whole, and at the same time to protect those who possessed greater saintliness from the temptations presented by those on a lower level of beatitude.

The Shakers' response to this difficulty was twofold. First, they established a highly authoritarian, theocratic polity. As they expressed it in a synoptic account of their theological principles:

> The Shaker institution being, as its subjects believe, *the kingdom of Christ's Second Appearing upon earth*, is not, therefore, a *democ-*

racy, it is a *theocracy.* Its leaders are . . . *appointed* to office. They
are *not* elected by majority votes of members. . . . The ORDER of
the leading and governmental authority is an infallible institution
. . . and elders . . . are the oracles of God; an authority that may not
be impugned. The true administration of this authority is not the
administration of man or woman, in the selfhood of mere human
capacity, but godliness through man and woman, each sex in its own
order, but a united twain.[3]

Secondly, they established a rigid and minute body of laws and regulations, which were intended to control the sexual lives of members totally
and to keep the sexes completely and absolutely separate except under
certain specified, and closely monitored, conditions, or under unavoidable circumstances. To the degree that it was humanly possible, these
regulations were enforced, and their observation assured, by the institution of auricular confession (in the separate sexual orders, of course),
control of reading matter, and the censorship of all correspondence. A
system of informers was also established so that those who refused to
confess would be turned in by others who had witnessed their trans-
gressions.[4] If regulations were not observed in any particular instance,
the offenders were subject to excommunication and expulsion from the
community.

In fact, the paradigm for the behavior and government of the Shakers
was the parental-offspring relationship. The centrality of parental, especially maternal, imagery to their system of thought (the fatherhood
and motherhood of the godhead) was reflected in the assumption of a
childhood model for behavior. Certainly on a psychological level there
was a direct connection as well: "virgin celibates" as prepubertal children. In the natural family, order, peace, and theological justification
were attained "by becoming like a little child, subject, innocent, and
obedient in all things, to those who are appointed by the gift and anoint-
ing power of God to be parents and shepherds in Israel . . . until this
state of childlike obedience is gained . . . there can be no real abiding
heaven in the soul."[5]

The rules and regulations established for the Shaker "children" were
quite detailed and in some cases even petty; but quite a number of them
bore directly or indirectly on the subject of sexual conduct. The overall
intent of their system of communal legislation was to maintain an atmosphere of virginal purity through a strict separation of the sexes. Self-
control, the crushing of the will, was difficult for individuals, who often
did not even suspect the pitfalls that awaited them. Shaker regulations
protected them and helped render them immune to temptation. Such a
set of detailed rules also relieved them of the necessity of thinking about

controlling their sexual natures and thus removed the possibility that, in grappling with sexual drives to subdue them, they would be overcome. All that was necessary to perfection was perfect obedience. The hierarchy of Elders, Deacons, and Trustees and the idea of "union" in "order," or strictly following the prescriptions laid out by the "lead," provided an environing structure of legislation that offered total security and freedom from anxiety in exchange for prescribed behavior.

Men and women were not permitted to talk to one another in private, to exchange presents, to walk or ride out together, or to visit each other's rooms. Touching the opposite sex was forbidden, even to the extent of handshaking. They were forbidden, of course, to room together; and although they took their meals at the same time, there were separate tables for men and women.[6] To better ward off any possible tactile or visual temptation, it was provided that "Brethren and Sisters should not pass each other on the stairs, if consistent to avoid it; but when in company with each other, the Brethren should go up stairs first, and the Sisters go down stairs first."[7] All altercations that arose between the sexes were referred to the Elders for adjudication. Under no circumstances was medical aid to be tendered a female by a male, except under the supervision of a nurse (always female). Significantly, in view of the fear of both male and female homosexuality noted in the preceding chapter, it was provided that "Brethren and Sisters should not dress in garments belonging to the opposite sex."[8]

These laws, as well as most other Shaker regulations, were the result of either oral tradition handed down from those who had been contemporaries of Ann Lee or the work of the Shaker Lycurgus, Lucy Wright (1760–1821), who had succeeded her as "Mother." A passage from a handwritten copy of one of the corpora of legislation attributed to Lucy Wright, and handed down from generation to generation of Shakers, summarizes the whole group of injunctions regulating the conduct of the sexes:

> We must not go into each other's apartments after our evening meeting except on some very needful occasion. The brethren must all leave their rooms while the sisters are doing the necessary chores therein, unless prevented by sickness or infirmity. Sisters must neither mend, nor sew buttons on brethren's clothes while they have them on. One brother and one sister must not be together alone, longer than to do a short—and necessary errand or duty—at any time; and must not have private talk together at all. Neither should brethren and Sisters touch each other unnecessarily.[9]

Another group of laws was directed solely at females, and its obvious intent was to protect feminine virtue. Women were strictly forbidden to walk out alone into the fields or to the barns, but were required to have a companion of their own sex. This rule, so reminiscent of the sororal regulations found among many orders of Roman Catholic nuns, seems to have been scrupulously observed. In most instances when reference is made to excursions of both men and women outside the community, the number of females participating is greater than the number of males. In the few instances when this is not so, the travelers are from the upper echelons of the Shaker hierarchy and therefore are allowed more personal freedom.[10] Young women were forbidden all access to the barns and stables; all labor performed by young girls was to be performed in their houses of residence; and young women were admonished to observe pudency in all their behavior. "They should not be allowed," warned Lucy Wright, "to tip back, nor sit cross-legged when about their work, or in company."[11]

The demographic composition of Shaker communities seems to have been carefully monitored to insure a numerical predominance of females in demographic units of all sizes. Throughout the period 1780–1895, the sexual composition of Shaker communities was exceptionally stable. On the largest demographic level, not one Shaker community seems to have had a larger proportion of men than women. Only on the level of the "Family" (several of which comprised each Shaker community) did men outnumber women, and then only infrequently. For the overall period, women made up 58 percent of Shaker societies, and men only 42 percent. There may have been a larger number of men than women when the societies were first being formed in the 1780s, but the high points of male membership were the 1830s and 1860s. In these decades the percentage of males, although still significantly lower than that of females, approached parity.[12]

Not only the fear of violation of female virginity but also the specter of homosexuality and masturbation loomed behind Shaker legislation. This is especially obvious in rules governing the protection of children. Children were, of course, sexually segregated as the adults were; men supervised the boys and women the girls. Children were never to accompany adults solely for companionship and should never be out of the sight of their caretakers. Older children were to be kept separate, as much as possible, from younger ones. The workshops of the adults and the barns and stables were off limits to children. They were allowed to be out at night only when performing some supervised task, and under no circumstances on Saturday night. Caretakers were "never [to] allow them to go into the water to wash, swim or whatever, unless you or some trusty person is present, that has come to years of understanding."[13] The point is made even more specific in a warning about the weekly bath: "but leave them not alone at such times, lest they tempt each other in some way."[14]

Discipline and regimentation were the keys to behavior both for children and adults, and many rules merely represented a subordination of individual will to communal policy. This was surely the justification for a rule that required children upon retiring for the evening to sit upright in a straight-backed chair without touching the back "for as long as caretakers deem proper."[15] But the border line between disciplinary regulations and those intended to order Shaker sexual life was often quite tenuous. This is evident in the rules governing behavior after retiring. Fear of masturbation and homosexuality clearly provided the impetus for their admonition to children that, "when you lie down to sleep, place yourselves strait with your hands laid pretty nearly together (not folded up) by the side of your head, but not under it. Never meddle with the one you sleep with, unless it be very necessary.[16] These injunctions were echoed in an appeal to children to "always keep your little hands clean from every filthy act; use no bad words, and keep your little consciences clear."[17]

As a rural people, the Shakers found the problem of bestiality of vital concern. In part, this was a reflection of their extreme frankness about matters sexual; but even more importantly, this particular form of sexual behavior was a wonderful metaphoric expression of one of their central doctrines: all sexual intercourse is brutish or animalistic; to indulge in sex at all is to render both oneself and one's sexual partner an animal.[18] Animals were not be kept as pets, were forbidden in living quarters, and could not be given names normally used for human beings.[19] Naturally, it would have been "contrary to order" to observe animals during the act of generation. The logic of Shaker "orders" would also have dictated an observation of the biblical commandment: "Thou shalt not let the cattle gender with a diverse kind" (Leviticus 19:19).[20] God herself had indicated that "all playing with or idolizing the brutal creation, is forbidden by my holy laws."[21] The equine order was particularly offensive, for "there has been much transgression, yea, sin & wickedness committed with that animal amongst my people. And I do require that all ye inhabitants of my Zion, should most use in your services, my horned kind, and use them according to my law."[22]

The venerated Mother Ann had repeatedly spoken out against animal aberrations in a manner which indicated that Shakers were not immune from this kind of temptation. She was especially concerned about feline and canine creatures: "Dogs and cats are unclean beasts, and full of evil spirits; therefore, if any of you, old or young, unite or play with them, you will be defiled."[23] This became an integral part of the regulations governing the relationship between animals and human beings. Children as well as adults were warned about animals. They were never too young to learn to "make no sport of them, and play not with them, and handle them not, at any time, except some immediate duty requires it, and you do it in obedience; and by no means handle cats and dogs."[24]

There remained one other problem to be dealt with in the body of Shaker rules and orders. This was the necessity of prohibiting exoteric contamination from individuals who did not subscribe to Shaker doctrine, but who nevertheless had some contact (however limited) with believers. It was partly for this reason that all contact between children taken into a Shaker community and their nonbelieving relatives was closely monitored. All interviews between children and such relatives were conducted in public buildings under the watchful eye of a Shaker Elder or Eldress. Children were never left alone with their relatives, nor were the latter permitted to enter the children's rooms except in cases of illness or extreme emergency.[25] Visitors were carefully watched during their stay; were only in rare instances allowed to stay overnight; and for the duration of their stay, were not allowed to wander about the grounds or go off alone for even the shortest period of time without giving notice of their intent.[26]

With increasingly successful economic production in the 1830s and 1840s, the Shakers were forced to take on hired hands to keep abreast of expansion. There was an ongoing debate about the wisdom of using outside, "worldly" labor, but the logic of the situation was inescapable. If they were to continue to progress and make a profit, they needed more labor. The problem was that progress achieved in such a way threatened the security of perfection. Material progress and spiritual progress, or "travel," as the Shakers liked to call it, were incompatible. Their response to this challenge was characteristic; they promulgated a body of regulations that insured maximum separation of saints and sinners, especially females of the former species and males of the latter. The handwritten laws of 1840 reflect this concern: if there must be hired men, "have them work by themselves attended only by those who are set in order for that purpose. . . . Never allow them to eat in the same room and at the same time with your younger brethren and sisters. . . . Also keep them in that place and order which is provided for them, while they are among you."[27]

This body of regulation recommended a standard of behavior that required superhuman control of the emotions. Shaker saints were to "abstain from all dalliance—shun lewd conversation, pictures, postures and literature having a tendency to stimulate the amative passion. . . . tolerate no impure thoughts";[28] "And when ye are together, and in any way begin to feel your nature's excited, withdraw immediately from each other's presence, and war against that filthy spirit."[29] It was humanly impossible to watch any group of people closely enough to insure complete adherence to the code. Moreover, the very stringency and ubiquity of these regulations continually called attention to sexual matters and may well have served to glamorize the deviant sexual behavior they were ostensibly designed to control. Ironically, at least for some Shakers, con-

scious restriction may have augmented rather than subdued sexual excitation. Just how closely, then, were these rules followed? There are two
kinds of information to which we can turn for an answer. The first is the
layout and architecture of the communities themselves; the second, the
journal kept by the Elders and Ministry and personal diaries.

Maximum separation of the sexes was achieved in the physical structure of the Shaker communities. In the South Family at Watervliet, New
York, for example, the grouping of all buildings was along an east-west
axis. In the center of the Family lay the group of buildings housing the
female workshops, the laundry, the sales shop, the canning shop, and the
separate dormitories for men and women. The dormitories were separated by a space of 55 feet, and a large tree on the north side of the
brothers' living quarters provided even further separation and privacy.
(This was an atypical domiciling pattern; it was more typical for common
brethren and sisters to share one large dwelling house. Only Elders and
Eldresses and members of the Ministry had sexually segregated dwelling
units, and even in their case this was not a universal practice.) Also
located in the center of the South Family was the office and visitors'
reception center. The interior of the building was divided into two parts,
one for men and one for women. To the northwest of the central, feminine area, separated from the former by a road 10 feet wide, lay another
smaller area, which housed the shops operated by males: the wagon
shed, ice house, stables, and garage. The poultry area, the original privies,
and the school buildings were located adjacent to the female quarters of
the Family. The cattle barn and farm outbuildings were to be found in the
southwest corner of the property, separated from the other communal
buildings by a small creek and a system of roads some 10 feet in width.
These buildings were set apart from the nearest building in which female
Shakers worked by 225 feet. The stables, on the opposite side of the
property, were 125 feet from the nearest building occupied by females.[30]

A less sophisticated drawing of the buildings of the Middle Family
of North Union, Ohio, provides corroborative evidence. No legend is
supplied, so we must perforce speak of the main axis of division as
horizontal. This axis divided the Family property almost exactly in half.
A vertical division provided by a broad public road, which intersected
the horizontal axis, served to divide the property into quarters. In the
lower left-hand quarter, the dwelling house (for both sexes) and the
female shops—cheese house, hospital, wash house, and dry house—were
located. In the lower right-hand quarter, in a neutral, or shared, area,
were the meetinghouse, schoolhouse, Elders and Eldresses' house, and
tool shed. In the upper left-hand quadrant lay the cattle barns and men's
shops. The upper right-hand quadrant contained the stables and wagon
sheds, the blacksmith shop, and the woolen mill.[31] Geographic separa-

tion of the sexes seems to have been quite strictly enforced. The less contact there was between the sexes, the easier it was to maintain discipline and order. It was much less difficult to prevent temptation than to arrest its progress once it was aroused.

In their domiciliary arrangements, the Shakers continued the policy of separation, even though both sexes normally slept in the same dwelling house. In most rooms for adults there were from two to six occupants of the same sex, each with a separate bed. Children usually slept two to a bed. Apartments for men and women were usually located at opposite ends or sides of the house and were separated by wide halls. In the main residence building at Mt. Lebanon, for example, there were separate stairways for men and women. The sisters' stairway was on the right-hand corner of the east side of the building; the brethren's on the left-hand corner. There were corresponding separate entrances to the building for the two sexes. The first floor was almost totally given over to the female order: on the right were the sisters' rooms, and on the left those of the deaconesses. There was a deacon's room on this floor, but it was cut off from the sisters' and deaconesses' rooms by the brethren's stairway. On the second floor, left-hand side, were the Elders' rooms; and on the right, the Eldresses'. The third floor was occupied on both sides of the building by brethren's rooms. A chapel and meeting room on the first floor were separated from the sisters' rooms by the sisters' stairway. Dining facilities were also located in this building. Separate tables were provided for men and women, with side tables for children. Two special dining rooms were set apart for hired farm hands and for visitors.[32]

The structure of the meetinghouse at Mt. Lebanon provides additional evidence of Shaker practices in separating the sexes and maintaining communal separation from "worldlings." It also attests to Shaker adherence to a rigid spatial arrangement of the sexes. Women were always placed on the left-hand side and men on the right-hand side in processions and seating arrangements.[33] There were three entrances on the south side of the meetinghouse: one for sisters, one for the Ministry, and one for the brethren (left, central, and right, respectively). On the left of the main entranceway was the sisters' cloakroom; on the right the brethren's. This was redemption order, however, not that of the worldly. On the eastern side of the building were the visitors' entrances, the men's to the *left* and the women's to the *right*. Shaker seating arrangements placed women on the left and men on the right, but in the visitors' balcony (east side), we again note an inversion—men on the left and women on the right.[34]

Even in death there was no respite from the rigorous separation of the sexes. In the Shaker cemetery in Harvard, Massachusetts, there are ten rows of graves set about eight feet apart. Beginning at the rear of the cemetery, there are three rows of women's graves, then a twelve-foot interval, then two rows of men's graves. A broad interval of sixteen feet separates the rear from the front portion. This is followed by two rows of men's graves, a nine-foot interval, and three rows of women's graves. J. P. MacLean, in his investigation of the burial ground at North Union, Ohio, discovered a similar division; females were buried on the north and males on the south side.[35]

It is an exaggeration, however, to say that men and women were always apart. There were two notable occasions when some mingling of the sexes was condoned. The first of these was in the worship service, especially the dance, which was so central a part of it. The other was during "union" or visiting meeetings. Even on these occasions, though, the relationships were continually controlled by prescribed ritual. In Shaker dances there were four types of formation: square, circular, linear or "march," and endless chain. But although male and female often came within close proximity during these terpsichorean rites of worship, they never touched. Dancing afforded an outlet for energies narrowly pent up by Shaker regimentation, and a supervised emotional release from the rigorously enforced separation of the sexes. This was true of the union meeting as well. In these meetings, an equal number of men and women (six to ten of each) gathered in one of the brethren's rooms. The pattern was a well-established one: "Visiting meeting in separate rooms, the Sisters visited the brethren and returned to the office, then . . . opened the partition and spend nearly an hour with the brethren, sing some, etc."[36] These meetings seem to have occurred only rarely; perhaps on special occasions. No doubt Shaker Elders were aware that they provided dangerous opportunities for "special love," as opposed to the general feeling of communal amicability and fraternal-sororal love they were intended to promote.

Even the diligence of the Elders, however, could not prevent some deviation from order on all levels of organization. In fact, in some instances there seems to have been a relaxation from the stringent requirements of Shaker regimentation, if not by, then at least with the cognizance of, the Elders. But for those who could not adjust to the rigors of Shaker life, dissociation was the only solution. It is a tribute to the genius of Shaker organization, and evidence of the ability of the individual Shaker to control and subdue his emotions, that the rate of apostasy from Shaker communities was only about 1 percent. At Mt. Lebanon and Watervliet, New York, in the period 1830–1915, for instance, the attrition rate upon membership through "going to the world," as it was called, averaged 32.7 individuals per decade. For individual Families, and for smaller societies like Canterbury, New Hampshire (1822–49), and Harvard, Massachusetts (1867–72), the attrition rate through apostasy averaged 6.45 people per decade. This would have been about 0.5 percent per annum of the total population of these communities.[37] Whenever we are given a reason for the defection, it is almost always sexual—an inability or unwillingness to bear the Shaker cross. The terms used to describe withdrawals are usually suggestive of a paranoiac fear of sexual beguilement. A case that occurred in October 1819 at Mt. Lebanon is illustrative: "Joel Wood and Clarissa Cogswell escaped together in the night between the 1st and 2nd instant." The apostatization of Joel was regretted, but as for Clarissa, "she was never a good Believer—she was considered a very disorderly, insinuating witch of a woman and proved to be Joel's ruin."[38] The same was true of excommunications. Henry Baker, who was involuntarily expelled in 1828, represented a threat to the peace, integrity, and moral standards of the community; he had been guilty of "disorderly, immoral and abusive conduct" and was unanimously excommunicated.[39]

What is most striking, though, when we examine the journals and diaries of Shaker leaders, is the relatively negligible amount of transgression of the rules, and the amplification of it in the minds of Elders and Eldresses. The tone of these manuscripts is one of pious self-justification. They are a practical demonstration of the necessity for the whole corpus of Shaker rules. This tone is evident in an entry in the Mt. Lebanon Ministry's Records for 29 May 1861, which deplores the flood tide of sensuality; with its "deep waters of sufferings and tribulation much apostasy, much weakness, darkness and loss, it requires exceedingly vigilant watchfulness and care on the part of Elders, to save and protect any of the young. . . . almost all outward conditions seem to favor and foster a worldly carnal sense and feeling."[40]

Certainly there was some justification for watchfulness, especially among the youths, or those in the most dangerous years from the onset of puberty to about twenty-five years. They were continually in danger of being misled. In one black week in 1846, for example, five young men and three young women went off to the world in what was characterized as "the largest defection in Shaker history."[41] No doubt is left as to the cause of this defection, for we are told that "poor Mary Wicks could hardly find words to express how awful it felt to her to lose her state of innocency which she had been brought up in. She said if someone would dig a hole in the ground and bury her therein it would be a heaven to her!!!"[42] An occasional wolf did get in among the fold and threatened to wreak havoc among the sexually inexperienced. We are told of a Canadian visitor and his son who were expelled from Mt. Lebanon in 1870, "after acting most rascally in trying to destroy some of the young females of the family."[43]

It was precisely with this prospect in mind that the regulations against associations with visitors and hired men were promulgated. Shakers in the individual Families, however, sought more gaiety and color in their lives and seem to have disregarded these separation orders—frequently to their regret. Warnings to various Families about their aberrant behavior occasionally appear in the written record. The Alfred, Maine, society was warned in 1861 about keeping hired men apart, "so as not to mingle, socially so common";[44] and the particularly wayward South Family at Mt. Lebanon was cautioned the following year about "entertaining the world among them for weeks in succession, as visitors."[45]

This was the more human, if less perfect, side of Shaker life, and it was not limited to relative newcomers or the lower echelons of Shaker society. For some, escape to a more tolerant atmosphere became imperative. Consider the case of Atha Holden, who had resided in the East Family at Mt. Lebanon from the age of five or six years. In the winter of 1861, aged forty-five years, she ran off precipitously "thro the snow which . . . [was] very deep and much drifted."[46] Even Elders and other trusted members of Shaker society went astray. In 1865 most of the leaders of the Groveland, New York, society apostatized; and among the Second and South Families at Mt. Lebanon there was "a great lack of gospel principles among Caretakers of children and others. The flesh is rampant, and purity and holiness couchant."[47]

Temptation recognizes no ranks or titles, and though Elders in most cases kept a firm hand on the reins of communal behavior and set a sterling example for common members to follow, the privileges and duties of their position may have rendered them in some ways even more vulnerable than the average Shaker. It was to them and their female counterparts that all confession was made; and they had many more opportunities than ordinary members to ride out beyond the confines of the Shaker communities, thus acquiring a greater contact with things worldly. The case of Elder John Cooper of South Union, Kentucky, may well be representative of the temptation that awaited Elders. Cooper had left Kentucky in 1877 to settle the business affairs of his brother in California. His action in leaving was "out of union" (he did not have the permission of the Ministry to go). The Ministry at Mt. Lebanon, which controlled the affairs of the entire eastern diocese of the Shaker church, reported that as a consequence, "he returned from California with a woman, whom he took with him from Philadelphia; his case looks hopeless, as a Shaker."[48]

Even among those who did not defect from Shaker ranks, there is evidence of less than strict adherence to established principles. Shaker correspondence gives us a fleeting glimpse of affection between individuals, which, if not an open threat to Shaker celibacy, certainly violated the prohibition on "special love." In a letter of 1832, for example, we read in a postscript: "N.B.—Olive says: I want my particular love and kind thanks to be given to Brother Elisha, and tell him I have improved in my health, and gained considerable strength by my journey. Also give him a pair of striped pants from the batch we send if any fit him."[49]

But Shakers would be more than human were they not subject to such minor lapses from discipline. Much more serious was the ideological challenge that threatened to overturn the whole structure of Shaker celibacy in the 1860s. To some extent, Shaker unrest echoed the general tone of restlessness and dislocation connected with the Civil War years in America. The 1860s saw a significant increase in the internal migration of the native-born, white population. The promise of prosperity, sparked by a steady and dramatic rise in the absolute wage rate between 1860 and 1865 (even though real wages declined), reinforced discontent and led to a restless, and in many instances frustrated, quest for economic success.[50]

To whatever extent this social atmosphere affected Shaker apostates in this period, the intellectual roots of this outbreak of discontent grew out of the spiritualist movement, with its contention not only that the spiritual and physical worlds were contiguous, but that there were points at which connections could be made between the two. This led to the doctrine of "affinities" of soul and "spiritual marriage." These were not new doctrines in the 1860s; but it was not until the 1850s that the Shakers began seriously and systematically to consider the relationship between their theology of continuous revelation through inspired visions and the broader spiritualist movement.[51] In some minds at least, this consideration seems to have led to some very unorthodox conclusions. In 1864 a group of believers at Mt. Lebanon began to advocate "purified generation, for Believers . . . they want to mingle flesh and spirit."[52] This heretical spirit still reigned among a certain group in 1867 when Shaker leaders described the even more radical conclusions of their challengers as "a spiritual condition in the Church much to be complained of, Viz., that it is practicable to separate from the union of the Household of Faith, in order to have more liberty between the sexes, and have less order, and yet find a spiritual protection from sin, and keep a justified conscience before God."[53] There was also trouble with the Hancock, Massachusetts; Watervliet, New York; and many other Shaker societies in 1867. A good part of the trouble at Hancock stemmed from the fact that the leaders, especially Bishop Pomeroy, were living in "the *old* way."[54] At Watervliet, a college-educated youth, William Bussell, who had been a Shaker for a decade, was trying to stir up speculation about the Shakers' sexual relationships. Other societies were riven by "false tenets in religion, and worldly theories and lusts . . . [which were] destroying souls in . . . many places."[55] Apparently the efforts of these "crazy, or lust cracked" people[56] were not unproductive, for there seem to have been an unusually large number of apostatizations and expulsions among the Shaker communities in the 1860s. In the period from July 1864 to February 1865, some twenty people left the various Shaker Families at Mt. Lebanon.[57] There is some indication that such tergiversation was also connected with awareness of other communal arrangements that were more closely attuned with the spiritual-wifery doctrines. We learn, for example, that an individual from the Oneida Community, probably Jonathan Burt, visited Mt. Lebanon from 1 to 3 September 1866. He is referred to fraternally as "Friend Burt."[58] William Hepworth Dixon, author of *Spiritual Wives* (1868), visited the same year from 13 to 15 August. In March of the next year, at a "reading meeting," the chapter on the Mormons from Dixon's *New America* was read.[59] As late as 1878, we read of a visit by Frederick W. Evans to the Oneida Community.[60]

But this is primarily a picture of what Shakers would have considered aberrant sexual behavior. There was intense pressure upon individuals to live up to the rigorous Shaker code. Many of those who could not or would not were expelled or ran off to the world. Others, who remained, were unable to withstand the pressure of the guilt they felt and went insane or committed suicide. In the years from 1833 to 1880, Shaker records for Mt. Lebanon mention seventeen cases of insanity, suicide, and attempted suicide.[61] The 1830s and 1870s were the decades of highest suicide and insanity rates. There obviously was an inordinate amount of strain and a gnawing feeling of uncertainty among Shakers in these two decades, for these were also the years of the highest apostasy rate. Of nine recorded cases of insanity, six were men and three were women. When causes were given for these derangements, they were of two types. Obviously, both stemmed from the religious-moral pressures of Shaker life. There were some who, like John Hobart, believed themselves not only saints, but angels with miraculous powers. Hobart was the victim of a monomaniac perfectionist dementia: he believed it was necessary for him to stab people so that he might subsequently exercise his miraculous powers of healing.[62] Others were more clearly deranged by overwhelming feelings of sin, inadequacy, failure, and guilt. James Chapman of the South Family exemplifies this group. He starved himself to death in 1872, as the result of "a kind of insanity, apparently from a guilty conscience."[63]

In these years there were also six suicides and two attempted suicides. If we consider these two groups together, five were male and three female. Of those who actually succeeded in ending their lives, however, there were an equal number of men and women. For the forty-eight year period 1833–80, then, the average annual suicide rate for Mt. Lebanon was 0.125/492. By contrast, the average annual rate for New England in the years 1856–80 was 6.85/100,000. Assuming that the suicide rate at Mt. Lebanon was representative of Shaker communities as a whole, it seems evident that the Shaker suicide rate was considerably higher than that of New England society in general. This is hardly surprising when we consider that Shaker society was composed of individuals deeply alienated from the values and behavior of nineteenth-century America. Their commitment to Shakerism was rooted in its radical rejection of the sexual morality of the world. When the oversight and regimentation of Shaker life failed to crush out sexual desire totally in individual cases, a sense of social disintegration, personal disorientation, and isolation generated by guilt and shame might well have led to profound despair (the condition Émile Durkheim called "anomie"), issuing in suicide.[64]

The sex ratio among suicide attempts indicates that the Shaker way of life caused a much greater degree of anxiety and frustration for males than it did for females. Motivations seem to have been much the same as the causes of insanity. Many suicides followed apostatization rather closely, and in several instances were accompanied by insanity.

Amy Bennett, for example, who had run off two months earlier, was listed in September of 1859 as "remaining in a deranged condition." The extreme strain of Shaker life on an individual of a sensitive disposition, which might well lead to overwhelming moral insecurity, is painfully evident in the official description of her case. She insisted on returning to her relatives "because she seems to think herself to be an awfully wicked creature and therefore not fit to remain with believers. . . . [yet she is] a faithful cross bearer. . . . It is evident that bodily infirmity is the cause of her present feelings."[65]

Among those who were able to live with the rigors of Shaker life (and the vast majority of Shakers fell within this category), what kind of sexual behavior do we find? Obviously, overt manifestations of sexual behavior are not to be found among "faithful" Shakers. They followed Ann Lee's dictum: "Put your hands to work and your hearts to God," thus sublimating sexual energies through labor. But as E. Hahn remarked, "When the exercise of the sexual function is prevented by celibacy, or even by castration, the most complete form of celibacy, the sexual emotions may pass into the psychical sphere to take on a more pronounced shape."[66]

This level of behavior in Shaker communities, which was manifested in their great spiritualist revival beginning in 1837, can be most cogently examined in an analysis of their reactions to visions and the "spiritual gifts" that were so much a part of them. The imagery of these visions and the symbolic character of the gifts that invariably accompanied them, as well as the behavior of those who were the intermediaries between the spiritual and physical worlds, tell us a great deal about Shaker sexual experience. The inspired were predominantly female, and rather young. Of inspired visions that were not accompanied by spiritual gifts, 67.5 percent were mediated by women, and only 33.5 percent by men. Female visionaries averaged 24.8 and male 37.5 years of age.[67] In visions accompanied by gifts, almost all the intermediaries were women. The established ritual of visions obviously required a female visionary. This position was an honorific one, and allowed certain liberties in behavior. In part the ritualistic structure of visions helps to explain why women found Shaker life more amenable than men. They had as a sexual outlet an integral part of Shaker religious ritual, not available to the brethren.[68] Men probably had more physical opportunities for the relaxation of tensions built up by the rigors of Shaker life. Their contact with the outside world, and consequent temptation, would therefore have been greater. All this would have added up to greater male dissatisfaction with Shaker life. The division of roles here is a familiar one: males are rational and more secular, females emotional and religious.

From the point of view of the young people who acted as intermediaries to the spiritual world, there were certain advantages in the ritualistic role. They were able to act out forbidden emotions by taking on the spirits of other cultures whose values were totally different, like the American Indian or polygamous Mohammedan culture. One young woman even assumed the spirit of Satan and, while under diabolic influence, "tried to get others to unite with her in opposition to the order of the gospel, and the opposing spirits caused something of a war among the Shakers."[69]

In those cases in which the spirits were male, of course, male Shakers manifested them. Evidently this business was limited to younger members of the community, for we learn that on 11 September 1842, all brethren and sisters under thirty-five were given permission to "take on" an Indian spirit.[70] Aside from the possibility of acting out repressed sexual feelings by assuming a completely different role under spiritual influence, inspired women who had gifts were occasionally allowed to break down some of the rigid sexual barriers. A group of sisters was allowed, for example, to enter the brethren's workshops in order to deliver spiritual messages.[71] Usually, only an Eldress on strict business could enter the men's shops. Visions frequently occurred in bed, at retiring time, or in the emotionally charged atmosphere of the meeting. Trances were a common aspect of these spiritual manifestations.[72] Many times young girls seemed to be inspired by the spirit of Ann Lee and were able to depict the grossest of sins, and indicate by name those guilty of them.

This inspiration provided the girls a special freedom. The case of three young women in 1838 is representative. Their gifts were specifically for one Gideon Cole and were delivered "after he had retired to rest, but he had to get up and receive what gift they had in Mother's name, which seemed to undermine him considerably." After the girls had cataloged his sins up to a period fifteen years before their births, "he became as simple and obedient as a child."[73]

The physical and psychical release of such a moment for these girls must have been tremendous. They were able to discuss with extreme frankness the various forms of sexual behavior forbidden them (a kind of vicarious verbal pornography) and at the same time project the guilt that would have been generated by merely thinking about, let alone publicly verbalizing, such matters onto an actual sinner. The exhilarant titillation of being in a man's room after he had gone to bed for the evening merely added to the enjoyment.

Other forms of physical release were provided by the trances that accompanied spiritual visions. Several young women, for example, "were frequently bent into hoops backward, inasmuch as that the tops of their heads actually pressed against the hollows of their feet!!!" In this manner they figured forth the sufferings of hell and " . . . will sometimes go, or rather roll from the top to the bottom of the stairs, bent as above described without receiving any injury whatever."[74] These girls seem to have used the excuse of possession by spirits, and perhaps self-induced trances, to exercise some power, to have some influence, and to escape, however momentarily, the rigors of Shaker life.

Given the highly ritualized quality of all such behavior, they were able to achieve personal, social, and sexual release through the mediating role. This was quite apparent in the Second Family at Mt. Lebanon, where in 1838, "seven of the young Sisters have been for a week past, unable to speak their own language except when in vision but they all speak flippantly in unknown tongues and seem to understand each other well. When they are asked questions in English they seem to understand, but they answer in some other tongue."[75] A certain quality of adolescent rebellion against the Shaker leadership as well as the formation of an exclusive peer group with an idiom and arcana all its own will be immediately recognized by those familiar with adolescent psychology.

The danger inherent in this kind of sexual behavior was that some people were not capable of keeping the worlds of fantasy and playacting apart from that of everyday behavior. It comes as no surprise to learn that three of the young women involved in visions and trances at Mt. Lebanon ran off to the world at the height of the spiritualist fervor. One of them, Elleyett Gibbs, ran off twice within a year. Her rationale for apostatization is clearly stated in the Shaker records: "Her plea for taking this awful step is, she is unwilling to live so strict a life as the gospel requires, that she had hurt the young and would most likely do them more hurt if she staid—She wanted the liberty of the world, etc."[76] There is some evidence that Shaker leaders feared that the youthful rebellion manifested in these visionary experiences would undermine social and sexual discipline in their communities as well. In 1839 there was great trepidation "that some of the Visionists have given away [sic] to a high sense and have measurably lost the fear of God—If so they are not fit representatives of Mother's Holy Spirit, and ought to be dismissed for a time, at least till they gain a better sense."[77]

The revelation entitled "A General Statement of the Holy Laws of Zion" (1840) prescribed the proper behavior for visionary "instruments." The fear that spiritual ecstasy will arouse carnal lust comes through clearly: "I do also require that all ye who have been chosen as instruments, should suffer and wade in *deep deep* tribulation, that your passions and your natural feelings may be under the greatest degree of mortification, that they may not blend, in any way, with my Spirit or gift to lead you astray."[78] This caution was necessary, for "the enemy has taken great advantage of souls, in many places, in this respect, of them that had been instruments through which my word of truth, and beautiful gifts have been conveyed."[79] From about 1840 onward, then, visions would be accompanied by gifts, but no longer by trances.

During the period 1842–57, Shaker visionaries produced a steady stream of spiritual gifts and inspired drawings. The gifts visions were less exclusive, more closely monitored by the Elders, and thus more socially useful in a communistic community. They were more "in union" with the established theological and sexual principles of the Shaker order. In fact, they offer us the best glimpse we have of publicly acceptable, officially sanctioned, Shaker sexual behavior. Shakers were definitely very strongly affected by their sexual drives, but refused to spiritualize or romanticize them in any way. In their visions, and especially the gifts that accompanied them, however, we see that their rejection of romanticism was only apparent. Their behavior, as exemplified in these visions, indicates a vacillation between a tough-minded, bellicose restriction of sexuality, and a yielding immersion in a syrupy, cloying romanticism. This accords with the pervasive strain of dualism so characteristic of their theological position. Such a schizoid response was psychologically and socially functional in Shaker communities, because it exacerbated extant feelings of guilt and worthlessness, and thus generated continual wariness of sexual feelings and continual striving for a perfection that remained always just beyond reach. It is not surprising, then, that sadomasochistic manifestations were not uncommon in these gifts visions.

The gifts, which were always spiritual (not material), were given through female mediums. On the one hand, they were restrictive and tended toward the quantification of the emotion of love. On the other, they were unrestricted and boundless, expressive of an infinity of love. Balls, boxes, rings, spools, and cups were common containers for spiritual love; all expressions of a quantification of emotion. Perhaps the most revealing symbol in this line, however, in view of Shaker adherence to the spermatic-economy system, certain overtones of which are reflective of capitalistic economic ideology, was the wallet. Roses, angels, hearts, and flowers, traditional romantic symbols, were also received as gifts of heavenly love.[80]

Expressive of unbounded love were the symbols of the fountain, the heaped-up measure, and the overflowing cup. The Holy Mount at Mt. Lebanon, which became a focal point of visionary experience in 1843–44, had as its central fixture a ritualized "fountain." The vision of Mariah Gillet was representative of this kind of imagery. She "said she had a fountain sufficient for all who wanted to partake—She said we might drink of it, and we might wash in it, all that chose. . . . We kneeled down and tried to drink and wash in Mother's fountain."[81]

More frequently encountered are the restrictive metaphors of love, occasionally intertwined with some of the romantic symbols. These visions were synecdochically expressive of the entirety of Shaker life. As one such vision was described, the young woman "said Mother encircled us with a chain, and if any of us broke one link, we might let in evil, etc., etc."[82] Chains, girdles (akin to chastity belts in this context), and swords were common images of this aspect of the visionary experience. Occasionally such gifts were sweetened by their presentation in the mixed metaphorical mode: transparent hearts suspended by chains, and baskets made of flowers filled with chains. The more characteristic expression was more direct, however, and therefore more blatantly repressive. In October of 1843, the Ministry, Elders, and spiritual leaders (all in the *male* order) made a pilgrimage to the Holy Mountain at Mt. Lebanon bearing one of the spiritual gifts the community had received—a "gold safety chain with locks." This they sedulously placed "around the outward enclosure of the Holy Ground."[83] They thus kept out the sinner and his evil, and kept the pure within. Those who remained within present the aspect of so many Marley's Ghosts walking the earth. Of course this is true only in a figurative or psychological sense; but what else are we to make of one Austin B., who received such a gift of chains?—one to bind him to the Ministry, one to bind him to the Elders, a third to bind him to the sisters and brethren, a fourth to encircle him totally and bind him to the Second Order, and those remaining to bind him to the whole church.[84]

Such close fettering is only a step away from a more overt sadomasochistic expression of feeling, and we find this boundary frequently crossed in Shaker religious-sexual life. These feelings were a complex expression of aggression against their own natures, which could never be irrevocably crushed out, as well as against non-Shaker individuals, who, because they enjoyed a freer sexual life, became objects of contempt to many Shakers. They also served as vicarious sexual experience of a voyeuristic variety. By identifying with individuals who experienced sexual extremes, and who were subsequently tortured or executed, they could experience passion followed by the inevitable and terrible retribution their consciences required, all by proxy. This latter sadomasochistic manifestation, probably the most complex in its operation, is most clearly illustrated in the Shaker use of martyrology. There is a certain gloating, soft-core pornographic quality to the description of the fate of the teen-aged Denisa, quoted from Wright's *Martyrology*. She was " 'given up to two libertines, to become the object of their lust: and having suffered under their brutality half the night, and being miraculously delivered, was afterwards beheaded.' "[85] Many of the stories about the life and sufferings of Ann Lee served the Shakers as a unique martyrological body of lore, which was treated in a similar manner.[86] Descriptions of those who apostatized and subsequently suffered for their sexual sins abound in Shaker records. These cases obviously served a similar function to that of the stories of martyrs.[87]

This element of Shaker emotional life found its reflection in the visions and in the folk-art drawings. The gifts that were presented by the visionaries were also, upon occasion, overtly sadomasochistic. The mixture of pleasure and pain is clear in a visionary gift of a rod, purportedly from Mother Ann. As Mother described her curious gift, "there was a pod of honey on the end of her Rod, and such as could bear scourging enough to break the pod could tase [*sic*] the honey."[88] On another occasion, the Elders were given "a large bundle of whips for the brethren and sisters to whip the devil with, when the Elders felt best to use them."[89]

Shaker inspirational drawings were apparently without exception the work of the sisterhood. There are no known examples of drawings executed by the brethren.[90] The symbols employed in Shaker drawings are highly stylized and present a vision of Shaker psychic life in microcosm. Natural images of growth—trees, bushes, flowers, plants, and very highly structured gardens—are common figures. These are expressive of the naturalistic world, a world of sex, reproduction, and growth. The orderly arrangement of these symbols suggests the need to contain, to control this world. Countering these images we have the iconographic representation of checks on nature and the implements of torture and retribution that await those who fail to observe such checks.

In a series of seven drawings (which may have been part of a larger roll), for instance, the sheets of paper are frequently divided by double horizontal lines. The "Walls of Zion" are often represented. Enclosed geometric figures, usually rectangles, are common. Axes, scythes, spears (sometimes shown piercing serpents), knives, "tomehacks," tongs, pincers, and gallows are repeatedly depicted. There are stylized angels, too, who resemble nothing so much as flowers in a flower pot. Perhaps these figures are intentionally naturalistic in representation, expressive of Shaker belief in the ubiquitous nature of sexuality. They do not seem to be in general, though, benevolent figures. A small circular book affords us further insight into these drawings, which are grounded in an inveterate paranoiac vision. In the text we are warned: "Behold the destroyer lieth in wait, the snare is set, the guns are ready and the trap devised by the cunning workman is nearly completed. The enemy, the enemy encampeth around thy lovely hill. Deceit destroyeth their countenances, and hypocrisy lieth deep in their hearts. They seek to do evil and they plot mischief against thee. These are those that encompass thee, that men call reprobates."[91]

An illustration of an angel is captioned "The Angel of Judgement" and is surrounded by a sickle and an ax. A figure of a gallows (another drawing with a similar gallows bears the inscription "Traitor") is placed opposite a cross with dots (ever watchful eyes?) on each of its four arms. The choice is clearly indicated: the cross or death; castration or chastity. This impression is heightened by a figure of a coffin near the bottom of the page, bearing the inscription in pidgin English, supposed to be characteristic of Indian spirits: "Let de dead be put in the box out ob my Zion."[92]

A series of inspired writings and drawings produced at Mt. Lebanon in the period 1842–59 employs similar imagery. One particularly striking drawing shows a crucified female figure. Running vertically on the two sides of the cross are the words: "But they must suffer Persecution / Like those who have gone Before." The female figure emphasizes both sexuality (the breasts are prominent and there are two spots of rouge on the cheeks) and spirituality (the figure is so ethereal that the cross can be seen through the body and its clothing). What a wonderfully apt pictorial expression of the doctrine that the body and its carnality have become the Shaker's cross! This is particularly true of the female body, because its part in the reproductive process is so much more elemental. Although crosses figure prominently in Shaker iconography, this is the only drawing of a crucified human figure that I am aware of. It is most significant that it is female.

Below the figure on the cross, a male and female, both dressed completely in black, are represented. The male figure has its left leg extended toward the woman, and one finger of its right hand is raised. The right hand of the man and the left hand of the woman are touching. The aspect of the figures suggests exhortation and perhaps aggression on the part of the male and, at the same time (given the strict Shaker separation of the sexes), a bond of peculiar intimacy. Below these figures double lines come together to form an inverted "v," which points directly toward the man and woman. On the two sides of the acute angle formed by these lines the words "Persecutors Rejoice in the Ruin of Souls" appear. Two black hands, one on each side of the "v," point to the two figures above. To the left of the male and female figures is another inverted "v" formed of double lines. On its sides the words "Falling Away from the Way of God" are written. On the extreme left margin of the page two smaller figures, dressed in black, one male and one female, can be seen.

The drawing has the appearance of an iconographic morality play. The central female figure, it would appear, is being tempted by the man in black. The two smaller figures are receding into the distance, carnal apostates, soon to pass off the page of Shaker history. Above all looms the figure of Ann Lee, the female Christ, who promises her faithful, in an affecting inversion of the male Christ's words at his sacrifice: "I never will Forsake Thee." The overall tone of the drawing is borne out by the text which runs across the very top of the page:

> O Zion, Zion, the day of thy trial hath come!!!
> Instruments [the spiritual visionaries] brought before
> publick Authority
> Some deny the work of God!!! Others stand boldly for it.
> *Persecution begins, And Some fall away from the Cross.*[93]

Yet these people, so fearful of contamination, so insecure in their perfection, because they chose to live celibate lives, could only secure members from the world. How were they to find suitable individuals? Rigorous selectivity would insure the continual progress of the race; a kind of anthropocentric prolepsis of Darwin's "natural selection." For individuals who believed in progress through control of the will, to the extent that even heredity could be shaped by the will if the proper attitude were maintained during intercourse, it was natural to think in eugenic terms. Of course this concern had to be somewhat ex post facto, as they had no children of their own. However, the ironic picture of Shakers speaking out in eugenic terms serves as a fitting representation of their concern and involvement with sex—at the same time feeling repulsed by it and needing to control and direct it. The Mt. Lebanon Ministry issued a eugenic warning to all Shaker societies "to let no slack witted nor maimed children enter the First Order of this first church upon earth because they could not come up to the requirements of such a forward order."[94] Their desire for control of the quality of human evolutionary progress, however, was not limited to selectivity of members. They warned the world that permanent progress was impossible as long as reproduction was uncontrolled. Men cried out against poverty, disease, and crime, but did nothing about them. Were "they afraid to advise unlucky mortals, who are morally and physically unworthy of multiplying God's image to abstain?"95

The Shakers' interest in eugenics was another manifestation of their aggressively postmillenarian attack on the sins of the flesh, but it was also a challenge to the world. Take up your cross, take control of the natural forces within you, and shape your own destiny and that of the human race as well. Either man or nature must be master. The irony of this position was that so much of their physical and psychic energy was devoted to the battle with their natures that they became as much obsessed with sex in their attempt to deny it as were libertines in their attempt to enjoy it.

Chapter 6 ❦ Renovated Woman: The Meaning of Shaker Ideology and Sexual Behavior from the Perspective of the Relationship between the Sexes

Aiunt enim dixisse Servatorem: "Veni ad dissolvendum opera feminae": feminae quidem, cupiditatis; opera autem, generationem et interitum [Verily, they say that the Savior said: "I have come to destroy the works of woman"; of woman and indeed of desire; moreover those works are generation and annihilation].

—Gnostic text, *Gospel of the Egyptians*

Per mulierem culpa successit,
per virginem salus evenit.
[Through woman sin came in; by means of a virgin deliverance followed].

—Episcopius to Siricius

*A*ndrew Jackson Davis (1826–1910), the popularizer of spiritualism, claimed that the accomplishments and significance of Ann Lee had been "revolutionary." As an inspired woman, she had led mankind "to perceive the plenitude of woman's nature, and the equality of her destiny."[1] Davis's evaluation has been widely accepted by investigators who have equated the separate sexual orders and strict dualistic division of Shaker society with equality of the sexes.[2] Certainly Lee was concerned with the plight of women in the marriage relation, and especially with the very real risks of pregnancy and parturition; but was the system she founded, or the direction it took under the guidance of her successors, one that accorded respect and an equal status to the feminine element? It is this question that we shall attempt to answer here in a final chapter on the Shakers.

In the early years of itinerancy, when Lee and her handful of disciples were traveling about the northeast, they had already taken an active stand on the abuse of women. Lee's personal experience and convictions were evidenced in her admonition to a destitute young mother, urging her to adopt chastity as a form of contraception: "When you had one, why did you not wait, and see if you was able to bring up that as you ought, before you had another? And when you had two, why did you not stop then? But now you have five! Are you not ashamed to live in the filthy works of the flesh? You must go and take up your cross, and put your hands to work, and be faithful in your business; clothe your children and keep them clean and decent, and clean up your house, and keep that in order."[3] Lee was concerned about the sexual and maternal servitude of women, but seems to have accepted much of the rest of the patriarchal system governing the relationship between the sexes. Ironically, her words of advice to other women belied her own experience and behavior toward her husband, Abraham Standley, for she consistently recommended female subservience. This ambiguity toward the value and position of women, which we see at the very outset of the Shakers' experiment, would continue to bedevil their thought and practice until the 1870s, when the argument began to broaden but reached no resolution.

From a strictly venereal point of view, Shakers saw woman as a victim, who was used by irresponsible men for their selfish pleasure. Their defense of women in this area was a direct function of their ideological position, which allowed sex for reproduction alone and denied pleasure any place in the sexual act. In all their attacks on marriage and sexual morality, they focus on the feminine condition; sexual crimes and immorality are what men do to women; women are the passive medium, not active participants. The key to the solution of these difficulties, therefore, is the male. It is he who is the selfish pleasure-seeker. Woman has a biological clock that indicates precisely the time of ovulation. The male violates the natural temporal order through his lust, and woman, in her subjection to him, becomes an unwilling vessel. All reform in sexual relations, therefore, is dependent upon prior male reformation and self-control.

From the feminine point of view, the Shaker solution to the plight of woman was unique and revolutionary; she had to sacrifice some of her femininity (her sexual nature) and become a "redeemed" woman. For

> tho all womankind have inherited their portion of the curse
> denounced upon the first woman; yet there has always been an

exception in favor of those virgin daughters who have wisely kept themselves from the contaminating corruptions of lust. They have been thereby, not only exempted from the pains and sorrows of childbirth, and preserved from those debasing pollutions, and that servile wretchedness, so common to those who subject themselves to the inordinate passions of man; but they have often been distinguished as peculiar objects of Divine favor.[4]

Women who had not strength enough to become "virgin celibates" became victims of lust, either under the sanction of, or without, matrimony. Shakers most frequently depicted woman's condition in the sexual relationship as servitude, prostitution, and rape. As early as 1823, they were arguing that marriage was legalized prostitution:

Is there any real difference between the married and the unmarried, either as to the nature of that propensity, the sensations excited by it, the effect it produces, or the gratification experienced in it? Does the marriage ceremony alter the nature of either? . . . Doubtless the sanction of a legal ceremony gives a licence which, assisted by the shades of darkness, removes all restraint from the feelings of those who do not look beyond it . . . so that they can now indulge their concupiscence in the dark without shame or remorse.[5]

The heart of the problem of marriage for the Shakers was the notion of control of the will. There was biblical and theological precedent for the submission of women to men, but if that submission were total, it would eliminate the possibility of progressive reform. The will of the female would always be subject to male determination, and the law of men sanctioned marriage. As antinomians as well as social dissidents, the Shakers opposed the law of man and felt that the human will could be free only in subjection to the divine.[6]

Their problem was how to afford the female the power of control over her own will without a male intermediary, while at the same time not completely overthrowing the established order of things. Because the attainment of perfection was so intimately related to the peculiar sexual system of the Shakers, the solution to their dilemma was not far to seek. They recommended the end of the double standard of morality, opposed prostitution and free love, and in general supported the female right to a voice in the determination of sexual morality and more especially in feminine sexual behavior.[7] At the same time, however, they insisted that the reproductive aspect of the marital relationship was primary, and that woman's conjugal role remained essentially generative. Thus, for example, they deplored the element of masculine force they found so characteristic of marital sex: "Woman should have full control of her own person, in every relation in life. It is her God given right. Only so, can she bring forth a free offspring. To usurp control to gratify libidinous passion is violating Divine law—is shocking to all refined sensibility—is an insult to woman and to intelligence and is not less than rape."[8]

For non-Shakers who indulged in connubial relations, Shakers sought to change the strictly sexual relation of female to male, but not their power relationships or their roles in any very significant way. The clearest passage expressing the tension in the Shaker mind between liberation from the male in a strictly sexual sense and subjection to the male in a social sense is from a prosopopoeia called "Wisdom's [the Female God-head's] Instructions to Females." The Female Spirit advises married women to

> honor thy husband that he may honor thee; yield and subject unto
> him, but go no further in sexual connexion than accords with the
> laws of God . . . respecting times and seasons. . . . O ye daughters
> of men, ye are called to be the glory of the man, the crown of his
> enjoyments, and the bright morning star of his existence. Ye are
> not called to become defiled and polluted, and to wallow in fleshly
> gratifications . . . in order to fulfill the marriage covenant, and rear
> up offspring to him, and become a crown of glory to his existence.[9]

Wisdom goes on to discuss the roles of females and, by implication, their dependency upon the ascendant male. The formula is a venerable one, recalling the seventeenth- and eighteenth-century virtues of the "good-wife" as presented in Puritan funereal eulogies of archetypal bourgeois women: diligence, cheerfulness, charity, nurturing qualities, discretion, thrift, and cleanliness; in short, "perform well your part which is allotted to you . . . discharging all the necessary duties which remain incumbent upon thee."[10]

Ostensibly, Shakers' concern with sexual intercourse and the marital relation seems incongruous with their profession of militant celibacy. Their solicitude about sexuality, however, was a logically consistent element of their total system of thought. It had its fundamental roots in the Shakers' relationship with the world. In the first instance, there was the question of conversion: bringing some individuals *from* the outside world into the virgin community. Secondly, there was the millenarian concern with the reform of a sinful world, the influence of the community *in* the world.

Converts to Shakerism were expected to go through a series of three progressive degrees, or Orders, before they could be accepted as full covenantal members. Each order required increasing renunciation of worldly ties and mortification of the prospective saint. In the Novitiate Order, for instance, although celibacy was expected of proselytes, they often continued to live with their families outside the community, and were not required to commit any of their personal property to the Shaker cause. The Junior Order, largely composed of those unhampered by family ties, resided in and consecrated some portion of its property to the community. The Senior, or Church, Order was fully consecrated to the Shaker movement, having dedicated all its property to the society.

It was among the proselytes, living outside the purview of Elders and Eldresses, and thus much less subject to direct Shaker control, that the most immediate threat of sexuality lay. The anxiety the Novitiate Order caused Shakers was evident in the official description of this Order: "Believers of this class are not controlled by the Society, either with regard to their property, children, or families; but act as freely in all these respects as the members of any other religious Society, and still enjoy all their spiritual privileges, and maintain their union with the Society; *provided they do not violate the faith, and the moral and religious principles of the institution.*"[11]

If it took the kind of minute regulation and vigorous oversight outlined in the previous chapter to keep fully covenanted Shakers on the straight-and-narrow path of virtue, it is hardly surprising that they should be greatly suspicious of backsliding among the neophytes who were not under strict and constant surveillance. When applied to the Novitiate Order, however, Shaker concern that sexual intercourse be limited to reproductive necessity seems to imply, despite assurances that new converts were subject to the rule of strict celibacy, that Shakers reluctantly accepted a progressive renunciation of sexuality.

The written record contains no reference to the conscious development of such a system of progressive steps toward celibacy, but the progressive renunciation of the world involved in the increasing economic commitment of the three Orders is structurally homologous. Furthermore, if this inference is correct, allowing the Novitiate Order to indulge in sexual reproduction would be functional within the Shaker system. Initially, it would allow a less abrupt transition from worldly sensuality to complete celibacy and would serve as a means of weeding out, preferably before they ever took up residence in a Shaker community, those who did not have sufficient faith and willpower to become full-fledged Shakers. In addition, those children produced by proselytes technically still in the world would become prospective Shakers should their parents ultimately reach the Junior or Senior Order. For a celibate society in which increase could come only through recruitment and conversion, this would not have been a negligible gain for tacitly allowing reproductive sexuality in the Novitiate Order.

In their attempts to have a reforming influence upon the world, Shakers sought to counteract the "unbounded abuse of the generative order, and its evil consequences on the race."[12] They did not expect all mankind to enter the regenerative order; most would no doubt remain in the generative. Marriage, in its own order, as long as intercourse was confined to a reproductive rather than an amative function, was acceptable to the Shakers. Those of superior spirituality, though, would progress toward the heavenly state while still in the flesh—to regenerated, celibate Shaker life. A certain inconsistency may be noted in the Shaker position at this point. Here was a radically celibate group devoting a sizable portion of its energy to the discussion of the sexual behavior of the unregenerate.

However, the Shakers' concern with the sexual behavior of nonbelievers was, as we shall see, primarily eugenic. They considered reproduction a necessary evil; there had to be generation (however much they might dislike it) before there could be regeneration. The demographic logic was simple. Without reproduction among the unregenerate (and probably the Novitiate Order as well), Shakerism as an institution would die out within a generation. Ironically, from a moral as well as a demographic point of view, the sinfulness of society was necessary to the continued existence of the community of perfected Shaker saints. Both eugenics and the demographic dependence of the Shakers on worldly reproduction were emphasized in a pamphlet on the marriage question written in the 1860s. The final paragraph provides a concise summary of Shaker attitudes: "It is not our work to improve generation. You that work at the business must do that. We want good *bricks*,—the very best that can be had, and sincerely wish you all success in improving them. We are not brick-makers, though we consider those that are, just as necessary in their place, if they do their work right. We are Master-builders, called to build in the temple of our God, and go no more out forever."[13]

Shakers' advocacy of celibacy as a form of contraception resulted from an anxiety about overpopulation, but more especially from an acute awareness of the physical risks pregnancy and childbirth represented for the female, and from eugenic concern for moral progress. Sexual abstention would insure the effective sterilization of "at least one-third of mankind, [who] through physical disease, weakness, disorganization, or mental disability are unfit to assume the responsibility of matrimony, unless at least, 'they keep the bed undefiled.'"[14]

On the level of male-female relations, the Shaker attitude toward birth control, insofar as it was concerned with eugenics, tended to support both the freedom and the bondage of women. When the rationale given for birth control was the risks sustained by women on account of too-frequent pregnancies, the intent was obviously to support the movement that favored the abolition of the double standard of sexual morality, and to afford women a greater voice in the determination of their fates through the control of their own bodies. When the rationale was strictly eugenic, however, although the end result from the sexual and medical point of view would be the same, there was a subtle difference from the social point of view. Birth control justified on the basis of the necessity of producing healthy, intelligent children required women who were healthy, intelligent mothers. The emphasis shifted from woman exploited by man for sexual reasons to woman the mother. She slipped back into her social, maternal role; no longer sexually used by man, she would be able to breed better children. Freedom from incessant pregnancies, and from the importunate demands of the male animal, made it possible for her to become a supermother, but a mother nonetheless. It was from this point of view that the Shakers opposed infanticide, abortion, and feticide.[15]

There remained the Malthusian justification for birth control, which became quite common in Shaker circles in the late 1860s and 1870s, but the basis of the argument remained the same; sexual intercourse perforce led to reproduction because that was the inherent end of the act. The only way to avoid reproduction, and thus population, was by completely renouncing sex. Woman could choose her role: mother or virgin celibate.

Shaker feelings about polygamy and the "complex marriage" of the Oneida Community were directly related to their concern with birth control. The "law of Nature—the use of marriage only for offspring" was of central importance. The Utah system they recommended, because the Mormons "marry a plurality of women, with the certainty that the violation of the same law will be in inverse ratio to the number of a man's wives."[16] Furthermore, by "dividing these passions among many wives, far less harm and brutality were done than very many a so-called christian enacts with one miserable woman, called by his name. . . . But while neither polygamy nor monogamy are in the least christian, monogamy, for the indulgence of libidinous passions only, is less so than polygamy."[17] But at Oneida, " 'unfruitful works of generation' [are] reduced to a science. . . . instead of using *marriage* . . . for the purpose of *increase only*, [they] seek how to use it *ad libitum*, and still be 'unfruitful.' "[18]

Here again, we have the sense of vacillation. Significantly, they ignore the fact that the Oneida system provides even greater protection for the health and constitution of woman by protecting her from unwanted pregnancies, and concentrate on the fact that the purpose of sex at Oneida was pleasure rather than reproduction. Woman's health must be protected, but her function remains that of a mother. There must be no compromise with "those in and out of the marriage relationship, who court the pleasures of sensuality, without the willingness to incur the responsibility of offspring."[19]

No single issue was more illustrative of the inveterate conservatism in male-female relations that characterized the Shakers' thought than their attitude toward divorce. Divorce, or at least de facto separation from spouses, was a problem they had to face from the very outset. They were determined that taking up the Shaker cross would not become for some merely an excuse for laying down a more onerous uxorial burden. Their membership rules provided that "no believing husband or wife is allowed to separate from an unbelieving wife or husband, except legally, or by mutual agreement. Nor can any person who has abandoned his or her partner, without just and lawful cause, be received into communion with the Society; and in case of separation between husband and wife, the latter must have a just and righteous share of all property in their possession."[20]

In all those states in which Shaker societies were located, with the exception of Ohio, New York, and to a limited extent Connecticut, the legislature passed laws that allowed divorce if one partner left the other to join a celibate religious organization. Kentucky passed the earliest such law in 1812 and retained it in the comprehensive divorce legislation of 1843, which remained in effect until the twentieth century. It permitted divorce for the party not at fault in case of his or her spouse's "uniting with any religious society whose creed and rules require renunciation of the marriage covenant, or forbid husband and wife to cohabit."[21] Similar anti-Shaker laws were passed in Maine in 1830, New Hampshire in 1842, and Massachusetts in 1850. In Connecticut, no specially directed legislation was required, because the "omnibus clause" of the 1849 law provided divorce for any conduct that "defeats the purpose of the marriage relation."[22]

Persecution from without forced the Shakers to take a stand on divorce; they sought to defend their communities from the opprobrium of being known as legalized divorce mills. The Shakers opposed state divorce legislation, not only because it was an attack upon the principle of freedom of religion insofar as it equated membership in a Shaker society with criminality and adultery, but also because it expanded the causes allowable in divorce suits and provided for separation *a vinculo matrimonii*. Abandonment, under which category joining a Shaker community fell, had to be uninterrupted for a period of from two to five years before an absolute decree of divorce was allowed. But, complained the Shakers, "if she or he for conscience sake, but enter the threshold of a Shaker church, although the party without the church is nurtured and guarded by the party entering and the whole society, during the membership, you allow no time for reflection and repentance. . . . with the Shaker, membership without conviction [of criminality]; is a good foundation for divorce."[23]

The Shakers seem to have preferred, from the period of their earliest concern with the matter, no separation at all; but if unavoidable, they favored separation *a mensa et thoro*:

> If a brother have an unbelieving wife, or a sister an unbelieving husband, and the parties can agree to live together in peace, they are not required to separate on account of their faith; but the believing husband is bound to take care of his unbelieving wife, to provide for her. . . . But if they cannot live together in peace, they may separate by mutual agreement, and divide their inheritance according to the principles of justice and equity. The society does not admit of a separation on any other conditions; unless the conduct of the unbelieving party be such that the believer . . . can be *fully justified, both by the laws of God and man, in a final separation*.[24]

Shakers were already considered antisocial radicals who discountenanced marriage and were misogynistic. But at least that was a personal preference; their separation from society and the unpopularity of their doctrines rendered them socially passive. If they advocated divorce and sanctioned laws that prescribed divorce to the aggrieved mate of a Shaker celibate, or allowed them to go unchallenged, they would become a positively antisocial force. They already had problems enough with persecution. Even if they had desired a liberalized divorce structure (and the evidence strongly suggests that they did not), it would have been perilously rash to have expressed it publicly. Their characteristic response, therefore, was to support a mutually accepted separation or, in cases of extremity, a legal one. They refused admittance to any who could not show evidence of one of these two types of separation. An entry in the official record for 20 July 1838, for example, notes: "The woman who came yesterday with 4 children, were [*sic*] sent back to day to wait till they get clear of bondage to that drunken man."[25] The essentially biblical conservatism of the Shaker attitude toward divorce was most neatly expressed in the midst of an attack on the unrighteousness of the world's sexuality. If the generative function were more controlled, it was argued, "divorces would be less frequent. And if the results of divorcement, as stated by one superior to Moses, were observed, there would be but few who would be willing to marry her who had been put away.[26] Note that it is only the female partner in a divorce action who is denied the right of remarriage in this statement. The division of property upon separation advocated by Shakers also argues a superior status for males. They recommended a divison of property in which eight shares went to the husband, four to the wife, two to each son, and one to each daughter.[27]

Inherent in Shaker theology and polity, however, was the *idea* of the equality of women. At all levels of the socioreligious organization, from the Trustees to the androgynous godhead, there were male and female representatives. It is in this pervasive sexual dualism that the argument for the equality of male and female originated.

There was some sporadic concern with women's rights in the 1850s, especially in the works of the universal reformer Frederick W. Evans, but the real expression of concern with this issue came in the 1870s and probably persisted, with somewhat abated fervor, into the twentieth century.[28] It seems apparent, then, that Shaker attitudes on the "woman question" paralleled the course of events in the world outside their communities. They followed the lead of feminine reformers rather than assuming a leadership role themselves. With the exception of the extraordinary interest in women's rights that affected a broad group of Shakers in the 1870s, the earlier expressions of feminism were isolated phenomena; and apart from Evans, whose interests were more catholic, Shakers were concerned primarily with sexual equality in religious life and ecclesiastical polity. Even at the height of accession to the feminist position, however, the inveterate theological assumption of female inferiority remained strong and often found expression in the same breath with concern for women's rights. Thus in the 1880s, for example, we find in an official propaganda tract a description of woman as "the glory and splendor of man, provided she has been redeemed from sin."[29]

From the early nineteenth century, there had been support among the Shakers for a broader female role in religious matters. Obviously, in a sect founded by a woman who claimed to be inspired by divine revelation, there was from the beginning an emphasis on the equality of women with respect to visions and revelations.[30] In fact, during the great eruption of spiritualism in the 1840s, most of the mediums were women. At religious meetings female speakers were not uncommon, and women also took the lead in pitching songs on occasion.[31] In ecclesiastical polity, authority was maintained in separate, parallel male and female orders. An incident that occurred in the 1850s is illustrative of how seriously the Shakers considered the strict separation and equality of the two orders. Philemon Stewart, Elder in the Second Family at Mt. Lebanon and a minor theological light among the Shakers, was removed from his position primarily because he sought to control the female order in that Family. "For a year or more past," we are told, "Elder Br. Philemon has repeatedly urged the necessity of quite a change or removal of the Female leaders in that family—(especially the Elder sisters), and others chosen to fill their place that would better harmonize with his peculiar views of progressive reform, or gospel increase as he would call it. This the Ministry could not accede to, not finding sufficient cause to do so."[32]

Stewart, in part as a result of his attempt to control an order in which his sex had no legitimate right, was further demoted from the First to the Second Order within a week of the termination of this incident.[33] There is little evidence of the equality of men and women, however, in any but religious terms. On the upper levels of the Shaker hierarchy, especially in the Ministry, there seems to have been more freedom. We find, for example, that members of the Ministry traveled together from one society to another in mixed groups of roughly equal male-female composition. In the 1850s we see one of these groups swimming together.[34] Shaker societies were thus divided horizontally according to sex and vertically according to religious prestige. Members of the Ministry had more privileges than any others in the Shaker community. Female members of the Ministry were therefore the most privileged Shaker women and enjoyed rights and freedoms not available to their less-elevated sisters.

Interest in political rights for women and a more intensive concern with the position of women in society did not find widespread expression until the 1870s. In 1871 we find a unique reference to an Elder's speech at a meeting on women's rights.[35] The official Shaker organ, which began publication in 1871 under the title the *Shaker,* was published from 1872 to 1875 under the title *Shaker and Shakeress.* A joint editorship was instituted for these years under Frederick W. Evans and Antoinette Doolittle. The paper became a mirror image of Shaker social relations. Each monthly issue was eight pages in length. With the exception of the masthead on the first page, the first half of the paper bore the inscription "Shaker And." At the head of the sheets in the second half the periodical title was completed by the word "Shakeress." All the articles and correspondence in the first half of the paper were by males, whereas those in the second half were by females.[36] With some surprise, outside observers noted that "of all places in the world," at Mt. Lebanon Shakers "have recognized the Woman's Rights doctrine by terming their paper *The Shaker and Shakeress.*"[37] Certainly the editorship of Evans, who was in the Shaker vanguard on the question of women's rights, contributed to the intensification of concern in this area in the 1870s. But the widespread nature of the concern, its sudden appearance and equally sudden demise, and its reflection in such a seemingly insignificant area as burial policy[38] argues for a broader base of support.

The *Shaker and Shakeress* and a number of books and pamphlets were concerned with voting rights for women, female inequality in the labor force, and female officeholders, as well as the problems presented by the sexual relationship in marriage and childbearing. But this was not an unqualified concern. It is necessary to understand the terms upon which Shakers recommended the tendering of political power to women. The tone of much of this literature was set in the *Shaker and Shakeress* for

1873. An order of celibates was the prerequisite for the achievement of political rights for women: "From its ranks, women-rulers—legislators, judges, juries, advocates, physicians, etc.—could be chosen, without being obnoxious to the charge, that the children at home were being neglected while they were caring for the children of the Republic."[39] Conjugal duties and motherhood took precedence over *all* rights that women might claim.

On the question of the vote for women, considered apart from female political participation, Shakers saw no such obstacles. They heartily recommended woman suffrage. Interestingly, this reform, which, unlike political officeholding, was advocated by Shaker women, was on occasion demanded as a right. A dialogue among six sisters, printed in the 1870s, took as its central concern the equality of women and the concomitant right to vote. The tone of this discussion, and on a broader level of most of the Shaker agitation for female suffrage, was evident in the words of one of the sisters:

> I rejoice that the time is approaching when the voice of *woman* will be heard in governmental affairs; when she shall help to enact laws that will bind Justice and Love in one inseparable bond; uplifting her sex from the thraldom of sensual and sexual sinfulness, into the untrammeled freedom of personal rights and privileges, such as *man* enjoys. Then shall a purer and more refining influence pervade the council halls of the nation, and a new epoch in civil history will hold a corresponding relation to the spiritual order under which we exist.[40]

The implication is clear: there are inherent, biologically determined differences between the sexes that render their psychological makeups totally different, yet at the same time complementary. Woman's strengths are in the religious and moral realms; she is a refiner, a savior, who will, through her own sufferings and bondage, redeem the fallen world of men. Woman is at once the reformed and the reformer. She is to be granted the vote not as a person with equal rights, but because she has become, through romantic mystification, a figure whose very alienation from the world of men will provide the impetus to reform.

Yet the traditional concern for woman the temptress died hard in Shaker communities; woman remained at once devil and demigod. No clearer expression of male distrust of women is to be found than Shaker attacks on fashion and female dress. In Shaker communities the dress and hairstyles of both men and women were very carefully prescribed. Regulations governing dress were virtually militaristic in their rigidity and concern for minute, apparently insignificant detail. In general, the rationale behind uniformity of dress was to maintain communal union; but in the case of women's clothing, concern ran deeper and revealed a totally different emphasis.

A European visitor to the Watervliet, New York, community in the early 1850s found a strong resemblance between the female Shaker costume and the habit of a cloistered religious order. It impressed him as "a sort of white Dutch hood, stitched in the back; blue or gray skirts with a short waist; over these, stiffly starched white breast-cloths, crossing over in front, covering the throat up to the chin, and hanging down three-edged more than half-way in the back; and final coarse stockings and heavy shoes. The costume is nothing less than unbecoming and gives to even the most youthful figure a grandmotherly and stiff (I should like to say wooden) appearance."[41]

Undoubtedly, the clothing of Shaker sisters was plain and serviceable: worsted and cotton gowns, cotton aprons and caps, worsted socks and stockings. The only undergarment recommended in an exemplary clothing list was the petticoat.[42] Nonetheless, "all who choose wear flannel or knit undergarments; corsets are discarded, and skirts are suspended from the shoulders."[43] All finery was to be shunned, including jewelry and watches. Unauthorized furbelows and gewgaws were "loudly disowned" by female Shaker leaders, who permitted

> no checked collars. No silk cushions, shoestrings, or bag strings. No silk bonnet strings for everyday. Homemade cloth is sufficient for bags. No frills, or ruffles in bonnets. No pearl buttons for collars. No green vales; no Bombazette aprons, or pressed shiny green aprons. No clasp garters. No bought striped gowns, with wider stripes than the good O.h.h. order stripe. If buttons are put on your gowns, cover, or, colour them like the garment. No writing or marking with red or other fine colours. . . . No dotting or dating. . . . No printing of names.[44]

The female fashion of hair dressing required Shaker sisters "to comb their hair clean, and straight back from the forepart of the head, and fasten it in a knot upon the back part with a pin made for that purpose. And to wear a straight plain muslin cap, which shall come so closely over the face as to conceal the hair entirely."[45] In view of the Shakers' essentially Pauline conception of women, it is not unreasonable to assume a connection between this mode of dressing the hair and the practice of female deference (see 1 Corinthians 11:4–10).

Apparently, not all women were satisfied with the established clothing regulations, and some of them may even have openly defied them. This opposition is not surprising, but the form it took is instructive in delimiting the essentially medial position Shakers took on the question of women's fashions. On the one hand, they had to guard against the world of *la mode*. The tendency of Shaker women to desire the accoutrements of this world was sadly lamented: "Why O why will we seek a Worldly look to mix in with the real Shaker appearance by making small our Waist and then with abundance of under clothing expand about the hips so that instead of being a blessing in Zion, our very appearance brings distress on the faithful and most of all upon our beloved Lead who have been striving to make us look pretty and bring us in Union. O may I never mar the Sacred Courts of Zion with Worldly fashions."[46]

On the other hand, care had to be taken lest in their rebellion against worldly fashion Shaker women adopt the dress associated with female reformers and free-love advocates. This mode was considered unfeminine. A narrow course had to be held between the covertly provocative fashion of the world and the radically antifeminine and immodest dress of the reformers. Shaker women would find peace in the modesty and moderation of Shaker dress. It was fervently to be hoped that "*never* may any of Mother's Children stoop so low as to wish themselves clothed in Bloomer Costume which originated among *Free Lovers*. . . . none of the hundreds who visit us who are almost entirely of the upper class of Society in the world ever dress in that manner and . . . [they] make very derogatory remarks concerning the character of those who wear it . . . . [no] real refined person can ever seek for such an adorning but would feel disgraced at the same in almost any Society."[47]

Shoes were also a mixture of serviceability and fashion. They were to be warm and made "to fit and not to cramp the feet," yet they were high heeled.[48] The photographic evidence indicates that the majority of Shaker women conformed in most essentials to the uniform dress code. Materials were not consistently drab, however, and bright calico prints and checked fabric were occasionally worn. It appears that when Shaker women deviated from the standard dress, they erred most frequently in the direction of a more feminine mode. Despite constant injunctions against "jewelry, ruffles, rosettes, travelling dresses, world's fashions," and so on,[49] in two photographs of women probably taken in the late 1860s or 1870s, we see a young woman with a pleated skirt and an overblouse trimmed with fringe and frogged fasteners, and an older woman with a plain skirt with fringed hem and a matching overblouse, also fringed. The elder woman wears an earring. Because earlier photographs show a more rigorous adherence to the uniform standard of Shaker dress, it would appear that there was a revolt against the female dress code during the late 1860s and early 1870s.[50]

But it was the rationale behind Shaker proscription of fashion in female dress that revealed the ideological basis of the system. This rationale was not present in prescriptions for male attire; the argument in this case was based solely upon uniformity. Furthermore, quite tellingly, the ideological crusade against fashion is largely confined to the 1870s. Apparently Shaker leaders realized the social aggression behind the desire for sartorial adornment and tried to institute measures that would reinforce communal cohesion. It was precisely those years in which women's rights were being openly advocated in Shaker publications that these innovations in fashion were being introduced, and Shaker Elders were not slow to note the connection between the two phenomena. Dress reform and women's rights are opposite sides of the same coin and reflect the deeply rooted tension in the Shaker mind about the status of women. Women needed to be saved from fashion in order to facilitate the salvation of mankind from sexual sin. Women who followed that meretricious mistress Fashion were a threat to society; they endangered the very morals of the men who were responsible for their fashionable enslavement. The way to reform the human race, then, was to start with woman. Make her pure, and man could not but be purified. The attack on fashion was a subtle renunciation by males of responsibility for the moral problems of the nineteenth century. "To our mind," a writer in the *Shaker and Shakeress* wrote, "*woman*, hampered with confining skirts, shrivelled and squeezed with pain producing ligatures, is so deformed that one would never imagine her part of that humanity that was 'created upright.' Submitting to fashion, which she despises, and which the better part of men also despise, but have not the strength to lift her above . . . evidences her weakness and imbecility."[51]

This was a relatively mild statement, implying that men and women may not even be members of the same species. Many statements of opposition to feminine dress saw the two sexes as bellicose combatants. Such was the somewhat tongue-in-cheek approbation afforded the witchcraft statute of James II, which provided severe penalties for "every woman who, by means of cosmetics, false hair, padding, stays, hoops, high-heeled shoes, or other feminine devices, should seduce and betray into matrimony any member of the opposite sex."[52]

The overtones of hostility and distrust of women, and the refusal to question the social mores that were the basis of this pattern of behavior, are indicative of the antifeminist and conservative rationale the Shakers employed in their attack on fashion. They opposed finery because it led to seduction, prostitution, and infanticide. The function of the plain dress was to keep woman's sexual nature under control and to keep her in her place. The real fear at the bottom of Shaker opposition to women's fashion, and the consideration that caused them to tergiversate on the question of women's rights, was their anxiety that liberation from established sexual mores (however bad they were) would lead not to a pure, celibate world, but to a world of sensual pleasure. It was for this reason that their attack on fashion sought to curb female sexual drives and to keep women rooted in a maternal role. This was not solely an attack of men upon women; apparently, many Shaker women feared their own sexual natures and adopted the same basic ideological position. But it was an attack upon femininity in that it was concerned only with women. There was no comparable attack on men's fashions.[53]

The prevalent division of labor in Shaker communities also belies the assumption that the predication of a dualistic godhead meant a correspondent change in male-female roles or provided any logical necessity for sexual equality. Aside from some sharing of labor in emergencies such as fire fighting, and large-scale tasks such as painting, women were strictly confined to domestic tasks. Even in a cooperative enterprise such as painting, functional boundaries were maintained: women painted the inside and men the outside of dwellings.[54] Women in the professional occupations seem to have been very rare. Antoinette Doolittle served as editress of the *Shaker and Shakeress* from 1873 to 1876; a woman served as a dentist at Mt. Lebanon in the late 1850s; and a few taught school in Shaker communities.[55]

In most cases, however, women performed feminine ascriptive tasks. They did the cooking, waiting on tables, cleaning, mending, tailoring, and laundry. The neat curtness of this division of labor was reflected in the observation that "females perform all kinds of household duties: cooking, washing, sewing, etc."[56] Household duties were rotated on a monthly basis, and laborsaving devices facilitated much of the heavier work in the laundry and ironing room, but no female servants were employed in Shaker communities to lighten the work load of the sisters, as hired men did that of the brethren. Men do not appear to have regularly assisted women, even in the more arduous aspects of their labor; but in the laundry, after the introduction of a steam washing machine in 1867, an "engineer" was present to run the machinery, a task that seems to have been considered beyond the female ken.[57]

In addition to their household chores, women were responsible for domestic industries and, after the middle of the nineteenth century, for the sale of their production in a community-based store. Women manufactured or processed herbs, medicines, lace caps, cane mats, soap, candles, preserved fruits and vegetables, and upholstery. At Mt. Lebanon, where female industry was more developed, the sisters' talents ironically served the painted jezebel of fashion, for they manufactured for sale "reticules, cushion baskets, . . . fur gloves, feather fans, . . . fur wristlets . . . [and] octagon poplar hearts."[58]

Women in Shaker communities were celibate mothers; their function was maternal vis-à-vis both children and adult males. Conversely, Shaker males had both a paternal and a puerile role. The paradigmatic basis for the relationship between the sexes was the adult-child relationship. The adult roles open to each sex were the traditional maternal and paternal ones. Men and women approached each other in either deference or precedence; they did not meet as equals. They were equals only in their separation. The emphasis on the importance of the maternal relationship in Shaker communities was underlined by the division of labor, and even more patently by the plan adopted for keeping clothing neat and orderly. Not only were women responsible for the care of the boys' clothing, but "each brother . . . has appointed for his convenience some sister to look after his individual necessities, as knitting, mending, general supervision of his clothing."[59] Upon occasion, women also brought dinner to the brethren who labored in the fields, but they seldom labored there themselves.[60]

Despite laborsaving devices and frequent rotation of labor, which elevated the condition of Shaker sisters above that of their less fortunate married counterparts, labor in these communities seems to have been very arduous for women. They had more mechanical assistance, yes; but the volume of work was multiplied many times, not only because of the larger scale of the Shaker Family in comparison to the average nuclear family, but also because of the hired men who boarded on Shaker property and the large number of annual visitors. The drudgery of life for these women may have been even greater prior to the middle 1860s, when they began to be provided with extensive mechanical assistance.

Yet perhaps increased mechanization raised false hopes among the sisterhood of a lightened burden of domestic labor and more leisure. If so, the increased use of hired help (male) in Shaker communities (and specifically their residence *in* the communities after the late 1860s) soon disabused them of this illusion and convinced them that greater mechanization only meant that greater efficiency and consequently increased productivity were expected of them. In any case, the only noticeable outbreak of discontent did not come until the 1870s, and was largely coincident with the wave of interest in feminism that swept through the eastern Shaker communities in that decade. An article entitled "Over-Burdened Shaker Societies," struck the keynote:

It is . . . well known that we keep no house servants; that our sisterhood is severely taxed with many household duties; while those serving in the culinary department of our *office* buildings are not only taxed to care for those calling on legitimate business but are unreasonably expected to cook, and otherwise care for a small army of *hirelings*! and when we say *unreasonably*, we mean that a due respect for the sister-hood of our faith would forbid any such use of the gospel sisters! . . . tired and jaded as the over-worked sisters are, *this company becomes very unwelcome.*[61]

This note was echoed in even more militant terms in a private letter from the same period: "It is a great drag and burden on Sisters in every place to be Servants to hirelings, and how long they will endure it without revolting we cannot say. But the sooner something is done to make a change the better it would be for Society's welfare, both physically and Spiritually."[62]

It was also in the 1870s that some breakdown in the division of decision making in Shaker societies became evident. Traditionally, males were responsible for business and temporal decisions, and both sexes met to resolve religious matters. In April 1872, both males and females were present at a Mt. Lebanon business meeting. In 1872 and 1874, joint education meetings were held at Mt. Lebanon. That these ventures were tentative and not thoroughly accepted by male Shakers is evident from a comment in the official record of Mt. Lebanon about women and finances. A meeting of the male hierarchy "had a consultation relative to Sisters holding some portion of the money to command."[63] This question does not seem to have been resolved, for there is no further mention of it in the record. The mere broaching of the subject, however, presented a challenge to the dogmatic assertion that sexual separation meant sexual equality. The old notion of orders so central to Shaker theology and ideology would not down. "Each sex works," it was argued, "in its own appropriate sphere of action, there being a proper subordination, deference and respect of the female to the male in his order, and of the male to the female in her order, so that in any of these communities the zealous advocates of 'woman's rights' may here find a practical realization of their ideal."[64]

It was this notion of "appropriate spheres" that was the nucleus of the Shaker system of adjustment. It received its most eloquent and extensive presentation during the 1870s as a kind of antidote to the noxious influence of overzealous feminist advocates, but it had been present in Shaker thought from the first. As official doctrine, it was subscribed to as heartily by women as by men. As Antoinette Doolittle explained female acceptance of the established pattern:

> We recognize the law of dependency running through all created things; the lesser leaning upon the greater—the weaker upon the stronger. Man is the lawful head, and is the representative of God in the male order, the Eternal Father, and will always have the supremacy. Woman, the representative of God in the female part of Deity, Mother, must act her part as co-worker, filling her sphere.

There is no bondage in the law of dependency, even as there is no
bondage in *any* of God's laws! for, without law, all would be
chaos.[65]

As the motif was most frequently employed in the 1870s, it became a tool
of resurgent evangelical feminism and served to link religious progress
and reform through the medium of women. This is to say not that there
were not more thoroughgoing arguments made on the woman question
among Shakers, but rather that they were buried amid a flood of counter-
ideology or, with more finesse, strategically placed in periodicals so that
a contrapuntal dialogue was established, a dialogue that good Shakers
could not fail to assess "correctly".[66]

Certainly the separation of male and female into rational-secular-
worldly and emotional-religious-domestic spheres was not unusual in the
romantic outlook of the mid-nineteenth century. But the vehemence
with which Shakers held that separation was unique. This sense of absolute, irrefragable separation was emphasized by Antoinette Doolittle: "If
woman would work successfully, she must keep within her own sphere.
The distinctive lines between the masculine and feminine are clearly defined. . . . The sea and land have their prescribed limits. So with man and
woman. Each should have full freedom to act in their own spheres."[67]
It was no accident that concurrently with an increased interest in the
woman question in the 1870s, the Shakers began to structure the system
of spheres along spiritualist lines, in a way that clearly expressed extant
power relationships in their hierarchical structure of sexual relationships.
Males were associated with the inner, higher, and spiritual spheres;
whereas females were found in the outer, lower, and material spheres.
Yet women were considered to be religious leaders, even the religious
saviors of men!

Shakers seem to have reconciled this contradiction by making a horizontal division into profane and sacred, which cut across the vertical
sexual division. Thus, woman is *socially* inferior to the male members of
the hierarchy, but is *religiously* superior to noncelibate (uninitiated) and
lower-echelon Shaker males. In her greater spiritual affinity as a medium
between the sublunary and celestial worlds, she is the source of vision, of
continued revelation. In her inspired capacity, she takes precedence in
the religious sphere even over the Elders; in social affairs, whatever her
rank, she remains subject to male control.

The key to the attainment of equality and liberation from sexual servitude for women in such a society, then, was the renunciation of their
sexuality; it was in essence becoming, with men, members of a new
species of neuter virgin celibates. "We wish to be clearly understood,"
cried a Shaker woman, "that self denial is the first, the second, and the

third requisite, by which one may attain to the position of a truly en-franchised woman."[68] It was this religious-sexual purity that redeemed woman and made it possible for her to regenerate man as well. That women should have accepted the sex roles and division of labor that existed in Shaker communities suggests that their more successful adaptation to the sexual system might have been merely a reflection of a greater general amenability or malleability; but it is undeniable that within the confines of the theological-sexual system, they had more to gain in the religious realm in which they exercised authority, and had at least symbolic preeminence, than did men.

The greater attractiveness of Shakerism to women is borne out by the sexual distribution of the withdrawal rate. Overall, women constituted 40 percent of total withdrawals and men 60 percent. It was extremely rare in Shaker demographic units of any size for the number of female to exceed that of male withdrawals. Male and female withdrawal rates at Mt. Lebanon differed by only 10 percent in the 1830s and 1850s, but in the 1840s men made up 65.5 percent and women 34.5 percent of those who left. From 1859 to 1874, males apostatized at a rate of 69 percent and females at a rate of only 31 percent.[69] The expulsion and excommunication rate also indicates greater female success in adapting to Shaker life. At Mt. Lebanon and Watervliet, New York, from 1828 to 1872, there were 23 expulsions, of which 19 were men. Of every 10 persons excommunicated, 8.2 were male and 1.7 female.[70]

The satisfactions that men derived from Shakerism were not uniquely related to the system itself. They could realize satisfactions of the same sort outside these communities, and could have conjugal lives as well. This is what made the life of the world so much more attractive, and life in a Shaker community so much more difficult, for them. This was not true for women. Sacrifice of the venereal relations was not without its compensations for women. It was an effective and acceptable form of birth control and preserved women from the risks of pregnancy and childbirth. Furthermore, although the woman still found herself subject to social controls and ideologically despised, she did achieve a preeminent spiritual power in the religious sphere.

Shakerism, in the broader context of nineteenth-century America, attempted to overcome the selfishness and licentiousness of worldly society through extreme mortification of the flesh. For Shaker brothers, celibacy provided the rationale for the masculine control of the threatening power of sexuality. For Shaker women, it meant the alienation of the womb and the consequent loss of moral and social power based on parturition, child rearing, and domesticity. Whereas the ideal "true woman" of nineteenth-century America had two primary sources of power—fecundity and sanctity, domestic and religious—celibacy limited feminine Shaker power to the religious sphere. Woman under Shakerism justified her claim to true womanhood not only, as with her unregenerate sisters, by her acceptance of a subordinate social role and by limiting her aspirations for power and achievement to her assigned sphere, but by physically renouncing her femininity.[71]

Once the beast that raged within woman, in the form of her seductive and reputedly excessive sex drive, was crushed out, she would become figuratively a female Christ. The renovated woman could achieve equality, but only in her appointed sphere. No real attempt was made to integrate the two spheres; the parallel male and female orders were to remain separate but equal for eternity. When the two orders or spheres impinged, the renovated woman remained as socially subordinate and powerless as her old irredeemable sisters who were untouched by the refulgent Motherhood of God.

Part III ❦ Celestial Marriage: Mormon Sexuality and Sex Roles in Ideology and Practice

Introduction 🜨 Sealed by the Holy Spirit: Joseph Smith and the Revelation on Plural Marriage

And there are none that do know the true God save it be the disciples of Jesus, who did tarry in the land until the wickedness of the people was so great that the Lord would not suffer them to remain with the people.

—Book of Mormon, Mormon 8:10

Beloved, believe not every spirit, but try the spirits whether they are of God: because many false prophets are gone out into the world.

—1 John 4:1

O n the evening of 21 September 1830, Moroni, the angel of the Lord, appeared to Joseph Smith, Jr., in a vision and prophesied that "all the proud, yea, and all that do wickedly shall burn as stubble: for they that come shall burn them saith the Lord of hosts, that it shall leave them neither root nor branch."[1] As the original text (Malachi 3:2–3) was reworked, there is a promise of the overthrow of the proud and wicked, not by Christ, but by a newly arrived group, which by implication is humble and righteous. This was precisely the tone and tenor of revelatory utterance that would have appealed to the twenty-five-year-old Joseph Smith. He had had his first revelation, which set him at odds with all established religions, in the spring of 1820. The reaction of the representatives of those religions was predictable; the adolescent Joseph was admonished, preached at, beseeched, and hounded until he felt mightily persecuted.[2] No doubt the social standing of the Smith family in Manchester, New York, combined with religious pressures to enter the ranks of the regenerated, contributed to his growing sense of paranoia.

Some indication of the fortunes of the Smith family can be gathered from its geographical mobility under Joseph Smith, Sr. Five generations of Smiths had been born in Topsfield, Massachusetts, since the seventeenth century. But Joseph, Jr., was born in 1805 in Sharon, Vermont; moved with his family at age ten to Palmyra, New York; and moved four years later to Manchester, New York.[3] The family apparently eked out a meager living by a combination of marginal farming, intermittent odd jobs, and manual labor. The restless mobility of the family suggests the instability of its tenure, as well as a relatively low level of economic capacity.

In an area where religious enthusiasms and superstitious folk beliefs went hand in hand, it was only natural for a boy to see visions and dream dreams. As one of ten children in a family living on the periphery of penury, Joseph Smith was motivated by forces of resentment against those more fortunate, ingrained cupidity, and an overweening desire to succeed. Although ill educated and temperamentally indolent, he seems to have possessed a native charm and cleverness that helped him achieve what the angel Moroni had prognosticated. He consistently took advantage of those who were proud or well-to-do but credulous, often ruining them in the process. The angel's prophecy had provided a perhaps only half-consciously perceived self-righteous justification for a paranoiac form of behavior grounded in vague delusions of grandeur. Certainly the reactions of his neighbors and those who had been duped, as manifested in a succession of lawsuits, only confirmed Smith's sense of persecution and increased his desire to triumph over his enemies.

His first trial, which grew out of his activities hunting for buried treasure on the property of Josiah Stowel, an affluent farmer in Chenango County, appears to have been in Bainbridge, New York, in 1826, when he was charged with being "a disorderly person and an impostor."[4] He was found guilty on 20 March 1826; his father lost his farm later that year. In January 1827, Joseph, Jr., eloped with Emma Hale, and they were married without her father's consent. On 22 September 1827, Joseph was given the Plates of Nephi, which in translation became the *Book of Mormon*, disparagingly denominated "The Golden Bible" by his detractors.[5]

The attempt to render the Smith family financially solvent is clearly behind both his money digging and the episode of the plates, and in each case he got an added sense of satisfaction from having humbled one of the proud ones of the world. His marriage to Emma Hale was certainly humbling to the pride of her father, Isaac Hale, a solid farmer, who considered Smith an itinerant ne'er-do-well. Smith may also have hoped to acquire some property by the marriage, and if the testimony of Isaac Hale is accurate, he seems to have in fact received a house, furnishings, and a few head of cattle.[6]

The Plates of Nephi and his divine appointment as custodian and translator thereof, however, provided Smith with both financial opportunity and the promise of elevation to a position of power and prestige, which appealed to his desire to see the mighty humbled, as well as his need for self-aggrandizement. It is instructive that he tells us that he did not acquire the sacred plates until 1827, although he had gone to the Hill of Cumorah to obtain them every year since 1820. Smith revealed the probable reason for his failure up to 1827 when he reported a visionary admonition of Moroni, "that Satan would try to tempt me (in consequence of the indigent circumstances of my father's family), to get the plates for the purpose of getting rich. This he forbade me, saying that I must have no other object in view in getting the plates but to glorify God, and must not be influenced by any other motive than that of building His kingdom; otherwise I could not get them."[7] The obsession of the Smith family with the monetary value of the plates and the paraphernalia found with them was explicitly revealed in the frank statement of Lucy Smith (Joseph's mother) about the breastplate of Nephi: "The whole plate was worth at least five hundred dollars."[8]

Once the plates had been translated, a publisher had to be found and, even more importantly, paid. Martin Harris, a wealthy farmer, was the man chosen to put up the requisite three thousand dollars. Harris's wife opposed the plan, and he himself appears to have had second thoughts, even though he is reputed to have said, " 'What if it is a lie; if you will let me alone I will make money out of it!' "[9] This statement suggests the way in which the translation scheme was initially presented to Harris. The refractoriness of Harris to Smith's blandishments was overcome by a revelation of the Lord, which represents the religious aspect of Smith's character of confidence man–victim. When individuals were not amenable to his charm or his appeal to their avarice, he became the fiery Old Testament prophet who threatened terrible retribution if the word of God, transmitted through him, were not obeyed. Thus, the prophet said to Martin Harris: "And again, I command thee that thou shalt not covet thine own property, but impart it freely to the printing of the Book of Mormon, which contains the truth of the word of God. . . . And misery shalt thou receive if thou wilt slight these counsels; yea, even the destruction of thyself and property. Impart a portion of thy property; yea, even part of thy lands, and all save the support of thy family. Pay the debt thou hast contracted with the printer. Release thyself from bondage."[10]

Further use of revelations in a manipulative way, which also corroborates the economic motivations behind the initial printing of the Book of Mormon, is not lacking. While Harris was trying to sell his property to raise printing costs, Smith purportedly had another revelation instructing him to send a delegation to Toronto to sell the Canadian copyright of the book. When the mission failed, Smith declared the vision uninspired by God.[11] In July of 1830, he received a revelation directed to Emma, his wife, obviously designed to keep her in her place, quiet her doubts, and assure her that God's prophet would provide support for her and his family: "And thou needest not fear, for thy husband shall support thee in the church; for unto them is his calling. . . . And verily I say unto thee that thou shall lay aside the things of this world, and seek for the things of a better. . . . Continue in the spirit of meekness, and beware of pride. Let thy soul delight in thy husband, and the glory which shall come upon him."[12]

When the Book of Mormon was finally published in 1830, the words "Author and Proprietor" appeared after Smith's name.[13] Subsequently, missionaries were sent out, among whose duties was to sell "the book." All of this activity, and the pretension of Smith himself, who sought not only financial security but also prestige for himself and his family, evoked the rage of his neighbors, who several times mobbed his house and on one occasion in 1832 tarred and feathered the man whom they considered an upstart and an impostor. These violent acts only accentuated the feeling of persecution under which Smith labored most of his life.[14]

Smith founded the Church of Jesus Christ of Latter-Day Saints on 6 April 1830. Initially, there were six members, but within a month some forty people, mostly from the vicinity of Palmyra, New York, had become Mormon adherents.[15] Despite the growth of the church, however, Smith was arrested for the second time in June of 1830, and again charged with being a "disorderly person." During this trial the first intimations of his sexual behavior came out. The two daughters of Josiah Stool [Stowel?] were questioned about Smith's behavior toward them "both in public and private." They denied any misbehavior, and Smith was acquitted.[16]

In later years, Brigham Young lent credence to the young Smith's reputation for amorous escapades when he claimed that Eli Johnson, one of the leaders of the mob that attacked Smith in 1832, wanted to have him castrated for putative intimacies with his sister, Nancy.[17] From 1832 on, Smith was involved in incessant imbroglios growing out of his sexual behavior. The magnitude of his sexual appetites was purportedly indicated in the phrenological chart published in the *Wasp* for 2 July 1842. The phrenologist, A. Crane, rated Smith eleven (on a scale from one to twelve) in amativeness and noted: "Extreme susceptibility; passionately fond of the company of the other sex."[18] Although the Revelation on the Eternity of the Marriage Covenant of 12 July 1843 officially authorized the practice of polygamy, Smith's opponents maintained that he actually had a revelation on polygamy and began practicing it in 1831, making it virtually coeval with the church itself.[19]

The records of the church for the period 1830–40, however, indicate a practice less organized—probably a form of spiritual wifery. Evidence for this position is provided by the record of the expulsions of Uriah and Lydia Anne Hawkins in 1837 for "unlawful matrimony" and of Sidney Roberts in 1840 for "saluting the sisters with what he calls a holy kiss."[20] There is little reason to doubt that Smith himself was involved in these affairs, or that he began the practice of polygamy at Nauvoo, Illinois, in the early 1840s, before his reception of the Revelation on Plural Marriage.

The revelation was a complex social and religious document, the main purposes of which appear to have been the regulation of a practice that threatened to get out of hand and the reconciliation of those who opposed such practices (chiefly women, and especially the Prophet's own wife) to the new doctrine. The recognition of, with an attempt to normalize, a rather tolerant standard of sexual behavior at Nauvoo is indicated in section 41: "And as ye have asked concerning adultery—verily, verily I say unto you, if a man receiveth a wife in the new and everlasting covenant, *and if she be with another man, and I have not appointed unto her by the holy annointing*, she hath committed adultery, and shall be destroyed."[21] Emma Smith is enjoined by the Lord, through the mouth of his Prophet, Joseph, to accept this kind of behavior, obviously a bitter pill to a proud woman. In an interesting passage, which indicates the prior practice of promiscuity by her beloved Joseph, she is admonished by God: "And let mine handmaid, Emma Smith, *receive all those that have been given unto my servant Joseph, and who are virtuous and pure before me*; and those who are not pure, and have said they were pure, shall be destroyed, saith the Lord God. . . . And again, verily I say, let mine handmaid forgive my servant Joseph his trespasses . . . and I, the Lord thy God, will bless her, and multiply her, and make her heart to rejoice."[22]

Emma was threatened with destruction if she failed to comply with this revelation, and in order to insure her compliance (as she was strictly forbidden to practice polyandry in article 54), Joseph sent the revelation to her by his brother Hyrum, noting in his autobiography that "I directed [William] Clayton to make out deeds of certain lots of land to Emma and the children."[23] Perhaps Joseph was offering his wife a property settlement as a tacit invitation to a quasi-legal separation, perhaps only a bribe to sweeten the gall the revelation contained, but we can only speculate.

Evidently the Prophet Joseph, who was a dashingly handsome man, took several other wives at Nauvoo. We need not give credence, however, to extreme estimates of his connubial plurality, most of which are based on the statements of his enemies.[24] In spite of his amorous tendencies, it does not follow that the Revelation on Plural Marriage was motivated solely by sexual desire. From a socioreligious perspective, maintaining control of a dangerously fractious situation seems to have been of prime importance. From a personal point of view, improving relations with Emma, "even the wife of my youth, and the choice of my heart,"[25] was of central importance.

Polygamy[26] offered Joseph certain opportunities beyond those of divinely legitimatized promiscuity. Although it is impossible to prove anything, owing to the secret nature of polygamous relationships prior to the publication of the revelation in 1852, it is quite possible that polygamy provided Joseph with a larger family than he might have had with the rather ill-fated Emma. Emma gave birth to eight children, four of whom were stillborn. A son, Don Carlos, died not long after birth. One of a pair of twins the Smiths adopted when their mother died in 1831 (the same year Emma gave birth to stillborn twins) died in 1832. Joseph had, then, only four children: three his wife bore and the one adopted twin. For a man from a large family who considered himself a biblical patriarch descended from Abraham, this must have been a rather disappointing production.[27]

In addition to an increased progeny, the system of polygamy as it evolved in its early years at Nauvoo, when it seems to have been little more than an institutionalized spiritual wifery, allowed Joseph to play his psychologically satisfying dual role of confidence man–prophet and victim of persecution. He could always claim to be the victim of vicious slander when (as in his final trial in Carthage, Illinois) he was indicted for "polygamy, or something else."[28] At the same time he could see the proud ones of the world cozened as a result of the secrecy of polygamy and his virtuous pretensions in his role of Prophet of the Lord. He apparently played the role of confidence man among his saints as well, for fully one-third of those women whose names became associated with his as plural wives were married. The others were daughters and sisters of his co-heirs to sainthood.[29]

The legacy of Joseph Smith, Jr., is a complex and enigmatic one. He was a man of great personal magnetism and expansive vision, a man whom loyal Mormons considered an inspired Prophet of the Lord. Non-Mormons, and those who had fallen away from the true faith, claimed that he was a counterfeiter, thief, lecher, and impostor. A man capable of inspiring unswerving loyalty and abiding faith in his followers, he was also a man of haughty pride and inordinate ambition. Misconstruing the extent of his power as a sectarian religious leader, he ran for president of the United States in 1844. In that same year, the nemesis of outraged unbelievers overtook him, fulfilling a threat against Mormonism made seven years earlier in an Ohio paper: "They lie by revelation, swindle by revelation, cheat and defraud by revelation, run away by revelation, and if they do not mend their ways, I fear they will at last be damned by revelation."[30] Joseph and his brother Hyrum, on 27 June 1844, were dragged from the Carthage, Illinois, jail and murdered by an incensed mob of Gentiles.

Joseph Smith, then, was a strange mixture of fiery Old Testament religious inspiration and frontier sharpness and chicanery. In his psyche a delicate balance was struck between a knowledge of his own guilt and the need to be considered innocent and saintly by his friends and neighbors. Years of experience had taught him that those whom he had duped and used would often be most vociferous in defending his innocence rather than risk the public derision that the exposure of their own folly might entail. The knowledge of his own guilt, however, necessitated some atonement, which he realized through his role of victim. And his church of Saints was created in his own image.

The experience of that church, scorned, contemned, cast out by a Christendom that found its doctrines inimical, and engaged for half a century in a pharisaical power struggle with the federal government and the minions of the Gentile churches, underscored the lessons inherent in the experiences of its martyr and founder. He had achieved a satisfactory integration of the contradictory elements of a paranoiac personality rendered acute by an existence on the periphery of social acceptability, but not without the aid of a transcendent power, a power he is supposed to have recognized in backhanded fashion in his statement of November 1843 that "GOD IS MY RIGHT HAND MAN."[31] That same centripetal egoism characterized his saints.

Chapter 7 ⚥ Sexual Resurrectionism: The Theological Foundations and Patriarchal Ideology of Mormon Polygamy

Not for the lack of clothing or of bread,
But for a husband—a man—a head!
To obviate reproach and share his name,
As to be single then will be a shame.

—Mormon poem

Such is polygamy, that she spawns warriors by the score,
Where none are prosecuted for that false crime, bigamy.

—Byron, *Don Juan*, canto 8, stanza 105

*I*n the summer of 1843, when Joseph Smith, Jr., sought enlightenment on the justification of the biblical polygamists, the answer he received was unequivocal; their acts had been directly ordained by God. The revelation he received was of central importance because its phrasing incorporated simultaneous polygyny into the theological structure of Mormonism from the very outset. Although opponents of Mormonism consistently asserted that polygamy was not an integral part of the Mormon religion, Mormons, during the period from 1852 to 1890, clearly considered it to be the very quintessence of their faith. John Taylor, third President of the church, made this point oracularly in 1882:

> It has been argued by those who are ignorant of the true nature of this doctrine, and how inseparably connected it is with all our hopes of eternal happiness in that world beyond the tomb, that this is not a part of our religion; that this system of marriage is not religion. . . . As a Church we have repeatedly testified in the most solemn manner

that the institution of marriage . . . has been revealed to us by the Almighty, and that it is part of our religion; that it is interwoven with our dearest and holiest hopes connected with eternity; and that—not from any lustful motives, but because we believe we should incur the eternal displeasure of our Heavenly Father if we did not comply with its requirements—we have espoused this doctrine.[1]

Salvation and the ultimate fate of both soul and body were completely dependent upon marital status and the proper arrangement of the sexual relation. Like the Shakers, the Mormons were "progressive perfectionists" and believed that moral progress would continue even after death. The hierarchical structure of their social and religious institutions reflected the degree of perfection, and thus the status attained, through enthusiastic participation in the institution of plural marriage. Whereas the Shakers had effectively pruned love of all its overt sexual manifestations by totally spiritualizing it, the Mormons attempted to strip it of all its nonsexual, spiritualized aspects; to reify it within the narrow limits of reproductive sexuality. They thus robbed love of all the attractions—companionship, loyalty, mutual respect—that were not directly related to reproduction. Shaker attitudes toward love were predicated upon their spiritualist theology. Mormon attitudes were equally rooted in their theological base, which was a thoroughgoing materialism.[2]

Mormon theological conceptions concerning the godhead are rudimentary, unsophisticated, and often contradictory. It is only when they are approached from the point of view of the polygamous marriage relationship that their underlying unity and whatever consistency they may have emerges. They range from a materialistic assertion of the Christian trinity to a more typical anthropomorphic polytheism; but whatever the particular manifestation of the godhead, Mormon interpretation tends to be pluralistic and somatistic. Not only is God a being of flesh and blood like men, but he is susceptible to the same passions and desires. Because Mormons considered sex the essence of human character, and sexuality properly understood the cause of the perfection of man, it was absurd to deny sex and sexuality to God:

> Or is that Being who by sexes works—
> Made a Creator by creation's scheme—
> Himself a sexless, and non-mated God?
> A "perfect man" and yet himself no man?[3]

If God possesses sexuality but there are only two materialized persons of the godhead, both male, we are faced with a theological problem. Either God is a homosexual, or we must have overlooked other manifestations of God. Because reproduction was the primary Mormon justification for sexual intercourse, the former alternative was doubly repugnant. Mormons solved their theological dilemma by positing feminine as well as masculine gods. Like the Shakers, they considered the godhead a sexual duality; but whereas the Shakers considered a bisexual God a logical necessity, the Mormons considered it primarily a physical necessity.[4] Celestial reproduction provided a bodily *pre*-incarnation:

> Fallen beings beget children whose bodies are constituted of flesh and bones, being formed out of the blood circulating in the veins of the parents. Celestial beings beget children, composed of the fluid which circulates in their veins, which is spiritual, therefore, their children must be spirits, and not flesh and bones. This is the origin of our spiritual organization in Heaven. The spirits of all mankind, destined for this earth, were begotten by a father, and born of a mother in Heaven, long anterior to the formation of this world.[5]

There is no logical necessity in the Mormon system, however, that precludes the gods from physical reproduction. Apparently convenience and rationalization are the only reasons for the observation of the boundaries separating the spiritual and material spheres. The desire to create in Christ both a perfect spiritual and physical man led to a unique deviation from the usual reproductive pattern. According to Mormon theology, "the Virgin Mary must have been, for the time being, the *lawful* wife of God the Father. . . . it was the personage of the Father who begat the body of Jesus; and for this reason Jesus is called 'the *Only* Begotten of the Father'; that is, the only one in this world whose fleshy body was begotten by the Father."[6]

Propagation was the essence of sexuality for Mormonism, and the sex drive was the divinely ordained mechanism that insured human observation of the biblical command to "be fruitful and multiply." Physical love and sex were therefore considered valuable and beneficial gifts that man had received at the hands of his gods. The duty of men and women during their earthly existence was to produce the maximum number of children possible; or, in Mormon terminology, to provide "tabernacles" for the vast numbers of preformed spirits. Polygamy was not merely a social arrangement but a religious necessity; it provided the means whereby human beings could accomplish the end for which they had been created. Perfect obedience and performance of one's terrestrial duty were the two keys to the attainment of progressive perfection and postmortem felicity.

The obvious implication of this position is that men, through progressive perfection, can enter the ranks of the gods. Joseph Smith made this point explicitly in his King Follett Sermon of 7 April 1844: "You have got to learn how to be gods yourselves," he told his audience, "and to be kings and priests to God, the same as all gods have done before you, namely by going from one small degree to another, from a small capacity to a great one; from grace to grace, from exaltation to exaltation, until you attain to the resurrection of the dead, and are able to . . . sit in glory, as do those who sit enthroned in everlasting power."[7] At death, men and women are awakened to a resurrection state that provides complete physical satisfaction in a celestial polygamic community. Bodies are merely translated from one medium to another, and all physical satisfactions and desires are retained: "When the sons and daughters of the Most High God come forth in the morning of resurrection, this principle of love will exist in their bosoms just as it exists here, only intensified according to the increased knowledge and understanding which they possess; hence they will be capacitated to enjoy the relationships of husband and wife, of parent and child, in a hundred-fold degree greater than they could in mortality."[8]

The hierarchy of the Mormon heavens was based almost entirely on marital status and demonstrated reproductive capacities:

> Except a man and his wife enter into an everlasting covenant, and be married for eternity while in this probation, by the power and authority of the Holy Priesthood, they will cease to increase when they die; that is, they will not have any children after the resurrection. . . . In the celestial glory there are three heavens or degrees; and in order to obtain the highest, a man must enter into this order of the priesthood [meaning the new and everlasting covenant of marriage] and if he does not, he cannot attain it. He may enter into the other, but that is the end of his kingdom: he cannot have an increase.[9]

Polygamists were able to become gods, kings who ruled over vast "kingdoms" composed of their many wives and children; the vision was one of a patriarchal paradise. Those who had married only one wife would have miniscule kingdoms, and consequently much less celestial authority and influence. Those who had never married, or who had failed to go through the endowment ceremonies, which secured marriage for "eternity" as well as for "time," were to be the servants of the gods forever.

The cosmography of the Mormons' universe was complicated by two aspects of their doctrine. The first was the centrality of stratification and a strong sense of individualism to their social and religious structure. They were not concerned with the problem of selfishness; in fact, their egocentricity was in direct contradiction to the dominant stance of much of liberal nineteenth-century thought. As one observer noted, "Not only do they admit, but they even advocate openly, that salvation is altogether a selfish matter; and Lorenzo Snow, an Apostle (!) publicly contended that

'God was the most intensely selfish being in existence.' "[10] Private property was at the very heart of Mormonism and applied not only to earthly goods and chattels but also to the vast spaces of the universe. Orson Pratt made this point most tellingly:

> Notwithstanding we have spoken of the saints jointly inheriting all things, yet there will, undoubtedly be strict and unchangeable laws regulating this divine inheritance, by which no one will be permitted to infringe upon the rights of others; these laws being established upon the strictest principles of justice and equity, from which there will be no deviation. Each will be appointed to take the immediate charge of particular or specified portions of the joint inheritance, over which he will more immediately rule . . . each will have his family and particularly kingdoms, and worlds assigned to him to govern and control . . . [the saints] will be unequal in regard to the extent of the allocated portions of the joint inheritance assigned to the management of each. This inequality probably arising from the nature of their callings and their righteousness in this life.[11]

The second element of doctrine that complicated the Mormons' picture of the universe was their insistence upon eternal procreation. Both the centrality of private property and an endless procreative order suggested the problem of scarcity. Economic and demographic expansion could not be infinite, for resources and space were limited, were they not? Mormon response to this philosophical dilemma was grounded in their frontier experience. They were a people of the wilderness; they were not bothered by the problems of the urbanized and increasingly industrialized East. Their problems were rather how to exploit with the greatest celerity and efficiency the arable land and mineral resources of their territory; and how to produce a devoted population to fill the seemingly vast space available to them, so as to prevent its loss to the Gentiles. Their cosmographic conceptions were cast in the same mold: "As soon as each God has begotten many millions of male and female spirits, and his Heavenly inheritance becomes too small, to comfortably accommodate his great family, he, in connection with his sons, organizes a new world, after a similar order to the one which we now inhabit, where he sends both the male and female spirits to inhabit tabernacles of flesh and bones."[12]

Mormons were obsessed with the quantification of life; they posited a plurality of wives, a plurality of gods, and a plurality of worlds. But the usufruct of these infinities, and the honors accruing to their possessors, were solely male prerogatives. Women were necessary to the procreative process and had therefore been initiated into the ranks of the gods, but they were of an inferior order.

The order of polygamous marriage was usually called "celestial marriage" by the Mormons, an indication that ideally the structure and functioning of the earthly marital relationship was predicated upon the presumptive divine model. Submission was the lot of Mormon women, and soteriological doctrine was employed to bring additional theological pressure to bear on them. Only married women could gain salvation, and they earned it through obedience and submission, not to God, but to their husbands. By this theory, women are justified before God, not by their own actions, but by the actions of their husbands, who stand as their surrogates before the Lord. Whatever status or glory a woman attains, either in this world or the next, is dependent upon the achievements of her husband. Man becomes the savior and even the god of woman. At the resurrection, if a woman's husband refuses to accept her into his kingdom, then she is forever excluded from heavenly bliss. In a body of rules recommended for the practice of celestial marriage, this principle is clearly set forth: "Let no woman unite herself in marriage with any man, unless she has fully resolved to *submit herself wholly* to his counsel, and let him govern as the head. It is far better for her not to be united with him . . . than to rebel against the divine order of family government, instituted for a higher salvation; for if she altogether turn therefrom, she will receive a greater condemnation."[13]

But this theological principle of a succedaneous male liability as the basis for female atonement cut two ways. Not only did it render women subordinate to men in the social and religious spheres, but it also absolved women from the ultimate responsibility for their actions. Ideally, women in Mormon theology were placed in the same category as children; both groups were at once innocent and morally incompetent to work out their own salvation. For this reason, and because of the extreme value they placed upon motherhood and the fact that they did not consider sex to be sinful, their view of the culpability of women for the Edenic disobedience (which constituted original sin) differed radically from widely accepted Christian interpretation. The Fall, they believed, had been perhaps the most propitious event in the history of mankind. Eve, in the act of taking the forbidden fruit, brought sin into the world; but by the very same act she made reproduction possible. Had it not been for that one hasty act, there would be millions of disembodied souls waiting in a purgatorial existence for a redemption that could come only through incarnation. From this point of view, Eve becomes a transcendent mother figure, her sacrifice of assured eternal life for the possibility of salvation for generations yet unborn a cosmic metaphor for the potential sacrifice of every mother undergoing parturition. Ironically, at the outset of her earthly career, woman had been a savior of the magnitude of Christ himself, but subsequent to her selfless sacrifice, she became unable to save even herself.[14] Exculpated from the guilt of original sin at the expense of her many capabilities, woman becomes primarily a reproductive drudge, her salvation and self-image completely bound up with the number of children she can bear. Even death lends no surcease to her labors, for heaven is also a male sinecure, and she can look forward not to an end of gestation but to an infinity of pregnancies.[15]

The social ideal of Mormon polygamy was integrally connected with this theological framework. Optimum social organization of the relationship between the sexes was patriarchally perceived. Women were considered chattels, rights to which had been vested by divine authority in their exclusive male proprietors. These rights were largely the result of righteous behavior on the part of male Mormons; women and children were the perquisites of power, purity, and prestige in the kingdom of God.

The covenant of God and man was an Old Testament one in which Abraham and Sarah were taken as prototypal models of behavior for the ideal polygamic family. Women were to be protected and controlled: protected against the threat to their virtue posed by anarchistic males who were excluded from the polygamic system, and controlled by their husbands lest their sexual drives lead them into dishonorable behavior. The ideological justification for this officious scrutiny of women's lives, exercised under the tutelage of their husbands, revolved around the question of the control of the will, a doctrine the Mormons shared with the Shakers and Oneidans.

For Latter-Day Saints, control of the will meant recognition of one's place in the religious hierarchy of the church and obedience to one's superiors. The passional life of the average Mormon was "controlled" by the earthly representatives of the divine power; he could not enter a marriage contract without the consent of his bishop and the First President of the church. As early as 1840, each Mormon purportedly took a secret oath, swearing "that I will never touch a daughter of Adam, UNLESS SHE IS GIVEN TO ME OF THE LORD."[16] The passion that received the most attention from Mormons, whether in men or in women, was sexual desire. Certainly, the officials of the church helped to control it through the institutionalization and routinization of the practice of plural marriage, but control over the seasons of matrimony and the number of a particular man's wives did not guarantee the individual's conquest of lust. Ultimately, although a minimum standard of public morality was insured by the church, individualism and personal responsibility (for males) remained the key to perfectionism and salvation. It was control of the will by the individual man that legitimized his claim to celestial marriage and his position of authority in his family, in society, and in the church. The realization that everything of value in their lives depended upon self-reliance and self-control generated a gnawing anxiety among Mormon men. As one Mormon leader expressed it, "I put a double guard over my evil passions that were sown thickly in my sinful nature. The passion most dreaded by me was the lust of the flesh; that I knew to be the worst enemy to my salvation, and I determined to master it. . . . that I might conquer and drive from my mind those besetting sins . . . which, if cherished or suffered to remain, would wound and grieve the Spirit and drive it away."[17]

Mastery of the flesh also meant mastery over women; the spirituality of the male was taken as the essence of his character, whereas women were characterized as more emotive, intuitional, and intrinsically sybaritic. The institution of marriage, as an instrument of social control, was regarded primarily as a means to control the primal urges of the female animal. Theoretically, polygamy was even better than monogamy from this point of view, because it provided the opportunity for a greater number of women to be matrimonially allied with men who were their moral superiors. Brigham Young, in his typically brusque and unrefined manner, made the connection between moral prestige and power in the family quite plain: "If I am thus controlled by the Spirit of the Most High I am a king, I am supreme so far as the control of self is concerned; and it also enables me to control my wives and children. And when they see that I am under the government and control of the Good Spirit, they will be perfectly submissive to my dictates."[18]

This kind of ideological adjustment of the marital relationship led to an intense concern with prescriptive sexual roles and a concomitant stress on the centrality of sexual "honor." "Honor" was equated on the female side with fealty, chastity, and fertility; on the male side with control, rationality, and virility. Roles were ideologically fixed; the pressures on both sexes to conform, and the terrifying realization that one's salvation was inextricably bound up with the behavior and ethical scruples of the other sex, only intensified the concentration upon sexual honor. For both men and women, their abilities and very character became totally subsumed under their physiological characteristics. Thus castration was considered a punishment only slightly less rigorous than death, for it as effectively destroyed the essence of the male personality. This was demonstrated by the examination required of candidates who wished to enter the arcane upper reaches of the Mormon hierarchy. The prospective member was disrobed and "conducted around, so that all the members of the lodge may be satisfied, by personal inspection, that he possesses the qualifications required in Deuteronomy, 23rd chapter and

1st verse."[19] Intelligence, capability, power, and self-control inhered in the testes, loss of which rendered a man effeminate, and by definition inferior. In 1847, for example, one Daniel Russell was "declared . . . unqualified to sit in council as he had lost his privy members & was an eunuch."[20]

For males, this inordinate concern with masculinity, which seems to have been indicative of the tension between a deep-seated insecurity and uncertainty about the male sex role and delusions of grandeur based on the assumption of male superiority, found expression in the classic Mormon fantasy—the monopolization of women. This fantasy was at once attractive and frightening, and seems to have served both as a utopian dream and a nightmare. It was most cogently expressed in a passage from a lecture on marriage delivered by Orson Hyde: "They [the Gentiles] may break us up, and rout us from one place to another, but by and bye we shall come to a point where we shall have all the women, and they will have none."[21]

The anxiety that underlay this vision of male power arose out of the perception of an ultimate demographic scarcity of females under polygamic conditions, and the realization that that scarcity would lead to keen competition between monopolizing and excluded males. The nature of woman, with her insistent, amoral sexual needs, further complicated the problem: "Women, in their yearning after the other sex and in their desire for maternity, will do anything to gratify that instinct of their nature and yield to anything and be dishonored even rather than not gratify it; and . . . they are not held accountable to the same extent as men are."[22]

The dilemma for the polygamous husband was how to satisfy his several wives' sexual needs so that they would not be readily responsive to the blandishments of single or monogamous Mormons or Gentiles, and at the same time keep his own passions under control so that reproduction and not pleasure remained the primary motivation for the sex act. Ironically, then, in an ideological structure that was predicated upon male dominance, although a double standard obtained, it was a reversal of that present in Gentile society. Men rather than women were forced to worry about the sexual satisfaction of their mates in order to keep them from infidelity.

During the 1850s, in the wake of the California gold rush, thousands of young men poured through Utah annually. These men were the physical embodiment of the subliminal fears that preyed upon the Mormon polygamist's mind. Their very presence exacerbated the concern over "women that will come into the Church and kingdom of God, and bring dishonor upon themselves, and endeavor to bring it upon the whole Church, by cohabiting with those cursed scapegraces who are passing through here to California, who make their boast of what they did in Great Salt Lake City. . . . [who] boast that you can get all you want for a dress pattern, or a yard of ribbon."[23]

Not surprisingly, women were considered temptresses in Mormon sexual ideology. Fortunately, however, in the institution of polygamy a means of social control was available that dealt specifically with this unfortunate aspect of woman's character. In the first instance, by placing women under the surveillance of their moral superiors, it sought to prevent them from exercising their wiles on innocent and unsuspecting young men. From the male perspective, it provided a sufficiently diversified sexual outlet to prevent those men with polygamous families from succumbing to feminine temptation.[24]

Outsiders frequently referred to polygamy as a libidinous sexual system, but its ideal purpose was to undergird the demanding and stringent Mormon moral code. Because the female was incapable of self-control she could be allowed only minimal sexual latitude, and that under immediate male supervision. Polygamy provided a social framework which offered the maximum assurance that women would be closely watched from birth to death, that the risk of the loss of grace by male Saints would be minimized, and that the destructive power of sex would be successfully contained; in short, that civilization would triumph over eros.

Ideologically, the erotic subjugation of women was an expression of the fear of human sexuality, which was translated, in a patriarchal system, into the need to dominate and control the sexual behavior of women. Certain Mormon men (and it must be remembered that polygamists never exceeded 15 to 20 percent of the male members of the church) were allowed broad erotic freedom, a freedom justified by the ideological perception of polygamy as institutionalized social control of women. As for the feminine Mormon population, "the emancipation of woman, or, in other words, the bestial theory of *free love* . . . if it were ever adopted and practiced by a nation, would produce the most disastrous and unnatural fruits it is possible to imagine; it would have the infallible result of causing degeneracy and would render that people totally extinct within a very few years."[25]

What we are really dealing with here is a rather disingenuous attempt to explain to devout Mormon women why they could not have the same sexual privileges as men; why polyandry could not be sanctioned as well as polygyny. This question was specifically addressed by Mormon authorities on several occasions; in the light of their theological and ideological presuppositions, their answer is not surprising. With one hand they held out an uncertain promise of sexual freedom for women in the next life, while with the other they absolutely forbade any concession to an extended erotic life for women in this life.[26]

The "great object" to which the life of woman was dedicated was motherhood, and any sexual practices that maximized childbearing were good, because "the spirits which are reserved have to be born into the world, and the Lord will prepare some way for them to have tabernacles. Spirits must be born, even if they have to come to brothels for their fleshy coverings, and many of them will take the lowest and meanest spiritual house that there is in the world, rather than do without, and will say 'Let me have a tabernacle, that I may have a chance to be perfected.' "[27] The one unpardonable sin for Mormons was the act of "murder, wherein ye shed innocent blood";[28] or, in practical terms, "foeticide, infanticide, and child-murder."[29] Some indication of the depth of feeling and aggression against women generated by this issue is suggested in John Taylor's emotional outburst: "We cannot have, and won't have . . . those who, by murder, stain their consciences and damn themselves forever. You sisters guard yourselves against these infamies, or you will sink yourselves down, down, down to pits of infamy and ruin, that you ever [*sic*] dreamed of."[30] Taylor personalized his tirade by referring to a Mormon woman who had had an abortion in a large eastern city in the 1850s: "I don't know when I felt such loathing for a human being in my life as I felt toward her. I would sooner have touched a rattlesnake than touched her hand."[31] Mormons certainly did not deny that pleasure was one of the purposes of sexual intercourse, for both men and women; they simply argued that it was a subordinate purpose. The right of women to gratification was theoretically as sacred as that of men, for "God has implanted, for a wise purpose, certain feelings in the breasts of females as well as males, the gratification of which is necessary to health and happiness, and which can only be accomplished legitimately in the marriage state."[32] The difficulty that provided the whole ideological justification for control of women's sexual behavior was their supposed lack of self-control; their tendency, "rather than being deprived of the gratification of those feelings altogether," to give way to "wickedness and licentiousness; hence the whoredoms and prostitution among the nations of the earth."[33] From the male point of view, the physiological function of polygamy was clearly to provide the sexual variety and frequency of intercourse requisite for male self-control. Physiologically, men seem to have been considered as prone to self-gratification as women, but the system of polygamy provided a male outlet that was not deemed an "immoderate and illegal gratification." Women had no similar outlet.

From a socioreligious point of view, polygamy was primarily a mechanism for masculine salvation. It obviated the difficulties and temptations of a monogamous relationship, wherein a "man must practice that which is vile and low, or submit to a system of repression; because if he be married to a woman who is physically incapable, he must either do himself violence or what is far worse, he must have recourse to the dreadful and damning practice of having illegal connection with women, or become altogether like the beasts."[34] Man, once he had been saved from masturbation, patronizing prostitutes, and homosexuality or bestiality, became the vehicle for the social and religious salvation of woman. Obviously the system of polygamy did not operate to maximize the sexual gratification of women, and when the institution was being considered from the standpoint of pleasure, certain grudging concessions to the female were necessary.

Although, as we have seen, simultaneous polyandry was ruled out, serial polyandry was relatively common and was built into the theological structure in the doctrine of marriage for "time" and for "eternity."[35] Although sex was proscribed during pregnancy, owing to Mormon subscription to the folk belief that the emotions and experiences of the mother during gestation would "mark" the fetus, on at least one occasion a Mormon church official recommended intercourse during pregnancy on the same basis, arguing "the propriety of gratifying women during pregnancy where it was right and consistent that they might not entail on their offspring unholy desires and appetites."[36]

But concern for female gratification in the sex act was motivated more by policy than by justice. Some concession to female sexual needs was necessary; otherwise, the defection of women from polygamous relationships, given any opportunity, would have been inevitable. Mormon women do not seem to have been inherently attracted to the doctrine of patriarchal marriage, a fact attested by the vast amount of apostolic energy expended in convincing, cajoling, cozening, and damning them into accepting it. Every theological and ideological screw was turned that might provide added pressure and thus conviction.

In this regard, Mormon use of the spermatic-economy ideology is instructive. They were generally opposed to its application to male sexual behavior, but they applied it freely to that of women. They simply reversed its implications so that it coincided with their own theological and ideological preconceptions. It thus provided another ground for prohibiting sex during pregnancy:

Nature has constituted women differently from men, and they are made for a different purpose. The vigor of the former lies in *the river of life which flows in her*, nourishing the embryo, giving birth to the child, and sustaining it at its mother's breast. When nature is not working to attain this heavenly end, she wisely and periodically comes to the aid of the female, to maintain purity and health in her *without exhausting the source of life*, until she reaches an age at which it becomes necessary for her to cease to be fertile, so that she can enjoy a more peaceful life in the bosom of her family circle.[37]

Mormons also used the doctrine to deny women the right to practice polyandry. Polyandrous marriage, through its effect on women, it was claimed, "deteriorates the vital power, and physical strength and longevity, and tends to weaken, lessen and destroy the human race."[38] Thus, in contradistinction to the Shaker and Oneidan use of the spermatic-economy doctrine, Mormons asserted that it was woman who was physically endangered by the sex act, and who consequently had to husband her nervous energy. Unfortunately, this belief was not linked with any concern for limiting the number of pregnancies a particular woman underwent. From the male standpoint, the doctrine's influence was totally denied. Heber C. Kimball, for example, advised gerontic apostles to "renew their age": "I have noticed that a man who has but one wife, and is inclined to that doctrine, soon begins to wither and dry up, while a man who goes into plurality looks fresh, young and sprightly."[39] The message was clear: sex was physically dangerous for the female, but not for the male.

But polygamy was not merely repressive; it was, viewed on the broadest level, a eugenic device, a utopian project, a means to universal reform. Its eugenic aspect is evident when we consider that under normal demographic conditions in nineteenth-century America, the ratio of men to women was about equal. Polygamy thus served as a kind of enforced birth control, or theologically based "sterilization" of the unregenerate. In that church approval was required before entering upon celestial marriage, selective breeding was largely in the hands of the Mormon hierarchy, which sought "a healthy, virile, and robust population" and believed that "our patriarchal marriage will rapidly give birth to a race of giants."[40]

As a utopian system of reform, Mormonism promised that the adoption of polygamy would instantaneously solve the "sexual question," and would thus prove to be the salvation of both men and women in this world and the next. A people who lived under patriarchal marriage

would have no institutions tending to licentiousness; no adulteries, fornications, etc., would be tolerated. No houses or institutions would exist for traffic in shame. . . . Wealthy men would have no inducement to keep a mistress in secret, or unlawfully. Females would have no grounds for temptation in any such lawless life. Neither money nor pleasure could tempt them, nor poverty drive them to any such excess, because the door would be open for every virtuous female to form the honorable and endearing relationships of wife and mother in some virtuous family.[41]

Ideally, then, polygamy was the way of salvation for both male and female Mormons; a social institution that insured both a plentiful supply of healthy Mormon babies and the subordination of erotic drives to community needs; and a utopian system of reform predicated upon an idealistic and optimistic belief in the potential perfectibility, if not of every man, at least of all those who "lived their faith" in the polygamic order. We must now examine Mormon behavior and practice to see how well their quixotic ideals coincided with the reality of celestial marriage.

Chapter 8 🎺 "Seven Women to One Man Shall Cling": The Ecclesiastical and Legalistic Aspects of Sexuality under Patriarchal Polygamy

And he [Solomon] had seven hundred wives, princesses, and three hundred concubines: and his wives turned away his heart.

—1 Kings 11:3

For he had built twelve pavilions, after the number of the months, each containing thirty private chambers, which thus numbered three hundred and three score, wherein he lodged his handmaids: and he appointed according to law for each one her night, when he lay with her and came not again to her for a full year.

—Richard Burton, *Book of the Thousand Nights and a Night*, vol. 2

lthough Mormon sources admitted that the Prophet received a preliminary revelation on the marriage question as early as 1832, they explicitly denied that it had been put into practice at that time. Despite these denials, however, Mormon social life in the 1830s was characterized by a practice akin to spiritual wifery, if not by institutionalized polygamy. By the early 1840s, though, the situation had changed. Construction of Nauvoo, the Mormon "city of beauty and repose," was well under way by 1841. Because all land was owned by the church, because the city maintained an independent militia and police force, and because the governmental hierarchy and that of the church were virtually coterminous, Nauvoo provided the Mormons with an exceedingly important precondition to the inception of the practice of polygamy—autonomy. Of the Nauvoo City Charter, passed by the Illinois legislature in 1839, a recent historian has noted: "The net result was not only to help protect the Mormons from legal persecution, real or imagined, but also to make 'outside' law enforceable in Nauvoo only if the city government concurred."[1] Even more importantly, their autonomous position provided Mormons for the first time the legal power to perform marriage ceremonies of both a religious and (in their capacities as justices of the peace) a secular nature. This power was essential to an orderly and ecclesiastically controlled system of polygamous marriage, as opposed to a rather disorganized practice of spiritual wifery.[2]

Mormon society matured under the Prophet's leadership at Nauvoo, and his stature as a religious and moral leader grew apace. It was natural that he should try to normalize and regulate sexual practices that threatened the stability of his kingdom and his reputation as the holy Prophet of the Lord. These efforts took two forms. The first was the excommunication of individuals who were proven guilty of seduction and adultery or, by 1844, of preaching polygamy.[3] The other was the establishment of a body of legislation directed against specific abuses, coupled with the semiofficial establishment of an antivice organization under the auspices of a woman's auxiliary society. In his journal, Smith described his central role in the legislative process of regulating sexual behavior through his influence over the city council. On 14 May 1842 he "advocated strongly the necessity of some active measures being taken to suppress houses and acts of infamy in the city; for the protection of the innocent and virtuous, and the good of public morals; showing clearly that there were certain characters in the place, who were disposed to corrupt the morals and chastity of our citizens, and that houses of infamy did exist, upon which a city ordinance concerning brothels and disorderly characters was passed, to prohibit such things."[4]

Earlier in 1842, the Prophet had organized the Female Relief Society, with his wife, Emma, as president. This group quickly assumed responsibility for policing the morals of Nauvoo and evinced an especial interest in adultery. But in this instance, Smith underestimated the zeal and fervor the women would bring to the job. He was in a tight spot; practicing polygamy, yet publicly committed to a crusade against vice, he was burning the candle at both ends. The ardor of the Female Relief Society burned so bright that he is said to have warned these pious women that "they must be extremely careful in all their examinations, or the consequences would be serious."[5]

In addition to the achievement of Mormon autonomy and the rather ill-fated attempt to regulate sexual behavior at Nauvoo, it seems likely that a third prerequisite for the transition from spiritual wifery to polygamy was achieved at Nauvoo: the arrival of large numbers of women who were single or separated from their husbands. The English mission had been established in 1837, but it was not until the early 1840s that the first fruits of Mormon missionary work in Great Britain began to be harvested. The years 1841–42 saw 2,749 people from Great Britain emigrate to Nauvoo.[6]

The demographic history of the Utah Territory bears out the contention that a ready supply, if not a surplus, of nubile females was a precondition for the effective practice of polygamy. According to the censuses taken in 1850, the initial sexual division of Mormon society was quite lopsidedly male; over 55 percent and probably closer to 60 percent of the enumerated population was male. In all Utah counties in that year, males were numerically superior to females. Of individuals aged twenty to fifty, males constituted 55 percent. Of unmarried persons in Weber County in 1850, eight of ten were male.[7] During the 1850s, however, concurrently with the abrupt rise in the incidence of plural marriage during the "reformation" of 1856–57, there was a correspondingly dramatic rise in the number of women entering Utah. Some observers estimated that the female percentage of the population of Utah in 1856 was as high as 54.75, but the Utah census for that year reported a female population that was 51.17 percent of the total. Women outnumbered men in ten of eighteen, or 55.56 percent, of the counties enumerated. By 1860, women still constituted 51 percent of the population aged fifteen to forty.[8]

From 1870 to 1890, while polygamy declined, the male percentage of the total population rose annually. In 1870, men outnumbered women in 71.34 percent of the counties in Utah. By 1880, although 51.94 percent of the total population was male, within the marriageable ages the division was much more equitable than it had been in 1850. By 1890, although there was still a considerable shortage of nubile females, the percentage of difference in this category had shrunk tremendously. When polygamy was officially renounced by the Mormon church, the sexual division of Mormon society very closely approximated that of American society as a whole.[9]

The problems Mormonism sustained with its missionary representatives indicate that these individuals were consciously attempting to build up just such a surplus of females as the order of celestial marriage required. These missionaries had such a disturbing tendency to concentrate their efforts on the conversion of females that several warnings were issued by the church to control the behavior of its representatives. Missionaries had to be advised against converting wives apart from their husbands and ordered, under pain of excommunication, not to marry young women whom they had recently converted.[10] The behavior of missionaries reflected their perception of the demographic situation in the areas from which they drew most of their converts (New England and Great Britain). One elder noted that "there is a great proportion of females over that of males, and there is a great proportion of males that are too wicked and corrupt to marry and raise up families; and the consequence is that a great proportion of your females are compelled to live single."[11]

This fantasy of an overwhelming surplus of unmarried women just waiting to be fulfilled by celestial marriage, coupled with the belief that male Mormons were Saints, who had been placed upon earth to redeem the souls of hopelessly lost females, led to behavior (in areas blessed with Mormon missionaries) that Gentiles considered indecorous at best, and often openly provocative. By 1861, Mormon authorities were forced to admit that the morality of missionaries was beyond their control. An editorial that appeared in the Mormons' English organ, the *Millennial Star*, admitted their "lustful and unvirtuous conduct . . . a sin that has been indulged in more frequently, probably, by such characters than any other. . . . The weakness, confidence, or ignorance of the opposite sex has been taken advantage of, and the result has been a withdrawal of the Spirit and a loss of that knowledge and certainty which enabled them to remain steadfast."[12]

The official policy of the church from 1844 to 1852, however, required the denial of polygamy as an aspect of Mormon dogma. This was done in order to protect Mormons from the wrath of their Gentile neighbors. It was discontinued only with the first public reading of the Revelation on Celestial Marriage in Utah on 29 August 1852.[13] It is the Mormons' experience in Utah, removed from the aegis of any state government, creating their own territorial legal codes, and developing an informal set of responses to the issues posed by polygamy, that we must examine if we are to understand the way polygamy functioned in practice from 1850 to 1890.

The unique nature of the Mormon experience, especially the clandestine nature of polygamy until 1852, reinforced the frontier predilection for immediate, extralegal, and highly personal solutions to disputes between individuals. It was not until March 1852, eighteen months after the organization of the territorial government of Utah, and a scant five months before the public acknowledgment of the polygamic doctrine, that a divorce law and laws defining the exact nature of, and providing punishments for, felonies were passed by the territorial legislature.[14] Traditional and informal ways of dealing with violations, however, continued as an ideal even after the passage of a body of legislation that sought to rationalize the criminal code. There were no effective statutory regulations governing sexual behavior among the Mormons until the

1860s; and even after their passage, tradition and ecclesiastical pressure often favored, and in some instances forced, the implementation of informal vigilante justice.

Especially in the years before the codification of criminal law in Utah, sexual behavior was primarily controlled by an inchoate body of ecclesiastical precept. Scant attention was given in the religious literature to the definition of terms or any discrimination of the relative seriousness of the various forms of sexual deviancy. Like other frontier Americans, the Mormons were forced back upon their moral presuppositions in an environment that did not yet provide socially ordained ethical guides to action. Unlike most other frontier Americans, however, the Mormons, because of the necessarily surreptitious nature of their polygamic system, were forced to rely longer on informal moral codes and vigilantism.[15] This fact, combined with the function of the church as interpreter and often executor of this rigorous moral code, and the customary precedence taken by the patriarchal hierarchs of the church over the common members in the monopoly of women, afforded this tradition both a deeper and a broader base in Utah than in other frontier areas. For the most part, the extralegal Mormon response to offenses of a sexual nature required a stringent penalty: either capital punishment or, in accordance with the Hebraic *lex talionis*, emasculation. Although some women were executed for adultery, in most instances the full force of public opinion seems to have been directed against the male offender. In a patriarchally organized community, any threat to the vested proprietorial rights a man enjoyed in his wives (especially prior to the public avowal of polygamy) represented a fundamentally anarchistic threat to the stability and very existence of Mormon society. For this reason, adultery, seduction, fornication, and incest were considered the most serious sexual offenses. All were threats to the authority of father or husband.

The vagueness of traditional conceptions of sexual deviancy and the theoretical assumption of the absolute right of the patriarch to his female chattels generated a great deal of anxiety about proper sexual behavior. Men believed that they could be killed or castrated for any sexual misdemeanor. The case of Mr. Long, who attempted to elope with a Miss Calkins in 1848, illuminates this pervasive attitude. Long was taken up by the Mormon police, roughly handled, and told, "We entend [*sic*] to learn you what it is to kidnap young girls in this place as you have done you now have got to atone for it now before you leave this place."[16] Long assumed he was to be killed, but he was released after manifesting complete contrition. John D. Lee, who, as a lower-echelon Mormon leader and enforcer, had good reason to know, maintained that even suspicion of adultery was likely to bring sudden death at the hands of Brigham Young's avenging vigilantes. In 1855, Lee was charged with "taking improper privileges" with a young woman. His fear of the consequences of mere suspicion, as recorded in his "confessions," was very real indeed: "For months I expected to be assassinated every day, for it was the usual course of the authorities to send an 'Angel' after all men who were *charged* or *suspected* of having violated their covenants."[17]

That such fears were not unfounded is evident in the case of Henry Jones and his mother, who were murdered by a group of Mormons in the spring of 1857. "Henry," we are informed, "had previously been emasculated on a charge of bestiality; now he and his mother were accused of incest, and shockingly murdered."[18] John D. Lee corroborates the continued use of castration and capital punishment as a means of regulating sexual conduct in Utah through the 1870s, and establishes the insidious manner in which the church employed the irrational fear this policy generated to manipulate its members. "The most deadly sin among the people," he writes, "was adultery, and many men were killed in Utah for that crime."[19] He further notes that "in Utah it has been the custom with the Priesthood to make eunuchs of such men as were obnoxious to the leaders. This was done for a double purpose: first it gave a perfect revenge, and next, it left the poor victim a living example to others of the dangers of disobeying counsel and not living as ordered by the Priesthood."[20]

Such executions and emasculations constituted a kind of ecclesiastical "reign of terror," for all such punishment "was then considered a religious duty and a just act. It was justified by all the people, for they were bound by the same covenants, and the least word of objection to thus treating the man who had broken his covenant would have brought the same fate upon the person who was so foolish as to raise his voice against any act committed by order of the Church authorities."[21]

In accordance with their policy of racial discrimination, the only other form of sexual misbehavior officially considered a capital offense by the church was miscegenation. God had promulgated a law with regard to the Negro: "If the white man who belongs to the chosen seed mixes his blood with the seed of Cain, the penalty, under the law of God is death on the spot. This will always be so."[22]

But not all cases of adultery were punished by death. The key to a particular instance of sexual deviancy seems to have been in the nature of the patriarchal system itself. Adultery committed with a married woman was the real threat. The seriousness of the offense was also dependent upon the position the husband or father of the feminine malefactor occupied in the ecclesiastical hierarchy, as well as upon that of the male offender. Fornication was seldom punished by death and in fact seems to have been frequently treated in jest rather than in earnest. In the Mormon camp during the hegira to Utah, an unmarried couple were discovered abed, and "a lot of boys upset the waggon, putting them to an uncommon nonpluss and disappointment."[23]

Hosea Stout, who served as a Mormon policeman in both Nauvoo and Salt Lake City, was alarmed at the laxness with which such misdemeanors were treated. As a literalist and an upholder of the strict letter of the law, he is illustrative of the official church position on sexual offenses. He refused to discriminate among adultery, seduction, fornication, and rape. In the case of several young couples who "had been out for fifteen nights in succession untill [sic] after 2 o'clock," he noted: "The crimes of these men were adultery or having carnal communication with the girls which was well known to many and the legal punishment was death."[24] Fortunately, although the pronouncements of the church were excessively moralistic, and the prescribed punishment for sexual offenses draconian,[25] in practice the judgments made by church officials (with the exception of cases in which the prestige or proprietary rights of the hierarchs themselves were challenged) were usually much more reasonable. In the case of these young couples, for example, the males were punished by whipping.

Another group of young men, who had offended against the rather puritanical sense of sexual proprieties held by the Mormons, and who had probably been guilty of fornication, was fined twenty-five dollars apiece and excommunicated. An older Mormon, who had been tried in a Gentile court and found guilty of adultery and fornication, was subsequently bailed out by his brethren "through sympathy."[26] Frequently, adulterers were excommunicated and their property forfeited. This was typically the policy of the church in instances in which the act did not trespass the patriarchal rights of another. In such cases, forfeiture of ecclesiastical and proprietorial rights was often temporary; reinvestiture was contingent upon the performance of matrimonial rites to sanction the sexual relationship. Brigham Young described this procedure best: "Brother John Holt had virtually cut himself off from the church by taking the woman he has with him and using her for a wife; therefore he must be [re]baptized and the woman also and then confer his ordination [to the priesthood and privilege of the church] and then Seal the woman to him and try how they for the future will carry Sail."[27]

Rape appears to have been considered largely a crime against women, and of least consequence of all sexual offenses. Rape, which involved a direct act of aggression against the proprietorial rights of father or husband, was subsumed under the categories of adultery and fornication. The trial of B. Covey for statutory rape is characteristic. He was brought to trial "for unlawfully sleeping with a girl less than Twelve years of age. It appeared that two girls about the same age lived with him both of whom he had thus defiled, which was abundantly proven. He was cut off from the church with this understanding, that his wives and children were under no more obligations to him."[28]

Both judicial and ecclesiastical punishment for rape was relatively mild. There is no reference to the death penalty for rape in any of the Mormon statements on sexual offenses. When judicial penalties for rape are compared to those for other crimes, they are revealed as inconsistently lenient. In 1876, for example, two men, who were side by side in the Utah penitentiary, were serving a simple one-year sentence and four years with hard labor. The former had raped a Danish widow, whereas the latter had robbed a bank. The proprietary basis of Mormon justice could not be more plainly manifested.[29]

On a popular level, however, the folk beliefs of Mormons on sexual deviance were much more in accord with the strictest pronouncements of the church. Orson Pratt gave enthusiastic vent to these feelings in 1854, when he wrote: "The people of Utah are the only ones in this nation who have taken effectual measures . . . to *prevent* adulteries and criminal connections between the sexes. The punishment in that territory, for these crimes [adultery, seduction, and prostitution] is DEATH TO BOTH MALE AND FEMALE. And this law is written on the hearts and printed in the thoughts of the whole people."[30] This was not an attitude that was embodied in the Utah legal code, but rather a deeply held belief of the people in the justice of a personal nemesis. Many cases of the murder of adulterers and seducers to vindicate the "honor" of sisters, wives, or daughters may be found in the history of the Utah Territory. The courts tended to exonerate the perpetrators of such crimes of passion in accordance with the popular will. Hosea Stout, who served on several juries trying such cases, commented on the characteristic case of M. D. Hambleton, who had murdered a Dr. Vaughan on account of the latter's supposed seduction of his wife: "His [Vaughan's] seductive and illicit conversation with Mrs. Hambleton was sufficiently proven that I was well satisfied of his [Hambleton's] justification as well as all who were present and plead to the case to that effect. He was acquitted by the Court and also by the Voice of the people present."[31]

In another similar case, the defense attorney declared it to be the "duty of the nearest kin to a female who was seduced to take the life of the seducer."[32] Stout's own comment on the case reveals the extent to which such a reaction and the subsequent acquittal of the accused had assumed the force of an unwritten law. "This is like to be a Precident [*sic*]," he wrote in his diary, "for any one who has his wife, sister, or daughter seduced to take the law into his own hands and slay the seducer and I expect it will go still farther."[33] In one instance, a woman who had been raped and apparently did not enjoy the services of a male guardian of her honor took her vengeance upon her defiler with an axe. There is no indication that the woman was ever made to answer for this murder.[34]

The Utah territorial legal code, which was promulgated in 1852 and was intended to rationalize the judicial system, only partly superseded the ecclesiastical mode and folkways that had previously constituted Mormon justice. In many ways it merely institutionalized legal attitudes and responses that had been informally held and practiced before that date. It outlawed adultery, seduction, rape, prostitution, and the exhibition or sale of pornography. Potentially, the stiffest penalties were reserved for adultery—a minimum of three years imprisonment and/or a fine of at least three hundred dollars—but the wording of the law was such as to protect Mormons who practiced polygamy from test cases brought by Gentiles in an effort to destroy celestial marriage. It was provided that "no prosecution for adultry [*sic*] can be commenced but on the complaint of the husband or wife."[35]

Rape received much greater consideration in the formal code than it had in the popular mind. The statutory age was set at ten years, and the minimum penalty for ravishment of an infant was ten years' imprisonment. Punishments for the rape of a woman were comparable, and the use of drugs and alcohol came under the cognizance of the act as methods of duress in attaining consent to sexual intimacy.

Prostitution, which Mormons consistently claimed was nonextant in Utah, was also regulated by the act. In fact, the basic assumptions behind the legal code are perhaps most clearly manifested in this section. Legally, the responsibility for prostitution fell squarely on the shoulders of men, or on the organized prostitution industry. Although they could be punished under a vague fornication clause, there was no specific provision to punish either those who frequented bordellos or the women who pandered to their needs and desires. Under the prostitution law, women were considered mere objects, movable property; in themselves they were legally nonpersons, morally neutral. Their masters determined their characters by the impress of their moral natures upon the remarkably plastic female nature. Therefore, both keepers of houses of prostitution and those who inveigled ingenuous young women there to begin careers of vice bore the brunt of legal punishment for prostitution. They were subject to a minimum jail sentence of one to five years and a fine of at least one to five hundred dollars.[36]

Instances of seduction continued to be lightly regarded under the new legal code, for it was provided that "if before judgment upon an indictment, the defendant marry the woman thus seduced, it is a bar to any further prosecution for the offence."[37] The code did, however, attempt to maintain a rigorous standard of morality in other respects. Exhibition-ism, which had plagued the Mormon paradise of Nauvoo, continued to be troublesome in Utah as well. Provisions were therefore made for the punishment of indecent exposure (including that of a disinterred corpse). A maximum fine of four hundred dollars was provided for printing, sell-ing, or exhibiting any pornographic book or picture.[38] Mormon society apparently enjoyed a typically lusty and wide-open frontier moral atti-tude, but church leaders sought to infuse a stricter and more refined code of conduct more in accord with the demesne of the divinely ordained Latter-Day Saints.

This struggle between popular moral beliefs and folk behavior and the desire of ecclesiastical authorities to raise the moral standard of the community found its classic expression in the question of the Mormon attitude toward divorce. The traditional attitude was set forth in the Book of Mormon: adultery was held to be the *only* acceptable grounds for legal separation.[39] But Mormons were faced with a terrible dilemma; they were caught between the logic of their ideological position and the pressures of their relationship to the Gentile world. Like all alternative socioreligious communities located in relatively close proximity to a more traditional social environment, the early Latter-Day Saints were consid-ered enemies of the integrity of local families, a source of easy divorce or separation for the discontented. They were forced, therefore, to take an official stand on divorce in the 1840s that was rather conservative: "we forbid that a woman leave her husband because he is an unbeliever. We also forbid that a man shall leave his wife because she is an unbeliever. If he be a bad man there is a law to remedy that evil. And if she be a bad woman, there is a law to remedy that evil. And if the law divorce them, then they are at liberty; otherwise they are bound as long as they two shall live, and it is not our prerogative to go beyond this; if we do it, it will be at the expense of our reputation."[40]

Even after the public announcement of polygamy, and the passage of a very liberal divorce law in Utah, spokesmen for the church continued to uphold the traditional attitude toward divorce. A polygamous system of marriage, it was argued, was not necessarily antithetical to the same regulations that govern monogamy. Under polygamy, a man "should not be considered divorced from either [of his wives], only through due course of law; and adultery should be the only crime, as our Savour [sic] has said, for which a man should be justified in putting away either of his wives."[41]

But both theological and legislative logic contradicted this apparently conservative stand. Theologically, the moral stature of a woman was totally dependent upon that of her husband. She was told that you can never obtain a fulness of glory without being married to a righteous man for time and for all eternity. If you marry a man who receives not the gospel, you lay a foundation for sorrow in this world, besides losing the privilege of enjoying the society of a husband, in eternity. You forfeit your right to an endless increase of immortal lives. And even the children which you may be favored with in this life will not be entrusted to your charge in eternity; but you will be left in that world without a kingdom—without any means of enlarging yourselves, being subject to the principalities and powers who are counted worthy of families.[42]

The logical consequence of this theological tenet was that if a man lost his justification, and his ability to provide both justification and sanctification for his wives and children, the latter were no longer under any obligation to him. The theoretical basis for marriage in the Mormon system was totally materialistic. It provided a transparent theological gloss for a strictly quid pro quo arrangement, which in its essentials was not much different from a *mariage de convenance* in the Gentile world. The crassness of monetary calculation was omitted, and the rewards sublimated to a "kingdom" in the next world, but the exchange value of female sexual service was essentially the same in both instances. If the male party to the contract proved unable or unwilling to fulfill his part of the agreement, it was necessary to provide a means of redress to the female. Divorce was the easiest solution. It was because he had forfeited his priesthood and been excommunicated, for example, that John D. Lee told his wives, "You are at liberty to get a bill [of divorce], or any other of my wives who do not wish to live with me can be free."[43]

In practice, on account of the dualistic Mormon marriage system (for time and for eternity), divorce in Utah fell into two categories, civil and ecclesiastical. Divorces granted by the probate court were capable of dissolving only the earthly tie, whereas the church could dissolve *all* marital ties. For Mormons, temple divorces were therefore more attractive. The effects of the system, according to one sociologist who studied Mormon polygamy, were salutary. "The Church," he writes, "was the main instrumentality through which divorces were arranged. . . . the process seems to have been comparatively easy, and no especial stigma attached to a divorced woman."[44] There do not appear to have been any restrictions placed upon the remarriage of divorced persons among the Mormons. Opponents of Mormonism, in fact, asserted that the ease with which divorce could be obtained by Mormons, and its more frequent use by women, meant in effect that the polygamous system of Utah included a kind of serial polyandry as well.[45]

Before the Mormons were geographically isolated, their position on divorce was quite conservative. After the public avowal of polygamy and the passage soon after of the Act in Relation to Bills of Divorce, however, the force of legislation was on the side of rapid and easy divorce. Like the Indiana divorce law of 1831, the Utah law contained an "omnibus clause," which allowed the probate court to grant a divorce "when it shall be made to appear to the satisfaction and conviction of the court, that the parties cannot live in peace and union together, and that their welfare requires a separation."[46]

The correlation between a rising incidence of polygamy and a wide-open divorce policy is very suggestive. Data on Box Elder County indicate that nearly three of every four divorce actions initiated during the period 1856–69 were undertaken by women. For the Utah Territory as a whole, 73 percent of all divorce actions in this period were initiated by women. These were precisely the decades of active expansion of polygamy, and the divorce rate was correspondingly low. In the 1870s, when polygamy was declining (it reached its nadir in 1881), the divorce rate was much higher, but only 37 percent of the actions were brought by women. The correlation between a high rate of plural marriage and a high female proportion among divorce plaintiffs suggests that to some extent the divorce system served, during these years, as a means of redress for women who were dissatisfied with the polygamic system, perhaps because they had been displaced in the affections of their husbands or in the control of their households.[47]

That this was clearly *not* the intent of the church was evidenced by the action taken by Brigham Young in 1854. He set a price of ten dollars on bills of divorce for time and fifty dollars for those for eternity. Most observers believed that his intention was to lower the divorce rate.[48] In view of Mormon sexual ideology, however, it is equally clear that he sought to limit the freedom of women to leave men who were faithful servants of the church. The whole matter of the availability of divorce to Mormon women, and its effect in mitigating the conditions of polygamic life for them, is much more complex and requires much more extensive treatment, but can be most cogently and effectively dealt with in connection with the evaluation of the system of polygamy in a later chapter. Divorce was the area of Mormon life bearing on sexuality, however, in which the conflict between popular beliefs and practices and ecclesiastical requirements was most blatant. It is to these beliefs and the informal sexual behavior of the Mormons that we must now turn our attention.

Chapter 9 🌱 Many Wives and Concubines: The Practice of Patriarchal Polygamy

By nature man is inclined to inconstancy in love, woman to constancy. The man's love diminishes perceptibly from the moment it has obtained satisfaction; almost every other woman charms him more than the one he already possesses; he longs for variety. On the other hand, the woman's love increases from that very moment.

—Arthur Schopenhauer, *The World as Will and Representation*

The enjoyment of women makes me more fervent in prayer.

—Mohammed

*T*hroughout the history of the Christian West, as a recent social historian has noted, "the open and legal possession of several wives permitted by polygamy has been strictly taboo. . . . such a practice has always seemed the acme of libertinage and has exercised a guilty fascination."[1] Traditionally, the opponents of Mormonism assumed that polygamy was the most degrading and oppressive form of slavery for women and that its only purpose was male sexual pleasure. As one of the numerous titillating bits of comminatory doggerel verse directed against the Mormons expressed it,

> He [the Mormon] took many wives, late and early,
> He traded in poor women's souls;
> Old Po-lig was a very fast fellow,
> Doing nothing by halves, but by wholes.[2]

Yet although strictly venereal motives provide a partial explanation of the attractiveness of simultaneous polygyny, it was much more complex, had many more ramifications, and ironically mirrored the practices quite common in a typically monogamous society in many ways. The practices under Mormon patriarchal-celestial marriage and their meaning for the sex roles of men and women are the subjects to be examined in this and the following chapter.

It is important to keep in mind at the outset that at any time only a minority of Mormons practiced polygamy, or actually "lived their faith," as they expressed it. The majority of people, not only resident in Utah, but members of the Latter-Day Saints, lived in monogamous relationships. Even among the 15 to 20 percent of those who actually practiced polygamy, however, the oriental harems fantasied by opponents of Mormonism were quite rare. At least half, and perhaps as many as two-thirds, of the polygamists in Utah had only two wives; less than 5 percent had five or more wives.[3]

Furthermore, polygamy as practiced by the Mormons was neither so free of restrictions nor so imbued with unalloyed amorous dalliance as its enemies supposed. Official church policy required the approval of any proposed match by the parents of the young woman in question, the woman herself, the first wife of the intended bridegroom, and the President of the church.[4] The essential approval was that of the church authorities; that of others was merely conventional and in some instances served as a way of placing additional obstacles in the way of those whom the church had decided should not marry. In fact, as a German observer noted, the approval of the first wife "is well-nigh a mere formality, for if she refuses, she will be expelled from the Church."[5] Those women who were in control of the situation, however, wisely employed the power thus tacitly invested in the first wife to exercise a degree of control over the choice of subsequent wives. They were in an excellent position to see that their husbands' future mates were both amenable and cooperative. It was thus in order to preserve domestic tranquility, as well as to provide a kind of social security for the less fortunate members of their families, that women sometimes recommended their sisters and mothers as polygamous wives for their husbands. Men of wisdom, who desired peace and comfort at home, frequently acquiesced in some degree of control exercised by the first wife over their choice of plural wives.

Given the right conditions, and within limits set by the church, women were afforded considerable freedom in courting and wooing. It was not uncommon for the first wife to make the initial overtures to a proposed plural wife, and in some instances her intercession served to assuage the diffidence of a rather self-conscious husband.[6] Courtships tended to be short and relatively businesslike, perhaps reflecting the desires of the first wife, who seems in some instances to have acted not only as an intermediary but also as a chaperon for her husband. The second wife of one polygamist described this kind of courtship: "He never went out with me unless Catherine [his first wife] was along, and used to bring us home together, leaving Catherine and taking me to my father's house. He always went right back home afterward."[7] Women were also sanctioned in taking an active, aggressive role in courtship on their own behalf: "among the Mormons the act of 'making love' . . . is not confined to the male portion of the Church; but . . . every unmarried woman has the same right, and she is expected to exercise it with the same freedom as the opposite sex, with this difference: that while the female is at liberty to decline an offer of marriage made by a man, he is not at liberty to decline an offer coming from a woman, against whose ability for childbearing there rests no well-grounded doubt."[8]

Such proposals were not always greeted with enthusiasm by the chosen swain, but refusal could bring public obloquy and loss of status. John Lee, who was married to several women at their behest, revealed both the reluctance with which polygamists took such women and the motives that prompted a young woman to prefer her suit.

> Jane Woolsy [his niece] . . . asked me to let her become a member of my Family. [I] Said, Jane, you are a young girl in the Bloom of youth. You can marry both young and middle aged. I am an old man, some fifty-five years of age. You certainly would be better satisfied with a young man. She replied, Uncle, you have almost raised me from a child. I love you more than any other man on Earth. I always loved you. *A home is what I want and a Kind Friend to protect me. You are the man of my choice and can furnish me the home I want.*[9]

There is nothing romantic or sexual in this young woman's proposal; Lee is for her primarily a father figure. Her motives are purely hard-headed. Her calculations lay bare one of the advantages the system of polygamy offered to women. In its ideal operation, unthwarted by ecclesiastical interference, Mormon polygamy allowed a woman to choose a husband (regardless of his marital status) who could provide for her in the style she desired. It would thus, in some instances, provide a kind of upward mobility for women, a chance to achieve a higher status (through their husbands) not available to their sisters who were bound to the monogamous system. Similar reasoning would dictate the selection of one's sister or mother as an additional wife for one's husband.[10]

The really difficult condition for a Mormon woman was widowhood. If she had been sealed to her first husband for eternity, all her subsequent children, regardless of their paternity, would accrue to the "kingdom" (progeny) of her eternal lord. The second husband could only be a "temporal" consort; under ecclesiastical law he was but a usufructuary of her fecundity. To obviate this difficulty, an elaborate system of proxy marriage was developed, which provided second husbands with the temporal delights of attractive and wealthy widows; assured the steady population increase that polygamy was theoretically designed to promote; "redeemed" the souls of those who had died spinsters or confirmed bachelors; and assisted in increasing the kingdoms of those temporarily unable to perform such services for themselves. Proxy marriages fell into four categories: (1) "glorifying proxy," or the marriage of a widow who had been married for both time and eternity to another; (2) "retroactive proxy," or the marriage (for time) of a living woman (widowed or unmarried) to a male who served as a succedaneum for a deceased Mormon to whom she was concurrently married for eternity; all children entered the kingdom of the eternal husband; (3) "redeeming proxy," or the marriage of a live surrogate in place of a deceased male in order to create a kingdom for him; and (4) "substitute proxy," the engagement to discharge the duties of father and husband to the children and wives of a departed missionary who expected to be absent for several years and didn't want the building up of his kingdom to suffer thereby.[11]

The system was intended to circumvent the excessively rigorous application of patriarchal principles by allowing female chattels to pass from one owner to another without the forfeiture of the original or prior claim to title of the first husband. It also solved another difficulty inherent in Mormon polygamy. Because the greatest female virtues were purity and fecundity, widows fell into the category of secondhand or salvage goods. The production of their wombs accrued to the original owner regardless of the level of investment of subsequent entrepreneurs. A man could not honorably be responsible for the soul of such a creature. The idea that responsibility for such a woman reverted to the first husband, who had "possessed" her virtue and whose kingdom her progeny augmented, provided a theological solution to this difficulty. The system of proxy marriages also served to relax the theological rigors of Mormonism. It allowed salvation for the unmarried through a postmortem nuptial ceremony. In this we can recognize a latitudinarian or universalist tendency in Mormon theology, which runs counter to the elitist and exclusionary formulation of Joseph Smith. From a more strictly social point of view, it also provided a system of social security for women whose "usefulness," from the standpoint of the religious community, had drastically depreciated with their loss of fertility. Many older women were married—sometimes the mothers of daughters married previously —not for sexual but for soteriological reasons. In 1861, for example, John D. Lee, aged forty-nine, married his nineteenth wife, of whom he wrote: "I was married to old Mrs. Woolsey for her soul's sake, and she was near sixty years old when I married her, I never considered her really as a wife. True I treated her well and gave her all the rights of marriage. Still I never counted her as one of my wives. That is the reason I claim *only eighteen true wives.*"[12] As a social institution the Mormon polygamous family, then, represented an expansion of the responsibility of the individual family, the basic social service unit of nineteenth-century American society. Many women were married not from passion but from principle.

From a passionate perspective, marriages before the mid-twenties were rare among Mormon males. Women entering polygamy were generally younger than men. They averaged twenty-two years of age at marriage, regardless of whether they were the first or one of the various plural wives. Males in polygamous relationships averaged twenty-six years of age at the marriage of the first wife, thirty-six at the marriage of the second, and forty-five at the marriage of the third.[13] This grouping suggests an economic rationale behind polygamous marriages. As the economic resources of a man increased and he could afford the expense consequent to additional wives and children (visible evidence of his glorification and sainthood), he might practice polygamy more vigorously and conscientiously. To the extent that women sought security and some degree of luxury within the polygamous system, it would have been only logical for them to have contracted marriages with Saints who were economically established and who could be expected to provide comfortably, if not handsomely, for their wives.

Clustering of male plural marriages in that part of the life cycle bracketed by the ages thirty-five to forty-five also suggests a correlation with the phenomenon that is today being called the "middle-age crisis."[14] Marriage in the late thirties or early forties to young women would have served to relieve males' anxieties about aging and loss of sexual potency. Fathering of children at a later age, made possible by sexual contact with younger women, who, unlike their first wives, had not yet passed the climacteric, would have provided visible proof of their undiminished vigor and potency. This pattern was even more marked among Mormons who married three or more wives. John D. Lee married three-fourths of his total wives during his thirties. Brigham Young, probably the most married man in Mormondom, married 80 percent of his wives in his forties. Hosea Stout, who had seven wives, married nearly three-fourths of them in his forties.[15]

Many Mormon males chafed under the burden of celestial marriage and were bored with the dutiful nature of this matrimonial form of salvation. The growing sense of confinement and lack of freedom the polygamous system represented for men; the desire to choose freely the wives of one's bosom and to bear responsibility for one's behavior to no one; and the desire for ever younger women are all clearly revealed in a dream of John D. Lee. It is the fantasy of an anarchic, sexually potent male, totally unbound by the social conventions that usually govern sexual life:

I had taken two young Women to wife. Both were sisters and appeared to be related to my wife Rachel, either her sisters or Daughters. I had bedded with both and they were lovely and charming. Especially the youngest one was neat and clean. It appeared that I obtained [them] legally, yet without the Knowledge of Pres. B[righam] Y[oung] and in fact I am not certain that my wife Rachel even was aware of My having them, as I introduced them to her and asked the youngest to embrace [her], which she cheerfully did to her astonishment with a Kiss. Intend[ed] to report what I had done to Pres. B. Y. as soon as an opportunity should present.[16]

In many ways the restrictiveness of the system was even more trying for women. As objects, or movable property, not only were they forbidden to have any contact with Gentiles, but their social relations with Mormon men were strictly circumscribed. That these restrictions were intended to protect the purity of Mormon women was evident in the reaction of one woman to her husband's parting injunction: " 'Don't have anything to say to anyone else while I am gone.' This astonished me, for I did not believe that he questioned my chastity."[17]

In instances of marriage to elderly women and widows, and to a lesser extent in all marriages, it was assumed that the male had married the woman out of the goodness of his heart. Such condescension should be rewarded by dutiful and respectful behavior from the female. If the marriage failed, it was commonly thought to be the fault of the wife.[18] As long as a man retained his "priesthood," or good standing in the church of the Latter-Day Saints, and his justification, his wives could not leave or divorce him without bearing the full brunt of responsibility for the separation. Such a system seemed particularly conducive to the abuse and victimization of women, as contemporary Mormon enemies never tired of pointing out.

In some cases the rhetoric of proprietorial polygamy was overzealously followed to its logical conclusion, and women became literally a marketable commodity. John D. Lee, for example, reported the overture of one Solomon Chamberlain, who offered him "another woman and four children who had been married to him for Terressa. I replied that I never bartered my wives or Family away like Stock, but if Terressa wanted to go back to him I should not object, yet I did not feel to drive her away contrary to her wish, and as for his other wife and four children, I did not want them."[19] This practice does not seem to have been a widespread one, however, and it was viewed with a great deal of hostility by the Mormon hierarchy. There were honorable and disreputable men among the Mormons just as there were among their Gentile enemies, but the *intent* of polygamy was not the systematic degradation of women; and the number of abuses of the system was probably commensurate with the number under the monogamous form of marriage. Mormon men, in fact, often shared the ideals of monogamous husbands in the treatment of their wives. Brutal physical abuse of women, for instance, was considered contemptible and pusillanimous by honorable Mormons. One witness to such an incident illustrates the feeling such behavior evoked: "Today witnessed the humiliating spectacle of seeing W. Camp thrash his wife. *This is the first time in my life I ever beheld such a sight.*"[20]

Polygamous husbands were considered to be under the same obligations to their plural wives as were monogamists to their single spouses. The ideal polygamous husband strove to achieve a balanced treatment of his wives. If one wife received a dress of a certain quality, all the others were theoretically entitled to a similar gift. This ideal was frequently ignored, however, and it was not at all uncommon to find a man being admonished for the "inequality that is in his Family." First wives proved especially difficult to control, and striking a satisfactory balance, which would afford each a sufficiency of supplies, attention, affection, and luxuries, remained one of the central problems of polygamous life. Human nature was not equal to the task of divine impartiality thus thrust upon it, and men's minds were naturally affected by the treatment which their several wives accorded them and the providence they exercised in the employment of their provisions.[21]

On the other hand, what was perceived in some instances as inequitable treatment of plural wives represented the different stages of the life cycle different wives were experiencing at a particular time. The prevalent domiciliary arrangement in Utah is a case in point. Three forms of housing arrangements were employed by polygamous families. All plural wives could live in the same house and share the same bedroom with the husband; all wives could live in the same house and have separate bedrooms; or each wife could have a separate establishment. Generally, the housing arrangement depended on the monetary resources available to the husband; but more significantly, it often represented the value a man placed upon a particular wife and the stage in the life cycle she had reached. Usually women began their polygamous married lives living in the same house with other wives, but by the time they had three or four children and were in their thirties, if they had been dutiful and made themselves agreeable to their husbands, they often had some form of independent establishment. Almost eight of ten plural wives seem to have achieved a residence apart from their husband's other wives at some point in their polygamic career; and two in ten enjoyed separate bedrooms. It was quite rare (perhaps one or two cases in a hundred) for all wives to occupy the same bedroom for any extended period of time.[22]

Opponents of Mormonism continually reiterated the horrors of polygamy for the first wife.[23] Certainly polygamous husbands had preferences among their wives, and in many instances the younger women, because they were sexually more active, received the greater part of a man's physical affection, and consequently all too often exercised an undue influence over the joint husband. But this picture is somewhat overdrawn. The value of a companion closer to one's own age and trust in the wisdom, counsel, and fidelity of an older wife often afforded her a position of great respect and deeper affection than the mere sexual capacities of her younger co-wives could command. Thus we find that sweet and romantic overtures were often made toward younger wives; especially during the early "honeymoon" years of marriage, they were afforded special privileges and exemptions. They might, for instance, be allowed to remain abed on a frosty morning while the husband hunted about for wood to kindle a fire.[24]

First wives, like "old marrieds" among monogamists, were not usually treated with such indulgence, but the depth of affection and loyalty expressed for them in many instances far surpassed that younger wives could expect. Shortly before his execution for his part in the Mountain Meadows Massacre, John D. Lee was imprisoned. When allowed to have a wife with him in his room, he asked his eldest wife, Rachel, to come. Throughout his diary, his most consistent and warmest expressions of affection are for Rachel. Typically, he describes their relationship as that of a devoted dyadic unit. His description of her greeting upon his return home after his first trial is characteristic: "She jumped off her Horse and Embraced me [in] her arms. We both stood Motionless for some time, being overcome with Joy."[25]

This impression is strengthened when we consider the relative lapse of time between marriages under polygamy. In many cases, especially among men who had more than three wives, the time lapse between the original marriage and the decision to enter polygamy was the longest in the plural marriage sequence. An interval of ten to fifteen years between the initial marriage and the first plural marriage was not uncommon. The average length of time between second and third marriages was six years, and the interval tended to become shorter with the increasing number of wives taken. In only a very limited number of cases did one plural marriage follow another at an interval of less than a year. The fact that the interval between succeeding plural marriages tended to become shorter suggests a tenderer concern for the feelings of the first spouse than for those of subsequent ones.[26]

The position of the first wife, though based on seniority, was buttressed by her legal standing. Although plural wives were of course considered legitimate under Mormon ecclesiastical law, their position was very tenuous under civil law (to the extent that it coincided with that of the rest of the nation). Despite the fact that Mormons were consciously trying to alter the established matrimonial pattern, they were afloat in a sea of monogamy, and their own upbringing and traditions were all monogamous. It is not surprising, therefore, that patterns of behavior under polygamy in many instances closely paralleled those of monogamy. Often the first wife occupied the role of official family hostess, and if she enjoyed a separate house, it was the social residence of the polygamous husband. It was also not uncommon for a man to leave all his property to his first wife. The Married Women's Property Act, passed by the territorial legislature in 1872, sought to prevent the recognition of the first wife's dower interest in her husband's property. Its effect seems to have been less thoroughgoing, however, than the legislators intended, for the practice of preferential treatment of the first wife continued.[27]

Plural wives were usually successful in getting their husband to give them title to their own homes before his death, and some women had considerable additional property at their disposal, but the typical pattern was the husband's engrossment of all property that came to the marriage by his wives. This was made much easier for him in that the nature of polygamy promoted competition for the time, attention, and favors of the husband. The more amenable one of his wives proved, the better her chances in the competition. Most polygamous wives, therefore, placed most of their property in the hands of their husbands.[28]

Because women were considered primarily objects of movable property, and because emphasis was placed upon new articles with a guarantee (virgins who promised to be fertile), one would expect to find the sexual morality of Mormons very rigid. This was not the case. Polygamy produced a tension in Mormon sexual morality. On one hand it emphasized virginity and proscribed all premarital sex. On the other, it emphasized a woman's fecundity and considered a barren first wife the chief raison d'être for polygamy. Among wives of childbearing age, breeding competitions were common.[29] Official church policy tended to favor purity above fertility and certainly in no wise overtly sanctioned sexual pleasure as a guide in matters of morality. Popular belief, however, reckoned motherhood above maidenhood and, despite denials, sanctioned sexual pleasure (especially for the male) as one of the ends of marriage.

Thus, we find a strict public adherence to the doctrine that all premarital sex was wrong, but at the same time it seems to have been quite common, especially among betrothed couples. Commission of adultery, assuming that such behavior would cause the authorities to sanction a fait accompli by forwarding the nuptials of the delinquent couple, was also common. Such behavior, however, did not take into account the depth of feeling that separated official church morality from popularly sanctioned moral behavior. The case of Robert Gillespie was indicative of the consequences that occasionally followed such behavior:

Gillespie wanted to be *sealed* to his sister-in-law, but for some reason his request was denied. He had known of others obtaining wives by committing adultery first and then being sealed to avoid scandal. So he tried it, and then went to the apostle George A. Smith, and again asked to be sealed to the woman; but George A. had a religious fit on him . . . so he refused to seal him or let him be sealed, giving as his reason for refusing, that Gillespie had exercised the rights of sealing without first obtaining orders to do so.[30]

But if the offender did not directly challenge the authority of the church, or if he were not in disfavor with Mormon hierarchs, such behavior would probably be ignored. The practice of engaged couples spending the night together was also common, although it may have been merely a continuation of the old New England custom of "bundling," which did not necessarily involve sexual intercourse. In some instances, a man made a "trial" of a woman for a limited period of time. Hosea Stout followed this procedure with his third wife: "Lucretia Fisher lived in the home two months before she was married to Stout. This plan was sometimes followed to see if two wives would be compatible, and also to determine whether or not the second was attracted to the husband sufficiently to become his wife."[31]

Since the average age of the male at first plural marriage was in the mid-thirties, simultaneous polygyny was not especially suited to providing an outlet for the male sex drive. During the period when male sexual desire was most insistent (between the ages of fifteen and thirty-five), the Mormon system would not have been any more physiologically satisfying than traditional monogamy. Furthermore, strict regulations forbade sexual intercourse during menstruation, gestation, or lactation. Masturbation was considered a heinous practice, contrary to nature, and consequently forbidden. Nevertheless, it was possible to follow this austere regimen with a relatively high degree of fidelity, while at the same time ensuring some sexual pleasure for the polygamous male, because a plurality of wives provided the possibility that some would be available when others were indisposed or under ecclesiastical taboo. Polygamy was the only moral way out of the sexual dilemma that faced man.[32]

Clearly inherent in the system was an assault on the romantic-love ideology which maintained that sexual attraction, reproduction, and companionship could all ideally be obtained in the unique person of the wife. Polygamy quite consciously strove to separate sexual pleasure from sexual reproduction, and sexual love in general from "spiritual love," or companionship. Such an intent only further increased the instability of the polygamous system. The disjunction between pleasure and reproduction served to separate those wives who were pregnant from those who were not, as well as separating males from females. The disjunction between sexual and spiritual love separated younger wives from the first wife. Sexual enjoyment was evidently a male prerogative; women provided sexual pleasure, but viewed in themselves were considered primarily breeders, or, in the case of older wives, burdens to be borne heavenward by dutiful Saints.

Indeed, pregnancy and childbirth were considered matters of concern only for females; and men do not seem to have been unduly concerned about whether their wives' health was endangered by pregnancy and parturition. As with Gentile society, birthing and its risks reached only the periphery of the male Saint's consciousness; it was not allowed to interfere with whatever important business was at hand. The behavior of Allen Frost was typical. When one of his wives was near her time, and illness presented an additional complication, he left home to work, "leaving some good nurses with her."[33] The child was stillborn. A year later, when his wife gave birth to a daughter, he revealed his impatience with the whole process of birth; it was a disturbance to an orderly, predictable male world: "My wife," he wrote, "being quite sick I was obliged to stay at home, Sisters Lewis, Brown, and Robertson came to assist her a little after several hours' severe labor she gave birth."[34] Three days later his wife was "very sick," and he had to get a nurse to stay with her so he could once again leave on business. It should not be inferred from this that Frost was particularly callous or indifferent toward the health of his wife. In each pregnancy he did provide nurses to assist at the birth. He did remain with her during an especially difficult parturition. It is possible that to have remained longer would have been rash, because the welfare of the entire family may have depended on his attending to his business interests. What comes out clearly in Frost's case, however, is the assumption that the male and female spheres are discrete, and that a woman's chief value lies in her fertility.

Despite her history of difficult births and his realization that his wife was "generally sickly" during childbirth,[35] Frost does not seem to have taken any measures to prevent future conceptions. Predictably, his wife died in childbirth in 1880. In this instance he remained with her through her trial and observed with matter-of-fact equanimity that "the case is something like this. When the child was born, *my wife was so thoroughly used up*, that no pains were produced to expel the afterbirth and [she] remained in that state 'til the womb contracted."[36]

A series of cruelly painful and dangerous births had left this woman utterly exhausted. Yet the patriarchal assumption that it was the function of a man's wives to populate his kingdom, in order to "glorify" the Saints, and the consequent Mormon proscription of birth control effectually prevented his taking steps to avoid the final insupportable pregnancy. His attitude toward the lot of women was evident when he wrote in conclusion that "she has suffered in the flesh, as a martyr. In weakness and pain she has brought forth children, and assisted in raising them in the way they should go. She has entered into her reward."[37]

The process of birth itself, and especially the lying-in chamber, was a largely female sanctum from which males were excluded. As with most of nineteenth-century America, "nurses" or midwives were a common feature of Mormon births.[38] Their presence was in part, however, a function of a family's financial status and of the difficulties that characterized a particular birth. Midwives charged a fee of $2.50 to $5.00 per case and often remained with the family as a "mother's helper" for several days, or until both mother and child no longer needed them. In a family like that of John D. Lee, which was relatively affluent by frontier standards, midwives were present as a matter of course. In less well-to-do families, like that of Allen Frost, however, midwives were called only after grave complications developed. The more informal "nurse," who might be only a neighbor woman with no particular training, was usually called first. When families of this socioeconomic level called a midwife, the woman was usually *in extremis*.

Describing the parturient experience of another of his wives, for example, Frost wrote: "She was in quite a dangerous position until nearly noon, for want of a skillful nurse."[39] In the case of the wife who died when she proved unable to expel the afterbirth, although three nurses were with her, the midwife was not called until nearly two days after the complication had been detected. More affluent families tended to send for a doctor if complications developed.[40] Normally, as in other strict patriarchal societies, no males other than the father of the child were admitted to the birth chamber. Folk belief, however, held that members of the highest, or Melchizedek, priesthood could heal all ills by the "laying on of hands." In some cases individuals who had enjoyed notable success in that line were called upon to facilitate childbirth, rather than nurses or midwives or, on occasion, in addition to them. One of the virtues of "priestly" attendance, of course, was that it was considered a religious duty of these hierophants, and as such was performed free of charge.[41]

When midwives were present at births, they administered an anodyne, most commonly lobelia, to ease the birth. Apparently, alternatives to the common dorsal position of delivery were resorted to in cases of difficult births. One eyewitness provided an account of such a case: "The midwife . . . put her over the back of a chair to help force the baby down. . . . It is reported that to make a delivery easier the mother should stay on her feet as long as possible."[42] The standing delivery, which employs the force of gravity as an aid to muscular contractions, was considered the most felicitous position for giving birth.

In cases of danger to the mother, even though Mormon society placed such high value on the number of a man's children, it seems to have been the practice of midwives to concentrate their efforts on saving the mother rather than the child. There is some evidence that the interests of midwives and husbands conflicted, and that husbands may not have shared the anxious concern of midwives for the life of the mother in preference to the life of the child. John D. Lee, for example, was terribly upset by the "carelessness and ignorance" of the woman who attended his wife during a miscarriage. The woman noted the sex of one fetus, but emptied the other into the fire in haste, because "the Mother being so ill at the time of the delivery . . . all attention was directed to her."[43]

The ideology of polygamy explicitly opposed birth control, but women as the victims of that system found ways to circumvent it. The folk pharmacopoeia included such putative abortifacients as baking-powder tablets, an infusion of an unidentified desert plant of yellowish inflorescence, and turpentine. One folklorist claimed that, for simple contraception, "the folk have long sustained their own concepts about the use of 'rhythm'. . . . It is said that the two weeks before menstruation one can become pregnant, and that the two weeks after one cannot. Another informant said that a woman is supposed to be able to get pregnant only two hours during any one month."[44]

Other solutions to the problem were available, and women of a more realistic bent realized that abstinence (enforced by the female) was the only effective method of contraception: "Stay single, or use twin beds, and you'll keep from having a baby. Just use gunpowder in a gun to prevent conception. Take saltpeter—eat the salt and leave the peter alone."[45] The existence of this body of folklore suggests that women were dissatisfied with their role as breeders and sought to protect themselves from being "used up" in childbirth. Quite significantly, *all* forms of birth control practiced by the Mormons, including that which was most widely used (total abstinence during a twelve- to eighteen-month lactation period), were controlled by the female. If any precautions were to be taken against pregnancy, the wife was the one who would take them; concern for birth control was largely a covert female activity. James Hulett, who interviewed seventy-eight members of polygamous families, found that many polygamists intentionally limited their families; they seem to have allowed a twenty-four-month interval between births. Hulett discovered "a widespread belief in the efficacy of lactation as a preventative of conception."[46] As Hulett notes, "The evidence on this point comes entirely from women informants, so it is impossible to say whether the men shared it."[47] Abstinence during the lactation period was, however, the official policy of the church.

It should be noted, however, that the system of polygamy itself and the regulations of sexual behavior it prescribed automatically established a kind of birth control. A polygamist with from two to seven wives, for instance, averaged 27.57 children. This meant an average of 6.45 children per woman.[48] From a more general perspective, it has been estimated that 50 percent of Mormon polygamous males sired fifteen or more children; 25 percent had twenty or more; 5 percent fathered thirty or more; and less than 2 percent produced forty and over. For wives in a polygamous family, this meant an average of 5.9 children per woman with a typical twenty-four month spacing. Monogamous Mormon women produced an average of between seven and eight children per woman with an average birth interval of thirty-three months.[49] As we have seen, for American society as a whole, fertility declined steadily after 1800. By 1860 women were bearing an average of 5.21 children. Both monogamous and polygamous Mormon women, then, had a higher fertility rate than the national average. Mormon fertility did not fall below the national average until a man had six or seven wives. This suggests that Mormons took the church's prohibition on birth control seriously and employed contraceptive techniques less frequently than non-Mormons.

A woman who entered a large polygamous household, then, could expect a shortened reproductive cycle, but a diminution in the total number of children she might expect to bear during her childbearing years. In fact, from the perspective of undergoing the risks of pregnancy fewer times, it made most sense to marry a man who already had several wives—preferably at least six. In a relationship with a man who had two wives, a woman could expect to bear an average of about 7 children; with a thrice-married man, an average of 8; and with a man with four wives, an average of slightly over 7. Married to a man with five or more wives, however, a woman could look forward to an ever-decreasing number of pregnancies with each new wife her husband took. For polygamists with five wives, each woman averaged 6 children; for those with seven wives, there were 4.43 children per woman.[50] In the case of Brigham Young, who had twenty-five wives and forty-four children, the average number of children per woman was 1.76, or 2.4 for those listed as of childbearing age.[51]

This was, of course, the ideal, and was not always consistently observed. One isolated piece of evidence suggests that the sexual pleasure of women may not have been totally ignored, or more probably that ingenious ways were found to avoid the prohibition of intercourse during pregnancy, lactation, and menstruation. Doubtless polygamy, girt about with the restrictions we have noted and positing reproduction as its primary goal, did not provide adequate sexual gratification for the average male practitioner who had only two or three wives. Two wives could easily be pregnant concurrently, and then, assuming he observed the injunction to avoid intercourse during gestation, he was reduced to the same condition as a monogamist. The erotic benefits of polygamy could only accrue to those who had a relatively large number of wives— probably less than 5 percent of those who practiced celestial marriage. That the majority of males found the system less than satisfying is clear from an admonition by Lorenzo Snow to "govern and restrain their passions," and his caution against the "baneful effects of the sin of masturbation or self-abuse destroying life and defeating the object for which God had given the fountain of life to the children of Men."[52] He concluded by pointing out the "*propriety of gratifying women during pregnancy* where it was right and consistent that they might not entail on their offspring unholy desires and appetites."[53]

If men were to secure gratification under plural marriage, there had to be some relaxation of the strict limitations placed on "seasonable" intercourse. Snow provided such a loophole. It is not surprising that the justification he provided placed the blame for violation of this ecclesiastical taboo on women. Fear of the power of the female sex drive was deep-rooted and provided a constant source of anxiety for polygamists. In this phobia we see a tacit admission that the female is also entitled to sexual pleasure, and a realization of the insufficiency of one man to provide such pleasure to a plurality of wives. Popular vigilante justice and the stringent legal sanctions Mormonism erected against adultery and seduction reflected these fears.

Women needed to be protected, nominally against their own desires and the anarchic threat of younger unmarried males, but in fact as property held in trust by their husbands. This kind of thinking was reflected in an elder's admonition to John D. Lee: "He . . . advised me to have my Indian girls, Alace and Alnora Married to me . . . in order to throw a shield of Protection around them, etc."[54] Young men were the primary threat to the honor of women in patriarchal households. Part of the problem was one of age, complicated by a system of marriage that a sizable proportion of women found unsatisfactory. Lee, who was a very acute observer, noted that in the town where he lived, "nearly 1/2 the women . . . are alienated in their feelings from their Husbands."[55] Lee's sixteenth wife, Mary Ann Williams, "for some cause became dissatisfied." It was evident to him that he "could not make her happy," so he asked her what she wanted to do. "She replied that she could love me and respect me as a Father but not as a husband; and that she wanted my oldest son for her companion and that she loved him more than any other Man that She ever saw."[56] He thus kept her from cohabitation with a Gentile; and since she remarried within his family, she might still swell the ranks of the old patriarch's kingdom.

Under such circumstances of strain and hostility, one would expect

Mormon patriarchs to be very exacting about woman's place in the home and very loath to allow her to pursue activities that took her out of the home and brought her into contact with young single men. Ideological statements about the respective roles of men and women were quite in accord with the doctrine of male and female spheres: "It is the calling of the wife and mother to know what to do with everything that is brought into the house, laboring to make her home desirable to her husband and children, making herself an Eve in the midst of a little paradise of her own creating."[57] But Eve found herself in the midst of a wilderness that required much hard labor to transform into a garden. The pressures of frontier life, especially under conditions of individual establishments for each plural wife, essentially replicated those faced by isolated nuclear-family groups. A shortage of labor, coupled with the need to maximize the labor that could be performed by each male in civilizing the western territory (Mormons pioneered not only throughout Utah but also in Arizona, New Mexico, Wyoming, and Idaho), often made it necessary for women to fill physically less demanding positions in older, established settlements.

None of these circumstances, however, decreased the emphasis on woman's domestic role. The wife's realm was generally called "inside discipline," whereas that of her husband was called "outside discipline." Children were raised in a sexually undifferentiated atmosphere until the age of eight, when they were expected to take their places in the sexually divided work force. Evidence for this kind of rigid sex-role division is abundant. One plural wife, for example, described her husband's system of labor organization as

> a definite division of labor by sexes. He operated according to the current ideas of what was "women's and girl's work, and what was men's and boy's work." For instance, none of his wives ever milked a cow, "picked up an axe," or worked much in the garden. The girls did all the milking and the boys did the garden work. Girls might be put to work pulling weeds in the garden, but ordinarily they spent their time in housework and did most of the sewing. Fruit picking and canning was women's work. The boys were put to work in the garden at five years of age, and had a lot of definite, systematic chores to do.[58]

This description is that of a highly organized and very efficient system of division of labor. It suggests a stable, well-integrated family structure. This was the ideal rather than the reality for most Mormon families. The point to be noted here, though, is that when at all possible, this was the preferred division of labor. Even in circumstances of high geographical mobility and consequent familial instability, the Mormon Eve was expected to carry her little corner of domestic paradise with her. On the wagon trains coming from Illinois, "the first duty of the Mormon women was, through all change of place and fortune, to keep alive the altar fire of the home."[59] When John D. Lee went off on an expedition to gather salt or lime, he took one of his wives with him to cook and wash for him and the hired men he had with him.[60]

In general, then, women were responsible for all aspects of domestic economy: housework, cooking, washing, tending the garden, and some light painting. Very few laborsaving devices were in use, but the burden of household chores was lightened somewhat by the widespread use of Indian women as servants.[61] Infrequently, Mormon women engaged in small-scale home manufactures that they sold at markets, but there does not seem to have been much time for this kind of occupation. Viewed from the point of view of labor organization under conditions of labor scarcity, polygamy provided a family with an adequate supply of labor to meet its own needs. Both the insistence upon large families and the plurality of wives insured a ready supply of labor. Women were expected to help men in the fields, especially during harvest time, and ironically the very insularity of Mormon families led to an expansion of women's responsibilities and capacities. Especially in outlying polygamous families in which the husband provided separate dwellings for his celestial wives, the women were frequently left to fend for themselves. They got a good deal of supervisory and administrative experience organizing the children into an efficient labor force to insure the day-to-day operation of the farm. Even when the husband was at home, the shortage of labor insured that the only responsible adult who could assist him in a given situation might often be his wife.

The most complete picture we have of a family of this type is that of John D. Lee. His wives helped clear fields and plant and harvest crops and oversaw irrigation. On one occasion, one of his wives helped build her own dwelling and daubed it with clay and mud in southwestern fashion. Another wife helped him gather salt, build a stone wall, set fenceposts, and build a fence.[62] These were rugged, hardworking women, who could take their places by the side of men and pull their shares of the load. Female members of the family stood up for family property and pride just as men did, and there was a frank respect for women's capacities in a rugged and hostile world. When Lee was trying to prevent a renegade band of Indians from killing one of his oxen, he found his wives by his side. "I looked around to see how things were," he wrote, "and I saw *seven of my Wives* standing with guns in their hands, ready to shoot if I was attacked."[63] One of the men present was unable to load his gun because he was so terrified, so one of Lee's wives did it for him. Clearly, women were schooled to defend themselves and their property during the frequent absences of their husbands.

It is not surprising with women of such fury and ruggedness that there should have been a movement among Mormons to expand the occupational spheres in which women moved. As with the Shakers, the movement for expanded occupational opportunities and women's rights among the Mormons coincided with the second wave of feminism in America, during the 1870s. The movement seems, however, to have been rather conservative in intent. This was evident in a speech Brigham Young gave in 1870 or 1871. "We believe that women are useful," he said, "not only to sweep houses, wash dishes, make beds, and raise babies, but that they should stand behind the counter, study law or physic, or become good bookkeepers and be able to do the business in any counting house, and all this to enlarge their sphere of usefulness for the benefit of society at large. In following these things they but answer the design of their creation."[64]

But why is such an enlarged "sphere of usefulness" required of women? The answer lies in the shortage of male labor available to subdue the wilderness. "The ladies can learn to keep books as well as the men; we have some few already, who are just as good accountants as any of our brethren. Why not teach more of them to keep books and sell goods, and let them do this business, and let the men go to raising sheep, wheat, or cattle, or go and do something or other to beautify the earth and help make it like the Garden of Eden, instead of spending their time in a lazy, loafing manner."[65] Yet although there was obvious contempt for the positions Young proposed that women be trained for, and even though they were clearly considered supplemental to women's domestic duties, which retained primary importance, the pressure of circumstances had forced a radical change in the traditional attitude of Mormons toward the economic role of females in society. Consider, for example, the "Fourteenth General Epistle of the Presidency," promulgated in 1856, which urged women to train their daughters to "sew, spin, and weave; to cultivate vegetables, as well as flowers; to make soap, as well as cakes and preserves; to spin, colour, weave, and knit, as well as to work embroidery; to milk, make butter and cheese, and work in the kitchen, as well as in the parlour."[66] There is no mention here of any feminine usefulness for anything beyond household-related tasks.

By the 1870s, however, women were being encouraged by the First Presidency of the church to take jobs outside the domestic sphere, albeit jobs of an inferior character. Once women entered the male work force, they could not be confined to jobs that required little skill, were low paying, or were considered unworthy of their male counterparts. By the mid-1870s, one observer noted that "they close no career on a woman in Utah by which she can earn a living."[67] In Salt Lake City, the chief telegrapher was a woman, and throughout Utah many women filled such posts. Two young women were working in the office of the church historian, two were lawyers, and two others had graduated from the Women's Medical College in Philadelphia and were practicing physicians. By the 1890s, a woman had been elected to the Utah Legislature, and was chairman of the Judiciary Committee in the house. In August of 1896, a Mormon was defeated by his wife in an election for a local office.[68]

The movement for women's rights in Utah was carried on concurrently with the expansion of women's roles in society. The two major achievements of the movement were the bill passed on 12 February 1870 entitled An Act Conferring upon Women the Elective Franchise and the Married Women's Property Act, passed in early 1872, which gave women the right to control their own property, so that "a plural wife occupied the anomalous position of *feme sole* as far as the law was concerned, and so could retain her property."[69] Both of these legislative enactments represented obvious benefits for women, but the issue is more complex than that. Both demand more detailed treatment than space allows here and are discussed more extensively in the final chapter on the Mormons.

In 1872 the *Women's Exponent*, the organ of the Female Relief Society, was founded. It defended polygamy and took a line on women's rights that patriarchs found satisfactory. The periodical was incorporated with Eliza Snow, the Mormon poetess, as president of the corporation. The position of the Female Relief Society was best expressed by Mrs. Sarah M. Kimball, who chaired the propolygamy meeting held in Salt Lake City in 1870. In her presidential address, she cried: "We are not here to advocate woman's rights, but man's rights. The bill in question [Cullom bill] would not only deprive our fathers, husbands, and brothers of enjoying the privileges bequeathed to citizens of the U.S., but it would deprive us as women, of the privilege of selecting our husbands; and against this we unqualifiedly protest."[70]

On the other side were those women who opposed polygamy, like Jennie Anderson Froiseth, the founder of the Women's National Anti-Polygamy Society and editor of the *Anti-Polygamy Standard* (begun in 1881). Like propolygamy women, they concentrated on the marriage issue and were little concerned with women's rights. They sought a return to the snug and cozy monogamous marriage in which woman's position was sharply defined, her roles traditionally established, and her position in the household undisputed.[71] In essence, the women of Mormondom were divided into hostile camps. They were unable to generate a dialogue centering upon issues of concern to women as women because of the overriding importance of the marriage question. Because the federal government chose to intervene legislatively and judicially in the social life of Mormon Utah, the issue became one of support for or opposition to the institution of polygamy. The First Amendment rights of Mormon men were under attack; and women divided, not over the question of women's rights (both pro- and anti-polygamy women were essentially conservative on this question), but over whether the rights of *men* were legitimate and should be defended.

The terms of the debate had not been chosen by women but were thrust upon them, and to some extent they were not even free to choose the side they supported. It took a great deal of courage, and no doubt a very deep sense of frustration and dissatisfaction with polygamy, for a woman practicing celestial marriage to enroll her name under the anti-polygamy banner; the Gentile world considered plural wives little better than prostitutes, and once separated from their husbands they could not expect to remarry and find support for their children.[72]

To a large degree, then, women were caught up in a national debate that transcended the territorial borders, questioned the very basis of the marital and family structures, and obscured the issues involved in the women's-rights movement. Ironically, it was these same national forces, and the reaction to them within the territory itself, that forced the more radical and beneficial changes in the rights and status of women. In a very real sense, women made positive gains in status and rights in Mormon Utah, but the driving forces behind those changes were men in the national legislature and in the Gentile clergy and the members of the Mormon hierarchy itself. Women were the pawns in a game of much wider scope than women's rights; the pressure of circumstances forced their masters to make changes in their condition that they had not initially intended to make.

Chapter 10 🐝 "Then Shall They Be Gods, Because They Have All Power, and the Angels Shall Be Subject to Them": An Evaluation of the System of Patriarchal Polygamy

Ayshat al-durrah murrah [The sister-wife hath a bitter life].

—Arab proverb

He didn't really want nine-hundred and ninety-nine wives, but in those days everybody married ever so many wives, and of course the King had to marry ever so many more just to show that he was the King. . . . Some of the wives were nice, but some were simply horrid, and the horrid ones quarrelled with the nice ones and made them horrid too, and then they would all quarrel with Suleiman-bin-David, and that was horrid for him.

    —Rudyard Kipling, "The Butterfly that Stamped," *Just So Stories*

*B*righam Young set the tone for the classic doctrine on the place of women in Mormon society, in his reaction to what he considered the extreme leniency of John D. Lee in pressing his monetary claims in a court action against a Mrs. Lytle. "Great God!" he exclaimed, "could women Tramel [*sic*] me in this manner? No! All their council [*sic*] and wisdom . . . don't weigh as much with me as the weight of a FLY TIRD [*sic*]. It is no woman's place to council her Husband & the moment a man follows a woman he is led astray & will go down to Hell unless he retracts his steps. I could have a perfect Hell with my wives were I to listen to them."[1]

Yet Mormons passed a divorce law (1852) that provided women much more control over their lives than was given by any other divorce statute of the nineteenth century, save only that of Indiana. Utah was among the first areas of the United States to grant female suffrage (1870);[2] and in the Married Women's Property Act of 1872, Utah took positive steps to insure women's rights to the retention of their property after marriage. All of this seems very paradoxical. In this chapter we examine woman's position in the religious life of Mormonism, the concern with fashion reform, and the genesis and use of female suffrage and the liberal divorce statutes in Utah, to afford a deeper understanding of the relationship between the sexes in Mormon society.

The position of the orthodox Mormon woman on the question of women's rights and status, typically very conservative, was exemplified by Eliza Snow's poem entitled "Woman":

And then the thought suggested to my view,
That woman's self might speak of woman too:
But not for "Woman's Rights" to plead or claim—
No! that in Zion, I should blush to name.[3]

She shared the fear of male Mormons that a crusade for women's rights would set the sexes against each other and lead to anarchy. She was therefore opposed to female agitation and striking out for rights. She urged women to place their trust in their male saviors; if "rights" were truly right, they would be recognized and implemented by God's Saints. In any case, it was duties that were of primary concern, not rights. An article that appeared in the *Salt Lake City Daily Telegraph*, entitled "Woman—Her Present and Possible Future," makes this point most succinctly: "It is the duty of women to reform and purify society ... and inculcate doctrines of purity and virtue into the minds of their children, instead of demanding more rights. Let them show themselves capable of approaching their duties to their families instead of clamoring for the elective franchise."[4]

Yet, within four years of the publication of this article, without any ostensible agitation or public consideration of the question, women could vote in any local, state or national election held in Utah! If female suffrage did not come about through female agitation, coupled with male reform, what was its provenance in Utah? This is a complicated and involved question, but one we must attempt to answer if we hope to understand the relationship between the sexes in nineteenth-century Mormon Utah.

The bill that conferred the right of suffrage upon woman was approved by the Utah Legislature on 12 February 1870. It was signed into law two days later by acting Governor S. A. Mann, a federal government appointee and a Gentile. This was indicative of federal support for the Utah law; and indeeed, Eliza Snow noted that the bill could not have been passed over an executive veto, because the territorial governor enjoyed absolute veto power.[5] In fact, the initial impetus for the suffrage bill had come not from Mormons, male or female, but from a group of Gentiles who recommended it as a facile solution to the last "relic of barbarism"— polygamy. The Radical Republican representative George W. Julian (1817–99) introduced a resolution to that effect in the House of Representatives on 15 March 1869. A few days later he championed a bill for the suppression of polygamy in Utah. Both bills were referred to the Committee on the Territories, and both were tabled.[6]

The assumptions behind the Julian resolution seemed to have been that polygamy was an institution which women found utterly oppressive and that the moral sense of women, being superior to that of men, would quickly outlaw the nefarious institution if given the chance. The resolution appealed to the Radical Republican style of thought, which perceived a superficial analogy between polygamy and Negro slavery, but had not the wit to reason that emancipated plural wives might show more loyalty to their husbands (as manumitted slaves had to their masters in many instances) than to those responsible for their liberation. From the Mormon point of view, the resolution represented a direct challenge. By granting female suffrage, they could meet their opponents head on; Mormon women would thus vindicate the polygamic system. Mormon women could effectively silence the antipolygamous Gentiles, by proving their base calumnies unfounded. Furthermore, with the continued migration of Gentiles to Utah, especially with the renascent interest in western mining that followed the Civil War and the completion of the Union Pacific in 1869, the introduction of female suffrage would swell the ranks of loyal Mormon voters and assure the election of Mormon candidates and their legal control of territorial policy.[7]

Intelligent observers of Utah affairs, and even those who understood the implications of the resolution, realized how futile it would be to pass it. Who could expect the women of Utah to admit indirectly, by voting against Mormon measures and candidates, that they were whores or concubines and their children bastards? The author of a short notice on the Julian resolution that appeared in the *New York Times* was astute enough to realize that the measure would have little effect on polygamy. "A Mormon's 'wives,' " he wrote, "are as much under his control as the negroes of a Southern planter were under their master's control in the days of slavery; and therefore the proposition which was yesterday introduced into Congress to give the ballot to the women of Utah as a means of abolishing polygamy, is not of much account. It is well enough to pass the resolution, but we don't believe it will ever be worth anything."[8]

No doubt J. H. Beadle was exaggerating when he contended that in the congressional campaign of 1872, between George Q. Cannon, who had four wives, and General G. R. Maxwell, a Gentile, not one woman voted for Maxwell.[9] Nevertheless, Beadle's statement reflected a widely held popular belief, among Gentiles and Mormons alike, about patriarchal control of the female vote. Bishop Henry Lunt gloatingly made the Mormon position clear. "We are now," he said, "and always shall be, in favor of woman suffrage. The women of Utah vote, and they never desert the colors of the church, and whatever they do here they will do everywhere our principles and our institutions spread."[10] From the Mormon perspective, the decision to implement female suffrage was political and pragmatic. It had little or nothing to do with women's rights. But was the national movement to institute woman suffrage in Utah as naive as many of its defenders implied?

A brief glance at the record of Rep. George Julian provides us with a surprising answer. Julian was a radical woman-suffrage advocate throughout his life. In 1868 he had proposed a constitutional amendment that would have conferred the suffrage on women. He brought two other resolutions before the House in 1869. The first, H.R. 67, sought to extend the suffrage in the District of Columbia, and the other, H.R. 68, proposed a similar extension for the territories. Both resolutions envisioned the incorporation of woman suffrage in areas that were not yet states as a means of promoting a broader movement for woman suffrage. In February of 1871, Julian introduced a resolution to allow Victoria Woodhull and Isabella Beecher Hooker to use the House chambers for an evening meeting to debate the constitutionality of woman suffrage.[11] Clearly, his intent in proposing a Utah woman-suffrage bill was to further the cause of woman suffrage. He could not hope to get much support for such a plan, so he appealed to the antipolygamist group, which enjoyed a far broader though more obtuse following.

Ironically then, the Utah woman-suffrage bill of 1870 was the result of the disingenuous proposal of a female-suffrage advocate couched in the rhetoric of the antipolygamy hysteria. His proposal met with congressional rebuff, but there were many legislators who cherished the hope that such a political device would destroy polygamy. The idea was taken up by Mormon legislators for political and ideological reasons that were largely shared by female Mormons.

Outside Utah the 1870 law was viewed by women's-rights advocates as a signal victory for their cause;[12] Mormon women considered it primarily a defense of polygamy and maintained that "the Church of Jesus Christ of Latter-Day Saints . . . [is] the only reliable safeguard of female virtue and innocence."[13] Mormon women were called to a messianic role; they could only be thankful to the men who had elevated the status of women. They concluded that "if it was Brigham Young who gave them that unparalleled power, no matter what should be declared by the enemy as his motive, then he has done more for women than any man living. But Mormon apostles and representatives executed this grand charter of woman's rights . . . [and are therefore] deserving the acclamations of the women of America."[14]

Women realized that the initial granting of female suffrage had been a political consideration having little to do with women's rights. Indeed, in March of 1886 they declared "that the suffrage [was] *originally conferred upon us as a political privilege*."[15] Once they had the right to vote, however, regardless of its origin, they were determined to retain it.

The men of Congress did not see the matter in quite the same light. Beginning in 1862 with the Morrill Anti-Polygamy Law, a whole series of bills had been introduced in Congress with but one purpose—to extirpate the "peculiar institution" of polygamy. Most of them included provisions (after 1870) to disenfranchise women. However, the Judiciary Committee Bill (S. 1540), sponsored in 1873 by the Radical Republican senator from New Jersey, Frederick T. Frelinghuysen (1817–85), was a direct congressional response to the Utah Women's Suffrage Act of 1870 and is the only one, therefore, that need concern us here.[16] Sections 5 and 7 of the bill sought to exclude women jurors, and section 18 proposed the termination of female suffrage. Fines and imprisonment were recommended as measures to insure that aliens and women did not exercise the right of suffrage (section 22), and the immigration of all aliens "living in bigamy or polygamy" was proscribed (section 15). The bill also undermined the position of Mormon women by providing for the repeal of An Act Concerning the Property of Married Persons (Utah, 1872). There was no debate or contention whatsoever regarding the provisions of this bill. The consensus seems to have been that the experiment George Julian had recommended had been a complete failure. Congress was disinclined to give credence to the claim of Mrs. Emeline B. Wells that although "it is currently reported that Mormon women vote as they are told by their husbands I most emphatically deny the assertion. . . . Our women vote with the same freedom that characterizes any class of people in the most conscientious acts of their lives."[17]

But the consciences of Mormon women had not vindicated the moral assumptions that Congress had harbored about the purity of womanhood. Their evangelical-romantic faith in the omnipotent power of women to reform all evils, to raise themselves and their masculine oppressors from the mire of polygamy, had not been justified. Was it possible that women did not find polygamy as degrading and oppressive as male congressmen did? Was it also possible that marital relationships, especially those involving children, were at once more resilient, more plastic, and more durable than these advocates of strict monogamy ever dreamed? These questions do not seem to have occurred to those who became the champions of monogamous civilization.

S. 1540 proposed another idealistic solution to the complex issue of polygamy, while at the same time somewhat vindictively denouncing the woman-suffrage solution earlier championed in Congress. The new way to salvation for Utah still lay through women, but now an extension of the divorce law of the territory was suggested. The critical section of the bill was section 11, which proposed

> that any woman now or hereafter holding the relation of spouse, or consort, and not that of a lawful wife, to any man who at the time cohabits with another woman as his wife, spouse, or consort, may file her petition in the district court . . . asking to be discharged from such relation, and . . . the said court may . . . adjudge and decree her discharged and freed from such relation as aforesaid, and may adjudge and decree to her the possession and control of her minor child or children, together with such portion of the estate and property of the said man to whom she held the said relation as shall, under all the circumstances, be equitable and just for the support of herself and minor child or children . . . and upon the entry of such decree the said woman . . . shall be a *feme sole: Provided, nevertheless,* That nothing in this section contained shall be construed to have the effect of recognizing the validity or legal effect of any dual or plural marriage, or to repeal any laws in relation to divorce; and nothing in this act shall be held to repeal, annul, or change any existing laws against polygamy or bigamy.[18]

The debate on this section of the bill was fierce even though trammeled by semantic fencing over the meaning of the terms "spouse" and "consort." Little concern was expressed for the plural wives in a polygamous relationship; the primary object sought was the protection of the rights of the first or "legal" wife. The position of the Congress would have been risible had it not been for the serious consequences their action might have had for polygamously married women in Utah. They sought to regulate and abate an institution that, from a legal point of view, did not exist. Most of the concern raised by the bill revolved about the assumptions that it would provide de facto legal recognition to polygamy and that it would create a strict parity among all the plural wives of one husband, thus undermining the proprietorial rights of the first or legal wife. Only one senator seems to have observed its effect upon plural wives and children. The proposed bill, he pointed out, "must bastardize the children. The very foundation of it is that the woman who seeks it, the woman who brings the suit is not a lawful wife but an unlawful one. . . . What is the child of an unlawful connection? He is not legitimate."[19]

The men and women who were involved in polygamous marriages were not considered honest human beings by these legislators. Congressmen were concerned only with the ideal of monogamy, not with protecting the rights of plural wives. Women were pawns in a struggle between two competing marital systems: first it was proposed that they be given privileges as inducements to proper behavior; then, when they failed to perform properly, Congress recommended that those privileges be taken from them. S. 1540 proposed to take away the rights of woman suffrage and the equal claim of every plural wife to her joint husband's property. In return for these sacrifices, polygamous women were given the opportunity to declare publicly that they were prostitutes, or at best concubines, and their children illegitimate! The only inducement to such rash behavior was the promise of a divorce from the husband and the payment of alimony and child support. The senators seem to have completely overlooked the existence of a liberal divorce statute in the Utah Territory (1852) and the fact that divorces were available to polygamous wives through the church, the proceedings of which were much more discreet and private. The effect of most such legislation, then, was to attack the virtue, character, and rights of plural wives, while mouthing the platitudes of deep concern about the oppression and enslavement of women. Congressmen did not overtly argue against the rights of women, but the effect of most anti-Mormon legislation was to limit very strictly the rights of Mormon women.

Perhaps the masculine fears generated by the woman-suffrage movement were partly responsible for this response. Here was a group of women who had the vote, could possess property apart from their husbands, and could relatively easily free themselves from a matrimonial bond they found onerous. These women had not behaved like "true women"; they had value systems that were different from those of the majority of *male* Americans. The whole Mormon experiment was a dangerous precedent and a direct challenge to the monogamous system; but the spectacle of women ignoring—flouting—a value system that was considered her biological destiny, inherent in the very blood that flowed in her womb, was most disturbing. The attempts of Congress to deal with Mormonism, therefore, insisted upon stripping women of the rights they had gained in Utah because they were not "respectable" women; they were deviants, who by their behavior had rendered themselves nonwomen. To deprive these women of rights they had been granted under Mormonism would at once remove a bad example from the purview of the woman-suffrage advocates and, it was hoped, lead to the reintegration of these deviant women into the ranks of good, true, moral women everywhere. Restrictive congressional bills were a way of achieving salvation for women (not only Mormon women) in an ethicotheological system whose terms were entirely male determined.

Mormons, for their part, used their wives as weapons against the Gentiles. This was especially true, as we have seen, of the woman-suffrage act of 1870. Another way in which Mormons used women's rights was to encourage proper behavior from polygamous wives. They were not so very different from their Gentile enemies in this respect. An excellent example of this was the way the divorce statute was used in Utah.

In Box Elder County, during the period 1856–69, nearly three-fourths of the divorce actions had been initiated by women. Although women remained in the majority, figures for the entire territory for the years 1867–86 indicate that only some 55.4 percent of the divorce actions were brought by women.[20] Divorces granted to women during these years were primarily for desertion, cruelty, or failure to provide. In the most nebulous area of the divorce code, "incompatibility of temper," 57 percent of the divorces were granted to men.[21] The liberal provisions of the Utah divorce law, in practice, do not seem to have benefited female as much as they did male Mormons. During this same period, the other frontier states of the West averaged 72 percent for female-initiated divorce suits. The New England states and New York averaged 70 percent, and Indiana, whose divorce law most closely paralleled that of Utah, averaged 71 percent.[22]

Although the intent of the law was liberal in Utah, federal interference, as in the case of woman suffrage and property rights, only served to render nugatory whatever efforts had been made to protect plural wives. The key decision in this realm came in 1874, when Congress passed a law providing that the defendant in a divorce action had the right to request the removal of the case from the probate court (the court of jurisdiction as provided in the 1852 Utah divorce law) to the district court, or from territorial to federal jurisdiction.[23]

On the face of it, this law appeared to be beneficial to plural wives, especially in light of the fate of territorial divorce legislation in the 1870s. The 1852 divorce statute contained an amorphous residence clause that allowed the granting of divorce to any resident or person "who wishes to become one." Procedures for notifying defendants of divorce actions pending against them were very sketchily set forth and even more desultorily observed. Decrees could be issued in the absence of the defendant at the discretion of the court. Consequently, during the years 1875–78, Utah became the mecca of those who sought immediate, marginally legal separation from their spouses. Most divorces in these years were granted to Gentiles, the overwhelming majority of whom had never even set foot in Utah. In Box Elder County, for instance, in the years 1874–76, 62 percent of the divorces granted were to individuals who did not reside in Utah and who were not members of the Mormon church.[24]

No self-respecting Mormon woman would have been likely to press her case in these courts during the years 1875–78. Of course, Mormons had the alternative of seeking church divorces. Although I have discovered no evidence of a higher percentage of women than men seeking such church actions, both the ideological assumptions of Mormonism, which rigorously insisted that a woman's salvation was totally dependent upon the moral condition of her husband and her obedience to him and that the marriage partners were linked together for eternity, and the fact that civil divorce could only reach marriages for time suggest the greater advantage to be gained, especially for women but certainly for all Mormons, in procuring church divorces. This predilection was partly countered by attempts of Mormon leaders to curb the divorce rate.

It would appear, then, that the federal government in the years 1873–74 was attempting to open another channel for the rescue of oppressed Mormon women, one that would be both morally beyond reproach and beyond the power of Mormon officials to hinder. The provisions of the Judiciary Committee bill (S. 1540) concerning the divorce law provided a new inducement to encourage plural wives to seek separation—the right to child support and alimony. Although this bill was not passed, it did give some indication of the tenor of congressional feeling on the matter. The position of Mormon opponents was clear, or so it appeared. If they controlled the judicial process, things might be different. The 1874 law, which provided for the removal of divorce actions from the probate courts, seemed to provide an impartial tribunal or, perhaps more accurately, an antipolygamy one. It was perhaps inevitable that in these years a test case would come before the courts, a case that revealed not so much the differences between Mormon and Gentile conceptions of marriage and divorce as the tragic position of Mormon women caught between the conflicting claims and expectations of two antagonistic groups of men.

The plaintiff in the trial was the beautiful and ambitious Ann Eliza (Webb) Young, who, though styling herself "wife number nineteen," was in fact Brigham Young's twenty-seventh wife. The defendant, of course, was the "Lion of the Lord," the richest and most powerful Mormon of his time. The suit, which was commenced on 28 July 1873, sought twenty thousand dollars in court costs plus, in Ann's own words, an agreement that "after our legal separation, he might be ordered to support myself and children suitably; and that for that purpose the sum of two hundred thousand dollars might be set aside from his estate."[25]

Ann Eliza was probably not the long-suffering martyr she claimed to be in her court appearances, but the progress of this protracted case made it quite obvious what Mormon women could expect both from the federal system of district courts in the territory and from the husbands they dared openly defy. The case also served resounding notice that the doctrine associated with the Freylinghuysen bill (S. 1540) was not widely accepted in Gentile circles and that the hopes of the more optimistic opponents of polygamy, who believed that a series of divorces and subsequent alimony payments would drive polygamists into bankruptcy and ruin, were totally groundless. In a case filled with irony, Ann Eliza, probably because she sought an impartial trial or anticipated a strong antipolygamy bias in the Gentile court, moved to have her case heard in the district court as early as 1873. The motion was denied, but with the passage of the federal law in 1874, removing divorce cases in Utah from probate to district court jurisdiction, and the parallel decision of the Utah Supreme Court in the case of *Cast* v. *Cast* in May 1874, it was inevitable that the case should be heard in the federal court.[26]

Brigham Young also requested that the case be heard by the district court in the summer of 1874. A series of federal judges made various tentative rulings on the case, but all faced a dilemma: they wanted to see polygamy destroyed (a desire that compassed the personal ruin of Brigham Young); yet at the same time, they refused to recognize the validity of any polygamous marriage. Brigham took full advantage of the confusion of the court. He claimed that Ann Eliza had never been legally divorced from her former husband and that he was at the time still married to his first or legal wife, Mary Ann (Angell) Young. As his claim was summarized by the plaintiff, "He admitted his marriage with me, after the custom of the Latter-Day Saints, but denied that the marriage was legal, in any sense of the laws of the land."[27]

In essence, his claims were a challenge to federal or civil authority; only the church would be recognized as the ultimate authority in matters of divorce and marriage. Furthermore, the affairs of the church were beyond the authority of civil and especially federal-Gentile officials. Ann Eliza had not been divorced by the church; therefore, her divorce was not valid in the church, and she could not be legally remarried under ecclesiastical sanction. Because a church marriage (assuming it were polygamous) was not recognized as legally valid by the U.S. government, the effect of Brigham's argument was that he was neither legally nor ecclesiastically married to Ann Eliza.

The final decision, which was handed down by Justice Schaeffer on 27 April 1877, was a savage attack upon women living in polygamy and left the plural wives of Utah without legal status and without *any* rights vis-à-vis their husbands. In this regard, although his rationale was different, the federal magistrate's opinion accorded with that of the polygamist. In the conclusion of his decision, Schaeffer wrote: "The plaintiff is not entitled to a decree of divorce. The alleged marriage was and is polygamous and therefore null and void. During the time the plaintiff was with the defendant as his polygamous wife she was serving him as a menial servant, and would be entitled to reasonable compensation for her services. But, having received in this instance in the form of alimony *pendente lite* more than such services are shown by the proof to be reasonably worth, she should go hence without further compensation."²⁸

The *New York Times* accurately noted the effect of this decision on polygamously married women of the territory. A woman in the position of Ann Eliza (in fact *all* plural wives), it was noted with mordant irony, "cannot obtain a divorce, because she was never legally married. . . . she was a wife *de facto*; she is denied a divorce and all other relief by the court, because she was not the wife *de jure*. So it seems that a woman may be married in point of fact, but not in law."²⁹ The *Times* correspondent concluded: "This decision . . . does, however, place a vast majority of Mormon women in the category of debased menials. They are entitled to wages; beyond this, they have no more rights in law than the inmates of a Turkish harem. Several thousand women, white, and of average intelligence, are remanded to the position of concubines with lawful claims for wages."³⁰

This was the kind of treatment Mormon women could expect at the hands of federal officials if they were intrepid enough to place their reputations on the line, open their private lives to public scrutiny, and suffer the obloquy of Gentiles and Mormon calumniation. Within the church of Latter-Day Saints, what degree of respect for their rights could plural wives expect? If they followed the dictates of the church they would be blessed, but only within the bounds set by the Melchizedek priesthood. Within the church, from its very outset, at least theoretically, women had been allowed to vote. They were, however, never allowed to become members of the priesthood.³¹ This was a doctrinal point and established practice from which Mormons did not deviate. They publicly proclaimed that "it is a fact well known, that we have not had a female preacher in our connection, for we do not believe in a female priesthood."³²

Even in church ceremonies and rituals the separation of the inferior female from the superior male was common practice. In the secret ritual of the endowment ceremony, for instance, it was asserted that men entered the temple first and were given arcane names that they were forbidden to reveal to their wives. Women were required to tell their secret celestial names to their husbands so that they could be claimed by their lords in the celestial world.³³ In religious matters, the counsel of women was considered of little value.

The real fear behind the Mormon attack on woman's central religious role among evangelical sectarians in the Gentile world was a concern lest women usurp the male role. Brigham Young expressed this fear most succinctly in his hackneyed assertion that "when you see a woman with ragged skirts, you may know she wears the unmentionables, for she is doing the man's business, and has not time to cut off the rags that are hanging around her. From this time henceforth you may know what woman wears her husband's pants."[34]

It was indeed in the field of women's fashions that the attitude of Mormon men toward women was most clearly expressed. Nineteenth-century sexual ideology held that women were only slightly lower than the seraphim, but their mode of dress and their actions showed them to be far from angelic. The attempt to control feminine fashion, in a society seeking to purify itself of all sin, was a major vehicle of suppressing asocial sexual behavior and insuring a tight control over community morality. Significantly, the major concern with women's fashion was in the 1870s and was coterminous with the concern over women's rights as manifested in suffrage, property holding, and divorce. Mormon attitudes toward fashion thus represented in microcosm their attitudes toward women and were eloquently expressive of the position and status of females in Mormon society.

Mormons, although concerned about economy, were more concerned with the seductive and contraceptive aspects of female fashion than anything else. In essence, the expense of clothing plural wives militated against the less affluent and tended to keep the monopoly of celestial wives among the more established members of the ecclesiastical hierarchy. Those who possessed the advantage of polygamy were not likely to democratize the system so that everyone could afford the status and beatitude of numerous wives.[35] The Mormon attack on fashion, therefore, concentrated on the sexually aggressive female and her challenge to patriarchal hegemony.

The typical literary device employed in attacks on fashion was counterpoint. Woman was contrasted with angel, real with ideal. This type of rhetoric is best exemplified by Brigham Young, who was greatly. allured by feminine dress and whose utterances exude an impotent rage at the teasing titillation of women beyond his power to control. In the mid-1870s, Young asked his hearers to consider an angel. "Do you think," he asked, "she would have a great, big peck measure of flax done up like hair on the back of the head? Nothing of the kind. Would she have a dress dragging two or three yards behind? Nothing of the kind. Would she have a great, big . . . a Grecian or Dutch—[the "Grecian bend"—an exaggerated bustle fashion]—Well, no matter what you call it, you know what I mean. . . . She would be neat and nice. . . . There is nothing needless about her."[36] He advised Mormon women to "Dress your children and yourselves in that comely, angelic manner that, were an angel to visit you, you would not feel ashamed."[37]

More explicitly, however, fashions were provocative and seductive. The aggressiveness of these attacks on fashion and the fear that lay behind them were clearly revealed in the journal entry of a simple Mormon: "Brother Brigham spoke of the folly and indecency of the present fashions, said that some of the Daughters of Zion acted like Damn Fools and the Whores of London or Paris would be ashamed to act like they did, said it would serve them right for someone to take a knife and slit their dresses from their navel to their knees."[38] Heber C. Kimball concurred. These "Gentile" fashions were the creations of "the ludest [*sic*] characters: they eminated [*sic*] from Hoarhouses [*sic*], Brothels, etc."[39]

All this concern about female fashion as a vehicle of seduction was largely a projection of male sexual aggression upon the objects of that aggression. As the knife imagery in the quotation from Brigham Young cited above indicates, much of the argument took on a vindictive tone; women who dared to dress provocatively would get what they deserved. Much of this rhetoric was the agonized cries of men who, under a strict patriarchal system, had assumed the role of moral arbiters for their society. They were obsessed with controlling their wills and subjugating their sex drives to rational control, and they found it increasingly difficult to do so. So women were admonished to be modest, in the futile hope that this would make it easier for the male to live up to his moral obligations. Such was the tenor of Brigham Young's appeal to the women of Mormondom: "if we ask you to make your dresses a little shorter, do not be extravagant and cut them so short that we can see the tops of your stockings. Bring them down to the tops of your shoes, and have them so that you can walk and clear the dust, and do not expose your persons. . . . conduct yourselves, in the strictest sense of the word, in chastity."[40]

Insofar as men's fashions were attacked (I have found only one case in which they were), the excesses involved were also blamed on the sexual aggression of women. Thus we find President Young inveighing against "those fornication pantaloons, made on purpose for whores to button up in front. My pantaloons button up here (showing how) where they belong, that my secrets, that God has given me, should not be exposed."[41] Modesty was all; impudence meant temptation and ultimately fornication, and was a direct threat to the stability of Mormon society. So, Brigham concluded, you must "keep your secrets secret, and hide your bodies and preserve your bodies. Now, if a whore comes along and turns up her clothes, don't turn up yours and go through the streets."[42]

Feminine fashions, Mormons felt, also represented a direct threat to established male-female role behavior. Women were expected to be primarily breeders; yet certain fashions they had adopted, it was felt, reduced their reproductive capacities. Behind this aspect of the male Mormon's reaction to female dress lay a nagging suspicion that women were using tight lacing as a contraceptive device. Was it possible that they really didn't want to be mothers? Such behavior would completely undermine the system of celestial kingdoms and postmortem power reserved for faithful male Mormons. This could not be allowed to happen. The fear of self-induced sterility, the ungodly thwarting of the divine purpose of sexual intercourse, was best expressed in John D. Lee's rendition of remarks Heber C. Kimball made in the late 1850s on women's lingerie: "Th[e]y lace themselves up and carry such a load of Peticoats [*sic*] across their hips that it destroys [the]ir Kidneys and the st[r]ength of their loins and causes them to dege[nera]te and thereby destroys their very existen[ce], which is [page torn] for without child[ren] [they soon would cease] [page torn]. [Su]ch folly and extravagance must be done away [with] and fashion after the order and council of Heaven [substituted], etc."[43]

If implied female renunciation of the maternal role roused Mormon wrath, the abortive attempt to introduce the bloomer costume in the 1850s was even less welcome. This represented an obvious manifestation of what Brigham Young so tritely termed "wearing the pants" in the family. As an eyewitness described the beginning of this fashion, "Today the first 'Bloomer' made her appearance flaunting through the streets puzzling the casual observer to properly determine the sex."[44]

In fashion, then, as in all other matters bearing upon women's role and rights in Utah, Mormon and Gentile men found themselves at odds on details but in perfect agreement on the ideal; woman was to be a true woman, a breeder, a nurturer, a force for purity and goodness in society. Though these terms were defined differently by Mormons and their opponents, the only really serious difference involved was that over the nature of the marriage relationship.

Mormon patriarchalism was more thoroughgoing than male dominance in nineteenth-century Gentile America, but it was largely a difference of degree rather than kind. Whereas the ideal true woman dominated domestic and religious life in Protestant America, Mormon women were excluded from the priesthood and stripped of the moral power derived from motherhood and piety. Mormonism followed the assumptions inherent in the relationship between the sexes in nineteenth-century America to their logical conclusion: because woman's main function was maternal and domestic, she should be confined to those tasks alone (or perhaps to tasks that would free male labor for more important pursuits); her energies should not be wasted on political or sacerdotal duties that were the proper masculine sphere. That polygamy endured for over half a century, until it was abolished as a doctrine of the Latter-Day Saints by the Woodruff Manifesto in 1890,[45] suggests that Gentile critics were both repelled and attracted by the "twin relic of barbarism" and that it was but a distorted mirror image of the imperfections inherent in their own sexual relationships.

Ironically, though women were ideologically excluded under Mormonism from the major sources of power they wielded in nineteenth-century America at large, they achieved significant gains under Mormon polygamy. Some gains were consciously granted as a means of combating Gentile opponents and correcting the abuses in the anomalous legal status of polygamy: female suffrage, the right of women to their property, and a relatively liberal divorce policy. Others were unconscious aspects of the marital system itself: the apparent decline in the maternal death rate in childbirth, a division of domestic labor, and the social security involved in provision for wives in their old age. Also, for women married to polygamists with over five wives, there was a decline (compared to the national average) in the average number of pregnancies a woman underwent.

But a polygamous wife had little chance to exert any power or agitate for rights. The treatment she could expect from Gentiles was much less attractive than her situation under polygamy. She had either to remain under polygamy as at best a breeder and a supplement to a scanty work force, and more frequently as an inferior, a seductive threat to male supremacy; or to declare herself a whore and her children bastards, and give up all hope of support and all legitimate claim to happiness and life itself. It is not surprising that Mormon women, caught between their polygamous lords and Gentile blandishments, should have chosen to remain subject "Angels," preferring the chthonic deities they served to what seemed to them a vast uncertain future in a godless and hostile universe.

Part IV 🌱 "In the Eden of Heart-Love": Sexuality and Sex Roles of the Oneida Community in Ideology and Practice

Introduction 🌿 The Perfect Love of God: John Humphrey Noyes, Founder of the Oneida Community

It is that we are never so defenseless against suffering as when we love, never so helplessly unhappy as when we have lost our loved object or its love.

—Freud, *Civilization and Its Discontents*

Let him that is pure in the flesh, not grow proud of it, knowing that it was from another that he received the gift of continence.

—New Testament Apocrypha: 1 Clement 17:38

*O*n 25 October 1847 the Windham County Court, meeting in Putney, Vermont, served a writ for the arrest of John Humphrey Noyes on two counts of adultery and "adulterous fornication." With the aid of his lawyers, Noyes and a small group of his Perfectionist followers fled to New York State, fearing the "outbreak of lynch law among the barbarians of Putney."[1] Some accused Noyes of cowardice, but a letter written by his wife, Harriet Holton, provides evidence that the situation of the Perfectionists in Putney was indeed ominous. "We were threatened with mobs," she wrote,

> and became a by word and the offscouring of the earth. . . . On the 26th of Nov. John left home and went to Brattleboro, purposing to make an offer to the people to give up his bonds [his brother-in-law, John R. Miller, had posted bail against his appearance in County Court in April], and stay in jail until his trial, and that there should be no further offence against the laws, if they would leave the remainder of our Association unmolested. Mr. Mead and Mr. Bradley, the lawyers to whom he made this proposal, said this course

would not answer, for Mr. and Mrs. Cragin [George and Mary] and some others were as obnoxious as himself. So he agreed that all persons who did not belong to Putney should leave, if they would let the remainder continue in peace. The leaders said they were satisfied with this move.[2]

Despite assurances to the contrary, the withdrawal of the central figures of the Putney Community did not appease the pious citizens of the town. Noyes received news of the state of affairs there in a letter from his brother, George: "We have been engaged in a frightful spiritual *melée*— Your departure was the signal for letting slip all the dogs of war. . . . no one is as yet hurt . . . [but] the real appetite for revenge still goes unfed— and hence the uneasy continuation of the excitement. . . . The only thing that will appease them henceforth will be our penitent return to the isolation of selfishness."[3]

Noyes's Putney Community, established in 1841, annoyed the orthodox townspeople because it violated both religious and social proprieties. It was particularly offensive to community moral standards because of its peculiar sexual arrangements, the system Noyes called "complex marriage," which was instituted among the communitarians in 1846. Complex marriage was a pantagamous arrangement whereby all the members of the community were considered united by marriage ties. The technique of "male continence" (discovered by Noyes in 1845), which prohibited male ejaculation during the sex act, assured virtually unlimited intercourse with no risk of pregnancy for the female. Such a frank attempt to institutionalize an erotic sexuality, to separate the "amative" from the "propagative" aspects of sex, as Noyes expressed it, naturally antagonized the local populace. It is hardly surprising that he was forced to flee Putney for New York State, where he established the Oneida Community (1848–79) on land in Madison and Lennox counties.[4]

"Father" Noyes played the central role in the shaping of the theological and ideological presuppositions upon which this theocratic utopian community was based. As a charismatic, elitist, and authoritarian leader, he had the dominant voice in decisions affecting the daily life and social practices of the community. It is therefore to the experience of John Humphrey Noyes that we must turn if we are to begin to understand the genesis and development of sexual ideology and behavior at Oneida.[5]

John was the middle child (b. 1811) in a family of nine; his father was forty-seven, his mother thirty, when he was born. His father, John, Sr., was a rather aloof, practical, serious man of affairs who established demanding standards of behavior for his sons and instilled in them an inveterate anxiety about temporal success. Although he was trained in the ministry, his faith became moribund, and the vital center of religion in the home became maternal. John Humphrey's mother, Polly Hayes, was a strong-willed, often overbearing Yankee woman, with a highly idealistic and deeply religious nature. She was the emotional mainstay of the family, especially when John, Sr., was away on business, or at Washington, D.C., during his service as a congressman (1815–17). He was away from home frequently during the formative early years of his son's life, and this absence, together with the presence of three elder sisters, must certainly have brought John very much under female supervision during his childhood.[6]

Noyes's father was not a particularly strong figure in the home, and his son does not seem to have been very close to him. Of the J. H. Noyes letters still available, a few are addressed to his elder sisters and more to his mother, but only two to his father. In a typical letter to his mother when he was ten years old, he wrote, "N.B.; tell Papa that I am studying Cicero and that I have got to the fourth book of Virgil. I must leave a little space for the news that the girls told me I must write."[7] This suggests that there was a very real distance between John Humphrey and his father, a distance bridged only by the intermediary function of his mother. There is also an almost pathetic attempt to impress the remote father figure with his scholastic progress and success, to demonstrate an achievement his father would understand. This desire to achieve was poignantly illustrated in the postscript to the same letter: "N.B.—Handwriting superexcellent."[8]

But it was largely a frustrated desire; the tension and distance between the elder Noyes and his son were exacerbated by the latter's choice of a religious career. Though his father apparently hoped John Humphrey would become a businessman and politician like himself, his mother hoped he would become a minister. Initially, even though there was an emotional distance between them, Noyes seems to have identified with his father. He attended Dartmouth (1826–29) and studied law with his uncle for a year; but after his conversion at a revival in 1831, he decided to become a minister. Significantly, he had attended the revival at his mother's request.[9] His decision to enter Andover Seminary in 1831 represented a victory for his mother's ideals and a rejection of his father's course.

Noyes's decision to follow his mother's wishes and his rejection of his father were the culmination of an internal struggle between faith (represented by his mother) and the world (represented by his father). In a postadolescent identity crisis, the revival meeting served as a rite of passage; Noyes turned his back on the values of the mundane father and embraced those of the celestial mother. His own account of the episode makes this apparent. "I looked upon religion," he tells us,

> *at least I endeavored to do so*, as a sort of phrenzy to which all were liable, and feared lest I should be caught in the snare. However, my

aversion to it was such, and my love of the pleasures of the world so strong, that I concluded to yield to the force of circumstances which seemed to summon me to the spot; and trusting in my own strength to resist the assaults of the Lord I attended the meeting. . . . I knew that Mother was exceedingly anxious that I should receive the word, but I told her plainly that she would be disappointed. She asked me why I went, and I replied, to please her.[10]

Obviously, Noyes had internalized many of the values of his father—worldliness, a certain canny wariness of religious cant, and a pragmatic outlook on life—but his decision to follow the path marked out by his mother represented a rejection of his father and an identification with his mother as a new, spiritual role model. It also represented a partial suppression of that part of his personality which he owed to his father's influence, which although never completely suppressed was effectively guided and controlled by the characteristics he derived from maternal influence. His struggle against the influence of his distant, demanding father was a formidable one, but it seems to have been facilitated by his turning toward his mother. In his confession of the struggle sustained to "get religion" he makes this evident. "The first duty which presented itself" (in humbling his pride to accept religion), he informs us, "was that of *overcoming my fear of man*, and though it was like cutting off a right hand God enabled me to resolve and execute the resolution of *communicating to Mother my determination.*"[11]

The distance between father and son and the awe and fear the paternal figure inspired in the son were further complicated by the character and habits of the elder Noyes. John, Sr., had returned from Washington, D.C., addicted to liquor, and gradually alcohol became a serious problem for him. A petition on behalf of the Noyes children living in Putney in 1837 suggests that his relationship to his children had become even more attenuated after his return from Washington. He was asked to stop drinking in order to avoid publicly disgracing the family. "We can by no means," the petitioners concluded, "feel that confidence in you as a counsellor and guide of the family which your former character was wont to inspire."[12]

Although we can only speculate, the crapulence of his father may well have made it virtually impossible for Noyes to identify with him effectively and to internalize his worldly, materialistic values. At the same time, failure to live up to his father's code, to "be a man" in his father's terms, could well have generated a dual sense of inadequacy and guilt. On the one hand, as a male, he identified with his father and shared the guilt of religious infidelity and drunkenness with him. A sense of failure and low self-esteem in his male identity may well have accompanied the consequent shifting of the burden of moral sustenance of the family to the maternal parent. On the other hand, he rejected his father's value system and identified with his mother as a responsible moral person. This identification made it impossible for him ever to satisfy his father's expectations, to be accepted as a competent adult male.

The crisis in the relationship between father and son came in the early 1830s. The conflict between his father's mundane pragmatism and the otherworldly idealism Noyes had derived from his mother was clearly the source of the difficulty. In a letter, Noyes addressed the distant, disapproving father figure:

> It is now years since I have had any claim upon you for support on the ground of relationship. What you have given I have received as a gratuity with thankfulness both to you and to my Father in heaven. If you are not interested in the object for which I live, I cannot ask or expect you to assist me. That object is that the will of God may be done on earth as it is in heaven. If the object is a good one and you consider me a person fitted to further it, you will not account money bestowed upon me as thrown away. It will not perhaps yield a profit so immediate and tangible as that of bank stock, but it will help the building of the kingdom in which you hope to dwell forever.[13]

Although his father continued to afford support, Noyes seems to have felt that he had been spiritually disowned. He noted in a letter to his mother that "Father fears to involve himself in my doings"; that, in effect, he had been disowned.[14] In 1837, living again under his father's roof, he revealed the agony and disappointment he felt at his father's refusal to accept him as a man on his own terms. "I am wintering at my father's," he wrote a Perfectionist friend, "on such terms as you may suppose must exist between me and an unbeliever, receiving friendly treatment as a man, but not known as a son of God, and a brother of the saints."[15] Noyes's feeling of rejection, of alienation from his father, made him more dependent on the female members of his family for emotional sustenance, and rather insecure in his sense of identity and autonomy.

Once his decision was made to follow his mother's wishes, rejecting the paternal role model, he readily conceived the idea that his pious mother had sinned greatly in marrying an unbeliever. For, "devout as she may have been herself. . . . she connected herself with an ungodly man, and so gave up half at least of the education of her children to the prince of this world. If she taught us to fear God, the partner she took taught us by example and precept to worship money and live for this world."[16] This attitude may well have been the result of his mother's own attitude toward her husband, which had been absorbed by the perceptive John Humphrey.

Noyes saw his father, then, as a man whom his devout mother could not (or at least should not) have respected. That part of himself which identified with his father, who represented the antithesis of his mother's ideal, was to be rejected at whatever cost, if he did not wish to risk losing his mother's respect and love. From the beginning, but especially after his effective disownment by his father, the strongest emotional ties of the young John H. Noyes were with his mother. His relationship to his mother was, not surprisingly, intensely Oedipal. He saw himself attempting to achieve autonomy from her while unable to overcome his need for her emotional support. Yet, though he needed her so desperately, he felt his desire for closeness frustrated by her refusal to accept him either as an adult or as a surrogate for his father as her moral superior.[17] It was probably his inability to identify with his father effectively, and his Oedipal feelings toward his mother, which later led Noyes to reject the procreative aspects of sexuality and which convinced him that virginity in both men and women was a desirable thing. This fastidiousness about sex is reflected in a comment about his boyhood friend, Kidder Green, whom he found "inclined to give way a little too much to the *libido corporis*."[18]

For a boy who was affectively close to his mother and whose father represented aggressive, amoral forces, the conception of a relationship with another male as purer and better than a heterosexual one was probably natural. At times, Noyes's relationships with other males, and his expressed feelings about them, seemed to border on a latent homosexuality. In the early years of Perfectionism, Noyes became close to several young men. He spoke figuratively of Chauncey Dutton going "hand in hand with me into the 'dark valley' of conviction," and asserted emotionally that "our hearts were knit together with a love 'passing the love of women.'"[19] Of James Boyle, another early associate, Noyes wrote: "I respected and loved him. . . . My feelings were especially tender in relation to him."[20] His relationship with David Harrison of Meriden, Connecticut, was apparently more substantial. Harrison left his wife and children to spend six weeks in a hotel in New Haven with Noyes. As Noyes disingenuously described the incident, "*He* proposed, without any suggestion from me to leave his family and go out with me."[21] They were, not unexpectedly, "in much outward contempt, but in much inward content. . . . We perceived," Noyes wrote, "much excitement and distress among many who beheld us in these strange circumstances; and especially among Harrison's friends and neighbors at Meriden. Many things were said and done to seduce or frighten us from what we knew to be the will of God."[22]

Noyes's relationship with his mother, the prototype for his relationships with other women, remained ambiguous. If she had compromised herself by marrying an infidel, how valuable was her ideal? Ironically, her guilt in her son's mind became greater than that of his rejected father. His closeness to her intensified his feelings of betrayal and convinced him that women were less moral than men. Noyes's authoritarian personality was at least in part a reflection of his realization that although he had pursued his mother's ideals in order to secure her affection, he could never be sure of her love. He remained at the core uncertain of the value of his choice of faith over the world. Consequently, he remained both emotionally dependent upon his mother and, because of his uncertainty of her love, rather afraid of her.

After attending Andover Theological Seminary for a year, Noyes transferred to Yale Theological School in 1832 to escape what he considered the complacency, the deadness of spirit, at Andover. He received his license to preach the next year and spent a trial period preaching at North Salem, New York. Upon his return to New Haven it became apparent that he held radical theological views, and on 20 February 1834 he publicly announced that he was radically perfect, incapable of committing sin. His license to preach was rescinded by Yale, but he continued to spread his doctrine from the pulpit of the New Haven Free Church and through itinerant preaching. Thus, New Haven Perfectionism was born.[23]

At the root of this Perfectionist theology (with its strident insistence on the worth and infallibility of the individual) was Noyes's uncertain sense of identity, as well as his lifelong struggle for autonomy from his family. This insecure sense of identity also contributed to his desire to avoid emotional dependency on woman in a sexual relationship.

His desire for autonomy assumed central importance in his life in 1833–34, when he was twenty-two years old. The crisis was intensified by the rejection by his father, by the ignominious loss of his license to preach, and by his relationship to his first convert to Perfectionism, Abigail Merwin. He felt strongly attracted to Abigail (eight years his senior), a pious, quick-witted woman. Just as in his relationship with his mother, he felt vulnerable. From Abigail, too, he hoped for love, but he hesitated to declare his feelings because he feared rejection. As a defense against this insecurity, he projected an extremely self-sufficient persona, masking his fears by an apparent indifference to others. In situations in which he had no need to fear the loss of others' loyalty through his own deep-felt inadequacies, he became autocratic. His relationship with Abigail reinforced his insecurity and the fear of rejection that had its origin in his relationship with his mother, and led to the establishment of a pattern that most of his interpersonal relations (whether with males or females) would thereafter follow—he had a neurotic, almost paranoiac, fear of betrayal.[24]

John probably never declared his love for Abigail, but he seems to have assumed that they were lovers. When he went to New York City in June 1834, Abigail and the members of her family withdrew from the Perfectionist church he had established in New Haven. In New York, John underwent a *Walpurgisnacht* struggle between flesh and spirit, all the while depending on God to provide. Abigail's brother-in-law, Everard Benjamin, paid John's final hotel bill and brought him back to New Haven. Abigail, although she accompanied Benjamin, did not reveal herself to John. Again he had been betrayed by a woman. There could be little doubt that Abigail was the force behind his "rescue," and as such represented a dire threat to his desire to be autonomous. His description of the episode is a very revealing one: "Her reasons for keeping her presence from my knowledge I never ascertained. The circumstances, however, chimed in suspiciously with the spiritual impressions which I received concerning her in N.Y., and I began to anticipate the division which followed."[25] Those "spiritual impressions" as he described them took on almost mythic overtones: "I saw her standing, as it were, on the pinnacle of the universe, in the glory of an angel; but a voice from which I could not turn away, pronounced her title—'Satan transformed into an angel of light.'"[26]

Abigail's marriage, early in January 1837, prompted John's famous "Battle Axe Letter" of 15 January 1837, in which he first set forth his theories on marriage. Concluding the letter, he gave notice that "my claim on her cuts directly across the marriage covenant of the world, and God knows the end."[27] In December of 1837, Abigail was separated from her husband. This served only to increase John's impression that God had intended her for him, but that some mysterious obstacle (her family, no doubt) had prevented their union. He wrote to her in an attempt to reestablish their relationship but she never replied.

Meanwhile, on the religious front, Noyes had established a Bible school in 1836 at Putney, Vermont, and was laboring to win converts to Perfectionism. And while his affairs of the heart were thus progressing unsatisfactorily, he was carrying on an intermittent battle for autonomy from his family. This struggle centered about his relationship with his mother and elder sister; and, significantly, it was coterminous with his difficulties with Abigail Merwin. The nature of the conflict was evident when he wrote his sister, Elizabeth:

> Let me ask now kindly and finally and once for all, Am I a boy or a man? . . . I pray you believe by the help of God that I can best manage my own matters, and let your hearts have peace. I perceive with pleasure and gratitude that my father is exempt from the charge implied in what I have said. . . . I ask Mother and all who sympathize with her in solicitude to inquire carefully before God

whether such solicitude is not selfishness. . . . I declare that the relation in which I stand to my friends at home has given me more trouble than anything else. It has long been my endeavor to avoid any explicit declaration of independence both for your sakes and mine. . . . I can receive no assistance which shall entitle anyone but Christ to mark the pathway for my feet. Yet you insist upon my coming home, and counsel me about getting a livelihood, as if dependence was the condition of your favor. (I speak only of my mother and sisters). Let me say now for your special notice, that family considerations have become with me subordinate to my relations to God, and if there is any conflict between them, the first will be sacrificed without faltering. I say to you as to all others, I am the Lord's freeman and, if you show me favor, let your motive be not parental or family affection but the love of God and the truth.[28]

As Noyes's insistence on attempting to revive his relationship with Abigail Merwin became somewhat indecorous with her marriage, his conflict with his mother intensified. Polly Noyes wrote a friend: "While Mrs. P was present, John took the occasion of something I said to reprove me sharply: told me that I was proud of many outward things about me, that almost everything I did was tinctured with vainglory, and concluded by saying that, if I did not loathe myself, he loathed and abhorred my spirit."[29]

On 28 June 1838, Noyes married Harriet A. Holton of Westminster, Vermont. She was relatively well-to-do and a faithful convert to Perfectionism, who had sent donations to the cause on several occasions. Noyes had made the direction of his thoughts on marriage and his conception of their relationship clear in his letter of proposal:

We can enter into no engagements with each other which shall limit the range of our affections as they are limited in matrimonial engagements by the fashion of this world. I desire and expect my yoke-fellow will love all who love God, whether man or woman, with a warmth and strength of affection which is unknown to earthly lovers, and as free as if she stood in no particular connection with me. In fact the object of my connection with her will not be to monopolize and enslave her heart or my own, but to enlarge and establish both in the free fellowship of God's universal family.[30]

In spite of this unorthodox declaration of affection, and her awareness and jealousy of his unremitting passion for Abigail Merwin, Harriet consented to marry him.[31]

After their marriage and Noyes's decision to begin his Perfectionist colony in Putney, Vermont, his struggle with his mother, played out on

the two levels of religious doctrine and familial authority, only intensified. In both cases power was at issue. This was evident in a reference he
made to his younger siblings:

> I have saved them from the world by disregarding Mother's advice
> and by teaching them to maintain their independence of her. . . .
> Many times I have found no way to lead on the children without
> requiring them to renounce her authority and make war on her. She
> has repeatedly withdrawn herself from me, and once at least made
> overtures of alliance to David Crawford and the church. She was
> in a state of rebellion against me when I married Harriet and com-
> menced permanent operations in this place. If her will had been
> done, I should have suppressed every strong feature of the gospel
> and remained in submission to the church; I should have avoided all
> the innovations which have given us our independent position and
> are leading us to the "new heaven and the new earth."[32]

The "worldliness" from which Noyes sought to save his younger sisters was of a decidedly sexual nature. All his elder sisters had followed
his mother's example and had married "worldly" men (i.e., had betrayed
him): Mary married a Unitarian minister; Elizabeth an infidel physician; and Joanna an irreligious West Indies merchant. Horatio, his elder
brother, had followed his father's lead and had become a bank teller.
Noyes wrote of his mother in terms revealing the depth of his distrust of
her and of all womankind, describing her marriage as a kind of prostitution: "By her own example she taught her daughters to sell themselves
to worldlings."[33]

He obviously sought not only to take the place of his father as the head
of the family (thus becoming symbolically dominant over his mother),
but also to assume some of the more strictly feminine prerogatives exercised by his mother. This was made clear in a letter he wrote to his
mother (25 February 1838) in which he declared that God "has set me to
reward you for your care over me by *changing places with you and
dealing with you as my little daughter.* . . . You must expect I shall affec-
tionately reprove you for thinking you know more than your father. . . .
I hope you will help your father in these efforts, like a dutiful daughter,
and not go about to hinder and vex him."[34]

Noyes sought, in an inversion of the evangelical child-rearing pattern,
to break his mother's will, to render her submissive to his will. In part
this was achieved by isolating her within the family; Noyes's control of
his younger siblings who remained at home made it possible for him to
produce a psychological state in his mother akin to the acute feelings of
separation and loss accompanying the death of a loved one.[35] In her
original confession of faith, Polly Noyes clearly revealed the harrowing
psychological quality of the experience she had been through:

It was not till after [2] or 3 months of entire separation from him and the other children that are at home that I received such evidence that the word of the Lord was in him as to make me willing to become as a child and receive his teaching and instruction and agree to receive him as a guide in spiritual [matters?]. I have no hesitation now in saying that the [word illegible] and decided measures he pursued with me was the only way that the [word illegible] could have been torn from my heart and I could ever have been made to see that my adherence to the old church from which I had received dominion was still holding an influence over me and the remains of a fleshy and carnal feeling were hindering me from laying hold of the new covenants which alone can establish us in righteousness. The sufferings and separation which I endured in the time, afford abundant evidence to my own mind at least that the testimony I now give to him is not the consequence of parental self-exaltation this I could not have known if I had not been made to pass thru this fiery trial nor could I have, as now I can testify that the Lord thru him [created] in me *the very spirit of submission which he so much insisted on in this and in some other things.*[36]

Noyes's concern with his younger sisters and his fear of their betraying him as his mother had done, in a definitely sexual way, can be seen as quite Oedipal when we realize that he recommended incestuous relationships at Oneida for better "scientific breeding." His sisters thus became surrogates for his mother in the originally Oedipal relationship. Noyes succeeded in controlling their matrimonial destinies and thus their loyalty, as well as that of his younger brother, George, for he selected husbands for his sisters and a wife for his brother.[37]

Although Noyes had become financially independent of his family through his marriage and his inheritance of a portion of his father's property in 1841, he continued to struggle with his mother as long as she lived. In 1847, when he was indicted for adultery, certainly an hour of great trial for him, his mother recanted her allegiance to Perfectionism. She was a recusant throughout her career at Oneida as well. Yet Noyes felt very deeply attached and attracted to her, and her refusal to accept him on his terms generated a feeling of rejection and consequent hostility, which was expressed as an inveterate distrust and, on a less conscious level, an actual hostility toward women. The problem of Abigail Merwin, which heightened these feelings, continued to haunt him after it was revived by the death of her estranged husband in 1845. As late as 1851, Noyes was still trying to get her to join him at Oneida.[38]

These two parallel struggles abated, but they had marked him for life. After such experiences the regularities of conventional married life were not possible for him. His psyche was torn by two role models that he considered to be diametrically opposed. His father represented the rough-and-tumble world of politics and business, a world that accepted the lusts of the body and subordinated the spirit to the flesh. His mother represented the ethereal ethical-religious world, a world of fine-honed morality and piety. Noyes seems to have most consciously identified with his mother's ideals. Yet his belief that she had betrayed her own ideals, coupled with the necessity of denying the validity of the role model offered by the parent of his own sex, created deep-seated feelings of ambiguity.

Feelings of contempt for his father would have led to feelings of contempt for that part of himself that was male and at the same time to feelings of hostility against those of the other sex who compelled him to renounce his father's values. Through a complicated process of psychological inversion, Noyes was able to cope with these ambiguities. He projected his fears and feelings of guilt about things of the flesh onto women, and they became ironically associated with sensuality, whereas the male was associated with morality and control.

Thus, his emotional need for women remained strong, yet his fear of them made him desire to remain independent. In this sense they represented mother figures to whom he was submissive. Certainly the practice of calling the women who cared for the men's clothes "mothers" was not an insignificant feature of Oneida life! On the other hand, as Noyes's conflict with his mother illustrates, he sought to appropriate feminine power in the family for himself. At Oneida this was accomplished in part by the system of "stirpiculture," in which population was very strictly regulated by John H. Noyes and other "elders" (almost exclusively male). As sexual beings, Noyes feared women both as sexually aggressive and as ego-crushing betrayers. His fear of failure with women, and of betrayal, was grounded in an innate reticence, reinforced by his experiences with the women in his life.

Throughout his life, Noyes was to vacillate between two poles of response to women. He either sought to dominate them (usually psychologically) or submitted to their emotional attraction while maintaining an independence rooted in profound distrust. The respective prototypes for this bipolar response to women were his relationship to his mother and his unrequited pursuit of Abigail Merwin. Already in his relationship with his wife, Harriet, he combined his divergent responses (domination and distrust) to the feminine nature. His discovery of a sexual arrangement by which to compass his ambiguous relationships with women came significantly in 1845, after the death of Abigail Merwin's husband. That system was "male continence," which became the official code of behavior that governed sexual practices at the Oneida Community.

Chapter 11 🦋 "Whosoever Is Born of God Doth Not Commit Sin; For His Seed Remaineth in Him": The Theological and Ideological Foundations of Oneida Sexual Behavior

Unto the pure all things are pure: but unto them that are defiled and unbelieving is nothing pure; but even their mind and conscience is defiled.

—Titus 1:15

Nam corpus muliebre minus dissipatur quam virile
[The expenditure of the body of woman is less than that of man].

—Hippocrates

John H. Noyes remained the guiding intelligence of the Oneida Community until its abandonment of the system of complex marriage (August 1879) and its subsumption into the joint stock company, Oneida, Ltd., in 1880. It was therefore from his experience, and its reflection in his thought, that the theological foundations of Oneida took form.

In Noyes's theological system, the godhead was at once dual and monistic: a unified, integrated essence, whose manifestations and operations were dual. Considered as essence, God was hermaphroditic, just as Adam, the first man, had been. God the Father manifested the male attributes of the godhead, whereas Christ, the Son, manifested the female attributes. This anthropomorphic dualism was of a distinctly sexual nature. The force that caused the worlds to turn was love; no functional difference was recognized between eros and agape; the expression of love at *all* levels was sexual. This meant that sex was purified, glorified, and deified in Oneida theology.

This emphasis on universal sexuality, combined with Noyes's need to find unity in a dualistic cosmos, led to a frankly acknowledged spiritualistic materialism, in which the spiritual and material worlds were not ineluctably sundered but impinged upon and interpenetrated each other unceasingly. "Spirit," as conceived by Noyes, was analogous to semen and in fact seems to have been thought of as the vital element, the power of life, in the sexual fluid of both men and women. "It is a *fluid*," he wrote, "having many of the properties of caloric, light, electricity, galvanism, and magnetism. . . . [These properties] are in some sense, connecting links between the material and spiritual worlds . . . spirit is in many respects like these fluids, and is as truly substantial as they."[1]

The significance of this doctrinal point for the emotional response of the Oneida Community to matters sexual was enormous. Given the very intimate participation of numinous essence in the phenomenological realm of the erotic life, the tendency of the theological superstructure was to sanctify sexual intercourse. The sexual act had all the significance of a sacrament, a eucharistic converse of spirits carried on through the forms (bodies) that manifested their irresistible force. This was even more clearly exemplified in Noyes's doctrine of the soul and the mythical origin of life on earth.

The first mortal soul was created by an act of sexual union between the transcendent godhead and the female aspect of the androgynous body of the prototypal man. The sexual nature of the act was unmistakable:

> The *vital fluid* from God entered into combination with Adam's body. . . . [It was] a mere fluid without definite form, and without material cohesiveness. If it had been instantly withdrawn, before a permanent union of it with matter was formed, it would doubtless have remained an incohesive fluid—an undistinguished part of the whole spirit of life. But as soon as it entered into combination with the dust-formed body, it received the shape and cohesiveness of that body—became partially indurate or congealed; so that it ever afterward retained a definite shape, and of course an identity separate from that of the universal spirit of life.[2]

If any doubt remained that this was a description of the intromission of the paternal spirit into the maternal matrix, and that its result was embryonic procreation of the pneuma, it was dispelled by the comment that Adam "was the immediate offspring of God."[3]

Spirits, and in fact all creation, were bisexual. All

> personal spirits are real things, having interiors and exteriors, attractions, receptivities, and capacities for combination. . . . From

this it results that individual spirits are capable of two distinct forms of compaction. They may be *filled*, and they may be *enveloped*. . . . The interior want, or the desire to be filled with life, is necessarily also a desire to envelop life; and on the other hand the exterior want, or the desire to be enveloped with life, is also necessarily a desire to fill with life. These two generic forms of desire are symbolized in the organization of the sexes. The desire to be filled and to envelop is female. The desire to be enveloped and to fill is male.[4]

It was this peculiar hermaphroditic vision of the universe that created the necessary condition for both a universal eros and a rationalization, or ordering, of the relationships among the multitude of sexual beings. An implicit evaluation of the contributions of the two sexes to the natural process, which equated their worth with physiologically determined characteristics, was an important corollary of this aspect of Oneidan theological dogma. For "it is obvious," Noyes continued, "that in all combinations, the interior life must be more compact and therefore stronger than the exterior. The female capacity is in its very nature negative. Weakness makes room for strength. Deficiency embraces fullness."[5]

In addition to asserting the inferiority of women, however, Noyes also very tellingly revealed a preference for a relationship bordering on the homosexual, which is of great importance in explicating his (and the community's) attitude toward women.

To begin with the higher forms of life, the Father and the Son are concentric spiritual spheres. Their relations to each other are those of male and female. The Father fills the Son and is enveloped by him. The Son envelops the Father and is filled by him. [The Son in turn] . . . came into the World that he might begin his work of concentration, by *introducing himself into the interiors of men*. To the Father he is the exterior female life, but to man he is the interior or male life. The Son is filled with the fulness of the Father, interiorly, and he seeks in man exterior development. And so in the whole succession of infoldings from the father outward, each spirit or sphere of spirits is filled by a more central life, and enveloped by a more external life; i.e., each life is female to the life in advance of it toward the centre, and male to the life behind it toward the circumference.[6]

The characteristic metaphorical expressions Noyes used to explicate the human-divine relationship were almost all sexual. In contradistinction to the usual tropical mode of Protestants, which establishes an analogy between birth and conversion, the Oneida system used puberty to express the emotional quality of conversion.[7] Children were, from this perspective, almost nonpersons; they were incapable of mature sexual love and, by extension, of a viable, intimate relationship with God. It was only the nubile beloved who could ardently say of the divine suitor, "If I have unfeigned, simple faith, he can fertilize me; the pollen of his Spirit can make me fruitful; but he will not give it to me except as I turn my face toward him and open myself to him. I am determined to keep my heart open to him and be humble for the sake of being fruitful, which is the joy of my life."[8]

Theologically, then, the divine-human relationship was cast in a traditionally male-female framework. Men, who experienced more direct and closer union with the godhead than women, achieved such beatitude only by accepting (for religious purposes) a submissive, passive female role. This was a direct expression of their centrifugal action with relation to the deity, their inferiority. It comes as no surprise, therefore, that the ambiguities such a homoerotic theology engendered, the expressed feelings of inferiority to a supreme male God, should have been projected upon the female whose sexual characteristics men had preempted to achieve a more satisfying union with the deity. The ascription of an inferior religious role to women was inherent in the whole hierarchical system of interior (superior) and exterior (inferior) life, but found its most extensive development in Oneida theology concerning the archetypal Edenic pair.

God created woman as a companion to man and so that he might have an erotic relation on the material plane. The separation into two beings of the unified sexual duality whose name had been Adam created a mundane interior-exterior (male-female) division which paralleled that of the heavenly sphere. It was this division that made possible the full outpouring of divine love upon humanity, for "Adam was the channel specially of the life of the Father, and Eve of the life of the Son." In the sexual act, "each reflects upon the other the love of God, each excites and develops the divine action in the other."[9]

Although in the state of innocence sexual intercourse was primarily a means of exaltation, with the Fall it became the chief means of reuniting sinful man with God. It became quite literally a sacrament: "With pure hearts and minds, we may approach the sexual union as the truest Lord's supper, as an emblem and also as a medium of the noblest worship of God and fellowship with the body of Christ. We may throw around it all the hallowed associations which attach to the festivities and hospitalities of Christmas and Thanksgiving. To sup with each other, is really less sensual than to sup with roast-turkeys and chicken-pies."[10]

But sexual intercourse in order to be holy had to be motivated by divine love, that is, love that sought ecstasy as a means of physical transcendence rather than love that used physical rapture as a "bait" to procreation. Like the Shakers, Noyes considered "untimely" generation the original sin. Eve, the "weaker vessel," had been tempted to a generative act by Satan. He was "the seducer of Eve, and the father of Cain."[11] Woman became in Noyes's system a creature to be feared; it was she who, through her lust, had let the force of evil into the world of men.[12]

The moral position of the female, in the theological system of John H. Noyes, was thus thoroughly undermined. As nurturer of the seed, woman possessed an enigmatic and ominously passive capacity that had to be carefully superintended. She was a neutral force, a conduit of semen, a retort in which any seed would germinate, and therefore a threat to the more energetic, vigorous goodness of the male saint. "Their goodness," Noyes wrote of women, "is negative, or perhaps we should say *receptive*, in distinction from that which is positive and active, and as such, is equally adapted to foster either good or evil influences from without."[13] If any doubt remained in the reader's mind about the nature and stature of woman, Noyes quickly sought to dispel it in his characteristically frank way: "In natural generation the Father gives his own image to the child, and the same mother may bear children of one complexion by one husband, and children of a different complexion by another. . . . Human nature is a female which conceives and brings forth sin or righteousness, according as it has Satan or God for its husband."[14] This argument is further underscored by Noyes's reworking of Paul's doctrine of "law" and "sin" in his contention that "the evil nature of the offspring in this case [the marriage of 'the law' and 'the sinner'] is not to be attributed to the husband [law] but to the wife [sinner]."[15]

The necessity for men to take on female characteristics in their intercourse with the spiritual worlds (both higher and lower) allowed men to project their guilt onto women. Because a psychological identification was set up between the perceived role characteristics of women in a male-female relationship and of men in a spiritual-mortal relationship, it became a simple matter to shift the burden of guilt for male transgression to women. A man had been "seduced by the devil"; he felt contempt for his own weakness and folly and projected that feeling upon the female. It required but one final turn of the screw to see the female not as a neutral but as an actively threatening force. On the psychological level, it was the acceptance of her sexual characteristics in man's religious role that allowed the devil entrance into human life. But even beyond this, she became metaphorically allied with Satan, "the great seducer of the world."[16]

The male had from the beginning been radically innocent, a victim whose sin had been "instigated, begotten, spiritually infused by . . . [the] tempter."[17] Woman was a similar seductive force, but of a physical rather than a spiritual kind; a temptress who figured forth the form of "Satan transformed into an angel of light." From this point of view, woman was an agent of Satan, and the seduction motif was expressed in more feminine terms, such as "beguilement." A common motif of this female seduction was the "destruction of the body"; the Samson and Delilah story was used as a cautionary tale.[18]

It became imperative, then, if salvation were to be achieved and life itself preserved, that the female be controlled, and conversely that the male exert control over his own emotions to prevent being seduced into sin by her. Self-control, or control of the will, thus became central to the theological system of Oneida. Oneida theology held that mankind could attain perfect freedom from sin; hence, Oneidans called themselves Perfectionists. Like the Shakers, they were "progressive perfectionists." Employing biological imagery of seeds, buds, and fruits, they held that every individual contained the potential for perfection: "Every believer in Christ may, in a valuable sense, claim to be perfect. He is perfect in the sense of having in him the germ of all righteousness . . . but he may at the same time be very *imperfect* with reference to the expansion of that germ into actual existence."[19]

Perfection resulted from a well-tended garden kept free of weeds and vermin; man's sexual nature was the key to perfection, but it must be pruned, fertilized, and fenced about, to help it achieve its proper and most perfect growth. It was this care of the perfumed garden of man's sexuality, the topiary aspect of Perfectionism, that provided the link between the strictly theological and the ideological aspects of Oneidan sexual attitudes.

The sexual ideology of the Oneida Community, male continence, was a unique intensification and modification of the spermatic-economy doctrine. Put into practice in 1846, it represented an even greater fear of debilitation, desiccation, or dementia arising through the loss of semen (the "vital" or "nervous" fluid distilled from the blood) than did the spermatic economy advocated by the Shakers or such secular reformers as Sylvester Graham.[20] In order to assure a conservation of "vital force," other sexual reformers insisted on limiting venereal contact between the sexes; but given the centrality and sacral nature of sex in Noyes's system, such a solution was unacceptable. Instead, he divided the sex act (viewed from the male perspective) into two parts, which he called "amative" and "propagative." The mere social act of sexual intercourse was healthy and joyful; only the procreative act rendered it insalubrious and destructive.

Noyes discovered a new technique of intercourse, which he called "male continence" (*coitus reservatus*), which provided for reservation of the semen in the sex act by prohibiting male orgasm. Women were encouraged to have orgasms, both because they could physiologically do so without entailing propagative consequences and, as we shall see later, because this brought them under the control of men. As Noyes described his system, "Sexual intercourse, apart from the propagative act . . . is the appropriate external expression of amativeness, and is eminently favorable to life. The contact and unity of male and female bodies developes and distributes the two kinds of life which in equilibrium constitute perfect vitality. Mere reciprocal communication of vital heat is healthful. . . . life passes by bodily contact."[21]

Life was equated with semen-blood-spirit-will. The heart, considered at once a physiological and a psychological organ, was the governing principle of the physical and spiritual life of man. Noyes reversed the typical assumption of his contemporaries that heart was female and head male. The heart was the vital link that ensured the unification within the body of man of the spiritual and material. This *"invisible organ, situated in the middle of the lower part of the breast,"* was the seat of the soul, that "perceiving, feeling, and willing substance" which guided choice.[22] On physiological grounds, therefore, Noyes considered the heart to be superior to the brain because it was the domain of the spirit and the seat and distributive agent of the will. "The spirit," Noyes wrote, is

> the *vital energy* that moves the internal organs and *impregnates the blood.* . . . The heart being the centre-point of all faculties of body and soul, is the special seat of personal consciousness—the thing commonly signified by the pronoun "I." In fact it is from this point that all growth and manifestations of life originally proceed, as the stalk and branches of a plant proceed from the germ. Of course all the powers that manifest themselves in the senses, nerves, brain, muscles, etc., were first in the heart.[23]

The heart, however, was only an agent, or perhaps a proximate cause, of the vitality and sensation of mind and body. The effective cause was a "subtle fluid, resembling electricity or galvanism."[24] The imagery Noyes employs in describing this fluid is a compound of the physical and spiritual, and clearly reflects his belief that sexual relationships were as subject to natural, physiological laws as the phenomena of electricity or magnetism.

The association of the willing substance with the life force, or semen, and the ideological importance of its control are even more graphically demonstrated when Noyes discusses spiritualism and animal magnetism. This nervous fluid emanating from the heart, the life force, "is greater in amount and power in some persons than in others, as some electrical machines generate the electrical fluid more abundantly than others."[25] Noyes saw the dominant partner in the sexual relationship in the role of the mesmerizer, who through his vigor and sexual potency "controlled" or dominated the will of his partner. In the sexual act, the passage of nervous fluid from one person to another followed the same essential laws of physics that required all fluids to seek a state of equilibrium. So, "by contact, or under other favorable conditions, the nervous fluid of a person whose vital powers are strong, may pass into and possess, more or less perfectly, the body of one whose vital powers are weaker. The senses and muscular powers of a person thus charged with the nervous fluid of another, are shut off more or less perfectly from the medium of their ordinary activity, viz., their own nervous fluid, and must act, if at all, in and by the nervous fluid of the magnetizer."[26]

Because Noyes believed that there was an exchange of vital energy in every sexual relationship, even if that exchange were made on a relatively spiritual level (assuming the male had no orgasm), there would have been a drain on the vital fluid of life in all such relationships. As his hypnotic metaphor indicated, the mere physical act of sexual intercourse was concurrently an exhilarating exercise of power and a deadly threat to the vitality of the more potent partner. In order to keep their supply of vitality or vital force at a constant level, all beings must be in spiritual contact with those above them. In sexual terms, as in his theological system, Noyes considered women the "weaker vessel," because although they possessed a vital fluid analogous to that of men, they lost a certain amount of it through orgasm.[27] Noyes frequently used the term "nervous fluid" for "vital fluid" or "vital force," thus underscoring the nineteenth-century association of nervous disorders with sex.

Women had less vital force and were thus more prone to nervous diseases, and would also have been considered weaker for that reason.[28] The difference was not a psychological one but a physiological one, grounded in the very biological difference between male and female. Women, unlike men, however, managed to recoup their losses (except those of the terrible drain of childbearing) through their sexual relationships with men. The terribly enervating and exhausting drain of parturition provided the ideological rationale behind birth control, which was so integral an aspect of male continence.

For males the situation was much more critical. Although sex was a divinely ordained sacrament, it was a most dangerous rite. Only a proper relation to God, and abstinence from orgasm, could save men from dehydration. God alone was self-sufficient, self-sustaining, and intarissable, constantly regenerating himself. His vitality was inexhaustible. Self-control and preparation were the keys to male participation in sex; they were the twin means of preventing exhaustion, desiccation, old age, and even death. If we keep in mind the significance of the heart in Noyes's physiological-psychological system, the sexual basis for the triumph over death becomes obvious: "The *direst* and at the same time the most common of all diseases in this world is the *withering of the heart*. As soon as the freshness and romance of youth is past, and men enter upon the serious warfare of life, they almost universally begin to be *seared and dry to the core.*[29] Only an intimate and unintermitted relation to God could assure the replacement of male vitality lost in even a nonorgasmic sexual act. It was at this point that the theological conception of a hierarchy of "interior" and "exterior" merged with the ideological necessity of a strict control of the will to generate both a heightened anxiety about the male predicament and a means of alleviating that tension.

Oneida theology posited that those beings who possessed interior life were by definition closer to God. The difficulty for the male, however, was presented by those beings of exterior life who tempted and seduced him away from his natural allegiance. Women threatened the autonomy and the very existence of man; only his strength of will could preserve him. Mental and physical health, therefore, came to depend on male superiority: "Our health and peace depend, not on communion with the external world, but on communion with the internal world. Thus we see that the overworked head gets into a false spiritual position, and the true order of our faculties is inverted. The world prevails over the head, and the head prevails over the heart, which is the same thing as having the child rule the woman and the woman the man."[30]

To prevent this inversion of the natural progression of moral superiority, Oneida ideology developed the concept of "ascending-descending fellowship." The "law of fellowship" required that all relationships, either with those above one in the hierarchy (ascending) or with those below one (descending), be controlled by the superior party to the relationship. "In the fellowship between man and woman, for instance, man is naturally the superior and his business is self-limitation. We hold that the male is not only responsible for his own limitation, but for that of the female."[31]

Children, who were spiritually deficient by definition, were "in a position where their fellowship ought to be almost exclusively in the ascending direction."[32] The nexus with God, or more properly the filial hypostasis of the deity, must first be assured before males could safely indulge in sexual intercourse: "It is man's business to take hold on Christ before he descends into woman's love at all. . . . I insist that all love, whether general or specific must have its authority in the sanctity and inspiration of the ascending fellowship. All love which is at work in a private corner, away from the general circulation, where there are no series of links connecting it with God, is false love; it rends and devours, instead of making unity, peace, and harmony."[33]

It was this aspect of Oneidan ideology that supported the reversal of the double standard of morality. Control of the sexual act was firmly vested in male hands, and as we shall see when we consider Oneida's sexual practices, specifically in John Humphrey Noyes's hands. Male control was necessitated by the fear of woman as a predatory, sexually aggressive being who, vampirelike, was capable of draining man of his vital fluid or, worse still, of emasculating him and leaving him spiritually, sexually, and socially impotent. In less emotional terms, women were equated with the physical world (body), and men with the spiritual world (soul). Just as the divine sexual dualism was transcended in a unified godhead with a definitely established order of precedence, so too a sexually divided mankind found a transcendent unity in the act of sexual intercourse; but only in a regulated intercourse in which each sex had its divinely ordained hierarchic position. The dreadful anxiety of the sexual act is reflected in Noyes's elevation of the principle of ascending-descending fellowship and its objective correlative, the regulation of inferior by superior, to the status of a universal physical law. This law, he tells us,

> is a principle which will finally have to regulate the relations between our souls and bodies. The soul must go down into the body and have fellowship with its pleasures just so far as God and the heavens send it and no farther; and the body must go down into the businesses and pleasures of the material world just so far as the soul sends it and no farther. The superior sending and limiting the inferior is the principle that starts from the example of the Father and the Son, and runs through all the descending links of celestial and terrestrial love.[34]

In less elevated terms, man must subject his will to God, before he can exercise his legitimate control over the life and body of woman.

The need for control, for limitation, for restriction of the sexual relation, which was central to Oneida sexual ideology, suggests a certain sense of guilt about the acknowledged pleasurable justification for intercourse that Noyes considered paramount. For men and women who had been reared in the Puritan tradition, pleasure could not be unequivocally accepted as a justification for anything. Pleasure might be an ancillary reward, but not an end in itself. The sense of guilt raised by Noyes's system and the need to find a more fundamental justification for sexual pleasure were assuaged by the system of male continence, which was quite literally a "labor of love," and by the community doctrine that love was the reward of labor. The official guidebook to the life of the community expressed this best: "The Association believes that . . . love is the appropriate reward of labor; that in a just spiritual medium, every individual, by the fixed laws of attraction, will draw around him an amount of love exactly proportioned to his intrinsic value and efficiency, and thus that all accounts will be punctually and justly balanced without the complicated and cumbersome machinery of bookkeeping."[35]

The very essence of pleasure is the service of self, if not at the expense of others, certainly with only adventitious concern for their enjoyment. Selfishness, then, is the very soul of pleasure. But selfishness is a highly antisocial form of behavior, obviously inimical to a communal life of "Bible Communism" like that of Oneida. The passage from the community guidebook suggests that selfishness would be controlled by a "natural," informal system of "bookkeeping," that "accounts" would be "balanced"; the community would help to make sex pleasurable by removing the guilt generated by self-gratification—but only if the individual followed the rules.

The system, as its name, "male continence," suggests, was primarily geared to the diminution of male guilt; men experienced a certain pleasure in intromission, but denied themselves orgasmic pleasure. They were thus performing a socially valuable act (as they afforded greater pleasure to women) and avoiding the guilt associated with selfish pleasure. To extend the economic metaphor, they were "paying" for the pleasure they received, by providing a "surplus" (the orgasmic pleasure of the female), while at the same time creating a "debit" on the female side of the ledger. The "indebtedness" of women was both a reason to fear her aggression against her creditors and a justification for the need to control her "economic"-sexual activity.

The very terms employed to refer to intercourse at Oneida, "personal fellowship" and "social fellowship," underscored the felt need to overcome the guilt associated with selfish pleasure. Fellowship was the key to the sexual life of the Oneida Community. The system of male continence was an attempt to socialize, to domesticate, sexuality and to employ it as a social bond. The male, as the nobler, superior partner, was called to altruism; a transcendently unselfish spiritual love was to take precedence over physical love. Thus, Noyes used masturbation as a symbol for asocial sexual behavior: "The discharge of the semen, and the pleasure connected with it, is not essentially social, since it can be produced in solitude. [In masturbation] . . . the pleasure of the act is not produced by contact and interchange of life with the female, but by the action of the seminal fluid on the internal nerves of the male organs. The appetite and that which satisfies it are both within the male, and of course the pleasure is personal, and may be obtained without sexual intercourse."[36]

Licentiousness, or the improper use of the sexual organs, was defined as "the *selfish* exercise of the sexual passion."[37] The very nature of the sex act as set forth by the male-continence doctrine, at the same time that it precluded male selfishness and antisocial behavior, insofar as it prescribed female orgasm, made the female the repository of self-regarding, licentious sexuality. The men of Oneida assured their own "perfection" by forcing women to commit the very sin they most dreaded to commit themselves.

Women were considered, then, thoroughly physical and egoistically sybaritic in their sexual desires. They represented a threat to the ideologically established definition of maleness not only in their ability to drain the vital force, the spirit, from men, but even more importantly in the potential for rebellion they had stored up, which might burst forth as a refusal to accept the full burden of guilt for human sexuality. In the former instance, they were portrayed as seductresses, insatiable and omnivorous sexual creatures. The selfish, uncontrollable desire of woman was embodied in her very approach to love. There were two opposing modes of loving: *"There is the love itself—a holy and a precious thing, and there is the love of being loved—a mean, greedy—a devouring passion where it exists without the act of loving, and where it demands so costly a thing as a human heart, with all its warm and generous affections, to satisfy the hunger of a selfish vanity."*[38]

Male love was noble, true, unselfish; female love base, physical, and selfish. When we recall the significance of the heart to Oneida ideology, the threat of the female is clear; she will physically enervate and morally debase the entrapped male.

Yet ironically, although male continence attempted to project the full weight of culpability for human selfishness upon women by its reification of their role in the sex act, men's concern for autonomy and the sanctity of the self was an even more consuming passion. To a degree, abstinence from orgasm (self-limitation) preserved the integrity of the self, and the special nexus with Christ preserved the self-sufficiency of vital force that inhered in the "heart" of the male. In Noyes's view, sex was a power struggle in which selfhood or autonomy was the goal. "Desire and its object may be called the *subjective* and *objective* means of happiness; and these two classes of means are concerned in every form of pleasure of which man is capable. As we love happiness, so we subordinately love the means of it. . . . all the *objective* means of sensual happiness—the outward material for the gratification of amativeness, alimentiveness, and the rest of the animal passions are procurable for money."[39]

The subjective (male) self, this passage suggests, converts the female into an object. There is an underlying anxiety that the male will also be objectified by the subjective (female) self in the act of lovemaking. By reserving his semen, though, by retaining at all times control of his will, the male is capable of maintaining his independence of all the objectifying power of the "other" in a relation that is "outward" and "material." The closest human relationship is thus subverted; it is controlled by the male with a single eye to his autonomous selfhood.

In any ideological system in which the sexual satisfaction of the female is considered important, there is bound to be anxiety about the ability of the male to provide it. The fear of being objectified by the female partner, of not being valued for those qualities that made up the "soul," or essence of a man, was a reflection of that anxiety. On a deeper psychological level, the whole system of male continence seems to have been a means of convincing the female of the devotion of the male. Beneath this need, as we suggested in the sketch of Noyes's development, lay a fear of the loss of affection, or anxiety about the male's ability to satisfy the sexual needs of the female.

One of the most revealing expressions of this fear (which characteristically linked *all* aspects of nineteenth-century reform activity with the peculiar sexual system developed at Oneida) was presented in an informal religious address given by John H. Noyes. There is nothing "more hopeless and heart-distracting," he said, "than to attempt . . . to gratify a propensity to universal philanthropy, by surrendering one's self to the various organizations, which occupy the field of human interests. Whoever makes this attempt will surely experience the worst woes of polygamy. He will find himself married to a dozen or more of independent and quarrelling wives. The most that he can do, will be to dally with them all. He can be a husband to none."[40]

The "heart-distracting" nature of the enterprise lay in the "surrendering of one's self," the vital force that constituted the essence of one's being: the conversion into a sex object. If this fear of sexual failure when bearing the relation of husband to many wives, which was objectified in the system of complex marriage, or pantagamy, as it was practiced at Oneida (where every man was married to every woman and vice versa), was one side of the nightmare the sexual ideology of Oneida evoked, the obverse of this anxiety was the concern lest dissatisfied women abandon men who were inadequate in their sexual performance. In a thoroughgoing materialist system, which provided for the resurrection of the body and the continual impingement of spiritual forces on the physical world, this latter anxiety assumed cosmic proportions. Oneida's spiritualist interpretation of the Sadducees's sophistic query to Christ (Matthew 22:23–30) was exemplary of this dread. In the case of a remarried widow,

> a woman . . . who has a living husband, may have two in the spiritual state, equally related to her, and as things appear now, equally accessible. What will those interested do with such a case? . . . in

this invasion of spirits there is coming in a class who cannot be held by human law. There is no legal redress to be had of them for any violation of the laws of marriage and society which they may choose to commit. If it is true, as seems to be the case, that the barrier between this world and hades is being penetrated, then a vast population is being let in upon us, who are entirely above human jurisdiction—all protection by statutes and penalties is at an end, and the world must revert again to the original law of nature, and the direct judgment of God.[41]

The frank acceptance of woman's sexuality and right to a satisfying sexual experience, combined with the normative judgment of woman such acceptance implied, apparently created great tension in the male mind. An inveterate fear of competition for affection (which was expressed in the monetary-economic terms used to refer to love at Oneida—sex as a reward for labor) intensified the fear of the anarchic, soul-devouring, and sperm-draining female. It was ultimately impossible, this fear indicates, to control the affections of the female, to watch them closely enough to forfend infidelity. Although Oneida sexual ideology could not vitiate the sexual anxiety the acceptance of the female sex drive aroused in man, it did offer the maximum potentiality for the control of feminine sexuality.

When we recall the Oneidan myth of Eve's seduction by the devil and the fear of the neutral moral character of the womb, the essential force behind the need for control assumes a deeper significance. The very reproductive capacity of women had to come under male (moral) control, if the generation of good Perfectionists were to go on apace. It was for this reason that the eugenic system, which Noyes called "stirpiculture," was instituted at the Oneida Community in 1867. Male control of the sex act insured his control of the seasons of impregnation and provided the opportunity to prevent any accidental conception. The key to selective breeding as practiced at Oneida was the selection of *fathers*. The statistical basis for concentration on male selection was Noyes's belief that males transmitted their characteristics more frequently than females in a ratio of fifty to one. "And although the female may produce very great results in the *second* generation—since any one of her *male* offspring taking her place, may produce *his* thousand, conveying her characteristics—yet it must ever remain true that the principal means of breeding choice stocks is by the selection of *males*."[42]

Female fertility bore a direct relation, according to Noyes, to *quantity* of increase, whereas male fertility bore more nearly on the *value* of the increase of a species.[43] A great deal of wishful thinking inheres in this system, but its significance lies in its insistence upon male control, even as it tacitly recognizes the genetic influence of the female in the second generation. Even at that distance, however, the protoplasmic germ must be protected from direct female influence; it is mediated through the woman's male descendant.

The eugenic system developed at Oneida was central to its sexual ideology. Its essentially male orientation (male continence combined with stirpiculture) made sure that not one drop of the precious "fluid of life" was wasted, and that the ambiguous reproductive potential of the female was sedulously supervised and properly channeled. It was, in fact, the link that provided the connection between individual and social improvement. Eugenic propagation insured procreative Perfectionism through the inheritance of learned characteristics, for "individual improvement must be the basis for improvement by inheritance. Persons must themselves improve, before they can transmit improvement to their offspring. If there is a rigorous law that people must be like their progenitors, then there is no hope for the improvement of humanity. But there is no such law. All the attempts to improve the lower animals are based on the principle that individuals can be improved, and can transmit improvement to offspring."[44]

If this were true, the sexual changes at Oneida could be seen as a means to broaden social reform. This was certainly the case with the social dimension of sexuality. Complex marriage, male continence, and scientific propagation were seen as a means of overcoming the sexual ills of the day: adultery, prostitution, obscenity, abortion, marriage, and divorce. Ordinary dyadic marriage relations were usually compared to slavery in Oneida publications, and the conjugal sex act was considered rape or at least violent sexual passion. Mormon polygamy, because it avoided exclusive possession (female, it should be noted!) of the spouse, was still a vicious system because it allowed legal ownership (by the male).

Adultery and divorce were opposite sides of the same phenomenon and could be solved by sexual reform based on pantagamy. Significantly, community doctrine tended to present its position in economic metaphors, ironically underlining the presuppositions about the sexual relation that, although they deplored them, they shared with the society they criticized. Their description of the therapeutic effect of complex marriage is characteristic: "The only way to prevent smuggling and strife in a confederacy of contiguous States, is to abolish custom-house lines from the interior, and declare free trade and free transit, collecting revenues and fostering home products by one custom-house line around the whole."[45]

The ideological-theological structure of Oneida thought was admirably suited to unite the contradictory needs and fears that men felt in their relationships with women. Sex was a very powerful physical drive, expressed metaphorically by chemical or magnetic attraction, the ardency of "white hot metal," or the impetuosity of a "damned stream."[46] Yet it was a force in need of the greatest control. The joy and burden of sexuality were dissolved as a colloidal suspension in the acid base of complex marriage, male continence, and stirpiculture, but the tension between the particles thus united remained. Oneida sexual ideology was an integration of anxieties and needs, but the tension of those suspended forces remained as the substrate that formed the basis for sexual relationships in the Oneida Community.

Chapter 12 🐝 "A Tide of Living, Healthful Love": Sexual Practices at the Oneida Community

Men feel a pleasure in remaining at table although they can no longer eat. Is it love? Is it simply recollection? Is it friendship? Is it something compounded of all these?

—Voltaire, "Love," *Philosophical Dictionary*

How manye myghte she have in mariage?
Yet herede I nevere tellen in myn age
Upon this nombre diffinicioun.
Men may devyne and glosen, up and down,
But wel I woot, expres, withoute lye,
God bad us for to wexe and multiplye;
That gentil text kan I wel understonde.
Eek wel I woot, he seyde myn housbonde
Sholde lete fader and mooder, and take to me.
But of no nombre mencion made he,
Of bigamye or of octogamye;
Why sholde men thanne speke of it vileynye?

—Chaucer, "Wife of Bath's Prologue," *Canterbury Tales*

*T*he discovery of male continence, the engine that ran the machinery of complex marriage and eugenics at Oneida, came in 1844, after John H. Noyes had been married for six years. During those years, his wife, Harriet, had experienced five pregnancies, all excruciatingly painful. Four of the children were premature and stillborn; only one survived. Noyes vowed that he would never again expose his wife to such "fruitless suffering." His solution to the problem was the separation of the "social" from the "propagative" function of sex. He tells us of his discovery: "I experimented on this idea, and found that the self-control which it required was not difficult; that my enjoyment was increased; that my wife's experience was very satisfactory, as it had never been before; that we had escaped the horrors and the fear of involuntary propagation."[1]

This new form of sexual relationship, instituted at Putney, Vermont, in 1846, required a change in the male role in the sexual act. It was the less demanding, self-sacrificing feminine mode of response that was required of the male; this was the "superior," the better, response. This was incisively expressed in a talk Noyes gave in 1847 entitled "An Overture," in which he contrasted what he called the "I spirit" with the "We spirit." In the light of Oneida ideology, the force of his address for sexual behavior is immediately apparent:

> Desire acted on by the I spirit is *greedy* . . . has an unnatural, feverish irritation about it. It has obstinate will, that won't be refused; there is no softness in it—no yielding, no accommodation, no dropping down into another's thoughts and interests, no harmony or communion with other desires. This is a morbid state of the passions. The *we* spirit is gentle and patient; and while at the same time it has a relish for pleasure . . . yet there is no sharp, severe will in it. It is healthful, happy in hope, content in the prospect of enjoyment. It is not greedy of action or of possession, but is made happy by hope. It prefers to wait on the execution of other folk's desires and wills.[2]

So male continence as practiced at Oneida was singularly dualistic in conception; it accepted the sexual mores of contemporary nonutopian society, which associated sexual pleasure with evil and condemned as basely physical any active venereal conatus, while at the same time maintaining that sexual pleasure was a God-given blessing. The male controlled the sex act, but did so by adopting a "feminine" role in intercourse; he subordinated his physical desires (the baser will) to the female's needs. The psychology of male continence is very complex and requires further explication, but in this chapter we shall be concerned primarily with its perceived physical benefits and its practical application.

In its initial phase, male continence grew out of the perception of the necessity for contraception based on Malthusian arguments and a deep feeling of compassion for the lot of women. Noyes attacked what he called "excessive and oppressive" and "random" procreation, yet he found all the proposed methods of birth control either physically wasteful (as was the case with the *coitus interruptus* recommended by Robert Dale Owen in his *Moral Physiology* [1837]) or emotionally stultifying (as he believed the celibacy advocated by the Shakers to be).[3]

Noyes was initially very interested in Shakerism and considered that system an honorable method of limiting reproduction. His own system, however, proposed

> to take the same power of moral restraint and self-control which Paul, Malthus, the Shakers, and all considerate men use in one way or another to limit propagation, and instead of applying it, as they do, to the prevention of the intercourse between the sexes, to introduce it at another stage of the proceedings, viz., *after* the sexes have come together in social effusion, and *before* they have reached the propagative crisis; thus allowing them the most essential freedom of love, and at the same time avoiding undesired procreation and all the other evils incident to male incontinence.[4]

Noyes's system of male continence insured "freedom of love" by adopting a position whose advocates, "while freely recognizing the right of men and women to limit the number of their progeny, consider that the sentimental character of intercourse is destroyed by the use of artificial agencies, and that higher emotions are repressed by the employment of mechanical measures."[5] Or, in less expansive phraseology, the available devices of birth control detracted from the pleasure of the sex act. In its simplest form, then, male continence hoped to achieve birth control while retaining the physical pleasures of intercourse. Yet, for the male, devoir took precedence over delight. His first responsibility was to the female and her protection against undesired pregnancies; his code was a demanding, gentlemanly one.

The initial object of male continence, therefore, was to prevent excessive propagation and male incontinence. From the perspective of woman, the goal was to reduce the *expenses* of sexual intercourse, which were enumerated by Noyes in 1853: "The infirmities and vital expenses of woman during the long period of pregnancy, waste her constitution. The awful agonies of childbirth heavily tax the life of woman. The cares of the nursing period bear heavily on woman."[6]

The male, as the impregnator of the female, was the aggressor, a threat to the very life of woman; his ability to impose upon and threaten the female under the guise of pleasurable intercourse had to be brought under control. Oneidans felt that sexual intercourse as it occurred in the world outside Oneida was a selfish, brutal act of rape by the male. The connection between intercourse and propagation removed the sex act from the category of "merely social actions" and was the basis of the double standard. Women were the victims of sex, yet they bore the brunt of the shame arising from bastardy.[7]

It was a leitmotiv of Oneida publications dealing with sexual relations that the marriage of the "world" was quite simply slavery, with the wife cast in the role of the planter's slave mistress. "The liberty of marriage, as commonly understood and practiced," therefore, "is the liberty of a man to sleep habitually with a woman, liberty to please himself alone in his dealings with her, [and] liberty to expose her to child-bearing without care or consultation."[8]

In an indirect sense, it was believed, male abstention from orgasm provided women with a greater degree of control over their bodies and destinies and liberated them from the sexual servitude of marriage. Male continence could not but be a salutary influence on the relationship between the sexes, for "any system which mitigates the miseries of matrimony by according to woman the control of her own body, with some right in limiting the number of her offspring, and determining their paternity, must be an improvement on the degrading influence which marriage brings to millions of people."[9]

Once male aggression had been brought under control and women felt secure in a greater measure of control over their lives, sexual intercourse would become the pleasurable social activity it was intended to be. But such prospective joy threatened the essence of communal life— pantagamy, or complex marriage. A system that valued sexual pleasure as an end in itself had to find some way to deal with the exclusive attractions, the "special attachments," in short, with the whole panoply of romantic love, which threatened to undermine the broader base of social affection inherent in pantagamy. The Oneida solution, based upon a complete reworking of the philosophical foundations of the idea of "love," involved overseeing all relationships between the sexes, and separating those who became too exclusively devoted to a single member of the opposite sex. The institution in 1867 of eugenic reproduction (significantly called "*scientific* propagation") and a concurrent frontal attack on the assumptions of romantic love on an ideological level, coupled with the assertion of an even more thoroughgoing romanticism as its ideal of physical love, were the means chosen to implement this vigilance.

The attempt was thus made to depersonalize love, to make it social rather than individual, while retaining the greatest possible reverence for the reified emotion perceived apart from any interpersonal relationship. The theory of love, which was the basis of the sexual system of Oneida, is quite reminiscent of the older Puritan tradition, which insisted that any two people could learn to love one another, given a mutual respect and the nurture of the germs of an incipient liking, and that therefore the choice of a marital partner should ideally be made upon rational rather than emotional grounds.[10]

John H. Noyes gave a classic statement of this theory of love in an article entitled "Falling in Love," which was both an attack on the romantic-love tradition as applied to individuals and an attempt to justify the control of sexual behavior at the Oneida Community by a group of elders, of which Noyes himself was the most prominent. He argued that "the whole domain of love is capable of being absolutely controlled by the will and the judgement; that it is possible for a person to become so enlightened, so well-educated . . . as to love only where it is wisest and best for him to love, and to reject and discard all appeals to the passions which will not stand the test of sound reason."[11]

Love at Oneida was not "free," and those who confused complex marriage with free love erred gravely in their conception. Especially with the young and immature, guidance and restraint in amorous attachments were of the utmost importance. How far removed from standard romantic-love dogma was this credo of the community: "We hold that the conduct of love between the sexes should be under the supervision of the best wisdom within our reach; that the whole theory of love should be reconstructed, and brought under the dominion of reason and conscience; that it should no longer be left a matter of unreasoning passion between immature youth of opposite sex, but should be studied by thoughtful persons, who have felt its emotions, and have obtained mastery over their own passions."[12]

And yet, controlled as it was in its choice of objects and its intensity toward any one individual, love at Oneida was ideally intended to be a continual honeymoon: frequent change of sexual partners would prevent boredom; the absence of unwanted children and the housing of all children in quarters apart from their parents would preclude juvenile interference in adult enjoyment of the company of the opposite sex; and the practice of male continence would remove the fear of pregnancy and allow for much more tenderness and amorous dalliance. "The theory of sexual interchange which governs all the general measures of the Community," we are told, "is just that which in ordinary society governs the proceedings in *courtship*. It is the theory of the equal rights of women and men, and the freedom of both from habitual and legal obligations to personal fellowship. It is the theory that love *after* marriage and always and forever, should be what it is *before* marriage—a glowing attraction on both sides, and not an odious obligation of one party, and the sensual recklessness of the other."[13]

The keys to sexual relationships at Oneida, then, were duty and control. Together they provided the preconditions that made pleasurable sexual intercourse possible within the context of a closely integrated communal society. Without them, intercourse remained flagitious, egocentric, and oppressive. Romantic love without the constraint of a reasoned control was asocial; guided by a duty to observe the health and welfare of one's partner, it became the ideal, a reflection of the divine origin of love. Sexual practices at Oneida were predicated on the desire to maximize sexual pleasure while at the same time proscribing any

anarchistic tendency in the pursuit of pleasure by the insistence upon
male self-control and limitation in the sexual act. Sex was to become a
force of "vital and social magnetism," which would cement the bonds of
communal loyalty, rather than an individual, private, or isolating act.[14]

Sexual practices at Oneida, or what Noyes called his "unfinished experiment in social science," grew out of the observation that the sex act
could be broken down into three parts. "It has a beginning, a middle,
and an end," Noyes wrote.

> Its beginning and most elementary form is the simple *presence* of
> the male organ in the female. Then usually follows a series of recip-
> rocal *motions*. Finally this exercise brings on a nervous action or
> ejaculatory *crisis* which expels the seed. Now we insist that this
> whole process, up to the very moment of emission is *voluntary*, en-
> tirely under the control of the moral faculty, and *can be stopped at
> any point*. In other words, the *presence* and the *motions* can be
> continued or stopped at will, and it is only the final crisis of emission
> that is automatic or uncontrollable.[15]

In view of Oneida spermatic-economy doctrine, it is not surprising
that Noyes should choose a hydrographic metaphor as the vehicle for his
most forceful expression of the technique of *coitus reservatus*, or male
continence. The passage indicates the pride in the skill the technique
requires, the craftsmanship of control that a contemporary gynecologist
called "an artistic fulfillment":[16]

> The situation (male continence) may be compared to a stream in
> three conditions, viz., 1, a fall; 2, a course of rapids above the fall;
> and 3, still water above the rapids. The skillful boatman may choose
> whether he will remain in the still water, or venture more or less
> down the rapids, or run his boat over the fall. But there is a point on
> the verge of the fall where he has no control over his course; and
> just above that there is a point where he will have to struggle with
> the current in a way which will give his nerves a severe trial, even
> though he may escape the fall. If he is willing to learn, experience
> will teach him the wisdom of confining his excursions to the region
> of easy rowing, unless he has an object in view that is worth the
> cost of going over the fall.[17]

Danger lurked in the hydrokinetic force, the "white water" of male
sexual fluid under excitation; the danger was acute, and Noyes conceded
that his system in the hands of a maladroit amateur could result in neuro-
genic disorders. The risk, however, was quite minimal if the system as
Noyes detailed it was followed, for only "a voluntary suppression of the
commencing crisis would be injurious. But . . . if a man, knowing his

own power and limits, should not even approach the crisis, and yet be able to enjoy the presence and the motion *ad libitum*," the sexual pleasure and physical safety of both partners would be assured.[18]

This was true, according to male-continence theory, because it was categorically possible to separate the generative and erotic aspects of human sexuality. The two levels of sexuality were conceived as related but distinctly separate in function and organization. From a biological standpoint, "the organs of propagation," Noyes wrote, "are *physiologically* distinct from the organs of union in both sexes. The testicles are the organs of reproduction in the male, and the uterus in the female. These are distinct from the organs of union."[19] The "organs of union" were the means of the spiritual pleasure of the sex act for the male, whereas the physical pleasure of sex was ineluctably tied to the reproductive organs. Women were physiologically different from men because they could receive orgasmic release through the "organs of union"; physical pleasure for them did not necessitate reproductive sexuality. This was the physical fact behind Oneida belief that women were subordinate to men. They were physically incapable of controlling their orgasmic response. It was also the fact that gave men power over women through their ability to provide erotic satisfaction for them while remaining above the physical level of response themselves.

In practice, the sex act was completely controlled by the male. No flirting, courting, or open demonstrations of affection were permitted in public. All solicitations for "personal fellowship" came from males (only one sexual experience being permitted per invitation), but provision was made in the early 1860s for a system of mediation, through which women could rebuff undesired suitors. A man "who wished to have intercourse with one of the opposite sex, usually sent a request through some third party, who was nearly always a woman. This third party was most frequently one of the more spiritual and leading members."[20]

According to one informant, however, the system was used more to control eugenically undesirable combinations than as a protection of the feminine right of refusal. Women were disciplined and pressure was brought to bear in cases of obdurate recalcitrance (as was true of male community members as well), by the system of "mutual criticism," a kind of proto–encounter-group therapy, in which an individual was publicly judged by his peers and frankly told of his faults, annoying habits, idiosyncrasies, and virtues. Women's power of refusal was limited to some extent by the status of the male who proffered intercourse. Retribution might follow an impolitic refusal: "If it were one of the leading members she was just as likely to be taken out of any responsible position she held at the time, and not be allowed to do anything until it was thought she had a good spirit and was humble."[21]

Although Oneidans were concerned about the perils of parturition, their primary anxiety in the sexual relationship revolved about the health of the male. This was reflected in complete male control of the sex act; he determined its frequency and its duration and controlled the orgasms of himself and his partner. The frequency of "amative" intercourse, according to a female member of the community, averaged two to three times per week. A more hostile estimate given by a woman who left Oneida in dissatisfaction maintained that there was "a great deal of complaint by the young women and girls . . . of too frequent demands upon them by the other sex. . . . I have known of girls no older than sixteen or seventeen years of age being called upon to have intercourse as often as seven times in a week and oftener, perhaps with a feeling of repugnance to all of those whom she was with during the time."[22]

Although the former estimate seems more accurate for the community as a whole, the latter reveals the effects of complex marriage on the younger women at Oneida. Sexual experiences ordinarily began for both boys and girls two or three years after the onset of puberty, or about seventeen years of age for males and fourteen or fifteen for females. In several instances, girls of nine or ten and boys of thirteen and fourteen were initiated into physical adulthood.[23] This radical foreshortening of the pregenital childhood years was based upon a forthright acceptance of human sexuality and the belief that sexual pleasure was the chief end of sexual intercourse, the birthright of every human being.

Because puberty brought sexual urges in its train, it was assumed that they would be satisfied one way or another. To prevent masturbation and to assure the socialization of the sexual instinct, children who had reached puberty were instructed in the practice of male continence.[24] The theory of ascending and descending fellowship was directly applied to sexual life at this point. For both ideological and pragmatic reasons, young people were initiated into the intricacies of sexual practice at Oneida by elder members of the opposite sex. Pubertal individuals were almost never allowed to have intercourse with their peers of the opposite sex. The goal was "to so arrange the sexual relations of the Community that every man and woman should have his or her heart anchored in the love of spiritual superiors and feel only a minor intensity of love, or at any rate a less uncontrollable kind of love, for spiritual inferiors."[25]

From a physical point of view, because the contraceptive aspect of male continence was essential, those who had not mastered the technique could not be allowed any physical intimacy with fecund females. In that sense there was a hierarchy of males that corresponded to their sexual experience and the degree of mastery they had attained in self-control. "It was very seldom," a former community woman related, that a young man under twenty years of age associated with a woman who had not passed the change of life, or who was not so near it that she would not be likely to become pregnant. . . . As to young women and girls—girls, after they were twenty or twenty-five years old, were allowed to associate with men who were not very much older than they were, but with the older ones, too. Girls under those ages did not, as a general thing, associate with men who were much under forty years, and then very seldom. They were considered better off, morally and physically, if they were sought by men fifty and seventy years of age, and in fact were put under moral pressure about it.[26]

Those males who were unable to control their ejaculations, or "leakers," as they were called in the community, were placed in the same category as young boys. Dr. Hilda Noyes reported that "the menstrating [sic] women declined them and those who had quick or uncontrolled emissions had to take women past the menopause."[27] Dr. G. E. Cragin corroborated this statement, also providing evidence of John Humphrey Noyes's central role in the initiation of female virgins at Oneida: "Girls were 'introduced' with great care, always by N[oyes] or a few older men. Very rarely were two young people allowed to have intercourse, as they naturally tended that way and would have divided the Community into two parties, old and young."[28]

The system was not foolproof and some "accidental" pregnancies resulted (in one instance the result of *coitus interruptus*), but the number of inadvertent fertilizations for the twenty-year period 1848–68 was estimated by Dr. Cragin at twelve.[29]

Despite the rigors of the practice of male continence, the sexual prerogatives afforded those most proficient in *coitus reservatus* seem to have kept accidents to a minimum. Observance of the requirements of the system was conscientious, and even such dodges as the practice of *coitus interruptus*, allowing ejaculation *ex vaginis*, followed by urination to evacuate the urethra of residual spermatozoa, and subsequent reentry and continuation of the sex act, were prohibited. If ejaculation occurred, whether within or without the female genital tract, the sex act was considered terminated, and no reentry was permitted.

Yet those who practiced this form of sexual relationship claimed that "intercourse brought relief to all" and, in a specific reference to young males, that "boys found relief in intercourse from symptoms of annoyance and passion."[30] But the "relief" of males differed significantly from that of females. Males were allowed release for the social emotions surrounding sexual attraction, but were barred from physical release.

Females were allowed relief on both levels. No doubt this was why masturbation, although common at Oneida, was more prevalent among boys than among girls. Self-stimulation among females was declared to be "quite rare." Physical release for men came primarily through nocturnal emissions.[31] It must be recalled here, however, that acceptance of the spermatic-economy doctrine provided a powerful psychological barrier that inhibited frequent male enjoyment of orgasmic sex. Dr. Theodore R. Noyes described the emotional effect of male continence and its satisfactions thus: "It gives rise to all those emotions which are refined and ennobling to both men and women, and reacts favorably upon the system of the male, by causing an active secretion and absorption of the seminal fluid."[32]

Physically, male continence served the needs of Oneida women admirably. Women were expected to have orgasms, and in the early years of the sexual experiment were evidently expected to have multiple orgasms, as in that period the duration of the sex act was *all night*. Oneidans "found after a while, danger in exhaustion from all night, so they were not allowed to sleep all night together." Intercourse was thenceforth limited to the period between ten and twelve P.M.[33]

Women do not seem to have been disturbed by the lack of physical mutuality in the relationship; apparently the psychological relief of freedom from anxiety about pregnancy more than compensated for any feelings of inadequacy their inability to provide orgasms in their partners might have entailed. Men, on the contrary, were herculean craftsmen of the sex act, who "prided themselves on bringing women to climax."[34]

The sexual position most commonly employed further allowed extensive clitoral manipulation, so that "the women were particularly satisfied by the long play."[35] This dorsal-ventral position was described by Dr. Hilda Noyes: "wife on side—upper thigh bent—husband enters from the rear, they play manually with each others [sic] genitals."[36] Oral-genital sex, especially cunnilingus, but occasionally fellatio as well, was practiced. It is probable that most sex acts took place by lamplight with both partners fully nude.[37]

From the point of view of contraception and relief from the burden of childbearing, the system was also beneficial to women. Birth-control practice at Oneida, when coupled with stirpiculture, apparently both lowered the average number of children born to each woman and lowered the female age at first conception. According to a gynecological sample taken in 1872, of the total number of women, 43 percent were childless, and the average number of children per woman was 1.38. If we consider only those women who gave birth *in* the community, the average number of children was 2.42 per woman. For those women whose childbearing years were over before they joined the community, the average was 3.12

children per woman. The average age of women who began their reproductive life at Oneida at the birth of their eldest child was twenty-four
years.[38] When we consider that these women had entered upon an active
sexual life at an average age of fourteen, and that they did not become
pregnant until they had been participating in complex marriage for about
9.4 years, it becomes evident that although they conceived their first child
earlier than women who had been married prior to entering Oneida,
they enjoyed a much longer period of erotic freedom before their first
pregnancy.[39]

And yet, as we have seen, some younger women felt the system made
undue demands upon their sexual natures. In fact, the available evidence
suggests that not only did men initiate all sexual intercourse, but they
also pressed women rather importunately, and subtly cajoled them, to
have sexual relations more often. The same woman who found solicitations too frequent claimed that "the sexual relations were encouraged
very much. The young women were always instructed that the more
unselfish they were in giving the men all the satisfaction they could in
that respect, the nearer they were to God. They were encouraged so
much that those in office would advise and urge it to both men and
women if they thought they did not care much for it."[40]

Her assertion is corroborated by the statement of Dr. G. E. Cragin that
"women's sex appetite grew with cultivation and use, but [was] always
less than men's."[41] This seems incongruous at first glance in view of
sexual practices at Oneida, but when we realize that women could refuse,
but not actively choose, sexual partners; that older men, higher in the
community hierarchy because considered closer to God, were recommended as ideal partners, especially for younger women; and indeed,
that the whole ideological background of these women prior to entering the community had frowned upon any manifestation of feminine
sexual desire, the lack of enthusiasm for complex marriage among the
female population is not surprising. By the mid-1870s a member of the
community remarked that there was "growing dissatisfaction among
women about Complex Marriage; young women especially disliked it—
'it was a man's plan, not a woman's.'"[42] Older men, of course, liked
the system, whereas "older women were accustomed to it, [and] young
people revolted."[43]

The system was indeed "a man's plan" in conception, execution, and
control. Certain women, especially those who were younger or found to
be more attractive, were overwhelmed with requests, whereas others
were left to take the leftovers of this sexual feast. Although sexual acts
tended to be marathons in the early years, this practice was discontinued
by the 1870s because it was "found that long continued intercourse was
injuring some men. After that couples [were] not allowed to stay together

all night. Must finish and leave."[44] The fact that intercourse was then limited, as we have seen, to a two-hour maximum may have been an additional cause of the dissatisfaction expressed by women about the male-oriented nature of complex marriage. Rigid limitation of the hours of intercourse was totally determined by male needs and had nothing to do with, and in fact took little or no cognizance of, female desires or needs.[45]

Some indication of female dissatisfaction with the system was also evidenced indirectly in the observation that lesbianism was condemned. No mention is made of homosexuality, either because there wasn't any, or more probably because it was assumed that male sexuality was carefully controlled (the superior godliness of males depended upon it), and any reference to homoeroticism would have been an open admission of the failure of the system. The reference to lesbianism, though it reinforces once again on a behavioral plane the ideological assumption of the uncontrollable sexuality of women, also indicates that at least some women were not erotically satisfied by the sexual system of Oneida and sought relationships with other women rather than those so closely and rigidly controlled by men in a male-dominated complex marriage. Furthermore, to the extent that lesbian relationships emphasize tenderness, companionship, and emotional warmth, feminine pairings may have provided women a closeness, an opportunity to give of themselves, that the sexual system of male continence denied them.[46]

Nevertheless, women's discontent was not manifested in overtly rebellious behavior or excessive apostatization. Throughout the thirty-two-year history of Oneida, there was a near parity in the ratio of adult members of one sex to those of the other. At almost any time in the community's history, however, the average percentage of women exceeded that of men by about 2 to 5 percent. This slight female surplus reflected the fact that for the period 1855–75, women comprised 57 percent of total adult accessions and only 44 percent of adult withdrawals. Females maintained numerical dominance chiefly because single and widowed women coming to Oneida considerably outnumbered males in these groups. Apparently women in these categories found the Oneida system (before any direct experience of it) attractive; subsequently, when they discovered its practical workings, some of them (especially younger, single women) became disenchanted. A higher percentage of females than males remained at Oneida, though, which suggests that for younger women without husbands and for widows, the social security provided by the communal life-style outweighed discontent with community sexual life.[47]

After 1867, when the eugenic experiment known as stirpiculture was begun, the scrutiny and control of sexual relations at Oneida became even more complete. The practice of *coitus reservatus* remained the only form of birth control, but the discovery of feminine syringes in the out-buildings of the community not long after the discontinuation of stirpi-culture indicates that women also employed some form of douching contraceptive method. This was most probably used in cases of "acci-dental" ejaculation during the eugenic years, because the essence of selec-tivity of parents was to avoid biological "accidents."[48] The presence of these syringes may also indicate a somewhat less than perfect adherence to the rigors of male continence by some male saints.

A sharp demographic change underlay the initiation of the stirpicul-tural system. Whereas in the years 1846 to 1854, almost 70 percent of Noyes's adherents were married, by the decade 1865–75, less than three in ten were married. In the period 1855–75, there was a steady increase in the number of new adherents who were either single or widowed. Between 1855 and 1865, almost 40 percent of the newcomers were single and slightly over one-quarter were widowed. In the next decade the per-centage of single newcomers exceeded 50, and the rate of more elderly widowed declined to just under 20 percent. Thus, the composition of the neophytic group tended to increase the number of single adults present in the community, thereby readjusting the ratio of married persons to total adult membership. The intention of producing genetically healthier chil-dren would have dictated the selection of healthier (which in most cases meant younger) parents, especially mothers. In this regard, it is signifi-cant that 61 percent of the single people and 95 percent of the widowed who entered Oneida in the decade 1865–75 were female. It appears to have been the result of conscious selection, therefore, that the percentage of single adults taken into the Oneida Community reached its highest level in the stirpicultural years between 1865 and 1875, and that in the same years the rate of widowed people taken in dropped 6 percent from its high in 1865.[49]

A domiciliary change followed the inception of selective breeding at Oneida, too. During the first two decades of community life, living quar-ters had been communal or semicommunal; in the early 1870s, separate rooms were available for most members. By 1870, four out of five adult Oneidans had separate beds; if they had bedmates, they were both of the same sex. "So," a statement from the *Oneida Circular* claimed, "instead of all huddling into one bed, as the story goes, we rather carry our refinement to the standard of royalty. The king has his own apartment, and the queen has hers. In the etiquette of high rank, it would be a vul-garity for husbands and wives to occupy the same bedchamber."[50] This represented an improvement on the early years of complex marriage, when certain rooms had been set aside for "social" purposes.[51]

Such living conditions meant that space was limited, and would have necessitated planning ahead and reserving space for sexual encounters. Certainly, in a community as small as Oneida, personal privacy was at a premium, but separate rooms must have made things a little easier for those with delicate sensibilities. Private rooms were especially necessary because the relationship of the stirpicultural parents was a closer and longer-lasting one. Whereas "amative" sexual encounters were limited to a single night, and circulation among all the members of the pantagamous community was strongly encouraged, "propagative" encounters allowed multiple visits (in most cases until impregnation was effected).[52]

The union was a much closer one, too, no doubt, because it was a more mutual and, after the approval of the Stirpicultural Committee had been obtained, a more spontaneous sexual experience. Propagative sexual relations under the selective breeding experiment provided the sole condition under which male orgasm in the sexual act was sanctioned. It was only in selective mating that the total self-surrender of both partners in a mutual giving was achieved. The conditions of propagative sexuality at Oneida were therefore much more equitable than those of amative sexuality. Ironically, then, although stirpiculture necessitated an additional body of rules and approval by a committee, the sex act itself was much freer than with merely social sexual relations.

Selection of partners for stirpicultural mating was done by John H. Noyes and a group of elders, who controlled the process rather closely.[53] But it was Noyes who exercised most of the control. The two pledges signed by the young men and women of the community in 1869 were indicative of his control of selective mating. Fifty-three females resolved

> that we do not belong to ourselves in any respect, but that we first belong to God, and second to Mr. Noyes as God's true representative. That we have no rights or personal feelings in regard to child-bearing which shall in the least degree oppose or embarrass him in the choice of scientific combinations. That we will put aside all envy, childishness, and self-seeking, and rejoice with those who are chosen candidates; that we will if necessary become martyrs to science, and cheerfully renounce all desire to become mothers if for any reason Mr. Noyes deems us unfit material for propagation. Above all, we offer ourselves "living sacrifices" to God and true Communism.[54]

Thirty-eight males signed a statement that asserted:

> The undersigned desire that you may feel that we most heartily sympathize with your purpose in regard to scientific propagation, and offer ourselves to be used in forming any combinations that may seem to you desirable. We claim no rights. We ask no privileges. We

desire to be servants of the truth. With a prayer that the grace of God will help us in this resolution, we are your true soldiers.[55]

The process of selection, however, was usually initiated by couples or individuals who desired to become parents. Noyes and the committee of elders could either approve or disapprove the suggested combinations. In cases of disapproval they would not infrequently suggest alternative combinations more in accordance with the ideals of selective breeding. In some instances, Noyes took the initiative to promote special "combinations" that were believed to be peculiarly felicitous for race improvement. The criteria for selection for fatherhood in the early years of the experiment were predominantly ideological. Those who most conscientiously observed the requirements of *coitus reservatus*, and who were considered the most advanced in Perfectionist religious ideals, were given priority in the mating process.[56]

For women, because healthy mothers were considered the sine qua non of eugenic propagation, the criteria for selection were more physical. Dr. Theodore R. Noyes, as a member of the eugenic committee, provides an eyewitness account of the feminine selection process:

> The Stirpicultural Committee was largely occupied in consideration of cases of women whose remaining child bearing years were getting few, and several times it was necessary to put these cases off and revert to younger candidates. There was some tendency to evil thinking on the part of the elder candidates that younger women were put forward, but we asserted our right to take those who were in their prime, which we took to be from 25 to 30. While 20 is too young as a rule, there are cases when no harm can possibly arise from bearing children at that age.[57]

Noyes's eugenic program sought to translate Perfectionism from an individual to a social basis: a reproductive Perfectionism that would render the kind of gymnastic logic which necessitated a Half-Way Covenant (1657) among the second generation of Puritans, to bring their children within the fold of the regenerate, unnecessary. Under a system of reproductive "progressive perfectionism," the children born of two sinless parents would progress even further beyond sinlessness. Oneidans contended that the Kingdom of God on earth had arrived on 1 June 1847. Perfectionists were, from that time onward, living in the "resurrection state," in which "they neither marry, nor are given in marriage" (Matthew 22:30). The manifestation of the Kingdom of God on earth justified the practice of complex marriage, and the conscientious application of the eugenic principles of stirpiculture, through a series of perfect matings, assured the progressive perfection of the citizens of that Kingdom while still in time. Sex and reproduction, therefore, were *the* agents of reform, or progressive perfection, in Noyes's system.[58]

It was not until later in the experiment that physical and mental characteristics began to take precedence over what were believed to be genetically transmitted spiritual-moral qualities. At this point genealogical and health records came to be of increasing significance to reproductive pairings. This raised the question of incest in a very immediate way. Noyes himself was quite well aware of this, and faced the problem squarely. Stirpiculture, he maintained, "is an attempt to create a new race by selecting a new Adam and Eve, and separating them and their progeny from all previous races. This process implies breeding in and in in two senses. First there must be, in the early stages, mating between very near relatives, as there was in Adam's family; and secondly there must be, in all stages, mating between members of the same general *stock* who are all related more or less closely."[59]

Participants claimed that they knew of no cases in which incestuous relations had occurred, but in view of Noyes's outlook, this does not seem very probable. A careful study of stirpicultural mating at Oneida makes the more likely contention that incest, though limited by the short time the experiment was pursued, was not uncommon. "In practice," we are informed, "such near relations as uncle and niece were twice paired; and it was further carried out in that a considerable proportion of the children have Noyes blood on one or both sides."[60] During the entire decade-long experiment in eugenics, fifty-eight children were born to forty fathers and forty-one mothers. Males were usually at least ten years older than females in all matings, the average ages for parents of each sex being twenty-five to sixty and twenty-three to forty years respectively.[61]

The success of the experiment was remarkable when the practical application of the method is considered. For the first two years of eugenic reproduction (which is the only period for which we have direct evidence provided by a participant), twenty men and twenty-four women were selected as breeders. In the course of two years, sixteen females, or 66.66 percent of the total group of prospective mothers, had been impregnated. The sex life of those selected as breeders was more intense than that of nonbreeders. For those who were chosen to be parents, the average number of sexual contacts *with each other* was about four per month. Because these contacts were most often confined to the period of estimated highest fertility, however, all four sexual experiences usually fell within a two week postcatamenial period.

For the "breeding period," therefore, one-half to two-thirds of the total sexual experience of an individual was with his or her stirpicultural mate. In order to avoid friction with those who were not chosen as breeders, all *males* were permitted to sire one child, but only the preferred "stirps" had more than one.[62] There does not appear to have been a corresponding concern that all *females* be allowed to become mothers. The concern of older women who were passed over by the selection committee has been referred to. It indicates that the stirpicultural system in practice did cause anxiety among some community women. No doubt the denial of devoutly desired and communally valued maternity would have led to feminine dissatisfaction with Oneida life. Deemphasis of the parental relation and communal child rearing, however, siphoned off most of the discontent generated by a frustration of the desire for maternity.

A child born in the community usually took the father's name, but occasionally the mother's or even the name of her husband was assumed. The child was cared for by its mother in her own room for a period of eight to fifteen months, but the nursing period rarely exceeded one year. At fifteen months the child was placed in a common nursery during the day, spending the night with its mother. The child gradually remained in the nursery for longer periods and at four years of age entered the children's department, separate living quarters for children. Child rearing and education under the Oneida system were communal responsibilities; the erotic and personal freedom of individual men and women was thus maintained despite communal reproductive needs. As one of the general principles of the community had it, "The love and care of children in parents should not supplant or interfere with their love as man and woman. Amativeness takes precedence of philoprogenitiveness, and parental feeling becomes a usurpation when it crowds out a passion which is relatively its superior."[63]

Nevertheless, the institution of increased reproduction under the stirpicultural program created more pressures on the practice of sexual communism and generated considerable individualistic sentiment. This threat to the communal sexual life was dealt with by the expansion of methods of control that had been developed early in Oneida history. These were propaganda; the system of "mutual criticism"; separation of those whose affections conflicted with communal needs or goals; and for incorrigibles, expulsion from the community. We can get some idea of the degree to which the ideals and full program of Perfectionist sexuality were internalized by community members by examining how and to what extent the latter three of these devices were employed.

The system of mutual criticism, or communal monitoring of behavior in an encounter-group situation, served largely as a measure of the effectiveness of community dogma. It also served indirectly to reinforce the communal belief system, by providing a forum for testimonials or "witness" by members. In practice, a rotating committee of four members "criticized" each member of the community in turn. After three months in office the committee was replaced, so that ideally everyone would be by turns critic and criticized.[64] The entire life of members of the community was thus under constant scrutiny from several perspectives simultaneously; it was very difficult for an individual to avoid exposure of any asocial actions or tendencies. Individuals were further encouraged to present themselves voluntarily for criticism, or to confess their faults and shortcomings.

Although mutual criticism was used as a disciplinary measure in the broadest sense, it often served to promote individual adjustments to the social necessities of sexual life at Oneida. It was widely employed to overcome "exclusive attachments" or "narcotic love" resulting from residual romantic-love notions. Sarah Bradley, for example, testified that criticism helped her overcome her false modesty and adjust to pantagamy. "I used to make a distinction," she related, "between brotherly love and the love which I had for my husband; but I was brought to see that there is but one kind of love in the kingdom of God."[65] One "A. S. B." was criticized "for a strong tendency to get into intimate relations with some one of her mates . . . to the exclusion of others. This tendency is quite strong, it was thought in most of that class of girls, as well as the habit of talking in a loose, unhealthy way about love. Recommended to them to be freer with those more spiritual and more experienced than they are, and more capable of benefitting them by sound doctrine and example."[66] A Mrs. "A." was criticized for "want of delicacy or refinement, & for being incautious in her dealings with young men."[67]

Criticism in these instances served to secure individual adherence to community sexual ideals and to adjust individual sexual needs and desires to the needs and requirements of the community. A more important use of criticism was to root out and destroy special attachments. With the beginning of the eugenic experiment this danger increased, and criticism for "exclusiveness" and "excessive philoprogenitiveness" became more frequent. The criticism of "F. W. S." and "T. C. M." is representative. A community record reports that their conduct "in continuing their intimacy after it had been partly censured by Mr. Noyes and the family, was spoken of this evening by Mr. Noyes, and severely reprobated by him and others. Their musical practice together has proved a snare to them by leading into false love and disrespect to the criticism of the Community; and rather than have this state of things continue, Mr. N. said he would rather sacrifice their music much as he appreciates it."[68]

Advice in the form of informal community criticism indicates the prevalence of asocial tendencies among parents, especially mothers. In 1864, Noyes admonished the community that "philoprogenitiveness is so strong a passion, particularly among women, that one who has had a family of her own needs rather to devote her after life to recovering herself from the disorders which it has brought upon her, than to continuing the cultivation of it by taking possession of the second generation."[69] Noyes felt that nuclear family sentiment inimical to communal family spirit was created with the expansion of reproduction provided for under eugenic mating. Looking back upon his noble experiment, he wrote that "it was 'first baby, then mother, then grandma, aunt, etc.' until a circle or family clique was formed. These small aggregations were the result of stirpiculture rather than the simple couple."[70]

But sexual relations between "simple couples" had proved only slightly easier to control than those of stirpicultural parents. Certainly if the sexual regulations provided in male continence, complex marriage, and stirpiculture had been uniformly followed, there would have been more difficulty with those who had actually produced children. But the romantic-love tradition and the monogamic bias never really died out at Oneida despite the heroic efforts made in behalf of pantagamy.

Most instances of individuals sent from the central community to one of the branch communities involved cases of exclusive love. No objective evidence exists on the frequency of such deviant behavior, but the testimony of a woman who withdrew from Oneida indicates that such exclusive attachments and subsequent separations were not uncommon. "Love affairs," she noted,

> were frequent and caused a great amount of trouble, sometimes causing one or both of the parties to leave the Community (of their own accord). It was generally like this: If a young couple loved each other and were intimate, so much that they did not care for others, they were severely criticized and separated, one being sent to Wallingford [Connecticut], and all correspondence forbidden. It was frequently the case with those who had children that they were getting too "special" to each other, and to the child. The consequence was that the child would be put into other hands, the father and mother separated, and one or both to have children by others.[71]

Indeed, all the cases of disciplinary action I have encountered in Oneida records involve some form of deviancy from the Oneida sexual code, most often the attempt to form sexual unions without the consent or prior approval of John H. Noyes. An individual was not allowed sexual liberty, Noyes tells us, "until he has decisively adopted our principles" and put himself "wholly in my hands," and "until he openly avows our principles and submits to my instructions."[72] That sexual disobedience prompted discipline was especially true of expulsion from the community, which was tantamount to excommunication. There are only three detailed accounts of expulsion, and all of them center about the question of sexual discipline.

The earliest of these cases occurred at the Putney community prior to the institution of complex marriage there. John B. Lyvere, a somewhat dissolute Perfectionist, wished to marry Almira Edson, characterized as "a coquette." Noyes forbade it, but the pair married secretly, and he expelled them from the community for insubordination to the "acknowledged head of the corporation." The nature of their refractoriness, beyond the threat to Noyes's authority, lay in a failure to internalize the sexual ethic that would soon come to be called complex marriage. They had not learned that "we ought to set brotherly love above sexual love, and that true love was not the blind instinct of brutes, but was founded on confidence and proportioned to worth."[73] In short, their sins were licentiousness, lack of self-control, evasion of the spiritual-sexual hierarchy doctrine, and perhaps worst of all, "special, false-love absorption."[74]

The next case was technically classified as "secession," but it is clear that it was in reality an exclusion of undesirable members. The family involved in this instance was that of Leander Worden. In 1854, Leander heard the Criticism Committee declare that his son, Wallace, "was guilty of licentious actions and foul talk with the children."[75] His wife, Keziah, had an egoistic, disobedient spirit. One of the central community members wrote of her: "Leander is just getting his eyes opened to the fact that she *is* and *has always been*, a very willful woman. She has been an active seducer of men and women. Leander has always been a complete victim of her *fascinations*."[76] She was blamed for the character flaw of Wallace; the responsibility "fell on Keziah as it always has, for having a loose, licentious spirit which was to blame for Wallace's diabolical spirit."[77] In February 1855 the Wordens were "advised" to leave the community.

The final case of expulsion occurred at Oneida before the institution of stirpiculture there and involved a William Mills, called "the human parasite" by Oneidans. His crime was the attempt to force his attentions on the women in the community, or failing that, to seduce young girls. When his sexual aggressions failed, Mills withdrew his two daughters from sexual intercourse with the men of the community. The essence of his transgression of the Oneida moral code was his persistent belief that women were personal property controlled by males; or, as Noyes expressed it, his entertaining "slaveholding principles concerning women." His deviancy was all the more dangerous because he had corrupted many of the young girls who had just reached menarche and rendered them as "willful" and "dissipated" as himself.[78]

In less refractory cases less rigorous forms of discipline, such as repentance and a publicly acknowledged, written confession, or complete social ostracism, were deemed sufficient. The exaction of a confession does not seem to have been used any more frequently than expulsion, but again the offenses meriting such action were sexual. In 1845, just prior to the inception of pantagamy, Mary Cragin and Abram C. Smith carried on an adulterous relationship without consulting Noyes. A written confession was drafted by Noyes, in which the two offenders admitted they were guilty of "licentiousness and deception."[79]

Social ostracism was practiced in the case of Tryphena Seymour. In 1851 she was declared a social deviant because she was "laboring under the spirit of diseased egoism, pride, and love of attention,"[80] and she was shunned by community members at Noyes's recommendation. The intent of this disciplinary action was to "starve Tryphena into submission to Henry [her husband], to give her the real prodigal son's spirit toward the Association so that she will be glad to come here and be a servant instead of wanting to be served."[81] Discipline was thus used to monitor community sexual life and to secure female assent to the ideologically established gender roles and sexual power structure of Oneida.

The record indicates, then, that serious disciplinary measures were only infrequently resorted to and that most instances of deviant behavior were handled by the ubiquitous practice of mutual criticism. Limited admissions and strict screening of candidates no doubt insured that, as far as was humanly possible, only those who seriously believed in Oneidan ideals and would therefore be likely to follow the directives of John H. Noyes were admitted. Regardless of his caution, however, petty dissatisfactions and jealousies seem to have been a daily part of life at Oneida. The very extent of the system of mutual criticism argues as much. Serious dissatisfaction, though, as the withdrawal rate suggests, was probably much more infrequent. For the years 1855–75, the average annual rate of withdrawal remained stable at around 3 percent. The fluctuation in the absolute rate of withdrawal (the differential between the rate of withdrawal and the rate of accession) suggests, however, that dissatisfaction with the sexual code at Oneida increased dramatically during the stirpicultural period. For the years 1855–65, the absolute withdrawal rate was only 0.3 percent, whereas during the next decade it increased to a full 1 percent.[82]

Propagative sexuality was at once potentially more satisfying and more frustrating. It exacerbated the problem of special or exclusive affections both by the intensity of the sexual relationship and by the additional emotional nexus provided by the child. Ironically, it was easier to renounce reproduction altogether than to allow it under strict genetic control. Under male continence, those who joined Oneida, like those who joined the Shakers, had to make a definite commitment to a system that set them apart dramatically from the world they had left. When reproduction was increased under stirpiculture, the Oneida system began to resemble that of the nonutopian world much more closely, and its regimentation appeared more galling.

The elitist nature of the selection process created invidious feelings, and the practice of propagative sexuality undermined the former emphasis on adult sexual relationships. Parenthood, even controlled parenthood, proved to have a romanticism of its own, creating a predilection for enduring monogamic pairings that undermined the carefully constructed system of "love among the Angels." The introduction of a numerically more significant second generation (with expanded eugenic reproduction), whose members were Oneidans by birth rather than by choice, also provided the possibility of a second-generation revolt against the principles consciously adopted by the first.

The experiment at Oneida was a noble one, and many of its goals were laudable, but the difficulties experienced, and the necessity for continual vigilance to keep the system functioning, indicate that Perfectionism could not in the end overcome human nature.[83] To the extent that the system worked (and it did so remarkably well for one generation), it was indeed, in the words of one community member, "a sharp-eyed love."[84] In attempting to create an "Eden of heart-love" where all could enjoy the "feast of joy forever,"[85] Noyes had attempted to create a considerate, unselfish, and totally socialized sexuality. He had tried to expunge the individual dimension of sexuality from the minds of people whose thoughts about sexuality had been shaped by the romantic-love notions of their era; but it was this irreducibly personal, narcissistic quality of sexuality that, from first to last, stemmed the "tide of living healthful love" and prevented the achievement of a completely harmonious sexual perfection.

Chapter 13 🜹 "Misbegotten Males": The Effect of Sexual Perfectionism on the Status and Roles of Women

Et quando natura non potest perducere ad maiorem
perfectionem, inducit ad minorem, sicut quando non potest
facere masculum, facit feminam, quae est "mas occasionatus"
[And when Nature cannot attain the greatest perfection,
it brings forth a lesser; just as when it is not able to produce
the masculine, it produces the feminine, which is a defective
male].

—Thomas Acquinas, *Summa theologica*

The reason is that the female is as it were a deformed male;
and the menstrual discharge is semen, though in an impure
condition; i.e., it lacks one constituent, and one only, the
principle of soul.

—Aristotle, *Generation of Animals*

*T*he Oneida Community presented a social alternative that comprised a unique religious position, the abolition of the family, free sexual association, birth control, eugenics, and the abolition of private property. As the elements of a voluntary society, all these changes in the social structure involved a reconsideration of the position and rights of women both as sexual and as social beings. Most contemporary observers concurred in the belief that the power and liberty of women had been greatly expanded at Oneida, but they differed as to whether such changes had increased the felicity of either the society or the women themselves. The indefatigable English traveler William Hepworth Dixon, for instance, who vacillated between admiration for the social system of the community and disgust with their sexual practices, believed that "the style of living at Oneida Creek gives a good deal of power to women, much beyond what they enjoy under law . . . all say they are happy in their lot."[1]

Opponents of Noyes's community agreed that woman's control of her life was greater there, but concentrated on the erotic freedom that Oneida provided. Mrs. S. T. Martyn, whose personal acquaintance with the Oneida Community must have been minimal, noted that the abolition of marriage was vociferously advocated by women; and yet from a moral point of view, "can a woman so far unsex herself as to promulgate a doctrine which, more than all others, degrades and debases her, and leaves her a defenseless prey to the passions and caprices of the stronger sex?"[2]

But in exactly what ways and to what extent did the Oneida Community offer women real alternatives in their societal and erotic lives? It will be the function of this chapter to attempt to answer this question through an examination of women's work and recreation, the theory of sexual roles as applied in the community, attitudes toward the women's-rights movement, changes in fashion and the ideological assumptions behind them, and a deeper analysis of the system of sexual behavior.

On the practical level of occupational roles, women at Oneida certainly enjoyed more freedom of choice than women outside the community. Because all tasks were apportioned to individuals on a rotating basis, no one was constrained to perform interminably duties he or she found personally repugnant. The percentage of women engaged in household and related duties fluctuated with the felt needs of the community (and, it will be argued, with increasing sensitiveness to women's rights in the 1870s); but these duties remained the primary female responsibility throughout the entire communal period. Even at the height of female employment in areas removed from the domestic sphere, no less than half the total number of women remained "communal housewives." Supervisory and responsible management positions, however, as well as heavy work about the kitchen, generally fell to the lot of men.

"Kitchen men" gathered wood and started the fires and performed any lifting or strenuous labor. The fine art of domestic management was also entrusted to capable male hands. Two women were responsible for the actual preparation of the food, and the twelve "table waiters" were females between the ages of twelve and thirty. Women cleaned the tables and stacked the dishes, and a man carried them out to the kitchen, where other women washed the dishes and silverware.[3] The situation was much the same in the laundry, except that the superintendent in that department was female. In both the kitchen and the laundry there were many steam-operated laborsaving devices, the heavier and more complicated of which were all tended by men. In the laundry, two men put the clothes into the washing machines, removed them, and hung them out to dry. Women operated the steam mangles used for ironing. For a time in the 1860s, two black women were employed two or three days a week to assist in the laundry, but by 1868 they had been dismissed for reasons of economy.[4]

Housecleaning, which raised in the minds of "the masculine part of the family," visions of "horrors," was completely abandoned to community women. "A certain portion of the women," an Oneida report notes, "are appointed to do the work of chambermaids, each having assigned to her the care of one or more rooms. The sweeping and mopping of the public rooms and halls is done by another corps."[5]

Indeed, the extent of female concern with domestic matters and the insufficiency of male assistance in this area led to a minor community crisis in the early 1860s, which very much resembled that which was to occur in Shaker communities in the 1870s. The vast influx of visitors to the community threatened to overburden Oneida women, and concern was expressed about how hospitality and the health of the domestic labor force might be reconciled. No evidence exists to indicate that the problem was solved by providing additional male assistance. On the contrary, the solution seems to have been found in increasing mechanization; delegation of a limited number of males to tend the machines; and by the mid-1870s, hiring some servants from outside the community. The case of the dishwashing machine, invented by the incorrigibly erotomanic William Mills, is indicative of this trend. The machine was introduced into Oneida about the time Mills entered the community. Mills himself worked in the kitchen, bearing primary responsibility for the maintenance and operation of the machine.[6]

Further indirect evidence of the mechanization of domestic labor in the 1860s as a solution to the problem of an overworked female labor force is provided by official community publications. The *Annual Reports* (1849–51), primarily designed as propaganda and information vehicles, say nothing at all about laborsaving devices. The compilation of material from these reports presented in *Bible Communism* (1853) mentions only one Singer sewing machine; but in the *Hand Book* of 1871, we find a fully steam-equipped kitchen and laundry in which machines are largely tended by men.[7] Servants also helped to lighten the domestic labor burden. By 1875, there were two men and five women employed in the laundry, three men and seven women in the kitchen, two men in the heating room, and two men in the tailor shop. All were outsiders.[8]

In the final area of domestic concern, care of children, women were again left virtually in sole possession of the field. Children resided in the Children's House with their teachers, who were also their caretakers. From the earliest years of the community, these teachers had been predominantly women. In 1871 the composition of this corps was over 80 percent female. Women served as children's attendants, however, for only very brief periods, "except in cases of special taste and qualification."[9] As with other departments of the domestic sphere, one man usually took charge of the overall operation of the Children's House.

Two other duties, although they involved adults as well as children, were exclusively female-ascriptive and essentially maternal in character. The first of these was nursing. The only reference we have to this aspect of Oneida life comes from the year 1864, during a diphtheria epidemic. The women drew up a petition, the gravamen of which was the need for male relief, as women bore almost the entire burden. The petition was approved, but the tone of the report indicates that this was rather irregular and that only special circumstances necessitated such action.[10]

The other exclusively female duty was more overtly maternal in character: "The clothes of each man and each child in the Community are given into the charge of some woman to mend and make. The women holding this position are called mothers to those whose clothes they care for."[11] Mending, darning, and sewing (even if done on a machine) were strictly female occupations. If women escaped the daily round of domesticity at Oneida, it was not because they shared their labors in that sphere with men, but rather because of mechanization, division of labor, domestic help, and the system of rotation of duties. Insofar as women participated in traditionally male kinds of tasks, they were "surplus labor," a group of women who could be spared to do something else once the domestic positions had been staffed.

The greatest expansion in female employment outside the domestic sphere came in the late 1860s and early 1870s. Although women comprised 13.11 percent of those reporting a nondomestic occupation in the early years of the community, by 1865 they had fallen to less than 6 percent of that group. In 1867, of seventy-one women able to work, twenty-nine, or 41 percent, were employed in some occupation other than housework. Of those in nondomestic occupations, nearly one of every four was in business and sales (they staffed the community store); two of three were artisans or craftsmen; and one in eight was in a professional category. This left 60 percent of the female work force in traditional household employments. The most significant change in the division of labor came, however, in the 1870s. In 1875, one of every five of those reporting a nondomestic occupation was a woman. Not only was there increased female participation in such occupations, but the sexual distribution of labor had changed dramatically as well. Slightly more than half of those in the business and office category were women in 1875, as were nearly 80 percent of the professional people.[12]

This broadening of female occupational roles seems to have resulted largely from the increasing economic success of the community in the post–Civil War period (and especially the expansion of the Oneida industrial base in 1866 to include the manufacture of silk thread) and from the beginning of stirpiculture in 1867. Its ideological basis (a commitment to women's rights) had been present in the community from the first, but it was greatly intensified in the 1870s, and its practical application was more conscientious than in the earlier years.

And yet, although the silk industry was predominantly staffed by female labor, the overwhelming majority of workers were hired girls and women from outside the community. Ironically, though the expansion of this industry offered additional occupational opportunities for Oneida women, it was not allowed to interfere with the performance of domestic duties. In 1868, for instance, when the silk industry was running at maximum capacity, it required a complement of sixty-seven workers. Of the total labor force, fifty, or nearly 75 percent, were "hirelings."[13] Women also worked in the other major Oneida industry, trap making; but they were confined to merely assembling chains, an occupation they shared in "boom" times with children.

The rationale that kept community women out of industrial labor on a larger scale was clearly set forth in an article that appeared under the title "Women's Work and Wages" in 1868. The peculiar nature of the almost physical relationship that linked the male and the machine, and the coarse masculine conviviality that pervaded the workplace, made woman an alien there and underlined her unsuitableness for industrial occupations. Women made inferior workers whenever they had to use machines, because

> women as a general thing, understand no more of the construction and general working of a machine than is absolutely necessary to run it; consequently, when any part breaks or gets out of order, they are forced to remain idle till a man comes along. Occasionally, it is true, some particularly enterprising female will attempt to repair a disabled machine; but she seldom does more than to repeat the last re-adjustment made by the foreman, with a ludicrous disregard to what the cause of the breakage may be. Then, too, women never work so steadily as men.[14]

In addition to women's basic physical and mental inferiority in machine industry, natural female delicacy, though in the long run it might provide a force for reformation of the male worker, was a decided disadvantage; contact with brutal men in a predominantly male environment posed a sexual threat to a chaste woman. Women would not be safe in a factory workplace until "man becomes a true friend of woman—a protector instead of a seducer. How many factories where men and women are employed are free from the stain of licentiousness? . . . How many girls would come out pure from such an ordeal?"[15]

Although this argument was clearly intended to apply to factories in the outside world, it was not without relevance to working conditions within the community. In 1874, Oneida hired between 25 and 30 seasonal agricultural laborers. Many of these, no doubt, were male. More particularly, in community factories in that year, a total of 203 hired laborers were employed. Of these, 98, or 49 percent, were male; 67 worked in the trap works, foundry, and machine shop. Hired men also worked in the silk works. Because, as we have seen, women did work in the trap manufactory when that branch of community business was swamped with orders, as well as in the silk factory, there would have been some danger of the contamination of pure Oneida womanhood by male "outsiders."[16]

Community women, then, were employed less frequently in industrial production than in other areas of community life. When they were used in the silk and other industries, it was ironically easier for them to attain managerial positions than to work in the production process. Exclusion of community women from the production process insured their purity; they would not come into contact with male hirelings who made the workshops a vulgar, threatening environment for women.

The belief that men were better and more valuable workers in machine industries was concretely applied to the silk industry. Although the community supported the policy of "equal pay for equal work," in practice women who worked in the silk factory received fifty cents less per diem than their male counterparts. In general, women do not seem to have been entrusted with the operation of complicated machinery in any branch of labor at Oneida. Even in strictly domestic labor, as we have seen, men ran most of the heavier and more complicated machines.[17] It was only very late in Oneida history (1871), during the efflorescence of women's rights, that this policy began to change.[18]

That this relative exclusion of community women from industrial labor was not based on any perceived or putative physical infirmity was attested by their participation from the earliest days in "bees" to harvest crops and perform whatever other jobs required additional labor. Gradually, as the economic base of the community changed from agricultural to industrial, hired workers from outside began to perform much of the labor in industry and to a lesser extent in agriculture. Woman's sphere thus became more constricted in the late 1850s and early 1860s, with the increased use of hired "worldlings" with whom it would have been unmeet for her to associate.

This trend in industry was reversed (to a limited extent) in the late 1860s and early 1870s by the rapid expansion and diversification of

Oneida production. In agricultural labor the trend was reversed primarily because of the institution of stirpiculture. Eugenic concern emphasized the health of parents (especially mothers) and the salutary influence of fresh air and outdoor employment. This emphasis was foreshadowed in a call for the creation of a "robust race of women" as early as 1859. "There is a keen appetite rising among us," one writer declared, "for having children . . . but if ladylike habits prevail, and the women grow delicate and feeble, our propagative prospects are very poor. Maternity requires rugged health. If our female branch is sickly, propagation that is worth anything is out of the question. All who are anxious we may advance in the direction of propagation should be equally anxious for the true development of the women."[19]

But physical development alone would insure only healthy births; it would not insure the presence of genetically transferred perfection. To insure a Perfectionist eugenics, the mental and spiritual qualities of the mother required development. Women needed to "feel that they are capable of development in a thousand ways apart from maternity. . . . If they are to be educated and act in the mental sphere, they cannot devote their life wholly to childbearing."[20] It was requisite that women become occupied in areas of concern outside the realm of domesticity and child rearing if they were to become physically and mentally acceptable mothers. The necessity of combating philoprogenitiveness and the maternal instinct (female selfishness) also conspired to promote a broadening of the occupational sphere of women. Physical culture encouraged female participation in agriculture, and the need to escape motherhood prompted participation in business and manufactures. The emphasis on mental and spiritual qualities, however, combined with the (male) fear of contamination of Oneida womanhood by "worldlings," meant that a very high percentage of women would be employed in business, professional, and managerial positions.

By the late 1860s, women were supervising certain operations. This was true not only of such traditionally female occupations as the fruit- and jelly-canning factory and the laundry but also of the satchel factory. A woman became assistant manager of the silk factory (in charge of hired girls) in 1867. Women also participated in all phases of the publication of the various community periodicals. From 1872 to 1875, a woman held the editorship of the Oneida Circular.[21] From about the middle 1860s, women were encouraged to enter the business and professional occupations in the community, and they became bookkeepers, stenographers, and record keepers in increasing numbers. In one instance a woman became a doctor; another was a dentist; and several others were teachers.

Women were not encouraged to enter sales, however, and seldom did so. In part this was another means of insuring minimal contact with men "of the world," and in part it reflected a deep-seated distrust of female capacity for business affairs. Women had a separate business meeting each month (they generally did not attend the male meeting), at which they discussed "dish towels and spoons, and general order about the house."[22] In important matters affecting the community, the decisions were in the hands of men. In March 1864, for example, when the question arose of allowing the railroad from Oneida to Hamilton right of way through their property, a meeting of men was held to determine the proper course of action.[23]

In the matter of recreation, women had been encouraged to participate in outdoor sports with men in the mid-1850s. A few women learned to play baseball in the 1850s, but they were not allowed to swim. In 1866 this partition between the sexes was breached. Oneidans clearly considered this but the beginning of a thoroughgoing reform of woman and her status and role in society. It was proposed that ultimately "girls shall have all the advantages of boys. . . . We have made a beginning in having our girls learn to swim. They have been admitted to a field there which has belonged to men alone, and it appears that they excel in swimming. They shall be admitted to all the sciences, to the whole course of education considered useful to men."[24] But physical culture must come first. Encouraging women to swim provided a starting point. In 1874, Turkish baths were built both at the central community and at the Wallingford, Connecticut, branch. From their inception, women were encouraged to use them both as an aid to health and a means of overcoming the infirmities of the body. Community practice in regard to the baths, as with swimming, however, provided separate hours for use by men and women.[25]

At the communal "bees," which were organized to expedite large jobs like picking strawberries; at concerts and lectures; and at general community meetings, the sexes mingled freely. Outdoor exercise was especially recommended for women, and they shared fully the community frenzy for croquet in the 1860s. It was Noyes's intention, in both work and play, to create a "vital society"; and the full participation and integration of females into all aspects of that society was of paramount importance. If such a society were to be achieved, however, a change in the accepted roles of men and women would be required, a change that went to the heart of social conceptions of masculinity and femininity.

One of the primary methods for achieving such role change was mutual criticism. The ideal of progressive perfection lay in adaptation to one standard of perfect character that combined the best traits of both sexes. As Noyes had admonished his followers as early as 1842, "Men have their peculiar vices, and women theirs; and in some things women must become more masculine, and men more feminine."[26] Mutual criticism served both to indicate character traits sadly in need of change, and to record approaches individuals felt they had made toward the ideal standard. One "A.," for example, was criticized for being "too *masculine*. He would be a better man if he were a little more of a woman: i.e., if his life instead of running so much into strength, ran more into delicacy, affection, amiability—qualities which peculiarly belong to the feminine nature."[27] It was said of "S." that he "has a great deal of what is usually termed manliness. He has encouraged the stern side of his nature, and discouraged the gentle side. He seems to be ashamed to show the softness and tenderness he feels. He needs to know that these two phases of character are not irreconcilable. They are in fact necessary complements of each other."[28]

Women seem to have been criticized in general for female frailty and excessive ardor in "social" matters—what was termed a "leap-year spirit." They were at the same time too feminine and too aggressively masculine. Men do not as a rule seem to have experienced comparable difficulties with femininity in their characters. Women were more frequently aware of a felicitous change of character, perhaps because ideologically they were considered less spiritually advanced than men and therefore had more room for improvement. Mary Cragin's experience was typical: "I have made the most improvement in overcoming effeminacy and false modesty, which was inherent in my nature, and fostered by education. . . . I find myself gaining in courage and true independence of character."[29] Other women testified that they had overcome bashfulness, melancholia, and hypochondria. All the typical maladies that women were heirs to in the romantic-love tradition came under attack under the influence of complex marriage and its disciplinary tool, mutual criticism.

The most concentrated reprobation, however, was mounted against what, from an ideological point of view, was considered the most dangerous and detrimental character trait—philoprogenitiveness. Because this failing was primarily associated with traditional feminine role expectations at Oneida, much of mutual criticism was directed at the reform of this basic female character flaw. The maternal instinct was considered merely a concentrated form of the special affection that Oneidans found so inimical to a vital, pantagamic society. It was indicative of the selfishness and egocentricity that characterized the relatively low level of female spiritual development. The use of mutual criticism to vitiate this stumbling block in the path of female perfection is symptomatic of the way in which ideological assumptions underlay most of the changes in concepts of femininity and sex roles at Oneida. The religio-sexual presuppositions that formed the foundation of all thinking about the relationship between the sexes insured that any reform of sex roles would require a change not so much *for* women as *of* women.

If progress toward the construction of a society that would insure both social and genetic purity were to be made, asocial female tendencies had to be rigorously controlled. A major part of the energy of the community was therefore directed toward the eradication, or perhaps more accurately the socialization, of the maternal instinct. George Cragin set the tone for much of this attack on woman's role as mother in 1845, when he wrote, "As a general thing *mothers* . . . have more life in their children than in their husband, or any other worldly object."[30] Women were peculiarly susceptible to the influence of the devil's "engine of philoprogenitiveness," and their seduction insured the betrayal of their own higher natures, their children, and their husbands.

In Oneida ideology, the servitude involved in maternity is not so much a physical state as a bondage of the spirit to the fiendish powers of selfishness and exclusiveness. The female struggle against philoprogenitiveness is the counterpart of the male struggle to master the procreative aspect of sexual intercourse. The attack on motherhood is the obverse side of the male subjection of his orgasm to the control of his conscious will. In both cases the end in view is the liberation of the will, hitherto incarcerated in a diabolical dungeon, by the exercise of spiritual power flowing from God. The drawback for the female in this struggle is the weakness of her will, or her remoteness from the source of spiritual power. Man can overmaster his will because he is in direct contact with God; woman can only do so in subjection to, or under the guidance of, man. This is why

> conjugal love has precedence of philoprogenitiveness, and should be preserved at all events. As Christ is the head of the male, and of the church, so the male is the head of the female. And as the church is subject to Christ, so the apostle enjoins that the female should be subject to the male. Therefore if it be possible for a case to occur in which duty to the husband and duty to the child come in competition, the latter must give place to the former inasmuch as the root and stock are of more importance than the branches.[31]

The spirit of "masculine independence" was not adopted without a struggle by Oneida women. They resisted the loss of power over their children and husbands that accompanied the death of philoprogenitiveness. The conflict centered on the process of child rearing and the procedures to be followed in the Children's House. As an Oneida publication described the problem: "The government of children forms one of the hardest knots of discord in common society, and is not without its difficulties in the Community. There are two poles of influence to be seen and conciliated, one represented by the father's exacting and truthful severity; the other by the mother's and grandmother's indulgent tenderness."[32]

The persistent undertone of maternal instincts formed a leitmotif in community life; in diminuendo during the 1850s, it reached a crescendo in the mid-1860s that continued into the 1870s. Noyes realized the danger maternal instincts posed to his system and took steps quite early in Oneida history to combat them. Many of his policies seem to have been a concession to what he reluctantly considered the inveterate nature of the maternal instinct, an attempt at once to gratify the instinct and to socialize it. One of the primary methods used was the employment of women in the Children's House (but, be it recalled, under *male* supervision), to oversee the process of child rearing.[33] Another important device was the appointment of "mothers" to care for the clothing of the men and children of the community. Expansion of maternal love to the entire community, or at least to children and men who were not directly related to her, undermined any tendency toward special or selfish philoprogenitiveness. This paralleled the attempt to prevent special love in the sexual relationships between men and women.

Two other important antimaternal measures were more actively aggressive and indicate the thoroughness of the campaign against motherhood. The first, which was begun in 1851, was intended to bear fruit in the second generation rather than among those who had come to Oneida as adults. This was the destruction of all the dolls in the community. The language used in reference to dolls reveals both the aggression generated in the community against children and the Oedipal foundation of it. Dolls were more than symbolic of maternal roles in Oneida life; in their ritualistic extirpation they functioned as scapegoats and surrogates for children of flesh and blood. This was evident in the chastising of young girls for "talking to them as though they were living children."[34]

The committee of three women that supervised the "doll-revolution" induced its young charges to sign a testimonial that clearly identified the reified maternal spirit and the objects through which it manifested itself with the supine and susceptible will of the female and the concupiscible beguilement of Satan. "We think that this doll spirit," the document concluded, "that seduces us from a Community spirit in regard to helping the family and that prevents us from being in earnest to get an education is the same spirit that seduces women to allow themselves to be so taken up with their children that they have no time to attend to Christ and get an education for heaven."[35]

The ritualistic nature of the "sacrifice" of dolls united the conflagration of the satanic spiritual force that mesmerized or magnetized the female with the martyrdom of female philoprogenitiveness and the redemption of the female through the burnt offering of the substitute "children." By extension, children cherished were a diabolical influence, whereas children renounced became a means of regeneration for their mothers. The solemnity of the rites of abolition reflected the psychological depths the ceremony was intended to plumb. Harriet M. Worden provides us an eyewitness account: "We all formed a circle round the large stove, each girl carrying on her arm her long-cherished favorite, and marching in time to a song; as we came opposite the stove-door, we threw our dolls into the angry-looking flames, and saw them perish before our eyes."[36]

Once the cherished objects had been abandoned, they were never again permitted in the community. But maternal instinct, which was symbolically sacrificed in 1851, would not down. In 1868, concurrently with the initiation of stirpiculture, mothers were required to give over the care of their children's clothes, which had hitherto been solely in their hands, to the attendants of the Children's House. The intent was to remove the last measure of control, the sole remaining link that fostered maternal selfishness; to completely communalize the children.[37] The episode is of a piece with the prohibition on dolls and stands as the culmination of the aggressive attack upon the role of the female as mother that went on unintermittingly at Oneida from 1850.

Women, however, do not seem to have welcomed wholeheartedly the freedom involved in the death of philoprogenitiveness and the change from monogamous to pantagamous marriage. When the community was on the verge of breakup in July 1879, Frank Wayland Smith, one of the "central members," reported to John H. Noyes that "there is among the young women a powerful sentiment in favor of marriage pure and simple. . . . A number of the young women . . . do not hesitate to say that they will have no children except by a husband to whom they have been legally married. The next class younger is still more set in this feeling. . . . The only feasible plan seems to be to modify into a Cooperative Society with familism and private purses."[38]

It is only within the context of culturally prepotent maternal instincts and the failure of complex marriage to root out the romantic basis of special affection that the Oneida position on women's rights and status can be understood. Questions of women's rights—the degradation of women, the necessity for equal educational opportunities for both sexes, the right of women to control their own bodies and sexual lives, and equal pay for equal work—were of central concern from the beginning of the community. As early as 1840, Noyes had covenanted with his wife to safeguard "*Health, Comfort, Economy and Woman's Rights*," in their housekeeping arrangements.[39] The position of the Oneida Community, however, was neither so simple nor so unequivocal. Ideological presuppositions affected the meaning attached to women's rights in practice, especially from the male point of view; and residual romantic notions and pronatalism inherited from a precommunal experience prevented the females from too importunately pressing their claims.

In certain peripheral ways a degree of respect was accorded women, but without materially altering their status in the community. This was true, for instance, in the mode of address in current use. Females were always referred to as "women" rather than "ladies," and all adult women were addressed as "Miss," with the exception of those who were very old, who were called "Lady." But this had reference only to the leveling of distinctions between women. Oneida policy on the relationship between male and female adhered to the more traditional doctrine of spheres, and was reflected in the maintenance of separate shelves of books for boys and girls in the Children's House.[40]

The male attitude toward women's rights may be surmised from the ideological position of the community. That attitude was essentially Pauline in nature, and it was indeed the thinking of Paul, filtered through the mind of John H. Noyes, that pervaded most aspects of the relationship between the sexes.[41] It will therefore be more fruitful to examine the feminine attitude toward women's rights, both because one would expect most resistance to Oneida ideology from women and because women had internalized community dogma to a somewhat lesser extent than men.

Apparently many women, especially younger women, were dissatisfied with the practice of complex marriage and male continence. They clearly considered the sexual ideology of Oneida male oriented and male dominated. A woman who left the community in the 1870s claimed that there was a great deal of discontent among the young women during that decade about the sexual system at Oneida. "Ten years before," she added, "they *felt* just the same, but partly in bondage to their religious beliefs about it, and partly from fear of criticism and the knowledge the relation with a loved one [special affection] would be broken up, they were quiet, and submitted."[42] A careful anthropological student of Oneida sexuality, who wrote in the 1890s, confirmed the "disinclination of many of the young generation to accept the peculiar tenets on which rested the whole system."[43]

Feminine discontent, then, was in part a persistent phenomenon, an obdurate adherence to the romantic-love tradition; and partly the result of the historical development of the community and its ideology, which reinforced the tendency to exclusive, noncommunistic love. The maturation of the second generation of Oneida women and the roughly coincident initiation of stirpiculture combined to render discontent more serious and widespread in the 1870s. It was clear that "the affection for individuals, engendered by living in pairs for stirpicultural purposes, was fatal in a number of cases to the love for all, regardless of person."[44]

Women were obviously cast in the role of rebels and underminers of the social order by the very assumptions of sexual ideology at Oneida. To what extent, in the area of women's rights, a matter directly related to their own interests, did they live up to their reputation? In general, women spoke out more about women's rights than did men, but their tone and the content of their utterances do not indicate any very serious divagation from the accepted community ideological position. The most typical female response to questions about the status of women at Oneida was complacency. Female testimony included in the official *Hand Book*, published in 1871, when agitation of female rights questions was at its highest in the community, reads like a lyrical panegyric of the communistic system. Woman found herself "the free and honored companion of man" in a society that "emancipates her from the slavery and corroding cares of a mere wife and mother."[45]

But apparently women were *not* concerned about equality with men, for "through it all, they have not ceased to love and honor the truth that 'the man is the head of the woman,' and that woman's highest, God given right is to be 'the glory of man.' "[46] Mutual criticism was employed to keep women from becoming too revolutionary in their pursuit of equality, and women participated in the process of socializing their rebellious sisters and helping them find satisfaction within the confines of the accepted communal mores. The criticism of Miss "M.," uttered by Mrs. "C.," illustrates this kind of behavior. "When she first came here," Mrs. "C." testified, "she had some ideas of women's rights which she will learn to be false."[47]

Those false ideas involved feminine self-assertiveness and failure to understand that the implementation of women's rights had been co-opted by the male hierarchs. Ironically, the ostensibly most submissive form of behavior, full acceptance of the traditional spheres doctrine of the outside world and a concomitant belief in female moral superiority, was actually the most subversive of Oneida values. Male control of the sociosexual system meant that women could rebel only by going outside that system, by asserting precommunal prerogatives associated with traditional monogamy and motherhood. It was primarily for this reason that such energetic efforts were made to control this kind of behavior at Oneida.

It was preferable that women accept their moral inferiority and acknowledge their indebtedness to the supererogation accomplished through excess male virtue for any advance in rights or status they gained. In that way, the male remained in full control of the overall reform process as well as the sex-specific reform necessary to elevate woman to equality with man. Certain concessions were granted to women in the way of rights, but they were always privileges granted by men; questions were decided chiefly on the basis of their effect upon the ideological system of male continence–stirpiculture, not according to their impact on male-female relationships.

Although there is no documentary evidence to support such a contention, the tone of community periodicals in the 1870s suggests that there was a very persistent "underground" demand for expanding the rights and enhancing the status of Oneida women. This discontent must have been much broader than the restiveness and dissatisfaction of younger women with Oneida sexual relations, discussed above. Official statements imply that general feminine discontent was met by partial concessions from the male leadership (which served to defuse the revolutionary potential of female dissent) and by "official" female statements of how good the position of women in the community really was. To the extent that the latter strategy was followed, it only opened the door, as we shall see, for female rebellion from another perspective—that of the true-woman ideology.

When the expansion of opportunities for women and female suffrage were broached at Oneida in the 1870s, the tone and tenor of the responses indicated a strict adherence to the idea that the two sexes possessed physiologically determined differences that were not susceptible to alteration, and that equality of status was therefore undesirable. In 1865, under a column of "Letters from Women," a piece entitled "Woman's Sphere and Influence" made the reality of the situation quite clear: "There is no gainsaying the truth that the position of woman is to be subordinate to man; this is her sphere, she can have no rights out of it, and all *her* duties are within the circle of *his*."[48]

The essentially conservative stand of Oneidans on women's rights was unequivocally established in a piece entitled "Woman's Rights," published in a community organ in 1876. In view of the dissatisfaction of Oneida women with the antiromantic and antimaternal policies carried out under complex marriage and stirpiculture, the echoes of the monogamic bliss of the true woman that ring throughout this piece may well have been closer to the hearts of Oneida women (especially younger women) than a more militant statement of desiderata would have been. "I believe woman's influence," the writer concluded, "in her divinely-ordained sphere to be unbounded, provided she be a true woman."[49] Ironically, the qualities of that woman were precisely those that suited her for maternal rather than communal responsibilities. In the midst of an article published in 1878, which referred to women in sororal terms and discussed the "working woman," the underlying assumptions about the status of women are patently obvious. "In the family," we are told, "woman is man's superior. Intuitively, she sees the fitness of things, and can act wisely and unhesitatingly. At all events, woman is instinctively progressive, and we dare not set the limits of her future agency in the elevation and refinement of the human family."[50] The inability to get beyond role stereotypes grounded in the maternal function of the true woman was also evident in the arguments for broadening the basis of female labor. If women were allowed in occupations formerly monopolized by men, they would bring those housewifely, maternal, and purifying influences into the dirty, irregular, impure world of male labor.

Oneida women were thus caught in an ideological cul de sac. When they thought to achieve equality with men, they only discovered that a dreadful, stifling, circumambient atmosphere kept the two spheres safely in their independent, though adjacent, orbits. Any progress toward a less procrustean role structure depended on a clear recognition of female inferiority and spiritual benightedness and of the spiritual superiority and condescending generosity of the male.[51] What woman required was not women's rights, but "womanly needs": "More than the need of suffrage, of reform, of privileges, we believe is the need of a change in woman herself. Badly as society is organized, we scarcely believe it excuses woman for being what she alas! too often is, vain, showy, careless of example and influence, falling far below her high ideals."[52]

Perhaps because of women's acceptance of their need for personal, sex-specific reform rather than societal reform, the organized women's movement received only a modicum of attention in community publications. It was no accident that it was not until 1878, only a year before the unique experiment at Oneida was dismantled, that a column entitled "Women's Topics," espousing a feminist point of view, appeared in a community publication (the *American Socialist*). Only then were discussions of women in nondomestic occupations, education, and politics more frequently undertaken. At the same time, the terms "sisters" and "sisterhood" in reference to women as a group with common interests began to be used.

Nevertheless, the concern appears to have been primarily exoteric; many, perhaps most women, seem to have been quite satisfied with their condition and status within the community, and even grateful to those whom they considered their munificent male benefactors. A statement written by a group of community women in early 1874 is indicative of this position:

> Our readers do not need to be informed that the Community took high ground on the subject of Women's Rights years and years ago. Curiously enough though, the movement did not originate with the women; nor was it urged forward by Women's Conventions or by the use of the ballot or any of the usual methods of insurrection. Yet certain it is that some way we have obtained our dearest rights and so have no occasion to get up meetings to talk about them as a separate concern. The spiritual and social questions that agitate women's meetings outside are freely discussed by us, but to confess the honest truth, we find ourselves criticizing ourselves oftener than we do the men.[53]

In general, the Oneida Community supported women's rights because they were considered antipathetical to the monogamous system. "Whatever may be the professed aim and object of this movement," they stated, "one thing is certain: its *result*, so far as it has any, must be against marriage. The things claimed and demonstrated to be the just rights of women, are wholly incompatible with their present domestic relations; and if they persist in the attempt to gain their rights, marriage must be subverted."[54]

Specific reforms, however, were considered on their individual merits. Consider the community attitude toward divorce, for example. Very little space was given to this reform, which was considered essential by many people involved in the crusade for women's rights, in the Oneida press. It was considered proof of the instability of the monogamous system as well as a life preserver for the moribund sexual arrangements of outside society. Oneida policy, therefore, either ignored the question totally or favored divorce solely on the grounds of adultery. The whole question was considered on an ideological rather than a pragmatic basis: would support for more lenient divorce laws aid the struggle against monogamic marriage, not would it benefit women who were the victims of that system?[55] A woman summed up the essence of women's rights attitudes in the community very neatly: "I am a woman's rights advocate. . . . The grand right I ask for women is to love the men and be loved by them. . . . It is but a cold, dismal right, in my opinion, to be allowed to vote, or to acquire and hold property. . . . I would rather be tyrannized over by him, than to be *independent* of him, and I would rather have no *rights* than be separate."[56]

Loved they were, at the expense of some tyrannizing; certainly they were not permitted to become so independent as to threaten the fine-honed edge of what was aptly called *male* continence. The chief example of how the potentially subversive feminine nature was controlled in its social manifestation was the measures undertaken for fashion reform at Oneida. Fashion reform demonstrates, probably more clearly than any other aspect of communal life, the presuppositions that generated most changes in the relationship of the sexes: reform mainly *of* the female, only secondarily *for* her, and very seldom *by* her.

The ironic vacillation between the overwhelming attractiveness of sex and the fear of the deceitful, seductive character of feminine wiles that appeared in all sexual interactions at Oneida also determined its approach to dress reform and fashion. Although logically it only made sense that women who labored alongside men should abandon certain of the more frivolous luxuries and fashions of the world, economic and, more importantly, sexual reasons were central to these changes.

The bloomer costume—a dress, the full skirt of which came to just two inches below the knee, and "pantalettes," or leggings, which stretched from the ankle to halfway above the knee—was adopted during the critical stage of early construction at Oneida, in which the women actively participated. This costume thereafter became characteristic of Oneida women and was consistently championed in community publications, where it was associated with a leveling, democratic influence.[57] Most of the cumbersome and fraudulently beguiling undergarments that were so much a part of the mystery of the middle-class woman at mid-century were abandoned with the long dress. Corsets and petticoats were not worn; the only undergarments women used were those common to children of both sexes—chemises and drawers. Neither the crinoline nor bustle fashion was ever adopted at Oneida. Such aids to the natural figure as "palpitating bosoms," "heavers," "plumpers," and "false calves" were considered dishonest; women were encouraged to remain "*genuine* from head to foot," even though such artificial assistance might have enhanced the appeal of some women in an age that preferred large breasts, wide hips, and rather heavy legs.[58]

The use of all cosmetics was discouraged as well; no rouge, toilet water, eyebrow coloring, or lip balm was employed. Occasional instances of the surreptitious use of hair dye to hide traces of grey were the sole exception.[59] Jewelry, though discountenanced as a violation of strict communism and a manifestation of selfish ostentation, was cherished by some of the women. The practice of women wearing their hair short, or "down in the neck," which was then the fashion for young girls, was adopted at the same time as dress and fashion reform. It represented both a voluntary renunciation of luxury and a necessity in a society that afforded little leisure time in which to brush and put up the hair.

All of this represents a reform in the role of women, a liberation from some of the more degrading, if not positively debilitating, aspects of femaleness, but for what end? The goal here, as with other reforms of the sexual relationship at Oneida, was prophylactic: to control the female and to protect the male from his own sexual desires, which threatened to be inordinately excited by feminine seductiveness. The adoption of the short dress and bloomer costume, of short haircuts, and of the rejection of cosmetics was an attack on the romantic-evangelical conception of woman as angel and savior; and by linking women with children (through their appearance), these devices expressed both women's dependence and men's desire for pure, virginal women, whose ambiguous fertility and minatory maternal instincts had both been effectively nullified.

The dress of the middle-class American woman of the Victorian era expressed her isolation from the world of toil and pain (her ethereal qualities), as well as her position as the goddess of the hearth. Her angelic nature was expressed in the lace that trailed about her sleeves and bodice and the lappets of her gown. Leg-of-mutton sleeves, in their most extreme extension, reached behind the wearer's back and flapped together, suggesting the wings of an angel. Crinoline fluctuated in popularity in the nineteenth century, but the hoop assumed its place in the 1860s, giving women a stature that was truly superhuman.[60] The change in women's attire at Oneida expressed a rejection of the apotheosis of woman as the moral arbiter of society and as the majestic matronly figure of awe in the home. The adoption of pantaloons and short hair, coupled with a short skirt (the costume of young children of both sexes at Oneida), underlined woman's need for guidance and control. Beneath the banner of reform, the aureole was wrested from the brow of woman, the crosier from her hand.

If women were spiritual children, it was but a short step to the emphasis on their physicality. Dress reform was thus commonly recommended as an enhancement of the physical charms of women. The point was made most tellingly in an article significantly entitled "Instinct Will Out." Woman's dress, it was argued, should "conform somewhat to Nature's outline in order to be beautiful. A tapering calf and small ankle are not indelicately included in the points of female beauty. What could worse misrepresent the outline of nature than the present cone-shaped skirt, widening as it descends from the hips, and belying even the existence of feet!"[61] The logic was circular: women required control because they were not spiritual enough to control themselves; yet the justification for providing that control over their external appearance was the need to render them more naturally physical. The system was a self-perpetuating objectification of the female. Control and power were the essence of the game. This was most clearly reflected in Oneida proscription of cosmetics, and especially in the adoption of a highly austere hairstyle.

Cosmetics as they were used in the nineteenth century both reinforced the wanness of the angelic woman and tantalizingly emphasized her sexuality. Powder was widely used at mid-century to increase paleness; and rouge kept two faint spots of pink in the cheeks, lest anyone think the lady was totally ethereal. Mouths were faintly painted into small rosebuds, at the same time symbolic of virginity and recalling Cupid, cherubic god of desire.[62] Proscription of this ritualistic mask helped insure that the male at Oneida would never fall at the feet of such a goddess of connubial bliss.

Hairstyles outside Oneida were an ambiguous expression of femininity. Hair was long, but usually worn braided, and wrapped in coils, with or without curls. The addition of large quantities of false hair was also quite common. A very strong sexual undertone is evident in these styles. Many of them resemble the external female genitalia. They suggest at once the power of virginity and the promise of fertility.[63] It should be noted in passing, in view of the importance of water imagery to the description of the technique of male continence (the exercise of self-control to insure that, metaphorically, the craft remains in "the still water above the fall"), that one of the most prevalent styles of coiffure in the period 1860–70 was popularly called "the waterfall."[64]

The element of sexual titillation and coquetry involved in these styles would have been rejected in Oneida tonsorial fashion because they seemed so representative of woman the deceiver and betrayer. The ideological basis for wearing the hair tightly braided and covering the back of the head was reinforced by phrenological thought, which located the seat of amativeness (the cerebellum) at the back of the head and base of the skull. After much dispute, it was agreed at Oneida that hair might be worn short (without the danger of women falling into licentiousness), because the dress covered the critical body parts![65]

The thrust of most attempts at equalization of the sexes at Oneida was to make woman "what she ought to be, a *female-man*."[66] This desire to make a woman into a man played an important role in the psychological dimension of Oneida sexual experience. On the one hand, men, who experienced great difficulty controlling their own sexuality, could deal with the anxieties generated by the fear of failure by projecting their own weaknesses and powerful desires onto women. Ironically, from this perspective, though women bore the stigma of guilt for male sin, they functioned as the very "saviors" that much of Oneida "reform" policy was designed to deny they were.

The aggressiveness of the male attack on femininity and women's position in society, as well as the basic insecurity of men, was most clearly expressed in a statement on high heels by Noyes's eldest son, a Yale-educated M.D.:

> Your trouble is that you are a *woman*, while you ought to be a man. Christ is a man, and a very strong man too. The word to us is, *Put on Christ*, and this word is to women as well as to men. The very thing you want is to get rid of your womanhood, which is your weakness. You think you are the "weaker vessel," but there is no "weaker vessel" in Christ. All are one; there is neither male nor female; all are strong; all are soldiers. So long as you count yourself a woman, bound to follow the fashions, tripping about in your high-heeled boots to prove yourself distinct from men, as the "weaker vessel" you will be weaker according to your faith. . . . Women must come up into unity with men, and men into unity with Christ. . . . Paul says, "put off the old *man* with his deeds." I say "Put off the old *woman*, with her deeds, which are a great deal worse!"[67]

It remains only for us to consider the deeper meaning of male continence in the struggle to restrain the "old woman." The system was wonderfully ambiguous. On one level it represented autonomy for the male, in that his sexual climax was overmastered by his own will. On another level it represented submission to the strictly animal nature of sexuality (which Noyes associated with women), in the form of the female orgasm. Although from one point of view a very significant gain in erotic freedom for women, such a system represents, viewed more intensively, an even more insidious dehumanization of women as sex objects. When male continence was conjoined with the eugenic system of stirpiculture in 1867, the arrogation of the female reproductive capacity to males afforded an even more complete expression of the control of the will (male) over the body and its sexuality (female).

In essence, the system, from a male point of view (and it was after all, called *male* continence), was a formula for transcendence: a sexual mysticism grounded in a thorough control of the will. The ideal was the total control of the body by the will. Only such transcendence of the physical legitimized the participation of the spiritual man in the sex act. As John H. Noyes expressed it, "Until the head [the seat of the senses] has found its strength in subjection to the heart [the seat of the will], it ought to be withdrawn from the poisonous influences of the external world."[68]

Transcendence in the Oneida system required of the spiritual man a certain inurement to discomfort if not actual pain, or in its more advanced form, the denial of pain by the conscious will. In this respect, male continence was simply one of a series of community schools that taught discipline and self-mastery. It is interesting to note in this connection that, although those not intimately familiar with sexual life at Oneida assumed that the practice was productive at least of discomfort if not of positive physical deterioration, only one old man seems to have ever publicly complained of any incommodious effect—a postintercourse pain in the testes.[69] Oneidans would have considered him an "old man" indeed!

But self-mastery did not provide the anxious male with enough control. As we have seen, he hoarded his physical-psychic energy and mistrusted the motives of his female associates. He feared the loss of control over his energy, his source of power. It was for this reason that he attempted so vigorously to direct the process of birth itself; if he could control the ambivalent power of female fecundity, the destiny of his seed, the spark of his energy, might be assured.[70] A system of eugenics and controlled mating made this possible. On a social level, the issue was the triumph of human energy over nature, order over chaos. As one community member told a reporter, the "final supremacy over nature lies in the full subjection of one's body to intelligent will."[71] The harnessing of male sexual energy would make it available to work *for* man instead of against him;

it would provide a powerful, natural civilizing and spiritualizing force. This striking prolepsis of Freudian sublimation theory was consciously employed as an argument for the Oneida system: "It . . . economizes the love principle. There need be no waste of it. It can all be turned to good account and made to bless the race incalculably. The entire power is confined for use—utilized as water is by a perfect dam—and made to turn machinery."[72]

This need for control expressed in the sex act was a reflection of the compulsive need for order that characterized the hierarchical presuppositions of Oneida sexual ideology. Any deviation of the stream from its bed, any attempt to tamper with the dam, but most especially any effort to replace the keeper of the floodgates was not only inimical to social order, but a criminal attack on civilization itself.[73]

Self-denial was at once the essence of civilization and the source of male power and prestige. It was "the great duty of self-denial, or the proper government of ourselves," which afforded "that spiritual power which man possesses, enabling him to subject all the faculties of his mind and body to a given object, [and it] is that which distinguishes him from the brute creation."[74] Ironically, although the system inculcated a supra-romantic approach to love (love of love itself, not of the individual beloved), and though it emphasized social duties, the key to its functioning was not universal in compass, but rather egocentric. Noyes had expressed this as early as 1835 in a letter to his mother. "I have learned," he wrote, "that the love of God, self-love, and the love of mankind are all one; that perfection, that is enlightened self-love, is and ought to be the mainspring of the human machine; that in blessing and perfecting myself I glorify God, and bless mankind. I have learned that perfect self-possession stands first in the list of blessings which God gives his sons, and that self-knowledge is the first lesson in their education."[75] This emphasis on the autonomous, self-sufficient will provided a counter, centrifugal force that offset the centripetal force of communistic love and society. It was concretely expressed in the system of male continence. Male abstention from orgasm meant a reservation of a part of himself from the female, a certain sense of disinterestedness that preserved his autonomy and his purity.

It was this conflict between the needs of the self and the ideals of the community that led to the breakup of the Oneida system of sexual adjustment and the reinstitution of monogamous marriage in 1879. Many observers blamed the "monogamous instinct" and maternal feelings, and certainly residual traces of their inherited ideological backgrounds were part of the cause; but this explanation overlooks the tension and anxieties inherent in the system of male continence–stirpiculture, which were more the fault of the male, in a male system, than of the female.[76] The system provided a channel for male attainment of perfection, but in its emphasis on female inferiority, and need of reform, it effectively shut women off from attaining an equal perfection.

The failure of the system was due not to outside interference or opposition but to the persistence or reemergence of precommunal value patterns and ideological assumptions and the inability to root out basic human selfishness, which provided an inherent vein of weakness in the rock on which the foundation of the edifice was constructed. The founding generation had been willing, on the whole, to subordinate itself to the ideological prescriptions of the community; but the younger generation, which led the revolt against the Oneida sexual system, had not been successfully indoctrinated with community norms. Apparently, the young people were not sufficiently sealed off from outside influences to preclude their perception that they were missing something. We can only speculate here, of course, but it seems likely that the elder generation had its misgivings about Oneida sexuality and that their ambiguities subtly transmitted to the communal children a sense of disquietude and uncertainty about complex marriage.[77] And certainly, both founding and second-generation members were subject to the strains and temptations to isolated romantic attachments that accompanied the beginnings of eugenic reproduction.

It was one of those little ironies of history that found John H. Noyes, who had metaphorically warned men against venturing in the sexual act too near the "verge of the fall where he has no control over his course," in the twilight of his career living in exile within sight of Niagara Falls, the most powerful rushing of waters in America.[78] There he sat, waiting to be washed over the precipice by the boiling rush of white water. The cultural and biological forces of sexuality he had tried to dam up in the toils of his sexual system had in the end burst their bonds and broken the man who would have mastered them.

Part V ❧ Distinguishing the Church from the World: Sectarian Communitarianism and Nineteenth-Century America

Chapter 14 🐍 "A Part of the Blest Family Above": The Maternal-Familial Paradigm of Utopian Society and Its Relation to Broader Cultural Patterns

*The male is born intellectual and the female volitional . . .
the male is born into the affection of knowing, understanding,
and of growing wise, and the female into the love of
conjoining herself with that affection in the male.*

—Emanuel Swedenborg, *Conjugal Love*

*Der Mann ist für das Weib ein Mittel: der Zweck ist immer
das Kind. Aber was ist das Weib für den Mann? Zweierlei will
der echte Mann: Gefahr und Spiel. Deshalb will er das Weib,
als das gefährlichste Spielzeug* [Man is for woman a means:
The end is always the child. But what is woman for man?
The true man wants two very different things: Danger and
sport. Therefore, he desires woman as the most dangerous
plaything].

—Friedrich Nietzsche, *Also Sprach Zarathustra*

*A*nxiety about sexual behavior, the family, and sexuality and sex roles, which was of such importance to the three utopian communities discussed in some detail in the preceding pages, was widely shared by the broader nineteenth-century American society. Although most areas of concern provided some evidence for at least a guarded optimism about continuing progress, moral life appeared not only refractory, but positively contradictory of the generally observable trend. Sexual problems were the resistant strain of an errant humanity that the universal solvent of perfection had not been able to expunge. As one historian of ideas expressed it, "while Americans felt deeply that they could look forward in the near future to an approximately perfect world under the beneficent influence of Christianity and democracy they realized sadly that no improvement was apparent in the area of sex; in fact, the growing cities with their blaring vice areas . . . gave the impression that conditions were getting worse."[1]

Communitarian societies provided one means of coming to grips directly with the intractable problems of sex. Their solutions proceeded on both the behavioral and the ideological levels; but it was the latter that was of fundamental importance, because it provided the sense of stability necessary for the acceptance of social change. Concern over the *legitimization* or *justification* of intercourse, which became highly self-conscious in the eighteenth-century antimasturbation literature and was reflected in the onset of the antiprostitution crusade in early nineteenth-century American culture, assumed increasing importance from the mid-1830s to the end of the century, and indeed on into the twentieth century.[2]

The period was one of ideological crisis generated by ambiguous feelings about behavioral change. People were alarmed by the fear that sexual morality was becoming looser and behavior less controlled; yet they were concurrently attracted and repelled by the argument that erotic sexuality quite apart from reproductive sexuality was, if not preferable, at least as valuable as reproduction devoid of any pleasurable intent. Out of guilt they lashed out at behavior that they, or their neighbors, or the family that occupied the adjacent pew on Sunday morning practiced even if they did not preach. Utopian societies that provided social alternatives to the hypocrisy of broader American society, insofar as they prescribed changes in the monogamous nuclear family structure, were viewed askance and provided excellent scapegoats for the anxieties and inveterate ambiguities that characterized the sexual morality of nineteenth-century Americans.

And yet, as seriously as both utopians and their critics took the changes that were instituted in sexual behavior in alternative societies, this study has indicated how very pervasive certain of the ideological patterns of nineteenth-century society were, even among groups that were avowedly hostile to the basic institutions society had traditionally employed to regulate the relationship between men and women. Though the reactions of these utopian societies to perceived changes in sexual mores varied, from Oneida's enthusiastic acceptance of eroticized sexuality to the Shakers' renunciation of all sexuality because it could not be freed of the impure dross of eroticism, they all accepted the ideological assumption that the erotic dimension was central to human sexual behavior. They did not as consistently accept the implications of this doctrine, but rather accepted it provisionally, and made whatever behavioral adaptations seemed necessary in view of changed sexual mores.

From the point of view of social theory, the sexual ideologies of these
utopians were strange mixtures of radical and reactionary elements. They
rejected the romantic-love tradition, the central social importance of the
nuclear family, and the matripotestal true-woman ideology. All of these
were themselves novel ideas, having arisen only in the very late eighteenth or early nineteenth centuries.[3] By the time this body of social ideas
became the focus of communitarian discontent, however, it had become
a frozen social orthodoxy, a body of norms prescriptive of Victorian
sexual behavior. Utopians were radical (and thereby made themselves
consummately obnoxious) in making conscious themes that were covert
in nineteenth-century American culture.[4] Thus, they called attention to
the cultural dilemma inherent in an ideology that insisted that intercourse should be used only for reproductive purposes, yet also maintained the romantic right to happiness in love. The covert acceptance, on
a behavioral level, of the erotic element of sexuality was frequently expressed in the advice literature of mainstream culture, too; but it was
always muted, its dangers clearly highlighted.

Take, for example, the physician George W. Napheys's admonition to
moderation in marital relations. He feared his readers might be losing
patience insofar as

> we are forever repeating and urging moderation, temperance, re-
> straint, self-denial—that if marriage is going to be one constant
> torment of Tantalus with the beaker of pleasure ever filled and ever
> presented to the thirsty lips only to be whisked away again at the
> next moment, leaving the ardent longings cruelly deceived, then that
> the charm of the condition is gone, and it is better and easier to
> deny one's self entirely than to irritate by half-indulgence. Or it may
> be thrown up to us that all this counsel is useless because men will
> *not* be moderate in lust, and will *not* practice self-restraint in order
> to spare feelings which they cannot understand, and a delicacy
> which they cannot appreciate, in a person over whom the law gives
> them, in this respect, an absolute power.[5]

Napheys goes on to argue that the moral commonplaces of Victorian
American culture, and more particularly his physiological prescriptions
for male hygiene, will provide an effective counter to the tendency to
sexual excess. But beneath the stereotypic rhetoric of this passage is the
less conscious expression of the power and more pertinently the attraction of erotic sexuality (for the author as well as the reader), and the
concession that erotic expectations arise from the inherent assumptions
behind the code of romantic married love. The Tantalus metaphor implies
the failure of the individual or social institutions (marriage, the family)
to restrain erotic sexuality. The imagery of the passage also suggests a

perhaps only half-conscious identification with temperance reform, and thereby a tacit concession that popular sexual behavior, in contrast to advice manuals, is governed by an intoxication of erotic desire. The role of the physician and marital advisor, then, is not to provide a social model through the reiteration of middle-class moral platitudes, but to attempt to change, and more especially to *restrain*, asocial behavior, to reform vice.

Utopians also sought to reform nineteenth-century sexuality, but their approach was more radical in several ways. First, they were highly self-conscious about the need for reform of the sexual relation; what remained largely unacknowledged in mainstream culture[6] was frankly discussed and criticized among Mormons, Shakers, and Oneidans. In the second instance, they considered reform from within the system impossible and self-defeating; cultural alternatives to monogamic, romantic love were requisite to any meaningful, enduring solution to the Victorian sexual dilemma. Finally, they insisted that significant reform of sexuality could be achieved only by concurrent behavioral and ideological change.

Nevertheless, although utopians openly admitted the dominance of erotic motives in nineteenth-century society as a whole, they attempted to limit (or to eliminate totally, in the case of the Shakers) their operation within their own social experiments. Recognizing that the discrepancies between ideology and sexual behavior were largely due to the inherent ambivalence of Victorian norms, they chose, unlike their noncommunitarian contemporaries, to abandon the norms. The social program of these three utopian communities was regressive with respect to both behavioral and ideological aspects of sexuality. Each sought to return to a preromantic era. For the Shakers, the sole justification for human sexual activity was procreative. Because their theology identified perfection with celibacy, they proscribed intercourse for both men and women. The Mormons, under the rubric of celestial marriage, attempted to limit all intercourse to the period of female fertility. At Oneida, although complex marriage allowed widespread sexual activity, orgasmic sex for the male was limited to self-consciously reproductive intercourse under the eugenic system of stirpiculture. Except at Oneida, then, and only under strictly controlled conditions there, physical pleasure and romantic love were deemphasized in the sexual lives of communitarians in these societies.

Ideologically, these utopians proposed alternatives that sought to return to what they considered the time-honored traditions of the patriarchally organized extended family. This involved a direct attack on the power and autonomy of women in the conjugal family. Utopian sexual ideology opposed the unique status and influence women achieved within the isolated familial unit in nineteenth-century American society, the social power Daniel S. Smith has called "domestic feminism."[7] Utopians looked to the future for the perfection of human sexual instinct and at the same time looked backward for the ideals that would serve as a model for the sexual beatitude of mankind. Thus, they sought to destroy the nuclear family with its selfishness, but only to employ its basic principles of organization on a more corporate social level. They sought to limit the exposure of women to the dangers of pregnancy and parturition while assuring as little change as possible in the authority and social roles of the respective sexes. They sought to adapt sexual practices to the pleasure principle, but even at Oneida were more concerned about containing than condoning erotic sexuality.

These alternative societies had discovered the ancient mystical truth that freedom comes only with self-denial; to be truly liberated from nagging sexual problems one must be in perfect control of the emotions at all times. Balance, order, control, and temperance were the keys. Having accepted the fact that the pleasure nexus was a primary justification for sexual intercourse, the task of the utopians was then to bring order out of sexual chaos, to stabilize the sexual relation. They were trying not to liberate sexuality but to overcome sexual excess, the "appalling licentiousness" of marriage.[8] Noyes continually denied that Oneida practice was free love, and the Mormons just as consistently denied that their system was spiritual wifery; and in these contentions they were quite correct. The sex act came under much closer surveillance, was girt about with a myriad of additional rules, and in short was subject to much greater societal pressure and control in these utopian societies than in society at large. A sense of the nirvana to be attained by self-denial or self-control pervades the inspirational literature of the Shakers. The end of Shaker life was a mystic *imitatio Christi*: "denying *self* of every actual and sensual gratification, as he did, [for thus he] released every member of his body from all the external obligations of those carnal ordinances."[9] The observation was made even more concisely in an Oneida Community publication: "Does anyone know the pleasure there is in self-denial—the happiness to be found in turning from a thing when you most enjoy it? Our life is one series of discoveries in this line."[10]

Certainly Oneida sexual practice as manifested in male continence followed this dictum. It was only within the narrow confines of a rigid system of control that sexual freedom (which meant chiefly freedom from anxiety about sexual problems, not sexual license) was possible for these seekers of perfection. Even the Mormons, who were hardly concerned with mystic transcendence, or indeed with spiritualized religious conceptions of any kind, were very careful to hedge their polygamous system about with regulations. In essence, the structure of simultaneous polygyny, like that of Oneida pantagamy and Shaker celibacy, seems to have been designed to provide assurance that a rigid moral code based upon self-control would be as scrupulously adhered to as possible.

Because the ideological position of all three communities maintained that self-control was a peculiarly male trait, they all agreed that in essence it was the male who should be responsible for moral control in matters sexual. To paraphrase the Oneida position, the male was responsible not only for his own limitation (self-denial), but for that of the female as well. This was a reversal of the romantic double standard, which considered woman the purer, more ethereal being. These utopians frankly acknowledged and had a visceral fear of female sexual drives and needs. At Oneida and in the Mormon Zion this feeling served as the rationale for an attack on the central soteriological role the female played in evangelical theological thought. They were reacting against that myth of femininity, emphasizing virginity and the moral power of woman, which found expression among the adherents of the "evangelical-woman" ideology.

One popular formulation of this viewpoint maintained that "women's influence" manifested itself through "ministering angels in female guise among us, all and about our paths, who sweetly serve to cheer and adorn life."[11] Through selfless devotion, "the female influence admirably serves to refine and temper," to lead heavenward the baser male, who would otherwise be "a brute indeed."[12] This apotheosis of woman was most beautifully expressed in Harriet Beecher Stowe's essay "The Blessed Woman" (1867). Reaffirming the feminization of Victorian American religion, she co-opted the saving grace of Christ as the essence of the female role. The unique purity, gentleness, and universal self-effacing love of Jesus was the product of his distinctive parentage: "It was the *feminine element exalted* and taken into union with divinity."[13]

Among the Mormons, the reaction to this evangelical ideology was most extreme. They overturned this matriotheism and set up a patriotheism in its place. Man became the savior of the female, who was impotent to control her own emotions and actions. A woman, reared in the evangelical tradition, was most conscious of the radical nature of the change Mormon theology had made in the moral and religious position of women. "I heard," she wrote, "that woman was an inferior being, designed by the Lord for the especial glory and exaltation of man. . . . He was to be her 'savior,' for he was all in all to her; and it was through him alone and at his will that she could obtain salvation."[14]

Essentially, the double standard of sexual morality associated with the romantic-love tradition was stood on its head in these utopian societies. The double standard remained, but its arbiter was no longer woman, but man. Having accepted the fact that the justification of sex might be erotic pleasure as well as, or even in preference to, reproduction, communitarians undermined the moral, religious, and social position of woman, whose emotions had been considered holy because they were relayed through the blood and nerves of her womb. She remained an emotional creature rather than a rational one; but as man was rendered bestial in an ideology that emphasized the pleasure bond, a rational animal that could control itself and its drives was preferable to an emotional one that could not. The adaptation made to a perceived change in sexual behavior was essentially conservative: to preserve the traditional double standard, but to alter its emphasis to permit the reestablishment of stability in the relationship between the sexes. Utopian ideological and behavioral change was undertaken largely to reaffirm order in a sexual situation that might easily have become anarchic.

Whether the sexual problem was considered from within or without an alternative society, the debate over woman's place in society was conducted largely by men. The change in women's moral and religious position in these three utopian societies represented the attempt to achieve autonomy from the female by giving dominance in these areas to the male. It was chiefly a question of the behavior to which men in these communities wished deviant, potentially destructive women to conform; it was not a matter of women contributing very materially to the shaping of their own destinies. The ideological foundation of all these utopian communities was patriarchal, not excluding the Shakers, despite their dual religious orders, which preserved equality in ecclesiastical polity only.

The attack on motherhood was clearly part of this male effort at control of women. It represented a further undermining on the social level of the ideology of feminine moral superiority. It was not, as might appear upon cursory examination of Mormon polygamous society or Oneida pantagamic practice, a reaffirmation or wholehearted acceptance of the pleasurable justification for sex; it was rather an attempt to control the social and biological power of woman by men who profoundly distrusted and dreaded her influence and believed that she was increasingly resorting to cold-blooded abortion and birth-control practices to frustrate the end of his seed and assure herself of pleasure without subsequent pain. All three of these utopian communities carried on a militant campaign against motherhood, but in different ways, and to different degrees.

Shakers emphasized that maternity was woman's punishment for her primeval seduction and that progressive perfection would create a race of virgin celibates in which the curse of motherhood would be overcome. In a celibate community no natural increase could be expected; Shaker societies could grow only through proselytism. In the earliest years of Shakerism women had shared in missionary labors, but by the time of the great Kentucky revival (1800–1808), only males were employed in this capacity.[15] The processes of birth and reproduction, the essential female physical functions, were devalued, and male social reproduction (through active conversion and apprenticing orphans), and the rebirth of souls in the deadness of sin, completely superseded them. Shaker Elders thus assumed the basic functions and prerogatives, in spiritualized and asexual form, of the maternal function.

At Oneida, the reproductive powers came under communal (predominantly male) control with the institution of stirpiculture in 1867. Mormons valued woman's propagative capacities, but insisted that her maternal role was subsidiary; a man's children were his chattels, his "kingdom," they belonged to him. Women only nurtured the seed; the maternal role in upbringing was de-emphasized. At Oneida and in the various Shaker communities, children were separated from their mothers at an early age in order to root out philoprogenitiveness.

Motherhood was a dangerous, asocial force; its essence was unalloyed selfishness; the function of a communitarian society was to control, to socialize, this instinct under male control. The interest of all three societies in eugenics was an extension of this drive to control the ambiguous maternal capacity. Control of the product of the female body, or to be more exact, the transmutation of the raw material of life (semen), they believed, would insure progressive perfection, and indeed the universal triumph of perfection.

In addition, conditions of life under utopian economic organization denied the male world of strife and competition associated with expanding business capitalism. Communistic cooperation among the Shakers and Oneidans more closely resembled the female world of household production. Under these conditions the male assumed many of the traditional female characteristics, and consequently he seems to have felt the need for a rigid ideological definition of the sexes in order to maintain a separate male gender identity.

On a broader social level, these communities became *almae matres* assuming generative and nurturing functions typically maternal. The utopian society usurped the functions of the ideal mother: her unselfishness, her moral guidance, her purity, and her religious power. These communities became the objective correlative of the motherhood they subverted; their function, like the maternal, was moral and prophylactic: "to foster tenderness of conscience, and so to regulate its balance that it swerves not amid the temptations of untried life. . . . to rivet principle that it may retain its integrity"[16]—in sum, to purify sex (love) and to help community members (children) to attain perfection. We need only recall the centrality of maternal imagery in these communities (for example, the use of the term "mother" as applied to those who darned and mended clothes at Oneida and the Shaker communities, and the parent-child paradigm adopted as roles for hierarchs and common members, respectively, in Mormonism and Shakerism) to realize how consciously this parallel was encouraged.

These communities reflected in their theological dimension the ideological attempt to control conception and birth as well. The traditional evangelical rebirth metaphor was merged with eugenic concern in which the community became a collective womb, a controlled environment for the conception and nurturing of perfect saints. The "true" birth was rebirth from the surrogate communal matrix; for this reason children were frequently considered virtually nonpersons. At Oneida this led to an emphasis on puberty—a physical expression of rebirth, a preparation for physical participation in the communal eugenic experiment—and the onset of the desire for autonomy from the parents, especially the mother, as a reification of the spiritual process of rebirth. Shakers emphasized the necessity for maturity in the perfect Shaker, and their difficulties with children who were apprenticed or left at their societies indicate that the puerile group found it difficult to accept the mother substitute offered them in the community structure and the dual Christology based on the apotheosis of *Mother* Ann Lee.

This aspect of community life was an inversion of the popular environmentalist argument, which held that the ambience of the womb, the emotions and psychological state of the maternal parent during the gestation period, would determine the destiny of the child. John Cowan, whose work was well known to all three utopian groups, gave this idea classic expression. "All the educational institutions in the world," he wrote, "all the benevolent, industrial, and reform societies—all the anti-tobacco advocates—all the temperance societies and all the divines in the world, combining and working harmoniously together, cannot do as much in a life time of effort in the elevation of mankind, as can a mother in nine months of pre-natal effort."[17]

Inasmuch as this argument typically placed responsibility for the character and spiritual development (the evolutionary development of the organism under eugenic conditions) upon the female, it clashed with the basic ideological assumptions of these utopians, that is, the potentially nefarious influence of the female both in conception and in nurture. It gave control of the evolutionary process over into the hands of that sex which had no self-control and could therefore not logically be expected to be capable of transmitting such control to its progeny. It undermined all hopes of progressive perfection from the outset. If, on the other hand, emphasis was put on the role of the male seed (spermatic economy) in the prenatal stage, and more particularly on the role of *postnatal* environment (the utopian community as mother), in the development of character and moral tone, this difficulty could be overcome; and the utopians could still maintain belief in an anthropocentric evolutionary process, which could be controlled and directed by *men*. The Mormon approach to this problem was somewhat different in particulars, but in effect the same. Mormons maintained that the maternal womb was the scene of evolutionary development, but asserted that it was of no value unless the woman was married to a godly member of the priesthood. In essence, they also emphasized postnatal communal influences in the perfection of children.

The emphasis placed upon the extended familial relationship by these communities, though in part a reaction against what they considered the breakdown of the nuclear family under the stress of industrialization and geographic mobility, and in part a means of assuring social cohesion and reinstituting the social security function of the family, was also an extension of the attack upon the position of women in the family. The problem with the conjugal nuclear family was, as we have seen, selfishness and the feeling of exclusive possession. Although this selfishness obviously applied to the husband as well as the wife, these communities consistently considered female selfishness, especially philoprogenitiveness, much worse both in kind and degree.

To achieve perfection it was necessary to break away from the maternal influence. The transition for utopians was geared to the life cycle; they sought autonomy from their families of origin and entered utopian communities, extended families of orientation. Thus we find that the founders of all three of these communities began with a nucleus of relatives, though usually not parents, of around the same age.

Ann Lee, for example, began her experiment with seven individuals. Four of them were members of her family: her husband, Abraham Standley; her brother, William; her cousin, Nancy Lee; and her adopted son, James Whitaker. John Humphrey Noyes commenced operations at Putney, Vermont, with his sisters, Charlotte and Harriet; his brother, George; his wife, Harriet Holton; and his mother, Polly. The latter was, however, as we have seen, very unreliable, a perpetual tergiversator. Noyes consciously expanded that familial nucleus by choosing husbands for his sisters (John C. Miller and John L. Skinner, respectively) and a wife, Helen Campbell, for his brother. The ages of this nuclear group averaged thirty-two years (with the exception of Noyes's lukewarm mother). Noyes himself was thirty-six when he founded the Putney community.

In the case of Mormonism, Joseph Smith began with a small coterie composed of his two brothers, Hyrum and Samuel; his wife, Emma Hale; and his parents. The younger members of the group averaged twenty-nine years of age. Smith was thirty. In addition to this nuclear group, another familial group, the Whitmers, supplied the remainder of the eight witnesses to the Plates of Nephi, upon which the Book of Mormon was purportedly based.[18]

Furthermore, most of those who came to these utopian communities came in related groups, although not often in integral families. In the three Shaker societies of Mt. Lebanon, Watervliet, New York, and North Union, Ohio, for instance, about 87 percent of the converted members in the years 1800–1860 were members of familial groups. At Oneida the overwhelming majority (75 percent) of individuals (even those over eighteen), who entered the association were members of family groups.[19] In that sense their critics were correct; the intent of these communities was to break up the traditional matri-central family and to reconstitute an extended family of choice.

Statements of the longing for, and the intention to create, an extended family situation in the social institution of the utopian community are quite common. Consider, for instance, the nostalgic feeling of the adult whose outlook is no longer consonant with that of his parents, and who acutely feels his exclusion and alienation from his family of origin, which pervades this statement by John H. Noyes: "Everybody remembers, away back in the beginning of life, a brief paradise that was good and pleasant and sweet because it held a company of brothers and sisters together in a unity. Communism of interests is realizing the charms of 'home sweet home,' and the world is dotted with little Communities that are the fountains of all good lives and fragrant memories."[20] The problem with most such communities was that they were only informal and not highly organized, and thus they were ephemeral. "They are always being broken up. They exist in most person's minds only as memories that increase the sadness of exile."[21]

It was this wistful evanescence that these utopian communities were intended to counteract. A manifesto published under the title "Program of the Millennium" set out as one of the primary goals of the Oneida Community "Dwelling Together in Association, or Complex Families."[22]

The emphasis was not on a family under parental guidance, but on an extended *sibling* family, in which the community, or more properly the theocratic communal hierarchy, would function in loco parentis. This was clear in Noyes's reference to a "company of brothers and sisters" and in his emphasis on the observation that families in the world were broken up and isolated by marriage, and that subsequently the members had nothing to do with one another.[23] The system of complex marriage adopted at Oneida made marriage a force for cohesion rather than disruption of familial ties, and in effect assured that everyone in the community would be related to everyone else through marriage.

The endogamous nature of the extended family was also indicated in Mormon thought. Mormons insisted that the marriage of believers be confined to members of the Latter-Day Saints, with the conscious intention of creating infinite kingdoms, or extended patriarchal families. Orson Pratt expressed this doctrine most concisely. *"Let them marry according to the holy order of God,"* he expostulated in addressing a group of Mormon women, "and begin to lay the foundation of a little family kingdom which shall no more be scattered upon the face of the earth, but dwell in one country, keeping their genealogies from generation to generation, until each man's house shall be multiplied as the stars of heaven."[24]

Shakers, too, although they shunned matrimony, sought to establish an extended family in their communities, in which "every member, both male and female, as brethren and sisters of one family, [would be] members of one joint body."[25] Shakers conceived their community as "a *Family*, living under the same roof as brothers and sisters."[26] Their goal was "to alter the form of human society, from the individual family relationship, to a community, embracing a number of families."[27] The motherhood of God, mediated through the dual communal order, stood in the place of the physical presence of the mother. "As it would be difficult," Antoinette Doolittle, editress of the chief Shaker organ, wrote, "to establish a perfect household in the *natural* order, without a *mother*, to counsel, guide and direct the inmates; so would it also be quite as impractical to organize and sustain a *spiritual* Family, or Church, without a *Mother's* influence and care."[28] Clearly, for Shakers militant celibacy was the key to their separation from their families of origin (as pantagamy was for Oneidans and polygamy for Mormons) and their association with a new fraternal-sororal family of choice or orientation.

From a broader social perspective, the extended familial nature of these utopian communities represented an attempt to reconstitute the family, or the closely knit community (the communal family), as the basic institution of social service. We have noted the practice among Mormon polygamists of marrying sisters, or mothers and daughters. Among the Shakers, the care of the aged and infirm and the taking in of orphans and unwanted children were integral parts of the organization. Oneida attracted numerous widows and individuals who were separated from their families, especially after the Civil War. This did not mean that these communities were charitable institutions or refuges for the unfortunate of the outside world. They were conceived of as tightly knit familial communities, militantly committed to progressive perfection.

The Shakers were most outspoken about their defense of this position, but the other two groups shared this attitude as well. A body of regulations published at Mt. Lebanon made the point quite plain. "Persons joining the Community," we are advised, "and living within the pale of its association, as partakers of its benefices in sickness and in health, who are possessed of property, and who do not feel prepared, and do not yet choose to consecrate some, are expected to contribute the interest of their property to the Community where they reside. . . . Without this proviso the society is liable, in some cases, to be very unjustly and unreasonably burdened."[29] Furthermore, "The doors of the Community are not open to any persons as a *merely charitable* institution. Nor is it anticipated that persons may spend their lives to an advanced and enervated enfeebled age in the worldly arena, and then throw themselves into the Community for care and support, by merely professing a faith in its cardinal principles. Such may receive a degree of union according to sincerity and faithfulness, and remain outside."[30]

Commitment not only to a new form of sexual and familial arrangement, but to a wholly different cultural outlook, was required of those who sought membership in these utopian communities. The very form of the societies and their emphasis on the closeness and durability of the social bond corresponded to a totally different conception of the self from that more generally accepted in nineteenth-century America. The whole social mythology of the self-made man was not only ideologically opposed, but practically overturned, in the social organization of these communities. The self was not considered sufficient and competent to any substantial achievement alone, but found its value only in a social context.

This was directly related to the emphasis placed upon control of the will and the concomitant socialization of the sexual instinct. Furthermore, to the degree that the self-made man was a fiction, even among those who professed to believe in that conception of egocentric selfhood; and to the degree that the seemingly autonomous and all-conquering male had really been "made" by a woman (that is, his moral foundations and character traits had been shaped by his mother), the rejection of this social myth was an expression on yet another level of the utopian attempt to undermine the religious, moral, and social power of the romantic-evangelical ideal of womanhood.

This sense of cultural alienation was reinforced by the attitude of outside society, which felt compelled to formulate new categories in order to deal with these utopian communities. Clearly, in a world of isolated individuals and the organized individualism of corporations, those who sought to achieve their goals collectively, who placed social values, control, and duty above self-realization and the pursuit of individual success, were viewed as anomalies. The clearest illustration of the reaction of outside society to this perceived cultural difference was the creation of new categories to deal with the Shakers and Mormons.

The bill passed by the Kentucky legislature in 1828 to regulate the economic and legal relations between the Shaker communities and the broader society is a case in point. It was entitled An Act to Regulate Civil Proceedings against Certain Communities Having Property in Common. It expressed a sense of the unique position of these communitarian societies between the standard economic and legal units of the individual and the incorporated group, and beyond the common social units of individual and nuclear family.

The law in question provided that Shaker communities could be sued as a unit for any demand exceeding fifty dollars, "without naming or designating the individuals of such community, or serving process on them."[31] The Shakers, on the other hand, could not sue; they had legal liabilities but no legal rights as a group. The key to the bill, apart from its obviously discriminatory nature, however, was the groping attempt to create some new category to encompass the phenomenon of the collective society. As the legal counsel retained by the Shakers saw the matter, the act "attempts to make them corporators against their consent."[32] It sought to separate the Shakers, as well, from the legally recognized category of religious institution, a noncivil body of Christians that could be sued as individuals but not as a church. In sum, the act was set forth on the assumption of partnership, yet it "refuses the partners *collectively or individually* to appear and defend themselves. It provides that no defence be received for them but from sworn agents or attorneys, who are, before they can safely take the oath, to have a power from every living partner, infant as well as adult."[33]

The anomalous legal position of the Shaker communities, neither fish nor fowl, was clear:

> When your laws do not allow this society to take and hold property as a community, when the law does not allow them the privilege of suing as a community for any contract, however fair on their part, or any outrage committed against their rights, however flagrant— is it not too cruel to be borne with, that you disable them to defend as individuals in courts of justice, and allow suits to be brought against them as a community, and allow judgments upon such suits to pass, on which not only the joint labor of the men, women and children may be seized and sold, but the individual property of both adults and helpless infancy. . . . Your law . . . entails upon women and children, born and to be born, debts to the extent of their joint interests in the common stock, and when that fails, to the extent of their property, which they may acquire by descent or purchase as individuals, in any period of their existence.[34]

Shakers were at once, then, both individuals and community, and yet really neither. They were an intermediate civil unit. This was clear in the divorce legislation passed by most of the states in which Shaker societies were located. Mere membership in a Shaker community was enough to subject the individual to divorce proceedings without the necessity of his even appearing in court. Members of communistic societies were at the same time both more and less than individuals in the eyes of the law.

A similar situation prevailed in the Mormon Zion. The whole series of laws enacted to combat polygamy was grounded in the belief that Mormonism was antirepublican, anti–laissez-faire. Did Mormons not seek to monopolize women? They were considered antiindividualists and yet not a civil or social unit within the commonly accepted definition of a territory. President Cleveland, in his first annual address (1885), noted: "Thus is the strange spectacle presented of a community protected by a republican form of government, to which they owe allegiance, sustaining by their suffrages a principle and a belief which set at nought that obligation of absolute obedience to the law of the land which lies at the bottom of republican institutions.[35] Utah, it was feared, would not remain a docile territory (an individual) or be incorporated as a state, but would seek some intermediate or, perhaps more accurately, transcendent position, as an independent polygamous community. Opponents of Mormonism trembled at the words of Bishop Henry Lunt:

> In some great political crisis, the two present political parties will bid for our support. Utah will then be admitted as a polygamous State, and the other Territories we have peacefully subjugated will be admitted also. We will then hold the balance of power, and will dictate to the country. . . . We possess the ability to turn the political scale in any particular community we desire. Our people are obedient. When they are called by the Church they promptly obey . . . [our organization] is the completest one the world has ever seen.[36]

Mormonism was a monster of fearful mien, fatal to individualism, yet somehow transcending all socially acceptable categories of collectivity; a creature of such hypertrophied elaboration as to threaten the existence of the republic itself. An anomalous institution, possessing at once economic, social, and religious dimensions and very much resembling Negro slavery, Mormonism was intolerable. The fear which generated the attempt to construct categories that would define and limit this creature was quite evident in the flood of petitions that poured into Congress in 1882 in support of one of these legal attempts at regulation, the Edmunds bill. One example will provide an adequate sense of the tenor of these petitions and of the emotion that led to federal laws regulating divorce proceedings and the recision of the right of female suffrage in Utah. The General Assembly of the Presbyterian Church delineated Mormonism's efforts to strengthen itself by immigration of the weak and ignorant from Europe and by despotic suppression of liberty among its votaries and victims. . . . For its own fortification, it is forcing its way from its original stronghold into adjacent territory, where, unobserved, it may take root, fastening on the land by finding quiet recognition in local laws. Its spirit grows, with age, no less hostile to the law of Christianity, to the instincts of morality, to the essential principles of civilization, and the existence of liberty for the people. It is condemned alike by the Church, by the State, by the family, and by the individual conscience. . . . It is growing, as slavery grew, from infancy to maturity of grasp upon the national life. The terrible conflict required for the extermination of one should sound timely warning as to the latent perils of the other.[37]

The steps taken to suppress the moral and political threat of polygamy fell short of open warfare (except for the brief Mormon War, 1857–58);[38] but they proceeded along general lines that paralleled those employed by state governments dealing with Shakerism. The rights of individuals were limited by federal legislation: the vote was taken from Mormon women; wives were required to testify against their husbands in polygamy prosecutions; the inheritance laws of Utah were altered to forbid the transmission of property to "illegitimate" children; and divorce proceedings came under federal aegis, a move that was intended to render them less liberal. On the other hand, the rationale behind this attack on individual rights was the need to overthrow a collectivity that in its cohesive success threatened the less-organized American republic.

There was a concomitant attack on certain corporate aspects of Mormonism only peripherally associated with polygamy, the institution considered of central importance in cementing communal loyalty and insuring separation from American institutions, in the Edmunds-Tucker bill of 1884. This was true of the provisions to remove textbooks with a Mormon bias from Utah schools (section 23), but even more so of the prohibition of the Perpetual Emigrating Fund Company, which had been organized to provide passage money for foreign Mormons en route to Utah. This article (section 15) provided that "it shall not be lawful for the Legislative Assembly of the Territory of Utah to create, organize, or in any manner recognize any *corporation or association* for the purpose of or operating to accomplish the bringing of persons into the said Territory for any purpose whatsoever."[39]

In a broader sense, the attempt to define the delineating line between the self and the community was reflected, in a progressive age, in the differing attitudes toward the methodology of reform adopted by utopians and by established American society. Both utopians and nonutopians viewed historical forces as operating through sexuality, but utopians considered the male, and their opponents the female, the chief agent of reform. As one of those who held the latter point of view felicitously expressed it, "All the social virtues and graces are so indissolubly linked with the domestic hearth and with woman, that all projected reforms should be social rather than civil."[40]

Ironically, although American political theory emphasized the place and value of the individual in this period, the general method of reform usually adopted was social or organizational in emphasis—the temperance, peace, and antislavery societies—and in the last extremity political—the Civil War and the legislative campaigns against Mormonism. Utopian societies, on the other hand, because they exercised a much more immediate control over the individual; because their goal was *perfection* rather than proximate progress; and because they sought to internalize principles of order, temperance, and self-control in their members, emphasized that social reform could only be achieved through the prior reformation of individuals. Whereas the general process of reform was to institute a *social* reform organization first, and have that organization gradually reform individuals, utopians sought through "total commitment and immediate reform" to amend the conduct of individuals, who would subsequently be able to correct the faults of society.[41]

The ambivalence of relying on "self-improvement" as a solution to a cultural decadence rooted in the egocentricity of the grasping self-made man of nineteenth-century business capitalism is evident. It should be emphasized, however, that utopian reform proceeded within the maternal paradigm. That is to say that, insofar as these communities had usurped the maternal role for the community as a whole, they thereby co-opted a feminine role in the reform process. The feminine approach to reform, grounded in the romantic and evangelical religious traditions, was a radical personalism, which sought to redeem individual character, rather than a concentration on social phenomena and institutionalized change.[42]

Sex was central to the reform process in these communities because it was both the most individual relationship and at the same time the basis for the most basic social unit. Sex was, therefore, the link between the individual and the social level of reform. The interest of all three of these communities in eugenics underscores this realization. Control of propagation provided the bridge, the transition, that made the socialization and the perpetuation of individual perfection possible. Furthermore, unlike many other proposed reforms, reform in sexuality, sexual behavior, the social organization of the sexual relation, and sex roles was an inherently social question (requiring fundamental change in the most elemental institutional forms of Western culture), in a way in which temperance reform and the graham bread crusade, for instance, were not. Part of the problem for reform groups had been, as historians have pointed out, how to link the individual and the social aspects of a particular reform movement.[43] Utopians sought to evade this difficulty by dealing with the smallest possible social units, individuals and conjugal pairs, thus beginning at the bottom rather than attempting change from the top, as so many reforms, like the peace movement or the antislavery crusade, for instance, did. Reform for utopians, as for nonutopians, was progressive and infinite, but utopians considered it largely a matter to be accomplished through internal rather than external means.

Some sense of the centrality of sexual reform as a prerequisite to social reform or to the progress of civilization, for these utopian societies, can be derived from an address of the Mormon elder Orson Spencer. "Domestic compact," he declared,

> is the first order of all social organization, and must even antecede all civil government, and contribute much to the genius and character of the same. It is the basis, upon which every superstructure of society must be reared. The laws regulating marriage and divorce, and the license of sexual intercourse, without any prescribed order of marriage at all, range in variety and discrepancy among different Christian nations. . . . If the intercourse of the sexes is not regulated in wisdom and purity, the result will be that every consequent branch and order of society will be vitiated thereby. First make the tree good, and the fruit will be also good.[44]

Reform of the personal scion, institutionalized in communal horticulture, would, in the course of time, result in the perfection of the species.

Chapter 15 🌱 "A Little World of Our Own": The Value and Function of Sectarian Utopianism in Nineteenth-Century American Culture

Doch hat noch niemand sich selber beherrscht; weil der opponierende Sklave immer mächtiger ist als der regierungsüchtige Herr. Jeder Mensch ist sich selber unterlegen [After all, no one has ever mastered himself; because the rebellious slave is always more powerful than the master who tries to govern him. Every man is subject to himself].

—Kurt Tucholsky, "Essay on Man"

Liberty means responsibility. That is why most men dread it.

—George B. Shaw, *The Revolutionist's Handbook*

*U*topians sought to achieve perfection or reform through a radical process of pruning and transplanting, to achieve a goodly harvest. Their programs were concrete rather than hortatory, and they attracted individuals who looked first to achieving perfection in their own persons as a prerequisite to reforming the mass of society. The approach to reform, therefore, was quite different in utopian societies. Were the fruits of this topiary model significantly different? Since their fruits were not only different in kind, but of a different order, we may best close this study with an examination of the changes in sexuality and sex roles these societies effected, not from a social point of view, but from the point of view of the individual men and women who became members of them.

In the final analysis, what were the advantages or disadvantages, for those individuals who sought to achieve progressive perfection, of the choice of life in one of these three utopian communities?

Of the three communities examined, the Shakers offered the greatest security and peace of mind on sexual questions. For those who were filled with a sense of shame and repugnance toward the physical sex act, and who were capable of internalizing the rigorous ethic of strict chastity, Shaker societies offered the maximum order and assurance of reinforced self-control. From this point of view, Shakerism represented the greatest possible freedom *from* sexual anxieties. Individuals who rejected adult sexuality, and who remained virgin celibates, were prepared to accept the child-parent paradigm that prevailed in the common member-Elder (Eldress) structure of Shaker society. They were also disposed to reject the romantic notions associated with love and motherhood, while retaining an adherence to the evangelical conception of the centrality of the feminine element in the religio-moral realm.

For women, the Shakers could offer a lightening of household drudgery through division of labor and laborsaving devices; a surcease from the risks and threat of pregnancy; release from a sexual obligation to husbands they often found loathsome; release from the cares and burdens of maternity; and an environment in which their physical needs would be met without the necessity of bartering their sexual favors in exchange.

Women found themselves controlled by men, who made all the important economic, political, and social decisions, but they had representatives of their own sex at all levels of the hierarchy. If sexual power relations were unaltered in Shaker society, at least the average woman had a buffer between herself and the masculine power structure. She was relieved from experiencing the duress or wrath of the masculine world directly. In effect, she did what the Eldresses and female Ministry told her to do; in any given instance her awareness of the ultimate source of a particular direction or regulation may not have extended beyond her immediate spiritual superior. In addition, the religious prestige and power of women in practice were elevated even beyond what was common in more orthodox evangelical religious sects. If not the savior of man, woman participated directly in the worship service and served as the primary link between the human and divine worlds. Women were by far the most frequent recipients of visions and gifts, in an ecstatic religious role that connected them directly with the ongoing prophetic tradition. They were the source of contemporary revelation, the essence of the vital heart of Shakerism.

To the degree that Shaker visions and gifts and the ecstatic emotional states that accompanied them served as a sexual outlet, women, who were predominant among the intermediaries, seem to have been able to achieve, within the rigid confines of the Shaker system, a greater degree of sexual satisfaction than men. Women were also, as we have seen, more satisfied with life in Shaker communities than were their male counterparts. This was reflected as well in withdrawals and expulsions, which were quite overwhelmingly male. In that the basis of Shaker economy was agricultural and small handicraft from the outset, no major changes in the roles of men and women in the division of labor were required; and for the most part, few were made. So, although the Shakers made a radical change in sexuality by completely eliminating sexual intercourse, sexual roles and power relationships remained much the same as in society at large.

From the male point of view, entering a Shaker society meant making a major change or commitment in the sexual realm; but all else remained essentially the same. He was relieved of the responsibility of caring for his own wife and children (assuming they also entered the Shaker fold), yet largely at the expense of assuming a more generalized responsibility for a much larger extended "family." The ultimate responsibility remained his. He was provided with a buffer against female sexuality and placed in an environment in which such temptations as private interviews, the titillation of female attire, and even the chance encounter were reduced to a minimum by careful social monitoring; but the one ultimately responsible for control, the final arbiter of his perfection, was no longer woman, but himself. In fact, he was also made responsible for the regulation and control of the female. The burden must have been hard to bear.

He shared with the female the sexual outlet and the restrained emotion of the terpsichorean Shaker ritual, but that aspect of Shaker worship provided less emotional release than the spiritualistic visions and gifts more readily available to the female. Finally, he found himself with increased responsibility for his own "travel," but with a greatly diminished sense of immediate power in his relationship with women. Only on the level of the Elders and Ministry was there direct contact between men and women in which power relationships could be expressed. The two totally separate orders served as buffers between the two sexes. Male satisfaction, beyond the assurance of self-control, would have been confined to the ideological level: the moral superiority of the male. This apparently provided small comfort for many men in the absence of more tangible benefits.

Mormon simultaneous polygyny, or celestial marriage, was a source of unending sexual anxiety for both men and women. For those who had been reared in a monogamous culture, adjustment to a new marital institution based on an ideology that sought to divest love of all its nonsexual, spiritual qualities (in short, its romantic aspects) proved most difficult.

Unlike the Shakers, Mormons sought to overthrow not only the romantic tradition of womanhood, but also the evangelical apotheosis of normative femininity. Although motherhood remained of paramount importance as the all-inclusive female role, the domestic moral power of the female was consistently subverted. It was no accident that the attack on women's fashions was most violent in Mormon Utah and the Oneida Community; it expressed a more thoroughgoing destruction of the social, moral, and religious power of woman than had been instituted in the Shaker communities.

A female's commitment to Mormonism meant a major change in her attitude toward marriage. She had to be willing to share her husband with an indefinite number of co-wives. Whatever romantic notions she might have about her personal claim to her *own husband* had to be waived. She assumed a primarily physical function, that of a breeder, a function that, at least from a theological point of view, was considered interminable. The essence of her position in society, the church, and the family was solely physical; she was reduced to the status of a breeding animal. Man was the savior, nay, even the tutelary god, of woman. No woman cometh unto the Father but through her husband.

There is ample evidence that many women did not respond favorably to the polygamic system and were consequently bullied into it by threats of abandonment, excommunication, and damnation. Even when women were aware of the existence of celestial marriage prior to their marriages to Mormons, many apparently felt that the bloom of early love would never fade and that *their* husbands would certainly not take other wives. Cruel disappointment awaited women who were fatuous or romantic enough to entertain such notions. If a man wanted to rise in the hierarchy of the church, he perforce had to "live his faith." If the figures cited by some Mormons are correct, as many as half the women married into polygamy may at times have been unhappy with the system.[1] Polygamy was very restrictive in its monitoring of female behavior. Women were not allowed to associate or even converse with Gentile men. The virtue of women was rigorously guarded, and consequently their freedom of movement was narrowly confined. The double moral standard was reversed, and men became responsible for female sexual behavior.

But polygamy was not without its advantages for women. As we have seen, the more wives a man took, the fewer pregnancies each woman underwent. Women generally began their reproductive cycle earlier and terminated it earlier than their monogamous sisters, so that whatever pregnancies were the lot of women, they at least bore them during their halest physical years. Quantitatively, Mormon plural wives could expect to have, on the average, one more child than their non-Mormon contemporaries. Significantly, however, their completed families averaged one or two children less than those of *monogamous* Mormon women. On the other hand, as diary accounts suggest, the reproductive emphasis of Mormonism and the physical availability of multiple wives may have meant that Mormon fathers valued the life of the child above that of the mother. For a healthy woman, who gave birth under optimal conditions, polygamy provided a minimum of risk; for an unhealthy woman with a history of parturient complications, it could be fatal. The universal Mormon prohibition on birth control had been initiated and was maintained by men; it was solely women, therefore, who adopted any contraceptive methods, and the fact that they did so indicates feminine dissatisfaction with the role of breeder, with the frequency of pregnancies, and especially with their number.

Because households tended to be of an extended nature (adult children usually remained on the homestead, frequently even after marrying), a woman could count on some reduction of her labors through an increased labor force, but not to a significant degree. Only those very few men, like Brigham Young, who maintained a joint establishment with all wives and children under one roof or those affluent enough to afford female Indian servants provided a truly relieving division of labor for women. Owing to the shortage of labor in the West, most women who lived in frontier settlements could look forward not only to performing their own duties, but in many cases to assisting their husbands (in the absence of hired hands) in male tasks. When their husbands were away, of course, which was more frequent with the increasing number of wives, and the prescribed missionary journeys required of those men who hoped to rise in the church hierarchy, women had to do all the work themselves.

In matters more strictly matrimonial, polygamy provided a woman the opportunity to select the man she felt would be able best to support her and make her happy—regardless of his marital status. For a woman who was willing to accept polygamy, therefore, the system provided a painless way of achieving social mobility. For many women the system also acted as a kind of social security insurance. Many men, out of a sense of duty, took older wives, women who had exceeded the climacteric and therefore were useless from a theological or ideological point of view. In some instances these women were the mothers of younger women who were already the wives of these men. Marriage of sisters served a similar function. It assured that one woman would not secure a better position for herself through marriage than her siblings. This whole pattern of behavior suggests the influence that a man's wives exerted over the selection of his subsequent mates. This was especially true of first wives. Women were thus often in a position to assure themselves that subsequent wives would be women they would find it possible to get along with. Especially after 1852, with the promulgation of the liberal divorce code in Utah, a form of redress was open to women who found polygamous marriage unacceptable. It also provided the possibility, for the woman whose sexual tastes were languishing in the monotony of polygamy and whose sexual needs were unfulfilled by the occasional visits of her lord to her bedchamber, of serial polyandry pursued sub rosa.

In terms of the rights of women, Mormon females enjoyed the right of suffrage from 1870 to 1884, and the right to own and retain title to their own property. These, as well as the liberal divorce policy, were decided advantages for women; but they had been granted, as we have seen, not primarily for the sake of women, but for political reasons bearing largely on the balance of power in Utah (the desire to retain Mormon control of the territory) and the desire to protect the institution of polygamy. In most areas of concern, a polygamous wife had little influence over her husband, and her isolation in relatively small (sometimes even nuclear) familial outposts on the frontier (for the Mormon familial demographic unit was the large, extended family *only from the point of view of the male polygamist*) prevented any very effective agitation for women's rights. Whatever rights a woman was granted were perquisites granted her by her husband for political reasons not immediately concerned with her welfare.

From the male point of view, polygamy offered the possibility of sexual variety, but most importantly it provided a means by which erotic and reproductive sexuality could be reconciled within a system of strict laws and regulations. In effect, the conduct of the husband with a particular wife was closely prescribed: no sex during pregnancy, menstruation, or lactation; and masturbation and birth control were forbidden. Polygamy provided more sexual partners so that a man could more conscientiously follow these regulations and yet enjoy a modicum of sexual pleasure. Polygamy was not a system of male sexual license. It was in some ways as restrictive for the male as it was for the female.

Because Mormon males did not normally embark on celestial marriage until they were in their mid-thirties, polygamy was no kinder to a man's sexual urges during the physiologically most demanding part of his life (from fifteen to thirty) than strict monogamy.[2] Furthermore, in order to take a plural wife, a man had to secure the approval of the intended's parents, his first wife, and the church authorities. He was not free to marry whomever he pleased whenever he pleased. The vigilance of fathers and husbands over the virtue of daughters and wives also helped to restrict his extramarital relationships. For those men who did not succeed in entering the Mormon hierarchy, who were not allowed to marry into polygamy, or were too young to have yet made their mark, polygamy served as a kind of eugenic sterilization. Since there was no surplus of women, these men often had to lead lives of enforced celibacy, at least for a time. For men, then, polygamy as a sexual system meant either a regulated marriage or exclusion from sexual life.

Polygamy increased the anxiety of men because with the reversal of the double standard they became totally responsible for the behavior of the female. Upon his good behavior and acceptance in the eyes of the church depended the salvation of all a man's wives and children. He spent much of his time worrying about the control of his women. In a system that amounted to an aristocracy of marriage, there was a great deal of pressure placed upon men to satisfy the needs of their wives. If they did not provide for their maintenance in the style to which they were accustomed, or if they were sexually unsatisfied, the specter of unmarried males or more capable polygamists always loomed in the background. If the ideological and theological structure of Mormonism were not sufficient, the very physical conditions of polygamy promoted anxiety, distrust, and distance between men and women in the sexual relation. Male satisfaction seems to have been primarily religious and ideological. Whatever enjoyment derived from sexual variety, or whatever assistance an extended family provided a man in lessening the burden of his labors, many polygamists seem to have come genuinely to regret their plural marriages.

The Oneida Community was in many ways intermediate between the Shakers' celibacy and Mormon polygamy. Oneidans regarded women as religiously inferior; but though they attacked the notion of romantic love, their emphasis on a pantagamic relationship *without children present* clearly indicated their emotional attachment to the romanticism of the honeymoon period. Oneida offered the maximum security for the male from sexual anxiety at the expense of orgasmic sexuality. Men who entered the community were placed in complete control of the sex act—its initiation, duration, and kind. With the institution of stirpiculture in 1867, males became responsible for the direct superintendence and control of the procreative power of women. Pantagamy in practice was designed to fulfill the physical needs of woman, to provide the physical prerequisite that made control of her possible. The system functioned to relieve male anxiety about the ambiguous fecundity of women, the necessity of female sexual fulfillment, and the danger of male sexual exhaustion.

Male continence was chiefly a male system that sought to diminish male guilt in the sexual act. Duty and control were the keys to the system. The socialization of sexual intercourse under the assumption that the erotic was its primary justification meant that as long as the individual followed the rules, the society would expunge his feelings of guilt. This was reinforced in the case of the male by the renunciation and self-control required to avert orgasm. His denial of the final pleasure of the sex act secured his social, religious, and moral superiority over the female.

The system afforded men the possibility of a wide variety of sexual partners within controlled conditions. It also assured that acts of "personal fellowship" would be unhindered by fears of contingent pregnancy or the presence of interfering children. For those who were central members, the system afforded the chance to associate sexually with the younger, more vigorous women and girls despite the differences in their ages. But the system was one of order and temperate control. Men could enjoy sexual relations only if the proposed match were approved by the community and the woman herself. Precautions were taken to assure the depersonalization of love: the use of older women as intermediaries so that there was no initial contact between the man and woman in question; and the use of mutual criticism to combat special attachments. Under stirpiculture, although relationships became more extended, to a degree more intimate, and presumably more pleasurable for the male, approval by the Stirpicultural Committee hemmed them in even more straitly.

For women, the Oneida system offered freedom from unwanted pregnancies and a much greater degree of control over the frequency of intercourse. It afforded her a sexual variety equal to that provided the male, and insofar as her orgasm was a matter of considerable attention by her lover, these encounters, it can be assumed, were generally pleasurable for her. Community pressures, however, prevented her from "playing favorites," and she was in some instances compelled, through the discipline of mutual criticism, to yield to the embraces of those she would rather have avoided. In some cases, eugenic control of reproduction left individual women with a feeling of unfulfillment. Apparently they were not permitted to bear as many children as they would have liked.

Positive efforts were made to change sex roles at Oneida, and these were not prompted, as in the Mormon community, by external pressures. Role change, however, affected women more frequently than men and seems to have been, to some extent at least, an expression of the inherent misogynistic tenor of social life at Oneida. This impression is strengthened when we note that although there was an expression at Oneida of concern for women's rights, especially in the 1870s, and although women began to enter jobs and occupations formerly monopolized by the male, much of this advance was due to the changeover from an agricultural to an industrially based economy there. Women succeeded primarily in the female industries—the silk thread, canning, and satchel factories.

"Rights" were granted to women as privileges by men, who had in mind not primarily the justice of feminine claims but the effects of ex-

panding female occupational roles and social participation on the ideological structure, most particularly the eugenic system of stirpiculture.
Yet, although Oneida sexual ideology was mainly designed to insure male
perfection and the transmission of that perfection to the next generation
through the male line, the physical and social benefits offered to women
were broader than in either the Mormon or the Shaker communities.

In essence, then, each of these utopian communities made honest attempts to deal with the host of problems raised by the ambivalence of the
romantic-love ideal as applied to ordinary marriage in the broader American culture. On the one hand, as sex-role expectations began to crystalize
in a highly self-conscious way, the purity and maternal character of
women was emphasized. At the same time, economic modernization in
the period 1780–1835, as Nancy Cott has pointed out, brought social
and economic changes that more sharply defined the distinction between
male and female spheres.[3] Men assumed primary responsibility for the
external, "instrumental" functions (politics, business, and public social
obligations), whereas women performed the internal, "expressive" functions (domestic duties, child rearing, and moral and religious tutelage).[4]

The sex-specific division of labor that was institutionalized in the cult
of domesticity was defined in the advice literature of mainstream American culture with a new rigidity in the years 1820–60. The obverse side of
the romantic ideal of marriage, however, emphasized affective closeness
in the conjugal relation. In the sentimental literature of the day women
were encouraged to give all for a "love without sex, [an] affection without passion."[5] Paradoxically, domesticity depended on the reproductive
function; but the true woman was supposed to remain ethereally pure.

Romantic love raised expectations of physical happiness in marriage,
while a cloying sentimentalism seemed to imply that platonic love and
parthenogenesis would satisfy the ideal woman. Victorian American culture provided conflicting signals on sexual morality. The strident insistence on the strict reproductive justification for intercourse ill concealed
a growing concern about erotic sexuality and anxieties about the permanence and suitableness of the "spheres" doctrine of sexual roles. Emphasis on the reproductive aspect of sex legitimized marital intercourse
and thus reinforced monogamous marriage and provided a socially acceptable rationale for behavior that might well be grounded in erotic
motivation. From the point of view of sex roles, the reproductive justification for intercourse reinforced pronatalist assumptions and legitimized
the cult of domesticity.

The utopian response to Victorian sexual anxieties was to reject the
romantic-love ideology and to provide a structured social environment
that offered alternative visions of the relationship between men and
women. The Shakers, Mormons, and Oneidans offered the promise of

order and stability in sexual life and some degree of freedom from anxiety about sexual problems. Their solutions, though quite different in conception, were all radical from the point of view of the broader American culture. They insisted upon the regulation, control, and perfection of the individual person. They were not radical in the sense that they permitted anarchistic licentiousness. They were *highly structured* social alternatives, not unthinking attacks on monogamous society.

Yet, in the end, their operation and practice were not so very different from those of the monogamous society whose values they tried so hard to transcend. Their ideological assumptions paralleled those of the patriarchal society they had come from, even though they attempted to overturn the very real advances in social power and moral prestige women had achieved in the romantic-evangelical tradition.[6] They did not set out consciously to change the structural assumptions that underlay the relationship between men and women; they merely sought to change the institutionalized manifestation of that relationship.

Their theological-ideological positions were consciously intended to *reinstitute* and *preserve* the kind of order and stability they saw as necessary in the sexual relationship, both in its physical and in its social dimensions. Social and political conditions forced changes in sexual roles and functions that were not initially intended. Yet in the final analysis, it was only the ideological structure that made it possible to accept these changes and the accompanying behavioral changes that were so much a part of the attempt to achieve a reordering, a normalization of sexual life, and to integrate them into a stable social order.

It is imperative to keep in mind that the three communitarian societies we have been concerned with were fundamentally religious movements. It was theology and religious inspiration that provided the foundation for their alternative systems of sexual behavior; their concepts of sexuality, sexual status, and gender roles; and their programs for the renovation of individual character and ultimately for broader social reform. Indeed, it seems likely that it was only the religious sanction, the conviction that their salvation depended on it, that led virtuous lower-middle-class women to violate ingrained sexual norms and behavior patterns and accept the pantagamous system of Oneida or Mormon polygamy.[7]

Theologically, the Shakers, Mormons, and Oneidans accepted the dualistic nature of God, positing both a male and a female godhead. They differed from other evangelical sects and antebellum adventist groups in that they consistently *institutionalized* this dualism in their social structure. Furthermore, except for the Shakers, they refused to accept the apotheosis of womanhood in the doctrine of the female savior[8] and uniformly established a theological and social hierarchy based on the superordination of the masculine manifestation of God.

Traditional historical discussions of nineteenth-century utopian communities have overlooked the implications of their sectarianism and have failed to evaluate them as emergent institutional alternatives with means and ends that differed significantly from those of mainstream society. Even recent accounts insist on applying the standards of institutional success developed for the instrumental, impersonal macro-institutions of American society as a whole to the intentionally affective, personalist micro-institutions of the communitarian movement.[9] Inherent in this traditional argument is a bias in favor of a linear conception of historical progress, a pragmatic impatience with social experimentation that is not readily absorbed into the extant institutional framework, and a refusal to consider these communities in the context of nineteenth-century utopianism. Such an approach obscures the aims and real significance of the historical communitarian movement.

To investigate whether the three communities discussed in this work were successful, then, we must not apply modern standards external to them. We must ask not whether they were successful in *our* terms, but whether in *their own* terms they provided individuals a choice, an alternative organization of the common value heritage of their culture.

A sectarian religious group, as Werner Stark has pointed out, "fulfills a function; not so much in public as in private life: it substitutes exaltation for depression, self-confidence for self-doubt and self-despair."[10] Communitarian sectarians were individuals suffering from anomie and alienation of a social, but even more importantly of a personal, nature. They were unable to cope alone with the anxieties of sociosexual life in Jacksonian America. Male communitarians were afraid of social and economic failure, and yet dreaded the brutal world of capitalist competition. They were fearful of their unaided ability to control their economic destinies or their sexual impulses.[11] The spermatic-economy doctrine they adopted was an expression on the sexual level of their need to forfend the exhaustion of their energy, and on the economic level of their obsession with husbanding their resources to assure financial security.

Female communitarians experienced anxieties generated by separation and loss (many were widows or single women cut off from their families). They feared that the institution of the family was crumbling and doubted their unaided capacity to transmit social and moral values to the rising generation.[12] They were at the same time doubtful of their ability to be the ideal, selfless, "cheerful giver" prescribed by the cult of true womanhood and apprehensive that the perceived decline of the family would force them to renounce the socially acceptable selfishness of romantic love and the cult of domesticity. Many, no doubt, questioned the value of motherhood (considering its very real physical risks) under these conditions.

Nineteenth-century sectarian utopians did not see the solution to social decay primarily as a function of the failure of social norms and institutions, but rather as a function of the breakdown of individual morality and the impotence of the individual will. The Shakers, Mormons, and Oneidans provided a primitive form of proto-psychoanalysis, an institutional way for society to deal with individual psychological problems. The system of mutual criticism at Oneida was the most clearly conceived and consistently institutionalized from this perspective, but Shaker auricular confession and the moral supervision of the Melchizedek priesthood among the Mormons served a similar function. The leaders of these three communities constructed unique philosophical-religious systems that answered certain of their personal needs and resolved some of their particular psychic tensions, but in doing so they appealed to other individuals who felt that Victorian American society did not have a place for them, did not answer their needs. That the answers communitarians found were antinomian and dissenting is hardly surprising in view of their alienation from mainstream society.

Because sects are notoriously volatile, it would be unreasonable to expect these sectarian communities to have lasted more than one generation. Most commonly a sect fulfills the needs of some of its members more successfully than those of others. Those whose needs are not met by the theological and social structure of the sect usually pass on to another sectarian movement that promises to satisfy their expectations or, alternatively, return to a more orthodox denominational faith. This fissioning process went on in each of these communities, as evidenced by expulsions and withdrawals. Among the Mormons a number of schismatic heretical movements arose: the Strangites, Morrisites, Godbeites, and Josephites (or Reorganites), all claiming to be the true heirs of the Prophet, Joseph Smith. Despite the natural sectarian tendency to dissolution, however, the shortest lived of these three communities was Oneida, which lasted thirty years. Shakerism flourished for a century, and Mormonism on a polygamic basis for fifty. Within the context of sectarianism, then, these communities were remarkably enduring and successful.

The success of the Shakers, Mormons, and Oneidans lay in their identifying the central socioeconomic problems of their age and providing solutions that a number of individuals found helpful in making an adjustment to a difficult and frustrating society. They provided a social and intellectual framework that allowed people to try answers other than those which American society rather uncertainly prescribed. That those answers and the values embodied in them were not those which ultimately triumphed in American society (they in a very real sense looked back to an idyllic past) is axiomatic in the very term "utopian" as applied to such communities.

But this perspective overlooks the value of a community that provides real alternatives for people: social and psychic reinforcement of their self-worth through association with like-minded individuals experiencing similar problems and ambiguities; time in which to come to know themselves and perhaps finally to achieve peace with themselves and a personally satisfactory adjustment of inner psychical needs and social necessity; and finally, renewed faith in themselves, a new sense of direction, and a strategy for surviving in the face of a mainstream society that they perceive as hostile and threatening.

The essence of the social value of the Shaker, Mormon, and Oneida movements lay in the establishment of a "vital community," a "true system of association" that aimed at overcoming "the falsehood of the present organization of society, with its isolated families and discordant interests."[13] The "new covenant" of perfection would insure that people would no longer be "*obliged* to remain as they are, and fight the battle with external necessities, each one by himself. . . . commencing with an inward defeat, compelled to remain isolated . . . find[ing] the circumference of outward evil out of all proportion to their inward ability."[14] Rather, communitarian sectarians would "come out from the world" and "form a little world of our own . . . a sort of mutual insurance," which, however, "does not *terminate* in isolation, because in God we find each other, and the perfection of unity and sociality must be the result."[15] That the loneliness, impotence, and alienation of man would fall away in a postmillenarian environment was a breathtakingly radical utopian conception. That it succeeded, even for a short period of time, for those who were able to make the total commitment of self required was a remarkable and noble achievement.

Afterword

That's right, you can't tell anyone here to do anything,
you can only ask them. But that's not efficient, he said. That's
right, it's not. WE ARE NOT INTERESTED IN EFFICIENCY.

    —Elaine Sundancer on "Saddle Ridge Farm" in
    Celery Wine

The Country, the land, intimate friendships—all these
spelled liberation, freedom from the old unhappy pattern;
they were desperate to start a newer and more fulfilling life
style. That desperation led them to move too quickly. Too
many years of wrong habits could not be resolved so easily.
Instead, seven desperate adults clung together, each shaking
from the weight of his own lack of clarity.

    —Richard Fairchild on the Harrad-based commune,
    Talsalsan, in *Communes U.S.A.*

*T*he first great wave of utopian communitarianism, which included the Shakers, Mormons, and Oneida Community, had broken by 1880. A reinforcing wave led to the foundation of nearly a hundred communities in the period 1873–95. But the real flowering of the communitarian spirit in American culture came only after nearly a century of relative dormancy. In contrast to the entire period of American history down to 1965, which produced an estimated six-hundred-plus communitarian societies,[1] the decade from 1965 to 1974 witnessed an incredible mushrooming communal movement, in which an estimated fifty thousand collective communities (exclusive of traditional religious orders), with as many as 750,000 members, were founded.[2] The average contemporary commune, however, has only 5 to 25 members; they are considerably smaller than nineteenth-century communes.

Modern communes are more diverse than their nineteenth-century counterparts; some are rural, some urban, and a few even suburban. They have been formed around a bewildering range of ideological foci, from flying saucer cults to drug detoxification; from women's or gay liberation to tarot lore and occultism. Unlike the earlier commune movement, however, many contemporary intentional communities are self-consciously single-issue organizations; they do not concern themselves with a broad spectrum of issues, and therefore member commitment is frequently very limited and insufficient to sustain an ongoing community. For the most part, only modern religious communes, like those of Sikh or Hare Krishna groups, are total institutions in the sense of the Shaker communities or the Oneida Community (which were also fundamentally religious).[3]

By and large the socioeconomic foundations of contemporary communalism are also radically different from the earlier movement. Although today's communards are characterized by anomie and rootlessness, their alienation is that of a privileged class (upper middle, upper) rather than the dissatisfaction and bewilderment of a dispossessed class (lower middle, lower). The new communards are, indeed, in the words of a recent student, "the children of prosperity."[4] Their revolt is grounded in disappointed expectations: American values, political and ethical, are hollow; the promise of prosperity and ease depends on mind-deadening, dehumanizing service to amoral corporate giants; and man in a materialist, technocratic, consumer culture has lost touch with his ability to feel and to respond spontaneously and, perhaps most importantly, with his desire, his need, for transcendence. It is not surprising, then, that the modern communitarian movement has been organized around three themes: political activism, psychedelic drugs, and the importance of self-realization. Thus, although both the classic nineteenth-century communitarian movement and its modern counterpart originated in a crisis of belief, an essentially normative alienation, their perceptions of the nature of cultural malaise and their methods of amelioration have been widely disparate.

Despite the involvement of the Mormon Brigade in the Mexican War, and Joseph Smith's bid for the presidency of the United States in 1844, the utopians we have been concerned with in this work were not particularly interested in political solutions. John Humphrey Noyes corresponded with William Lloyd Garrison on the question of religious anarchism, and the Shakers, of course, were pacifists. Each of these groups sought spiritual transcendence not through releasing the self from outer restraint, but through bringing individual selfishness in all its forms under the conscious control of the will.

It is proper that we should ask, in view of the differences between nineteenth- and twentieth-century communitarianism, about the relationships of the sexes in modern communities. Sexual practices in contemporary alternative communities range from celibacy and strict monogamy to polygamy, casual promiscuity, and homosexuality. In some instances, like the Skinnerian community, Twin Oaks, in Virginia, or the Oz commune in Pennsylvania, several different modes of sexual behavior are found within the same community.

A thorough study of modern communitarianism in all its geographical, ideological, and social diversity remains to be written. The large numbers, geographic dispersal, and in many cases aggressively antiintellectual stance of modern communes make this a formidable task. The most recent study of modern communitarianism, Hugh Gardner's *The Children of Prosperity*, however, provides a detailed and thoughtful analysis of thirteen rural communities. In these communities women are primarily confined to the traditional household roles.[5] Gardner underscores the difficulties inherent in the relationship between the sexes in the modern religious-rural commune by citing the example of the Maharaj Ashram. The wife of the leader of the movement, in reaction to the subordinate status of women in the community, founded the "Grace of God Movement of the Women of America." The goal of this "feminist" movement, was to "restore woman to her rightful status . . . where woman will once again be known as the living goddess and put back on her pedestal in the hearts of all men and all mankind the world over."[6] This modern reaction to the women's liberation movement parallels that of Oneida women to male superordination and the external women's movement in the 1870s. In both instances women rebelled against a theologically grounded assumption of female inferiority by reasserting the traditional moral and cultural prerogatives of femininity.

Other observers feel that women in modern communes have achieved considerable gains. As one of these writers, who bases his conclusions largely on the Twin Oaks community, concludes, "overall, from a strong women's liberation perspective, there is still something to be desired in many alternative culture communes, but in contrast to the establishment, at least, the equalitarian atmosphere is striking."[7] Only a detailed, in-depth study comparing the anarchistic and the religious, the urban and the rural manifestations of the modern communitarian movement can provide a comprehensive vision of the status and role of women in twentieth-century utopian culture. Such a study remains to be done. Yet whatever the extent of change in the relative status and gender roles of men and women in the modern communal movement, it is clear that for a culture of affluence and narcissism, as for a culture of scarcity and self-control, anxieties and ambivalence remain central to questions of sexuality and sexual identity.

Notes

Introduction

1. John H. Noyes, *History of American Socialisms*, pp. 21–29.
2. The quotation is from B. F. Telft, "Progress and Society," *Ladies' Repository* 8 (June 1848): 186, quoted in James Moorhead, *American Apocalypse*, p. 5. For a more detailed discussion of millennialism, see also Norman Cohn, *Pursuit of the Millennium*; and Ernest L. Tuveson, *Redeemer Nation: The Idea of America's Millennial Role* (Chicago: University of Chicago Press, 1974).
3. For an excellent and detailed discussion of the commitment process in communitarian societies, see Rosabeth M. Kanter, *Commitment and Community*, pp. 61–138.
4. The standard treatise on religious perfectionism is Benjamin B. Warfield's *Perfectionism*, 2 vols. (New York: Oxford University Press, 1931). Werner Stark argues in *The Sociology of Religion*, 2:93–95, that religious sectarians, because of their hatred of their persecutors, rarely concern themselves seriously with the salvation of the world. With American utopian societies the case seems to be rather that they admit the possibility of achieving and maintaining a state of total purity only in a sequestered communal setting. Withdrawal from the world is the precondition for perfection.
5. For a highly readable, though sensationalist, survey of the connection between antinomianism and sexual irregularity, see William Hepworth Dixon, *Spiritual Wives*. Stark, *Sociology of Religion*, 2:190–91, cites the Russian sects of the Khlysty and Skoptsy as examples of the "dionysiac" and the "self-destroyers," respectively. They correspond to the antinomian sexual responses we have identified as sexual regulation and total rejection. Stark also points out that during the period 1830–40 there were unconnected but parallel outbreaks of perfectionism in East Prussia and Wales as well as the United States (p. 237).
6. See, for example, Arthur Bestor, *Backwoods Utopias*; V. F. Calverton, *Where Angels Dared to Tread*; Alice Felt Tyler, *Freedom's Ferment*, pp. 86–226; and Maren Lockwood Carden, "The Experimental Utopia in America."
7. Four recent attempts to accomplish such a "re-vision" of utopian societies in historical perspective from outside the historical discipline are John A. Hostetler, *Communitarian Societies*, an anthropological study; Kanter, *Commitment and Community*, a sociological perspective; John M. Whitworth, *God's Blueprints*, a sociological study; and William M. Kephart, *Extraordinary Groups*, also a sociological work. A work that makes no pretense of dealing with historical communities, but rather confines itself to contemporary movements, reveals the basis for this new consciousness of social alternatives and a more sympathetic understanding of their goals: Andrew Rigby, *Alternative Realities*. A psychological study, also not historically oriented, is Adam Curle, *Mystics and Militants*. The most recent sociological account, which limits itself to modern rural communes, is Hugh Gardner, *The Children of Prosperity*. A strictly historical account that is partially informed by this change of viewpoint (although it remains fundamentally concerned with more traditional political issues) is Michael Fellman, *The Unbounded Frame*. Laurence Veysey's *The Communal Experience* takes full advantage of the new consciousness of alternative cultural models.
8. The work in question is Raymond Muncy's *Sex and Marriage in Utopian Communities: Nineteenth-Century America*. The book attempts to discuss a large number of utopian

societies and thus provides at best a sketchy treatment of its subject. Muncy seems totally unaware of the ideological dimensions of sexuality and presents a survey of these communities that seems grounded in little more than voyeuristic curiosity. His own ideological stance and real concern in the book, as well as his inability to recognize the integrity and essential seriousness of several key figures, mar any attempt at the presentation of the fullness and depth of the sexual lives of these communitarians. He is decidedly antifeminist, if not positively misogynistic, and his evaluation of the "liberating" nature of utopian life for females, and his readings of the motives of women like Ann Lee and Margaret Fuller, consequently suffer greatly. He ends his volume with what I take to be his primary interest throughout—a consideration of the reasons for the failure of all these utopian communities—and thus he reveals a shortsighted and limited definition of "success," which is insensitive to the qualitative ways in which such experiments may have affected nineteenth-century American society, totally apart from their quantitative or temporal "failure," as well as his fundamental commitment to the status-quo theory of consensus history, which holds that whatever is, and manages to survive, is good.

9. This discussion is based on the sociology-of-knowledge approach of the Frankfurt School as presented in Karl Mannheim's *Ideology and Utopia*, pp. 88–108. For a more recent approach to political ideology, see Alexander J. Groth, *Major Ideologies: An Interpretative Survey of Democracy, Socialism, and Nationalism* (New York: John Wiley & Sons, 1971), pp. 2–23.

10. Mannheim, *Ideology*, p. 40.

11. Ibid.

12. J. E. Crowley, *This Sheba, Self*, p. 2.

13. See Christopher Lasch, *The Culture of Narcissism*, p. 127. For a more detailed analysis of contemporary sexual ideology, see ibid., pp. 187–206.

14. See Nancy Cott, *The Bonds of Womanhood*, pp. 36–75. David H. Fischer, in "The Vital Revolution," found that the years 1780–1820 saw major changes in demographic indicators of sexual behavior (fertility and premarital pregnancy). He characterized this as a period of "deep change." On the association of the home with a retreat, a refuge, see Kirk Jeffrey, "The Family as Utopian Retreat from the City: The Nineteenth-Century Contribution," in Sallie Teselle, ed., *The Family, Communes, and Utopian Societies*, pp. 21–43.

15. Lawrence Stone, *The Family, Sex and Marriage in England, 1500–1800*, p. 321. David Fischer, "The Vital Revolution," found premarital pregnancy rates rising dramatically in the late eighteenth century, but peaking at about 30 percent in 1800. Daniel Scott Smith, "The Dating of the American Sexual Revolution: Evidence and Interpretation," in Michael Gordon, ed., *The American Family in Social-Historical Perspective*, pp. 321–35, found that premarital pregnancy peaked in the years 1761–1800 and subsequently began to decline. See ibid., tab. 1, p. 323.

16. Lawrence Stone documents this change for the English experience. See his *Family, Sex and Marriage*, pp. 250–335. For an early nineteenth-century American statement on the desirability of romantic love in marriage as a means of preventing adultery, see Thomas Branagan, *The Excellency of the Female Character Vindicated*, p. 185. On the increasing value of the individual child, see Stone, *Family, Sex and Marriage*, pp. 400–415. Decline in the birthrate and in average household size is documented in Wilson H. Grabill, Clyde V. Kiser, and Pascal K. Whelpton, "A Long View," in Gordon, *American Family*, pp. 374–96. James W. Reed in *From Private Vice to Public Virtue*, pp. 3–5, notes the same demographic trend and makes a very convincing argument for the influence of contraception on steadily declining fertility after 1800. On changing attitudes toward children as reflected in child-rearing practices, see Philip J. Greven, Jr.,

Child-Rearing Concepts, 1628–1861 (Itasca, Ill.: F. E. Peacock, Publishers, 1973), pp. 4–6. On the liberalization of divorce laws, see George E. Howard, A History of Matrimonial Institutions, 3:3–160; and William L. O'Neill, Divorce in the Progressive Era, pp. 1–3.

17. The doctrine of the "true woman" was first given serious attention in Barbara Welter, "The Cult of True Womanhood, 1820–1840." On the anxiety about sexual excess in Victorian advice literature, see Daniel Scott Smith, "Family Limitation, Sexual Control, and Domestic Feminism in Victorian America," pp. 50–51; Charles E. Rosenberg, "Sexuality, Class, and Role in Nineteenth-Century America," pp. 136–39; and G. J. Barker-Benfield, "The Spermatic Economy."

18. Herbert Ross Brown, The Sentimental Novel in America, 1789–1860, p. 366. The ironic ambiguities of Victorian sexual attitudes were also underlined by Edward D. Branch, The Sentimental Years, 1836–1860 (New York: Appleton-Century Co., 1934).

19. Smith, "Family Limitation," p. 53. Other historians who share this perspective on female assertiveness within the home include Carroll Smith-Rosenberg, "The Hysterical Woman"; Kathryn K. Sklar, Catharine Beecher; Ann Douglas, The Feminization of American Culture; James Reed, Private Vice, pp. 55–56; and Cott, Bonds of Womanhood. The latter provides a succinct historiography of changing perceptions of "woman's sphere" in the writings of recent feminist historians (pp. 197–99).

20. Nineteenth-century advice literature generated a vast bibliography. Representative works include William A. Alcott, The Young Wife; Timothy Shay Arthur, Advice to Young Ladies on Their Duties and Conduct in Life; and John Cowan, The Science of a New Life. It should be noted that criticism ostensibly directed toward women often reveals as much if not more about men's anxieties and guilt feelings concerning their own failures to attain the ideal standard of masculine behavior. Some authors more forthrightly concentrated their attention on the male audience. Exemplary of this subgenre was John Todd's The Student's Manual.

21. Stowe's novel entitled Pink and White Tyranny was published in 1871. The quotation is from Douglas, Feminization, p. 8.

22. Smith, "Family Limitation," pp. 42–52.

23. Douglas, Feminization, pp. 30–35, 42–47, 72–85, 102–20. See also Barbara Welter, "The Feminization of American Religion, 1800–1860"; Gail Parker, ed., The Oven Birds, pp. 13–20; and Catharine Beecher, A Treatise on Domestic Economy, pp. 9–12, 145–46.

24. On matriarchy and the feminization of Christ, see Welter, "Feminization of American Religion," pp. 310–12; Douglas, Feminization, pp. 48–50; and Parker, Oven Birds, pp. 24–29. For Stowe, see below.

25. Harriet B. Stowe, Religious Studies, Sketches, and Poems (1867; reprint ed., New York: A.M.S. Press, 1967), p. 36. The canonization of selfless domestic virtue was expressed in Stowe's 1864 essay "The Cathedral," which was published in the Atlantic Monthly. In this piece not only does woman become the patron saint of pure, evangelical Christianity, but her virtue merges with the church itself. On a subconscious level, woman has become the church. This essay has been conveniently reprinted in Parker, Oven Birds, pp. 203–14.

26. On illness as an outlet for female aggression and an ironically acceptable means of assertiveness, see Smith-Rosenberg, "Hysterical Woman," pp. 654–55; Parker, Oven Birds, pp. 32–33; and Douglas, Feminization, pp. 90–92. The latter draws a parallel between typically feminine illnesses and the peculiar susceptibility of the ministerial class to tuberculosis (p. 90).

27. Cott, Bonds of Womanhood, p. 196.

28. On organized feminism, or what Daniel Scott Smith calls "public feminism" as distin-

guished from the "domestic feminism" we have discussed above, see Aileen S. Kraditor's Introduction to *Up from the Pedestal* (Chicago: Quadrangle Books, 1968), pp. 13–21; and the rather more popular account of Miriam Gurko, *The Ladies of Seneca Falls*. On free love, see Hal D. Sears, *The Sex Radicals*. For a reading of the English experience of feminism and free love, see J. A. Banks and Olive Banks, *Feminism and Family Planning in Victorian England*; and Constance Rover, *Love, Morals and the Feminists*. The only book to deal specifically with communitarian sexuality is Muncy, *Sex and Marriage in Utopian Communities* (see n. 8, above).

29. Data on occupational backgrounds may be found in J. P. MacLean, *The Society of Shakers*, pp. 88–104; and *First Annual Report of the Oneida Association*. Data on the religious composition of these communities was collated, for the Shakers, from *Testimonies concerning the Character and Ministry of Mother Ann Lee*; *Testimonies of the Life, Character, Revelations, and Doctrines of Our Ever Blessed Mother Ann Lee*; and [Philemon Stewart], *A Sacred and Divine Roll and Book*, pp. 282–402. Data for the Mormons is from Andrew Jensen, *The Latter-Day Saints Biographical Encyclopedia*; and for Oneida, from the *First Annual Report*, p. 1; and "Oneida Association, Jan. 1, 1849, Family Register." All of these percentages are based on a total of all members in the community for which previous religious affiliation is given. They therefore exclude children born into the sects and those who chose not to provide biographical information on their religious antecedents. One problem in dealing with the religious antecedents of these communitarians is inherent in the tendency to sectarian radicalism. When social discontent and spiritual longing are not satisfied in one sect, individuals go on to more extreme positions in hopes of achieving peace of mind, a sense of self-worth, and social acceptance. (Stark, *Sociology of Religion*, 2:287–300, has an interesting discussion of sectarian fission.) Approximately 20–25 percent of the membership of the Shakers and Oneida Community had this kind of questing religious background. One would expect Mormon religious experience to have followed the same pattern, but the scattered and uneven nature of the sources does not allow an accurate projection. For those Shakers and Oneidans who experienced several conversions, I have taken the last religious affiliation prior to communal association as definitive. In any case, in almost every instance, previous conversion experience was confined to the evangelical denominations; therefore, for our purposes, we do not lose anything by concentrating on the most recent conversion prior to choice of a perfectionist utopian doctrine. Another difficulty in dealing with communal source materials is the difficulty of determining the level of unconcern or even aggressively antireligious animus in the background of community members. Shaker and Mormon sources give us no hint of this kind of discontent. In the "Oneida Family Register" a level of between 3 and 4 percent is indicated. In view of Oneida's emphasis on education and rationality, I would expect the level of precommunal infidelity to be considerably higher there than in either the Shaker or Mormon instances. The Mormon experience presents a special problem in regard to religious origins because of the increasing level of immigrant membership after 1840. In order to maintain conceptual consonance with the other two communities, I have considered the religious backgrounds only of American-born Mormons.

30. Timothy L. Smith has pointed out that in the middle years of the nineteenth century the four denominations that contributed the most members to these communities made up over 70 percent of the total number of Protestants in America. These were also the denominations that were most prone to a belief in perfectionism, which each of these communities pushed to a radical degree that was inimical to the established denominations. See Smith's *Revivalism and Social Reform in Mid-Nineteenth-Century America*,

pp. 22–24. On the prevalence of revivalism and missionary activity in the dominant denominations, see ibid., pp. 39–41, 60–62; and Whitney Cross, *The Burned-Over District*, pp. 21–35, 55–78.

31. The missionary thrust of Mormonism is widely known. The best discussion of Shaker revivalism is Richard M'Nemar [McNemar], *A Brief Account of the Entrance and Progress of What the World Calls SHAKERISM, among the Subjects of the Late Revival in Ohio and Kentucky*, which may be found in his *The Kentucky Revival*, pp. 73–108. The Oneida Community was much less concerned with face-to-face proselytism, although many early converts were made through personal contact with John H. Noyes. After about 1850, Oneida spread the gospel largely through its printed organs. For a general description of evangelical Protestantism, see Smith, *Revivalism and Social Reform*, pp. 60–61; and Cross, *Burned-Over District*, pp. 45–50, 135–37.

32. On the feminization of evangelical Protestantism, see Smith, *Revivalism and Social Reform*, pp. 80–85, 141–45, 170–76; Cross, *Burned-Over District*, pp. 35–38, 84–88; and Douglas, *Feminization*, passim.

33. Freud's psychological theories grew out of nineteenth-century cultural assumptions. To the extent that they seek to delineate the connections between individual psychological development and the collective mind of the Victorian era, his methods and approaches are immediately relevant to a study of nineteenth-century culture. On the cultural relativism of psychology, Christopher Lasch writes: "Every age develops its own peculiar forms of pathology, which express in exaggerated form its underlying character structure. In Freud's time, hysteria and obsessional neurosis carried to extremes the personality traits associated with the capitalist order at an earlier stage in its development—acquisitiveness, fanatical devotion to work, and a fierce repression of sexuality" (*Culture of Narcissism*, p. 41). These are the areas of concern most important to an investigation of nineteenth-century sexuality.

34. Essentially, the argument put forth here is that we are dealing with the determination of particular social and behavioral phenomena by several distinct wishes, needs, or desires. Some of these, no doubt, remain unconscious, although they play their part in the behavioral manifestation. We thus have a psychic "over-determination" of behavior. Freud used this concept specifically with respect to dreams, but the element of wish fulfillment in the utopian impulse is so strong as to present a parallel to the dream state. See *The Interpretation of Dreams* (1900), pp. 208–16, 225–38, 442–43, 497–514, in A. A. Brill, ed., *The Basic Writings of Sigmund Freud* (New York: Modern Library, 1938).

35. See Neil Smelser, "The Value-Oriented Social Movement," in *Theory of Collective Behavior* (New York: Free Press, 1963), chap. 10, pp. 313–81. The movements we are concerned with also involve behavioral change and so also fall under Smelser's category of "The Norm-Oriented Movement" (chap. 9, pp. 270–312). An interesting and exceptionally fruitful application of Smelser's categories of determinants of social development to modern communal experience may be found in Gardner, *Children of Prosperity*, pp. 10–21.

Chapter 1

1. Benjamin Nelson, "Self-Images and Systems of Spiritual Direction in the History of European Civilization," in Samuel Z. Klausner, ed., *The Quest for Self-Control: Classical Philosophies and Scientific Research* (New York: Free Press, 1965), pp. 49–103 (quotation from p. 69).

2. Michael Zuckerman, "The Fabrication of Identity in Early America," p. 185.

3. Ibid., p. 212. Susan Sontag, *Illness as Metaphor*, confirms this contention in her analysis of the cultural perception of disease, arguing that "it is with T.B. that the idea of individual illness was articulated" in the latter half of the eighteenth century (p. 30). By the nineteenth century, tuberculosis, with its romantic associations, was *the* disease of Western culture.

4. Jonathan Edwards, "Miscellanies," quoted in Roland A. Delattre, *Beauty and Sensibility in the Thought of Jonathan Edwards: An Essay in Aesthetics and Theological Ethics* (New Haven: Yale University Press, 1968), p. 36.

5. Ibid.

6. Ibid., pp. 6–9.

7. See Crowley, *This Sheba, Self*, pp. 78–102. One of the most important English moralist schools, under the aegis of Lord Anthony Ashley Cooper, third Earl of Shaftesbury (1671–1713), who had been educated under the tutelage of John Locke, was called the Benevolists. Shaftesbury's most influential essay, "An Inquiry concerning Virtue or Merit" (1699), provided the philosophical basis for the acceptance of self-interest as the ground of virtue and the belief that man's innate "moral sense" (an affection for virtue) would act as a sufficient check to social egoism. For a further discussion of Shaftesbury's contribution to the development of the tradition of self-interest, see Crowley, pp. 18–20.

8. James Madison, *Federalist*, no. 10, in Paul L. Ford, ed., *The Federalist: A Commentary on the Constitution of the United States* (New York: Henry Holt & Co., 1898), pp. 58–59. The quotation on ambition is from *Federalist*, no. 50, p. 344. Classical statements of the self-interest school are to be found in Bernard de Mandeville's *The Fable of the Bees; or, Private Vices, Publick Benefits* (1732), and Adam Smith's *Wealth of Nations* (1776).

9. See Robert H. MacDonald, "The Frightful Consequences of Onanism: Notes on the History of a Delusion," *Journal of the History of Ideas* 28 (1967): 423–31.

10. See *Oxford English Dictionary*. Logan Pearsall Smith noted in *The English Language* (1912) that the word "self" was not compounded as a prefix in English much before the late sixteenth or early seventeenth century (cited in Zuckerman, "Fabrication of Identity," p. 187 n). Owen Barfield, *History in English Words* (London: Faber & Faber, 1926), argued that the Reformation ushered in a whole crop of "self" words. John Locke was responsible for the popularization of the terms "consciousness" and "self-consciousness," and it is from the late seventeenth century, then, that we can date the birth of the concept of modern self-consciousness. At that point the focus of consciousness shifted from the cosmos to the individual human being (ibid., pp. 165–66).

11. Timothy Flint, *Biographical Memoir of Daniel Boone*, p. 12. A second edition of the work was published in 1856 under the title *The First White Man; or, The Life and Exploits of Col. Daniel Boone* (Cincinnati: Applegate & Co.). For a discussion of the ambiguities of the frontiersman myth in Cooper's Leatherstocking series, see R. W. B. Lewis, *The American Adam* (Chicago: University of Chicago Press, 1955), pp. 98–105; and David W. Noble, *The Eternal Adam and the New World Garden* (New York: Grosset & Dunlop, 1968), pp. 8–24. For a discussion of the obverse side of the myth, see Marvin Meyers's discussion of Cooper's Effingham novels in *The Jacksonian Persuasion* (New York: Vintage Books, 1957), pp. 74–100.

12. Flint, *Daniel Boone*, p. 41.

13. On Jacksonian ambivalence, see Meyers, *Jacksonian Persuasion*, pp. 33–56. Perceptive analyses of the mythic expression of nineteenth-century cultural ambivalence may be found in Lewis, *American Adam*; Henry Nash Smith, *Virgin Land: The American West as Symbol and Myth* (Cambridge: Harvard University Press, 1950); and Leo Marx, *The*

Machine in the Garden: Technology and the Pastoral Ideal in America (New York: Oxford University Press, 1964).

14. Flint, *Daniel Boone*, p. 64.

15. Ibid., pp. 107, 71.

16. Mitford M. Matthews, ed., *Dictionary of Americanisms on Historical Principles*, 2 vols. (Chicago: University of Chicago Press, 1951). See also John G. Cawelti, *Apostles of the Self-Made Man*, p. 85.

17. Cawelti, *Apostles*, p. 54. For a provocative discussion of the social and ethical content of the self-made-man doctrine, see Irvin G. Wylie, *The Self-Made Man in America* (New York: Free Press, 1954).

18. Quoted in Stephen P. Andrews, *Love, Marriage, and Divorce and the Sovereignty of the Individual*, p. 50.

19. Ibid., pp. 69–70, 74, 80.

20. Robert V. Remini, *The Revolutionary Age of Andrew Jackson* (New York: Harper & Row, 1976), p. 6. For another statement of the seriousness of the problem of the self in nineteenth-century America, see "The Selfish Faculties," *American Phrenological Journal and Repository of Science, Literature and General Intelligence* 14 (July–Dec. 1851): 55–56.

21. See Matthews, *Dictionary of Americanisms*.

22. William Chambers, *Things As They Are in America*, p. 183.

23. Frederick Marryat, *A Diary in America with Remarks on Its Institutions*, p. 351.

24. Ibid.

25. Ibid., pp. 351–52. For other statements by foreign travelers on the appallingly self-willed nature of American children, see Anthony Trollope, *North America*, 1:152; Frances Trollope, *Domestic Manners of the Americans*, pp. 67, 212–13; and Isabella Bird, *The Englishwoman in America*, p. 350. For a rarer expression of the opposite viewpoint, approving American "free and easy" child-rearing practices as conducive to increased affection and closer interrelationship in the companionate family, see Harriet Martineau, *Society in America*, pp. 310–11.

26. Michael Roland, trans., *Sarmiento's Travels in the United States in 1847*, p. 207.

27. Thomas Hamilton, *Men and Manners in America*, p. 74. Michael Chevalier described the self-willed American pioneer as a man who is "occupied entirely with himself, and cares nothing for others" (*Society, Manners, and Politics in the United States*, p. 212).

28. Marryat, *Diary*, p. 352. For material documenting the change in emphasis in American child-rearing concepts from "breaking the will" in the seventeenth century to a more indulgent mode in the 1820s and 1830s, see Greven, *Child-Rearing Concepts*, pp. 113–81.

29. For a description of the importance of the will in American political life, and of Andrew Jackson as the heroic embodiment of the power of the will, see John W. Ward, *Andrew Jackson: Symbol for an Age* (New York: Oxford University Press, 1962), pp. 153–80. American ambivalence toward the "self-willed" is discussed in ibid., pp. 181–204. Irvin G. Wylie discusses the importance of the will to American economic and social life in *Self-Made Man*, pp. 40–55.

30. Temperance tract no. 51, reprinted in the collection *Temperance Tracts Inspired by the National Temperance Society and Publication House* (New York: J. N. Stearns, [ca. 1867]), pp. 1–2 of pamphlet. See also Alfred Taylor, *Our National Curse*, pamphlet no. 1 in ibid., p. 3; and William Parker and Joseph Parrish, *The Curability of Drunkenness: A Scientific View of the Question*, pamphlet no. 82, in ibid., pp. 4–5.

31. The phrase "slaves of fashion" was quite common. One example may be found in F. Saunders, *About Woman, Love, and Marriage*, p. 222. The comparison of marriage to slavery was also widely current. See Andrews, *Love, Marriage, and Divorce*, p. 10. The

most thoroughgoing use of the slavery metaphor in relation to the feminine condition was Sarah M. Grimké, *Letters on the Equality of the Sexes and the Condition of Woman*, passim.

32. Noah Webster, *An American Dictionary of the English Language* (Springfield, Mass.: George and Charles Merriam, 1850), p. 1265.

33. Ibid., p. 1004. Note the use of "self-love," which makes a mental connection between selfishness and masturbation.

34. On the cult of Byron, see Harvey Wish, *Society and Thought in Early America: A Social and Intellectual History of the American People to 1865* (New York: Longmans, Green, 1950), pp. 239–41, 473. The literary aspect of the vogue of Byron in America is chronicled in William E. Leonard, *Byron and Byronism in America* (Boston: Nichols Press, 1905). The classic expression of dissatisfaction with the stance of the Byronic hero and Don Juanism was Harriet Beecher Stowe's *Lady Byron Vindicated: A History of the Byron Controversy from Its Beginnings in 1816 to the Present Time* (Boston: Fields, Osgood, & Co., 1870). On the connection between revivalism and perfectionism, see Smith, *Revivalism and Social Reform*, pp. 140–47. The connection between Transcendentalism and romantic revivalism is made by John L. Thomas in "Romantic Reform in America, 1815–1865," *American Quarterly* 17 (1965): 656–81.

35. William E. Channing, *Self-Culture: An Address Introductory to the Franklin Lectures, Delivered at Boston, September, 1838* (Boston: Dutton & Wentworth, 1838), pp. 11, 12–13.

36. Ibid., p. 16.

37. Ibid., p. 17. See also the article entitled "Self-Culture" in the *American Phrenological Journal and Repository of Science, Literature and General Intelligence* 14 (July–Dec. 1851): 60–61. See also the article of the same title by Laura E. Lyman in ibid., 48 (July–Dec. 1868): 50–51, 127–28; and "Self-Help," ibid., pp. 55–56.

38. J. E. Crowley notes in *This Sheba, Self* that from the latter half of the eighteenth century, the greatest sin for evangelical Protestants was selfishness. For evangelicals, as for liberals like Channing, selfishness became the root and head of all sin, an insidious perversion of the moral faculties that "was most to be feared when it was least evident" (ibid., p. 67). Charles Grandison Finney in his classic discourse on revival methods, reprinted in *Finney on Revival* (Minneapolis: Dimensions Books, n.d.), stresses self-examination (p. 17) and the individuation of approach to sinners (pp. 68–69). The key to successful revivalism is to turn the mind away from the self and its gratification. Of those who are moved, yet remain in sin, Finney writes pointedly: "It is common for persons in such cases to *keep their eyes on themselves*; they will shut themselves up, and keep looking at their own darkness, instead of looking away to Christ. Now, if you can *take their minds off from themselves*, and get them to think of Christ, you may draw them away from brooding over their own present feelings, and get them to lay hold on the hope set before them in the Gospel" (p. 70). Through the aid of Christ they will realize that "self-denial is a condition of discipleship" (p. 32). The victory over self, sought through transcendence by liberals and through mortification by evangelicals, leads in both cases to the reaffirmation of social responsibility through the duty of self-control.

39. The phrase was brought to the attention of historians by Barbara Welter in "The Cult of True Womanhood, 1820–1840." The phrase was, as she indicates, ubiquitous, but it was part of a broader usage of the term "true," which had additional ramifications for nineteenth-century America, as we shall see in the next chapter. Smith, *Revivalism and Social Reform*, pp. 22–23, 142–43; and Cross, *Burned-Over District*, p. 38, point out the predominance of women in evangelical religious life.

40. Arthur, *Advice to Young Ladies*, p. 242.

41. Ibid., pp. 246–47.
42. Ibid., p. 247. My emphasis.
43. In the first of the Alger tales, *Ragged Dick*, published seriatim in *Student and School-mate* in 1856 (it was not published in book form until 1867), we find the protagonist doubly orphaned. His mother died when he was three, and his father either deserted the family or died at sea some years earlier. The people Dick's family boarded with adopted him, but the woman died when he was seven, and her husband went West, leaving Dick on his own. Nevertheless, from the moment we meet the orphaned bootblack we know that he has great self-possession and a firm set of values. He is characterized as "manly and self-reliant," "a boy of energy and industry" (p. 46), who declares: "You don't catch me stealin'" (p. 39; all quotations cited here are taken from *Ragged Dick and Mark, the Match Boy* [New York: Collier Books, 1962]. Where do these values so germane to the middle-class work ethic come from? Dick's first patron, the pious Mr. Greyson, provides the answer when he says to Dick: "You evidently have some good principles to start with as you have shown by your scorn for dishonesty" (p. 133). Mark Talbot, hero of the third novel in the series, *Mark, the Match Boy* (1867), makes the point more directly when he says to a pal: "It was my mother told me I ought always to tell the truth" (p. 283). Earlier, he has told the greedy woman who claims to be his guardian in order to appropriate the few pennies he makes selling matches: "Mother told me never to beg if I could help it" (p. 247).

Being abandoned and without parental affection or a comfortable home generates a drive to establish a stable home for oneself, which is clearly one of the forces that Alger feels motivates the ambition to succeed. Home is essential as a retreat from temptation and thus a bastion of virtue; but for boys who would become upwardly mobile, it must be a fraternal home without a mother. This male-bonding relationship is the most common domiciling arrangement in the Alger books. Dick and Henry Fosdick board together in *Ragged Dick*; Mark Talbot comes to live with them in *Mark, the Match Boy*; Mark and Ben Gibson go to live with Mark's uncle, the bachelor Hiram Bates, at the end of the latter book; and Tom Grey and Mr. Mordaunt share rooms in *The Western Boy* (1873). Boys who have succeeded prove their worth, legitimize their rise in station, by acting as guardians and patrons of younger boys who are "struggling upward" (the relationship of Dick and Henry Fosdick in *Ragged Dick*; of Dick and Mark Talbot in *Mark, the Match Boy*; and of Mr. Mordaunt and Tom Grey in *The Western Boy*). There is clearly a homosexual undertone about these relationships. Boys who *have* parents, especially mothers, are the unfortunate ones in Alger's world. If they are poor, they are forced to support their mothers (like Tom Wilkins in *Ragged Dick*; this relationship is perverted in the case of Mark Talbot and "Mother" Watson in the same book). If they are middle class, they are frequently imbued with aristocratic pretensions and a fatuous superciliousness that enervates their moral fiber (like Roswell Crawford in *Ragged Dick*, whose mother has raised him since his father's death; or Jasper Grey in *The Western Boy*, raised by his father after his mother's death).

Boys with parents are uniformly the villains in the Alger tales. They inherit their parents' worst traits, are prevented from undergoing the empirical testing of their values, and are thus denied the opportunity of creating their own characters out of the stuff of parental precepts of virtue and personal experience. In this sense the Alger cycle represents an inversion of the Leatherstocking myth. The hero reenters the (urban) wilderness, not to preserve his virtue intact, but to try it, to temper it; and to reemerge not the unspoiled, solitary innocent, but a man of character and self-reliance, with a firm sense of social obligation. John Cawelti has commented on the ineffectual mother figure in Alger and has suggested that the books may have been read by boys "as phantasies of father elimination" (*Apostles*, pp. 114, 123). His more extended discussion of this juvenile morality genre (pp. 102–25) is excellent. For another penetrating discussion of the Alger books, see R. Richard Wohl, "The 'Rags to Riches' Story: An Episode in Secular Idealism," in Reinhard Bendix and Seymour Lipset, eds., *Class, Status, and Power: Social Stratification in Comparative Perspective* (Glencoe, Ill.: Free Press, 1953), pp. 501–6. An interesting and provocative study of the man behind the myth is John Tebbel, *From Rags to Riches: Horatio Alger and the American Dream* (New York: Macmillan, 1963).

44. Arthur, *Advice to Young Ladies*, p. 230.

45. James Foster Scott, *The Sexual Instinct*, p. 419. My emphasis. In a discussion of gonorrhea, he condemns "coitus per rectum" and "buccal intercourse," noting that the latter is a "beastly and unnatural perversion" (p. 314).

46. Cf. Hawthorne's story "Egotism; or, The Bosom Serpent" (1846).

Chapter 2

1. The word used in this sense seems to have been introduced by Royall Tyler in the phrase "true blue" in *The Contrast* (1790). See Matthews, *Dictionary of Americanisms*.

2. *Marriage Present*, p. 39. See also pp. 23–29 for additional expressions of the hierarchical structure of the family and society.

3. Ibid., p. 36.

4. Neil Harris, *Humbug: The Art of P. T. Barnum* (Boston: Little, Brown, 1973), p. 77. For a broader exposition, see "The Operational Aesthetic," in ibid., pp. 59–90. On "confidence" terms, see Matthews, *Dictionary of Americanisms*; and Webster, *American Dictionary* (1850), p. 1179.

5. Marryat, *Diary*, p. 456. The reference to the Boston sign is from the same page. Other examples of this concern may be found in Trollope, *North America*, 1:138–40, 162; and Martineau, *Society in America*, pp. 35–36. For a more charitable construction of American behavior, see Hamilton, *Men and Manners in America*, pp. 146–47.

6. Bird, *Englishwoman in America*, p. 326. The term "almighty dollar" seems to have arisen in the 1830s and is sometimes attributed to Washington Irving (see Eric Partridge, *A Dictionary of Slang and Unconventional English*).

7. Bird, *Englishwoman in America*, p. 326.

8. Marryat, *Diary*, p. 458. He goes on to record three "Yankee" jokes, which are clearly in the indigenous, hyperbolic idiom familiar to students of the tall tale, but which bear out his contention beautifully (pp. 458–60).

9. The term "confidence woman" does not appear to have been current until the late 1880s. See Matthews, *Dictionary of Americanisms*. The extreme concern with the "confidence game" and the belief that the century was in reality false and counterfeit were indicated as well in Edgar A. Poe's tongue-in-cheek essay "Diddling Considered As One of the Exact Sciences," in which he provides the following definition of man: "Man is an animal that diddles, and there is no animal that diddles *but* man." Both aspects of the Barnum phenomenon as noted by Neil Harris—the hoax and the explication of delusion—are represented in Poe's work. Cf. his "The Balloon Hoax" and "Maezel's Chess Player."

10. See Webster, *American Dictionary* (1850), pp. 1218, 1224. The titillating sense of a striptease and the lure of the vaguely forbidden (veils were frequently associated with the meretricious enjoyments of Moslem polygamy) and obscene were also implied in the use of this metaphorical expression. The veil metaphor, so prevalent from 1830 to 1880, was used in a dual way. The crimes and enormities of one's opponents were continually being "unveiled" in rather bold and coarse descriptions, whereas the

lasciviousness inherent in such voyeuristic literary behavior was "veiled" in slang phrases, euphemisms, and circuitous locution. Examples of this rhetorical device and its synonyms abound: Ann E. Young, *Wife Number Nineteen . . . a Complete Exposé of Mormonism*; E. S. Goodrich, *Mormonism Unveiled*; Mrs. Thomas B. H. Stenhouse, *Exposé of Polygamy in Utah*; John D. Lee, *Mormonism Unveiled*; John B. Ellis, *Free Love and Its Votaries; or, American Socialism Unmasked*; Hubbard Eastman, *Noyesism Unveiled*; William J. Haskett, *Shakerism Unmasked*; Mary M. Dyer, *The Rise and Progress of the Serpent from the Garden of Eden . . . : With a Disclosure of Shakerism, Exhibiting a General View of Their Real Character and Conduct*; and John Woods, *Shakerism Unmasked*. For a specific use of the veil symbol in relation to deviant sexual practice, see John C. Bennett's description in *History of the Saints*, pp. 220–23, of the hierarchical structure of the Mormon polygamic "seraglio." On the first level women wear a white veil (symbolic of their relative purity); on the second, they are called "Saints of the Green Veil" (experienced, lusty women; cf. the phrase "give a green gown," meaning "to deflower," current from the seventeenth through the nineteenth centuries [see Partridge, *Dictionary of Slang and Unconventional English*, under "green"; and the extensive entry under "greens" ("venery, to have sexual intercourse") in J. S. Farmer and W. E. Henley, *Slang and Its Analogues*]; and on the third "Saints of the Black Veil" (those totally abandoned to lechery). Cf. also the use of the veil symbol in Nathaniel Hawthorne's short story "The Minister's Black Veil," which first appeared in the *Token* in 1836.

11. See Webster's *American Dictionary* (1850), under "real," p. 914.

12. Alexander Walker, *The Ladies' Guide to Perfect Beauty: Being a Complete Analysis and Classification of the Elements, Nature, Standard, Causes, Anatomy, Species, Defects, and Effects of Beauty in Women; also, External Indications or the Art of Determining the Precise Figure, the Degree of Beauty, the Mind, the Habits, and Age of Women, notwithstanding the Disguises of Dress*, p. 329. The repetition of the chapter title in the title of the book indicates the importance of this section (pp. 329–39) to the overall purpose of the book. Walker's position as an M.D. and LL.D. suggests the connection between the health of the body and that of the soul, which was frequently employed in arguments to keep women within their prescribed sphere and to encourage them to live up to male expectations of their behavior. Like most of this literature, this work was written by a man, from the male perspective, and with male readers in mind. The essential object of the work is to allow a poor fellow to have a reasonably accurate conception of the goods on the market (in an age rather prudish about nudity), before he barters away his life and soul for the delusion of attractive packaging.

13. Ibid., p. 331. See also John Cowan's warning to "avoid being misled through extravagance of ornament" (*Science of a New Life*, p. 54).

14. Cowan, *Science of a New Life*, p. 54.

15. Walker, *Ladies' Guide to Perfect Beauty*, p. 181. My emphasis.

16. Ibid., pp. 181–82. My emphasis. See also the use of "ideal" and "real," "natural" and "social," in the discussion of aesthetics in the plastic arts and literature in Scott, *Sexual Instinct*, pp. 161–65.

17. William L. Langer, "Checks on Population Growth: 1750–1850," *Scientific American* 206, no. 2 (Feb. 1972): 92–99. For the American experience, see Fischer, "The Vital Revolution," and *Growing Old in America*, pp. 99–108. Fischer suggests that another reason for the decline in mortality may be biological—a decline in the virulence of contagious diseases (see *Growing Old*, p. 106). On the causes of the increase in life expectancy, see Thomas McKeown and R. G. Brown, "Medical Evidence Related to English Population Changes in the Eighteenth Century," *Population Studies* 9 (1955): 119 ff.; and Thomas McKeown, *The Modern Rise of Population*, pp. 91–151.

McKeown argues most convincingly that improved medical practice and the development of new drugs had very little influence on demographic change in the modern Western world. He establishes the predominance of improved hygiene and nutrition as causes of the eighteenth-century population explosion. Decline in fertility was also related to the rise of the companionate family and the emphasis on the unique value of each child, developments described in the previous chapter. As industrialism progressed, the labor value of a large family began to be outweighed by the necessity in a modernized society for increasing education. Large families came to be seen as a drain on the family's economic resources and a threat to its social mobility and pretensions to status. James Reed discusses this question in *Private Vice*, p. 22.

18. Langer, "Checks on Population Growth," pp. 92–95. On the agricultural revolution, see Paul W. Gates, *The Farmer's Age: Agriculture, 1815–1860* (New York: Holt, Rinehart & Winston, 1960). On transportation, George R. Taylor's *The Transportation Revolution, 1815–1860* (New York: Holt, Rinehart & Winston, 1951), is still the best. Estimates of population increase are taken from Samuel E. Morison, Henry S. Commager, and William E. Leuchtenberg, *The Growth of the American Republic*, 6th ed. (New York: Oxford University Press, 1969), p. 861.

19. On the development of contraceptive devices, see Reed, *Private Vice*, pp. 13–17. A German gynecologist, Friedrich A. Wilde, had invented a cervical cap in 1836, but the modern flexible rubber diaphragm was probably invented by Edward Bliss Foote in the late 1850s. He called his device a "womb veil" (Reed, *Private Vice*, p. 16). On Foote's contribution to contraceptive technology and the birth-control movement, see also Sears, *Sex Radicals*, pp. 195–97. The diaphragm does not appear to have been widely used in conjunction with a spermicidal jelly until about 1880. See also Norman E. Himes, *Medical History of Contraception*, pp. 187, 211; and Scott, *Sexual Instinct*, pp. 315–16. On the relationship between the development of the biological sciences and the control of venereal diseases, see J. Walter Wilson, "Biology Attains Maturity in the Nineteenth Century," in Marshall Clagett, ed., *Critical Problems in the History of Science* (Madison: University of Wisconsin Press, 1962), pp. 401–18 (see especially p. 413); and William A. Locy, *Biology and Its Makers* (New York: Henry Holt & Co., 1915), p. 254. In the 1870s one observer maintained that 80 percent of all married women had gonorrhea; a more conservative estimate had it that 20 percent of "good, moral" women and 66 percent of "lewd" women were its victims (see Scott, *Sexual Instinct*, p. 381).

20. Wilson, "Biology Attains Maturity," p. 413.

21. Milton Rugoff, *Prudery and Passion*, p. 165. Increasing concern with birth control is also evidenced by the works that were wholly or primarily concerned with the issue of contraceptive necessity and technique. Among these were Richard Carlile, *Every Woman's Book; or, What Is Love?* (London: Richard Carlile, 1826); Robert Dale Owen, *Moral Physiology* (New York: Wright & Owen, 1831), which went through ten editions by 1858; Charles Knowlton, *Fruits of Philosophy* (New York: n.p., 1832); A. M. Mauriceau, *Married Woman's Private Medical Companion* (New York: n.p., 1847); J. Soule, *Science of Reproduction and Reproduction Control* (Cincinnati: n.p., 1855); Russell Thacher Trall, *Sexual Physiology* (New York: Miller, Woods, 1866); and Cowan, *Science of a New Life* (1869). For purposes of demonstrating the historical scope of the early concern with contraception the first editions of these works have been cited here. Many of these books, however, are rare, and therefore the editions I have consulted are usually later impressions. James Reed points out that though confusion reigned triumphant in the theoretical basis for the "rhythm method," Frederick Hollick had by 1850 developed a system that was effective for a woman with a regular menstrual cycle (*Private Vice*, pp. 11–13). In the 1830s contraception was practiced

widely, the two preferred methods being withdrawal (*coitus interruptus*), advocated by Owen, and vaginal douching, recommended by Knowlton.

22. Rugoff, *Prudery and Passion*, pp. 277, 318–19. See also *Congressional Globe*, 38th Cong., 2d sess., 1864–65, pt. 1:661; and ibid., 42nd Cong., 2d sess., 1871–72, pt. 3: 2648. Hal D. Sears discusses the development of the antipornography crusade in *Sex Radicals*, pp. 70–71.

23. Figures for 1830 may be found in Sidney Ditzion, *Marriage, Morals, and Sex in America*, pp. 108–9; and John R. McDowall, *Magdalen Facts*, no. 1 (Jan. 1832), p. 69. The figure for 1890 is, I assume, an approximation; it comes from Scott, *Sexual Instinct*, p. 197. In 1831, an informant told Alexis de Tocqueville that there were some two thousand prostitutes in Boston (*Journey to America*, ed. J. P. Mayer, Alphabetical Notebook no. 2, p. 223).

24. See U.S. Department of the Interior, Federal Bureau of the Census, *Eleventh Census of the United States: 1890*, Population, "Progress of the Nation," table: "Relative Proportions of Females to Males, by States and Territories: 1890, 1880, and 1870," p. lxxxi. For an example of the attacks on individuals and institutions involved in the crusade against vice, cf. McDowall's *Magdalen Facts*, no. 1 (1832), pp. 63–71.

25. James C. Mohr, *Abortion in America*, pp. 3–19.

26. John Duer, Ben F. Butler, and John C. Spencer, *Revised Statutes of the State of New York* (1828–46), 2:779; Mohr, *Abortion*, pp. 25–27.

27. For a discussion of the increased incidence and visibility of abortion after 1840, and its prevalence down to 1880, see Mohr, *Abortion*, chap. 4, pp. 46–85. He states, on the authority of Dr. Elisha Harris, registrar of vital statistics for New York City during this period, that fully one in five pregnancies in the city was terminated by abortion in the 1850s. For the figures of the Special Committee on Abortion, and doctors' estimates of the appeal of abortion to the married, see Scott, *Sexual Instinct*, pp. 259, 263, 273, 296. For an expression of Scott's belief that abortion is directly related to pleasurable sex apart from pregnancy, see pp. 287, 302. Despite these fears, there do not appear to have been a very large number of convictions for abortion in New York City. In 1859, for example, a projection based on quarterly statistics would indicate that there were about eight convictions for the year. Comparable figures of ninety-two convictions for indecent exposure and fifty-six for "insulting" women in the street provide some measure of comparison. (See Samuel B. Holliday, *The Lost and Found; or, Life among the Poor* [New York: Phinney, Blakeman, & Mason, 1860], p. 337.)

28. Quoted in Mohr, *Abortion*, p. 130. For the New Hampshire and Wisconsin laws, see ibid., pp. 133–35, 139–41. For the 1846 New York law, see Duer et al., *Revised Statutes*, p. 779. For a discussion of the anticontraceptive legislation in New England, see Carol F. Brooks, "The Early History of the Anti-Contraceptive Laws in Massachusetts and Connecticut."

29. Quoted in Mohr, *Abortion*, p. 216. For the course of abortion legislation in these two decades, see ibid., pp. 226–45. That the enforcement of legislation did not necessarily coincide with its enactment is evidenced by the fact that in the 1880s, New York courts were still operating under the interpretation of the 1830 abortion act, which recognized the legality of abortions (even with the ensuing death of the quickened fetus), upon the conditions that they be recommended by two physicians and be necessary to the preservation of the life of the mother. For cases at law, see *Reports of Cases in Law and Equity in the State of New York* (New York: Banks & Brothers, 1859–), Barbour (1859), 2:217; Thompson and Cook (1874), 2:212–15; Hun (1877), 16:113–21; and Hill (1883), 3:92–94. See also Frank Brightly, *A Digest of the Decisions of All the Courts of the State of New York from the Earliest Period to the Year 1892*, 1:598. The earliest and most celebrated case in New York, the Mme. Restell (Ann Lohman)

conviction (1848), was based on the standard of the quickened fetus (see Barbour [1859], 3:217).

30. Cf. George E. Howard, *A History of Matrimonial Institutions*, 3:3–160.

31. Quoted in Andrews, *Love, Marriage, and Divorce*, p. 157.

32. Carroll D. Wright, *Report of the Commissioner of Labor, 1889: A Report on Marriage and Divorce in the U.S., 1867–1886*, pp. 197–201.

33. Ibid., p. 201. O'Neill, *Divorce in the Progressive Era*, estimates that the "migratory" divorce rate was only about 5 percent. This seems to be a reasonable estimate.

34. Wright, *Report on Marriage and Divorce*, pp. 144, 148.

35. Ibid., pp. 170–71. If we omit the southern states from consideration (where divorces were predominantly granted to men), 70 percent of *all* divorces were granted to women (see ibid., Statistical Tables, pp. 214–977).

36. Data interpolated from "Statistical Study of the Marriage of Forty-seven Women," in Clelia D. Mosher MSS, Stanford University Archives. These women were solidly middle class. Almost all of them were college educated or had attended college. They were from both urban and rural backgrounds, and their husbands ranged from professionals to farmers. It was Carl Degler who first called the attention of historians to this rich source on sexual practices in the latter half of the nineteenth century, in his article "What Ought to Be and What Was."

37. See Knowlton's *Fruits of Philosophy*, p. 54.

38. The term "spermatic economy" is taken from G. J. Barker-Benfield's seminal article, "The Spermatic Economy." This piece was instrumental in calling the attention of social historians to the pervasiveness of this ideology. The doctrine seems to have been derived from the work of the Swiss physician Samuel Tissot, who claimed that the loss of one ounce of semen was the equivalent, in the body's physical economy, to the loss of forty ounces of blood. Spermatic economy was peculiarly suited to a society that was agonizingly guilty about erotic sexuality, because Tissot was one of the founders of the modern antimasturbatory movement as well. His work *L'Onanisme* (Lausanne, 1760) was widely accepted as the authoritative treatment of masturbation in Europe. It was translated into English in the final quarter of the eighteenth century and was published in an American edition under the title *A Discourse on Onanism* (New York, 1832) (see Sears, *Sex Radicals*, pp. 207, 310, n. 4). For a discussion of Sylvester Graham and Thomas Low Nichols, who also were advocates of spermatic economy, but whose theoretical formulations differed significantly from Tissot's, see Stephen Nissenbaum, "Careful Love," pp. 160–65, 251–53. Spermatic economy will be discussed in more detail below when we consider the three utopian societies. It seems to have been the dominant sexual ideology for much of the nineteenth century. An extreme statement of this view can be found in Cowan, *Science of a New Life*, pp. 120–21, 344–45, in which the author maintains that no passage of the seed is ever necessary and asserts that nocturnal emissions are therefore a disease (unnatural). The more liberal viewpoint is exemplified in the seminal-repletion school, of which Knowlton, *Fruits of Philosophy*, pp. 16–17, 54–55, offers a fine example.

39. Saunders, *About Woman, Love and Marriage*, p. 228.

40. See George Bancroft, *A History of the United States* (Boston: Charles Bowen, 1834), 1:3–4.

41. See *Oxford English Dictionary*.

42. Quoted from the *New York Tribune* in Saunders, *About Woman, Love and Marriage*, p. 287.

43. Ibid., p. 288.

44. Ibid.

Chapter 3

1. Claude Lévi-Strauss, *The Savage Mind* (Chicago: University of Chicago Press, 1968), pp. 94–95.
2. The religious groups most energetic in their attacks on Oneida and the Mormons were the Methodist-Episcopal, Baptist, and Presbyterian churches. In the petition campaign of 1882, spawned by the introduction of the Edmunds bill in Congress, nearly 90 percent of those petitions that can be clearly identified as to religious source are Methodist-Episcopal and Baptist. Presbyterians made up just over 10 percent. (See *Congressional Record*, 47th Cong., 1st sess., 1882, 13, pts. 1–7). The chief critics of Oneida, from 1867 to 1879, were Presbyterian and Methodist-Episcopal. Baptists were less troublesome.
3. An examination of the authorship of the books written against a particular group bears out this conclusion. With respect to the Shakers, of the eighteen books employed, thirteen, or 72 percent, were written by men (see also the testimonials included in Mary Dyer, *The Rise and Progress of the Serpent*, passim; the majority of affidavits are by men).

   In a sampling of fifty-seven anti-Mormon books, males accounted for forty-six, or 82 percent; and a collation of material from the *Congressional Record* indicates that in the antipolygamy petition campaign of 1882, over 95 percent of the petitions were authored by men. Charles A. Cannon, in an article in the *Pacific Historical Review* 63 (1974): 61–82 entitled "The Awesome Power of Sex: The Polemical Campaign against Mormon Polygamy," contends that both authors and readers of antipolygamy literature were largely female (p. 73). Though it is true, as Leonard J. Arrington and John Haupt pointed out in "Intolerable Zion: The Image of Mormonism in Nineteenth-Century American Literature," *Western Humanities Review* 22 (1968): 243–60, that 56 percent of the anti-Mormon *novels* were written by women, this does not seem to have been the case with nonfictional works. Furthermore, the problem becomes more complex with the fictional mode when we consider a work like that attributed to Mary E. V. Smith. In the first place, although ostensibly nonfiction, it contains patent misinformation about Mormonism and highly colored romantic fantasy tinged with latent sadomasochism. More importantly, however, in its first two editions (1859 and 1870), it appeared under the name of Nelson W. Green. Its initial title was *Fifteen Years among the Mormons: Being the Narrative of Mrs. Mary Ettie V. Smith*. It did not appear under her own name until the third edition (1876), when it was entitled *Fifteen Years' Residence with the Mormons, with Startling Disclosures of the Mysteries of Polygamy*. What part did Green play in its authorship? Was he primarily responsible for its content, or did it merely appear beneath his name in order to secure ready access to a publisher as a nonfiction work?

   The anti-Oneida production was much slimmer and more scattered. I have been able to locate only five books that deal at all extensively with the community. All of these were authored by men.
4. See Constance Noyes Robertson, *Oneida Community: The Breakup*, p. 76.
5. Eastman, *Noyesism Unveiled*, p. 402.
6. See David B. Davis, "Some Themes of Counter-Subversion: An Analysis of Anti-Masonic, Anti-Catholic, and Anti-Mormon Literature." Note that Davis considers the Mormons under the same polemical literary mode as the Catholics. Freud discussed the projection mechanism in *Totem and Taboo* (1913): see Brill, *Basic Writings of Sigmund Freud*, pp. 854–56.
7. David R. Lamson, *Two Years' Experience among the Shakers*, p. 198. The subtitle of this work indirectly alludes to Catholicism, with references to "confession" and "in-

quisition." Anti-Mormon sources recalled the rash of exposés of nunneries in American popular literature in the 1830s (see n. 17 to this chapter, below). Critics of polygamy maintained that there was a secret "Mormon seraglio" divided into three orders or degress (see n. 15 to this chapter, below, for the parallel male hierarchy). The first order was called the "Cyprian Saints"; the second, the "Chambered Sisters of Charity"; and the third, the "Cloistered Saints," or "Consecrates of the Cloister." The system was most exhaustively described in the very colorful and highly imaginative work of the Mormon apostate John C. Bennett, *History of the Saints*, pp. 220–25. It is also mentioned in Benjamin G. Ferris, *Utah and the Mormons*, pp. 218–19. Opponents of the Shakers maintained that they "castrated all their males . . . stripped and danced naked in their night meetings, blew out the candles and went into a promiscuous debauch.—And . . . the fruits of their unlawful embrace, they concealed by the horrid crime of murder" (M'Nemar [McNemar], *Kentucky Revival*, p. 95).

8. Haskett, *Shakerism Unmasked*, p. 146.

9. Ferris, *Utah and the Mormons*, p. 238. See also J. B. Turner, *Mormonism in All Ages*, pp. 75–78.

10. Phrases quoted from Eastman, *Noyesism Unveiled*, p. 183.

11. The phrase "Yankee Mahometanism" is from William Jarman, *U.S.A.*, p. 25. The reference to Oneida "harems" is found in Eastman, *Noyesism Unveiled*, p. 242. One of the most popular anti-Mormon tracts, a novel comprising a tissue of semipornographic fantasies and pure fabrication, entitled *Female Life among the Mormons* (1855), was entitled *Les Harems du Nouveau Monde* (1869) in its French edition and *Los Serralos del Nuevo Mundo: Vida de la Mujer entre los Mormones* (1879) in its Spanish edition.

12. Jarman, *U.S.A.*, p. 116.

13. Eastman, *Noyesism Unveiled*, p. 85.

14. On the psychological dynamics of cathexis and wish fulfillment, see Freud's *Interpretation of Dreams* (1900), in Brill, *Basic Writings of Sigmund Freud*, pp. 225–37, 497–518, 537–45. Freud applied his analysis to daydreams as well as dreams during sleep. The fantasies we are dealing with here fall into the former category.

15. John H. Beadle, *Life in Utah*, pp. 491–92. The hierarchy of the church of the Latter-Day Saints was divided into two "priesthoods," membership in which was restricted to white, male saints. The lower order was called the Aaronic and the upper the Melchizedek priesthood. The Melchizedek order was subdivided into three estates or degrees; the Second Estate was the middle step. The biblical basis for this dual priesthood is Heb., chap. 7; in the Book of Mormon, its foundation is Alma 13:1–19.

16. The best example of this type of work, which provides examples of *all* these devices, as well as illustrations in the form of harrowing etchings, is Jarman, *U.S.A.* For the Shakers, Dyer's *Rise and Progress of the Serpent*, with its graphic eyewitness accounts; and for Oneida, Ellis's *Free Love and Its Votaries*, with its line drawings, are the primary examples.

17. The anti-Catholic tradition is best represented by Maria Monk, *Awful Disclosures*; and Rebecca T. Reed, *Six Months in a Convent* (Boston, 1835). *Female Life among the Mormons*, by Maria Ward (perhaps the pseudonym of Mrs. Benjamin G. Ferris?), is the closest parallel to this type of sensationalist fiction, of which it is a direct imitation. The gothic tradition of Charles Brockden Brown, especially in *Wieland* (1798) and *Ormond* (1799), is clearly in the background of this work, as is the sentimental pornography and proto-romanticism of the Richardsonian tradition, as represented by *Clarissa* (1748). The pornographic tradition of George Lippard—best manifested in his *The Monks of Monk Hall* (1844) and *New York: Its Upper Ten and Lower Million* (1853)— particularly the sadism so rife in the former, also served as models for this genre of popular literature.

18. Haskett, *Shakerism Unmasked*, p. 58.
19. Ibid., p. 56. See also Thomas Brown, *An Account of the People Called Shakers*, p. 335. For a veritable catalog of Shaker tortures and atrocities, see *Shaker Examination before the New Hampshire Legislature*, pp. 5–45. For Mormon examples, see Ward, *Female Life among the Mormons*, pp. 32, 429.
20. The metaphorical use of Negro slavery to express the condition of women seems to have come most immediately from the women's-rights tradition, more especially the generative work of Sarah M. Grimké, *Letters on the Equality of the Sexes*. One of the earliest uses of the phrase "white slave" seems to have been in John R. McDowall's *Magdalen Facts*, no. 1 (Jan. 1832), p. 63. See also the play of that title (1857) by Bartley Campbell.
21. Lamson, *Two Years' Experience*, p. 171. The reference to "Negro-stealing" is found on p. 184, and a reference to the "slavery of Shakerism" on p. 176.
22. Jarman, *U.S.A.*, p. 6. See also ibid., pp. 124–25, 127. For a description of the Oneida Community as one large "brothel," see Eastman, *Noyesism Unveiled*, p. 281.
23. Dyer, *Rise and Progress of the Serpent*, p. 22. See also ibid., pp. 20, 23, 46–47, for other condemnations of Ann Lee as a syphilitic whore and bawd.
24. John C. Bennett, *The History of the Saints*, p. 257. The term "American Mahomet" is found in the subtitle of Charles Mackay's *The Mormons or Latter-Day Saints*; and the epithet "Bigamy Young" is from the subtitle of Will Cooper, pseud. [William C. Carman], *Rattling, Roaring Rhymes on Mormon Utah and Her Institutions*.
25. See Eastman, *Noyesism Unveiled*, pp. 20, 56, 87, 241–42.
26. *Shaker Examination before the New Hampshire Legislature*, p. 23. A veiled allusion to lesbianism is also clearly intended here. The jealousy of the first woman, who resents the substitution of the inanimate object for the physical closeness of another human being, implies the existence of lesbian sexuality among the Shakers. Thus, this passage provides a dual animadversion on female Shaker sex life.
27. Dyer, *Rise and Progress of the Serpent*, p. 197.
28. Lee, *Mormonism Unveiled*, p. 286. Snow was bishop of the church at Manti, San Pete County.
29. For a metaphorical expression of the fear of race suicide, see the critique of Oneida social practice in Eastman, *Noyesism Unveiled*, p. 290. Indirect evidence for the attack on Oneida sexuality as productive of nervous disorders and sterility may be found in Theodore R. Noyes, "Report on Nervous Diseases in the Oneida Community," which it was considered politic to append to John H. Noyes's *Essay on Scientific Propagation*, pp. 30–32. The irrationality of this fear is clear when we remind ourselves that the Mormons could hardly have been said to favor *any* limitation on family size. In fact, they opposed the use of any contraceptives and saw polygamy as a means of increasing the population of Saints. In practice, however, Mormon polygamy under demographic conditions of a shortage of women probably meant fewer children, as some men were forced to lead celibate lives while others had several wives. The total number of children a polygamist produced with any given wife did not always equal the average number of children produced in a monogamous marriage.
30. William Hepworth Dixon, *White Conquest*, 2:302.
31. The term is from Mrs. Lydia H. Sigourney, *Letters to Mothers*, p. 273.
32. William H. Dixon, *New America*, p. 455. Note Dixon's belief that those providing birth-control devices and abortions are predominantly female.
33. Both the tendency toward erotic sexuality in marriage and its essentially masculine foundation were emphasized in the observation of the Oneida Community doctor, Theodore R. Noyes, that "it is highly probable that much evil which results in ordinary married life is due to a struggle with the orgasm for the purpose of prolonging the pleasure of the act" (quoted in John H. Noyes, *Essay on Scientific Propagation*, p. 31).

34. Bennett, *History of the Saints*, p. 221. The phrase "Female Roosters" is from Jarman, *U.S.A.*, p. 107. Cf. also the character of the Amazonian frontierswoman Mrs. Bradish, in Ward's *Female Life among the Mormons*, especially pp. 56, 106, 114, 119, 242–43, 258.

35. Ferris, *Utah and the Mormons*, pp. 306–7. Cf. President Cleveland's attack on polygamy cited in William A. Linn, *The Story of the Mormons*, pp. 588–89. "Artemus Ward," pseud. [Charles Farrar Browne (1834–67)] attacked the sexual forwardness of Shaker "old maids" from the perspective of the droll old bachelor in *Artemus Ward: His Book*, p. 101.

36. Ellis, *Free Love and Its Votaries*, pp. 177–78.

37. Ibid., p. 118.

38. *Artemus Ward: His Book*, p. 23. He commented adversely on the appearance of Mormon women on p. 101 and on that of Oneida women on p. 90.

39. Ibid., p. 122. Beneath the bantering chaff, as is usual with Ward, there is a serious core. The sense of ambiguity is established at the outset with the use of the word "angle," which suggests two lines (of behavior) diverging from a point (woman). These two lines are angel (angle) and devil, which becomes apparent toward the end of the passage. The sexual aggressiveness of the female is underscored by the phrase "get into pantyloons" with its parenthetical qualification. "Get into" was a low colloquialism for "to have intercourse with" from the eighteenth century (cf. the twentieth-century expression "get into her pants"). The use of "rites" ironically suggests the codified, Christian rules (or roles) rejected by such women and, when linked to the reference to devils near the end of the passage, indicates that the new roles of behavior suggested for women are considered elements of the black arts. These new roles are expressive of forbidden desires to be avoided ("no-shuns"). The use of "emfatic" reinforces the unattractiveness of such "masculine" women, and the spelling of "noosance" indicates the author's belief as to what the fate of such social rebels should be.

40. Edward T. Coke, *A Subaltern's Furlough*, 1:203.

41. *Shaker Examination before the New Hampshire Legislature*, p. 6.

42. Ibid.

43. J. M. Coyner, comp., *Handbook on Mormonism*, p. 14. Another statement of this position may be found in Bennett, *History of the Saints*, p. 56.

44. The phrase is from Charles E. Rosenberg, "Sexuality, Class, and Role in Nineteenth-Century America," p. 139. The "Christian gentleman" is described as "an athlete of continence, not coitus, continually testing his manliness in the fire of self-denial." Just as it was self-denial and the reproductive gloss that "justified" sexual intercourse for such a man, it was selflessness and charitable instincts that "justified" his economic and (on a national level) his rapacious political pursuits.

45. Ellis, *Free Love and Its Votaries*, pp. 167–68.

46. Article in opposition to the Oneida Community by L. W. Hall in the *Syracuse Courier* for 15 Feb. 1879, reprinted in Robertson, *Oneida Community: The Breakup*, p. 81. My emphasis.

47. Beadle, *Polygamy; or the Mysteries and Crimes of Mormonism*, p. 357.

48. Ibid., p. 356.

49. Dixon, *White Conquest*, 2:310.

50. Dixon, *New America*, pp. 428–29.

51. Cowan, *Science of a New Life*, p. 303.

52. Dixon, *New America*, pp. 426–27.

53. Ibid.

54. Quoted in C. P. Lyford, *The Mormon Problem*, pp. 66–67.

55. Eastman, *Noyesism Unveiled*, p. 290.

56. Broadside: "To the Patriotic Citizens of America," reprinted in Coyner, *Handbook on Mormonism*, p. 94. My emphasis.

57. Coyner, *Handbook on Mormonism*, p. 13. The "Twin Sister" reference is to the Republican party's 1860 platform, which termed slavery and polygamy the "twin relics of barbarism."

58. These terms are found in Robertson, *Oneida Community: The Breakup*, p. 80. See also Eastman, *Noyesism Unveiled*, p. 60.

59. On the Shakers, see Haskett, *Shakerism Unmasked*, pp. 146–47. On Oneida, see Eastman, *Noyesism Unveiled*, pp. 123–24; and Ellis, *Free Love and Its Votaries*, pp. 121–22.

60. "One of the People," *An Appeal to the American Congress*, p. 6.

61. Ibid., p. 7.

62. Ibid., p. 9.

Part II, Introduction

1. The Shakers were the spiritual descendants of a radical religious sect, the French Prophets of the Cevennes, which appeared in London in 1706. The proto-Shaker group in England, the Shaking Quakers, was founded in Manchester in 1747 by Jane and James Wardley. Ann Lee had a vision convincing her that sex was the root of all evil in 1770, and the Shakers emigrated to America under divine guidance on the *Mariah* in 1774. The first Shaker settlement was established at Watervliet, N.Y., in 1776; by 1836 there were eighteen Shaker communities. Shakerism began to decline in the late 1860s, although it maintained its theological and intellectual vitality under the leadership of Elder Frederick Evans into the 1890s. By the twentieth century, Shakerism was clearly moribund. Today there are only two active Shaker communities: Canterbury, N.H. (founded 1792), and Sabbathday Lake (New Gloucester), Me. (founded 1794). The last surviving Shaker brother died in 1961; there are now nine Shaker sisters, ranging in age from forty-nine to eighty-nine, living in the two remaining societies. Since 1961 the Sabbathday Lake community has published the *Shaker Quarterly* in order to keep Shaker doctrine alive; sisters from the Canterbury society have participated in seminars to arouse public interest in Shaker art, craftsmanship, and traditions since the 1950s.

The standard sources on Shaker history from within the movement are *Testimonies of the Life, Character, Revelations, and Doctrines*; *Shakers: Compendium*; and *A Summary View of the Millennial Church or United Society of Believers*. The best secondary accounts are Edward D. Andrews, *The People Called Shakers*; Marguerite F. Melcher, *The Shaker Adventure*; and Henri Desroche, *The American Shakers*. Of these, the latter is by far the most probing and perceptive. There is also a twenty-five-minute documentary film, *The Shakers in America*, which was produced in 1975 by Vincent R. Tortora. The Shakers also figured in the literary production of William Dean Howells (1837–1920): "A Shaker Village" (1876); *The Undiscovered Country* (1880); "A Parting and a Meeting" (1890); and *The Day of Their Wedding* (1896) all feature Shakerism more or less prominently.

2. *Testimonies of the Life, Character, Revelations, and Doctrines*, p. 3.

3. *Shakers: Compendium*, p. 122. My emphasis.

4. *Shaker* 1 (Jan. 1871–Dec. 1871): 11. See also [Paulina Bates], *The Divine Book of Holy and Eternal Wisdom*, pp. 560–61, 564–66.

5. *Shakers: Compendium*, p. 122; Brown, *Account of the People Called Shakers*, p. 313; *Summary View*, p. 6. Because Lee was illiterate and left no written records, much of the information we have concerning her life is derived from oral tradition that eventually

found its way into written sources either as "testimony" (statements by her contemporaries about her life) or "visions" (supposedly spiritual in nature), which so closely paralleled the testimonies as to make their rooting in the same oral tradition unmistakable.

6. [Bates], *Divine Book of Holy and Eternal Wisdom*, p. 564.

7. Ibid., p. 565.

8. *Testimonies of the Life, Character, Revelations, and Doctrines*, p. 47.

9. *Summary View*, p. 16.

10. Ibid.

11. Ibid., p. 41.

12. *Shakers: Compendium*, pp. 161–65. See also Desroche, *American Shakers*, pp. 49–53.

13. See Theodore Schroeder, "Shaker Celibacy and Salacity Psychologically Interpreted," pp. 800–805; and Desroche, *American Shakers*, p. 30. Both accept the existence of an "Electra complex."

14. *The Testimony of Christ's Second Appearing*, p. xxvi.

15. Desroche, *American Shakers*, pp. 44–45.

16. *Testimonies of the Life, Character, Revelations, and Doctrines*, p. 212. This highly sensual imagery describing the relationship with Christ was, of course, not unique to Lee. The devotional ecstasies of female Catholic saints, whose religious predilections were highly mystical and imbued with asceticism, provide a tradition for Lee's spiritual visions. Perhaps the best known of these ecstatic Catholic saints was St. Teresa de Cepeda (1515–82), founder of the reformed Carmelite order, the Descalzos (Barefoots). She called herself Teresa de Jesus, to signify the closeness of her relationship with Christ. As his Bride, she claimed that all her actions were dictated by Christ through the medium of her mystical visions. The ecstatic trances that accompanied these visions were frequently described by Teresa in erotic imagery. She believed, for example, that a pain she experienced during her trance had been induced by an angel who had pierced her with a lance tipped with fire. The phallic thrust of this figure is clear. The most graphic representation of the erotic ecstasy of this episode in her life is a life-size baroque sculpture by Gianlorenzo Bernini (1598–1680) entitled *The Ecstasy of St. Theresa* (1645–52), in the Cornaro Chapel, Sta. Maria della Vittoria, Rome. For a concise account of her life, see Alban Butler's *Lives of the Fathers, Martyrs, and Other Principal Saints*, 2 vols. (New York: P. F. Collier, n.d.), 2:519–45.

17. *Testimonies of the Life, Character, Revelations, and Doctrines*, pp. 212–13.

18. Ibid., p. 226.

19. Ibid.

20. Ibid., p. 251.

21. Ibid., p. 296.

22. Ibid., p. 303.

Chapter 4

1. *A Concise Shaker Catechism*, p. 6. See also Giles B. Avery, *Sketches of Shakers and Shakerism*, pp. 44–45.

2. *Shakers: Compendium*, p. 106.

3. Ibid., pp. 107–8. On breeding and horticultural experiments, see Tyler, *Freedom's Ferment*, p. 161; and Rufus Bishop, A Journal or Register of Passing Events (Mt. Lebanon), entry for 28 Oct. 1858.

4. *Testimony of Christ's Second Appearing*, pp. 462–63.

5. Ibid., pp. 7–8.

6. Ibid., pp. 48–49.
7. Ibid., p. 28.
8. *Summary View*, p. 276.
9. H. L. Eads, *Shaker Sermons*, p. 51.
10. Frederick W. Evans, *Autobiography of a Shaker*, p. 133.
11. *A Shaker Letter: H. L. Eads to Mrs. E. D. S.*, p. 5; see also p. 50. The connection between the sex drive and alcoholism was even more clearly delineated when Shakers urged wives to discontinue intercourse with their husbands in order to end intemperance. (See "Temperance," *Shaker and Shakeress* 4 [1874]: 33.)
12. *Shaker* 7 (1877): 85. See also Eads, *Shaker Sermons*, p. 176; and J. M. Peebles, *Oriental Spiritualism from the Spirit of Mother Ann Lee*, p. 7. The scriptural reference implicit here is to Col. 2:21 ("touch not, taste not, handle not"). For a less restrictive interpretation of this passage, see 1 Tim. 4:1–5.
13. *Testimony of Christ's Second Appearing*, p. 74.
14. Eads, *Shaker Sermons*, p. 171.
15. [Bates], *Divine Book of Holy and Eternal Wisdom*, p. 561.
16. *Testimony of Christ's Second Appearing*, p. 67.
17. This is patently the intended meaning in these passages when they are considered in context. Deut. 23:12–13 deals with the establishment of a latrine outside the confines of the camp; and Lev., chap. 15, is concerned with "the uncleanness of issues"—those of wounds, diseases, nocturnal emissions, and menstruation. Verse 18 seems to imply that the male "issue," as it is rejected by the female subsequent to intercourse and comes in contact with bedclothes, etc., must be cleansed away. But again, it is the bodily secretion itself, *not the act of sexual intercourse*, that is involved in the taboo in question. The Mosaic law and its taboos were favorite themes of Shaker literature. Cf. *Shakers: Compendium*, p. 64; and Evans, *Autobiography*, pp. 141–60. It should be pointed out in this context, however, that there was a long history of the confusion of leprosy and syphilis in the popular mind. In 1303, for example, Gordino described an epidemic of "lepra," a highly contagious infection acquired venereally, often appearing congenitally. His description fits syphilis more than leprosy, which is not transmitted venereally and is never congenital. John E. Lobdel and Douglas Owsley have pointed out that the spirochete *Treponema pallidum*, or *Spirochaeta pallida*, which is the active agent of syphilis, often produces a pathological bone condition called periostitis gummosa. This condition is characterized by the secretion of gummy, gelatinous masses that eat deep pits or furrows into the bone. "Some European 'leper' burial grounds," they emphasize, "have yielded many skeletons with the deep worm-like lesions suggestive of syphilis" ("The Origins of Syphilis," p. 77). Finally, with the advent of mercury treatment for venereal diseases in the latter half of the eighteenth century, the incidence of leprosy in Europe declined dramatically (ibid., p. 78). Certainly by the nineteenth century any medical basis for the association of leprosy and syphilis had been eroded away, but it is quite possible that the Shakers continued an older folk tradition that irrationally equated the two diseases.
18. Evans, *Autobiography*, pp. 179, 152.
19. *Summary View*, pp. 165–66.
20. Evans, *Autobiography*, p. 148; [Bates], *Divine Book of Holy and Eternal Wisdom*, p. 606. See also *Shakers: Compendium*, p. 87.
21. Evans, *Autobiography*, p. 20. See also the discussion of emasculation in R. W. Pelham, *A Shaker's Answer to the Oft-Repeated Question, "What Would Become of the World If All Should Become Shakers?"* (1868), reprinted in Avery, *Sketches of Shakers*, pp. 31–46 (see p. 37).
22. *Summary View*, p. 166.

23. *Shaker* 1 (1871): 30; *Testimonies of the Life, Character, Revelations, and Doctrines*, p. 304.
24. "The Believers' Appeal," reprinted in Brown, *Account of the People Called Shakers*, p. 369. See also [Bates], *Divine Book of Holy and Eternal Wisdom*, p. 618.
25. *Summary View*, p. 126.
26. Joseph Meacham, *A Concise Statement of the Principles of the Only True Church*, pp. 24–25. See also Brown, *Account of the People Called Shakers*, pp. 41–42, 65.
27. Eads, *Shaker Sermons*, p. 64.
28. Quoted in Brown, *Account of the People Called Shakers*, p. 111 n. My emphasis. Interestingly, fear of homosexuality helps to explain in part the Shakers' scatological association of filth and ordure with sex.
29. Ibid., p. 74.
30. See Albert Barnes, *Notes, Explanatory and Practical on the First Epistle of Paul to the Corinthians*, 3d ed. (New York: Harper & Brothers, 1847), p. 116, nn.
31. [Bates], *Divine Book of Holy and Eternal Wisdom*, p. 514.
32. *Testimony of Christ's Second Appearing*, p. 59.
33. Shaker hymn, "Christian Names and Deeds," quoted in Haskett, *Shakerism Unmasked*, p. 276. See also *Summary View*, p. 166.
34. *Shakers: Compendium*, pp. 53–54.
35. The polarity of concepts typically associated with male and female was "Father and Mother; Being and Willing; Truth and Love; I Am and I do; Spirit and Matter; Religion and Science" (*Shaker* 1 [1871]: 33).
36. *Testimony of Christ's Second Appearing*, pp. 548–51. Significantly, the Shakers considered seriously the story of Celsus the Epicurean that Mary was pregnant by Pantheras, a Roman soldier, at the time of her espousal to Joseph. See ibid., pp. vii, 169; and [Bates], *Divine Book of Holy and Eternal Wisdom*, p. 490.
37. *Summary View*, p. 38.
38. [Bates], *Divine Book of Holy and Eternal Wisdom*, pp. 534–35. Ann Lee, through her unique position as *the* female Christ occupied an unchallenged position, justified through the ascription to women in general of an inferior social and (to a lesser extent) religious role. Because much of Shaker theology was elaborated only after the death of Lee, however, it is possible that its patriarchal structure may have represented a denial of its original principles. In that case, the continued reference to Lee as the female Christ (apart from maintaining the tradition and unique theological position of the sect) may have served largely to conceal the co-optation of real social and religious power by the masculine order.
39. *Testimony of Christ's Second Appearing*, p. 436. See also *Summary View*, pp. 218–19, 230–31.
40. [Stewart], *Sacred and Divine Roll and Book*, pp. 89–90.
41. *Summary View*, p. 217.
42. [Bates], *Divine Book of Holy and Eternal Wisdom*, p. 539 n. This appears to have been the orthodox nineteenth-century understanding of 1 Cor. 11:7. Albert Barnes (1798–1870) notes that "glory" means "the honour, the ornament, etc. She was made *for* him; she was made after he was; she was taken from him. . . . All her comeliness, loveliness, and purity are therefore an expression of his honour and dignity, since all that comeliness was made of him and for him" (*Notes . . . on the First Epistle of Paul to the Corinthians*, p. 222 n). Barnes was a Presbyterian minister around whom the early controversy between the Old and New Schools coalesced. He was expelled from his pulpit by the Synod of York in Oct. 1835. His rustication, which lasted a year, resulted from his advocacy of libertarian theology (denying original sin) in his sermon "The Way of Salvation."

43. Evans, *Autobiography*, p. 201.
44. Barker-Benfield, "Spermatic Economy," p. 49. It was natural that a celibate group should adopt such a system of ideas, because it so closely paralleled the feminine fears associated with male threats to their virginity. The term "virgin celibates" used by the Shakers to describe themselves makes this connection obvious. For a statement of the female fear of the male as a destroyer, see the poem by a Shaker woman quoted in Hervey Elkins, *Fifteen Years in the Senior Order of Shakers*, p. 8.
45. *Oxford English Dictionary*, definitions 1 and 3.
46. Brown, *Account of the People Called Shakers*, pp. 74–75.
47. *Public Discourses Delivered at Union Village*, p. 22.
48. Article signed "O. C. H.," *Shaker* 1:63.
49. Cowan's work is cited with approval in *Shaker* 7:6. Andrew Jackson Davis is quoted in Avery, *Sketches of Shakers*, pp. 27–30, and with special reference to the spermatic-economy ideology on pp. 36–37, 40.
50. A. G. Hollister, *Mission of Alethian Believers*, p. 7.
51. Evans, *Autobiography*, p. 112. See also *Testimony of Christ's Second Appearing*, pp. 30, 41–42.
52. Frederick W. Evans, *The Shaker System*, p. 5.
53. See [Bates], *Divine Book of Holy and Eternal Wisdom*, pp. 520–21; *Summary View*, p. 137; *Testimony of Christ's Second Appearing*, p. 70; Daniel Fraser, *Longevity of Virgin Celibates*, p. 6; and Calvin Green, *The Law of Life*, pp. 8–9.
54. *Testimony of Christ's Second Appearing*, p. 60. For a statement of the doctrine of "times and seasons," see *Summary View*, pp. 146–47, 175–76.
55. [Bates], *Divine Book of Holy and Eternal Wisdom*, p. 530. See also [Stewart], *Sacred and Divine Roll and Book*, p. 170; *Summary View*, pp. 138–41; and *Testimony of Christ's Second Appearing*, pp. 42, 67, 72–73.
56. See Fraser, *Longevity of Virgin Celibates*, p. 6; Avery, *Sketches of Shakers*, pp. 40–41; and William Leonard, *A Discourse on the Order and Propriety of Divine Inspiration and Revelation*, p. 15.
57. For an excellent statement of the phrenological doctrine of cerebellum (animal) vs. cerebrum (spiritual) areas of the brain, see the article "How to Be an Angel," *Shaker* 2 (1872): 73.
58. [Bates], *Divine Book of Holy and Eternal Wisdom*, p. 413. See also the Shaker poem "Sin of Wastefulness," in "E. W. (C. S.)," *A Little Selection of Choice Poetry New and Old, Doctrinal and Devotional*, inside rear cover.
59. For a discussion of Shaker craftsmanship and theory of artistic creativity, see Edward D. Andrews and Faith Andrews, *Religion in Wood*, pp. ix, 19–20.
60. Avery, *Sketches of Shakers*, pp. 38–39.
61. Ibid., p. 25.
62. Ibid.

Chapter 5

1. Shakers had abandoned the use of all distilled liquors as early as 1824, and by 1844 had discontinued the use of fermented liquor, pork products, and tobacco (see Avery, *Sketches of Shakers*, pp. 7–8).
2. *Summary View*, p. 320.
3. Avery, *Sketches of Shakers*, p. 9. This information is more strongly set forth here, but agrees in essence with that included in all the Shaker covenants. The first written covenant was that of New Lebanon (1788), but *The Covenant or Constitution of the*

Church at Hancock (1830) served as a model for almost all later ones and can stand as an exemplum. The assumption of a kind of "apostolic succession" for the Ministry is clear in art. 1, sec. 3, "Of the Gospel Ministry." Secs. 4 and 5 describe the power of the Ministry and the subordination of the common members thereunto. Art. 4, "Of the Eldership," establishes the supremacy of the Elders in the individual Families; and Art. 6, sec. 3, "Obligations of the Members," asserts the subjection of individual members to the established hierarchical power structure. (The edition I have used is bound with John S. Williams, *The Shaker Religious Concept*.)

4. A direct connection between oral confession and Shaker authoritarianism is made in *Summary View*, pp. 291, 299–300; and in H. L. Eads, *Shaker Sermons*, p. 206. See also Lamson, *Two Years' Experience*, pp. 164–65. Censorship of reading matter is advocated in *Authorized Rules of the Shaker Community*, rule 1, p. 12, and rule 3, p. 16; and in Elisha D. Blakeman, *The Youth's Guide in Zion*, p. 7. Further evidence is provided by Hervey Elkins in *Fifteen Years*, pp. 101–3. Elkins claims to have left the Shakers because he was forbidden to study, a pursuit that represented a direct opposition to the authority of the Elders, who would allow no newspapers, magazines, or books into the society without prior inspection. Elkins also mentions censorship of mail. On this matter, see also "Information for Inquirers," point 12, inside back cover of *Shaker Church Covenant* (point 11 prescribes auricular confession); *Shaker Examination before the New Hampshire Legislature*, p. 54; and Haskett, *Shakerism Unmasked*, pp. 131–32. Reference to the "informer" system is made in *Authorized Rules*, rule 4, p. 8.

5. [Bates], *Divine Book of Holy and Eternal Wisdom*, pp. 383, 390. Compare this to Ann Lee's statement to children, found in *Summary View*, p. 31.

6. *Shakers: Compendium*, p. 39; Avery, *Sketches of Shakers*, p. 12. See also *Authorized Rules*, p. 16; and "Orders for the Church of Christ's Second Appearing," pp. 29–30.

7. *Supplementary Rules of the Shaker Community*, rule 1, p. 1. These rules, although published in the 1890s, were traditional, as they show up in the account of Elkins, *Fifteen Years* (1853), pp. 25–30; and in that of Haskett, *Shakerism Unmasked* (1828), pp. 165–85. There is also a reference to reading them (although they may not have been printed at that time) in Rufus Bishop, A Daily Journal of Passing Events, entry for 3 July 1839. They were to be read in all Shaker Families in the period from July to November. They agree in most particulars with the "Millennial Laws, or Gospel Statutes or Ordinances" (1845), which are reproduced in the appendix to Andrews, *People Called Shakers*, pp. 243–89.

8. "Orders for the Church," p. 30. The rule on Elders as umpires is found in *Authorized Rules*, p. 9; and medical regulations are in "Orders for the Church," p. 18.

9. "Elder Brethren Orders" (Mt. Lebanon), section entitled "Mother Lucy's Rules."

10. For the rule, see *Supplementary Rules*, p. 1; and "Elder Brethren Orders." On strict observation of the rule, see Maria Julia Neal, ed., *Journal of the Eldress Nancy*, 1:73–74, 2:155, and passim; Giles B. Avery, Minister's Journal, p. 409 (1885); and Bishop, Daily Journal, entries for 9 and 24 Jan. 1831 and passim. See also *Testimony of Christ's Second Appearing*, p. 512 n. It seems to have been common to have more women than men present at funerals as well. See A Diary Kept by the Elder Sister, entries for 1 July 1868 and 12 May 1870. In the case of excursions by the Ministry or Elders, there was usually an equal number of men and women (reflecting Shaker insistence upon corresponding numbers of males and females in leadership positions *in their separate orders*). See Bishop, Journal or Register, entry for 13 July 1857. For photographic evidence of adherence to the principle of female plurality on outings among the common Shakers, see the photograph of the South Family, Mt. Lebanon, returning from meeting (Elmer R. Pearson, ed., *The Shaker Image*, fig. 12, p. 31). In

each of the wagons there are two males sitting in front driving and four sisters in the rear.

11. *The Gospel Monitor*, p. 20. This work is supposed to have been a transcription by Lucy Wright (d. 1821) of moral regulations uttered by Ann Lee (d. 1784) and communicated by revelation to an unidentified "instrument" who copied them down. The book was kept in manuscript form by the Elders at Mt. Lebanon and was used as a guide to Shaker behavior. No doubt it represents oral tradition handed down from Ann Lee to Lucy Wright and passed on in the female Order from generation to generation. (See Mary L. Richmond, comp., *Shaker Literature: A Bibliography*, 2 vols. [Hancock, Mass.: Shaker Community, 1977], 1:99). The barn and work regulations are in ibid., pp. 12–13. It is also observed that "apparel should be modestly and properly adjusted" in "Elder Brethren Orders."

12. *Testimonies concerning the Character and Ministry of Mother Ann Lee* yields figures for male and female testimonials of 77.25 and 22.0 percent respectively. These figures obviously exaggerate the communal sex ratio, but they do suggest that there were more males than females in Shaker societies in the 1780s. At Watervliet in 1834 and 1835, females exceeded males by 10–11 percent (Bishop, Daily Journal, entries for 6 Feb. 1834 and 7 Mar. 1835). A general estimate for the years 1839–49, for all the New York societies, stated that women exceeded men by 10 percent (*New York Legislative Assembly Committee on the Subject of the Shakers*, p. 5). Each Shaker community was subdivided into two or more smaller administrative units called "Families," which might have as many as one hundred-odd members. They were usually named according to their geographical relationship to the meetinghouse.

13. *Gospel Monitor*, p. 21. For other regulations, see ibid., pp. 12, 19, 36. Separation of the sexes among children is specifically detailed in "A General Statement of the Holy Laws of Zion," p. 72. Obviously the fear of pederasty is behind some of these regulations. There is an additional reference to the prohibition on watching the copulation of animals and a reiteration of other animal regulations in Haskett, *Shakerism Unmasked*, p. 168.

14. *Gospel Monitor*, p. 23.

15. Ibid., p. 35.

16. Ibid., p. 33.

17. Ibid., p. 37. Pubertal children posed an especial problem for the Shakers, and it comes as no surprise to learn that the adult population proved more stable in the long run than the juvenile. Melcher, *Shaker Adventure*, pp. 254–55, estimated that only one child in ten reared in a Shaker community went on to become a member as an adult. When the Seventh Census was taken in New York, 76.7 percent of the population of Mt. Lebanon was over eighteen years of age. The fundamental orientation of Shaker communities was toward adults (see MS Census, 1850, for Mt. Lebanon, New York).

18. On this point see *Testimonies of the Life, Character, Revelations, and Doctrines*, p. 303.

19. *Authorized Rules*, p. 15; *Supplementary Rules*, p. 2; "Orders for the Church," pp. 49–50.

20. These rules are cited in Haskett, *Shakerism Unmasked*, p. 168.

21. "General Statement of the Holy Laws," p. 49.

22. Ibid., pp. 49–50.

23. *Testimonies of the Life, Character, Revelations, and Doctrines*, pp. 279–80.

24. *Gospel Monitor*, p. 36.

25. Ibid., p. 23.

26. Lucy Bowers, *Concise Statements concerning the Life and Religious Views of the Shakers*, p. 17.

27. "General Statement of the Holy Laws," p. 30. See also "Orders for the Church," p. 61.

Some intimation of the debate about the wisdom of employing hired men may be gathered from "Orders for the Church," pp. 12, 30; Avery, A Register of Incidents and Events, p. 81, entry for 28 July 1861; and letter from "E. T." and "P. R." to Elders, 4 Aug. 1878, re boarding hired men outside the society for the common welfare, "both physically and Spiritually." There was some class conflict involved here as well. The hired men were used chiefly as day laborers; they do not seem to have been employed in the industrial ventures of the Shakers. Their function was to free Shaker men to work in the industrial, semiskilled trades rather than at manual labor. They were the *Gastarbeiter* of the communistic societies. See Bishop, Daily Journal, entries for 4 Dec. 1830, 30 Apr. 1836, and intermittently whenever mention is made of hired men.

28. A. G. Hollister, *"In the Day Thou Eatest,"* p. 8.

29. "General Statement of the Holy Laws," pp. 45–46.

30. U.S. Department of the Interior, Historic American Buildings Survey, Survey N.Y. 3272, "Group Plan of Buildings of the South Family of Shakers, Watervliet, Albany Co., N.Y.," reproduced in John Poppeliers, ed., *Shaker Built: A Catalog of Shaker Architectural Records from the Historic American Buildings Survey* (Washington, D.C.: U.S. Dept. of the Interior, 1974), p. 77. There was one school in most Shaker communities, but there were separate school terms for the two sexes. Boys usually attended the winter session so that they would be free to help with planting and harvesting, whereas girls, whose occupations were more likely to be indoor, attended the spring term (see Diary of Martha Anderson, pp. 185, 232, entries for 1 May 1866 and 19 Nov. 1866. Separate hours were reserved for the two sexes for singing school as well (see Avery, Register of Incidents and Events, p. 620, entry for 23 Feb. 1874).

31. J. P. MacLean, *The Society of Shakers*, drawing entitled "Plan of Location of Buildings of Middle Family," p. 56. *Shakers: Compendium*, p. 40, confirms the existence of separate workshops for the two sexes.

32. U.S. Department of the Interior, Historic American Buildings Survey, Survey N.Y. 3298, "Main Residence—Mt. Lebanon, N.Y.," Shaker MSS, New York Public Library. Lamson in *Two Years' Experience*, p. 42, maintains that men and women entered the dining room from separate doors.

33. See Bishop, Journal or Register, p. 13, entry for 16 June 1850, describing a procession up the Holy Mount; "Orders for the Church," p. 57; and *Testimonies of the Life, Character, Revelations, and Doctrines*, p. 342. In a woodcut showing a procession to the Holy Mount at Mt. Lebanon, it is obvious that males walked on the right and females on the left (fig. 7, "Mountain Meeting," facing p. 52, in Edward D. Andrews, *The Gift to Be Simple*).

34. U.S. Department of the Interior, Historic American Buildings Survey, Survey N.Y. 3254, "Mt. Lebanon Meeting House," Shaker MSS, New York Public Library. Brethren were always on the right as you faced them from the front entrance to a building or room. See the wood engravings of Joseph Becker from *Leslie's Popular Monthly* (1885), reproduced in figs. 8 (facing p. 53) and 16 (facing p. 101) in Andrews, *Gift to Be Simple*. See also Lamson, *Two Years' Experience*, p. 60. In the light of Shaker belief that women were idealized in the outside world, is it farfetched to see their right-left division as a statement of their desire to overturn such idealization, or even as a statement of the subordination of the feminine to the masculine order? This impression is strengthened by the fact that right (male) was considered superior to left (female) in the Shaker ruling on placement of hands. When hands were folded, the right thumb was always to be uppermost. Also, when walking, the first step had to be made with the right foot. See *Gospel Monitor*, pp. 30–31; Haskett, *Shakerism Unmasked*, pp. 177–78; and Lamson, *Two Years' Experience*, p. 44. The right shoe was always to be put on first.

35. MacLean, *Society of Shakers*, p. 67. At Harvard, Mass., there were a few instances in

which men and women were buried side by side. Most of these cases come from the 1870s, and none come from outside the period 1874–1912. I believe, as I attempt to show in the next chapter, that this is a reflection of the feminist movement in Shaker society and, therefore, the exception that proves the rule. Infrequently, and only with special permission of the Elders, a husband and wife might be buried side by side. See Bishop, Journal or Register, entry for 18 Dec. 1858.

36. A Diary Kept by the Elder Sister, entry for 26 Nov. 1871. Significantly, Shakers referred to any kind of relaxation from the rigor of their daily life as an "outlet" or "release-ment," thus demonstrating their awareness of an oppressive feeling of enclosure. See Bishop, Journal or Register, entries for 1 and 3 Apr. 1857.

37. New Lebanon figures based on a collation of data from North Family Book of Records; Avery, Minister's Journal, and Register of Incidents and Events; Diary of Martha Anderson; Bishop, Daily Journal; and Covenant or Constitution of the United Society in the Town of New Lebanon (1830), with signatories through 1911. Material on the smaller communities was drawn from A Diary Kept by the Elder Sister; and *Shaker Examination before the New Hampshire Legislature*. This figure is probably too low as a measurement of total apostasy. In the first place, we cannot be sure that all departures were recorded by the authorities. Furthermore, recorded departures seem to have been largely confined to those in the Gospel Order; and therefore those who had more recently associated with the Shakers, the Novitiate Order, who were much less commit-ted to Shakerism than the full-fledged members, do not as a rule appear in these figures. Children who were removed by their parents prior to coming to the age of consent are also excluded from these accounts. If we were to add the loss of membership from these two sources, the percentage would rise dramatically. But there seems little rationale for following this procedure. To calculate church membership we would hardly consider those who had not yet been confirmed in the faith. The same principle applies here. Making allowance for the inaccuracy of the figures given in Shaker accounts, then, their communities were still remarkably stable. The apostasy rate was probably well under 5 percent, which, in a society with a prevailing mobility rate of over 20 percent (see Chapter 2, p. 45, above; and n. 50 to this chapter, below), made the Shakers a very stable society.

38. Records Kept by Order of the Church, 1780–1855, p. 57, entry for 27 Oct. 1819.

39. Ibid., pp. 83–84.

40. Avery, Register of Incidents and Events, p. 74.

41. Bishop, Daily Journal, entry for 11–14 Sept. See separate entry for 14 Sept. as well.

42. Ibid. For further apostatizations of youth, see Avery, Register of Incidents and Events, pp. 230, 232, entries for 19 and 31 Jan. 1865; and Bishop, Daily Journal, entry for 16 Jan. 1837.

43. Avery, Register of Incidents and Events, p. 458, entry for ? Mar. 1870. See also entry for 31 Jan. 1865.

44. Ibid., p. 81, entry for 28 July 1861.

45. Ibid., p. 109, entry for 26 Jan. 1862.

46. Ibid., p. 56, entry for 30 Jan. 1861.

47. Ibid., p. 237, entry for 17 Feb. 1865. For Groveland, see p. 244, entry for 4 May 1865. For apostatization of trustees, see also ibid., pp. 228, 525, entries for 2 Jan. 1865 and 27 Sept. 1871. Children's caretakers were apparently quite prone to apostatization as well. See ibid., p. 48, entry for 17 Dec. 1859.

48. Avery, Minister's Journal, p. 168, entry for 15 Oct. 1877.

49. Olive Spence and Susanah Ellis to Eldress Esther, New Lebanon, 6 Aug. 1832. Other examples may be found in Eliza Ann and Betsy Bates to Eldress Lydia and Sister Polly, Mt. Lebanon, 13 Dec. 1863; and Sister Molly to Sister Esther Bennett (Watervliet),

South Union, Jasper, Ky., 18 Dec. 1818. The latter is concerned with particular affection between two sisters. Note that women wrote only to women. Except for formal letters to the Elders, correspondence between the sexes was forbidden.

50. On the internal migration rate, see Social Science Research Council, *The Statistical History of the United States* (Stamford, Conn.: Fairfield Publishers, 1965), p. 41, ser. C1–14, "Native Population, by Residence within or outside State, Division, and Region of Birth, by Color, 1850–1950." On social conditions and wage rates during the Civil War, see J. G. Randall and David Donald, *The Civil War and Reconstruction*, 2d ed. (Boston: D. C. Heath & Co., 1961), pp. 480–86.

51. This was largely the work of the great Shaker reformer Frederick W. Evans. Evans, of course, considered that aspect of spiritualism which supported spiritual marriage to be spurious. See Evans's *Tests of Divine Inspiration*. A second edition was issued under the title *Shaker Communism* in 1871.

52. Avery, Register of Incidents and Events, p. 206, entry for 15 May 1864. A slip of paper interleaved in Avery, Minister's Journal, indicates that the fervor for spiritual wifery affected Union Village, Ohio; Harvard, Mass.; and Canterbury and Enfield, N.H. The dates for the references are 17 July and 1 Nov. 1864. The fact that Avery should have felt it necessary to include such a reference in a journal begun a decade later, indicates the depth of feeling stirred by this issue.

53. Avery, Register of Incidents and Events, p. 314, entry for 3 Feb. 1867.

54. Ibid., p. 316, entry for 18 Feb. 1867.

55. On Watervliet see ibid., p. 319, entry for 15 Mar. 1867. On other societies, see ibid., p. 316, entry for 20 Feb. 1867.

56. Bishop, Daily Journal, entry for 29 Aug. 1837.

57. Avery, Register of Incidents and Events, p. 233, entry for 5 Feb. 1865.

58. Ibid., p. 329, entries for 18–23 May 1866.

59. Diary of Martha Anderson, pp. 214–15, 210–11, 264, 266, entries for 13 and 15 Aug. 1866, 1 and 3 Sept. 1866, and 25 and 29 Mar. 1867.

60. Avery, Minister's Journal, p. 189, entry for 20 Mar. 1878. Apparently others accompanied Evans: see North Family Book of Records, p. 139, entry for 22 Feb. 1878. Avery himself wrote to Oneida about financial matters, indicating a closer connection in 1883: see Minister's Journal, p. 388, entry for 31 Dec. 1883. In the *Shaker* 1 (1871): 15, there is a laudatory article on the Shakers by John Humphrey Noyes.

61. See Bishop, Daily Journal, entries for 8 Mar. 1833, 31 Mar. 1834, 28 Mar. 1838, 13 Aug. 1839, 18 Nov. 1846, 29 Mar. and 18 Dec. 1857, and 6 Sept. 1859; Avery, Register of Incidents and Events, pp. 47, 252, 527, 550, 558, 631, entries for 7 Dec. 1860, 7 and 8 Aug. 1865, 7 Oct. 1871, 12 Apr. and 27 June 1872, and 3 July 1874; and Avery, Minister's Journal, pp. 201, 275, entries for 8 June 1878 and 5 Jan. 1880.

62. Avery, Register of Incidents and Events, p. 47, entry for 7 Dec. 1860.

63. Ibid., p. 559, entry for 27 June 1872.

64. The general New England suicide rate has been calculated from Ruth S. Covan, *Suicide* (New York: Russell & Russell, 1965), tab. 1, facing p. 8. If we render the Shaker figures in the same order of magnitude as those for New England as a whole, we would have an average suicide rate of 25.43/100,000, which is nearly four times that of the general New England average. This is possible, in the light of the rates for Protestants in four of the larger German states in the second half of the nineteenth century, which averaged 19.97/100,000 (calculated from Covan, *Suicide*, tab. 6, p. 38). This data suggests that during the nineteenth century, Protestants, especially radical sectarians among them, were particularly prone to suicide. We should be careful of making a direct statistical analogy, however, between Europe and America, for in the same period the average suicide rate for European Jews was 16.82/100,000 and for Catholics 10.65/100,000.

This is an order of two to one, rather than the four to one the Shaker average represents, in comparison to the New England averages. In statistical terms, the relative population of the Shaker communities was so small that expansion of their rate to make it comparable with the regional or national rate involves inherent statistical distortion. From the point of view of statistical theory this sample would yield an accuracy on statistical probability of suicide of 0.33. This would translate into an annual suicide rate of 8.4 for Mt. Lebanon as compared to 6.85 for New England as a whole. In view of the higher suicide rate among Protestants observed above, it would be most interesting to compare the Shaker rate with that of other nineteenth-century evangelical or, better yet, radical sectarian groups. When we consider attempted as well as achieved suicides, the Shaker rate of about two male to one female coincides with that observed for the principal European countries from 1831 to 1871. The correlation is much closer in the available figures for Massachusetts (1851–70), Rhode Island (1866–80), and the rest of New England (1876–80), which indicate a lower proportion of females to males than the European evidence. The New England statistics yield a ratio of 23–39.6 female to 100 male suicides (Covan, *Suicide*, pp. 306–8). On anomic suicide, see Émile Durkheim, *Suicide: A Study in Sociology* (New York: Free Press, 1951), pp. 241–76.

65. Bishop, Journal or Register, entries for 9 July and 6 Sept. 1859.
66. Quoted in Havelock Ellis, *Studies in the Psychology of Sex* (1905; reprint ed., New York: Random House, 1942), 1, pt. 1: *Auto-Eroticism: A Study of the Spontaneous Manifestations of the Sexual Impulse*, p. 311. Lee's aphorism on work is traditional. For another statement on sublimation, see [Bates], *Divine Book of Holy and Eternal Wisdom*, p. 608. It dovetails marvelously well with the spermatic-economy doctrine.
67. This data has been collated from [Stewart], *Sacred and Divine Roll and Book*. It covers the Mt. Lebanon; Watervliet, N.Y.; Hancock, Mass.; and Enfield, N.H. communities.
68. There was also a class of ritualistic behavior called "testimonies," which appear in several printed sources. These were merely recitations of actual experiences, written in a rational mode of exposition. Very little sexual releasement could be expected from this kind of religious behavior. Interestingly, in a work like [Stewart], *Sacred and Divine Roll and Book*, 78 percent of the testimonies were presented by males, and 22 percent by females. Ages of those offering testimonies average 50.25 years for men and 43 years for women. See also "A Record of Messages from the Spiritual World, 1841–45," in which all the intermediaries are women.
69. Bishop, Daily Journal, entry for 11 Nov. 1838. On the assumption of Indian spirits, see "Sayings of the Prophetess Anna, Miriam, and Deborah"; and Bishop, Daily Journal, entry for 4 Sept. 1845. For the assumption of other spirits, see ibid., entries for 8 Jan. and 1, 2, 7, and 10 Feb. 1843.
70. Bishop, Daily Journal, entry for 11 Sept. 1842.
71. Ibid., entries for 22 Feb. and 8 Nov. 1841.
72. Ibid., entries for 4, 14, and 24 Jan. 1838.
73. Ibid., entry for 7 Feb. 1838. See also entry for 24 Jan. 1838, on exposing sinners.
74. Ibid., entry for 2 Sept. 1838.
75. Ibid., entry for 17 Apr. 1838.
76. Ibid., entries for 6 June 1838 and 3 Aug. 1839 (quotation from the latter date).
77. Ibid., entry for 27 Apr. 1839.
78. Quoted in Edward D. Andrews and Faith Andrews, *Visions of the Heavenly Sphere*, p. 14.
79. Ibid.
80. For quantified imagery, see Bishop, Daily Journal, entries for 1 Mar., 12, 13, and 15 Apr., and 5 May 1839; and Philemon Stewart, *A Closing Roll from Holy and Eternal Wisdom*, p. 39. For romantic imagery, see Bishop, Daily Journal, entries for 18 Dec.

1838 and 5 May, 23 June, and 18 Aug. 1839. The specific reference to the wallet as a container of spiritual love, which makes the psychological link between the economic and emotional spheres metaphorically plain, is to be found in ibid., entry for 3 Nov. 1839. The Shaker dance in its choreographic patterns is also illustrative of the restrictive-permissive dichotomy of Shaker sexual life. The dance figures themselves, close geometrical ones, are expressive of restriction, limitation, binding, and enclosure; whereas the approach and retreat of the sexes, always near, but never touching, expresses the simultaneous attraction and repulsion that characterized the Shaker sexual attitude. For additional examples of Shaker use of romantic-love symbols, see Shaker Autograph Album (New Lebanon, 1881–83); Autograph Album of Isabella Graves, South Family, Watervliet (1872–93); and Autograph Album Kept by Frieda (1881–98). The latter two are especially interesting. Both are bound in maroon velvet. Isabella's is full of nineteenth-century seals of cherubim, roses, violets, and others bearing inscriptions such as "with love" and "friendship." Frieda's is also filled with romantic stickers—beautiful birds, butterflies, flowers, etc. Shakers also produced small inspired books, handwritten on paper in the form of embellished hearts.

81. Bishop, Daily Journal, entry for 20 Oct. 1839. For fountain imagery, see also ibid., entry for 16 Apr. 1849; Andrews, Gift to Be Simple, fig. 7, "Mountain Meeting," facing p. 52; and Lamson, Two Years' Experience, pp. 60–65. For other expressions of the bounteous perception of love, see Bishop, Daily Journal, entries for 15 Dec. 1838 and 21 July 1839.

82. Bishop, Daily Journal, entry for 18 May 1839.

83. Ibid., entry for ? Oct. 1843. For mixed metaphorical presentation, see ibid., entries for 10 Mar. and 2 Nov. 1840. For other metaphorical representations, see ibid., entry for 29 Oct. 1839. In 1845 a heavenly visitor presented the Christmas gifts in one Shaker community: "The brethren and sisters formed a circle in their respective parts of the room, while the Angel bound each circle with a chain of love, fastened by the clasp of obedience." It was a chain of celibate love, one that kept the sexes in their segregated orders (quoted in Andrews and Andrews, Visions of the Heavenly Sphere, p. 27).

84. Bishop, Daily Journal, entry for 14 Nov. 1840.

85. Testimony of Christ's Second Appearing, p. 370. The fate of Theodora, essentially the same as that of Denisa, is recounted on the same page.

86. See Summary View, pp. 8–9; and Testimonies of the Life, Character, Revelations, and Doctrines, pp. 3, 47–48, 67–68, 95–98, 100–115, 140–45, 157–65, 184–95.

87. Olive Warner, who apostatized in the early nineteenth century, "went off . . . to the brothel in Boston, & rotted alive, as it were, with the venereal disease" (Testimonies of the Life, Character, Revelations, and Doctrines, p. 396). The kidnap motif so often found in Shaker literature also served a similar function. See Bishop, Daily Journal, entries for 6 Aug. 1833, 14 Jan. 1834, 16 Nov. 1836, 17 Feb. 1840, 7 Apr. and 18 Nov. 1846, and 15 Mar. 1847; and Avery, Register of Incidents and Events, pp. 18–19, 101, 335, entries for 27 Feb. 1860, 5 Dec. 1861, and 11 July 1867.

88. Bishop, Daily Journal, entry for 26 June 1839.

89. Ibid., entry for 14 Aug. 1844.

90. Andrews and Andrews, Visions of the Heavenly Sphere, p. 62.

91. "Sayings of the Prophetess," p. 8.

92. Ibid., p. 56. See also "The Word of the Savior by Signs"; and the collection of MS Shaker drawings in the New York Public Library Shaker MSS Collection. The word "traitor" as it appears in the drawing analyzed is clearly used by the Shakers to refer to those who betray their standard of sexual behavior. For example, speaking of the original transgression, they ask: "Was he [Adam] not condemned as a traitor?" (Testimony of Christ's Second Appearing, p. 35; my emphasis).

93. This series of drawings and writings is cited in the "Check List of Shaker Inspirational

Drawings" appended to Andrews and Andrews, *Visions of the Heavenly Sphere*, pp. 119–22. The drawing analyzed in the text is reproduced there on p. 122. The Mt. Lebanon series of drawings is located in the Western Reserve Historical Society, Cleveland, Ohio. The pages of the drawings are numbered 27–41, and the drawing discussed in detail in the text is on p. 30 of the MS. The tone of all the drawings and writings in this series is apocalyptic. The admonition "Zion is ravished continually by the unclean" appears on p. 32 of the MS. Also specified are dungeons (MS p. 35); showers and rivers of blood (MS p. 38); terrible winds, hail, fire, and earthquakes (MS p. 39); "the Sun clothed in Sackcloth and the Moon in Scarlet" (MS p. 40); and "awful judgements without ceasing" (MS p. 40).

94. Bishop, Daily Journal, entry for 25 Nov. 1840. See also entry for 13 July 1853. Shakers, for eugenic reasons, often refused to take in foundlings, and for this reason, as well as economic necessity, did not consider their communities to be charitable institutions. See ibid., entry for 26 Jan. 1841; *Shaker* 1 (1871): 25; and Avery, *Sketches of Shakers*, p. 20. In the 1870s, Shaker leaders were quite aware of Darwin's work, although like almost everyone else they interpreted it to suit their own needs. See *Shaker and Shakeress* 5 (1875): 89, wherein Frederick W. Evans cites "the Darwinian law of brute force."

95. *Shaker* 7 (1877): 25. For further expressions of eugenic concern, see Avery, *Sketches of Shakers*, p. 21; C. E. Sears, *Shakers: A Short Treatise on Marriage*, p. 11; Fraser, *Longevity of Virgin Celibates*, p. 6; Hollister, *Mission of Alethian Believers*, p. 2; and *Testimony of Christ's Second Appearing*, pp. 36–37.

Chapter 6

1. Pamphlet entitled "Ann Lee," in Avery, *Sketches of Shakers*, p. 27.
2. See Desroche, *American Shakers*, pp. 139–40 (chap. 5 is called, significantly, "Distinguishing between the Church and the World: Ascetic Feminism"); William A. Hinds, *American Communities*, p. 104; and Tyler, *Freedom's Ferment*, pp. 148–49.
3. *Testimonies of the Life, Character, Revelations, and Doctrines*, p. 313.
4. *Summary View*, p. 132 n. Desroche affirms that Shaker women were expected to renounce their sexuality in order to achieve religious status. See *American Shakers*, p. 140.
5. *Summary View*, p. 140. See also *Shakerism: "The Possibility of the Race,"* p. 11; and *Shaker* 1 (1871): 48.
6. Cf. *Summary View*, p. 180.
7. For opposition to prostitution, see ibid., pp. 137–39, 163; and [Bates], *Divine Book of Holy and Eternal Wisdom*, pp. 518–19. On the double standard and free love, see Evans, *Autobiography*, p. 87; Evans, *Tests of Divine Inspiration*, pp. 87–88, 90; and *Shakerism: "The Possibility of the Race,"* p. 11.
8. Green, *Law of Life*, p. 11. See also *Summary View*, p. 55.
9. [Bates], *Divine Book of Holy and Eternal Wisdom*, pp. 516–17.
10. Ibid., p. 517. For an earlier statement of the traditional "mistress of the house" conception, see *Summary View*, pp. 28–29.
11. From *A Brief Exposition of the Established Principles and Regulations of the United Society of Believers*, quoted in Hinds, *American Communities*, pp. 91–92. My emphasis.
12. Pelham, *A Shaker's Answer to the Oft-Repeated Question, "What Would Become of the World If All Should Become Shakers?"* (1868), reprinted in Avery, *Sketches of Shakers*, pp. 31–46 (quotation from p. 46).
13. Ibid., p. 46. The centrality of this pamphlet to the Shaker corpus is evidenced by the fact

that it had gone through three editions by 1874 and was reprinted in Avery's work in 1884.

14. Sears, *Shakers: A Short Treatise on Marriage*, p. 10. For other statements of Shaker advocacy of celibacy as a form of contraception, see E. Myrick, *The Celibate Shaker Life*, pp. 1–2; Daniel Fraser, *Is Celibacy Contrary to Natural and Revealed Law?* Fraser, *Longevity of Virgin Celibates*, p. 6; and Pelham, *A Shaker's Answer to the Oft-Repeated Question*, pp. 33–46.

15. See *Shaker and Shakeress* 4 (1874): 36; and Evans, *Autobiography*, pp. 56–57, 84.

16. Evans, *Autobiography*, p. 88. For the Malthusian justification for birth control, see ibid., pp. 215–16; and Avery, *Sketches of Shakers*, pp. 32–34, 37.

17. "Polygamy-Monogamy," *Shaker* 7 (1877): 87. On Shaker preference for polygamy, see also Evans, *Autobiography*, p. 219; and [Bates], *Divine Book of Holy and Eternal Wisdom*, pp. 520–21.

18. Evans, *Autobiography*, pp. 87–88. An additional statement of Evans's opposition to spiritual wifery and the Oneida system will be found in his *Tests of Divine Inspiration*, pp. 87–88, 90.

19. Sears, *Shakers: A Short Treatise on Marriage*, p. 6.

20. *Shakers: Compendium*, p. 43.

21. Howard, *History of Matrimonial Institutions*, 1:54.

22. Ibid., p. 13. For the Massachusetts law, see pp. 7–8; for the New Hampshire, p. 12; and for the Maine, p. 17. That these laws were part of a broad persecution and legal delimitation of the Shaker societies is quite clear when we consider that three of the states that passed such laws—New York, Kentucky, and New Hampshire—were among the most conservative on the divorce issue. As noted previously, New York divorce law allowed absolute separation only in cases of proven adultery throughout most of the century. Mere adherence to Shakerism, though, was taken as grounds for separation in this anti-Shaker legislation, and technically the injured party could sue for divorce immediately. There is no provision in this legislation for discriminating among the three Orders of Shakerism or adjudging the degree of commitment of resources or the extent of an individual convert's observance of strict celibacy. According to the wording of these laws, Novitiate members, who retained control of all their economic resources and continued to live with their spouses but wished to limit (though perhaps not discontinue altogether) sexual relations, could be cited as defendants in divorce proceedings. Though anti-Shaker divorce legislation allowed immediate separation upon a husband or wife's adherence to Shaker principles, a waiting period of two to five years was legally required in cases of simple abandonment. Many people whose spouses were impotent or chronically ill or refused all sexual relations as a result of some phobia, trauma, or mental imbalance found no recourse in the divorce laws of these states. They lived celibate married lives with no hope of divorce. Association with a Shaker community, however, in and of itself was enough to justify divorce. On the legal delimitation of Shaker communities see *Memorial of Stanton Buckingham, Stephen Wells, Justice Harwood, and Chauncey Copley*. In 1849 and 1850 the Trustees of Mt. Lebanon and Watervliet were required to make reports to the New York Legislature, and that body put out a report on the Shakers (Legislative Document 198) in 1849. In 1849, as part of a broader effort to redefine the status and prerogatives of Shaker communities, the New York Legislature passed An Act to Amend an Act in Relation to Certain Trusts, Passed April 15, 1839, which only then made the hereditary transfer of authority and property rights from one Shaker Trustee to another legal (*Laws of the State of New York, Passed at the 72nd Session of the Legislature, Jan. 2–Apr. 11, 1849* [Troy, N.Y.: Albert W. Scribners and Albert West, 1849], p. 528). Shakers were being harassed by the legislative body in New Hampshire in 1828 and 1846, and in Kentucky in 1831 and 1846. In

the latter state, the 1846 debate centered about the divorce laws of 1842 and 1843. In the 1831 debate, the corporate status of Shaker societies was at issue, as well as the 1812 divorce statute. See *Some Account of the Proceedings of the Legislature of New Hampshire in Relation to the People Called Shakers in 1828; Account of Some of the Proceedings of the Legislatures of Kentucky and New Hampshire, 1828, etc. in Relation to the People Called Shakers;* and Robert Wickliffe, *The Shakers: Speech of Robert Wickliffe in the Senate of Kentucky, Jan. 1831.*

23. Wickliffe, *The Shakers: Speech,* p. 29.

24. *Summary View,* p. 55, my emphasis. It is noted that the Shaker position is based on 1 Cor. 7:12–16.

25. Bishop, Daily Journal, entry for 20 July 1838.

26. Ruth Webster, "The Family Relation," *Shaker* 3 (1873): 39. The implied scriptural reference here is Matt. 5:31–32.

27. *Some Account of the Proceedings of the Legislature of New Hampshire,* p. 6.

28. See Evans, *A Short Treatise on the Second Appearance of Christ in and through the Order of the Female,* pp. 14–15; and *Shakers: Compendium,* pp. 34, 53–54.

29. Giles Avery, *Eine Kurtze Beschreibung des Glaubens und Praktischens Lebens der Verein,* p. 6. My translation. That "man" does not refer to "humankind" in this quotation is evident from the biblical allusion inherent in the passage. The quotation is a Shaker gloss on 1 Cor. 11:7–10. Shaker interpretation seems to have agreed with orthodox Christian exegesis of the day: cf. Alexander Cruden, *A Complete Concordance to the Holy Scriptures of the Old and New Testament; or, A Dictionary and Alphabetical Index to the Bible* (New York: M. W. Dodd, 1868). Under the heading "woman," Cruden remarks: "Woman was created to be a companion and assistant to man: She was equal to him in that authority and jurisdiction that God gave them over all other animals: But after the fall God made her subject to the government of man" (p. 691).

30. See *Summary View,* p. 214. On Shaker visions, revelations, and inspired drawings, see Chapter 5, above, pp. 105–12.

31. Bishop, Daily Journal, entry for 11 June 1837.

32. Ibid., entry for 23 Oct. 1858.

33. Ibid., entry for 28 Oct. 1858.

34. Ibid., entries for 13 and 23 July 1857.

35. A Diary Kept by the Elder Sister, entry for 27 Sept. 1871.

36. In 1876 the title of the periodical reverted to the *Shaker,* and in 1878 the journal took the title the *Shaker Manifesto.* Significantly, with the change in title in 1876, the central concern of the articles shifted from the woman question and social concerns in general to theological and ecclesiastical, and ultimately to socialist, discussion. The extent to which Shakers went to maintain a strict division between the male and female sections of the *Shaker and Shakeress,* and thus at least the illusion of equality through separation, is evident in a short note in vol. 3 (1873), requesting all contributors sign their full names, "which will determine whether the writer is male or female" (p. 32).

37. Quoted in *Shaker and Shakeress* 3 (1873): 36.

38. It will be remembered that Shakers began to bury men and women side by side in the 1870s, a suggestion that at least on the ritualistic level certain prescribed sexual divisions were beginning to break down.

39. *Shaker and Shakeress* 3:41. Evans had taken the same position in his *Autobiography,* pp. 197–98, 223.

40. Martha J. Anderson, and Charlotte Byrdsall, *Social Gathering,* pp. 16–17. See also Bowers, *Concise Statements,* p. 6; Ruth Webster, *The Second Eve,* pp. 5–7; and N. Briggs, *God Dual,* pp. 3–5.

41. Morris Busch, *Travels between the Hudson and the Mississippi*, p. 71. The more severe breastcloths described by Busch were called "neck handkerchiefs" by the Shakers. Cf. "List of Instructions for Clothing Young Females." By the latter half of the 1860s these shawl-style bibs had been replaced by cape-style bibs, usually of a material that matched the rest of the dress. As opposed to the earlier mode, which presented a sharply triangular or square base emphasizing angularity, the new fashion had a more graceful curve and softer line.

42. "List of Instructions for Clothing." The list was designed to serve as a guide for females under twenty-six years of age.

43. Bowers, *Concise Statements*, p. 8.

44. "List of Instructions for Clothing." For objections to jewelry, see Avery, Minister's Journal, p. 209, entry for 21 July 1878; and Elkins, *Fifteen Years*, p. 29. Green veils were the mid-nineteenth-century equivalent of sunglasses. They were also proscribed in Bishop, Daily Journal, entry for 8 Apr. 1840.

45. Lamson, *Two Years' Experience*, p. 39. Photographic and graphic evidence supports this contention. In the recent collection *The Shaker Image*, edited by Elmer R. Pearson, virtually all the photographs of Shaker sisters (all are post-1860) show them wearing the characteristic cap. Their hair is pulled back tightly and is almost completely concealed by the head covering. Most of the pictures of males, on the other hand, show them without their hats. Their hair is cut, in conformity with Shaker regulations, square across the forehead, with the sideburns trimmed even with the bottom of the ear. In the rear, however, their hair is allowed to grow down to the shoulders and hang free (for a description of Shaker regulations for male hair styles and clothing, see Lamson, *Two Years' Experience*, pp. 38, 60). There are two photographs of women in the New York Public Library Shaker MSS Collection; in both cases the hair is done up under the cap and does not hang loose at all. In Andrews, *Gift to Be Simple*, see figs. 1 and 17.

46. MS Sheet on the Dress of Believers, New York Public Library Shaker MSS Collection.

47. Ibid.

48. Bowers, *Concise Statements*, p. 8. Elkins, *Fifteen Years*, p. 30, observed the high-heeled style in Shaker communities in the 1850s.

49. Avery, Minister's Journal, p. 209, entry for 21 July 1878.

50. The two photographs referred to in the text are from the small collection in the New York Public Library Shaker MSS Collection. It should perhaps be noted that Shaker Millennial Laws forbade possession of photographs or display of *any* pictures whatsoever (including the inspired drawings discussed in the preceding chapter): "No Maps, Charts, Pictures nor paintings should ever be hung up in retiring rooms; and no pictures paintings or likenesses, as Deguerotypes [*sic*] etc. set in frames or otherwise should ever be kept by Believers" (*Rules and Orders for the Church of Christ's Second Appearing*, quoted in Pearson, *Shaker Image*, p. 16). These injunctions are also found in *Orders concerning the Furniture of Retiring Rooms* (broadside circular: n.p., n.d.). Pearson's collection provides additional evidence of feminine concern for adornment in this period. Fig. 78, p. 102, shows a young Shakeress whose characteristic short cape is embellished with two rows of elaborate fringe. Her skirt is drawn in at the waist and pleated. Sister Emma Neale's shirtwaist is made of a dark material with small white dots and decorated with vertical bands of satin ribbon; her collar is of fine-point lace (fig. 144, p. 139). No doubt in fashion, as in other aspects of life, Eldresses were allowed more latitude than the common sisterhood, but their deviances from the sartorial norm were of the same kind. A photograph of Eldress Anna Case, for instance, shows a dark sateen fabric with a small light-colored floral design (roses?) printed on it; running across the front of the dress, at about the level of the clavicle, is a semicircle of black, intricately worked lace, which resembles nothing so much as a lace necklace (fig. 42, p.

78). Eldress Clymena Miner sports a breast pin with a jewel or cameo, attached to her dress by a long chain; she also has a metal collar-clasp that serves as neck jewelry (fig. 149, p. 141). Finally, Eldress Sarah Ann Collins is wearing a pleated crepe cape, a pleated skirt emphasizing her narrow waist, and form-fitting leather gloves (fig. 151, p. 143). All of the photographs cited seem to be mid-Victorian, roughly contemporaneous with those referred to in the text (1865–75). For earlier photographs showing more conformity to the uniform standard of Shaker dress, see Pearson, *Shaker Image*, passim.

51. E. H. Webster, "Is Woman a Slave?" *Shaker and Shakeress* 3:13–14. Opposition to women's fashions on the grounds of their impracticability and the necessity of reform for the attainment of equality are rare in Shaker literature. For an example of this argument, see Betsey Johnson, "Dress Reform," *Shaker and Shakeress* 3 (1873): 86.

52. *Shaker and Shakeress* 3:47.

53. For an attack on fashion because it served as a preventative against motherhood, see *Shaker and Shakeress* 4:65.

54. On women assisting with fire fighting, see Diary of Martha Anderson, p. 125, entry for 3 July 1865. On painting, see ibid., pp. 106, 108, entries for 12 and 17 May 1865; and Bishop, Daily Journal, entry for 10 Sept. 1838. On exceptional occasions women helped the brethren in the fields, but this was not the usual practice. See Neal, *Journal of the Eldress Nancy*, 2:143–44, 166, entries for 1 July 1863 and 27 Oct. 1863. Women also gathered and stacked firewood, but this was considered an ancillary task to kitchen and household duties. See Bishop, Daily Journal, entries for 21 Oct. 1834, 5 and 6 Apr. 1838, 15 Apr. 1853, and 12 Apr. 1854.

55. On the female dentist, see Bishop, Daily Journal, entry for 26 Feb. 1839. Women served as nurses, but not doctors. See ibid., entry for 23 Aug. 1839.

56. Avery, *Eine Kurtze Beschreibung des Glaubens*, p. 3. My translation. See also Evans, *Autobiography*, p. 240; Avery, *Sketches of Shakers*, p. 7; Mary A Doolittle, *Autobiography*, p. 39; Haskett, *Shakerism Unmasked*, p. 165; and Elkins, *Fifteen Years*, p. 129.

57. See "Washing Day among the Shakers," *Shaker* 7:36. On monthly rotation, see Diary Kept by the Elder Sister, passim; and Diary of Martha Anderson, passim. See also Evans, *Autobiography*, pp. 261, 265, 271. For an illustration of the South Family's laundry at the Enfield, Conn., community, see Pearson, *Shaker Image*, fig. 28, p. 67. "General Statement of the Holy Laws" gives a rather hysterical injunction against hiring worldlings as servants. That this was specifically a measure designed to protect *male* Shaker purity from temptation by the wiles of worldly females becomes quite apparent when we consider that hired *men* were involved in all the processes of Shaker agriculture and were employed to aid in building and to facilitate heavy work in the communities.

58. The fashionable list is from Avery, Minister's Journal, p. 298, "Review of 1880." See also Diary of Martha Anderson, pp. 27, 44, 47, entries for 30 and 31 Dec. 1863 and 3 and 13 Apr. 1864; and Avery, *Sketches of Shakers*, p. 7. It is possible that the feminine revolt against the rigors of the Shaker dress code derived in part from an expansion of female industry in the communities into areas related to the market for fashionable women's apparel. Shaker women who began to manufacture these items might well have begun to wonder why their use was forbidden them.

59. *Shaker* 7:14.

60. Bishop, Daily Journal, entry for 15 Aug. 1836.

61. *Shaker* 7:79. Ann Oakley, *The Sociology of Housework* (New York: Pantheon Books, 1974), chap. 2, "Standards and Routines," pp. 100–112, suggests that standards are a highly individual matter for housewives. In a communal setting, however, standards of cleanliness and uniformity of quality in diet are independent of the individual woman and would have a multiplier effect on male expectations when laborsaving devices were

introduced. Much greater uniformity and much more rapid routinization would be expected of communal "housewives" than of women isolated in nuclear family environments. Thorstein Veblen, *Theory of the Leisure Class* (1898; reprint ed., New York: Mentor Books, 1953), suggests that increased use of laborsaving devices leads to higher standards of cleanliness and that therefore woman's work load in the home is not lessened by such devices but merely becomes more ceremonial in character and more removed from productive labor; i.e., becomes drudgery (pp. 55–56).

62. "E. T. and P. R." to "Elders," 4 Aug. 1878. "P. R." and "E. T." to Eldress Lydia and Sister Polly, Mt. Lebanon, 23 June 1878, recounts the breakdown of a woman's health owing to excessive work in the kitchen.

63. Avery, Minister's Journal, p. 121, entry for 2 Oct. 1876. On male control of business decisions, see Bishop, Daily Journal, entry for 18 Jan. 1846 re a public meeting concerning legislative persecution of the Shakers (all males attending); and Journal or Register, entry for 5 Mar. 1855. On female participation in decision making in the 1870s, see Diary Kept by the Elder Sister, entry for 23 Apr. 1872; and Avery, Register of Incidents and Events, pp. 569, 640, entries for 23 Sept. 1872 and 28 Oct. 1874.

64. "Shakers," reprinted from the *New Haven Daily Press* in *Shaker and Shakeress* 5 (1875): 4.

65. *Shaker* 1:21. Earlier statements of this idea abound. For example: *Summary View*, pp. 92–93; and [Bates], *Divine Book of Holy and Eternal Wisdom*, p. 153.

66. For examples of such techniques, see *Shaker and Shakeress* 4:4–5. On facing pages we have (1) letter from the Daughters of Zion in New York to Frederick W. Evans, taking a militant stand on women's rights with no leader or attempt to catch the eye employed; and (2) an article entitled "The Voice of Woman," with the entire title set in capitals, which talks of "redemption for Woman!" and ends with a plea for woman to reform herself, observe her duties (sphere), and become a savior of man (p. 5). On pp. 54–55 of the same volume, a similar technique is used. An article entitled "Woman's Sphere" is one of the most inclusive attacks on that doctrine and in effect counters the basis for the "spheres" ideology (p. 54). On p. 55 we find a letter to "Eldress A." supporting the doctrine of spheres. Throughout the 1870s, the word "spheres" occurs as frequently in references to woman's social position as the word "motherhood" occurs in references to her religious manifestation.

67. *Shaker and Shakeress* 5:5.

68. Asenath C. Stickney, "The Shaker Woman's Rights," *Shaker and Shakeress* 4:53.

69. Collation of data from North Family Book of Records, 1814–1910; Avery, Register of Incidents and Events, and Minister's Journal; Diary Kept by the Elder Sister; Bishop, Daily Journal; Diary of Martha Anderson; Covenant or Constitution of the United Society in the Town of New Lebanon, (1830), with signatories through 1911; and *Shaker Examination before the New Hampshire Legislature*.

70. See Records Kept by Order of the Church, 1780–1855; Avery, Register of Incidents and Events; Bishop, Daily Journal, vols. 1 and 2, and Journal or Register; and Diary of Martha Anderson.

71. For a statement that reflects the sentiments expressed in this paragraph, see A. G. Hollister, *Divine Motherhood*, p. 4.

Part III, Introduction

1. Joseph Smith, *History of the Church*, 1:12 (hereafter cited as *History of Church*).

2. Ibid., pp. 5–8.

3. Ibid., p. 2. All told, the elder Smith moved his family nineteen times in ten years (see Stanley P. Hirshson, *The Lion of the Lord*, p. 14).

4. Fawn M. Brodie, *No Man Knows My History*, app. A, "Documents on the Early Life of Joseph Smith," p. 427. Joseph's employment by Stowel (spelled "Stoal") is mentioned in Lucy Smith, *Biographical Sketches of Joseph Smith, the Prophet*, pp. 90–93, but no mention is made of the trial.

5. *History of Church*, 1:15–18; Smith, *Biographical Sketches*, pp. 93–99. The background and early life of Brigham Young, who emerged as the successor to the title of Mormon Prophet after the death of Smith in 1844, was strikingly similar. He was born in 1801 in Whitingham, Vt., the ninth of eleven children. Three years later his father was dispossessed when the side he supported in a land dispute lost out in court. The family went to Sherburne, N.Y., and after scant agricultural success, to Pine Grove, N.Y., in 1812. Brigham's father, unsuccessful as a farmer, was a religious exhorter on the side. Brigham and his brothers worked at odd jobs, performed manual labor, and hunted and fished to help the family make ends meet. In this environment of frontier poverty, of scrounge and scramble, Brigham found time for only eleven days of formal schooling. His mother died when he was fourteen, and all the children were sent to live with different families. Working for little more than his board, Brigham lived with a succession of families. He married in 1823. His conversion to Mormonism came in April 1832. (This outline of Young's life is based on Hirshson, *Lion of the Lord*, pp. 5–8.)

6. Brodie, *No Man*, p. 439.

7. *History of Church*, 1:14.

8. Smith, *Biographical Sketches*, p. 107.

9. Affidavit of Abigail Harris, reprinted in app. A in Brodie, *No Man*, p. 437.

10. *Doctrine and Covenants of the Church of Jesus Christ of Latter-Day Saints*, sec. 19, entitled "A Commandment of God and not of Man, Revealed through Joseph, the Seer, to Martin Harris" (Mar. 1830), pp. 119–20.

11. M. R. Werner, *Brigham Young*, p. 39. Material quoted from *Address to Believers in Christ*, a pamphlet by David Whitmer, one of the original three witnesses of the Plates of Nephi.

12. *Doctrine and Covenants*, sec. 25, pp. 136–37.

13. Mormon sources assert that this was in accord with copyright law and that Smith's name appeared thus only to protect the book from piracy, but I have been unable to corroborate the statement. See *History of Church*, 1:58 n; and Ivan J. Barrett, *Joseph Smith and the Restoration*, p. 100.

14. On early attempts at the sale of the Book of Mormon, see Smith, *Biographical Sketches*, pp. 152–54; and Werner, *Brigham Young*, p. 68. On the mobbings, see Smith, *Biographical Sketches*, pp. 143–50, 192–95.

15. In Jan. 1831 the Mormons left the vicinity of Palmyra and went to Kirtland, Ohio. After the failure of a highly speculative, and only marginally legal, wildcat banking venture (the Kirtland Safety Society and Anti-Banking Company) in 1838, the Saints moved farther west to Far West and later Independence, Mo. In Sept. 1839 they decided to plant their Zion on a malarial spit of land jutting into the Mississippi, which Joseph Smith named Nauvoo—he claimed it meant "Beautiful Place" in Hebrew. It was here that the Latter-Day Saints would begin the construction of their temple. Rumors of polygamy, political tyranny, and unscrupulous land speculation invested the Mormon stronghold. After the death of the Prophet (June 1844), the Mormons were again forced to flee the self-righteous wrath of the Gentiles.

If Joseph Smith was the Moses of Mormondom, Brigham Young was its Joshua. He led his people on the hegira that would end in September of 1848 in the Great Salt Lake Basin. The Mormons had found an isolated Zion, a place of solace, but the practice of polygamy, officially announced in 1852, continued to embitter their relations with the Gentile world until the practice was outlawed by the Woodruff Manifesto in 1890.

Today the Latter-Day Saints have a worldwide organization; from 1965 to 1975 the Mormon conversion rate was 80,000 annually, and at present some 2.5 million people revere Joseph Smith as the Prophet of the Lord.

Material on the Mormon movement as a whole is rather sketchy, and much of it is forensic rather than analytical and therefore of little use to the historian in reconstructing a balanced overall picture of Mormonism. For the early years, the best primary source is Joseph Smith's seven volume *History of the Church of Jesus Christ of Latter-Day Saints*. Edward W. Tullidge's *History of Salt Lake City* (original ed., 1850) provides detail on the Utah polygamous period. The best secondary sources are Brodie, *No Man*; Robert Flanders, *Nauvoo*; Hirshson, *Lion of the Lord*; and Thomas F. O'Dea, *The Mormons*. The Mormons have figured prominently, not to say egregiously, in fictionalized accounts. To cite only the more notable examples: Mark Twain's *Roughing It* (1875); Arthur Conan Doyle's *A Study in Scarlet* (1887); Zane Grey's *Riders of the Purple Sage* (1912); and Irving Wallace's *The Twenty-Seventh Wife* (1961).

16. *History of Church*, 1:90–91.

17. Brodie, *No Man*, p. 119. In 1838, Oliver Cowdery, who had served as amanuensis to Joseph Smith during the translation of the Book of Mormon, was excommunicated for charging the Prophet with adultery (see *History of Church*, 3:16).

18. Quoted in *History of Church*, 5:53.

19. See Orson F. Whitney, *The Mormon Prophet's Tragedy*, p. 34; B. H. Roberts, *The Rise and Fall of Nauvoo*, p. 114; and Oliver H. Olney, *The Absurdities of Mormonism Portrayed*. In later years, Elder Orson Pratt, one of the Council of the Twelve Apostles (the highest order of the Melchizedek priesthood), confirmed that the Prophet had received the Revelation on Plural Marriage as early as 1831 and that he began to practice it actively as early as 5 Apr. 1841. See *History of Church*, 5:xxix–xxxii.

20. *History of Church*, 2:54; 4:237.

21. *Doctrine and Covenants*, sec. 132, art. 41, p. 470. My emphasis. The passage seems to imply that under the new dispensation, women may be given a certain license that will exculpate them from the onus of adultery by religiously sanctioning it. The same is true of men. See art. 43, p. 470.

22. Ibid., arts. 52 and 56, p. 472.

23. *History of Church*, 5:507. Conveniently, the Lord stayed the hand of the impulsive Prophet, for in art. 51 of the revelation, Emma is commanded to "stay herself, and partake not of that which I command you to offer her; for I did it, saith the Lord, to prove you all" (*Doctrine and Covenants*, p. 471). In art. 57, Joseph is warned not to "put his property out of his hands, lest an enemy destroy him" (p. 472).

24. See Brodie, *No Man*, app. C, "The Plural Wives of Joseph Smith," which lists forty-eight women. Many of the details in these lists are drawn from unreliable sources, hostile to the Mormons. The problem of drawing up an accurate list in the face of such biased data (either violently pro or con Mormon) seems insurmountable.

25. *History of Church*, 5:107. This phraseology, which came to be accepted as the ritualistic form of address for first wives of polygamists, suggests that Joseph was already involved in polygamous relationships before the revelation was announced.

26. It should be noted that we are technically speaking of simultaneous polygyny when we refer to Mormon polygamy, as the Mormons did not countenance polyandry, although they did allow serial monogamy for women.

27. See Brodie, *No Man*, pp. 54, 110, 120, 122, 257, 327. See also Brodie's comments on the paucity of evidence that Joseph ever fathered children by women other than Emma Hale Smith (pp. 344–47, 460–62). Presumably a larger family was also an attraction of polygyny for women. Cf. the Revelation on Plural Marriage, arts. 55 and 56, wherein

the Lord promises Joseph to "multiply him, and give him an hundred-fold in this world, of fathers and mothers, brothers and sisters, houses and lands, wives and children" (*Doctrine and Covenants*, p. 472).

28. *History of Church*, 6:405.

29. See Brodie, *No Man*, pp. 457–88.

30. The quotation is from a letter from Warren Parrish to the Painesville (Ohio) *Republican*, which was printed in that paper in Feb. 1838. It is quoted in Hirshson, *Lion of the Lord*, p. 28. When Joseph and Hyrum were murdered, they were in prison for the destruction of the press and the consequent silencing of the *Nauvoo Expositor*, an apostate paper.

31. Quoted in I. Woodbridge Riley, *The Founder of Mormonism*, p. 329.

Chapter 7

1. James R. Clark, ed., *Messages of the First Presidency of the Church of Jesus Christ of Latter-Day Saints*, 2:345.

2. David B. Davis points out the Mormons' interest in science, their consequent materialism, and their conflict with other religious sects in "The New England Origins of Mormonism."

3. Edward W. Tullidge, "Marriage," reprinted in the *Latter-Day Saints' Millennial Star* 19 (1857): 656.

4. See G. D. Watt, J. V. Long, et al., eds. *Journal of Discourses Delivered by Brigham Young*, 19:269, 26:214 (hereafter cited as *Journal of Discourses*); and Edward W. Tullidge, *The Women of Mormondom*, pp. 192–94.

5. "The Pre-Existence of Man," *Seer* 1, no. 3 (Mar. 1853): 37.

6. *Seer* 1, no. 3, p. 158.

7. Sermon reprinted in *History of Church*, 4:302–17. See pp. 305–6, especially the section entitled "God an Exalted Man" (quotation from p. 306).

8. *Journal of Discourses*, 13:187. On the resurrection of the body, see also the *Seer* 2 (1854): 273–80.

9. Clark, *Messages of the First Presidency*, 1:181.

10. John Hyde, Jr., *Mormonism*, p. 54. See also the *Seer* 2:264, 290–93. John Hyde, a Mormon schoolmaster, apostatized in 1857. He had been a faithful Mormon for a number of years, although he does not seem to have participated in "celestial marriage." In the *New York Herald* of 1 Dec. 1857 he recommended the institution of martial law in the Utah Territory, the use of federal troops and volunteers from California and Oregon against the Saints, and the outlawing of polygamy and the exile of all known polygamists (see Hirshson, *Lion of the Lord*, pp. 173–74). Hyde's book was the most popular anti-Mormon treatise of the decade. His descriptions of ceremonies, rituals, and theology, if somewhat colorful, are usually relatively accurate. His assessments of personalities, especially that of Brigham Young, whom he utterly loathed, and his discussions of the activities and motives of church officials, are much less trustworthy.

11. *Seer* 2:288.

12. Ibid., 1:37.

13. Ibid., p. 175. My emphasis. See also Jarman, *U.S.A.*, p. 70; and Tullidge, *Women of Mormondom*, p. 488. William Jarman, an Englishman, claimed to have been a Mormon for about a decade. His account is the most vituperative and pornographic of the anti-Mormon tracts. The fact that excerpts and illustrations from his book appeared in the *Police Gazette* in the early 1880s is indicative of the audience for which the work was intended. Great care is required in using *U.S.A.* as a source on Mormon life, and in

all instances it should be checked against a more positive vision of Mormonism, or certainly against a more objective account. The work of Edward W. Tullidge is a more positive source. Tullidge, another English Saint, adhered to the heretical Godbeite sect of Mormonism (which denied the legitimacy of Brigham Young's succession to the mantle of the martyred prophet, Joseph Smith) in 1869, and was summarily excommunicated. He later recanted and was readmitted to the church. A litterateur and editor, he became the most prominent early church historian. He fully accepted the divinely ordained system of polygamy and was one of its most eloquent defenders. His work is useful as a frank statement of the patriarchal presumptions of Mormon polygamy and as a source of biographical and genealogical material (see Ray B. West, *Kingdom of the Saints*, p. 296).

14. See Tullidge, *Women of Mormondom*, pp. 171–81, 189–91, 200. Significantly, Mormons allocated the role of women in redemption to the distant and mythic past, whereas men possessed the keys to future perfection and salvation. This conception, involving the necessity of female sin as essential to the drama of human salvation, recalls the Miltonian conception of the necessity of original sin. See Arthur O. Lovejoy, "Milton and the Paradox of the Fortunate Fall," in his *Essays in the History of Ideas* (Baltimore: Johns Hopkins Press, 1948), pp. 277–95.

15. Orson Spencer, *Letters Exhibiting the Most Prominent Doctrines of the Church of Jesus Christ of Latter-Day Saints*, p. 220.

16. Bennett, *History of the Saints*, p. 276. John C. Bennett was an Ohio physician, self-styled military genius, dashing ladies' man, and unabashed frontier rogue, who admittedly converted to Mormonism to achieve political power and wealth in 1840. He acted as Joseph Smith's closest advisor and confidante for two years. After a falling-out with Smith, he was excommunicated in 1842. His book was the first of those making the accusation of polygamy against Mormon leaders to gain widespread attention. After his break with Smith, Bennett styled himself Professor of Mid-Wifery and the Diseases Peculiar to Women and Children at the Cincinnati "University of the Literary and Botanico-Medical College." In 1846 he joined the heretical movement of the pseudo-Mormon prophet James J. Strang and temporarily convinced the descendants of the Prophet Joseph to recognize the legitimacy of Strang's claim to the prophetic tradition. Always on the periphery of the Mormon movement, Bennett appeared again during the Mormons' troubles with the federal government in the 1850s, when he petitioned Stephen A. Douglas to intercede with President Buchanan: Bennett proposed that he be appointed commander of a legion to be dispatched to crush the Mormon menace through force of arms. (This outline of Bennett's career is based on Hirshson, *Lion of the Lord*, pp. 39, 47, 74–75, 174.) Bennett has all the charlatan's charm, so his book must be used by historians with great circumspection.

17. Lee, *Mormonism Unveiled*, p. 100. John D. Lee was a loyal Mormon for three decades and a bodyguard first to Joseph Smith and then to Brigham Young. This work was a kind of deathbed confession, written while he awaited execution for his part in the Mountain Meadows Massacre (Sept. 1857), in which a wagon train of 120 Gentile immigrants was ambushed and massacred by a combined force of Indians and Mormons. Lee had been acquitted of any involvement in a first trial in which church authorities apparently shielded him. He was abandoned by President Young and the church in his second trial and bore complete responsibility for this craven deed, in which, undoubtedly, the highest-ranking Mormon officials, including Young, were deeply implicated. Lee's confessions were marketed by the Gentile press as part of the anti-Mormon sensationalist literature, and some passages suggest that they may have been ghostwritten to conform to this literary tradition. The events and interpretations provided in this work and in *The Mormon Menace* (1905), a later, revised edition, can

be checked against Juanita Brooks's two works on Lee: *John Doyle Lee: Zealot, Pioneer, Builder, Scapegoat* (Glendale, Calif.: Arthur H. Clark, 1962); and *The Mountain Meadows Massacre* (Norman: University of Oklahoma Press, 1962). They can also be checked against Lee's diaries for the years 1848–76, *A Mormon Chronicle*, edited by Robert G. Cleland and Juanita Brooks (hereafter cited as *Mormon Chronicle*).

18. Sermon, "The Gospel: One Man Power," reprinted in *Journal of Discourses*, 13:272. See also *Seer* 1:159.

19. Bennett, *History of the Saints*, p. 275.

20. Juanita Brooks, ed., *On the Mormon Frontier*, 1:275, entry for 25 Sept. 1847.

21. Lecture entitled "The Marriage Relation" (1854), reprinted in *Journal of Discourses*, 2:83.

22. *Journal of Discourses*, 13:207. The sexual passion seems to have continually plagued Mormon males, and being both attracted and repelled by its power and allure, they likened it to feces. They described those so in need of sexual gratification as to be under woman's complete control in scatological terms. One example will suffice: "They live in filth and nastiness, they eat it and drink it, and they are filthy all over" (*Journal of Discourses*, 4:50).

23. Ibid., 2:86–87.

24. On woman as temptress, see *Seer* 1:124; and *Mormon Chronicle*, 2:171–73.

25. L. A. Bertrand, *Mémoires d'un Mormon*, p. 177. My translation. It is significant that Bertrand should use the term "amours libres" (free love) to designate the state of female erotic freedom. The usage serves to underscore the extent to which Mormons considered polygamy a means of controlling eroticism rather than providing it free rein. "Abâtardir" ("to cause to degenerate") also means "to bastardize" and indicates that the fear of female betrayal, of cuckoldry, is behind the perceived necessity for controlling women. Bertrand, a French convert to Mormonism, left his wife and children behind and came to Utah in the 1850s. He spent four years in the Mormon Zion. His book is generally descriptive and straightforward. Much of his account is directly drawn from Mormon sources, which are quoted at length in his text.

26. See Bertrand, *Mémoires*, pp. 198–99; and *Seer* 1:154. See also *Journal of Discourses*, 13:195. Bertrand gives a more concisely typical Mormon argument against polyandry: fear that woman without proper control would become a prostitute. Mormons also opposed polyandry because they felt it was an indirect form of birth control.

27. *Journal of Discourses*, 3:264. On woman's role as a breeder, see ibid., 11:270–71, 338–39; and Spencer, *Letters Exhibiting the Most Prominent Doctrines*, p. 239.

28. *Doctrine and Covenants*, sec. 132, pt. 27, p. 468. It is highly significant that this injunction against the murder of innocents appears in the midst of the Revelation on Plural Marriage, thus giving added credence to the assumption that feticide and abortion are being obliquely interdicted.

29. *Journal of Discourses*, 26:219. See also John A. Widtsoe, ed., *Discourses of Brigham Young*, p. 305.

30. *Journal of Discourses*, 25:354.

31. Ibid. See also ibid., 17:101, 23:238, 26:219.

32. Ibid., 13:195.

33. Ibid.

34. Ibid., p. 206. For another statement of the role of male gratification as the justification for polygamy, see *Seer* 1:124.

35. *Journal of Discourses*, 16:177.

36. Diary of Charles Walker, 1855–1902, p. 40, entry for 3 Nov. 1883. On the general belief of "marking" children in the womb, see Bergen Evans, *The Natural History of Nonsense* (New York: Alfred A. Knopf, 1946), pp. 113–16; and Havelock Ellis, *Studies*

in the Psychology of Sex, 2, pt. 1: "The Psychic State in Pregnancy," pp. 218–26. For the specifically Mormon belief, see Spencer, *Letters Exhibiting the Most Prominent Doctrines*, p. 233; *Mormon Chronicle*, 2:26–27, 115; and the *Millennial Star*, 2 June 1860, p. 213.

37. Bertrand, *Mémoires*, p. 200. My translation and emphasis. See also ibid., p. 194; Jules Remy and Julius Brenchley, *A Journey to Great Salt-Lake City*, 2:101–2; and *Millennial Star*, 2 June 1866. Jules Remy and Julius Brenchley were French travelers who visited Salt Lake City in 1860 and whose work was the result of a journal they kept during their stay. They depended largely on lapsed Mormons and Gentiles for their information. Nevertheless, their account is not exceptionally biased and does provide an insightful reading of Mormon society. Their vision of Mormon children bears the usual European animus against the lack of discipline and ill-mannered deportment of American children (2:175).

38. *Journal of Discourses*, 19:270.

39. Quoted in Lee, *Mormonism Unveiled*, p. 26.

40. Bertrand, *Mémoires*, p. 208. My translation. On the enforced celibacy of neophytes and "unproven" Mormons, see also Richard Burton, *The City of the Saints*, p. 432; and *Seer* 1:110. Sir Richard F. Burton (1821–90), linguist, translator, explorer, and proto-anthropologist, was deeply interested in sexuality, especially its polygamous manifestations. He is most noted for his translation of the Arabic masterpiece *The Book of the Thousand Nights and a Night* (1885–88) and of the classical Arabic manual on the art of love, *The Perfumed Garden of Sheikh Nefzawi* (1886). He traveled in Utah in 1860. His experiences and observation of polygamy in the Middle East colored his vision of the Mormon system. He is perhaps too sanguine about the potential of polygamy for securing social stability and morality among a people to whom it was a novel experiment rather than a traditional way of life: he does not have a grasp of the historical realities of the Mormon situation. His feeling is shared, however, by the Mormons themselves, but more clearly out of a utopian vision of celestial marriage.

41. Burton, *City of the Saints*, p. 438. See also Spencer, *Letters Exhibiting the Most Prominent Doctrines*, pp. 210–11; Tullidge, *Women of Mormondom*, pp. 385, 396; and Remy and Brenchley, *Journey*, 2:116–17, 160.

Chapter 8

1. Flanders, *Nauvoo*, p. 99. See also pp. 92–94, 98–102.

2. In Kirtland, Ohio, Mormons were not allowed legally to perform marriage ceremonies because they were not considered ordained ministers in that state (see *History of Church*, 2:408; and Brodie, *No Man*, p. 183). The first records of marriages and sealings I have encountered are those of the Nauvoo Temple, dated early in 1846. For these marriage records, see Stanley S. Ivins MSS, 4:259–67, 5:203–8.

3. See Edwin D. Follick, "The Cultural Influence of Mormonism in Early Nineteenth-Century America," p. 113. Yet at the same time, Smith was also indirectly sanctioning polygamy. A work was issued in Nauvoo under the imprimatur of "Joseph Smith, Printer," in 1842. The pamphlet was by Udney Hay Jacob (an "Israelite and a Shepherd of Israel" [i.e., a Gentile]) and was entitled *An Extract from a Manuscript Entitled the Peace Maker, or the Doctrines of the Millennium: Being a Treatise on Religion and Jurisprudence, or a New System of Religion and Politicks*. It was a frank defense of polygamy, and Jacob was, and remained, an orthodox Mormon (see Hirshson, *Lion of the Lord*, pp. 41–42). In the ensuing uproar generated by the pamphlet, Smith was forced to repudiate it publicly, but that did not deter him from a clandestine practice of polygamy.

4. *History of Church*, 5:8. For additional "moral" activity, see ibid., 7:282; and Brooks, *On the Mormon Frontier*, p. 65, entry for 17 Sept. 1845. The direction of some of this moral crusade was evident in the case of the City of Nauvoo v. Orsimus F. Botswitch, which came before the courts on Monday, 26 Feb. 1841. Botswitch was brought to the bar on complaint of Joseph's brother, Hyrum, "for slanderous language concerning him [Hyrum] and certain females of Nauvoo" (see *History of Church*, 6:225).

5. *History of Church*, 6:570. He gave a further warning against "overmuch zeal" on 25 May 1842 (ibid., 5:19–20).

6. M. Hamlin Cannon, "Migration of English Mormons to America"; see table on p. 441. By 1864 six of every ten Mormon immigrants came from New England, New York, or Great Britain, whereas less than 1 percent came from other parts of the United States. The only statistics I have been able to locate on emigration from Great Britain that provide a sexual breakdown are for the spring of 1861 and cover only three ships. The total emigration figures for these ships were 930 males (47 percent) and 1,042 females (53 percent). Of those whose country of origin was within the British Isles, there were 668 females (52 percent) and 617 males (48 percent). The highest percentage of females was found within the Scandanavian group, where there were 321 females (55 percent) and 266 males (45 percent). Only three countries, Ireland, Germany, and the United States, showed more males than females emigrating during this season. (These figures are extrapolated from Burton, *City of the Saints*, p. 300.) Burton accepts the Mormon claim that female immigrants exceeded male: see ibid., p. 430. By far the largest bodies of emigrants to the United States in 1842 (the only full year for which I have been able to locate statistics) came from Liverpool, where the most active Mormon mission had its headquarters. It should be remembered that Martha Brotherton, who first gave the alarm about Mormon polygamy, was an Englishwoman. In the United States from 1810 to 1860, there was a surplus of women between the ages of sixteen and forty-five in the New England area and generally between the ages of twenty and thirty in New York. These were the areas from which Mormon converts most frequently came. See U.S. Department of the Interior, Federal Bureau of the Census, Censuses for 1810–60. This data is only suggestive, but it does indicate a direction for further research that might prove fruitful.

7. U.S. Department of the Interior, Federal Bureau of the Census, *Seventh Census, Population Schedules*, p. lxxxvi, tab. 59, "Proportion of White Males to Females for 1850"; and "MS Census for Weber County, 1850," Ivins MSS, 5:283. In this respect the early history of Utah seems to have followed the pattern of other western frontier areas.

8. The highest estimate is from Burton, *City of the Saints*, p. 228. Other estimates are from Utah Census for 1856, as found in *Bancroft Scraps, Utah Miscellany*, 21:475, abstracted from Ivins MSS, 3:241–42; and U.S. Department of the Interior, Federal Bureau of the Census, *Eighth Census, Population Schedules*. In larger Utah cities, women outnumbered men by about 3 percent.

9. See U.S. Department of the Interior, Federal Bureau of the Census, *Compendium of the Eleventh Census*, table, "Relative Proportions of Females to Males, by States and Territories, 1890, 1880, and 1870," p. lxxxi; U.S. Department of the Interior, Federal Bureau of the Census, *Compendium of the Ninth Census*, tabs. 48, "Sex of the Aggregate Population with General Nativity, 1870," and 49, "Sex of the White Population with General Nativity, 1870," pp. 546–47. See also Stenhouse, *Exposé of Polygamy*, p. 181; and U.S. Census for 1880, abstracted in Ivins MSS, 4:84. Fanny Stenhouse was the wife of Thomas B. H. Stenhouse, a Scottish journalist who edited the *Salt Lake City Telegraph*. He had been a member of the Mormon church from the mid-1840s until his excommunication for insubordination and adherence to the Godbeite heresy in 1869. He had been the president of the Latter-Day Saints' Swiss and Italian Mission and briefly served as church spokesman in Washington, D.C. The

Stenhouse's daughter was married to Brigham Young's son Joseph in the mid-1860s. Thomas Stenhouse, with the consent of his wife, had unsuccessfully attempted to enter polygamy in the late 1850s. The Stenhouses produced several books after their expulsion from the church. Fanny's books were rather sensationalist and played up the polygamy issue: *Exposé of Polygamy in Utah* (1872), *"Tell It All"* (1875), and *An Englishwoman in Utah* (1880). Thomas's book, *The Rocky Mountain Saints* (American ed., New York: D. Appleton & Co., 1873), was one of the more scholarly and well-written accounts by ex-Mormons (see Hirshson, *Lion of the Lord*, pp. 233–36, 295–96). One needs to be especially careful with Mrs. Stenhouse's work because she is dealing with nearly a quarter of a century of her life that has been embittered by excommunication. She was with Thomas on his missionary journeys and had the opportunity to observe the behavior of missionaries at first hand; one wonders if she is indirectly discussing the behavior of her own husband here.

10. On the behavior of missionaries, see Lee, *Mormonism Unveiled*, p. 166; Stenhouse, *Exposé of Polygamy*, p. 22; and Clark, *Messages of the First Presidency*, 1:157. (A statement about separating wives and husbands, which appeared in a letter from the Prophet to Parley Pratt, was published in the Liverpool, England, periodical the *Millennial Star* in Nov. 1842.)

11. *Journal of Discourses*, 5:12, remarks made on 31 May 1857. There was, indeed, a surplus of women of marriageable age in both Great Britain and New England in the 1850s. If we consider the number of single and widowed persons between the ages of fifteen and forty-five years of age in the English population in the two censuses of 1851 and 1861, we discover an abrupt increase in the female component of this category. The increase is well beyond the expected natural increase derived from general population expansion and may have reflected a decline in the male population in this age bracket as a result of the military actions consequent to empire building—the Crimean War (1853–56), the great Indian Mutiny (1857–58), and the struggles with the Chinese during the T'ai P'ing Rebellion (1850–64). In any event, whereas there were 1,200 more single males than females between the ages of fifteen and forty-five in 1851, there were 80,700 more females in this group in 1861. When we examine the widowed in this age bracket, we find a similar situation. In 1851 there were 78,000 more females in this group; in 1861 the female surplus was 129,000. Between 1856 and 1857 the annual number of marriages remained virtually unchanged, and between 1857 and 1858 there was a decline of 4,711. In 1861 there was another decline (see *Papers of the Royal Commission on Population*, vol. 2, *Reports and Selected Papers of the Statistics Committee* [London: Royal Stationery Office, 1950], pp. 199–209).

For the New England states in this period there was also a surplus of women of marriageable age. In the six New England states in 1840, there were 113,433 more women than men between the ages of fifteen and fifty. In 1850, except for New Hampshire and Vermont, where there was a near parity in the sex ratio, New England showed a surplus of women in all except the thirty-to-forty age group. In the 1860 census, New Hampshire and Vermont also showed a surplus of marriage-age women. For the United States as a whole in these years, however, there was a slightly larger number of men than women. It was only with the 1870 Census, which reflected the carnage of the Civil War, that females outnumbered males in the total population (abstracted from the U.S. Censuses, 1840, 1850, 1860, and 1870). This surplus of marriageable females, however, was not inordinate—certainly not of the magnitude suggested by the Mormon elder quoted in the text. Women comprised only 50.01 percent of the single English population between fifteen and forty-five in 1851; in 1861 they made up 52.23 percent of the total. (There was a phenomenal number of unattached widows in England during this period, however. The female percentage of the widowed group for this age class was 66.7 in 1851 and shot up to 73.4 in 1861.) In the age category fifteen to fifty for the six New England states, there was a slight preponderance of females in the period 1850–70. In 1850 females in New England made up an average 50.23 percent of the total population of this age classification; in 1860 the figure was 51.35 percent, and in 1870, 50.86 percent. Only in Vermont were there fewer women than men of this age group from 1850 to 1870, and there women comprised 49 percent of the total.

12. Editorial, "Power of the Elders for Good or Evil—Unvirtuous Conduct, Marriage, etc.," *Millennial Star* 23 (1861): 154. Elders were specifically cautioned against "marrying," "covenant-making," and "courting by letter or otherwise," as acts "offensive in the sight of Heaven and good men," in their character as missionaries (ibid., p. 155). If this demographic evidence concerning widows in Great Britain is correct, they must have represented a particularly sore temptation for Mormon missionaries there.

13. The revelation was not acknowledged in the *Millennial Star*, the Mormons' English publication, until 1863. See vol. 15 (1863): 1–64, which reprints the entire *Deseret News Extra* edition on the revelation (14 Sept. 1852).

14. J. H. Beadle, *Polygamy*, p. 457, supports the claim that the Mormons enacted a particularly harsh adultery law in 1852. See also *Acts, Resolutions, and Memorials Passed at the Several Annual Sessions of the Legislative Assembly of the Territory of Utah from 1851 to 1870 Inclusive*, pp. 49–53. John H. Beadle was a Gentile journalist in Salt Lake City who spent much of his time exposing the political corruption and tyranny of the Mormon hierarchy. He assisted Bill Hickman, former Mormon Danite, or avenger, in preparing his biography (see n. 17 to this chapter, below). On Beadle, see Hirshson, *Lion of the Lord*, pp. 309–10. Beadle, despite the title of his work, is not overly concerned with the sexual aspects of Mormonism, and his account is generally less sensationalist than those of other Gentiles or apostates. Nevertheless, his evidence should be accepted only when it bears out trends corroborated by independent and less-biased sources.

15. The Massachusetts Bay Colony under Governor John Winthrop (1629–49) was governed by a paternalistic theocracy that depended on informal magisterial interpretation of a vaguely defined, uncodified common-law tradition. Winthrop resisted the codification of law for the Puritan colony because he feared a written body of legislation. Not until 1641, with the adoption of Nathaniel Ward's *Body of Liberties*, did Massachusetts Bay get a written code of law. The Puritans, however, unlike the Mormons, were building a patriarchal judicial tradition from the outset, a tradition almost medieval in its dual magisterial and sacerdotal administration, its dual civil and ecclesiastical jurisdiction. The Mormons were typical of nineteenth-century western frontier areas not only in their insistence on informal, traditional, clear-cut codes, but also in their tendency to demand precipitate justice for wrongdoers. Violent action by those wronged was the essence of the code of the vigilante.

In Montana the two primary periods of vigilante justice were Dec. 1863 to Mar. 1867 and Apr. to July 1884. Vigilantism was resorted to in the first instance to bring order to the lawless gold-mining camps, especially in the Bannack and Virginia City areas. In the latter instance, it was employed to rid the territory of horse thieves and rustlers. But whereas, in Utah, informal codes and summary vigilante justice functioned as the whole body of the law from 1848 to 1852, in Montana vigilante justice was limited to specific epidemic lawlessness. In the mining camp era, for example, vigilante justice was provoked by the vicious Henry Plummer gang. The reign of informal law enforcement seems to have lasted only long enough to wipe out the last member of the gang. Vigilante justice in Utah was more generalized and not directed toward any such specific, limited objective. On vigilantism in Montana, see Michael P. Malone and

Richard B. Roeder, *Montana: A History of Two Centuries* (Seattle: University of Washington Press, 1976), pp. 61–64, 122–24; Paul C. Phillips, ed., *Forty Years on the Frontier as Seen in the Journals and Reminiscences of Granville Stuart* (Glendale, Calif.: Arthur H. Clark Co., 1957), pp. 195–210; and Hoffman Birney, *Vigilante* (Philadelphia: Penn Publishing Co., 1929).

16. Brooks, *On the Mormon Frontier*, 1:297, entries for 13–14 Jan. 1848.

17. Lee, *Mormonism Unveiled*, p. 278. The "Angels" were the handpicked avengers of Brigham Young. See William A. Hickman, *Brigham's Destroying Angel* (New York: G. A. Crofutt, 1872). Usually, in Mormon parlance, "violating of covenants" referred to adultery, but sexual misbehavior of *any* kind could come under that heading. The textual justification for capital punishment is to be found in the Book of Mormon, 2 Nephi 10:15–16.

18. Beadle, *Polygamy*, p. 145. For men who lose only their testes *after* the onset of puberty, there is no loss of ability to perform sexual intercourse. To the extent that erotic desire is a mental function, there might well be little diminution of the sex drive. In fact, in the seraglios of the Near East, the eunuch was reputedly preferred by the hetaerae because "his *erectio et distensis penis* was that of a boy before puberty and it would last as long as his heart and circulation kept sound. Hence the eunuch who preserves his penis is much prized in the Zenanah where some women prefer him to the entire man, on account of his long performance of the deed of kind" (Richard Burton, *The Book of the Thousand Nights and a Night* [Privately printed by the Burton Club, 1885], 2:50, n. 3).

19. Lee, *Mormonism Unveiled*, p. 282.

20. Ibid., p. 284.

21. Ibid., p. 283. Lee gives descriptions of murder and emasculation on pp. 282–86. Cases in which less stringent punishments were meted out are described on pp. 274–76.

22. *Journal of Discourses*, 10:110, statement made in Salt Lake City Tabernacle by Brigham Young, 8 Mar. 1863. The prohibition on blacks in the ranks of either the Aaronic or Melchizedek priesthoods continued unabated from 1842 to 1978. Although this exclusionary policy may have begun informally as early as 1834, it did not become dogma until the publication of Joseph Smith's *The Pearl of Great Price* (1851). The passage from this treatise justifying racial discrimination is Abraham 1:21–27. The basis for exclusion was that commonly adopted by southern apologists for chattel slavery: racial inferiority stemmed from the curse of Cain, transmitted by Noah's son, Ham, through the progeny of his wife, Egyptus. For a full discussion of the genesis of the traditional Mormon policy of Negro exclusion (and, curiously, only blacks of American descent have been excluded), see Stephen G. Taggart, *Mormonism's Negro Policy*. The policy came to an end with the revelation of 9 June 1978; President Spencer W. Kimball announced that henceforward "all worthy male members of the Church may be ordained to the priesthood without regard to race or color." On 12 June 1978, the first black man was ordained to the priesthood of the Latter-Day Saints. For the text of the revelation, see the *New York Times*, 10 June 1978, p. 24, cols. 1, 2.

23. Brooks, *On the Mormon Frontier*, 1:160, entry for 7 May 1846.

24. Ibid., p. 190, entry for 4 Sept. 1846.

25. In 1866, Brigham Young recommended that Congress pass a law "making it death for any man to hold illicit intercourse with any woman but his lawful wife" (*Journal of Discourses*, 11:261). See also "Did Jesus Do Away with the Law That Put Adulteresses to Death?" *Millennial Star* 28 (1866): 790. As late as 1883, a prominent spokesman for the church could publicly recommend capital punishment for seducers: see *Journal of Discourses*, 24:224, speech of George Q. Cannon, 20 June 1883.

26. The case of the five men who were fined and excommunicated is found in Brooks, *On the Mormon Frontier*, 2:343, entry for 25 Feb. 1849. The case of the older Mormon is in ibid., p. 387, entries for 7–9 Jan. 1851.

27. *Mormon Chronicle*, 1:94, entry for 24 Feb. 1849. See also Brooks, *On the Mormon Frontier*, 1:303, 2:611; and Lee, *Mormonism Unveiled*, pp. 275–77.
28. Brooks, *On the Mormon Frontier*, 1:304, entry for 11 Mar. 1848.
29. *Mormon Chronicle*, 2:434–35, entries for 10–11 Mar. 1876.
30. Orson Pratt, in *Seer* 2 (1854): 223. See also ibid., p. 222; and *Journal of Discourses*, 24:224. The Mormon predilection for capital punishment for these sexual offenses was apparently derived from the Mosaic law (cf. Lev. 20:10). In view of the common polygamic practice of marrying sisters or mothers and daughters, however, the incorporation of this particular portion of the Hebraic tradition into unofficial ecclesiastical precept is highly ironic: Lev. 20:11–12, 14, 19–21, is a statement of the forbidden degrees of consanguinity, violation of which constitutes incest. Verse 14 specifically prohibits sexual intercourse with both mother and daughter under pain of death.
31. Brooks, *On the Mormon Frontier*, 2:396, entry for 17 Mar. 1851. See also Diary of Allen Frost of Kanab, Utah, and Snowflake, Ariz., 5:27, entries for 28 Nov. and 18 Dec. 1886.
32. Brooks, *On the Mormon Frontier*, 2:407, entry for 18 Oct. 1851. Brigham Young supported this position only when the deed was done upon discovery of the adulterous couple *in flagrante delicto*, but argued that, if not caught in the act, they should be dealt with more leniently (*Journal of Discourses*, 3:247).
33. Brooks, *On the Mormon Frontier*, 2:408. This tendency to retributive justice in cases of adultery and seduction was not unique to Mormons. They shared it with other Americans of the second half of the nineteenth century. Cf. David B. Davis, *Homicide in American Fiction, 1798–1860* (Ithaca: Cornell University Press, 1957), pp. 181–84. He specifically links such behavior with the male's fear of loss of status and with the concept of female as possession (pp. 183, 208–9). Parley P. Pratt, a Mormon apostle, was murdered in 1857 by an irate Gentile whose wife he had seduced (Werner, *Brigham Young*, pp. 405–6). In that the patriarchal attitudes Mormons shared with the rest of nineteenth-century American society were strengthened by Mormon ideology, however, this tradition was more readily and thoroughly accepted in the folk behavior of the Latter-Day Saints than in society at large.
34. Brooks, *On the Mormon Frontier*, 2:595, entry for 14 Apr. 1856.
35. *Acts, Resolutions, and Memorials*, chap. 22, "An Act in Relation to Crimes and Punishment," sec. 31, p. 53.
36. Ibid., secs. 19, 33, and 34, pp. 52–53. This is apparent when we compare the antiprostitution section with the antigambling section. Both persons actually engaging in gambling and those operating gambling establishments are specifically made subject to punishment. See ibid., secs. 38 and 39, p. 53.
37. Ibid., sec. 21, p. 52.
38. Ibid., secs. 32, 35, and 37, pp. 52–53.
39. Cf. 3 Nephi 12: 31–32. The entire chapter is a direct plagiarism of Matt., chap. 5. Interestingly, Smith omits the covert castration reference contained in verses 29–30 and substitutes a vague threat of hell. This suggests a more tolerant attitude toward adultery in the early church than was later prevalent.
40. Clark, *Messages of the First Presidency*, 1:157, letter from Joseph Smith to Parley P. Pratt.
41. *Seer* 1 (1853): 127. The Utah Act in Relation to Bills of Divorce closely parallels the Indiana Divorce Law of 1831, drafted by Robert Dale Owen, in grounds allowable, the existence of an "omnibus clause," and the provision for absolute divorce only.
42. *Seer* 1:140. See also "Be not Overcome of Evil," *Millennial Star* 25 (1863): 83.
43. *Mormon Chronicle*, 2:151, entry for 19 Dec. 1870. Lee had been excommunicated for his part in the Mountain Meadows Massacre of 1857. See also ibid., 1:275, entry for 2 Oct. 1860.

44. James E. Hulett, "The Sociological and Social Psychological Aspects of the Mormon Polygamous Family," p. 256.
45. See Stenhouse, *Exposé of Polygamy*, pp. 173, 176; and Hyde, *Mormonism*, p. 80. John Lee tells us of the necessity of a bill of divorce, but no other preconditions for remarriage of divorced parties (*Mormon Chronicle*, 1:258, entry for 4 June 1860).
46. *Acts, Resolutions, and Memorials*, p. 49.
47. Marriage data based on Stanley S. Ivins, "Notes on Mormon Polygamy," pp. 311–12, and MS Census for Weber County, 1850, and 1860 Census for Utah, in Ivins MSS, 5:283. On divorces, see Box Elder County, Utah, Clerk's Office Probate Court Record Book "A," 5 Mar. 1856–26 July 1869; Record Book "B," 24 Nov. 1874–Nov. 1876; and Record Book "C," 12 June 1876–Mar. 1883, collected in the Ivins MSS, 4:245–49.
48. See Remy and Brenchley, *Journey*, 1:149; and Hyde, *Mormonism*, p. 80. Fifty dollars in cash was a considerable amount of money in a frontier territory lacking a ready supply of coin.

Chapter 9

1. John Cairncross, *After Polygamy Was Made a Sin*, p. 1.
2. "Old Po-lig on His Last Legs," in Cooper, *Rattling, Roaring, Rhymes*, p. 139. The colloquial tone, imbued with bad puns and double entendres, is evident from the title. Cooper's book is typical in the scurrility and covert obscenity of its offerings. Note, for example, the double entendre in the last line of the stanza quoted. The term "pol-lig," while apparently a contumelious epithet, is a fusion of two common slang terms, "pol" or "poll"—a woman, especially a prostitute (ca. 1860)—and "lig"—a bed (ca. 1720–1840). An alternate reading may be derived from "pole"—the penis or, as a verb, to fuck—and "lig-by"—a bedfellow. "Lig" in a nautical sense may also mean "a weighted fishhook." "Fast" in this context obviously means dissipated. So the term "po-lig" can connote that Mormon women are whores, or that Mormons (as "fishermen" [cf. Matt. 4:19]) baited their "hooks" to catch prostitutes (in this sense a nautical flavor is present throughout: cf. the folk expression, "there are many fish in the sea," and "fish"—the pudenda [ca. 1850]). Clearly the low colloquial sense is maintained throughout the alternative readings that the purpose of polygamy is strictly sexual. The implication is also quite obvious: it is women who are attracted to this system, which is little better than public prostitution. (See Eric Partridge, *A Dictionary of Slang and Unconventional English*.)
3. Ivins, "Notes on Mormon Polygamy," p. 314. See also Hulett, "Mormon Polygamous Family," p. 17; and Ruth Kauffman and Reginald Kauffman, *The Latter-Day Saints*, pp. 220–21. Estimates of the numbers of Mormons practicing polygamy vary, but Thomas F. O'Dea's assertion that polygamists did not exceed 8 percent of the Mormon population is certainly too low (see his *Mormons*, p. 246). This chapter is based largely on Hulett's study of polygamous families and on the diaries of John D. Lee, Hosea Stout, and Allen Frost. Both Stout and Lee were in the top 5 percent of polygamists; Stout had six wives and Lee nineteen. Lee was also among the approximately 10 percent of polygamists who married sisters, having married the three Woolsey sisters and their mother. Allen Frost was a more typical polygamist, with three wives. Although other journals and diaries were consulted, these provide the most extensive information on the personal and sexual lives of Mormon polygamists. All are multivolume, and together they cover the entire polygamous period, 1848–96. Although these journals reflect the attitudes and behavior of the most frequently married polygamists most

clearly, they do provide an adequate vision of the system as a whole. Insofar as anti-Mormons tended to base their attacks on the supposed behavior of the most egregious cases of extended polygamy, an examination of the actual attitudes and behavior of this group serves as a useful corrective to traditional assumptions about the nature of celestial marriage.

4. Stenhouse, *Exposé of Polygamy*, p. 70.

5. Theodor Olshausen, *Geschichte der Mormonen oder Jungsten Tages Heiligen in Nordamerika*, p. 176. My translation. On the requirement of the approval of church authorities for plural marriages, see also Levi Savage, Jr., *Journal, 1852–1902*, p. xiv.

6. See the testimony on courting in Hulett, "Mormon Polygamous Family," pp. 208–9.

7. Ibid., p. 215.

8. Nelson W. Green, *Fifteen Years among the Mormons*, pp. 89–90. For further evidence on this point, see Young, *Wife Number Nineteen*, p. 297; Olshausen, *Geschichte*, p. 177; and Hulett, "Mormon Polygamous Family," pp. 194, 212–13, 225.

9. *Mormon Chronicle*, 2:76, entry for 5 June 1867. My emphasis. For another case of "female initiative," see ibid., 1:141, entries for 2 and 4 Jan. 1858.

10. For sisters marrying the same man, see Hulett, "Mormon Polygamous Family," pp. 212–13; and Lee, *Mormonism Unveiled*, pp. 50, 199, 288. For the marriage of the mothers of plural wives, see Lee, *Mormonism Unveiled*, p. 288; and *Mormon Chronicle*, 1:10–11. Among the putative wives of Joseph Smith there were six pairs who were either sisters or mother and daughter. See Brodie, *No Man*, pp. 457–58.

11. This classification system is reported in Remy and Brenchley, *Journey*, 2:151–52. On the difficulties facing widows, see Hulett, "Mormon Polygamous Family," p. 191 n.

12. Lee, *Mormonism Unveiled*, p. 289.

13. Collated from Hulett, "Mormon Polygamous Family," p. 131. The figure on average male ages is from Ivins, "Notes on Mormon Polygamy," p. 314. For the town of Kanab, Utah, estimates are somewhat lower than those given here. Dean L. May, "People on the Mormon Frontier," argues that women averaged nineteen and men twenty-nine at marriage (p. 182).

14. Cf. Edmund Bergler, *The Revolt of the Middle-Aged Man* (New York: A. A. Wyn, 1954), pp. 203–78; and Barbara Fried, *The Middle-Age Crisis* (New York: Harper & Row, 1976), pp. 98–134.

15. Lee, *Mormonism Unveiled*, p. 289; Linn, *Story of the Mormons*, p. 580; and Brooks, *On the Mormon Frontier*. Levi Savage, who had three wives, married the last two in his forties. See Savage, *Journal*, xiv–xv.

16. *Mormon Chronicle*, 2:367, entry for 22 Sept. 1875. Mormons also considered younger women easier to control. See advice of Brigham Young to Lee in ibid., p. 89, entry for 16 Nov. 1867.

17. Sarah S. Leavitt, *Journal*, p. 31.

18. See *Mormon Chronicle*, 1:9, 12, entries for 16 and 22 Mar. 1848.

19. Ibid., p. 283, entry for 25 Nov. 1860.

20. Brooks, *On the Mormon Frontier*, 2:627–28, entry for June 1, 1857.

21. *Mormon Chronicle*, 2:95, entry for 6 Jan. 1868. See also ibid., p. 26, entry for 18 Aug. 1866.

22. Hulett, "Mormon Polygamous Family," pp. 42–48.

23. See Young, *Wife Number Nineteen*, pp. 142–60, 468–70; and Stenhouse, *Exposé of Polygamy*, pp. 70–75, 120–27.

24. *Mormon Chronicle*, 2:96, entry for 29 Jan. 1868.

25. Ibid., p. 277, entry for 26 July 1873. See also ibid., pp. 343, 392, entries for 9 Aug. and 19 Nov. 1875.

26. Hulett, "Mormon Polygamous Family," p. 19. Ivins estimates the number of polyga-

mous marriages that succeeded previous ones by less than one year at about 10 percent of the total ("Notes on Mormon polygamy," pp. 314–15).

27. On the Married Woman's Property Act, see Hulett, "Mormon Polygamous Family," pp. 85 n, 120 n. He cites the law from S. R. Thomas et al., *The Compiled Laws of Utah*, vol. 2 (1888), sec. 25284. See also Savage, *Journal*, p. 170, entry for 7 Sept. 1888.

28. See Hulett, "Mormon Polygamous Family," pp. 80–85, 112, 148.

29. Ibid., pp. 288, 367.

30. Lee, *Mormonism Unveiled*, p. 275. Gillespie was arrested, stripped of his property, and driven from Utah. Lee commented, "Many such cases came under my observation" (ibid., p. 275).

31. Brooks, *On the Mormon Frontier*, 1:21 n. Lucretia came to live with Stout on 14 Feb. 1845 and married him on 20 Apr. 1845 (p. 35). On the practice of engaged couples, see *Mormon Chronicle*, 2:427–28, entry for 12 Feb. 1876. On the New England practice of "bundling" in the seventeenth and eighteenth centuries, see Henry R. Stiles, *Bundling: Its Origin, Progress, and Decline in America* (Albany: J. Munsell, 1869).

32. Remy and Brenchley, *Journey*, 2:102 n, 109. The phrasing in reference to masturbation reads: "ac pro nefandu pollutione habitur [and indeed they consider defilements (pollutions) heinous]" (p. 102 n). Mormons still adhere to a strict sexual code today. A recent student has pointed out that "premarital and extramarital sex relations are frowned upon, along with abortions, masturbation, indecent language, immodest behavior, birth control, and divorce" (William M. Kephart, *Extraordinary Groups*, p. 221). A contemporary Mormon, Mrs. Rhea A. Kunz, who has a polygamous background on both sides of her family, underscores the fact that reproduction was considered *the* justification for intercourse in the Mormon system. "The first principle of purity," she says, "the strictest law, is one that many women who enter plural marriage do not understand. A man shall not even approach his wife for sex unless she invites him, and then only when it is time to have another child" (*New York Times*, 9 Oct. 1977, p. 80, col. 4).

33. Diary of Allen Frost, 1:31, entry for 28 July 1874.

34. Ibid., p. 92, entry for 6 Aug. 1875.

35. Ibid., pp. 92, 225, entries for 9 Aug. 1875 and 27 Mar. 1878. May, "People on the Mormon Frontier," p. 182, points out that the incidence of childbirth-related deaths among the Mormons (1 death per 175 children born, or a rate of 57.1/1,000) was lower than the national average.

36. Diary of Allen Frost, vol. 2, entry for 23 Jan. 1880. The phrase "used up" became common in popular parlance in about 1850 to mean "tired out" or "utterly exhausted." It also was used to mean "bankrupt." (See Eric Partridge, *Dictionary of Slang and Unconventional English*.)

37. Diary of Allen Frost, vol. 2, entry for 28 Jan. 1880. Cf. *William Clayton's Journal*, p. 20, entry for 15 Apr. 1846. Frost appears to have been an orthodox Mormon from this point of view. Mormon doctrine maintained that female sexuality followed the natural rhythm of conception, pregnancy, and birth. The cycle was governed by a natural balance of feminine energies that insured her healthful performance of the maternal function "without exhausting the source of life" (Bertrand, *Mémoires*, p. 200). In the case of Frost's unfortunate wife, the system had gotten out of balance and broken down.

38. See G. J. Barker-Benfield, *The Horrors of the Half-Known Life*, pp. 61–62, 80–81. The polygamous wife (one of four) of John Hafen provides some corroborative detail on the birth of her last child in 1893: "Aunt Mary Bunker, wife of the Bishop, was the acting mid-wife of the town. She came the customary ten days to bathe the baby while I was in bed. . . . As soon as his father learned of the birth, he came down to Bunkerville. I have never had a doctor at the birth of any of my children, nor at any other time for that

matter, and I have never paid more than five dollars for the services of a mid-wife" (from *Memories of a Handcart Pioneer: With Some Account of Frontier Life in Utah and Nevada* [1938], excerpted in Christine Fischer, ed., *Let Them Speak for Themselves*, pp. 101–8 [quotation from p. 105]).

39. Diary of Allen Frost, 5:50, entry for 3 May 1887. Some idea of the relative status of Frost and Lee can be derived from a comparison of the number of their wives: Lee had nineteen, whereas Frost had three. On Lee's use of midwives, see *Mormon Chronicle*, 1:241, entry for 9 Mar. 1860. Data on midwives' fees is from Thomas E. Cheney, ed., *Lore of Faith and Folly*, p. 115.

40. Diary of Allen Frost, vol. 2, entry for 23 Jan. 1880. For the use of a physician in a case of birth-related complications, see *Mormon Chronicle*, 1:224–25, entry for 4 Dec. 1859 (miscarriage). In this case the period of waiting before summoning the doctor was five days.

41. See *Mormon Chronicle*, 2:128, entry for 22 Nov. 1869.

42. Cheney, *Lore*, p. 229. The woman in question was delivered by a midwife in twelve out of thirteen pregnancies. *Lobelia inflata* is an antispasmodic, emetic, and expectorant (cf. *Webster's New International Dictionary*, 2d ed.; and Harold N. Moldenke, *American Wild Flowers* [New York: D. Van Nostrand Co., 1949], p. 244).

43. *Mormon Chronicle*, 1:275, entry for 30 Nov. 1859.

44. Cheney, *Lore*, p. 228.

45. Ibid.

46. Hulett, "Mormon Polygamous Family," p. 37.

47. Ibid. See examples of family planning he cites on pp. 37–38.

48. Ibid., pp. 19–31. May, "People on the Mormon Frontier," p. 182, gives a figure of 8.9 children per woman as the *average* completed Mormon family size.

49. Average number of children in polygamous families based on Ivins, "Notes on Mormon Polygamy," p. 318. Birth intervals are my own calculations based on Hulett, "Mormon Polygamous Family," pp. 19–31. See also Stenhouse, *Exposé of Polygamy*, p. 61; and Lee, *Mormonism Unveiled*, p. 50. On monogamous Mormons, see Ivins, "Notes on Mormon Polygamy," p. 318; and *Memory Book of Moroni Gerber and Emily Jane Jacob*, pp. 3–8. The national fertility figure is taken from Reed, *Private Vice*, p. 4; Reed in turn derived the figure from Ansley J. Coale and Melvin Zelnik, *New Estimates of Fertility and Population in the United States* (Princeton, N.J.: Princeton University Press, 1963), pp. 36, 40. By 1900, when polygamy ceased to prevail in Utah, the average number of children per women for America as a whole was 3.56. By the end of the Mormon polygamous period, then, the gap between Mormon and national fertility was probably even greater than in 1860.

50. Hulett, "Mormon Polygamous Family," pp. 16–19, 31–38.

51. Linn, *Story of the Mormons*, p. 580.

52. Diary of Charles Walker, p. 40, entry for 3 Nov. 1883.

53. Ibid. My emphasis.

54. *Mormon Chronicle*, 1:214, entry for 5 Aug. 1859. This fear was not unfounded. Cf. the seduction of a "Lamanite Girl" by a "young man" in ibid., p. 86, entry for 8 Sept. 1867. It was not uncommon for Mormons to marry Indians. See ibid., 1:214, entry for 10 Mar. 1860; Beadle, *Polygamy*, p. 451; and Joel H. Jackson, *A Journal or Sketch of the Life of Joel Hill Jackson*, p. 13.

55. *Mormon Chronicle*, 1:176, entry for 13 July 1858.

56. Ibid., p. 191, entry for 18 Jan. 1859. "According to family tradition," notes Juanita Brooks, "Lee released Mary Ann from the union because she refused to allow him to consummate the marriage" (ibid., p. 324, n. 45).

57. Widtsoe, *Discourses of Brigham Young*, p. 307.

58. Hulett, "Mormon Polygamous Family," p. 303. See also pp. 290–91, 296, 301.
59. Thomas L. Kane, *The Mormons*, p. 46. See also *Mormon Chronicle*, 1:46, 79, entries for 27 June and 19 Sept. 1848.
60. *Mormon Chronicle*, 2:124, entries for 17 Sept. and 2 Nov. 1869.
61. For women in typically feminine ascriptive tasks, see ibid., 1:144, 249, 257, 289; 2:279–81, 299, entries for 11 Jan. 1858; 5 Apr., 28 May, and 31 Dec. 1860; 30 July, 3, 4, and 6 Aug., and 19 Sept. 1873. Technically the status of the Indian women was that of domestic servants, but most of them had been purchased by their employers and were therefore chattels. On Lee's ownership of Indian servants, see ibid., 1:149, 167–68, entries for 5 Feb. and 5 and 10 June 1858.
62. Ibid., 1:93, 162–63, 216, 237, 277; 2:199, entries for 8 and 14 May 1858, 18 Aug. 1859, 25 Feb. and 18 Oct. 1860, and 27 May 1872. On small-scale home manufacture, see ibid., 1:97, 101, entries for 1 Mar. and 12 May 1849.
63. Lee, *Mormonism Unveiled*, p. 204.
64. Widtsoe, *Discourses of Brigham Young*, p. 335.
65. Ibid., p. 337.
66. Clark, *Messages of the First Presidency*, 2:208–9.
67. E. D. Kane, pseud. [William Wood], *Twelve Mormon Homes Visited in Succession on a Journey through Utah to Arizona*, p. 5.
68. On the telegraph, see ibid., pp. 4, 126; on the women in professions, see Tullidge, *Women of Mormondom*, pp. 524–25; and on the election of women, see Beadle, *Polygamy*, p. 603. For women as lawyers, see Thomas G. Alexander, "An Experiment in Progressive Legislation," p. 27. In another case, in 1896, Dr. Martha Hughes Cannon defeated her husband, Angus M. Cannon, in an election on the local level.
69. Hulett, "Mormon Polygamous Family," p. 85 n. For the text of the franchise bill, see *Acts, Resolutions, and Memorials*, sec. for 1870, p. 8.
70. Tullidge, *Women of Mormondom*, p. 381. See also pp. 394, 400. On the *Women's Exponent*, see ibid., p. 520.
71. See Jennie Anderson Froiseth, ed., *The Women of Mormonism*, p. 385. For attitudes of this group toward polygamy, see ibid., pp. 37–38, 127, 191–92, 279. The Utah Anti-Polygamy Society was organized in 1878. Cf. Gustave O. Larson, *The "Americanization" of Utah for Statehood*, p. 87.
72. Cf. *Memorial of the Mormon Women of Utah to the President and the Congress of the U.S.*

Chapter 10

1. *Mormon Chronicle*, 1:7, entry for 11 Mar. 1848.
2. Although women were not allowed to hold elective office in Utah in the 1870s, three successive sessions of the legislature passed bills to delete the word "male" from the qualifying statute, only to have them vetoed by the governor. The effect of allowing women to hold office would have been to allow more Mormon candidates to stand for the same office. The intent of these bills does not seem to have been egalitarian. Cf. Elizabeth C. Stanton, *Eighty Years and More: Reminiscences, 1815–97* (1875; reprint ed., New York: Schocken Books, 1971), pp. 286–87.
3. The poem was published in the *Millennial Star* 19 (1857): 79–80.
4. Reprinted in ibid. 28 (1866): 204.
5. See Tullidge, *Women of Mormondom*, p. 502. A committee of women was appointed to express the gratitude of Mormon women for the action of Governor Mann. Eliza Snow's attitude indicates the deep-seated belief among Mormon women that Mormon

men were not very enthusiastic about woman suffrage, and that passage of the bill had little if anything to do with recognizing the validity of the concept of equal rights for women.

6. The women's suffrage bill was H.R. 68, and the one for the suppression of polygamy was H.R. 93. See *Congressional Globe*, 41st Cong., 1st sess. and appendix, 1869, pp. 73, 84; and ibid., 3d sess., 1870–71, pt. 2:966.

7. Alan P. Grimes reaches similar conclusions about the political origin of woman suffrage under polygamy: see *The Puritan Ethic and Woman Suffrage* (New York: Oxford University Press, 1967), pp. 40–44.

8. *New York Times*, 16 Mar. 1869, p. 4, col. 6.

9. Beadle, *Polygamy*, p. 439. Beadle argued that the idea that woman suffrage would overturn the polygamous system was "self-complacent folly." Of all places, Utah, with its unflinching patriarchal control of women, provided the least promising environment for female political rights. Under such conditions, he argued, it would be absurd to think that women "could be anything else than just what men choose to make them" (pp. 430–31).

10. Quoted in Coyner, *Handbook on Mormonism*, p. 74. See also Beadle, *Polygamy*, p. 439. Cannon returned the compliment by urging that woman suffrage be extended "to the entire republic." See Tullidge, *Women of Mormondom*, p. 550.

11. For Julian's other suffrage proposals, see *Congressional Globe*, 41st Cong., 1st sess. and appendix, 1869, pp. 73, 84. His plan to grant female suffrage in the District of Columbia was taken up by Representative Sargent in 1871. See ibid., 3d sess., 1870–71, pt. 1:659. On Julian's proposal to allow the suffrage delegates to use congressional meeting rooms, see ibid., pt. 2:1000–1001. See Elizabeth C. Stanton, Susan B. Anthony, and Matilda Joslyn Gage, eds., *History of Woman Suffrage*, 2:325, for the text of the three bills proposed by Julian. He had also been an early advocate of granting suffrage to the freedmen, and his advocacy of female suffrage displays a notable consistency of thought. The Radical Republicans' leaders, especially Charles Sumner and Benjamin Wade, were also considered stout champions of woman suffrage. See ibid., 2:322–25.

12. The ties between Mormon women and the National Suffrage Association continued to be strong. In 1887, when the Edmunds-Tucker bill, which ended woman suffrage in Utah, was being debated, the national organization sprang to the defense of Mormon women's rights. Cf. Stanton, Anthony, and Gage, *History of Woman Suffrage*, 3:937–40. This did not mean, however, that the women of the National Suffrage Association favored polygamy.

13. Tullidge, *Women of Mormondom*, p. 385. The phrase "true women" was included in the salutation of a petition to "Mrs. President Grant" from Mormon women (ibid., p. 528).

14. Ibid., p. 550.

15. Quoted in Grimes, *Puritan Ethic and Woman Suffrage*, p. 40. Emphasis mine.

16. S. 1540 was presented on 26 Feb. 1873. See *Congressional Globe*, 42d Cong., 3d sess., 1873, pt. 2:1780–81. The phrase "peculiar institution" as applied to polygamy is from the speech of Senator Thurman of Ohio, where it appears several times.

17. Quoted in Stanton, *Eighty Years*, p. 287.

18. *Congressional Globe*, 42d Cong., 3d. sess., 1873, pt. 2:1780. The complexity of the issue seems to have eluded those who sought the demise of the institution, but in fact they were reenacting the whole course of the debate and legislative attempts to end the system of slavery. The specter of another civil war loomed behind the feeble attempts of congressmen to deal with polygamy.

19. Ibid., p. 1801, speech of Senator Casserly of California.

20. See Wright, *Report on Marriage and Divorce*, tab. 4, "Duration of Marriage before

Divorce for Divorces Granted from 1867 to 1886, by Specific Causes—Utah," pp. 748–51.
21. Ibid.
22. Ibid., pp. 602–769.
23. See William A. Richardson, ed., *Supplement to the Revised Statutes of the U.S.: Forty-third to Fifty-first Congress Inclusive* (Washington, D.C.: Government Printing Office, 1891), vol. 1 (1874–91), p. 49. The act in question was passed in the Forty-third Congress on 23 June 1874. The relevant section was chap. 469, sec. 3, par. 1.
24. For the text of the 1852 law, see *Acts, Resolutions, and Memorials*, pp. 49–50. A brief account of the "divorce brokerage" carried on between eastern lawyers and Mormons can be found in Howard, *History of Matrimonial Institutions*, 3:131–33. Corroborative figures can be found in Wright, *Report on Marriage and Divorce*, pp. 203–6, 415–17. See also Ivins MSS, 4:245–49.
25. Young, *Wife Number Nineteen*, p. 555. Mrs. Ann Young was a young divorcée with two children when Brigham Young married her. They had been married two years when she brought suit against him on the grounds of failure to provide. For other accounts of this case, see Linn, *Story of the Mormons*, pp. 572–73; Wallace, *The Twenty-Seventh Wife*, pp. 359–69; and Werner, *Brigham Young*, pp. 330–33.
26. Young, *Wife Number Nineteen*, p. 558.
27. Ibid., p. 559.
28. Quoted in the *New York Times*, 28 Apr. 1877, p. 2, col. 2. Ann Eliza had been granted alimony for the duration of the trial by Judge James B. McKean in 1875 (see Young, *Wife Number Nineteen*, p. 561).
29. *New York Times*, 2 May 1877, p. 4, col. 4.
30. Ibid.
31. Tullidge, *Women of Mormondom*, p. 509. Cf. *Doctrine and Covenants*, sec. 28, art. 13, p. 141.
32. *Times and Seasons* 1 (1840): 46. Today, women are still excluded from the ranks of the priesthood, and Mormons have been foremost among those actively opposing the Equal Rights Amendment. In fact, through the church's influence on its members, Mormons have succeeded in preventing the ratification of the ERA in three states in which they comprise a sizeable proportion of the population—Utah, Arizona, and Nevada. See the *New York Times*, 5 May 1978, p. A16, cols. 1–6; 18 June 1978, p. 1, cols. 2–4, p. 49, cols. 1, 2, 6; and 26 Nov. 1978, p. 36, col. 1.
33. Coyner, *Handbook on Mormonism*, pp. 28–29.
34. Quoted in Jarman, *U.S.A.*, p. 115.
35. May, "People on the Mormon Frontier," pp. 179–80, contends that wealth was especially concentrated among the heads of polygamous families. The median income for nonpolygamous heads of households was $389 annually; for polygamous heads, $670.
36. *Journal of Discourses*, 16:21, speech entitled "Assistance of the Ladies, etc.," delivered 7 Apr. 1873.
37. Ibid., 19:65, speech delivered 24 July 1877.
38. Diary of Charles Walker, p. 29, entries for 13 May and 11 June 1876. The phallic aggression of the knife slitting the outer integument from navel to knee is obvious. The aggressive desire of "retributive" rape lurks just below the surface here.
39. *Mormon Chronicle*, 1:139.
40. Widtsoe, *Discourses of Brigham Young*, p. 334.
41. Cooper, *Rattling, Roaring Rhymes*, pp. 94–95.
42. Ibid., p. 95. All of the material quoted in the text at nn. 40–42 is also to be found in a somewhat more expurgated version in *Journal of Discourses*, 14:21, address entitled "Fashions of the World," delivered 6 May 1870.

43. Quoted in *Mormon Chronicle*, 1:140. Much of this argument had been borrowed from similar attacks appearing in the Gentile press, but Mormon theology and patriarchal ideology intensified it considerably.
44. Brooks, *On the Mormon Frontier*, 2:441–42, entry for 12 July 1852.
45. President Wilford Woodruff announced the end of Mormon polygamy on 25 Sept. 1890. In his address he upheld the ideal of polygamy but declared that the church could no longer sanction its practice. For the text of the Woodruff Manifesto, given out as a prophetic revelation, see Joseph Fielding Smith, *Essentials of Church History*, pp. 494–95. Six years later Utah entered the Union as the forty-fifth state. Fundamentalists, however, continued to practice polygamy, claiming that President John Taylor, Woodruff's predecessor, had called together five devoted followers just before his death in 1887 and had required them to promise to uphold the practice of celestial marriage at all costs. In the mid-1940s a surprise raid in three states netted a number of polygamists. Fifteen were arrested in Salt Lake City alone. There were further raids in the fifties, sixties, and seventies. The last man convicted of polygamy left a Utah state prison in 1969. (See Kephart, *Extraordinary Groups*, pp. 232–34.) At the present time, there are an estimated twenty to thirty thousand polygamists in the American West. They have settled in single family groups, small communes, or large extended families. The largest such group of thirty-five hundred polygamists is located in Colorado City (formerly Short Creek), Ariz. There are small settlements in Utah and Montana and three colonies in Mexico. Their religious organizations are sectarian groups such as Ervil le Baron's Church of the Lamb of God, or his brother Joseph's Church of the First Born of the Fulness of Times. One such group of Fundamentalists, as they prefer to call themselves (they are referred to as "pligs" by their enemies) in Davis County, Utah, is an economic cooperative reputed to be worth some $20–$30 million. (See *New York Times*, 9 Oct. 1977, p. 1, cols. 1, 2; p. 80, cols. 3–6.)

Part IV, Introduction

1. John H. Noyes to Larkin G. Mead (his lawyer and brother-in-law), Brooklyn, 4 Apr. 1852, quoted in George W. Noyes, comp. *John Humphrey Noyes and the Putney Community*, p. 302.
2. Harriet A. Noyes to Simon Lovett, Bristol, Wis., dated Putney, Vt., 27 Jan. 1848, p. 2. Noyes's letter to Larkin Mead, cited in the preceding note, contained a five-point defense of his decision to flee Putney. For the full text of the letter to Mead, see Constance Noyes Robertson, *Oneida Community Profiles*, pp. 10–11.
3. This letter was written sometime between the end of Oct. 1847 and 27 Jan. 1848. The portion quoted here appears as an extract on pp. 3–4 of the letter from Harriet A. Noyes cited in the preceding note.
4. The Putney Community in its original phase lasted from 1841 to 1848; Oneida as a communal society practicing complex marriage, male continence, and (after 1867) the eugenic system called "stirpiculture" extended from 1848 to 1879. In 1879 the Oneida Community became a joint-stock company, and monogamous marriage was reinstituted. The primary business of the corporation under the leadership of Pierrepont Burt Noyes, the son of John Humphrey, was silver-plated flatware. Oneida silver is still produced and widely valued for its quality. Today, the grounds of the Oneida Community are the home of surviving relatives of the original communards; and the main building, the Mansion House, houses a museum and collection of the printed works of the community. The site is today called Kenwood, N.Y.
5. My interpretation of Noyes agrees in its broad general outlines with that presented in Robert Thomas's excellent psychobiography of Noyes, *The Man Who Would Be*

Perfect. The interpretation here is derived from a seminar paper I wrote in 1973–74, however, and was developed independently of Thomas's discussion. For Thomas's analysis, see *The Man Who Would Be Perfect*, pp. 1–19, 42–84. The bulk of this section on the Oneida Community (the succeeding three chapters) was written in 1975–76.

A second important source on the life of John Humphrey Noyes is Robert Allerton Parker's *A Yankee Saint*, which remains essential because Parker was the last person to have access to the archives and documents of Oneida, as well as to Noyes's personal papers (in 1934–35), then in the possession of John Humphrey's son, George Wallingford Noyes. These materials were subsequently destroyed. For the early period of Noyes's life and the course of the Putney Community, George W. Noyes's *Putney Community* is invaluable. On the Oneida Community, the essential sources are Maren Lockwood Carden's *Oneida* and Constance Noyes Robertson's *Oneida Community: An Autobiography* and *Oneida Community: the Breakup*. Records were carefully kept of all stirpicultural matings and of all sexual encounters in the community, and in addition there was a large quantity of documentary, diary, and epistolary material written by individual members. As far as I have been able to ascertain, the community records of the sexual experiment were destroyed by George W. Noyes in the 1930s. The bulk of the personal material remained at Kenwood, N.Y., in the Oneida, Ltd., vaults. In the late 1960s or early 1970s, in order to protect individuals' families, all this material (a whole truckload) was taken to the dump and burned. The documents necessary for a detailed reconstruction of everyday life under the Oneida sexual experiment were thus destroyed. Many questions that might have been answered will remain unanswered; much of what the Oneida sexual experience was like for the people involved will remain a mystery. The only literary work I have encountered that directly treats Oneida is Lawrence Langer and Armina Marshall, *Suzanna and the Elders: An American Comedy* (New York: Random House, 1940), a short dramatic piece based, it would appear, on Parker's *Yankee Saint*. George Bernard Shaw in *Man and Superman* (1902) referred to the Oneida Community in the appendix section entitled *The Revolutionist's Handbook and Pocket Companion* by John Tanner, M.I.R.C. (Member of the Idle Rich Class); the portion on Oneida is called "The Perfectionist Experiment at Oneida Creek."

6. George W. Noyes, comp., *The Religious Experience of John Humphrey Noyes*, pp. 2–7. Noyes's father was a state legislator from 1811 to 1814, but the sessions were held in Brattleboro, which was close to home. John, Sr., retired from business in 1821.

7. Letter dated Amherst, 26 May 1821, quoted in ibid., p. 11. See also Noyes, *Putney Community*, pp. 91, 96.

8. Noyes, *Religious Experience*, p. 11. See also ibid., p. 23, for an extract from Noyes's college journal, entry for 1 Apr. 1830, and a letter to his father dated 31 Mar. 1829.

9. Parker, *Yankee Saint*, p. 17.

10. Noyes, *Religious Experience*, pp. 35–36. My emphasis.

11. Ibid., p. 37. My emphasis.

12. Noyes, *Putney Community*, p. 92.

13. John H. Noyes to his father, New Haven, 8 Oct. 1834, quoted in Noyes, *Religious Experience*, pp. 171–72.

14. John H. Noyes to his mother, New Haven, 2 Nov. 1834, quoted in ibid., p. 172.

15. MS copy of the "Battle Axe Letter."

16. Noyes, *Putney Community*, p. 96.

17. See Karen Horney, "The Dread of Woman."

18. Noyes, *Religious Experience*, p. 13.

19. John Humphrey Noyes, *Confessions of John H. Noyes, Part I: Confessions of Religious*

Experience, pp. 16, 11. Noyes's phraseology echoes David's lament over the slain Jonathan, 2 Sam. 1:26. Cf. also 1 Sam. 18:1–3.
20. Noyes, *Confessions*, p. 24.
21. Ibid., p. 67.
22. Ibid. In 1843, Noyes, in an article entitled "A Word of Warning," advised Perfectionists that "brotherly love" must precede "sexual love." In such love "we shall not prefer one sex to another." In "Imposition of hands, kissing, washing feet, leaning on the breast, etc. . . . there is not less occasion and there is more authority for these practices between men and men, than between men and women" (*Perfectionist and Theocratic Watchman* 5 [1845–46]: 34).
23. Perfectionism was a development of New Light Calvinism as it was taught at New Haven Theological Seminary through the works of Nathaniel W. Taylor, Wesleyan Methodism, and the evangelical revival tradition. It was a form of antinomianism, maintaining that for those who had achieved perfection (absolute sanctification), both civil and ecclesiastical law had become superfluous. Perfectionists did not maintain that their adherents *would* not sin, but rather that they were incapable of *willing* sin; and therefore even though they might in fact backslide, they were not morally responsible: they were not *guilty* of sin. Perfectionists began their organized religious activity at the Free Church in New Haven in 1834.
24. See Noyes, *Confessions*, passim. See also Theodore W. Adorno et al., *The Authoritarian Personality* (New York: W. W. Norton Co., 1950), pp. 337–41.
25. Noyes, *Confessions*, p. 47.
26. Ibid., p. 42. The scriptural reference here is to 2 Cor. 11:14.
27. MS copy of "Battle Axe Letter." This letter was sent to his friend David Harrison "in the nakedness of privacy." Harrison, however, showed it to other Perfectionists, among whom was Simon Lovett. He in turn showed it to Elizabeth Hawley, who sent it to Theophilus Gates, publisher of an antimarriage paper, *Battle Axe and Weapons of War* (hence the letter's popular name). The letter appeared anonymously and was initially attributed to another Perfectionist, James Boyle. Noyes acknowledged authorship in the Sept. 1837 issue of the *Witness* (p. 49), q.v. He claimed that the letter was based on 1 Cor., chap. 7, and that there was nothing in it not contained in the source. The phrase "nakedness of privacy" is from Noyes's letter to William Lloyd Garrison, Ithaca, N.Y., 15 May 1838, asking him to reprint Noyes's acknowledgement of the "Battle Axe Letter" in the *Liberator*, because that paper reached a larger audience. The letter to Garrison is reprinted in the *Witness* 1, no. 7 (23 Jan. 1839): 51.
28. Noyes, *Religious Experience*, pp. 172–74. Letter dated 11 Dec. 1834.
29. Ibid., p. 314. Letter dated Jan. 1837.
30. Noyes's letter to Harriet is dated Putney, 11 June 1838. It is reprinted in Noyes, *Putney Community*, pp. 17–18. For an account of Harriet's background and antecedents, see Robertson, *Autobiography*, pp. 7–8.
31. In a letter dated Westminster, Vt., 24 June 1838, Harriet referred to Abigail with misgivings: "I might fear she would be the object of my envy. . . . If my fate be that of the Empress Josephine, the Lord will give me a heart to rejoice and say Thy will be done" (quoted in Noyes, *Putney Community*, p. 22). Josephine (1763–1814) was married to Napoleon Bonaparte in 1796; in view of the Noyes's marriage, which produced but one live birth out of five pregnancies in six years, the fact that the Bonapartes' marriage was childless adds poignant if unconscious prescience to Harriet's comment. Her conscious reference in the allusion to Josephine was obviously to the fact that her marriage with Napoleon was dissolved in 1809 as a result of her infertility. Clearly, Harriet feared that Noyes would set her aside in order to marry Abigail. Apparently, her fears were groundless, for Noyes wrote in 1874 that "I never knew

woman sexually till I was married, . . . I never knew any woman but my wife until we entered into complex marriage in 1846—which was eight years after my first marriage, twelve years after my conversion to holiness. . . . in this second marriage I have not been unfaithful, either to the expressed terms of the first, or to the wishes of my partner, I can honestly boast of a clear matrimonial record" (John Humphrey Noyes, *Dixon and His Copyists*, p. 7).

32. Noyes, *Putney Community*, pp. 96–98, from a paper entitled "Pride of Motherhood," ca. 1845.

33. Ibid., p. 96.

34. Quoted in ibid., pp. 27–28. My emphasis. See also ibid., p. 30.

35. On the reaction of survivors to the death of a family member, see Elisabeth Kübler-Ross, *On Death and Dying* (New York: Macmillan Co., 1969), chap. 9, "The Patient's Family," pp. 157–80.

36. "Original Confession of Polly Hayes Noyes." The MS was found in late 1968 in a wall at the rear of the barn in the John Noyes, Sr., house, Locust Grove, Kimball Hill, Putney, Vt. It is now located in the Putney Historical Society. My emphasis.

37. On incest, see John Humphrey Noyes, *Essay on Scientific Propagation*, p. 10. On Noyes's selection of mates for his younger siblings, see Anita N. McGee, "Dr. Anita N. McGee's Interviews at Kenwood, N.Y., Aug., 1891," n.p. (hereafter cited as "Anita N. McGee's Interviews").

38. On Noyes's mother as a recusant, see Noyes, *Putney Community*, pp. 336–37. Although her initial conversion to Perfectionism came in 1841, when Polly Noyes penned her "Original Confession" in 1846 she noted: "When William was here in autumn as he probably informed you, I was in a state of open rebellion against John. I can give it no softer name as it now appears to me to have been wholly the result of some misconception, [as] was my want of faith and a spirit of submission which is willing to receive the truth however horrifying it may be to the natural feelings of [*sic*] the maxims of the world." She was a hard woman to keep under conviction.

Chapter 11

1. John Humphrey Noyes, *The Berean* (1847), pp. 55–56. "Caloric" was a supposed form of matter to which the properties of heat and combustion were ascribed (see *Webster's New International Dictionary*, 2d ed).

2. Noyes, *Berean*, pp. 57–58. My emphasis.

3. Ibid., p. 58.

4. Ibid., pp. 487–88.

5. Ibid., p. 488.

6. Ibid., pp. 488–89. My emphasis.

7. Ibid., pp. 248–51.

8. John Humphrey Noyes, *Home Talks*, ed. Alfred Barron and George Noyes Miller, p. 165.

9. *Bible Communism*, p. 44.

10. Ibid., p. 56.

11. Noyes, *Berean*, p. 101. Cf. *Bible Communism*, p. 51, for a statement of propagation as original sin.

12. Noyes, *Berean*, p. 114.

13. Ibid., p. 113.

14. Ibid., pp. 114–15. See also p. 113.

15. Ibid., p. 163. Cf. Rom., chap. 7.

16. Ibid., p. 125.
17. Ibid.
18. Ibid., p. 485. See also pp. 115, 118, 163, 412.
19. Noyes, *Home Talks*, pp. 153–54.
20. Sylvester Graham and Thomas Low Nichols shared Noyes's belief that postcoital debilitation resulted not from the simple loss of semen, but from the expenditure of vital or nervous energy inhering in the fluid (see Sears, *Sex Radicals*, p. 207).
21. "Bible Argument: Defining the Relations of the Sexes in the Kingdom of Heaven," appendix to *First Annual Report of the Oneida Association*, p. 29.
22. Noyes, *Berean*, p. 60. For the connection between blood and semen, see John Humphrey Noyes, *The Way of Holiness*, p. 209. Noyes considered the heart not so much a physical body organ as a psychological-religious one. His training in evangelical Protestantism, with its belief in the paramount importance of religious experience generated by emotional response (especially as propounded in the works of Jonathan Edwards), was probably responsible for his particular conception of the importance of the heart.
23. Noyes, *Berean*, pp. 64–65. My emphasis. See also *First Annual Report*, p. 14; and Noyes, *Way of Holiness*, pp. 34, 206–7.
24. "Animal Magnetism," *Perfectionist and Theocratic Watchman* 5 (1845–46): 15.
25. Ibid. See also Noyes, *Berean*, p. 66.
26. *Perfectionist and Theocratic Watchman* 5:15. Edward Bliss Foote shared this electromagnetic vision of sexuality. He believed that chemical electricity was generated by the contact of the acidic skin of the penis and the alkaline lining of the vagina. This electricity stimulated the genital organs and was conducted by the pubic nerves. There was also frictional electricity generated by the rubbing together of the glans penis and the clitoris. Thus, both the male and female stood to lose vital electromechanical energy in the act of intercourse. It must have been this thought that was in Noyes's mind, too, but it did not find coherent expression in any of his writings. On Foote's conception of sexual intercourse, see Sears, *Sex Radicals*, p. 187.
27. There is a long physiological tradition which maintains that there is a female ejaculate expelled from the urethra (*sic*) during intercourse that is analogous to male semen. Though for much of human history both males and females were thought to ejaculate, the debate over the physiology of reproduction, and the corresponding truncation of the term "semen" so that it referred only to the male sexual fluid, led to a denial of female ejaculation in twentieth-century gynecological thought. The process of redefinition of the sexual functions of the sexes in the reproductive process began with Regnier de Graaf (1641–73), the Dutch anatomist who discovered the Graafian vesicles (or follicles) of the ovary. He concluded that male semen was essential to procreation and that the female contribution was only the ovum; no female sexual fluid was required for reproduction. The discovery by Anton van Leeuwenhoek (1632–1723) of the spermatozoa in the male semen confirmed de Graaf's discoveries and led to an increased denigration of the female ejaculate. The cultural denial of the female ejaculate is underscored by the etymological development of the word "semen," which is derived from the Greek γυνή (seed), a female root. Gradually, in conjunction with the investigations of biologists and microscopists, the term came to be used to refer solely to the male sexual fluid. The first clear example of this androcentric usage provided in the *Oxford English Dictionary* is from 1725. Apparently, by the eighteenth century, then, the cultural denial of the female ejaculation had triumphed both medically and linguistically. By the end of the nineteenth century, because female sexual fluid was nonfunctional reproductively and had no word in the language to describe it, it came to be associated with physical and mental disease—especially hysteria. For a more detailed treatment of this question, see J. L. Sevely and J. W. Bennett, "Concerning Female

Ejaculation and the Female Prostate"; the outline of the medical and linguistic repression of the female ejaculate given above is largely based on pp. 15–17. For the Aristotelian discussion of semen, see *Generation of Animals*, bk. 1, secs. 2–22.

28. Noyes took great pains to dispel the notion that male continence would lead to nervous disorders among the men. See John Humphrey Noyes, *Male Continence*, pp. 23–24; and Noyes, *Essay on Scientific Propagation*, appendix by T. R. Noyes entitled "Report on Nervous Diseases in the Oneida Community," pp. 26–32.

29. "Cure for Old Age," *Spiritualist Magazine* 2 (1847–48): 43, my emphasis. See also Noyes, *Male Continence*, p. 21; and *Bible Communism*, pp. 46, 51.

30. Noyes, *Home Talks*, p. 91.

31. Ibid., p. 205.

32. Ibid., p. 206.

33. Ibid., pp. 207–8.

34. Ibid., pp. 208–9, address entitled "The Law of Fellowship."

35. *First Annual Report*, p. 15. See also *Bible Communism*, p. 12; and *Spiritual Moralist* 1, no. 2 (25 June 1842): 12.

36. Noyes, *Male Continence*, p. 15.

37. *Spiritual Moralist* 1, no. 1 (13 June 1842): 5.

38. *Spiritual Magazine* 2 (1847–48): 331. See also *Oneida Circular*, n.s. 3 (1866–67): 158.

39. Noyes, *Berean*, p. 472.

40. Ibid., p. 445. For a statement of Noyes's belief in the right of women to sexual enjoyment, see his criticism of Emanuel Swedenborg's doctrine of concubinage in Noyes, *Putney Community*, pp. 181–82, reprint of the article "Swedenborg on Mistress-Keeping and Concubinage" (*Perfectionist*, 31 Jan. 1846). For Swedenborg's doctrine, see *The Delights of Wisdom Pertaining to Conjugal Love, After Which Follow the Pleasures of Insanity Pertaining to Scortatory Love* (1768; reprint ed., New York: American Swedenborg Printing and Publishing Society, 1910), nos. 462–77, pp. 434–66.

41. *Third Annual Report of the Oneida Association*, pp. 26–27. The Sadducees's questions are to be found in Mark 12:18–25 and Luke 20:27–36.

42. Noyes, *Essay on Scientific Propagation*, p. 10. My emphasis.

43. Ibid., p. 12.

44. Noyes, *Home Talks*, p. 141. Noyes is assuming a kind of moral Darwinism here.

45. *Bible Communism*, p. 58. For other commercial metaphors, see ibid., pp. 88–91, 102, 110, 125–28; and Noyes, *Home Talks*, p. 64, where Noyes speaks of salvation in economic-sexual terms of assuring oneself that "income" exceeds "expenses." The slavery metaphor for marriage and its analogue, the ownership metaphor, are also grounded in a commercial vision of the social relationship of the sexes. See *Bible Communism*, pp. 125–28, 84. Opposition to prostitution is expressed in ibid., p. 38; and in the *Oneida Circular* 4 (1867–68): 67. Antiabortion and antidivorce statements are to be found in ibid., pp. 58, 87, 95; and in *Bible Communism*, p. 38.

46. See *Bible Communism*, pp. 32, 37; and Noyes, *Home Talks*, pp. 96, 340.

Chapter 12

1. Noyes, *Male Continence*, p. 13. Noyes obviously means that the act was more enjoyable to both partners because a psychological burden, fear of pregnancy, had been lifted from their minds. In light of the insistence on female orgasm at Oneida, though, it is possible that he means that his wife first experienced an orgasm after the beginning of male continence. We can only speculate on this point, but it is possible that Noyes was a premature ejaculator.

2. *Spiritual Magazine* 2 (1847–48): 275.
3. Noyes, *Male Continence*, p. 18. For Noyes's attack on Owen, see the polemical *Dixon and His Copyists*, p. 34. For his gentle rebuff of Shakerism, see *Bible Communism*, p. 50. For the influence of Malthus and an additional rejection of Owen, see "Malthus and Owen," *American Socialist* 2 (1877): 172.
4. Noyes, *Male Continence*, pp. 10–11. Harriet Holton, in a letter to Noyes shortly before their marriage (dated Westminster, Vt., 24 June 1838), referred to "the spirit I have been under which forbids me to marry," but noted that she would discuss the matter with Noyes when they next met. Noyes replied (letter dated Putney, Vt., 25 June 1838) that he was not sure of the degree to which she had "imbibed the spirit of Shakerism, but I will say frankly, that there may be no mistake between us, that so far from regarding the act of sexual enjoyment as in itself unholy, I am sure that there is no sacrifice except that of the heart that is more acceptable to God." (These letters are reprinted in Parker, *Yankee Saint*, pp. 63–64; and in Noyes, *Putney Community*, pp. 22–23.) A letter from Noyes's sister, Harriet H. Skinner, Putney, Vt., 29 Oct. 1847 (after the inception of complex marriage there), refers to her brother's definitive rejection of Shakerism (see Noyes, *Putney Community*, p. 285). See also *Oneida Circular*, n.s. 3 (1866–67): 202–4. For attacks on Shakerism as a "primrose path" as opposed to the "strait gate" of male continence, see "A Visit to Watervliet," p. 7, and "Shaker Communism," p. 74, in ibid. For early statements about Shakerism by Noyes, see "A Word of Warning," *Perfectionist and Theocratic Watchman* 5 (1845–46): 34, in which Shakers are characterized as "licentious spirits"; and "Marriage," in *The Berean*, p. 431.
5. "Restricting of Population," *American Socialist* 2:235.
6. *Bible Communism*, pp. 45–46.
7. Ibid., pp. 52–53.
8. *Hand Book of the Oneida Community*, p. 55. See also appendix to *Bible Communism* entitled "Colloquy between Judge North, Major South, and Mr. Free Church," pp. 125–28. There is a certain ambiguity in the continual comparison of marriage to slavery in Oneida publications. It is an expression on the one hand of the guilt the male feels over a relation he believes is characterized by extreme interpersonal aggression on his part. But this conceals a haunting fear, as Winthrop Jordan has shown in *White over Black* (Baltimore: Penguin Books, 1971), pp. 150–54, of revolt of the oppressed, which is grounded in sexual aggression. In the case of women, the revolt is adultery, promiscuity, and prostitution growing out of a suppression of female erotic needs. The insecurity of the male in a "worldly" marriage relationship is made clear when, in a passage written late in the Civil War, the two estranged parts of the nation are considered male (the North) and female (the South): these are respectively "Uncle Sam" and "Aunt Sam." Oneida assumptions about sexual precedence and gender role expectations are clear when the writer declares: "The South has always been the conspicuous or woman part of the nation. The North, on the other hand, has represented the male element. It has furnished the power, and done the hard work of the nation." It is hoped that, with the termination of the war, "Uncle Sam will become what he should have been from the first—*the head of the family*; and Aunt Sam, subordinately refined and receptive, will be the glory of her husband" (*Oneida Circular*, n.s. 1 [1864–65]: 65–66). What a perfect figurative expression of Oneidans' feelings about the battle between the sexes!
9. Alan Estlake, *The Oneida Community*, p. 80.
10. For an Oneida expression of rationally controlled love, see "A Heart Story," *Oneida Circular*, n.s. 4 (1867–68): 100. For the Puritan conception, based on the belief that one should not love the creature above the Creator, see J. T. Johnson, "The Covenant Idea and the Puritan View of Marriage," *Journal of the History of Ideas* 32 (Jan. 1971):

107–18. There was also an attempt in nineteenth-century marriage manuals to promote the growth of rational love in marriage over romantic love based on a premarital attachment. See Michael Gordon and M. Charles Bernstein, "Mate Choice and Domestic Life in the Nineteenth-Century Marriage Manual," p. 668.

11. John Humphrey Noyes, "Falling in Love," *American Socialist* 3:125.

12. Ibid.

13. *Hand Book of the Oneida Community*, p. 55. See also Noyes, *Male Continence*, pp. 11–12; and *First Annual Report*, pp. 48–49.

14. See "Bible Argument," in *First Annual Report*, p. 31. See also "Internal Life of the Oneida Community," written "By a Member," p. 7 n, in the McGee MSS.

15. Noyes, *Male Continence*, pp. 8–9.

16. See Ely Van de Warker, "A Gynecological Study of the Oneida Community," p. 785.

17. Quoted in ibid., pp. 787–88. When we consider the theological context of the Oneida Community, it is clear that the "fall" metaphor also conveys intentional echoes of the biblical "fall of man." As in the primeval garden, woman is the temptress. Sandor Ferenczi, the Hungarian Freudian, analyzed the same orgasmic crises in *Thalassa*. In the terminal phase of the sex act, he contended, "there then occurs the final and decisive battle between the desire to give away and the desire to keep the genital secretion itself. ... In fine, therefore, the entire genital warfare rages about the issue of giving up or not giving up a secretory product the escape of which from the male body is permitted by the terminating ejaculation, thus freeing the man from sexual tension, but in a way which at the same time safeguards the security and welfare of this secretory product inside the body of the woman. This safeguard, however, may clearly be assumed to constitute an identity between the sex secretion and the ego, so that we should now have a three-fold identity in connection with coitus: identity of the whole organism with the genital, identity with the partner, and identity with the sexual secretion" (pp. 17–18). In the case of Noyes's male continence, an overdeveloped sense of the identity between the self and the sexual secretion prevented any transcendence of the self in the sex act through an identification with the partner. Wilhelm Reich in his *Function of the Orgasm* made a similar division of the sex act into three parts. For a brief statement of Reich's division, see *Selected Writings: An Introduction to Orgonomy* (New York: Farrar, Strauss, & Giroux, 1960), pp. 43–50. The practice of *coitus reservatus*, employed primarily as a contraceptive measure, was later advocated by Elmina Slenker, under the name "Alphaism" in the 1880s (see Sears, *Sex Radicals*, pp. 206–7); and Alice B. Stockham, under the rubric "Karezza" in the 1890s (see her *Karezza*).

18. Noyes, *Male Continence*, p. 9. (This treatise was subtitled "Self-Control in Sexual Intercourse" in its first edition [1866]). Such close approach to orgasm as to make it difficult to restrain was listed as the "abuse" of male continence ([Anita N. McGee], Oneida Community: Interview of R. L. D. and Mr. and Mrs. George W. Noyes, in McGee MSS). The myth persisted outside Oneida that the peculiar sexual practices of the community produced impotence in men and sterility in women. Dr. Theodore R. Noyes examined the semen of Oneida men and discovered a normal presence of viable zoosperms even in men sixty-five to seventy years old. Dr. Van de Warker's examination of the women of Oneida in the autumn of 1877 disproved the assumption of their sterility. T. R. Noyes's "Report on Nervous Diseases," published in 1875 as an appendix to J. H. Noyes's *Essay on Scientific Propagation*, and Van de Warker's investigations denied the presence of any neurotic symptoms that could be traced to the sexual life of Oneidans. A brief reference to T. R. Noyes's spermatic lucubrations is to be found in [McGee], Oneida Community: Interview of R. L. D. and Mr. and Mrs. George W. Noyes. Norman Himes has explained the physiological basis of male continence that helped to protect the male: "Too close an approach to the climax is

intentionally avoided, and, as it is not so commonly understood about this method, detumescence takes place intravaginally, until normal circulation is restored. It is claimed by the adherents of male continence that, when detumescence takes place inside rather than outside, there are no harmful effects, nervous or otherwise" (*Medical History of Contraception*, pp. 269–70).

19. Noyes, *Male Continence*, p. 15.

20. [Henry J. Seymour], *The Oneida Community: Replies by One of the Surviving Members*, pp. 6–7. On male initiative, see Van de Warker, "Gynecological Study," p. 792; "The Oneida Community: Its Motives Pure," reprinted from the *New York World* (26 July 1871) in *Oneida Circular*, n.s. 4:167; and "Anita N. McGee's Interviews," sheets entitled "Stirpiculture." Prior to the 1860s, intermediaries were not used. This meant that in the early period of complex marriage (for about fifteen years after its beginning in 1846), sexual proposals were made on a one-to-one basis: see "Anita N. McGee's Interviews." On flirting in public, see Pierrepont Noyes, *My Father's House*, p. 131. See also Estlake, *Oneida Community*, pp. 63–64; and "Oneida Community," reprinted from the *New York Tribune* in *Oneida Circular*, n.s. 4:63.

21. Van de Warker, "Gynecological Study," p. 790. See also ibid., p. 792.

22. Ibid., p. 789. For the more conservative estimate, see "Anita N. McGee's Interviews." Dr. George E. Cragin gave an estimated average frequency of intercourse of two to four times per week (ibid.).

23. The information on male and female ages at the beginning of active sexual experience is from "Anita N. McGee's Interviews" and is attributed to Mrs. Herrick. Although Mrs. Herrick seems to have considered the age of puberty for males to have been about seventeen years, physicians of the day established the age at fourteen or fifteen (see George H. Napheys, *The Transmission of Life*, p. 21). Knowlton, *Fruits of Philosophy*, established the same age for feminine puberty (p. 23); it seems likely, though, that girls would have reached puberty between twelve and fourteen in the nineteenth century.

24. See the statement of Mrs. Herrick in "Anita N. McGee's Interviews"; and Van de Warker, "Gynecological Study," p. 789. See also "Mills among the Girls," *Oneida Circular*, n.s. 1:354. Late in the history of Oneida, Noyes realized that young girls "desired amativeness expressed by companionship, kissing, embracing, &c. but that intercourse was only indifferent or repugnant," so he raised the ages for female sexual initiation. Individual development became the primary criterion. See "Anita N. McGee's Interviews." The change probably came in the 1870s. Cf. Noyes's statement of 1865, which reiterates the doctrine of the earliest possible sexual experience, in *Oneida Circular*, n.s. 1:355.

25. F. W. Frankland to Anita N. McGee, New York, 13 June 1894. See also *Third Annual Report*, p. 19. Ideologically, there was no urgent need to control love in the ascending direction. In fact, because the flow of vital energy or "magnetic force" was from superior to inferior ("interior" to "exterior"), whether in a physical or a spiritual relationship, one could only truly "let oneself go" without fear of loss or desiccation in an "ascending" relationship. The danger lay in "descending" relationships (from the male point of view, *all* male-female relations), which had to be carefully controlled.

26. Quoted in Van de Warker, "Gynecological Study," pp. 790–91. See also "Women in the Commune," *Oneida Circular*, n.s. 3:109.

27. "Interview of Dr. Hilda Noyes, Sept., 1926, by Robert L. Dickinson," in his Notes on the Oneida Community, p. 3. See also: Van de Warker, "Gynecological Study," pp. 803–4; and Estlake, *Oneida Community*, pp. 54–55.

28. "Anita N. McGee's Interviews." This Oneida practice recalls the medieval custom of the *jus primae noctis*, which provided for the deflowering of a new bride by the feudal lord. The practice seems to have been fairly common in medieval Europe; it was known

as *jus cunni* in France, *marchette* in England, and *cazzagio* in the Piedmont. It appears to have been the survival of a very ancient cultural rite that occurred in many widely scattered cultures and was connected with the widespread male fear of intercourse, especially with a virgin. This fear derived from a belief that the violated maiden would retaliate, or perhaps from the ancient blood taboo (which identified the maiden blood with malignant, impure menstrual blood). Male fear of offending the essence of femininity found expression in mythic cycles focusing on the themes of the "poison damsel" (see Nathaniel Hawthorne's "Rappaccini's Daughter") and the "vagina dentata" (see the Waspishiana and Taruma Indian legends). Taboos of separation of the sexes seem to derive from the same source. A milder form of the *jus primae noctis* is found in many cultures, which forbid the consummation of a marriage for a certain stipulated period. The fear of abridging virginity is again underscored, because invariably the taboo on intercourse lasts longer if the woman is a virgin than if she is a widow. The ancient roots of this cultural manifestation go back to a period before mankind practiced systematic agriculture. In hunting and gathering societies, man had to learn which plants were poisonous and to be avoided and which were to be used for food. Strangers or specially appointed tribesmen seem to have been employed in this often fatal process of experimentation. Out of this background arose the almost universal rites associated with the "first fruits," which were dedicated to the gods or ancestors in order to propitiate either evil influences within the vegetal products themselves or the deities who were responsible for their growth. A direct connection between the floral and faunal worlds is perceptible in the mythic tradition that maintains that certain plants spring from human blood and house the spirits of the dead. The transition from plant lore to blood taboo is clear here. The survival of this ancient tradition is clear in the practice of the *jus primae noctis* and in the fear of the virgin female that lies behind it. On the *jus primae noctis*, see G. Rattray Taylor, *Sex in History* (New York: Vanguard Press, 1954), p. 31; Ernest Crawley, *The Mystic Rose* (New York: Meridian Books, 1924), 1:230–38, 2:66–95; Edward A. Westermarck, *The History of Human Marriage* (London: Macmillan and Co., 1921), 1:166–95; and Sigmund Freud, "The Taboo of Virginity." On the mythic conceptions surrounding the "poison damsel" and the "vagina dentata" see Wolfgang Lederer, *The Fear of Women*, chap. 6, "A Snapping of Teeth," and chap. 7, "Poison Damsels and Other Lethal Ladies"; Robert Gessain, "'Vagina Dentata' dans la Clinique et la Mythologie," *Psychoanalyse* 3 (1957): 247–95; and N. M. Penzer, *Poison Damsels* (London: Chas. J. Sawyer, 1952). On "first fruits," see James G. Frazer, *The Golden Bough* (London: Macmillan and Co., 1955), 3:5, 21; 4:102; 5:280, n. 1; 6:191; 7:235; 8:6, 48–137. On plants springing from human blood, see T. F. Thiselton-Dyer, *The Folk-Lore of Plants* (London: Chatto & Windus, 1889), pp. 10–17, 309–11.

29. "Anita N. McGee's Interviews."
30. Testimony of Dr. G. E. Cragin and Mrs. Herrick, respectively, quoted in ibid.
31. Testimony of G. E. Cragin, quoted in ibid.
32. Noyes, *Essay on Scientific Propagation*, appendix, "Report on Nervous Diseases," p. 31. Ironically, male continence from this perspective is the ultimate in autoeroticism. By reserving the semen that is *internally* secreted through sexual stimulation during intercourse, the male in a sense impregnates himself.
33. Testimony of Dr. Cragin in "Anita N. McGee's Interviews." Reference to the limitation of intercourse to 10:00–12:00 P.M. is found in Dickinson, Notes on the Oneida Community, p. 1.
34. Evidence of Dr. T. R. Noyes, in Dickinson, Notes on the Oneida Community, p. 3.
35. Ibid.
36. Ibid.
37. For presumptive evidence of nudity and illumination during sex acts, see Noyes's

comments in *Bible Communism*, p. 61; and "Shaker Communism," *Oneida Circular*, n.s. 3:74.
38. Van de Warker, "Gynecological Study," tab. 1, "Antecedent Conditions," p. 795.
39. Ibid.
40. Quoted in ibid., p. 789.
41. Quoted in "Anita N. McGee's Interviews."
42. Ibid.
43. Ibid. See also Noyes, *Home Talks*, p. 257, an address called "Old Age Played Out."
44. "Anita N. McGee's Interviews." On the "surplus" attention allotted some women, see "Woman in the Commune," *Oneida Circular*, n.s. 3:109; "Success a Duty," ibid., p. 117; and the criticism of Mrs. "R.," ibid., 26 Mar. 1863, quoted in Robertson, *Autobiography*, p. 142.
45. Dickinson, Notes on the Oneida Community. In the testimony of Dr. Cragin in "Anita N. McGee's Interviews," the danger of "exhaustion" is given as the reason for the temporal limitation of intercourse.
46. Reference to the condemnation of lesbianism at Oneida is found in Dickinson, Notes on the Oneida Community. A current study of homoerotic sexuality published under the auspices of the Kinsey Institute contends that the lesbian experience emphasizes emotional closeness rather than genital sexuality. See Alan P. Bell and Martin S. Weinberg, *Homosexualities*, pp. 69–72, 93–102, 113–15, 217–28.
47. Data collated from Eleanor Meyers, "Oneida Community"; Anita N. McGee, "An Experiment in Human Stirpiculture," author's personal annotated copy, p. 392; *First Annual Report*, p. 1; "Oneida Association Family Register"; Noyes, *Putney Community*, pp. 390–93; [C. A. W.] "Community Journal" (1864), pp. 31–36; Charles Nordhoff, *The Communistic Societies of the United States*, pp. 262–64; John Humphrey Noyes, *History of American Socialisms*, p. 641; Hinds, *American Communities*, p. 121; and *Oneida Circular*, 13 Mar. 1867 and 21 Nov. 1870, quoted in Robertson, *Autobiography*, pp. 162–63, 89.
48. See Dickinson, Notes on the Oneida Community. The use of condoms by men was specifically denied. Abortion was not practiced at the community, either. See Van de Warker, "Gynecological Study," p. 790; and "The Oneida Community: Its Motives Pure," *Oneida Circular*, n.s. 4;167.
49. Figures derived from Noyes, *Putney Community*, pp. 390–93; "Oneida Association Family Register"; and Meyers, "Oneida Community," pp. 193–210. The decline in the percentage of married couples at Oneida was attested to by Theodore R. Noyes, who claimed in 1880 that prior to the breakup of the community, only twenty-five couples were married. This was about 23 percent of the total adult population. Cf. McGee, "An Experiment," p. 324.
50. *Oneida Circular*, 6 June 1870, quoted in Robertson, *Autobiography*, pp. 88–89. The shift to separate rooms for most community members was a function of both the increasing affluence of the community and its changing demographic composition under the system of stirpiculture. In the very beginning of Oneida life (1849), with the erection of the original Mansion House, domiciliary arrangements had resembled those in Shaker communities. On the third story of the central community building were the sleeping apartments for married couples and single females; the garret provided lodging space for the unmarried males and young boys (*First Annual Report*, p. 5). By 1855, Oneidans admitted that they were overcrowded, but felt that lack of space provided an ideological advantage: "Smallness of space has served as a compress on excessive individuality" (*Oneida Circular*, 25 Oct. 1855, quoted in Robertson, *Autobiography*, p. 33). Building expansion allowed more individuals to have rooms of their own, in accordance with their enunciated principle: "We believe in the right of retirement as one of the most

sacred rights of existence" (*Oneida Circular*, 6 June 1870), quoted in Robertson, *Autobiography*, p. 88. The fact that about one person in five regularly shared a bed with someone else, however, indicates that conditions of crowding persisted at Oneida throughout its history. Mrs. Herrick testified that the "number of rooms per person varied according to space at command" ("Anita N. McGee's Interviews"). Personal taste and disposition also played a part in the assignment of rooms, for we are told that most individuals in 1870 had separate bedrooms "as far as agreeable." Perhaps those who wished to mortify their selfishness most completely, or those who (like the lesbian couples referred to above) preferred the company of the same sex, chose to have roommates.

51. Statement of Mrs. Herrick in "Anita N. McGee's Interviews."

52. On the intensity of the propagative relationship, and the allowance of "exclusive cohabitation" for reproduction in some cases, see A. N. McGee to J. B. Herrick, Washington, D.C., 6 Aug. 1891, p. 2.

53. These "central members" seem to have been uniformly male except for a brief fifteen-month interim period from Jan. 1875 to Apr. 1876, when a Stirpicultural Committee composed of six men and six women directed the process. See Robertson, *Autobiography*, p. 339; and McGee, "An Experiment," p. 321. There appears to have been some relaxation of the rigors of the stirpicultural system toward the end. See Theodore R. Noyes to Anita N. McGee, New York City, 13 Sept. 1891, p. 10.

54. Robertson, *Autobiography*, p. 338. See also Parker, *Yankee Saint*, p. 257.

55. Robertson, *Autobiography*, p. 338; Parker, *Yankee Saint*, p. 257.

56. See [McGee], Oneida Community: Interview of R. L. D. and Mr. and Mrs. George W. Noyes; and "Anita N. McGee's Interviews."

57. Theodore R. Noyes to Anita N. McGee, 13 Sept. 1891, p. 12.

58. On Oneida doctrine concerning the arrival of the Kingdom of God, see Noyes, *Putney Community*, p. 255. In the "Battle Axe Letter," Noyes had made it quite clear that under civil law the marriage system of the world would obtain until the resurrection: "God has placed a wall of partition between male and female during the apostasy, for good reasons, which will be broken down in the resurecion [*sic*] for equally good reasons. But woe to him who abolishes the law of apostasy before he stands in the holiness of the resurecion" (MS copy). The Walls of Jericho fell in the summer of 1847. On the Puritan doctrine of the Half-Way Covenant, see Robert G. Pope, *Half-Way Covenant: Church Membership in Puritan New England* (Princeton: Princeton University Press, 1969).

59. Noyes, *Essay on Scientific Propagation*, p. 12. In view of Noyes's Oedipal relationship with his mother, the realities of Adam's family, in which only sons were born, make it interesting to speculate on how far Noyes might have carried his belief in incest as a eugenically acceptable practice. On the later concern with physical and mental qualifications of parents, see "Anita N. McGee's Interviews," statement of Dr. Cragin; and McGee, "An Experiment," p. 322. The first evidence of genealogical concern I have encountered is "A Study in Genealogy," *American Socialist* 2:122.

60. McGee, "An Experiment," p. 321. Noyes himself noted that "breeding in and in means incest" (*Essay on Scientific Propagation*, p. 10).

61. See "Anita N. McGee's Interviews"; and McGee, "An Experiment," p. 322, marginal notes. Noyes himself fathered eight of the "stirpicults."

62. See Noyes, *Essay on Scientific Propagation*, appendix, "Report on Nervous Diseases," p. 31; and [McGee], Oneida Community: Interview of R. L. D. and Mr. and Mrs. George W. Noyes. In the latter, Anita N. McGee estimates that the timing of intercourse for mating couples at Oneida would have allowed sex only *after* the period of maximum fertility, almost in "the so-called 'safe period.'" On the permission of all males to have one child, see Noyes, *My Father's House*, p. 10.

63. From the *Oneida Circular*, 29 Jan. 1863, quoted in Robertson, *Autobiography*, p. 319. See also Theodore R. Noyes, "Children in the Oneida Community," *American Socialist* 4 (1879): 45; McGee, "An Experiment," p. 322; "Anita N. McGee's Interviews"; and *Hand Book of the Oneida Community*, p. 21.

64. *First Annual Report*, p. 11. See also *Mutual Criticism*, p. 18. Significantly, Noyes himself was never criticized. See Theodore R. Noyes to Anita N. McGee, 13 Sept. 1891, p. 2.

65. *First Annual Report*, p. 49. See also the statements of George W. Noyes and Susan C. Hamilton (ibid., p. 51), which also indicate the acceptance of complex marriage through the exercise of mutual criticism. The term "narcotic love" occurs in "Essay on Love," *Oneida Circular*, n.s. 4:410.

66. [C. A. W.], "Community Journal" (1863), p. 5, entry for 5 Jan.

67. Ibid., p. 12, entry for 24 Jan.

68. Ibid. (1864), p. 13, entry for 17 Feb. See also ibid. (1863), p. 34, entry for 12 May, case of Mrs. "S. B." and Mr. "D."; and *Daily Journal of the Oneida Community* 1, no. 1 (14 Jan. 1866): 44. On separation of "special" couples, see also Carden, *Oneida*, pp. 58–60; Noyes, *My Father's House*, pp. 8–9; and [C. A. W.], "Community Journal" (1864), entry for 27 Aug. p. 66.

69. *Oneida Circular*, n.s. 1:52.

70. "Anita N. McGee's Interviews."

71. Quoted in Van de Warker, "Gynecological Study," p. 790. See also *Oneida Circular* n.s. 2 (1865–66): 116.

72. John H. Noyes to Harriet H. Skinner re John H. Miller, ca. 1 Aug. 1846, reprinted in G. W. Noyes, *Putney Community*, p. 202.

73. Noyes, *Putney Community*, p. 51.

74. *Oneida Circular*, n.s. 3:317.

75. Quoted in Robertson, *Oneida Community Profiles*, p. 91.

76. Ibid., p. 88. The letter was written by George Cragin. Essentially, the problem with Keziah seems to have been her dominance over her husband, her refusal to play a subordinate female role. Leander had a reputation at Oneida for "lacking manliness." He seems generally to have been a failure, economically and socially. He was among the group who "accidentally" fathered children at Oneida (ibid., p. 91).

77. Ibid., pp. 91–92. The date for their expulsion is given on p. 92.

78. "The Human Parasite," *Oneida Circular*, n.s. 1:274; "Mills among the Girls," ibid., p. 354. For full coverage of the episode, see ibid., pp. 274–89, 290, 314, 353–55. Presumably, Mills had raised the young girls' romantic expectations and thus rendered them less submissive to Noyes's personal claims to their maidenheads.

79. Ibid., 3:158. See also Noyes, *Putney Community*, pp. 42–43. For additional cases of this type, see ibid., pp. 140–44, 384.

80. Quoted in Robertson, *Oneida Community Profiles*, p. 87.

81. Ibid. This case of shunning recalls Noyes's alienation of the affections of his siblings from his mother in order to break her resistance to his religious and moral authority (see above, Introduction to Part IV).

82. Collated from Meyers, "Oneida Community," pp. 193–210. This was the case despite a great rise in the influx of new members—from 6.4 to 9.6 persons per annum. The lower figures for the earlier period may also reflect a higher retention rate for community members owing to an unwillingness of some people to leave Oneida during the uncertainties and dislocation of the Civil War. At least they were safe within the confines of the community, even if they were not always happy.

83. The final decision of the community to abandon complex marriage and "Bible Communism" and to divide into a joint-stock corporation was partly the result of a process of internal autocatalytic fissioning brought about by the activities of one J. W. Towner.

Towner and a group of his followers who entered Oneida with him had been at the free-love commune at Berlin Heights, Ohio, and attempted to establish an alternative power locus at Oneida. Towner demanded government by committee. An Administrative Council was accordingly established, and on 22 June 1879, Noyes left the community for Niagara Falls. The Agreement to Divide and Reorganize was adopted 31 Aug. 1880. Thus, the end of the unique system of sexuality and of economic communism was to some extent the result of the failure of central control. (See Anita N. McGee to J. B. Herrick, with his answers, Washington, D.C., 6 Aug. 1891, p. 1; and Theodore R. Noyes to Anita N. McGee, 13 Sept. 1891, pp. 3–9.)

84. The phrase is from "Murder of the Unborn," *Oneida Circular*, n.s. 4:58.

85. These phrases are from a community hymn quoted in Nordhoff, *Communistic Societies*, p. 299. "Love among the Angels" was the title of a poem printed in the *Oneida Circular*, n.s. 1:397. Noyes himself realized the pressure his system placed upon the individual, especially under stirpiculture. See his statement that "breeding from the best means *intolerable* discrimination—*suppression* for some, and large liberty for others" (*Essay on Scientific Propagation*, p. 10; my emphasis).

Chapter 13

1. Dixon, *New America*, p. 422.

2. Quoted in Eastman, *Noyesism Unveiled*, p. 295. Among contemporary students of communitarian movements, Rosabeth Moss Kanter has argued that Oneida provided substantial gains in rights and status for women. She considers women's position in nineteenth-century communal societies more equitable than in contemporary "hippie communes." (See "Family Organization and Sex Roles in American Communes," pp. 287–305, in her *Communes: Creating and Managing the Collective Life*.) On the other hand, Patrick W. Conover, "An Analysis of Communes and Intentional Communities with Particular Attention to Sexual and Genderal Relations," maintains that nineteenth-century communes were less successful than their twentieth-century counterparts in achieving gender equality (p. 462). My own feeling is that *neither* communal movement has been notably successful, or even ideologically consistent, in its pursuit of sexual equality.

3. "Community Housework," *Oneida Circular*, n.s. 4 (1867–68): 342–43.

4. On the operation of the laundry and laborsaving devices, see *Hand Book of the Oneida Community*, pp. 10, 13; and "Community Work," *Oneida Circular*, n.s. 4:351. On hired women, see *Oneida Circular*, 1 Oct. 1863 and 30 Mar. 1868, quoted in Robertson, *Autobiography*, pp. 226, 296.

5. *Oneida Circular*, n.s. 4:355. Male reaction to housecleaning can be found in the *Daily Journal of the Oneida Community* 1 (1866): 230.

6. On overworked women, see *Oneida Circular*, 9 July 1863, quoted in Robertson, *Autobiography*, p. 71. On 4 July 1863, 1,500 to 2,000 people visited the Oneida Community. See also "Mills among the Girls," *Oneida Circular*, n.s. 1 (1864–65): 354.

7. Reference to the sewing machine is on pp. 15–16 of *Bible Communism*. In the *Hand Book of the Oneida Community*, see pp. 10, 13. In the bakery, the large oven was operated by a man, too.

8. Nordhoff, *Communistic Societies*, p. 263.

9. See *First Annual Report*, p. 7; Noyes, *My Father's House*, pp. 47, 78, 90; and Robertson, *Autobiography*, p. 325.

10. [C. A. W.], "Community Journal" (1864), entry for 26 Jan.

11. *Oneida Circular*, n.s. 4:355. See also ibid., 7 Dec. 1868, quoted in Robertson, *Autobiography*, p. 306.

12. Data collated from New York State Census, Town of Lennox, Madison County, 1855, 1865, and 1875, as reproduced in Meyers, "Oneida Community"; and *Oneida Circular*, 15 Mar. 1867, quoted in Robertson, *Autobiography*, p. 304.

13. "Financial Report for 1868," *Oneida Circular*, 11 Jan. 1869, quoted in Robertson, *Autobiography*, p. 255. In 1874 there were seventy-five hired women and girls working in the Oneida silk factory and another thirty-five working in the subsidiary establishment at the branch community in Wallingford, Conn. (see Nordhoff, *Communistic Societies*, p. 263).

14. *Oneida Circular*, n.s. 5 (1868–69): 39, article signed "K."

15. Ibid.

16. Nordhoff, *Communistic Societies*, p. 263. This fear of contamination by "worldlings" extended to children as well. Pierrepont Noyes recalled that community children were forbidden to even talk to hired men, or "outsiders" (see *My Father's House*, p. 25). Clearly, for women, the problem of contamination was a combination of the factory environment (considered particularly masculine by Oneidans) and the increased potential for the interaction of pure Oneida females with vulgar male "outsiders." The fact that there were hired *male* servants working in household-related areas did not seem to disturb (male) Oneidans' sensibilities. Domestic labor was the female sphere, and Oneida men did not want to be employed there. On the other hand, as a peculiarly feminine realm, domestic employment would presumably work to the improvement of male hired hands, whereas the masculine factory environment would work to the detriment of Oneida womanhood. The ideological acceptance of traditionally ascriptive sex-role tasks is clear here.

17. On the equal-pay doctrine, see "A Worldly Example," *Oneida Circular*, n.s. 4:234.

18. See *Oneida Circular*, 5 Jan. 1874, quoted in Robertson, *Autobiography*, p. 310. See also *Oneida Circular*, 10 Feb. 1873, in ibid., p. 308.

19. *Oneida Circular*, 26 May 1859, quoted in Robertson, *Autobiography*, p. 341.

20. *Oneida Circular*, 10 Jan. 1870, quoted in Robertson, *Autobiography*, p. 345.

21. *Oneida Circular*, n.s. 4: 62; ibid., 8 Apr. 1867 and 10 Feb. 1873, in Robertson, *Autobiography*, pp. 244–45, 308–9. The woman who edited the *Circular* was Harriet M. Worden.

22. *Oneida Circular*, n.s. 1:20. On bookkeepers, see Meyers, "Oneida Community." According to the 1875 New York State Census, three of eight women in the business and office category were employed as bookkeepers in that year. There is no record of female bookkeepers before the 1870s.

23. [C. A. W.], "Community Journal" (1864), p. 25, entry for 24 Mar. See also ibid. (1863), p. 41, entry for 1 June.

24. *Oneida Circular*, 6 Mar. 1866, in Robertson, *Autobiography*, p. 302. Cf. *Daily Journal of the Oneida Community* (1867), entries for 3 and 26 July, quoted in Robertson, *Autobiography*, pp. 202–3.

25. *Oneida Circular*, 18 Jan. 1875, in Robertson, *Autobiography*, pp. 170–71.

26. Extract from the notebook of Harriet Noyes, reprinted in the *Oneida Circular*, n.s. 3 (1866–67): 295.

27. *Mutual Criticism*. pp. 49–50.

28. Ibid., p. 54. Leander Worden, it will be remembered, had the opposite problem (see Chapter 12, at n. 75, above). Henry Seymour, husband of Tryphena, had similar difficulties stemming from the failure of an assertive masculinity (see Chapter 12 above; and Constance N. Robertson, *Oneida Community Profiles*, pp. 87–88).

29. *First Annual Report*, p. 43. The term "leap-year spirit" was used in criticism of girls and young women in 1864. Cf. [C. A. W.], "Community Journal" (1864), p. 57, entry for 18 July. Significantly, men who might have been considered to have too much of the feminine in their characters (like Henry Seymour and Leander Worden) were criticized

for "lacking manliness." Women, on the other hand, were criticized for usurping the male role, *not* for lacking *femaleness.*

30. "A Hint to Parents," *Perfectionist and Theocratic Watchman* 5 (1845–46): 14.

31. "Woman's Slavery to Children," *Spiritual Magazine* 1 (1846): 110. The scriptural reference here is to Eph. 5:22–24. For a statement by a young mother who found the system liberating, see *Oneida Circular*, 23 June 1873, in Robertson, *Autobiography*, p. 354.

32. *Oneida Circular*, 5 Nov. 1863, quoted in Robertson, *Autobiography*, p. 320.

33. During Pierrepont Noyes's childhood (the 1870s), "Pappa" William Kelley was the head of the Children's Department. He saw to it that the children marched to the dining hall in an orderly two-by-two formation. Kelley was responsible for the discipline and whipping of disobedient or insubordinate children.

34. *Oneida Circular*, 19 Oct. 1874, quoted in Robertson, *Autobiography*, p. 332. For additional attacks on motherhood, see [C. A. W.], "Community Journal" (1863), p. 73, entry for 22 Oct.; and ibid., (1864), p. 43, entry for 27 May.

35. Robertson, *Autobiography*, p. 332.

36. Ibid., p. 333.

37. See *Oneida Circular*, 15 June 1868, in ibid., pp. 323–24.

38. Frank Wayland Smith to John H. Noyes, 19 July 1879, quoted in Robertson, *Oneida Community: The Breakup*, pp. 128–33. The portion cited in the text is from pp. 130, 132. For further corroboration of this attitude, see Frank W. Smith's journal entry for 5 Feb. 1879, quoted in ibid., pp. 91–92.

39. *Oneida Circular*, 4 Nov. 1872, quoted in Robertson, *Autobiography*, p. 308.

40. See *Oneida Circular*, n.s. 4:167; Noyes, *My Father's House*, p. 29; and *Daily Journal of the Oneida Community* 1 (1866): 286.

41. Noyes's debt to Paul is clear in his theological tract *The Berean.* Sec. 21, "Paul's View of the Law," pp. 203–16, establishes the basis for Oneida Perfectionism. In the key passage for Perfectionist thought, Rom., chap. 7, the fulcrum of the argument involves marriage law. Sec. 42, "Marriage," pp. 431–40, discusses the sexual question more directly. Pauline doctrine is specifically discussed on pp. 434–35. See also [John Humphrey Noyes], *Paul's Prize.*

42. Quoted in Van de Warker, "Gynecological Study," p. 789.

43. Anita N. McGee, "Oneida Community History, Aug., 1891," p. 2. See also J. W. Towner to Anita N. McGee, Santa Ana, Calif., 1 Nov. 1894.

44. Anita N. McGee to Theodore R. Noyes, Washington, D.C., 12 Nov. 1891, p. 2.

45. *Hand Book of the Oneida Community*, p. 27.

46. Ibid.

47. George W. Noyes, *Putney Community*, p. 109. Cf. the statement that the Oneida Community did not believe in the equality of men and women in *Hand Book of the Oneida Community*, p. 29.

48. *Oneida Circular*, n.s. 2:3.

49. *American Socialist* 1 (1876): 103.

50. Ibid. 3 (1878): 165, article signed "G. C. [George Cragin?]." See also ibid., p. 159; *Oneida Circular*, 29 Jan. 1866, in Robertson, *Autobiography*, p. 302; and Noyes, *Berean*, pp. 19, 51, 412.

51. On the salvation of women by men's grace, see Noyes, *Way of Holiness*, p. 226.

52. *American Socialist* 1:19.

53. *Oneida Circular*, 1 Jan. 1874, quoted in Robertson, *Autobiography*, p. 297. See also "Suffrage for Women," *Oneida Circular*, n.s. 3:77.

54. *Third Annual Report* (1851), p. 27.

55. On divorce attitudes, see *Bible Communism*, p. 84; *Oneida Circular*, n.s. 3:1–2, 4:87, 95; and ibid., 1 Jan. 1853, in Robertson, *Autobiography*, p. 279.

56. *Oneida Circular*, 23 Jan. 1858, quoted in Robertson, *Autobiography*, p. 300. See also *Oneida Circular*, 18 Mar. 1872, in ibid., p. 284.

57. See *American Socialist* 1:30; *Oneida Circular*, n.s. 1:75; and [C. A. W.], "Community Journal" (1864), p. 54 entry for 6 July.

58. See Oneida Community, Ltd. Laundry List; *Oneida Circular*, n.s. 5:12; and *Oneida Circular*, 10 Jan. 1870 and 3 Apr. 1871, in Robertson, *Autobiography*, pp. 306–8. In part the Oneida prohibition on corsets and other common feminine undergarments paralleled contemporary admonitions against tight lacing in advice manuals of the day. The Oneida argument, however, grew out of community ideology which held that tight lacing of corsets tended to constrict the heart and thus to dry up the amative propensities of women. On the other hand, because the heart was considered the seat of the will at Oneida, constriction of that organ rendered women incapable of adult self-control. See "The Smothered Heart," *Oneida Circular*, n.s. 4:140.

"Palpitating bosoms" was probably a reference to what in the twentieth century came to be called "falsies." "Bosom" was used specifically to refer to the space between the breast and its covering, and after 1849, "to palpitate" meant "to vibrate or quiver." The intent of the device was to give the impression of the presence of full, firm breasts. "Heavers" most likely was a reference to either a brassiere with a powerful upward and forward thrust or, again, a heavily padded one ("heavers" was a slang term referring to the breasts from the seventeenth to the nineteenth century). "Plumpers" were devices of whalebone used to expand the skirt at the hips, to give the impression of greater girth. "False calves" is self-explanatory. (See *Oxford English Dictionary*, and Eric Partridge, *Dictionary of Slang and Unconventional English*.) For a recent discussion of the development of fashion in lingerie and feminine undergarments, see Elizabeth Ewing, *Dress and Undress*, or the more popular treatment in *The Undies Book* (New York: Scribners, 1976), by Nanette Rothacker.

59. *Oneida Circular*, n.s. 5:12.

60. Cf. Elisabeth McClellan, *History of American Costume*. J. C. Flügel has commented on the way in which the crinoline fashion was a symbol of female domination: see his *The Psychology of Clothes*, p. 47.

61. "About Dress," *Oneida Circular*, n.s. 1:148. See also *Bible Communism*, pp. 61–62; and "Oneida Short Dress," *Oneida Circular*, n.s. 3:13.

62. See Maggie Angeloglou, *A History of Make-up*, pp. 96–100; and Richard Corson, *Fashions in Makeup from Ancient to Modern Times*, pp. 318–50.

63. See Richard Corson, *Fashions in Hair: The First Five Thousand Years* (New York: Hastings House, 1965), for illustrations.

64. McClellan, *History of American Costume*, p. 486. This fashion would have been doubly obnoxious to Oneida ideology because it employed masses of artificial hair. A frame of horse hair was attached to the back of the head by an elastic device, the back hair was brushed smoothly over this base, and the ends were caught up underneath the frame. In view of Oneida reworking of phrenological doctrines of sexuality, such a mode of dressing the hair would have been rejected as applying too much pressure and generating excessive heat in those parts of the brain in which the sexual instinct had its seat. To allow such a fashion of hairdressing, in their minds, would only render female sexuality more uncontrollable than it already was.

65. This account of the beginnings of the short-hair fashion is found in the *First Annual Report*, p. 9. Cf. 1 Cor. 11:4–14. For a more detailed account of "amativeness" and the cerebellum, see O. S. Fowler, *Human Science; or, Phrenology* (Philadelphia: National Publishing Co., 1873), pp. 679–86.

66. *Bible Communism*, p. 62.

67. *Oneida Circular*, n.s. 5:77. For additional comments on the shoe question, see *Oneida Circular*, 15 Feb. 1855 and 30 Nov. 1868, in Robertson, *Autobiography*, pp. 299, 306.

The former reference specifically mandates shoe reform "if women wish to get rid of effeminacy."
68. Noyes, *Home Talks*, address entitled "Hygiene for the Head," p. 93. The mysticism evident in the community was reflected in the religious experience of Noyes himself. Cf. Noyes, *Confessions*, pp. 13, 37, 62–63.
69. The report on the old man's discomfort is found in Dickinson, Notes on the Oneida Community. On the eradication of pain and discomfort by sheer willpower, see "The Use of Anaesthetics in Dentistry," *Oneida Circular*, 6 Aug. 1866, and *Oneida Circular*, 17 Feb. 1873, both quoted in Robertson, *Autobiography*, pp. 162, 169; Noyes, *Confessions*, pp. 62–63; and *Bible Communism*, p. 18.
70. Cf. Noyes's use of Mark 4:26–29 in *The Berean*, p. 251. For the psychological basis of this fear, see Ferenczi, *Thalassa*, pp. 17–18.
71. *Oneida Circular*, n.s. 4:62. See also *Witness* 1, no. 2, quoted in Eastman, *Noyesism Unveiled*, pp. 117–19.
72. "A Plea for Communism," *Oneida Circular*, n.s. 4:286.
73. See Noyes, *Confessions*, p. 39; and *Perfectionist* 2 (1835): 8.
74. "Self-Denial," *Spiritual Magazine* 1:68. Though it might appear that the article refers to man in the generic sense, the scriptural citation accompanying the article dispels this belief. Matt. 10:37–39 is cited, the context of which is the injunction of Christ to his disciples to "take up the cross." See also Noyes's reading of Swedenborgianism in its use of "man" in a similar way in *The Berean,* p. 87.
75. J. H. Noyes to his mother, Milford, 9 Sept. 1835, quoted in Noyes, *Religious Experience*, pp. 234–35.
76. We have already commented on the male orientation of male continence and stirpiculture. Significantly, the very terms used to describe the sexual arrangement indicate this. "Male continence" is self-evident in this regard. The term "stirpiculture," however, which comes from the Latin root "stirps," meaning "root" or "stock," may also mean the generation and raising of *male* offspring. When we recall the relative weight attached to male and female in the genetic transferal of traits, can we doubt that this was the tacit intention of the system? Interestingly enough, that is the way the system worked, too: of the fifty-six children who survived infancy (all the result of stirpicultural reproduction), thirty-two, or 57 percent, were male, and twenty-four, or 43 percent, were female (see McGee, "An Experiment," p. 322, marginal notes).
77. The ambivalence of the elder generation about community sexuality is indicated by the decision to discontinue the Oneida sexual experiment in Aug. 1879. Theodore R. Noyes tells us that, with the sole abstention of William A. Hinds, "NO ONE VOTED TO CONTINUE COMPLEX MARRIAGE. . . . SEVERAL MEMBERS HAD CEASED TO PRACTICE COMPLEX MARRIAGE MONTHS BEFORE" (Noyes to Anita N. McGee, 13 Sept. 1891, p. 9). Furthermore, as Maren Carden has pointed out, there had been no stirpicultural matings since the latter part of 1878, nearly a year earlier (*Oneida*, p. 103).
78. See Noyes, *My Father's House*, p. 267.

Chapter 14

1. Robert E. Riegel, "Changing American Attitudes toward Prostitution (1800–1920)." See also Arthur A. Ekirch, *The Idea of Progress in America, 1815–1860* (New York: Columbia University Press, 1944), pp. 132–65, 252–67.
2. See Riegel, "Changing American Attitudes," p. 443; and Robert H. MacDonald, "The Frightful Consequences of Onanism: Notes on the History of a Delusion," *Journal of the History of Ideas* 28 (1967): 423–31.

3. See Stone, *Family, Sex and Marriage*, pp. 8–9, 320–24; Douglas, *Feminization*, pp. 8–15; and Welter, "The Cult of True Womanhood."

4. On the concept of covert culture, see Bernard Bowron, Leo Marx, and Arnold Rose, "Literature and Covert Culture," *American Quarterly* 9 (Winter 1957): 377–86; and Arnold M. Rose, *Theory and Method in the Social Sciences* (Minneapolis: University of Minnesota Press, 1954), chap. 21, "Popular Logic in the Study of Covert Culture." The Bowron, Marx, and Rose article specifically calls attention to covert responses to sexuality in relation to the Kinsey Report (p. 377).

5. Napheys, *Transmission of Life*, p. 177. The passage is full of theological overtones. Tantalus is the prototypical Adamic figure, a demigod who revealed the secrets of the gods to men. He was responsible for the original sin (erotic sexuality in this context), punishment for which is visited upon his descendants. And yet it was Tantalus, according to Pindar, who brought to earth the delights of paradise—the nectar and ambrosia of the gods. There is a Christian echo of the paradisiacal state in the reference to the "beaker ever filled" (Ps. 23:5). The connection between divine inebriation and sexual pleasure is also made clear on this level of the passage. The negative connotations here imply that the seeker after sexual pleasure is as much an addict as the alcoholic inebriate. On another level, Tantalus was reputed (according to Diodorus Siculus) to have killed his son, Pelops, cut him up, and served him to the gods. In the context, this may be an oblique reference to abortion or infanticide. Regardless of the negative allusions in the passage, which in any case are offset by a primitive Edenic eroticism, the final sentence concedes the impotence of Victorian romanticism and the power of the true woman to restrain elemental sexuality. The covert expression of the male's inability to control his sex drive without external coercion (Tantalus is supposed to have been, in one version of the myth, immured beneath Mt. Sipylus or, more commonly, plunged into the River Hades up to his chin) is clear in this passage. Marriage only tempts to excess, so it too is an ineffectual means of restraint. The mechanism of restraint must be external to the individual, to marriage, or to the family. That mechanism, it would appear, is the ideological structure of spermatic economy, or sexual temperance. Napheys's misgivings about that ideology's effectiveness are also suggested on the metaphorical level. Like Tantalus, the married man is always tempted to reach out for the fruit that social norms prescribe should only be enjoyed in moderation. The seminal fluid of the ideal husband, because retained, provides a continual reminder of a sexual indulgence he, like Tantalus, again, must continually deny himself. Thus, like Tantalus, he is at the same time restrained from, but continually tempted to, sensual delights. The temperance phrase "touch not, handle not" expressed the feeling conveyed by the Tantalus imagery applied to sexuality. On a broader social level, historians have pointed out the connection between male sexual self-control and the drive to an ordered, disciplined personality to achieve success in the marketplace. (See Smith, "Family Limitation," p. 50.) In this respect it is interesting to note that Tantalus was the son of Zeus and Pluto (Wealth), daughter of Himantes. He was the very prosperous king of Sipylus in Lydia and on intimate terms with the gods. Translating this into a general nineteenth-century context, he was successful and politically and socially powerful. That Tantalus loses all his wealth and station and finds his person physically restrained, tortured by unfulfillment, suggests that Napheys has doubts about the efficacy of personal virtue to the achievement of individual success; or, more probably, in view of the other levels of metaphorical meaning in this passage, that because unaided man is incapable of self-restraint, his potential for the legitimization of power, wealth, and success is severely limited. (On Tantalus, see E. Cobham Brewer, *A Dictionary of Phrase and Fable*; and Michael Grant and John Hazel, *Gods and Mortals in Classical Mythology* [Springfield, Mass.: G. C. Merriam Co., 1973], pp. 371–72, 377.)

6. I am excluding active reformers from the mainstream culture here. Reformers were as much a minority as were utopians, and in many ways it makes more sense to group reformers and utopians together than to subsume the former under the category of a more inclusive social unit. For a comparison of the utopian approach to reform and that of meliorative reformers, see pp. 286–87 and 298–300 above.

7. Smith, "Family Limitation," pp. 45, 53. The existence of a halcyon era when extended familial patterns prevailed seems to have been a creation of the sentimental nineteenth-century imagination. Family historians today agree, as Peter Laslett has pointed out, that the conjugal or nuclear family has been the standard familial form since the late sixteenth century (see Laslett, "The Comparative History of Household and Family," in Gordon, *American Family*, pp. 19–33). William Goode called the extended family "the classical family of Western nostalgia" (cited in ibid., p. 29). For a nineteenth-century statement of the extended family myth, and its use as a utopian, millennial panacea of reform, see Alcott, *The Young Wife*, p. 333.

8. The phrase is from George Bernard Shaw. See Daniel H. Lawrence, ed., *Bernard Shaw: Collected Letters, 1874–97* (New York: Dodd, Mead, & Co., 1965), p. 780.

9. *Testimony of Christ's Second Appearing*, p. 74.

10. *Oneida Circular*, 12 Aug. 1872, quoted in Robertson, *Autobiography*, p. 207.

11. "Woman's Influence," in *The American Book of Beauty*, ed. by "A Lady," p. 87.

12. Ibid.

13. Harriet Beecher Stowe, *Religious Studies, Sketches, and Poems* (1867; reprint ed., New York: A. M. S. Press, 1967), p. 36. My emphasis. This passage reflects the increasing feminization of Christ in the Christology of the nineteenth century.

14. Stenhouse, *"Tell It All,"* p. 343.

15. On male missionary dominance in the great era of frontier revivalism, see M'Nemar [McNemar], *Kentucky Revival*, p. 74.

16. Sigourney, *Letters to Mothers*, p. 15.

17. Cowan, *Science of a New Life*, p. 137.

18. Four witnesses were Whitmers and one was Hiram Page, who had married a Whitmer sister. The other three witnesses were Hyrum and Samuel Smith and Joseph Smith, Sr. Oliver Cowdery, one of the original three witnesses (who saw the pristine plates before a second revelation was vouchsafed for the eight additional witnesses), married another Whitmer sister, Elizabeth, in 1832.

19. Shaker figures collated from the *Shaker Manifesto* 8 (1878): 68; "Original Covenant of North Union, Ohio," reproduced in MacLean, *Society of Shakers*, p. 39; Avery, Register of Incidents and Events, pp. 98–225; and Dyer, *Rise and Progress of the Serpent*. Oneida material collated from Meyers, "Oneida Community."

20. Noyes, *Home Talks*, p. 310.

21. Ibid., p. 311.

22. See "Best Friend of Family Affection," *American Socialist* 3 (1878): 348.

23. Ibid.

24. Quoted in Stenhouse, *"Tell It All,"* p. 65. Indeed, the centrality of genealogical study to Mormonism is revealed in the vast literature on families and the intense interest in preserving family records. For a description of the steel and waterproof concrete-lined bunker sunken eight hundred feet beneath a solid granite slab, capable of withstanding the severest nuclear explosion, which serves as the genealogical storehouse of the Mormon church, see Kephart, *Extraordinary Groups*, p. 223.

25. *Testimony of Christ's Second Appearing*, p. 503. Of fourteen families that entered the Watervliet, N.Y., society in the years 1800–1803, the average number of family members was nearly 8.5. Only ten individuals, or 8 percent of the total entrants, came without other family members (see *Shaker Manifesto* 8 [1878]: 68).

26. *Shaker and Shakeress* 3 (1873): 27.
27. Daniel Fraser, *A Letter Touching Important Principles*, p. 5.
28. *Shaker and Shakeress* 4 (1874): 13.
29. Avery, *Sketches of Shakers*, p. 20.
30. Ibid.
31. *Investigator; or, A Defence of the Order, Government and Economy of the United Society Called Shakers against Sundry Charges and Legislative Proceedings*, p. 10.
32. Wickliffe, *The Shakers: Speech*, p. 18.
33. Ibid., p. 17. My emphasis. The bill was subsequently (1832) declared unconstitutional in the Kentucky Circuit Court (see ibid., p. 2). New York State passed a bill entitled An Act in Relation to Certain Trusts (15 Apr. 1839), which sought to regularize the heritable transmission of community property through a succession of Shaker trustees and at the same time limit the economic activities of these societies. Again, Shakers were placed between the individual (by joint inheritance) and the corporation (by the limitation of their economic resources by law). See *New York Legislative Assembly Committee on the Subject of the Shakers*, p. 10.
34. Wickliffe, *The Shakers: Speech*, pp. 13–14.
35. Albert E. Bergh, ed., *Grover Cleveland: Addresses, State Papers and Letters* (New York: Sun Dial Classics, 1908), p. 73.
36. C. P. Lyford, *The Mormon Problem*, pp. 63–64.
37. *Congressional Record*, 47th Cong., 1st sess., 1882, 13, pt. 1:367.
38. The standard account of the military confrontation between the Latter-Day Saints and the federal government is Norman Furniss, *The Mormon Conflict, 1850–59* (New Haven: Yale University Press, 1960).
39. Both the Edmunds bill (1882) and the Edmunds-Tucker bill (1884) are reprinted in full in Ellen Dickinson, *New Light on Mormonism*, pp. 150–60 (quotation from p. 157; my emphasis).
40. Saunders, *About Woman, Love and Marriage*, pp. 165–66. See also Hyde, *Mormonism*, p. 295.
41. My argument on individual, antiinstitutional reform proceeds from the outline laid out in John L. Thomas, "Romantic Reform in America, 1815–1865," *American Quarterly* 17 (1965): 656–81 (quotation from p. 661).
42. This tradition was not unique to communitarians. John G. Cawelti has pointed out in *Apostles of the Self-Made Man* (pp. 88–98) that Transcendentalist social perfection as represented by Ralph Waldo Emerson also emphasized the precedence of individual self-improvement over the reform of social institutions. For a discussion of the evangelical-feminine technique of reform, see Douglas, *Feminization*, pp. 157–58; and Cott, *Bonds of Womanhood*, pp. 96–97.
43. See, e.g., Tyler, *Freedom's Ferment*; Aileen S. Kraditor, *Means and Ends in American Abolitionism: Garrison and His Critics on Strategy and Tactics, 1834–1850* (New York: Pantheon Books, 1969); and William H. Pease and Jane H. Pease, "Anti-Slavery Ambivalence: Immediatism, Expediency, Race," *American Quarterly* 17, no. 4 (Winter 1965): 682–95.
44. Spencer, *Letters Exhibiting the Most Prominent Doctrines*, pp. 207–8. Arthur Ekirch has noted the "radical programs of progress" associated with anarchism and utopian socialism, but he overlooks the fact that these communities often saw not too much, but too *little*, order in the social institutions of society at large. See his *Idea of Progress in America, 1815–1860*, pp. 149–50.

Chapter 15

1. Cleland and Brooks, *Mormon Chronicle*, 1:176, entry for 13 July 1858.
2. See Alfred C. Kinsey et al., *Sexual Behavior in the Human Male* (Philadelphia: W. B. Saunders Co., 1948), chap. 7, "Age and Sexual Outlet," pp. 218–62.
3. See Cott, *Bonds of Womanhood*, pp. 46–55.
4. For this distinction between male and female roles, see Talcott Parsons and Robert F. Bales, *Family, Socialization, and Interaction Process*, pp. 151–52.
5. Herbert R. Brown, *The Sentimental Novel in America, 1789–1860*, p. 366.
6. See Parker, *Oven Birds*, pp. 13–14; Douglas, *Feminization*, pp. 110–15; Smith, "Family Limitation," pp. 40–57; and Cott, *Bonds of Womanhood*, pp. 153–54, 168, 204–5.
7. Stanley P. Hirshson makes this argument about Mormon women and polygamy in *Lion of the Lord*, pp. 45–46.
8. For the evangelical belief in a dualistic godhead and the necessity for a female savior, see Welter, "Feminization of American Religion," especially pp. 310–11.
9. For recent accounts exemplifying this approach, see Muncy, *Sex and Marriage in Utopian Communities*, epilogue; and Thomas, *Man Who Would be Perfect*, pp. 165–66, 175–76. For a statement of the earlier approach, see Arthur Bestor, "Patent Office Models of the Good Society: Some Relationships between Social Reform and Westward Expansion," in *Backwoods Utopias*, pp. 250–52.
10. Stark, *Sociology of Religion*, 2:159.
11. Thomas, *Man Who Would be Perfect*, pp. 59–67.
12. Ibid., pp. 119–24.
13. "Utility of Combination," *Spiritual Magazine* 2 (15 May 1847): 131.
14. Ibid., p. 132.
15. Noyes, *Home Talks*, address entitled "The Revival of Faith," p. 285; see also pp. 286–87.

Afterword

1. This estimate is based on a meticulous study of premodern American communes by Foster G. Stockwell, cited in Gardner, *Children of Prosperity*, p. 13.
2. This estimate was made by Judson Jerome in *Families of Eden: Communes and the New Anarchism* (New York: Seabury Press, 1974), pp. 15, 18. He provides a profile of the average communitarian member on pp. 19–24. For those who are interested in modern communities, the Center for Communal Societies at Indiana State University, Evansville, maintains a collection of materials on over seventy communes, both rural and urban.
3. Hugh Gardner divides contemporary communes into two types—anarchistic-libertarian and religious-authoritarian. The latter type has proved to be the longest lived. In the 1960s religious communes were a decided minority, but in the spiritually adrift 1970s they have come to be more common than the anarchist mode (see *Children of Prosperity*, p. 243). Veysey, *Communal Experience*, pp. 3–15, 449–59, makes essentially the same division of the modern communal movement. On the question of commitment in modern intentional communities, see Kanter, *Commitment and Community*, pp. 165–212; and Gardner, *Children of Prosperity*, pp. 218–38. I do not intend to imply here that only religious cults can be total institutions; certainly Synanon is a total institution. It remains true, however, that most communities that function as total institutions are religiously based.

4. This is the title of Hugh Gardner's book. Conover, "Analysis of Communes," calls the new communitarians "the children of affluence" (p. 455).

5. Gardner, *Children of Prosperity*, pp. 45, 57, 115, 125, 132. Veysey, *Communal Experience*, p. 466, also found that sex roles remained traditionally defined in modern rural communes, as did Kanter, "Family Organization," pp. 304–5.

6. Quoted in Gardner, *Children of Prosperity*, p. 132.

7. Conover, "Analysis of Communes," p. 460. See also "Judith," "Some Views from Women in Communes," *Communities* 7 (1974): 11–13.

Bibliography

General Background Sources

MS AND PRIMARY SOURCES

Abdy, E. S. *Journal of a Residence and Tour in the United States*. 3 vols. 1835. Reprint. New York: Negro Universities Press, 1969.

Alcott, William A. *The Young Husband; or, The Duties of Man in the Marriage Relation*. 1841. Reprint. New York: Arno Press, 1972.

————. *The Young Wife; or, Duties of Woman in the Marriage Relation*. 1837. Reprint. New York: Arno Press, 1972.

Alger, Horatio. *Ragged Dick and Mark, the Match Boy*. 1867. Reprint. New York: Collier Books, 1962.

Andrews, Stephen P. *Love, Marriage, and Divorce and the Sovereignty of the Individual*. 1853. Reprint. New York: Source Book Press, 1972.

Arthur, Timothy Shay. *Advice to Young Ladies on Their Duties and Conduct in Life*. Philadelphia: J. W. Bradley, 1860.

The Battle Axe and Weapons of War 1, nos. 1–4 (July 1837–Aug. 1840).

Beecher, Catharine. *A Treatise on Domestic Economy*. 1841. Reprint. New York: Schocken Books, 1977.

Beecher, Henry Ward, and Brady, James T. *Address on Mental Culture for Women*. New York: E. D. Barker, 1859.

Billington, George. *The Women of New York; or, The Underworld of the Great City*. 1869. Reprint. New York: Arno Press, 1972.

Bird, Isabella L. *The Englishwoman in America*. 1856. Reprint. Madison: University of Wisconsin Press, 1966.

Black, J. Watt, ed. *Selected Obstetrical and Gynecological Works of Sir James Y. Simpson*. New York: D. Appleton & Co., 1871.

Branagan, Thomas. *The Excellency of the Female Character Vindicated: Being an Investigation Relative to the Cause and Effects of the Encroachments of Men upon the Rights of Women, and the Too Frequent Degradation and Consequent Misfortunes of the Fair Sex*. 2d ed. Philadelphia: J. Rakestraw, 1808.

Brightly, Frank. *A Digest of the Decisions of All the Courts of the State of New York from the Earliest Period to the Year 1892*. 5 vols. Albany: Banks & Brothers, 1893.

Britton, S. B. *Man and His Relations: Illustrating the Influence of the Mind on the Body; The Relations of the Faculties to the Organs, and to the Elements, Objects and Phenomena of the External World*. New York: W. A. Townsend, 1864.

Brown, W. K. *Gunethics; or, The Ethical Status of Women*. New York: Funk & Wagnalls, 1887.

Busch, Morris. *Travels between the Hudson and the Mississippi, 1851–52*. Translated by Norman H. Binger. Lexington: University of Kentucky Press, 1971.

Chambers, William. *Things As They Are in America*. 1854. Reprint. New York: Negro Universities Press, 1968.

Chevalier, Michael. *Society, Manners, and Politics in the United States: Letters on North America*. 1837. Reprint. Gloucester, Mass.: Peter Smith, 1967.

Coke, Edward T. *A Subaltern's Furlough: Descriptive of Scenes in Various Parts of the U.S.,
Upper and Lower Canada, New Brunswick, and Nova Scotia during the Summer and
Autumn of 1832.* 2 vols. New York: J. & J. Harper, 1833.

Cooper, James Fenimore. *Notions of the Americans Picked Up by a Travelling Bachelor.* 2
vols. 1825. Reprint. New York: Frederick Ungar Publishing Co., 1963.

Cowan, John. *The Science of a New Life.* 1869. Reprint. New York: Cowan & Co., 1874.

De Tocqueville, Alexis. *Journey to America.* Edited by J. P. Mayer; translated by George
Lawrence. New Haven: Yale University Press, 1959.

Dixon, William Hepworth. *New America.* Philadelphia: J. B. Lippincott & Co., 1867.

_____. *Spiritual Wives.* 2d ed. Philadelphia: J. B. Lippincott & Co., 1868.

_____. *White Conquest.* 2 vols. London: Chatto & Windus, 1876.

Duer, John, et al., comps. *Revised Statutes of the State of New York.* Vol. 2 (1828–46).
Albany: Weare C. Little & Co., 1846.

Dunning, William, comp. *Domestic Happiness Portrayed; or, A Repository for Those Who
Are, and Those Who Are Not Married.* New York: Charles Spalding, 1831.

Emerson, Joseph. *Female Education: A Discourse Delivered at the Dedication of the
Seminary Hall in Saugus, Jan. 15, 1822.* Boston: Samuel T. Armstrong & Crocker &
Brewster, 1822.

Emerson, Ralph Waldo. "Woman: A Lecture Read before the Woman's Rights Convention,
Boston, Sept. 20, 1855." In *Complete Works of Ralph Waldo Emerson.* Vol. 11–
12:405–26. New York: William H. Wise, 1929.

Flint, Timothy. *Biographical Memoir of Daniel Boone, the First Settler of Kentucky.*
Cincinnati: N. & G. Guilford, 1833.

Geddes, Patrick, and Thompson, J. Arthur. *The Evolution of Sex.* New York: Scribner &
Welford, 1890.

Grimké, Sarah M. *Letters on the Equality of the Sexes and the Condition of Woman:
Addressed to Mary S. Parker, President of the Boston Female Anti-Slavery Society.*
1838. Reprint. New York: Burt Franklin, 1970.

Grund, Francis J. *The Americans in Their Moral, Social, and Political Relations.* 2 vols.
1837. Reprint. New York: Johnson Reprint Corp., 1968.

Hamilton, Gail, pseud. [Mary Abigail Dodge]. *Woman's Wrongs.* 1868. Reprint. New
York: Arno Press, 1972.

Hamilton, Thomas. *Men and Manners in America.* 1833. Reprint. New York: Russell &
Russell, 1968.

Hinds, William A. *American Communities.* 1878. Reprint. New York: Corinth Books,
1961.

Knowlton, Charles. *Fruits of Philosophy: An Essay on the Population Question.* 3d ed.
1853. Reprint. London: Freethought Publishing Co., 1878.

"A Lady." *The Young Lady's Mentor: A Guide to the Formation of Character, in a Series of
Letters to Her Unknown Friends.* Philadelphia: H. C. Beck & Theodore Bliss, 1853.

"A Lady," ed. *The American Book of Beauty, or Token of Friendship: A Gift for All
Seasons.* Hartford: Silas Andros & Son, 1849.

Laws of the State of New York Passed at the 83rd Session of the Legislature. Albany:
William Gould, 1860.

Marriage Present. Boston: James B. Dow, 1834.

Marryat, Frederick. *A Diary in America with Remarks on Its Institutions.* 2 vols. 1839.
Reprint. New York: Alfred A. Knopf, 1962.

Martineau, Harriet. *Retrospect of Western Travel.* 3 vols. 1838. Reprint. New York:
Greenwood Press, 1969.

_____. *Society in America.* 1837. Reprint. Gloucester, Mass.: Peter Smith, 1968.

Monk, Maria. *Awful Disclosures of Maria Monk, As Exhibited in a Narrative of Her*

Sufferings during a Residence of Five Years as a Novice, and Two Years as a Black Nun, in the Hotel Dieu Nunnery at Montreal. New York: Howe & Bates, 1836.

Mosher, Clelia D. "Statistical Study of the Marriage of Forty-seven Women." Clelia D. Mosher MSS, Stanford University Archives, Stanford, Calif.

Napheys, George H. *The Transmission of Life: Counsels on the Nature and Hygiene of the Masculine Function.* 2d ed. New York: Rufus C. Hartranft, 1878.

Nordhoff, Charles. *The Communistic Societies of the United States; from Personal Observation: Including Detailed Accounts of the Economists, Zoarites, Shakers, the Amana, Oneida, Bethel, Aurora, Icarian, and Other Existing Societies, Their Religious Creeds, Social Practices, Numbers, Industries, and Present Condition.* 1875. Reprint. New York: Hillary House, 1962.

Noyes, John Humphrey. *History of American Socialisms.* 1870. Reprint. New York: Hillary House, 1961.

Owen, Robert Dale. *Moral Physiology; or, A Brief and Plain Treatise on the Population Question.* 10th ed. 1858. Reprint. London: Holyoake & Co., 1859.

Phelps, Almira H. L. *The Female Student; or, Lectures to Young Ladies on Female Education: For the Use of Mothers, Teachers, and Pupils.* Boston: Crocker & Brewster, 1836.

Pike, J. G. *Persuasions to Early Piety, Interspersed with Suitable Prayers.* New York: American Tract Society, n.d.

Report of the Judiciary on the Petition of George Powlesland for Divorce (in Assembly, 9 Feb. 1855). State of New York, No. 83.

Report of the Judiciary on the Petition of John Black and William H. Pillow for a Divorce of the Marriage Contract (in Assembly, 30 Jan. 1849). State of New York, No. 66.

Roland, Michael, trans. *Sarmiento's Travels in the United States in 1847.* Princeton: Princeton University Press, 1970.

Saunders, F. *About Woman, Love and Marriage.* New York: G. W. Carleton & Co., 1868.

Scott, Franklin D., trans. and ed. *Baron Klinkowström's America, 1818–20.* Evanston: Northwestern University Press, 1952.

Scott, James Foster. *The Sexual Instinct: Its Use and Dangers as Affecting Heredity and Morals Essential to the Welfare of the Individual and the Future of the Race.* New York: E. B. Treat & Co., 1899.

Sigourney, Mrs. Lydia H. *The Girl's Reading Book in Prose and Poetry for Schools.* New York: Turner & Hayden, 1846.

————. *Letters to Mothers.* 2d ed. New York: Harper & Brothers, 1839.

Stanton, Elizabeth C.; Anthony, Susan B.; and Gage, Matilda Joslyn, eds. *History of Woman Suffrage.* 3 vols. 1882. Reprint. New York: Arno Press, 1969.

Todd, John. *The Student's Manual: Designed by Specific Directions to Aid in Forming and Strengthening the Intelligence and Moral Character and Habits of the Student.* Northampton, Mass.: Bridgman & Childs, 1861.

————. *The Sunset Land; or, The Great Pacific Shore.* Boston: Lee & Shepard, 1870.

The Token: A Christmas and New Year's Gift. New York: D. Appleton & Co., 1857.

Trollope, Anthony. *North America.* 2 vols. Philadelphia: J. B. Lippincott & Co., 1863.

Trollope, Frances. *Domestic Manners of the Americans.* 1832. Reprint. New York: Vintage Books, 1949.

Vivian, H. Hussey. *Notes of a Tour of America.* 1878. Reprint. New York: Arno Press, 1974.

Walker, Alexander. *The Ladies' Guide to Perfect Beauty: Being a Complete Analysis and Classification of the Elements, Nature, Standard, Causes, Anatomy, Species, Defects, and Effects of Beauty in Women; also, External Indications or the Art of Determining the Precise Figure, the Degree of Beauty, the Mind, the Habits, and Age of Women,*

notwithstanding the Disguises of Dress. New York: Derby & Johnson, 1861.
Ward, Artemus, pseud. [Charles Farrar Browne]. *Artemus Ward: His Book.* New York: Carleton, 1862.
Wright, Carroll D. *Report of the Commissioner of Labor, 1889: A Report on Marriage and Divorce in the U.S., 1867–1886; Including an Appendix Relating to Marriage and Divorce in Certain Countries in Europe.* Washington, D.C.: Government Printing Office, 1891.

SECONDARY SOURCES

Angeloglou, Maggie. *A History of Make-Up.* New York: Macmillan Co., 1965.
Athansiou, Robert, et al. "Sex." *Psychology Today* 4, no. 2 (July 1970): 39–52.
Banks, J. A., and Banks, Olive. *Feminism and Family Planning in Victorian England.* New York: Schocken Books, 1964.
Bardwick, Judith M. *Psychology of Women: A Study of Bio-Cultural Conflicts.* New York: Harper & Row, 1971.
Barker-Benfield, G. J. *The Horrors of the Half-Known Life: Male Attitudes toward Women and Sexuality in Nineteenth-Century America.* New York: Harper & Row, 1976.
––––––. "The Spermatic Economy: A Nineteenth-Century View of Sexuality." *Feminist Studies* 1 (1972): 45–74.
Bell, Alan P., and Weinberg, Martin S. *Homosexualities: A Study of Diversity among Men and Women.* New York: Simon & Schuster, 1978.
Berger, Bennett M.; Hackett, Bruce M.; and Millar, R. Mervin. "Child Rearing Practices of the Communal Family." In *Communes: Creating and Managing the Collective Life,* edited by Rosabeth M. Kanter, pp. 356–64. New York: Harper & Row, 1973.
Bestor, Arthur. *Backwoods Utopias: The Sectarian Origins and the Owenite Phase of Communitarian Socialism in America: 1663–1829.* 2d ed. Philadelphia: University of Pennsylvania Press, 1970.
Bogue, Donald J. *The Population of the United States.* Glencoe, Ill.: Free Press, 1959.
Brill, A. A., ed. *The Basic Writings of Sigmund Freud.* New York: Modern Library, 1938.
Brooks, Carol F. "The Early History of the Anti-Contraceptive Laws in Massachusetts and Connecticut." *American Quarterly* 18 (1966): 3–23.
Brown, Herbert R. *The Sentimental Novel in America, 1789–1860.* Durham, N.C.: Duke University Press, 1940.
Calverton, V. F. *Where Angels Dared to Tread.* New York: Bobbs Merrill Co., 1941.
Carden, Maren Lockwood. "The Experimental Utopia in America." *Daedalus* 44 (1965): 401–18.
Cawelti, John G. *Apostles of the Self-Made Man: Changing Concepts of Success in America.* Chicago: University of Chicago Press, 1965.
Cohn, Norman. *Pursuit of the Millennium: Revolutionary Millenarians and Mystical Anarchists of the Middle Ages.* New York: Oxford University Press, 1970.
Conover, Patrick W. "An Analysis of Communes and Intentional Communities with Particular Attention to Sexual and Genderal Relations." *Family Coordinator* 24, no. 4 (Oct. 1975): 453–64.
Corson, Richard. *Fashions in Makeup from Ancient to Modern Times.* New York: Universe Books, 1972.
Coser, Rose L., ed. *The Family: Its Structure and Functions.* New York: St. Martin's Press, 1964.
Cott, Nancy. *The Bonds of Womanhood: "Women's Sphere" in New England, 1780–1835.* New Haven: Yale University Press, 1977.

Cross, Whitney. *The Burned-Over District: The Social and Intellectual History of Enthusiastic Religion in New York, 1800–1850.* Ithaca, N.Y.: Cornell University Press, 1950.

Crowley, J. E. *This Sheba, Self: The Conceptualization of Economic Life in Eighteenth-Century America.* Baltimore: Johns Hopkins Press, 1974.

Curle, Adam. *Mystics and Militants: A Study of Awareness, Identity, and Social Action.* London: Tavistock Publishers, 1972.

Davis, David B. "Some Ideological Functions of Prejudice in Ante-Bellum America." *American Quarterly* 15 (1963): 115–25.

———. "Some Themes of Counter-Subversion: An Analysis of Anti-Masonic, Anti-Catholic, and Anti-Mormon Literature." *Mississippi Valley Historical Review* 47 (1960): 205–24.

Degler, Carl. "What Ought to Be and What Was: Women's Sexuality in the Nineteenth Century." *American Historical Review* 79 (1974): 1467–90.

Ditzion, Sidney. *Marriage, Morals, and Sex in America: A History of Ideas.* New York: Bookman Associates, 1953.

Douglas, Ann. *The Feminization of American Culture.* New York: Alfred A. Knopf, 1977.

Egbert, Donald D., and Persons, Stow, eds. *Socialism and American Life.* 2 vols. Princeton: Princeton University Press, 1952.

Engels, Friedrich. "Beschreibung der in Neuerer Zeit entstanden und noch Bestehenden Kommunistischen Ansiedlungen." In *Karl Marx-Friedrich Engels Werke.* Vol. 2:521–35. Berlin: Dietz Verlag, 1962.

———. *The Origin of the Family, Private Property, and the State: In the Light of the Researches of Lewis H. Morgan.* 1884. Reprint. New York: International Publishers, n.d.

Erasmus, Charles J. *In Search of the Common Good: Utopian Experiments Past and Future.* New York: Free Press, 1977.

Ewing, Elizabeth. *Dress and Undress: A History of Women's Underwear.* New York: Drama Book Specialists, 1978.

Fellman, Michael. *The Unbounded Frame: Freedom and Community in Nineteenth-Century American Utopianism.* Westport, Conn.: Greenwood Press, 1973.

Ferenczi, Sandor. *Thalassa: A Theory of Genitality.* 1938. Reprint. New York: Norton, 1968.

Fischer, Christine, ed. *Let Them Speak for Themselves: Women in the American West, 1849–1900.* Hamden, Conn.: Archon Books, 1977.

Fischer, David H. *Growing Old in America.* New York: Oxford University Press, 1977.

———. "The Vital Revolution: Demographic and Social Change in American Society, 1750–1850." Paper read at the Sturbridge Village Conference on the Family in the Process of Industrialization, April 1978.

Flügel, J. C. *The Psychology of Clothes.* London: Hogarth Press, 1930.

Freud, Sigmund. *Civilization and Its Discontents* (1930). In *The Complete Psychological Works of Sigmund Freud.* Vol. 21:59–145. London: Hogarth Press, 1957–61.

———. "On the Universal Tendency to Debasement in the Sphere of Love" (*Contributions to the Psychology of Love,* no. 2, 1912). In *Complete Psychological Works of Sigmund Freud.* Vol. 11:179–90.

———. "Sexuality in the Aetiology of the Neuroses." In *Complete Psychological Works of Sigmund Freud.* Vol. 3:263–85.

———. "A Special Choice of Object Made by Men" (*Contributions to the Psychology of Love,* no. 1, 1910). In *Complete Psychological Works of Sigmund Freud.* Vol. 11:165–75.

———. "The Taboo of Virginity" (*Contributions to the Theory of Love,* no. 3, 1918). In

Complete Psychological Works of Sigmund Freud. Vol. 11:193–208.

————. *Three Essays on the Theory of Sexuality.* New York: Avon Books, 1962.

Gardner, Hugh. *The Children of Prosperity: Thirteen Modern American Communities.* New York: St. Martin's Press, 1978.

Goergen, Donald. *The Sexual Celibate.* New York: Seabury Press, 1974.

Gollin, Gilliam L. "Family Surrogates in Colonial America: The Moravian Experiment." In *The Nuclear Family in Crisis: The Search for an Alternative,* edited by Michael Gordon, pp. 44–58. New York: Harper & Row, 1972.

Gordon, Michael, ed. *The American Family in Social-Historical Perspective.* New York: St. Martin's Press, 1973.

Gordon, Michael, and Bernstein, M. Charles. "Mate Choice and Domestic Life in the Nineteenth-Century Marriage Manual." *Journal of Marriage and the Family* 32 (1970): 665–74.

Grabill, Wilson H.; Kiser, Clyde V.; and Whelpton, Pascal K. *The Fertility of American Women.* New York: John Wiley & Sons, 1958.

Gurko, Miriam. *The Ladies of Seneca Falls: The Birth of the Women's Rights Movement.* New York: Macmillan, 1974.

Hare, E. H. "Masturbatory Insanity: The History of an Idea." *Journal of Mental Science* 108, no. 452 (Jan. 1962): 1–21.

Himes, Norman E. *Medical History of Contraception.* 1936. Reprint. New York: Schocken Paperback, 1970.

Holliday, Robert C. *Unmentionables: From Figleaves to Scanties.* New York: Roy Long & Richard R. Smith, 1933.

Holter, Harriet. *Sex Roles and Social Structure.* Oslo: Universitetsforlaget, 1970.

Horney, Karen. "The Dread of Woman: Observations on a Specific Difference in the Dread Felt by Men and by Women Respectively for the Opposite Sex." *International Journal of Psychoanalysis* 13 (1932): 348–60.

Hostetler, John. *Communitarian Societies.* New York: Holt, Rinehart, & Winston, 1974.

Howard, George E. *A History of Matrimonial Institutions, Chiefly in England and the United States, with an Introductory Analysis of the Literature and the Theories of Primitive Marriage and the Family.* 3 vols. 1904. Reprint. New York: Humanities Press, 1964.

Huber, Joan, ed. *Changing Women in a Changing Society.* Chicago: University of Chicago Press, 1973.

Hunt, Morton M. *The Natural History of Love.* New York: Alfred A. Knopf, 1959.

Kanter, Rosabeth M. *Commitment and Community: Communes and Utopias in Sociological Perspective.* Cambridge, Mass.: Harvard University Press, 1972.

————. "Family Organization and Sex Roles in American Communes." In *Communes: Creating and Managing the Collective Life,* edited by Rosabeth M. Kanter, pp. 287–307. New York: Harper & Row, 1973.

Kephart, William M. *Extraordinary Groups: The Sociology of Unconventional Life-Styles.* New York: St. Martin's Press, 1976.

Komarovsky, Mirra. "Cultural Contradictions and Sex Roles." *American Journal of Sociology* 52 (1946): 184–89.

Lasch, Christopher. *The Culture of Narcissism: American Life in an Age of Diminishing Expectations.* New York: W. W. Norton & Co., 1978.

————. *The World of Nations: Reflections on American History, Politics, and Culture.* New York: Vintage Books, 1962.

Lawrence, Donald H., ed. *Bernard Shaw: Collected Letters, 1874–97.* New York: Dodd, Mead & Co., 1965.

Lea, Henry C. *History of Sacerdotal Celibacy in the Christian Church.* 3d ed. 2 vols. New York: Macmillan Co., 1907.

Lederer, Wolfgang. *The Fear of Women.* New York: Grune & Stratton, 1968.

Lobdel, John E., and Owsley, Douglas. "The Origin of Syphilis." *Journal of Sex Research* 10 (1974): 76–79.

McClellan, Elisabeth. *History of American Costume, 1607–1870.* New York: Tudor Publishing Co., 1969.

McKeown, Thomas. *The Modern Rise of Population.* New York: Academic Press, 1976.

Mannheim, Karl. *Ideology and Utopia: An Introduction to the Sociology of Knowledge.* New York: Harcourt, Brace, & World, 1936.

Melville, Keith. *Communes and the Counter-Culture: Origins, Theories, and Stages of Life.* New York: William Morrow & Co., 1972.

Mohr, James C. *Abortion in America: The Origins and Evolution of National Policy, 1800–1900.* New York: Oxford University Press, 1978.

Moorhead, James. *American Apocalypse: Yankee Protestants and the Civil War, 1860–69.* New Haven: Yale University Press, 1978.

Muncy, Raymond. *Sex and Marriage in Utopian Communities: Nineteenth-Century America.* Bloomington: Indiana University Press, 1973.

Nissenbaum, Stephen. "Careful Love: Sylvester Graham and the Emergence of Victorian Sexual Theory in America." Ph.D. dissertation, University of Wisconsin, 1968.

O'Neill, William. *Divorce in the Progressive Era.* New York: New Viewpoints, 1973.

Parker, Gail, ed. *The Oven Birds: American Women on Womanhood, 1820–1920.* New York: Anchor Books, 1972.

Parsons, Talcott, and Bales, Robert F. *Family, Socialization, and Interaction Process.* New York: Free Press, 1955.

Reed, James W. *From Private Vice to Public Virtue: The Birth Control Movement and American Society since 1830.* New York: Basic Books, 1978.

Reich, Wilhelm. *The Function of the Orgasm: Sex Economic Problems of Biological Energy.* New York: Noonday Press, 1942.

————. *The Sexual Revolution: Toward a Self-Governing Character Structure.* 1945. Reprint. New York: Octagon Books, 1971.

Remini, Robert V. *The Revolutionary Age of Andrew Jackson.* New York: Harper & Row, 1976.

Riegel, Robert E. "Changing American Attitudes toward Prostitution (1820–1920)." *Journal of the History of Ideas* 29 (1968): 437–52.

Rigby, Andrew. *Alternative Realities: A Study of Communes and Their Members.* London: Routledge & Kegan Paul, 1974.

Rosenberg, Charles E. "Sexuality, Class, and Role in Nineteenth-Century America." *American Quarterly* 25 (1973): 131–53.

Rover, Constance. *Love, Morals and the Feminists.* London: Routledge & Kegan Paul, 1970.

Rugoff, Milton. *Prudery and Passion.* New York: G. P. Putnam's Sons, 1971.

Ryan, Mary P. "American Society and the Culture of Domesticity, 1830–1860." Ph.D. dissertation, University of California at Santa Barbara, 1971.

Schroeder, Theodore. "Erotogenic Interpretation of Religion." *Journal of Religious Psychology* 7 (1914): 23–44.

Sears, Hal D. *The Sex Radicals: Free Love in High Victorian America.* Lawrence: Regents Press of Kansas, 1977.

Sevely, J. L., and Bennett, J. W. "Concerning Female Ejaculation and the Female Prostate." *Journal of Sex Research* 14 (1978): 1–20.

Seward, Georgene H., and Williamson, Robert C., eds. *Sex Roles in Changing Society.* New York: Random House, 1970.

Shaplen, Robert. *Free Love and Heavenly Sinners: The Story of the Great Henry Ward Beecher Scandal.* New York: Alfred A. Knopf, 1954.

Sklar, Kathryn K. *Catharine Beecher: A Study in American Domesticity.* New Haven: Yale University Press, 1973.

Smith, Daniel Scott. "Family Limitation, Sexual Control, and Domestic Feminism in Victorian America." *Feminist Studies* 1 (1973): 40–57.

Smith, David E., and Sternfield, James L. "Natural Child Birth and Co-operative Child Rearing in Psychedelic Communes." In *The Nuclear Family in Crisis: The Search for an Alternative,* edited by Michael Gordon, pp. 196–203. New York: Harper & Row, 1972.

Smith-Rosenberg, Carroll. "The Hysterical Woman: Sex Roles and Role Conflict in Nineteenth-Century America." *Social Research* 39 (1972): 652–78.

Smith-Rosenberg, Carroll, and Rosenberg, Charles. "The Female Animal: Medical and Biological Views of Woman and Her Role in Nineteenth-Century America." *Journal of American History* 60 (1973): 332–56.

Smith, Timothy L. *Revivalism and Social Reform in Mid-Nineteenth-Century America.* New York: Abingdon Press, 1957.

Sontag, Susan. *Illness as Metaphor.* New York: Farrar, Straus & Giroux, 1978.

Speert, Harold. *Iconographia Gyniatrica: A Pictorial History of Gynecology and Obstetrics.* Philadelphia: F. A. Davis, 1973.

Spitz, René. "Authority and Masturbation." *Psychoanalytic Quarterly* 21 (1952): 490–577.

Stark, Werner. *The Sociology of Religion.* 6 vols. Vol. 2, *Sectarian Religion.* Vol. 5, *Types of Religious Cultures.* New York: Fordham University Press, 1967, 1971.

Stekel, Wilhelm. *Bi-Sexual Love.* 1922. Reprint. New York: Emerson Books, 1944.

Stern, Karl. *The Flight from Woman.* New York: Farrar, Straus, & Giroux, 1965.

Stone, Lawrence. *The Family, Sex and Marriage in England, 1500–1800.* New York: Harper & Row, 1977.

Strong, Bryan. "Toward a History of the Experiential Family: Sex and Instinct in the Nineteenth-Century Family." *Journal of Marriage and the Family* 35 (1973): 457–66.

Symonds, Alexander; Moulton, Ruth; and Badaraco, Marie R. "The Myth of Femininity: A Panel Discussion." *American Journal of Psychoanalysis* 33 (1973): 56–57.

Taeuber, Conrad, and Taeuber, Irene. *The Changing Population of the United States.* New York: John Wiley & Sons, 1958.

Teselle, Sallie, ed. *The Family, Communes, and Utopian Societies.* New York: Harper & Row, 1972.

Troeltsch, Ernst. *The Social Teachings of the Christian Churches.* 2 vols. London: George Allen & Unwin, 1931.

Tyler, Alice Felt. *Freedom's Ferment: Phases of American Social History from the Colonial Period to the Outbreak of the Civil War.* New York: Harper & Row, 1944.

Veysey, Laurence. *The Communal Experience: Anarchistic and Mystical Counter-Cultures in America.* New York: Harper & Row, 1973.

Vincinus, Martha, ed. *Suffer and Be Still: Women in the Victorian Age.* Bloomington: Indiana University Press, 1972.

Watts, Alan W. *Nature, Man and Woman.* New York: Pantheon Books, 1958.

Welter, Barbara. "The Cult of True Womanhood, 1820–1840." *American Quarterly* 18 (1966): 151–74.

―――. "The Feminization of American Religion, 1800–1860." In *Insights and Parallels: Problems and Issues of American Social History,* edited by William L. O'Neill, pp. 305–31. Minneapolis: Burgess Publishing Co., 1973.

Whitworth, John M. *God's Blueprints: A Sociological Study of Three Utopian Sects.* London: Routledge & Kegan Paul, 1975.

Wilcox, Walter F. *Studies in American Demography.* New York: Russell & Russell, 1971.

Wylie, Irwin G. *The Self-Made Man in America: The Myth of Rags to Riches.* New York: Free Press, 1954.

Young, Wayland. *Eros Denied.* New York: Grove Press, 1964.

Zirkle, Conway. "The Early History of the Inheritance of Acquired Characteristics, and of Pangenesis." *Transactions of the American Philosophical Society* 35, pt. 2 (1946): 141–46.

Zuckerman, Michael. "The Fabrication of Identity in Early America." *William and Mary Quarterly* 34 (1977): 183–214.

Shaker Sources

MS SOURCES

Autograph Albums: Shaker MSS Collection, New York Public Library (hereafter NYPL).
Shaker Autograph Album. New Lebanon, 1881–83.
Autograph Album of Isabella Graves. South Family, Watervliet, 1872–93.
Autograph Album Kept by Frieda. 1881–98.

Avery, Giles B. Minister's Journal. Mt. Lebanon, 1 Jan. 1874–15 Jan. 1890. Shaker MSS Collection, NYPL.

———. A Register of Incidents and Events: Being a Continuation from Other Records Kept by the Ministry. New Lebanon, 20 Oct. 1859–21 Dec. 1874. Shaker MSS Collection, NYPL.

Bishop, Rufus. A Daily Journal of Passing Events. 2 vols. Vol. 1, 1 Jan. 1830–18 May 1839. Vol. 2, 19 May 1839–1 Jan. 1850. Shaker MSS Collection, NYPL.

———. A Journal or Register of Passing Events. 2 Jan. 1850–19 Oct. 1859. Shaker MSS Collection, NYPL.

Book of Mystic Letters and Drawings Revealed by Isabella L. Shaker MSS Collection, NYPL.

Counsel and Instruction Given by Mother Lucy, for the Use and Benefit of Those Who Are Called to Bear Temporal Burdens throughout Zion's Habitations: Written by Inspiration. Wisdom's Valley [Mt. Lebanon], 5 Oct. 1844. Shaker MSS, NYPL.

Covenant of Novitiate Members of the South Family of the United Society of Shakers of New Lebanon. (1874–99.) Shaker MSS, NYPL.

Covenant or Constitution of the United Society in the Town of New Lebanon. (1830, with signatories through 1911.) Shaker MSS, NYPL.

A Diary Kept by the Elder Sister. Harvard, Mass., 19 July 1867–29 Apr. 1872. Shaker MSS, NYPL.

Diary of Martha Anderson. Mt. Lebanon, 1 Aug. 1863–30 Apr. 1867. Shaker MSS, NYPL.

"Elder Brethren Orders." [Ca. 1858.] Shaker MSS, NYPL.

Experience of Thankful E. Goodrich. Shaker MSS, NYPL.

"A General Statement of the Holy Laws of Zion." New Lebanon, 10 May 1840. Shaker MSS, NYPL.

The Gospel Monitor. Mt. Lebanon, 1 Mar. 1841. Shaker MSS, NYPL.

The Holy Law of the Almighty concerning the Sabbath, and the Birthdays of Our Holy Savior and Blessed Mother Ann: Given to the Ministry through Divine Inspiration. Holy Mount [Mt. Lebanon], 26 Feb. 1841. Shaker MSS, NYPL.

Indenture. 28 Aug. 1876. Shaker MSS, NYPL.

Letters: Shaker MSS, NYPL.
To Sister Esther Bennett, Watervliet, from Sister Molly, South Union, Jasper, Ky. 18 Dec. 1818.

To Eldress Esther, from Olive Spence and Susanah Ellis, New Lebanon. 6 Aug. 1832.

To a Sister in Groveland, from Hannah and Elsey, Sodus, N.Y. 12 Feb. 1837.

To Charlotte, Lydia, and Eliza Ann, from Eliza, Sodus, N.Y. Feb. 1837.

To Elder John, from C. G. [Calvin Green], New Lebanon. 8 Nov. 1847.

To Brother Malachi Sanford of Groveland, from Brother Elisha D. Blakeman. 13 Apr. 1851.

To the Elders of Groveland from the Ministry of Watervliet. 29 Aug. 1860.

To the Elders at Groveland from the Ministry of New Lebanon. 30 Oct. 1860.

To the Elders at Groveland from the Watervliet Ministry. 6 Mar. 1861.

To Eldress Lydia and Sister Polly, from Eliza Ann and Betsy Bates, Mt. Lebanon, 13 Dec. 1863.

To the Ministry at Mt. Lebanon, from Pleasant Hill. 9 Feb. 1869.

To Sister Polly, from Mary A. Gillespie, West Gloucester. 9 Aug. 1869.

To "My Gospel Parents," from Maria Cady, Enfield, N.H. 1 Mar. 1870.

To Eldress Lydia, Wisdom's Valley, from the Ministry of Mt. Lebanon. 25 June 1870.

To Eldress Lydia and Eldress Abigail, from Elder Daniel and Elder Giles, Mt. Lebanon. 19 Nov. 1871.

To the Elders of Groveland, from "E. T. V." and "P. R.," Watervliet. 14 Jan. 1872.

To the Elders at Groveland, from "E. T. V." 19 Dec. 1875.

To Eldress Lydia and Sister Polly, from "E. T." and "P. R." 7 May 1877.

To Eldress Lydia and Sister Polly, from "P. R." and "E. T.," Mt. Lebanon. 23 June 1878.

To Elders, from "E. T." and "P. R." 4 Aug. 1878.

To Eldress Lydia, from "E. T." and "P. R." Mt. Lebanon. 21 Sept. 1879.

To Eldress Lydia and Sister Polly, from "E. T." and "P. R." 30 Sept. 1879.

From Daniel Offord with Reply by Koresh [Cyrus R. Teed], Mt. Lebanon. 16 Nov. 1892.

To Sister Marilla, from Ann Eliza. 22 Oct. ?.

To Brother Daniel, Groveland, from the Elders of Watervliet. N.d.

To The Elders from "P. R." N.d.

"List of Instructions for Clothing Young Females, According to Mother Lucy." New Lebanon, 1840. Shaker MSS, NYPL.

Miscellaneous MS Items: Shaker MSS, NYPL.

    Shaker MS Drawings.

    Poem by "Caroline."

    A Poem of Life's Journey: By a Sister in the Body. In Answer to the Questions of the 24th. By "Ann."

    Untitled Poem.

    Shaker Photographs.

    Song—"Banishing Feeling." Mt. Lebanon, 1890.

    MS Sheet on the Dress of Believers.

North Family Book of Records. Mt. Lebanon, 1814–1910. Shaker MSS, NYPL.

"Orders for the Church of Christ's Second Appearing." Mt. Lebanon, 1887. Shaker MSS, NYPL.

"A Record of Messages from the Spiritual World, 1841–45." Shaker MSS, NYPL.

Records Kept by Order of the Church, 1780–1855. [Mt. Lebanon.] Shaker MSS, NYPL.

Roll of Confessions of Faith. New Lebanon, 6 July 1841. Shaker MSS, NYPL.

"Sayings of the Prophetess Anna, Miriam, and Deborah." 21 June 1843 (Circular Book). Shaker MSS, NYPL.

Shaker Diary, 1885. [Gathering Family?] Mt. Lebanon. Shaker MSS, NYPL.

Supplement to the Holy Laws of Zion. Shaker MSS, NYPL.
"The Word by the Savior of Signs." (Cut Out and Folded Out Message: Revelation with Inspired Illustrations.) Shaker MSS, NYPL.

PRIMARY SOURCES

Account of Some of the Proceedings of the Legislatures of Kentucky and New Hampshire, 1828, etc., in Relation to the People Called Shakers. New York: Egbert, Hovey, & King, 1846.
Allen, Catharine. *The Questions of the Day.* Mt. Lebanon, N.Y. [Title page missing, 1870s?]
Anderson, Martha J., and Byrdsall, Charlotte. *Social Gathering: Dialogue between Six Sisters of the North Family of Shakers, Mt. Lebanon, N.Y.* Albany: Weed, Parsons, & Co., 1873.
Authorized Rules of the Shaker Community: Given for the Protection and Guidance of the Members in the General Societies. Mt. Lebanon, N.Y.: n.p., 1894.
Avery, Giles B. *Eine Kurtze Beschreibung des Glaubens und Praktischen Lebens der Verein. Gesellschaft Gläubiger in Christs Zweiten Erscheinung Gewöhnlich gennant "Shakers."* Union Village, Ohio: Carl Julius, Printer, 1888.
—————. *Sketches of Shakers and Shakerism: A Synopsis of the Theology of the United Society of Believers in Christ's Second Appearing.* Albany: Weed, Parsons, & Co., 1884.
[Bates, Paulina.] *The Divine Book of Holy and Eternal Wisdom, Revealing the Word of God, out of Whose Mouth Goeth a Sharp Sword.* Canterbury, N.H.: Published by the United Society Called Shakers, 1849.
Blakeman, Elisha D. *The Youth's Guide in Zion, and Holy Mother's Promises: Given by Inspiration at New Lebanon, N.Y., Jan. 5, 1842.* Canterbury, N.H.: n.p., 1842.
Blinn, Henry G. *A Christian Community.* East Canterbury, N.H.: n.p., n.d.
Bolton, Aquilla. *Lines in Verse about the Shakers.* New York: William Taylor & Co., 1846.
Bowers, Lucy. *Concise Statements concerning the Life and Religious Views of the Shakers.* Mt. Lebanon: n.p., n.d. [post-1850].
A Brief Account of the Shakers and Shakerism: Several Pages of Music Are Also Added Which Have Never Before Been Published. Canterbury, N.H.: n.p., n.d.
A Brief Exposition of the Established Principles and Regulations of the United Society of Believers Called Shakers. New York: Edward O. Jenkins, 1851.
Briggs, N. *God Dual.* N.p., n.d. [ca. 1870s or 1880s].
Brown, Thomas. *An Account of the People Called Shakers: Their Faith, Doctrines, and Practice, Exemplified in the Life, Conversations, and Experience of the Author during the Time he Belonged to the Society, to Which Is Affixed a History of Their Rise and Progress to the Present Day.* New York: Parker & Bliss, 1812.
Bushnell, Richard. *Shakers.* N.p., n.d.
Circular concerning the Dress of Believers from the Ministry at New Lebanon. N.p., 1866.
A Concise Shaker Catechism, Containing the Most Important Events Recorded in the Bible: Also a Short Sketch of the Lives of Our First Elders or Parents, Mother Ann, Father William, and Father James. Shaker Village, N.H.: n.p., 1850.
Cottrell, Rachel. "Shaker Death Records." *New England Historical and Genealogical Register* 115 (1961): 32–45, 118–35.
The Divine Afflatus: A Force in History. Boston: Rand, Avery, & Co., 1875.
Doolittle, Mary A. *Autobiography of Mary Antoinette Doolittle, Containing a Brief His-*

tory of Her Early Life prior to Becoming a Member of the Shaker Community, Also an Account of Her Life and Experience among the Shakers. Mt. Lebanon, N.Y.: n.p., 1880.

————. *Thoughts concerning Deity.* N.p., n.d.

Dyer, Mary M. *The Rise and Progress of the Serpent from the Garden of Eden to the Present Day: With a Discourse of Shakerism, Exhibiting a General View of Their Real Character and Conduct from the First Appearance of Ann Lee: Also the Life and Sufferings of the Author.* Concord, N.H.: Privately printed, 1847.

Eads, H. L. *Expression of Faith: A Discursive Letter.* Orange, N.J.: Chronicle Book & Job Printing Office, 1875.

————. *Shaker Sermons: Scripto-Rational–Containing the Substance of Shaker Theology Together with Replies and Criticisms Logically and Clearly Set Forth.* Shakers, N.Y.: The Shaker Manifesto, 1879.

Elkins, Hervey. *Fifteen Years in the Senior Order of Shakers: A Narrative of the Facts concerning That Singular People.* 1853. Reprint. New York: A. M. S. Press, 1973.

Evans, Frederick W. *Autobiography of a Shaker and Revelation of the Apocalypse.* 2d ed. 1888. Reprint. Philadelphia: Porcupine Press, 1972.

————. *Christ.* [Broadside from the *Berkshire County Eagle*, n.d.]

————. *Confession of Sin.* N.p., n.d.

————. *Lecture: Delivered in Taylor's Hall, Amenia, N.Y.* [*Amenia Times Extra*, n.d.]

————. *Liberalism, Spiritualism, Shakerism.* N.p., n.d.

————. *One Hundred Years of Shaker Life: Centennial of a Communism of Peace.* N.p., n.d. [ca. 1885].

————. *Religious Communism: A Lecture Delivered in St. George's Hall, London, Aug. 6, 1871.* London: J. Burns, 1871.

————. *Resurrection.* N.p., n.d.

————. *Robert G. Ingersoll for 1892.* Mt. Lebanon, N.Y.

————. *Shaker Essay.* N.p., n.d.

————. *Shakers' Sabbath Composed of Seven Days.* N.p., n.d.

————. *The Shaker System, and a Lecture Delivered at Randolph, Cattaraugus Co., N.Y., Dec. 9, 1877.* Albany: Weed, Parsons, & Co., 1877.

————. *A Shaker's Views on the Land Limitation Scheme and Land Monopoly, and Mormon Prosecution.* N.p., n.d. [ca. 1887].

————. *A Short Treatise on the Second Appearance of Christ in and through the Order of the Female.* Boston: Bazin & Chandler, 1857.

————. *A Suggestion.* N.p., n.d.

————. *Tests of Divine Inspiration; or, The Rudimental Principles by Which True and False Revelation, in All Eras of the World, Can Be Unerringly Discriminated.* New Lebanon: United Society Called Shakers, 1853.

"E. W. (C. S.)." *A Little Selection of Choice Poetry, New and Old, Doctrinal and Devotional.* Watervliet, Ohio: n.p., 1835.

"E. W. H." *Thoughts Suggested by the Question–"What Induced You to Join the Shakers?"* N.p., n.d.

Fraser, Daniel. *Analysis of Human Society: Declaring the Law Which Creates and Sustains a Community Having Goods in Common.* N.p., n.d.

————. *The Divine Procedure in the Affairs of Man.* [From the *Shaker Manifesto*, post-1877.]

————. *The Divinity of Humanity: The Cornerstone of the Temple of the Future.* Boston: Rand, Avery, & Co., 1874.

————. *Is Celibacy Contrary to Natural and Revealed Law?* N.p., n.d.

————. *A Letter Touching Important Principles.* N.p., n.d.

————. *Longevity of Virgin Celibates*. N.p., n.d. [post-1880].

————. *The Music of the Spheres*. Albany: Weed, Parsons, & Co., 1887.

————. *Shakerism*. N.p., 1886.

————. *Theocratic Government Is Self Government*. Mt. Lebanon: n.p., 1894.

————. *Theology: Facts for Christendom*. N.p., n.d.

The Gospel Monitor: A Little Book of Mother Ann's Word to Those Who Are Placed as Instructors and Caretakers of Children; Written by Mother Lucy Wright, and Brought by Her to the Elders of the First Order, on the Holy Mount, March 1, 1841. Copied by Inspiration at Mother Ann's Desire, March 2, 1841. Canterbury, N.H.: n.p., 1843.

Green, Calvin. *The Law of Life: Extracts from a Writing Received in the Name of the Prophet Joel, at Mt. Lebanon, N.Y., Jan., 1841*. Mt. Lebanon: A. G. Hollister, 1901.

Green, Calvin, and Wells, Seth Y. *A Brief Exposition of the Established Principles and Regulations of the United Society of Believers Called Shakers*. Albany: Hoffman & White, 1834.

————. *A Brief Exposition of the Principles and Regulations of the United Society of Believers*. East Canterbury, N.H.: n.p., 1895.

Grossvenor, Lorenzo D. *A Concise Answer to the Inquiry, Who or What Are the Shakers*. N.p., 1849.

Haskett, William J. *Shakerism Unmasked; or, The History of the Shakers; Including a Form Politic of Their Government as Councils, Orders, Gifts, with an Exposition of the Five Orders of Shakerism, and Ann Lee's Grand Foundation Vision in Sealed Pages with Some Extracts from Their Private Hymns Which Have Never Appeared before the Public*. Pittsfield, Mass.: B. H. Walholey, 1828.

Hollister, A. G. *Divine Motherhood*. N.p., 1887.

————. *Government*. Mt. Lebanon: n.p., 1894.

————. *"In the Day Thou Eatest."* N.p., n.d.

————. *Mission of Alethian Believers, Called Shakers*. N.p., n.d.

————. *Witness of Daniel Fraser*. N.p., n.d.

Important Rules Necessary for Everyone to Observe. [Broadside, n.d.]

Investigator; or, A Defence of the Order, Government and Economy of the United Society Called Shakers against Sundry Charges and Legislative Proceedings: Addressed to the World by the Society of Believers at Pleasant Hill, Kentucky. Lexington, Ky.: n.p., 1828.

Kenworthy, John. *Marriage*. N.p., n.d.

Lamson, David R. *Two Years' Experience among the Shakers: Being a Description of the Manners and Customs of That People; the Nature and Policy of Their Government; Their Marvellous Intercourse with the Spiritual World; the Object and Uses of Confession, Their Inquisition; in Short, a Condensed View of Shakerism As It Is*. 1848. Reprint. New York: A. M. S. Press, 1971.

Leonard, William. *A Discourse on the Order and Propriety of Divine Inspiration and Revelation, Showing the Necessity Thereof, in All Ages to Know the Will of God*. Harvard, Mass.: United Society, 1853.

————. *Of a United Inheritance in All Things in Order to Support a True Christian Community*. Harvard, Mass.: United Society, 1853.

Lomas, George A. *The Life of Christ Is the End of the World*. Albany: The Shakers, 1869.

————. *Plain Talks upon Practical Religion: Being Candid Answers to Earnest Inquirers*. Albany: Van Benthuysen, 1873.

McNemar, Richard. *A Concise Answer to the General Inquiry, Who, or What are the Shakers*. Union Village, Ohio: n.p., 1825.

M'Nemar [McNemar], Richard. *The Kentucky Revival; or, A Short History of the Late Extraordinary Out-Pouring of the Spirit of God, in the Western States of America* . . .

  with a Brief Account of the Entrance and Progress of What the World Call
  SHAKERISM, among the Subjects of the Late Revival in Ohio and Kentucky. 1808.
  Reprint. Cincinnati: Art Guild's Reprints, 1968.

Meacham, Joseph. *A Concise Statement of the Principles of the Only True Church,*
  According to the Gospel of the Present Appearing of Christ as Held and Practiced by
  the Followers of the Living Saviour at New Lebanon. New Gloucester, Me.: n.p.,
  1847.

Memorial of Stanton Buckingham, Stephen Wells, Justice Harwood, and Chauncey Copley,
  Trustees of the United Society of Believers Called Shakers, Residing at Watervliet, to
  the Senate of New York. Watervliet, N.Y.: n.p., 18 Mar. 1845.

Myrick, E. *The Celibate Shaker Life.* N.p., n.d.

Neal, Maria Julia, ed. *Journal of the Eldress Nancy: Kept at the South Union, Kentucky,*
  Shaker Colony, Aug. 15, 1861–Sept. 4, 1864. 2 vols. Nashville, Tenn.: Parthenon
  Press, 1963.

New York Legislative Assembly Committee on the Subject of the Shakers. No. 198 (2 Apr.
  1849).

North Family, Mt. Lebanon. *Present Day Shakerism.* N.p., n.d.

Offord, Daniel. *Seven Travails of the Shaker Church.* Mt. Lebanon: n.p., 1889.

The Orthodox Trinity with a Few Remarks upon Certain Doctrines Connected Therewith.
  N.p., n.d.

Peebles, J. M. *Nihilism, Socialism, Shakerism: Which?* N.p., n.d.

————. *Oriental Spiritualism from the Spirit of Mother Ann Lee.* N.p., 1877.

Pelham, R. W. *Shakers: A Correspondence between Mary F. C. of Mount Holly City and*
  Shaker Sister Sarah L. of Union Village. Cincinnati: P. T. Schultz, 1869.

————. *The Shaker's Answer to a Letter from an Inquirer.* 2d ed. Cincinnati: Joseph B.
  Boyd, 1868.

The Present Truth for the Honest Inquirer. Miamisburg, Ohio: *Bulletin* Steam Press, 1885.

Public Discourses Delivered at Union Village, August, 1823. N.p.

Rathbun, Valentine W. *Some Brief Hints of a Religious Scheme, Taught and Propagated by*
  a Number of Europeans, Living in a Place Called Nisquenia in the State of New York.
  New York: n.p., 1783.

Report of the Trustees of the United Society of Shakers in the Town of New Lebanon,
  Columbia County, New York. Senate (New York) no. 89. 19 Mar. 1850.

Report of the Trustees of the United Society of Shakers in the Town of Watervliet, Albany
  County, New York. March 1850.

Sears, C. E. *Shakers: A Short Treatise on Marriage.* Rochester: *Daily Democrat,* 1867.

————. *Shakers: A Treatise on the Second Coming of Christ.* Rochester: *Daily Democrat,*
  1867.

————. *Shakers: Duality of the Deity; or, God as Father and Mother.* Rochester, N.Y.:
  Daily Democrat, 1867.

Shaker 1–2 (Jan. 1871–Dec. 1872); 6–7 (1876–1877).

Shaker and Shakeress 3–5 (1873–75).

Shaker Church Covenant. Shaker Village, N.H.: n.p., 1889.

Shaker Examination before the New Hampshire Legislature, November Session, 1848,
  Including the Testimony at Length, Several Extracts from Shaker Publications, the Bill
  Which Passed the House of Representatives, the Proceedings in the Pillow Case:
  Together with the Letter of James W. Spinney. Concord, N.H.: Ervin B. Tripp, 1849.

Shakerism: "The Possibility of the Race"–Letters of "A. B. B." and F. W. Evans. Mt.
  Lebanon: Office of the *Shaker,* 1872.

A Shaker Letter: H. L. Eads to Mrs. E. D. S. South Union, Ky.: n.p., 1880.

Shaker Manifesto 8 (1878).

"Shaker Records of Harvard, Mass." *New England Historical and Genealogical Register* 61 (1907): 341–46.

Shaker Sermon: Delivered Sept. 12, 1886 at the Funeral of John Greves, Mt. Lebanon. N.p., 1886.

Shakers: Compendium of the Origin, History, Principles, Rules, and Regulations, Government, and Doctrines of the United Society of Believers in Christ's Second Appearing, with Biographies of Ann Lee, William Lee, James Whittaker, John Hockness, Joseph Meacham, and Lucy Wright. 5th ed. New York: D. Appleton & Co., 1859.

Some Account of the Proceedings of the Legislature of New Hampshire in Relation to the People Called Shakers in 1828. N.p.

Some Thoughts of the Gloomy Cloud That Hangs over New England by the Numerous Errors in Doctrines As Well As Schools of Instruction Such As the Universalist, Hopkinsians, Arminians, and Shakers. Boston: privately printed, 1793.

Stewart, Philemon. *A Closing Roll from Holy and Eternal Wisdom, Mother Ann, Father William, and Father James, to the Children of Zion: Part I. And Part II: A Sacred Covenant of Our Heavenly Parents, Sent Forth upon Earth to Their Children, at the Close of Their Late Manifestation (on the Holy Mount of God), for the Purification of Zion and the Inhabitants Thereof. Given by Inspiration, in the Church of the Holy Mount of God at New Lebanon, Dec. 31, 1843.* Canterbury, N.H.: n.p., 1843.

[Stewart, Philemon.] *A Sacred and Divine Roll and Book: From the Lord God of Heaven to the Inhabitants of Earth: Revealed in the United Society at New Lebanon, Columbia County, State of New York, United States of America.* Canterbury, N.H.: printed by the United Society, 1843.

A Summary View of the Millennial Church or United Society of Believers (Commonly Called Shakers), Comprising the Rise, Progress, and Practical Order of the Society; Together with the General Principles of Their Faith and Testimony: Published by Order of the Ministry, in Union with the Church. Albany: Packard & Van Benthuysen, 1823.

Supplementary Rules of the Shaker Community. (These are Published to Encourage the Spirit of Carefulness.) Mt. Lebanon: n.p., 1894.

Testimonies concerning the Character and Ministry of Mother Ann Lee and the First Witnesses of the Gospel of Christ's Second Appearing, Given by Some of the Aged Brethren and Sisters of the United Society: Including a Few Sketches of Their Own Religious Experience. Albany: Packard & Benthuysen, 1827.

Testimonies of the Life, Character, Revelations, and Doctrines of Our Ever Blessed Mother Ann Lee, and the Elders with Her; Through Whom the Word of Eternal Life Was Opened in This Day of Christ's Second Appearing: Collected from Living Witnesses. Hancock, Mass.: J. Talcott & J. Deming, Juns., 1816.

The Testimony of Christ's Second Appearing; Containing a General Statement of All Things Pertaining to the Faith and Practice of the Church of God in This Latter Day. 2d ed. Albany: E. & E. Hasford, 1810.

To the Senate of New York: The Memorial of Stephen Buckingham, Stephen Wells, Justice Harwood, and Chauncey Copley, Trustees of the United Society of Believers Called Shakers, Residing at Watervliet in the County of Albany. 18 Mar. 1845.

Vincent, Henry. *Henry Vincent's Visit to Mt. Lebanon.* Albany: Chas. Van Benthuysen, 1868.

Webster, Ruth. *The Second Eve.* N.p., n.d.

Wells, Seth Y., and Silliman, Benjamin. *Thomas Brown and His Pretended History of the Shakers: Correspondence between Seth Y. Wells of Shakers', New York, and Professor Benjamin Silliman of Yale University.* N.p., n.d. [correspondence dated Nov. 1823].

Western Review. 10 Jan. 1812–17 Oct. 1813.

White, Anna. *The Motherhood of God*. N.p., n.d.

Wickliffe, Robert. *The Shakers: Speech of Robert Wickliffe in the Senate of Kentucky, Jan. 1831*. Frankfort, Ky.: A. G. Hodges, 1832.

Williams, John S. *The Shaker Religious Concept* (bound together with *The Covenant or Constitution of the Church at Hancock* [1830]). Chatham, N.Y.: Shaker Museum Foundation, 1959.

Woods, John. *Shakerism Unmasked; or, A Narrative Shewing the Entrance of the Shakers into the Western Country, Their Stratagems and Devices, Discipline and Economy; Together with What may Seem Necessary to Exhibit the True State of That People*. Paris, Ky.: Office of the *Western Observer*, 1826.

SECONDARY SOURCES

Andrews, Edward D. *The Gift to Be Simple: Songs, Dances and Rituals of the American Shakers*. 1940. Reprint. New York: Dover Publications, 1962.

————. *The People Called Shakers: A Search for the Perfect Society*. 1953. Reprint. New York: Dover Publications, 1963.

Andrews, Edward D., and Andrews, Faith. *Religion in Wood: A Book of Shaker Furniture*. Bloomington: Indiana University Press, 1966.

————. *Visions of the Heavenly Sphere: A Study of Shaker Religious Art*. Charlottesville: University of Virginia Press, 1969.

Desroche, Henri. *The American Shakers: From Neo-Christianity to Presocialism*. 1955. Translated and edited by John K. Savacool. Amherst: University of Massachusetts Press, 1971.

MacLean, J. P. *The Society of Shakers: Rise, Progress, and Extinction of the Society at Cleveland, Ohio*. Columbus, Ohio: Fred J. Heer, 1900.

Melcher, Marguerite F. *The Shaker Adventure*. Cleveland: Case Western Reserve University Press, 1941.

Pearson, Elmer R., ed. *The Shaker Image*. Boston: New York Graphic Society, 1974.

Rourke, Constance. "The Shakers." In *The Roots of American Culture and Other Essays*, pp. 195–237. New York: Harcourt, Brace & Co., 1942.

Schroeder, Theodore. "Shaker Celibacy and Salacity Psychologically Interpreted." *New York Medical Journal* 113 (1921): 800–805.

Mormon Sources

MS SOURCES

Diary of Allan Frost of Kanab, Utah, and Snowflake, Ariz. (Mar. 1866–Sept. 1896). 6 vols. Princeton University Microfilm Library.

Diary of Charles L. Walker, 1855–1902. Photolithograph. Princeton University Library.

Stanley S. Ivins MSS. Princeton University Microfilm Library.

PRIMARY SOURCES

Acts, Resolutions, and Memorials Passed at the Several Annual Sessions of the Legislative Assembly of the Territory of Utah from 1851 to 1870 Inclusive. Salt Lake City: Joseph Bull, 1879.

Bard, Richard. *Mormonism Pulled Down: The Kingdom of the Church Set Up and the Pope*

Dethroned. Omaha: Omaha Steam Printing Establishment, 1870.

Beadle, John H. *Life in Utah; or, The Mysteries and Crimes of Mormonism: Being an Exposé of the Secret Rites and Ceremonies of the Latter-Day Saints, with a Full and Authentic History of Polygamy and the Mormon Sect from Its Origin to the Present Time.* Philadelphia: National Publishing Co., 1870.

————. *Polygamy; or, The Mysteries and Crimes of Mormonism: Being a Full and Authentic History of This Strange Sect from Its Origin to the Present Time.* Philadelphia: National Publishing Co., 1904.

Bennett, John C. *The History of the Saints; or, An Exposé of Joseph Smith and Mormonism.* Boston: Leland & Whitney, 1842.

Bertrand, L. A. *Mémoires d'un Mormon.* Paris: E. Denton Libraire, Palais-Royal, n.d.

A Book of Commandments. Independence, Mo.: W. W. Phelps & Co., 1833.

Brooks, Juanita, ed. *On the Mormon Frontier: A Diary of Hosea Stout, 1844–1861.* 2 vols. Salt Lake City: University of Utah Press, 1964.

Burton, Richard F. *The City of the Saints and Across the Rocky Mountains to California.* New York: Harper & Brothers, 1862.

Busch, Moriss. *Geschichte der Mormonen Nebst einer Darstellung Ihrer Glaubens und Ihrer Gegenwärtigen Socialen und Politischen Verhaltnisse.* Leipzig: Ambrosius Abel, 1869.

Campbell, Alexander. *Delusions: An Analysis of the Book of Mormon; with an Examination of Its Internal and External Evidences and a Refutation of Its Pretenses to Divine Authority.* Boston: Benjamin H. Green, 1832.

Chamberlain, L. T. *Mormonism and Polygamy: An Address Delivered in the Broadway Church, Norwich, Conn., Feb. 19, 1882, by the Pastor.* N.p.: published by request.

Clark, James R., ed. *Messages of the First Presidency of the Church of Jesus Christ of Latter-Day Saints (1833–1964).* 2 vols. Salt Lake City: Bookcraft, 1965.

Clayton, William. *William Clayton's Journal: A Daily Record of the Original Company of Pioneers from Nauvoo, Ill., to the Valley of the Great Salt Lake.* Salt Lake City: Deseret News, 1921.

Cleland, Robert G., and Brooks, Juanita, eds. *A Mormon Chronicle: The Diaries of John D. Lee, 1848–1876.* 2 vols. San Marino, Calif.: Huntington Library, 1955.

Cooper, Will, pseud. [William C. Carman]. *Rattling, Roaring Rhymes on Mormon Utah and Her Institutions, Life among the Rocky Mountain Saints, the Land of Many Wives and Much Silver; or, The Follies and Crimes of Bigamy Young and His Pol-Lig Divines.* Chicago: Union Publishing Co., 1874.

Correspondence between Joseph Smith, the Prophet, and Col. John Wentworth (Editor of the Chicago Democrat and Member of Congress from Illinois); Gen. James Arlington Bennett; and John C. Calhoun (Senator from South Carolina): In Which is Given a Sketch of the Life of Joseph Smith, the Rise and Progress of the Church of Latter-Day Saints, and Their Persecutions in the State of Missouri, with the Peculiar Views of Joseph Smith in Relation to Political and Religious Matters Generally, to Which Is Added a Concise Account of the Present State and Prospects of the City of Nauvoo. New York: John E. Page & L. R. Foster, 1844.

Coyner, J. M., comp. *Handbook on Mormonism.* Salt Lake City: Handbook Publishing Co., 1882.

Cradlebaugh, John. *Utah and the Mormons: Speech of the Honorable John Cradlebaugh of Nevada on the Admission of Utah as a State, Delivered in the House of Representatives, Feb. 7, 1868.* N.p.

Dickinson, Ellen E. *New Light on Mormonism.* New York: Funk & Wagnalls, 1885.

Doctrine and Covenants of the Church of Jesus Christ of Latter-Day Saints: Containing the Revelations Given to Joseph Smith, Jun., the Prophet, for the Building Up of the

Kingdom of God in the Last Days. Salt Lake City: Deseret News, 1876.

Doctrine and Covenants of the Church of Latter-Day Saints, Carefully Selected from the Revelations of God. Kirtland, Ohio: F. G. Williams & Co., 1835.

Enring, Heinrich. *Ein Wort der Vertheidigung oder Antworten auf Fragen in Betreff der Lehrer der Kirche Jesu Christi der Heiligen der Letzten Tage.* Berne: J. U. Stucki, 1875.

Etzenhauser, R. *From Palmyra, N.Y., 1830, to Independence, Mo., 1894.* Independence: Ensign Publishing House, 1894.

Evans, R. C. *Forty Years in the Church: Why I Left It.* Toronto: n.p., 1920.

Ferris, Benjamin G. *Utah and the Mormons: The History, Government, Doctrines, Customs, and Prospects of the Latter-Day Saints from Personal Observation during a Six Months' Residence at Great Salt Lake City.* New York: Harper & Brothers, 1854.

The Fireside Visitor; or, Plain Reasoner 1, nos. 1–3 [only three numbers published; n.d., ca. 1850s or 1860s].

Froiseth, Jennie Anderson, ed. *The Women of Mormonism; or, The Story of Polygamy As Told by the Victims Themselves.* Detroit: C. G. G. Paine, 1882.

Goodrich, E. S. *Mormonism Unveiled: The Other Side from an American Standpoint.* Reprinted from the *Chicago Times,* 1884.

Green, Nelson W. *Fifteen Years among the Mormons: Being the Narrative of Mrs. Mary Ettie V. Smith.* New York: H. Dayton Publishers, 1859.

———. *Mormonism: Its Rise, Progress, and Present Condition, Embracing the Narrative of Mrs. Mary Ettie V. Smith, etc.* Hartford: Belknap Press, 1870.

Hyde, John, Jr. *Mormonism: Its Leaders and Designs.* 2d ed. New York: W. P. Fetridge & Co., 1857.

Jackson, Joel H. *A Journal or Sketch of the Life of Joel Hill Jackson.* N.p.: privately printed, n.d.

Jacques, John. *Catechism for Children, Exhibiting the Prominent Doctrines of the Church of Jesus Christ of Latter-Day Saints.* Salt Lake City: Deseret News Co., 1848.

Jarman, William. *U.S.A.: Uncle Sam's Abscess or Hell upon Earth.* Exeter, Eng.: H. Ledve, 1884.

Kane, E. D., pseud. [William Wood]. *Twelve Mormon Homes Visited in Succession on a Journey through Utah to Arizona.* Philadelphia: n.p., 1874.

Kane, Thomas L. *The Mormons: A Discourse Delivered before the Historical Society of Pennsylvania, March 26, 1850.* Philadelphia: King & Baird, 1850.

Latter-Day Saints' Messenger and Advocate 1 (1844).

Latter-Day Saints' Millennial Star 19–26 (1857–66).

Leavitt, Sarah S. *Journal.* N.p., 1911.

Lee, John D. *The Mormon Menace: Being the Confession of John Doyle Lee, an Official Assassin of the Mormon Church under the Late Brigham Young.* New York: Home Protection Publishing Co., 1905.

———. *Mormonism Unveiled; or, The Life and Confessions of John D. Lee: Embracing a History of Mormonism from Its Inception Down to the Present Time, with an Exposition of the Secret History, Signs, Symbols, and Crimes of the Mormon Church.* St. Louis: Byron, Brand & Co., 1878.

Letters of Oliver Cowdery. Kirtland, Ohio: published in the *Messenger and Advocate,* 1834–35.

Lyford, C. P. *The Mormon Problem: An Appeal to the American People.* New York: Phillips & Hunt, 1886.

Mackay, Charles. *The Mormons or Latter-Day Saints: A Contemporary History—With Memoirs of the Life and Death of Joseph Smith, the "American Mahomet."* London: Office of the National Illustrated Library, 1857.

Memorial of the Mormon Women of Utah to the President and the Congress of the U.S.:

The Outrages of Which They Complain—The Justice They Demand (6 Apr. 1886). Washington, D.C.: n.p., 1886.

Memory Book of Moroni Gerber and Emily Jane Jacob. N.p., n.d.

Nauvoo Expositor 1, no. 1 (Friday, 7 June 1844) [only issue ever published].

Olney, Oliver H. *The Absurdities of Mormonism Portrayed: A Brief Sketch.* Hancock Co., Ill.: n.p., 1 Apr. 1843.

Olshausen, Theodor. *Geschichte der Mormonen oder Jungsten Tages Heiligen in Nordamerika.* Göttingen: Vandenhoeck und Reprecht's Verlag, 1856.

"One of the People." *An Appeal to the American Congress: The Bible Law of Marriage against Mormonism.* N.p., n.d.

Partridge, George E., ed. "The Death of a Mormon Dictator: Letters of Massachusetts Mormons, 1843–1848." *New England Quarterly* 9 (1936): 583–617.

Pratt, Orson, ed. *The Doctrine and Covenants of the Church of Jesus Christ of Latter-Day Saints: Containing the Revelations Given to Joseph Smith, Jun., the Prophet, for the Building Up of the Kingdom of God in the Last Days.* 1880. Reprint. Westport, Conn.: Greenwood Press, 1971.

Remy, Jules, and Brenchley, Julius. *A Journey to Great Salt-Lake City, with a Sketch of the History, Religion, and Customs of the Mormons and an Introduction on the Religious Movement in the U.S.* 2 vols. London: John E. Taylor, 1861.

Savage, Levi, Jr. *Journal, 1852–1902.* N.p.: John Savage Family Organization, 1966.

Seer 1 (1853); 2 (1854).

Sessions, Patty. "Midwifery." *Our Pioneer Heritage* 2 (1959): 11–13, 60–69.

Smith, Joseph. *The Book of Mormon: An Account Written by the Hand of Mormon upon the Plates Taken from the Plates of Nephi.* 1830. Reprint. Salt Lake City: Church of Jesus Christ of Latter-Day Saints, 1964.

————. *History of the Church of Jesus Christ of Latter-Day Saints.* 7 vols. Salt Lake City: Deseret Book Co., 1956.

Smith, Lucy. *Biographical Sketches of Joseph Smith, the Prophet.* 1853. Reprint. New York: Arno Press, 1969.

Smith, Mary E. V. *Fifteen Years' Residence with the Mormons, with Startling Disclosures of the Mysteries of Polygamy.* Chicago: Phoenix Publishing Co., 1876.

Spencer, Orson. *Letters Exhibiting the Most Prominent Doctrines of the Church of Jesus Christ of Latter-Day Saints.* 5th ed. Salt Lake City: Deseret News, 1874.

Stenhouse, Mrs. Thomas B. H. *An Englishwoman in Utah: The Story of a Life's Experience in Mormonism.* London: Sampson, Low, Marston, Searle, & Rivington, 1880.

————. *Exposé of Polygamy in Utah—A Lady's Life among the Mormons: A Record of Personal Experience as One of the Wives of a Mormon Elder during a Period of More Than Twenty Years.* 2d ed. New York: American News Co., 1872.

————. *"Tell It All": The Story of a Life's Experiences in Mormonism: An Autobiography.* Hartford, Conn.: A. D. Worthington & Co., 1875.

Stenhouse, Thomas B. H. *The Rocky Mountain Saints.* 1873. British ed., London: Ward, Lock, & Taylor, 1874.

Strang, Mark A., ed. *The Diary of James J. Strang (1831–36).* East Lansing: Michigan State University Press, 1961.

Times and Seasons 1–3 (Nov. 1839–Oct. 1842).

Tucker, Pomeroy. *Origin, Rise and Progress of Mormonism.* New York: D. Appleton & Co., 1867.

Tullidge, Edward W. *History of Salt Lake City.* Salt Lake City: Star Printing Co., 1886.

————. *The Women of Mormondom.* New York: Tullidge & Crandall, 1877.

Turner, J. B. *Mormonism in All Ages; or, The Rise, Progress, and Causes of Mormonism;*

with the Biography of Its Author and Founder, Joseph Smith, Junior. New York: Platt & Peters, 1842.

Ward, Maria. *Female Life among the Mormons: A Narrative of Many Years' Personal Experience by the Wife of a Mormon Elder Recently from Utah.* New York: J. C. Derby, 1855.

Watt, G. D.; Long, J. V.; et al., eds. *Journal of Discourses Delivered by Brigham Young, His Two Counsellors, the Twelve Apostles and Others.* 26 vols. Liverpool, Eng.: George Q. Cannon, 1854–86.

Whitmer, David. *An Address to All Believers in Christ, by a Witness to the Divine Authenticity of the Book of Mormon.* Richmond, Mo.: D. Whitmer, 1887.

Whitney, Helen Mar. *Plural Marriage As Taught by the Prophet Joseph.* Salt Lake City: n.p., 1882.

Whitney, Orson F. *"The Mormon Prophet's Tragedy": A Review of an Article by the Late John Hay, Published Originally in the* Atlantic Monthly *for December 1869 and Republished in the* Saints Herald *of June 21, 1905; the Reviewer Orson F. Whitney.* Salt Lake City: Deseret News, 1905.

Widtsoe, John A., ed. *Discourses of Brigham Young, Second President of the Church of Jesus Christ of Latter-Day Saints.* Salt Lake City: Deseret Book Co., 1925.

Woodruff, Wilford. *Leaves from My Journal.* 4th ed. Salt Lake City: Deseret News, 1909.

Young, Ann E. *Wife Number Nineteen; or, The Story of a Life in Bondage: Being a Complete Exposé of Mormonism, and Revealing the Sorrows, Sacrifices, and Sufferings of Women in Polygamy.* 1875. Reprint. New York: Arno Press, 1972.

SECONDARY SOURCES

Alexander, Thomas G. "An Experiment in Progressive Legislation: The Granting of Woman Suffrage in Utah in 1870." *Utah Historical Quarterly* 38 (1970): 20–30.

Arrington, Leonard J., and Haupt, Jon. "Intolerable Zion: The Image of Mormonism in Nineteenth-Century American Literature." *Western Humanities Review* 23 (1968): 243–60.

Barrett, Ivan J. *Joseph Smith and the Restoration: A History of the Church to 1846.* Provo, Utah: Young House, 1973.

Brodie, Fawn M. *No Man Knows My History: The Life of Joseph Smith, the Mormon Prophet.* 1945. Reprint. New York: Alfred A. Knopf, 1971.

Cairncross, John. *After Polygamy Was Made a Sin: The Social History of Christian Polygamy.* London: Routledge & Kegan Paul, 1974.

Cannon, Charles A. "The Awesome Power of Sex: The Polemical Campaign against Mormon Polygamy." *Pacific Historical Review* 63 (1974): 61–82.

Cannon, M. Hamlin. "Migration of English Mormons to America." *American Historical Review* 52 (1946–47): 436–55.

Cheney, Thomas E., ed. *Lore of Faith and Folly.* Salt Lake City: University of Utah Press, 1971.

————. *Mormon Songs from the Rocky Mountains: A Compilation of Mormon Folksong.* Austin: University of Texas Press, 1968.

Clignet, Remi. *Many Wives, Many Powers: Authority and Power in Polygamous Families.* Evanston, Ill.: Northwestern University Press, 1970.

Davidson, Levette J. "Mormon Songs." *Journal of American Folklore* 58 (1945): 273–300.

Davis, David B. "The New England Origins of Mormonism." *New England Quarterly* 26 (1953): 147–68.

Eriksen, Ephraim E. *The Psychological and Ethical Aspects of Mormon Group Life.*

Chicago: University of Chicago Press, 1922.

Faull, George L., comp. *Inside Mormonism*. Joplin, Mo.: College Press, 1969.

Flanders, Robert B. *Nauvoo: Kingdom on the Mississippi*. Urbana: University of Illinois Press, 1965.

Follick, Edwin D. "The Cultural Influence of Mormonism in Early Nineteenth-Century America." Ph.D. dissertation, St. Andrew's Collegiate Church College, 1958.

Gallichan, Walter M. *Women under Polygamy*. New York: Dodd, Mead, & Co., 1915.

Gardner, Hamilton. "Communism among the Mormons." *Quarterly Journal of Economics* 37 (1922): 134–74.

Hill, Marvin S., and Allen, James B., eds. *Mormonism and American Culture*. New York: Harper & Row, 1972.

Hillman, Eugene. *Polygamy Reconsidered: African Plural Marriage and the Christian Churches*. Maryknoll, N.Y.: Orbis Books, 1975.

Hirshson, Stanley P. *The Lion of the Lord: A Biography of Brigham Young*. New York: Alfred A. Knopf, 1969.

Hulett, James E. "The Sociological and Social Psychological Aspects of the Mormon Polygamous Family." Ph.D. dissertation, University of Wisconsin, 1939.

Jensen, Andrew. *The Latter-Day Saints Biographical Encyclopedia*. 6 vols. Salt Lake City: Deseret News, 1901.

Kauffman, Ruth, and Kauffman, Reginald. *The Latter-Day Saints: A Study of the Mormons in the Light of Economic Conditions*. London: Williams & Norgate, 1912.

Lambert, A. C. *The Published Editions of the Doctrines and Covenants of the Church of Jesus Christ of Latter-Day Saints in All Languages, 1833–1950*. N.P.: privately printed, 1950.

Larson, Gustave O. *The "Americanization" of Utah for Statehood*. San Marino, Calif.: Huntington Library, 1971.

Larson, T. A. "Woman Suffrage in Western America." *Utah Historical Quarterly* 38 (1970): 7–19.

Linn, William A. *The Story of the Mormons: From the Date of Their Origin to the Year 1901*. New York: Macmillan Co., 1923.

McNiff, William J. *Heaven on Earth: A Planned Mormon Society*. 1940. Reprint. New York: Porcupine Press, 1972.

May, Dean L. "People on the Mormon Frontier: Kanab's Families of 1874." *Journal of Family History* 1 (1976): 169–92.

Mormonism and the State of Utah: Origin and History of Mormonism: And Social, Political, and Religious Conditions in Utah Arising from Mormon Influence As Described in a Collection of Articles Thereon. Cleveland: n.p., 1961.

O'Dea, Thomas F. *The Mormons*. Chicago: University of Chicago Press, 1957.

Parkin, Max H. "Conflict at Kirtland: A Study of the Nature and Causes of External and Internal Conflict of the Mormons in Ohio Between 1830 and 1838." M.A. thesis, Brigham Young University, 1966.

Prince, Walter F. "Psychological Tests for the Authorship of the Book of Mormon." *American Journal of Psychology* 28 (1917): 373–89.

Riley, I. Woodbridge. *The Founder of Mormonism: A Psychological Study of Joseph Smith, Jr*. London: William Heinemann, 1903.

Roberts, B. H. *The Rise and Fall of Nauvoo*. Salt Lake City: Deseret News Press, 1900.

Smith, Joseph Fielding. *Essentials of Church History*. 22d ed. Salt Lake City: Deseret Book Co., 1971.

Taggart, Stephen G. *Mormonism's Negro Policy: Social and Historical Origins*. Salt Lake City: University of Utah Press, 1970.

Wallace, Irving. *The Twenty-seventh Wife*. New York: Simon & Schuster, 1961.

Werner, M. R. *Brigham Young*. New York: Harcourt, Brace & Co., 1925.

West, Ray B.*Kingdom of the Saints: The Story of Brigham Young and the Mormons*. New York: Viking Press, 1957.

Oneida Community Sources

MS SOURCES

[C. A. W.] "Community Journal." 1863–64. Mimeographed.

Dickinson, Robert L. Letter to Anita N. McGee, dated 27 Sept. 1924. Typescript in Anita N. McGee MSS, Kinsey Institute, Indiana University.

————. Letter to Anita N. McGee, dated New York City, 22 Dec. 1924. Typescript in McGee MSS.

————. Letter to Anita N. McGee, dated 26 Feb. 1925. Typescript in McGee MSS.

————. Notes on the Oneida Community, Sept. 1926. Typescript in McGee MSS.

Frankland, F. W. Letter to Mrs. Anita N. McGee, dated New York City, 30 Apr. 1894. Typescript in McGee MSS.

————. Letter to Anita N. McGee, dated New York City, 15 May 1894. Typescript in McGee MSS.

————. Letter to Mrs. Anita N. McGee, dated New York City, 13 June 1894. Typescript in McGee MSS.

————. Letter to Mrs. Anita N. McGee, dated New York City, 17 Dec. 1894. Typescript in McGee MSS.

————. Letter to Anita N. McGee, dated New York City, 26 Mar. 1895. Typescript in McGee MSS.

Herrick, J. B. Letter to Mrs. Anita N. McGee, dated Kenwood, N.Y., 16 Aug. 1891. Typescript in McGee MSS.

Hinds, William A. Letter to Mrs. Anita N. McGee, dated Community, N.Y., 9 June 1888. Typescript in McGee MSS.

————. Letter to Mrs. Anita N. McGee, dated Community, N.Y., 20 June 1888. Typescript in McGee MSS.

————. Letter to Mrs. Anita N. McGee, dated Wallace, N.M., 13 Dec. 1888. Typescript in McGee MSS.

McGee, Anita N. "An Experiment in Human Stirpiculture." *American Anthropologist* (Oct. 1891): 319–25. Author's personal annotated copy. McGee MSS.

————. "Dr. Anita N. McGee's Interviews at Kenwood, N.Y., Aug., 1891." Typescript in McGee MSS.

————. Letter to J. B. Herrick, dated Washington, D.C., 6 Aug. 1891. Typescript in McGee MSS.

————. Letter to J. B. Herrick, dated Washington, D.C., 14 Aug. 1891. Typescript in McGee MSS.

————. Letter to J. B. Herrick, dated Washington, D.C., 23 Aug. 1891. Typescript in McGee MSS.

————. Letter to William Hinds, dated Cleveland, Ohio, 15 Aug. 1888. Typescript in McGee MSS.

————. Letter to George Miller, dated Washington, D.C., 3 Sept. 1891. Typescript in McGee MSS.

————. Letter to Theodore R. Noyes, dated Washington, D.C., 12 Nov. 1891. Typescript in McGee MSS.

————. "Oneida Community History, Aug. 1891." Typescript in McGee MSS.

[McGee, Anita N.] Oneida Community: Interview of R. L. D. [Robert Latour Dickinson] and Mr. and Mrs. George W. Noyes. Typescript in McGee MSS.

Noyes, Harriet A. Letter to Simon Lovett, Bristol, Wis., dated Putney, Vt., 28 June 1847. Noyes Papers, Putney Historical Society, Putney, Vermont.

———. Letter to Simon Lovett, Bristol, Wis., dated Putney, Vt., 27 Jan. 1848. Noyes Papers.

———. Addenda to Letter of 27 Jan. 1848, dated Putney, Vt., 28 Jan. 1848. Noyes Papers.

———. Letter to Simon Lovett, dated Oneida Castle, 11 June 1848. Noyes Papers.

Noyes, John Humphrey. "Battle Axe Letter" to David Harrison of Meriden, Conn., dated 15 Jan. 1837. MS copy in Constance Noyes Robertson MSS, Syracuse University.

———. Letter dated 1843. Robertson MSS.

———. Letters (two undated), signed "N." Robertson MSS.

———. "The Rights of the Human Mind," MS Paper dated 1 July 1851, signed "N." Robertson MSS.

[Noyes, John Humphrey.] "The Surrender of Our Talents to God," unsigned letter, dated Brooklyn, 7 July 1851. Robertson MSS.

Noyes, Theodore R. Letter to Anita N. McGee, dated New York City, 13 Sept. 1891. Typescript in McGee MSS.

"O." "The Kiantone Valley and the Association of Beneficents." Typescript in Robertson MSS.

"Oneida Association, Jan. 1, 1849, Family Register." Mimeographed. Noyes Papers.

Oneida Community, Ltd., Laundry List. Robertson MSS.

"Original Confession of Polly Hayes Noyes." Dated 1846. MS in Noyes Papers.

Towner, J. W. Letter to Anita N. McGee, dated Santa Ana, Calif., 1 Nov. 1894. Typescript in McGee MSS.

———. Postcard to Anita N. McGee, dated Santa Ana, Calif., 20 Oct. 1894. Typescript in McGee MSS.

PRIMARY SOURCES

American Socialist 1–4 (1876–79).

Bible Communism: A Compilation from the Annual Reports and Other Publications of the Oneida Association and Its Branches; Presented in Connection with Their History, a Summary View of Their Religion and Social Theories. Brooklyn: Office of the *Circular*, 1853.

Cochrane, Elizabeth [Nelly Bly]. *Outline of Biblical Theology Extracted from a Letter by a Lady to the New York World of June 2, 1889.* N.p.

[Cooley, Benjamin F.] *A Summary Exposition of the Social Theory of the Dissenters, Called Perfectionists, Which Theory Is Called by Them the Bible Argument: Showing the Relation of the Sexes in the Kingdom of Heaven on Earth, unto Which Some of Them Profess to Have Been Attained, Especially Those of the Oneida Association in the State of New York.* Worcester, Mass.: n.p., 1850.

Daily Journal of the Oneida Community 1, no. 1 (14 Jan. 1866).

Eastman, Hubbard. *Noyesism Unveiled: A History of the Sect of Self-Styled Perfectionists with a Summary View of Their Leading Doctrines.* Brattleboro, Vt.: published by the author, 1849.

Ellis, John B. *Free Love and Its Votaries; or, American Socialism Unmasked: Being an Historical and Descriptive Account of the Rise and Progress of the Various Free Love Associations in the U.S. and of the Effects of Their Various Teachings upon American Socialism.* New York: U.S. Publishing Co., 1870.

Estlake, Alan. *The Oneida Community: A Record of an Attempt to Carry Out the Principles of Christian Unselfishness and Scientific Race-Improvement.* London: George Redway, 1900.

First Annual Report of the Oneida Association: Exhibiting its History, Principles, and Transactions to Jan. 1, 1849. Oneida, N.Y.: Leonard & Co., 1849.

Hand Book of the Oneida Community: Containing a Brief Sketch of Its Present Condition, Internal Economy, and Leading Principles. Number Two. Oneida: Office of the *Oneida Circular,* 1871.

Meyers, Eleanor. "Oneida Community." *National Genealogical Quarterly* 54 (1966): 193–210.

Mutual Criticism. Oneida: Office of the *American Socialist,* 1876.

New Covenant Record and Advocate of Freedom from Sin, from Sectarian Legality, Usurpation, and Delusion 2, no. 6 (18 Dec. 1835), no. 9 (16 Mar. 1836).

Noyes, John Humphrey. *The Berean: A Manual for the Help of Those Who Seek the Faith of the Primitive Church.* Putney, Vt.: Office of the *Spiritualist Magazine,* 1847.

———. *Confessions of John H. Noyes, Part I: Confessions of Religious Experience, Including a History of Modern Perfectionism.* Oneida Reserve: Leonard & Co., 1849.

———. *Dixon and His Copyists: A Criticism of the Accounts of the Oneida Community in "New America," "Spiritual Wives," and Kindred Publications.* 2d ed. Oneida: Oneida Community, 1874.

———. *Essay on Scientific Propagation with an Appendix Containing a Health Report on the Oneida Community.* Oneida: Oneida Community, 1875.

———. *Home Talks by John Humphrey Noyes.* Edited by Alfred Barron and George N. Miller. Oneida: Oneida Community, 1875.

———. *Male Continence.* 2d ed. Oneida: Office of the *American Socialist,* 1877.

———. *Salvation from Sin: The End of Christian Faith.* Oneida: Oneida Community, 1876.

———. *The Way of Holiness: A Series of Papers: Formerly Published in the* Perfectionist *at New Haven.* Putney, Vt.: J. H. Noyes & Co., 1838.

[Noyes, John Humphrey.] *Paul's Prize: Report of a Home Talk by John H. Noyes.* N.p., n.d.

Noyes, Theodore R. *Health Report of Oneida Community Children.* Oneida: n.p., 1878.

Oneida Circular. N.s. 1–5 (1864–69).

Perfectionist 1 (20 Aug. 1834–July 1835); 2 (15 Aug. 1835–20 Nov. 1835); 3, nos. 1–24 (15 Feb. 1843–1 Feb. 1844).

Perfectionist and Theocratic Watchman 4 (22 Mar. 1845–14 Feb. 1846).

Second Annual Report of the Oneida Association Exhibiting Its Progress to Feb. 20, 1850. Oneida Reserve: Leonard & Co., 1850.

Seymour, Henry J. "The Oneida Community: A Dialogue." N.p., n.d.

[Seymour, Henry J.] *The Oneida Community: Replies by One of the Surviving Members, to the Interrogatories of a French Political Economist* [M. Fabre]. Kenwood, N.Y.: n.p., 1897.

Smith, D. E., photographer. *Photographic Views of the Oneida Community.* [Eight Stereoscopic Views, 1870s.]

Spiritual Magazine 1 (15 Mar. 1846–15 Feb. 1847); 2 (15 May 1847–5 Aug. 1848).

Spiritual Moralist 1, no. 1 (13 June 1842), no. 2 (25 June 1842).

Third Annual Report of the Oneida Association Exhibiting Its Progress to Feb. 20, 1851. Oneida Reserve: Leonard & Co., 1851.

Van de Warker, Ely. "A Gynecological Study of the Oneida Community." *American Journal of Obstetrics and Diseases of Women and Children* 17 (1884): 785–810.

SECONDARY SOURCES

Achorn, Erik. "Mary Cragin, Perfectionist Saint." *New England Quarterly* 28 (1955): 490–518.
Bartell, Gilbert D. "Group Sex among the Middle Americans." *Journal of Sex Research* 6 (1970): 113–30.
Carden, Maren Lockwood. *Oneida: Utopian Community to Modern Corporation.* Baltimore: Johns Hopkins Press, 1969.
Case, Richard G. "The Oneida Community Lives on in Spirit." *Syracuse Herald American Empire* (Sunday magazine), June 1970.
Constantine, Larry L., and Constantine, Joan M. *Group Marriage: A Study of Contemporary Multilateral Marriage.* New York: Macmillan, 1973.
Denfield, Duane, and Gordon, Michael. "The Sociology of Mate Swapping." *Journal of Sex Research* 6 (1970): 85–100.
Hawkins, Charles H. "The Erotic Significance of Contraceptive Methods." *Journal of Sex Research* 6 (1970): 143–57.
Kephart, William. "Experimental Family Organization: An Historico-Cultural Report on the Oneida Community." *Journal of Marriage and the Family* 25 (1963): 261–71.
Noyes, George W., comp. *John Humphrey Noyes and the Putney Community.* Oneida: n.p., 1931.
————. *The Religious Experience of John Humphrey Noyes, Founder of the Oneida Community.* New York: Macmillan Co., 1923.
Noyes, Hilda H., and Noyes, George W. "The Community Experiment in Stirpiculture." *Eugenics, Genetics and the Family* 1 (1923): 374–85.
Noyes, Pierrepont. *My Father's House: An Oneida Boyhood.* New York: Farrar & Rinehart, 1937.
O'Neill, George C., and O'Neill, Nena. "Patterns in Group Sexual Activity." *Journal of Sex Research* 6 (1970): 101–12.
Parker, Robert Allerton. *A Yankee Saint: John Humphrey Noyes and the Oneida Community.* New York: G. P. Putnam's Sons, 1935.
Ramey, James W. "Communes, Group Marriage, and the Upper Middle Class." *Journal of Marriage and the Family* 34 (1972): 647–55.
Robertson, Constance Noyes. *Oneida Community: An Autobiography, 1851–1876.* Syracuse: Syracuse University Press, 1970.
————. *Oneida Community Profiles.* Syracuse: Syracuse University Press, 1977.
————. *Oneida Community: The Breakup, 1876–1881.* Syracuse: Syracuse University Press, 1972.
Sellers, Charles C. *Theophilus the Battle Axe: A History of the Lives and Adventures of Theophilus Ransom Gates and the Battle Axes.* Philadelphia: Patterson & White Co., 1930.
Seymour, Henry J. *Letter to the Outlook.* Kenwood, N.Y.: n.p., 1903.
Sibley, Mulford Q. "Oneida's Challenge to American Culture." In *Studies in American Culture: Dominant Ideas and Images,* edited by Joseph J. Kwist and Mary C. Turpie, pp. 41–62. Minneapolis: University of Minnesota Press, 1960.
Smith, James R., and Smith, Lynn G. "Co-Marital Sex and the Sexual Freedom Movement." *Journal of Sex Research* 6 (1970): 131–42.
Stockham, Alice B. *Karezza: Ethics of Marriage.* N.p.: Alice B. Stockham & Co., 1896.
Thomas, Robert. *The Man Who Would Be Perfect: John Humphrey Noyes and the Utopian Impulse.* Philadelphia: University of Pennsylvania Press, 1977.

Index